Captain J. C. Dunn D.S.O., M.C. and Bar, D.C.M. was Medical Officer of the Second Battalion His Majesty's Twenty-Third Foot, The Royal Welch Fusiliers. A courageous soldier and an impressive man, he was mentioned by both Robert Graves and Siegfried Sassoon in their famous books with respect and admiration. Compiling *The War the Infantry Knew 1914–1919* was a labour of love and Captain Dunn did not name himself as the editor. He died in 1955.

Keith Simpson was a Senior Lecturer in War Studies and International Affairs at the Royal Military Academy Sandhurst from 1973–1986. He is the author of two books on the British Army and the First World War and has written a history of the German Army. He is now Member of Parliament for Mid Norfolk. Keith Simpson is married and lives in Norfolk.

The War the Infantry Knew
1914 - 1919

A Chronicle of Service in France and Belgium

with

The Second Battalion

His Majesty's Twenty-Third Foot,

The Royal Welch Fusiliers:

founded on

personal records, recollections and reflections,

assembled, edited and partly written

by

One of their Medical Officers.

ABACUS

ABACUS

First published in Great Britain by P. S. King Ltd 1938
in a private edition
This edition first published in Great Britain
by Jane's Publishing Company Limited 1987
Published in Cardinal by Sphere Books Ltd 1989
Published by Abacus in 1994
Reprinted 1997, 1998 (twice), 1999, 2001, 2003, 2004,
2009 (twice), 2012 (twice)

Text copyright © The Royal Welch Fusiliers 1987
Introduction © Keith Simpson 1987

Photographs 1, 2, 3, 4, 5, 6, 7, 8, 9, 10, 11, 12, 14, 15, 19, 23, 25
and 31 are by courtesy of the Royal Welch Fusiliers.
Photographs 13, 16, 17, 18, 20, 21, 22, 24, 26, 27, 28, 29 and 30 are
by kind permission of the Trustees of the Imperial War Museum, London

A CIP catalogue record for this book
is available from the British Library.

ISBN 978-0-349-10635-9

Printed and bound in Great Britain by
Clays Ltd, St Ives plc

Papers used by Abacus are from well-managed forests
and other responsible sources.

MIX
Paper from
responsible sources
FSC® C104740
www.fsc.org

Abacus
An imprint of
Little, Brown Book Group
100 Victoria Embankment
London EC4Y 0DY

An Hachette UK Company
www.hachette.co.uk

www.littlebrown.co.uk

PREFACE

War will always interest men.

There is no end to the output of books about the Great War. Setting aside technical books, most of them have come from writers whose emotions have been quickened by the penitential mood that follows all great wars, or from writers turning to account that mood and the relaxation of age-long, wholesome usages needful to community life, which is another common sequel of great popular upheavals. A picture of the War from the front-line standpoint, made without afterthought, will neither tickle a taste for foulness nor slake a thirst for pomp if it is drawn from what was seen and felt, and noted, at the time. War in the battle-zone between antagonists of equal tenacity and resource is prolonged drudgery— that is what many people say about life in general—but drudgery with fearful moments; and, as in everyday life, there is very much that is trivial, or seems so. War is neither a glitter of high lights nor a slough of baseness, it calls forth the best that is in the human spirit : its worst aspects are found far from the battle-line.

This Chronicle is offered as an authentic record of the comings and goings, the chances, deeds and moods of the Second Battalion of His Majesty's 23rd Foot, the Royal Welch Fusiliers ; it tells of blissful and what were counted hum-drum days as well as of fevered hours and minutes. To begin with it was an abstract of day-to-day notes made during the long middle period of the War ; two narratives from diaries of the early weeks were the first additions, then a collection of still clear memories was wrought in, and an outline of the last phase was joined on. Yielding to the wish of a few interested correspondents I set myself the task of welding the parts in narrative form and of finding witnesses to fill serious gaps. Contributions, long and short, have come from some fifty sources in the course of years. The bulk of the story consists of notes which, though expanded later, were made within twenty-four hours, at most, of the events described; contemporary letters, operation orders, messages, and Battalion Intelligence maps which have escaped destruction have been drawn upon. Someone with first-hand knowledge has given the detail of each incident or phase, or has added to it, and readers with equal knowledge may have checked it. A sentence may be a compound of three sources. Plain has been preferred to coloured in the telling of incident. Guess-work has not been taken. Vagueness or omission is not owing to want of candour, but to want of evidence: distance has made it difficult to trace or tap likely witnesses; many men will talk, and talk vividly, but not write. The ambit of anyone's observation is limited, especially during action. At all times food and warmth occupy much of the front-line man's thoughts—indeed, the private soldier's thoughts, as one of them wrote, are largely bounded by these needs; and when things are moving his load or peril engrosses him. Impressions of happenings are consequently blurred, they become mingled, and are soon lost by the great majority of men. The facts about which witnesses have written or spoken are stated on their authority, but quotation marks have been used sparingly because the original text is seldom given in its verbal integrity, although the idiom of most sources is in great part original and the tone altogether so. The brevity, inconstant tense, and disjointedness of diaries have not been quite expunged.

The actions and locations of other units are sketched sufficiently to introduce the action of the Battalion which followed, or as part of its coincident action; but, since it is seldom easy to learn what other units really did, the sketches are not always to be taken as conclusive: even within a unit a carried story may take on a twist.

Events are dealt with at greatly varying length, chiefly owing to a relatively unequal supply of data. Tactical importance and length of treatment have no relation here. In war incidents and events may signify much to a battalion, and be of no account in the operations of an army: sometimes a few men do a great thing unwittingly. A sense of proportion can be had only by comparison with large-scale accounts; such a comparison is beyond the intended scope of these personal impressions and reflections. Nowhere has the story been adjusted to any official view; it remains throughout a series of records of individual observation and, in the main, of common outlook and talk in billet and trench. The views are mostly repetitions of casual talks, of gossip during reliefs and at other times when news was exchanged; they reflect front-line knowledge and attitude, and express its mood. As a consequence lower and higher staffs may object to various statements, to some of which there is necessarily another side. Divergences from official reports may be found in several passages. Recorded history, which is mostly of official origin, is not always a recital of what happened—there are many reasons for that.

My service of nearly three years with the Battalion, or in its Brigade, was a time of trench warfare with eruptions of great violence, of waning morale, of increasing vexation and heartache. This is largely a record of a long spell of duty done in the face of difficulty and discouragement which, perhaps, demanded more leading and gallantry than actions of which more has been heard, more made. The Battalion was always used late in action. Attacks had to be made with the knowledge of others' failures, and over their dead. Such a lot called for a full measure of steadfastness and devotion, and yielded no redeeming spectacular repute. What was achieved is made radiant in my memory by the gay self-sacrifice of junior officers and of non-commissioned officers; by the resource and cheerfulness in discomfort of the men of our Old Army, and their prompt answer to every call, confident in themselves and in each other: beside them the Territorial and New Army personnel had the native virtues common to all, good nature and endurance.

CONTENTS

		PAGE
GLOSSARY	. . . .	xi
SKETCHES FROM MAPS	. . . .	xiii
CONTRIBUTORS	. . . .	xv
ACKNOWLEDGEMENTS	. . . .	xvii
INTRODUCTION	. . . .	xix

CHAP.

I. JULY–AUGUST 21st, 1914 1
    Mobilizing—Base Duty.

II. AUGUST 22nd–SEPTEMBER 5th, 1914 17
    Retreat.

III. SEPTEMBER 6th–OCTOBER 5th, 1914 49
    Recoil to the Aisne.

IV. OCTOBER 5th–NOVEMBER 15th, 1914 68
    Race for the Sea—La Cordonnerie.

V. NOVEMBER 16th, 1914–AUGUST 17th, 1915 . . . 95
    Houplines, Bois Grenier—Work and Play.

VI. AUGUST 18th–OCTOBER 15th, 1915 141
    Béthune–La Bassée—Loos.

VII. OCTOBER 16th, 1915–APRIL 8th, 1916 164
    Béthune–La Bassée—Working.

VIII. APRIL 9th–JULY 6th, 1916 192
    Béthune–La Bassée—Eruptions.

IX. JULY 7th–AUGUST 29th, 1916 222
    Somme–Ancre—High Wood.

X. AUGUST 30th–NOVEMBER 11th, 1916 256
    Somme–Ancre—Rest and Activity, Morval—Lesbœufs.

XI. NOVEMBER 11th, 1916–MARCH 17th, 1917 . . . 282
    Winter on the Somme.

CHAP.   PAGE

XII. MARCH 12th–APRIL 16th, 1917 306
     A Chapter in a Subaltern's Life.

XIII. APRIL 10th–JUNE 30th, 1917 324
     Arras—Hindenburg Line.

XIV. JULY 1st–SEPTEMBER 20th, 1917 362
     Echoes of Old Wars—Nieuport.

XV. SEPTEMBER 21st, 1917–JANUARY 26th, 1918 . . . 390
     The Ypres Salient—Polygon Wood, Messines, Pass-
     chendaele.

XVI. JANUARY 27th–MARCH 31st, 1918 439
     All Welsh—Bois Grenier.

XVII. APRIL 1st–AUGUST 22nd, 1918 461
     Ancre—In Wait.

XVIII. AUGUST 23rd–NOVEMBER 11th, 1918 510
     Going over Old Ground and New—Across the Sambre.

XIX. NOVEMBER 12th, 1918–JUNE 6th, 1919 571
     Going Home.

APPENDIX 585

INDEX 589

SKETCHES . . . . *at end*

GLOSSARY

A.A.&Q.M.G. Assistant Adjutant and Quartermaster-General : the chief administrative officer of a division ; deals with drafts, honours, leave, provisions, quarters, stores.

A.D.M.S. . . Assistant Director of Medical Services : the principal (administrative) medical officer of a division.

Axing . . . a R.W. term for peevish fussing.

Berm . . . a strip at the surface of a trench kept clear (supposedly) of the out-thrown soil of the parapet or parados.

Boxed. . . cut off by shells ; box-barrage.

B.M. . . . Brigade Major : the operations officer of a brigade.

B.G.G.S. . . Brigadier-General, General Staff : the chief operations officer of a Corps.

Camouflet . a charge exploded in a counter-mine to wreck enemy work.

Chesses . . planks laid on pontoons (*q.v.*) to make the surface of a bridge.

C.O. . . . Commanding officer of a unit.

Corduroy . . trunks of trees or logs laid side by side on spongy ground to make a firm surface.

Cosh . . . a wooden truncheon with a spiked iron head.

C.Q.M.S. . . Company Quartermaster-Sergeant : indents on, and collects from, the Quartermaster everything on issue to his company.

C.R.A. . . Officer Commanding Royal Artillery—of a division.

C.R.E. . . Officer Commanding Royal Engineers—of a division.

C.S.M. . . Company Sergeant-Major.

C.T. . . . communication trench.

D.A.D.O.S. . Deputy Assistant Director of Ordnance Supplies—of a division : issues clothing, ammunition, and other stores, but not rations, to the Quartermasters of units on indent.

Derbyite . . a volunteer conditionally exempt from calling up for training and service.

F.O.O. . . Forward Observing Officer : spots for the artillery and checks the shooting.

Formation . a brigade or larger mixed body able to operate independently.

G.H.Q. . . . General (or C.-in-C.'s) Headquarters : may mean the place, the Staff as a whole, or one of its offices, according to the context.

> (Army, Corps, Division, Brigade, and H.Q. have like shades of meaning.)

G.O.C. . . General Officer Commanding—a division in this text.

G.R.O. . . General Routine Order : issued by G.H.Q. (*q.v.*).

G.S.O. . . General Staff Officer of a division for operations (O. or 1), Intelligence (I. or 2), Training (T. or 3).

G.S. wagon . General Service—a 4-wheeled, 2-horse—wagon.

G.S.W. . . gunshot wound—is used of any missile wound.

H.E. . . . high explosive—of various composition.

M.G. . . . machine-gun : hence Machine-Gun Corps, M.G.C.

M.G.G.S. . . Major-General, General Staff : the chief operations officer of an Army, or next in rank to the Chief of Staff at G.H.Q. (*q.v.*).

O.C. . . . Officer Commanding—a battalion, battery, company or detachment.

Pontoons . . commonly boats or cylinders of metal moored across a stream as the supports of a bridge (see Chesses).

Red Cap . . worn by the police of a garrison or division, hence military policeman.

Red Tab . . a strip of Royal Scarlet worn on the coat lapel by Staff Officers.

R.F.C. . . Royal Flying Corps—later R.A.F., Royal Air Force.

R.Q.M.S. . Regimental Quartermaster-Sergeant : next in rank to the R.S.M. (*q.v.*) and chief of the Quartermaster's staff.

R.S.M. . . Regimental Sergeant-Major : the senior non-commissioned officer.

R.T.O. . . Railway Transport Officer.

Small Arms . rifle, Lewis gun and M.G.

S.A.A. . . small-arms ammunition.

S.C. . . . Staff Captain : the administrative officer of a brigade.

Train . . . the transport of a brigade, division or other formation : it does not include the transport of a battery, battalion or other unit.

Unit . . . *e.g.* a battery of artillery, battalion of infantry or company of Royal Engineers.

18-pounder . the British field-gun.

13-pounder . the British horse-artillery gun.

·75 . . . . the French field-gun.

·77 . . . . the German field-gun.

SKETCHES FROM MAPS

These are mainly freehand sketches, so scale is only approximate. Sheet 1 is reproduced with the permission of John Bartholomew & Son, Edinburgh; all the other Sheets are reproduced from Ordnance and Official History Maps with the permission of the Controller of H.M. Stationery Office. To these thanks are due, also to A. L. Kent, Esq., formerly of the Royal Welch Fusiliers, for much-needed technical advice and generous help in making ready the sketches for printing.

1. The Channel: B.E.F. Area of Operations, Chief Bases and Communications (diagrammatic).
2. Mons to the Aisne—Retreat.
3. Retreat continued: Recoil: Move to Flanders.
4. St. Omer–Laventie.
5. Armentières–Béthune.
6. La Cordonnerie–Fauquissart.
7. Bois Grenier (Wez Macquart).
8. Béthune–La Bassée.
9. Cambrai and Cuinchy Trenches, 1915.
10. Givenchy Trenches, 1915–16.
11. Amiens–Péronne–Bapaume–Doullens.
12. Middle Somme and Ancre.
13. High Wood–Lesbœufs.
14. High Wood, July 25th, 1916.
15. Morval–Lesbœufs, 1916–18.
16. Arras–Doullens.
17. Gommecourt: Cojeul and Sensée Valleys, Hénin.
18. Hindenburg Line–Croisilles.
19. Nieuport: Dunkirk–Passchendaele.
20. Ypres–Messines.
21. Polygon Wood, September 26th, 27th, 1917: Ypres Salient.
22. Ancre, Albert.
23. Ancre—Two Raids.
24. Ancre Crossing.
25. Lesbœufs–Sailly-Saillisel, September 1st, 1918.
26. Le Cateau: Villers-Outreaux, October 8th, 1918.
27. Forest of Mormal–Aulnoye.

CONTRIBUTORS

ROYAL WELCH FUSILIERS

AINGE, D. A. L., Lieutenant
ATTWATER, A., Captain
BERNERS, R. A., Brigadier-General
BLAIR, H., Captain
BOREHAM, A., Regimental Sergeant-Major
BRIERCLIFFE, R. D., Captain
CHARLTON, G. H., Lieutenant-Colonel
CHICK, F., Captain
CLEGG-HILL, The Hon. C. R., Brevet Lieutenant-Colonel
    —Viscount Hill
COCKBURN, J. B., Colonel
CRABTREE, C. P., Lieutenant
CRAWSHAY, C. H. R., Lieutenant-Colonel
CROCKETT, H. L., Captain
DAVIES, G. H. PICTON, Captain
EVANS, HOWELLS, Captain
EVANS, LLEWELYN, Captain
FLETCHER, W. G., 2nd Lieutenant
FOX, W., Captain
GEIGER, G. J. P., Major
GREAVES, E. J., Captain
GREAVES, RALPH, Lieutenant
HIGGINSON, J. V., Captain
HOLMES, W. G., Major-General
HUGHES, F. M., Lieutenant
JONES, C., Lieutenant and Quartermaster
JONES, CUTHBERT, Captain
JONES, E. R., Chaplain
JONES, W. MORGAN, Signaller
KEARSLEY, E. R., Major
KENT, A. L., Corporal
KIRKBY, W. W., Captain
MOODY, P., Captain
MORGAN, D. ROBERTS, Captain
MOSTYN, Bart., Sir PYERS, Captain
NICKSON, J. E., Captain
NORMAN, C. C., Brigadier
OWEN, C., Brigadier-General
POWELL, F., Regimental Quartermaster-Sergeant

RADCLIFFE, H. DELMÉ, Lieutenant-Colonel
RADFORD, N. H., Captain
RICHARDS, F., Private
RICHARDSON, —, Lieutenant
ROBERTS, Owen M., Lieutenant
RODERICK, P. B., Regimental Sergeant-Major
SASSOON, S. L., Captain
STOCKWELL, C. I., Brigadier-General
TURNER, H., Lieutenant
WARD, V. W., Lieutenant
WILLIAMS, O. DE L., Brigadier-General
YATES, H., Major

ROYAL FIELD ARTILLERY

GREEN, G. R. A., Major

ROYAL FUSILIERS

ARMOUR, R., Regimental Sergeant-Major
FYSON, H. H., Captain
MODERA, F. S., Major

THE CAMERONIANS

DOCHERTY, C., Company Sergeant-Major
SMITH, H. C. HYDE, Lieutenant-Colonel

5TH SCOTTISH RIFLES

COLTART, J. S., Captain
CROMBIE, —, Captain
KENNEDY, A., Colonel
McKAY, D., Private
SMITH, —, Lance-Corporal
SPENS, H. B., Colonel
SPENS, T., Captain

All dates and places have been checked with Regimental Records, and a few Orderly Room details have been taken from Records.

ACKNOWLEDGEMENTS

I was fortunate enough to purchase a copy of *The War the Infantry Knew* for £1.00 in a second-hand bookshop in Edinburgh in 1974. At the time I did not realize what a rare volume I had acquired, until my friend and colleague John Keegan fell upon it and spoke eloquently and enthusiastically about its importance. Since then I have had reason to refer to it on numerous occasions when writing about the British Army and the First World War.

It has taken several years to arrange a reprint of *The War the Infantry Knew*, and in doing this I found that I have been on the trail of the elusive, anonymous editor, Dr. Dunn. On 6 June 1948 Dunn formally transferred the copyright of *The War the Infantry Knew* to the Colonel of the Royal Welch Fusiliers and his successors. The present Colonel of the Royal Welch Fusiliers, Brigadier A. C. Vivian, C.B.E., A.D.C., has kindly given permission for this reprint. Major Tim Herbert, Regimental Secretary, Brian Finchett-Maddock, Curator of the Regimental Museum and Norman Holme, Regimental Archivist, have given me considerable assistance. Lieutenant-Colonel Richard Sinnett has generously shared with me his own knowledge of regimental history. Recently, Beryl Graves kindly donated Dunn's letters to her late husband to the Regimental Archives. Siegfried Sassoon's poem, 'A Footnote on the War (On Being Asked to contribute to a Regimental History), is taken from *The War Poems* Faber and Faber 1983, by kind permission of Sir Rupert Hart-Davis and George Sassoon. Others who have assisted me include Brigadier L. C. Dunn, Anne-Lucie Norton, Alistair Mackenzie, Peter Scott, Rod Suddaby and Mike Willis. Whilst a member of the Department of War Studies and International Affairs, R.M.A. Sandhurst, I benefited from many delightful and informative conversations with my friends and former colleagues John Keegan and Richard Holmes.

The primary sources used for the introduction to *The War the Infantry Knew* include the Dunn–Sassoon and the Dunn–Graves

correspondence held in the Archives of the Royal Welch Fusiliers
at Caernarvon, and the Dunn–Blunden correspondence held at
the Harry Ransom Humanities Research Center, The University
of Texas at Austin, U.S.A. Dunn was a prodigious correspondent who wrote over three hundred letters to his aunts during the
First World War. He kept a form of diary throughout the war,
and this, combined with his letters provided the basis for most of
the chronicle from August 1915 to May 1918. But it would appear
that neither the letters nor the diary have survived. Dunn was a
meticulous man, and in his very detailed will there is no mention
of these documents. His solicitor confirms that there were no
such letters or a diary found amongst his effects at the time of his
death. Probably he decided to destroy them, for as he wrote to
Graves on 25 October 1925, 'My diary contains many odd
jottings—too intimate to show anyone.' In the introduction, I
have attempted to unmask Dunn's anonymity to reveal a complex man, and explain his motives in compiling *The War the
Infantry Knew*.

Little Sandhurst   **Keith Simpson**
December 1986

INTRODUCTION

In the autumn of 1938 a book was published by P. S. King Ltd., entitled, *The War the Infantry Knew 1914–1919* A Chronicle of Service in France and Belgium with the Second Battalion His Majesty's Twenty-Third Foot, The Royal Welch Fusiliers: founded on personal records, recollections and reflections, assembled, edited and partly written by One of their Medical Officers. An expensive book at 21s., and with a limited edition of five hundred copies, nevertheless, it was enthusiastically reviewed in the national, regional and military press. On 23 January 1939, Llewelyn Wyn Griffith, author of *Up to Mametz* (1931), himself a former temporary officer in the Royal Welch Fusiliers, described *The War the Infantry Knew* in a BBC broadcast about 'Wales and New Books,' as 'one of the finest of all War books.' The consensus of opinion was that it was one of the very few books to really explain the everyday lives, events and feelings of the infantry during the First World War. The limited number of copies printed and the onset of another World War soon relegated *The War the Infantry Knew* to a scarce military classic. A reprint of *The War the Infantry Knew* is to be welcomed not only because it is a fascinating account of the history of a Regular infantry battalion during the First World War, but also because that battalion was fortunate in having within its ranks at one time or another three quite remarkable literary figures.

At the time of publication in 1938 of *The War the Infantry Knew*, the Royal Welch Fusiliers were well known through the literary endeavours of a number of distinguished men of letters and former professional soldiers who had served in one or other of its forty-two battalions during the First World War. Both Siegfried Sassoon and Robert Graves served with the Royal Welch Fusiliers, and personalities and incidents relating to the Second Battalion are to be found in Sassoon's *Memoirs of a Fox-Hunting Man* (1928) and *Memoirs of an Infantry Officer* (1930), and in Graves' *Goodbye to All That* (1929). The Second Battalion was fortunate also in having in its ranks one of the few pre-war Regular private soldiers who wrote his memoirs. Private Frank Richards' *Old Soldiers Never Die* (1933) is a marvellous account of life with the battalion seen from the perspective of a working-class Welsh private soldier. In 1936 he was to publish *Old Soldier Sahib*, and account of his service with the Second Battalion before the war in India and Burma.

Although published anonymously in 1938, for anyone who had read either Graves or Richards, it was possible to identify the editor of *The War the Infantry Knew*, who had modestly described himself as 'One of their Medical Officers,' as Captain James Churchill Dunn, D.S.O., M.C. and Bar, D.C.M., R.A.M.C. In *Goodbye to All That*, Graves had described Dunn as a 'hard-bitten man,' and that, 'the men were rather afraid of him, but had more respect for him than anyone else in the battalion.' Graves believed, 'he was far more than a doctor; living at battalion headquarters he became the right-hand man of three or four colonels in succession. When his advice was not taken this was usually afterwards regretted.'[1] Frank Richards wrote of Dunn, 'he was the bravest and coolest man under fire that I ever saw in France. . . . I always thought he was more cut out for a general than a doctor and that he certainly would have made a better one than most of those who were in France.'[2] Both Graves and Richards claim that Dunn temporarily "resigned" from the R.A.M.C. and took command of 2/R. Welch Fusiliers on 26 September 1917 when most of the battalion's senior officers had been killed or wounded. Sassoon referred to Dunn as "Munro" in *Memoirs of an Infantry Officer*, and described his modesty and dislike of publicity, writing, 'the Doctor is a man averse to the idea of being applauded in print, and he would regard any reference to his local renown as irrelevant to this narrative.'[3] And so it was Dr. Dunn, only a temporary officer in the R.A.M.C. and "attached" to the 2/R. Welch Fusiliers who was to painstakingly compile *The War the Infantry Knew*.

Dunn's father, Richard, came from a large family of Lanarkshire Coal Masters, and he emigrated to New Zealand in the 1860s where he married an Irish girl. James Dunn was born at Churchill, near Auckland, New Zealand, on 24 February 1871. Within three or four months Dunn's parents were killed during a

Maori uprising, but baby Dunn was discovered by a neighbouring sheep farmer, and sent back to Scotland to be brought up by his two spinster aunts. Dunn was educated at Hamilton Academy, Glasgow Academy and Clifton Bank, St. Andrews. In 1888 he began his medical studies at Edinburgh University, qualifying M.B. C.M. in 1893, having studied at Leipzig and Vienna in 1892. In 1897 he gained the additional qualification M.D. from Edinburgh, having spent the intervening years as a Research Assistant in Glasgow. Dunn then moved to London serving as a House Physician and later as Resident Medical Officer at the St. Pancras North Dispensary. It was whilst he was in London that he volunteered for military service during the South African War. As he later explained in a letter to Sassoon, 'In "Black Week" of December 1899 I quitted a scientific and mildly musical set [West London Medical Surgical Society] to enlist in the Yeomanry for service in South Africa.'[4]

It might appear strange that with his medical qualifications, Dunn did not volunteer for service as an army doctor, but he decided to join the Yeomanry and serve as a combatant soldier out of a sense of patriotism and adventure. Dunn served for over a year in South Africa as a trooper in the Montgomeryshire Yeomanry and was awarded the D.C.M. for bravery. In a history of the Montgomeryshire Yeomanry, Dunn is erroneously listed as having received a commission in the Army Medical Corps,[5] when in fact he served for a few months at the end of the war as a Civil Surgeon with the South African Field Force.

By 1903 Dunn was back in London working as a physician in a Lambeth hospital. In 1908 he received a Diploma in Public Health from the University of Cambridge. Before 1914 his address was Portland Square, London, where probably he was taking in private patients. After the outbreak of the war in August 1914, Dunn took several months to put his affairs in order before volunteering, at the age of forty-three, for military service. On 18 January 1915 he was commissioned as a temporary lieutenant in the R.A.M.C., and on 23 July 1915 he was posted to the 19th Field Ambulance, 19th Brigade in France. On 7 November 1915 he succeeded Captain Harbison as Regimental Medical Officer (R.M.O.) to the 2/R. Welch Fusiliers, a position he was to hold until he was temporarily incapacitated by gas on 22 May 1918.

After recovering from this in June 1918 Dunn asked to be transferred to another battalion as he could not work with the new
acting Commanding Officer, Dunn served, somewhat unhappily, with a Service battalion of the East Yorkshire Regiment in
the 31st Division until the end of the war.

Following the Armistice, Dunn returned to civil practice, moving to Glasgow to live with his aunts, and there he served as a
member of a Pensions Appeal Tribunal for those claiming War
Disability, and he gave evidence in 1922 to the War Office Committee Enquiry into "Shell Shock." Dunn continued to live in
Glasgow during his retirement, considered something of a local
celebrity, not least because of his association with the Royal
Welch Fusiliers. He maintained a lively correspondence with
many former members of the Regiment, and died aged eighty-
four on 30 March 1955.

James Churchill Dunn was a more complex man than he
superficially appeared. From Graves' description of him as a
'hard-bitten man' and his decorations for bravery, one might
suppose him to have been a tough, grizzled and somewhat
unsympathetic and reactionary man. And yet the portrait photograph of him in uniform taken at the end of the war reveals a
sensitive, intelligent face, rather drawn after his experiences,
partially obscured by a handle-bar moustache. Dunn was a loner,
who had been brought up by his spinster aunts, and he was to
remain a bachelor throughout his life. As he wrote to Edmund
Blunden following the death of his second aunt in 1939, 'Now I, a
solitary by nature, am learning what a width there is between
being alone & being lonely.'[6] Dunn was very conscious of being
brought up and moulded by these aunts and he felt drawn to
Sassoon, erroneously believing that he likewise had no memory
of his parents, writing to him. 'What I am is largely (how largely?)
the finished whole of "Aunt".'[7]

Llewelyn Evans, who served as a junior officer with the 2/R.
Welch Fusiliers, described Dunn in the regimental obituary as,
'reserved, reticient, and typically "Scotch," [who] made friends
warily; but once his friendship was won it was generously given
and sedulously maintained.'[8] This reserved, unassuming image
appears to be reinforced by Dunn's desire to remain the anonymous editor of The War the Infantry Knew, going so far as to restrict

his own named appearance to but three entries in the index. And yet this reserved, reticient, somewhat unemotional image is contradicted by Dunn's forceful and barbed opinions expressed in his surviving correspondence with Graves, Sassoon and Blunden. He preferred anonymity as editor as he genuinely abhorred publicity, and because he was very sensitive to the fact that he had only been an "attached" officer with the Royal Welch Fusiliers, and therefore felt constrained in expressing his opinions and making judgements in public about the regiment and its members.

This underlying passion and energy is reflected in Dunn's physical courage and the active role he took as R.M.O. He had been awarded the D.C.M. during the South African War, and this combined with his service as a ranker undoubtedly impressed all ranks of the 2/R. Welch Fusiliers. During his thirty months as R.M.O., Dunn was awarded a Mention in Despatches, the M.C. and Bar, and the D.S.O. The citations he received were for outstanding bravery in attending wounded under fire with complete disregard for his own life. Dunn's physical courage and the awards he received as an R.M.O. were not unique in the R.A.M.C. Dunn belonged to a generation which expected and valued physical courage above all other qualities, and during the First World War R.M.Os. served at the front and were expected to move forward with the firing line. Dunn was no laggard in this respect, but even amongst a generation of R.M.Os. who were noted for their physical courage, Dunn had a reputation for being always in the firing line, and, furthermore, going out patrolling and at times engaging in activities which were not really compatible with his non-combatant status.

As R.M.O. Dunn did not serve continuously in the forward trenches. He was attached to battalion HQs, and for quiet periods lived with the HQs staff to the rear of the trench system. But Dunn was frequently out visiting the companies and platoons, and was invariably present during a raid, bombardment or attack. During an attack the R.M.O. would organize the Regimental Aid Post in the front line, which might be sited in a dug-out, a cellar, in a sunken road, support trench or even a shell-hole. There, in theory, the R.M.O. attended the sick and wounded brought in by the regimental stretcher bearers. In practice, Dunn, like other

R.M.Os. did not wait for the wounded to be brought in, but went forward with orderlies and stretcher bearers tending to the wounded under fire. Dunn was very fortunate, in that, apart from the effects of gas in May 1918, he was never wounded during thirty months service with the 2/R. Welch Fusiliers. To others, Dunn appeared a calm and stable figure, moving with ease amongst the horrors and carnage of war. Sassoon recalled going up the line on 16 April 1917 and meeting Dunn who, 'was strolling along the trench with the detached air of an amateur botanist.'[9] Richards observed of Dunn's behaviour during an attack on 27 May 1917, that, he 'had been wandering about no-man's land attending to the wounded and doing what he could for them. How he didn't get riddled was a mystery. Some of the men who did not know him so well as the rest of us were saying that he was fed up with life and was doing his level best to get killed.'[10]

Dunn rejected the assertion made by Graves that he had assumed temporary command of the 2/R. Welch Fusiliers on 26 September 1917. In a letter to Graves on 16 November 1929 Dunn wrote that the description of his activities on that day in *Goodbye to All That* showed that, 'Legends are always livelier than fact.'[11] But whatever motive lay behind Dunn's protestations, there appears to be little doubt that effectively he did take command for a few hours. Richards confirms Graves' account, and in a letter to Sassoon on 1 March 1929, Dunn admitted to having fired a machine gun on that day, writing, 'I was the "unskilled enthusiast" of p. 343 of the RWF history.' ['when the medical officer got up, Williams, who had remained in command of his company, was sent to hospital. Colquhoun, whose wound was not severe, remained longer and directed an unskilled enthusiast how to handle an abandoned German machine gun, until it jammed.'][12] These unofficial combatant activities would appear to be confirmed by Richards' claim that when "Tibs" Crawshay, the C.O. of the 2/R. Welch Fusiliers, was wounded on 25 January 1917, whilst out on a night patrol with the aim of capturing a German patrol in no-man's land, he had been accompanied by Dunn. Dunn does not include his own participation in the day's entry in *The War the Infantry Knew*.[13]

Dunn's age, experience, physical courage and strength of

character made him an influential figure within the battalion. Amongst the rank and file, neither "Old Sweats" nor young conscripts could attempt to "swing the lead" with Dunn, whilst numerous young officers during and after the war, including both Graves and Sassoon, turned to him for advice and comfort. Dunn was old enough to be their father, and as a bachelor he took pleasure in their comradeship and sexless love. Although Dunn dismissed Graves' claim that, 'he became the right-hand man of three or four colonels in succession. When his advice was not taken this was usually afterwards regretted,'[14] nevertheless, through his position as R.M.O. and his personality Dunn was influential.

Dunn's experience as R.M.O. of the 2/R. Welch Fusiliers was moving and vivid and remained with him to the end of his life. At the age of seventy-one he wrote to Graves, 'My time with the R.W.F. remains a live experience; faces & figures are remembered, but the names attached to them keep dropping off.'[15] It was through compiling *The War the Infantry Knew*, or 'the chronicle,' as he was to call it, that Dunn was able to use his wartime observations and experiences and to bring to life the 2/R. Welch Fusiliers.

The origins of *The War the Infantry Knew* lay in the preparations made during the 1920s for the Regimental History of the Royal Welch Fusiliers. A regimental committee under Lieutenant-Colonel C. I. Stockwell was appointed in 1925 to gather material and select an editor to write the volume on France and Flanders. Dunn enthusiastically became involved in collecting material on the Second Battalion because of his length of service with them and the fact that he had kept diaries and notes at the time. Within a few months Dunn was criticising the way in which the material was being acquired and the shortcomings of an early draft. In October 1925 he submitted to Stockwell a suggested syllabus for the Second Battalion section which forcefully and clearly outlined his approach to writing a regimental history. Dunn argued that what was required was as much personal recollection as possible from as many officers, N.C.Os. and other ranks, Regular and Temporary of both Regular battalions. 'If only they will realise that nothing is too trivial to send in, the mass will yield some gems and alot of illuminating observations that otherwise will be

lost, but, by inclusion, will make a real biography—that is what is
wanted—of two battalions that were living things and that still
live.'[16] He was critical of other regimental histories which merely
documented events and were very selective in fact and comment,
and failed to explain what "ordinary trench life" was really like.
He stressed the need for a wide perspective of the war as seen by
an infantry battalion, including details of trench life, raids and
battles, billeting, delousing, the local population, types of
recruits, morale, rations, humour and entertainments.

Dunn was fearful that the brilliant military record of the First
Battalion would detract from the less conspicuous role of the
Second, which had, nevertheless, displayed, 'a maximum of
endurance and sacrifice and a minimum of spectacular renown.'[17]

Dunn had written to many former officers, N.C.Os. and other
ranks who had served in the Second Battalion soliciting diaries,
letters, notes and comments. As he explained in a letter to Graves,
'The idea is to make the history something between a popularly
written text book that can be used for purposes of instructing
recruits, & a real good story of the life lived by the men from
mobilisation to armistice. There cannot be too many
contributors—my fear is that Stockwell is not going to cast his net
nearly wide enough—but individual contributors are to be treated
as raw material for an edition to put into good narrative form.'[18]
Dunn contacted more and more veterans as he began to fill in the
gaps of the weeks, months and years of the war attempting to
relive the history of the Second Battalion. In February 1926 Dunn
wrote to Sassoon asking him for an account of his short period of
service with the battalion in March–April 1917. Initially, Sassoon
felt unable to respond, and instead wrote the poem, 'A Footnote
on the War' (On Being Asked to Contribute to a Regimental
History).[19]

> A Lenten blackbird singing in the square
> Has called me to my window, Thence one sees
> Sunshine—pale shadows cast by leafless trees—
> And houses washed with light. One hears out there
> A Sunday-morning patter of pacing feet,
> And Time, in drone of traffic, drifting down the street.
> When I was out in France, nine years ago,
> The Front was doubly-damned with frost and snow:
> Troops in the trenches cowered on the defensive,

While the smug Staff discussed the Spring Offensive.
Rest-camps, though regions where one wasn't killed,
Were otherwise disgusting: how we hated
Those huts behind Chipilly! Drafts we drilled
Were under-sized arrivals from belated
Chunks of the population wrongly graded
As fit for active service. No one cursed
The weight of an equipment more than they did,
Poor souls! I almost think they were the worst
Soldiers who ever gulped battalion stew;
And how they fired their rifles no one knew.

We'd got a Doctor with a D.S.O.
And much unmedalled merit. In the line
Or out of it, he'd taught the troops to know
That shells, bombs, bullets, gas, or even a mine
Heaving green earth toward heaven, were things he took
For granted, and dismissed with one shrewd look.
No missile, as it seemed, could cause him harm.
So on he went past endless sick-parades;
Jabbed his inoculation in an arm;
Gave "medicine and duty" to all shades
Of uninfectious ailment. Thus his name
Acquired a most intense, though local fame.

Now here's his letter lying on my table,
Reminding me that, by some freak of chance,
He sauntered through three years of gory France
Unshot. And now, as amply as he's able,
He's quietly undertaken to compile
His late battalion's history. Every mile
They marched is safely stored inside his head . . .
I visualize the philosophic smile
That mask his wounding memories of the dead.
He asked me to contribute my small quota
Of reminiscence, What can I unbury? . . . .
Seven years have crowded past me since I wrote a
Word on a war that left me far from merry.
And in those seven odd years I have erected
A barrier, that my soul might be protected
Against the invading ghosts of what I saw
In years when Murder wore the mask of Law.

Well—what's the contribution I can send?
Turn back and read what I've already penned
So jauntily. There's little left to say . . .
I'm not the man I was. Nine years have passed;
And though the legs that marched survive today,

My Fusiliering self has died away;
His active service came and went too fast.

He kept a diary. Reading what he wrote
Like some discreet executor I find
The scribbled entries moribund—remote
From the once-living context of his mind.
He wrote as one who craved to leave behind
A vivid picture of his personality
Foredoomed to swift extinction. He'd no craft
To snare the authentic moments of reality;
His mind was posing to be photographed:
"*If I should die*". . . . His notebook seldom laughed.

The distant Doctor asks me to report
That morning "when the Bosche attacked the Block,"
When my detachment functioned to support
Some Cameronians who had "got the knock" . . .
Our own artillery fire was dropping short;
A sniper shot me through the neck; the shock
Is easy to remember. All the rest
Of what occurred that morning has gone west.
"The battle and the sunlight and the breeze;
Clouds blowing proud like banners;" lines like these
Were written in the way by many a poet
Whose words range false, although he didn't know it.
The battle and the breeze were up that morning
For my detachment, stiff and chilled and yawning,
When out from underground they swore and stumbled;
The sun shone bright; intense bombardments grumbled,
And from their concrete-nests machine-guns rattled—
In fact the whole Brigade was properly embattled.

But how can I co-ordinate this room—
Music on piano, pictures, shelves of books,
And Sunday morning peace—with him for whom
Nine years ago the world wore such wild looks?
How can my brain join up with the plutonian
Cartoon? . . . The trench; and a fair-haired Cameronian
Propped in his pool of blood while we were throwing
Bombs at invisible Saxons . . . War's a mystery
Beyond my retrospection. And I'm going
Onward, away from that Battalion history
With all its expurgated dumps of dead:
And what remains to say I leave unsaid.

Almost immediately Sassoon relented and sent Dunn a twelve-page account, taken from his diaries. This was to form unedited, eventually, Chapter XII of *The War the Infantry Knew*, entitled, 'A Chapter in a Subaltern's Life.' By the time it was published Sassoon had incorporated it into *Memoirs of an Infantry Officer*.

Based on individual contributions submitted to him, and his own diaries, Dunn produced a manuscript of 70,000 words on the Second Battalion. The "Regimental Mandarins" gave Dunn permission to publish his manuscript on the Second Battalion, but after the regimental history was finished, the only condition being that his work was not to be called a "history." Dunn forwarded his manuscript to Dudley Ward, the editor of the regimental history. But when the volume was published in 1928, Dunn was bitterly disappointed. Although some of his material had been used, Dunn claimed that the history was full of factual errors, and that Ward had failed to use the best contributions. Dunn blamed the "Regimental Mandarins," commenting tartly, 'No men could have done worse staff work on a book of intense interest,' and writing of Ward, that he was, 'a good natured, lethargic grand man with no literary or technical qualification.'[20]

Sassoon asked Dunn if he could see the manuscript, and Dunn replied, 'The only notes I have are a diary I alone can decipher and the (a) disjointed notes, (b) drafts & (c) more carefully compiled portions of what I sent to Ward. More than half is reliably my own, the rest I collected. My intention is to rewrite to please myself, including matter it was useless or impolitic to submit for the purpose of a regimental history for contemporary publication. For instance you will see that personalities were almost entirely omitted, whether for praise or blame.'[21] Sassoon passed on sections of Dunn's manuscript to Edmund Blunden, author of *Undertones of War* (1928), who had served as a temporary officer with the 11/R. Sussex Regiment. He wrote to Dunn full of enthusiasm for what he had read and imploring him to publish the manuscript notes. Blunden wrote that both he and Sassoon, 'independently felt that they constitute easily the best record of the B.E.F. experiences, from the B.E.F. point of view, that has yet been made; and a very little modification and abbreviation of the mechanical & "family" details so necessary to those who were there, or in a similar history, will make them a book that anybody may read with pleasure and advantage. The elements in which you excel are (1) general knowledge of war and peace, providing an immense quantity of illustration and reflection (2) detachment, which even in the most shattering moments kept your long view of things clear, & made you "take notes" (3) a thorough comprehension of the rank and file (4) extreme accuracy and suitability of expression. Pardon me for raining my jargon on you; even now I haven't displayed all that I felt of admiration and gratitude.' Dunn pencilled against this, 'Blunden ought to blush with me at this para.'[22] And well he might have under the circumstances.

Although Blunden genuinely believed that Dunn's manuscript deserved to be published on merit, he had another purpose in mind in writing such a flattering letter of encouragement. A month before, on 18 November 1929, Robert Graves' *Goodbye to All That* had been published. Immediately it caused a storm of personal, literary and historical controversy.[23] Sassoon's first reaction at seeing an advance copy sent to him by Blunden, was one of hysterical rage. He was furious that Graves had included an unpublished poem without his permission and had publicised intimate details about his mother and his own breakdown during the war. Because of the breach of copyright, Jonathan Cape the publishers had to withdraw as many copies as they could of the first edition and remove Sassoon's poem. Blunden was motivated probably by envy of Graves which prompted him to encourage Sassoon's righteous indignation. In the bitter recriminations between Sassoon and Graves, Blunden was anxious to enlist the support of Dunn who was mentioned in *Goodbye to All That*. In the same letter of encouragement to Dunn, Blunden wrote of Graves, that, 'it's a crying shame that a man who had been regarded as a very fine specimen of a Modern Poet should now associate that title in the public mind with his latrine bucket.'[24]

Eventually, Dunn was only too willing to take the part of Sassoon and Blunden against Graves. Dunn had been sent an advance copy of *Goodbye to All That*, and was not impressed by what he had read. He wrote a long letter to Graves on 16 November 1929 pointing out a number of factual errors and gently chiding him for hyperbole. It was not an unfriendly letter, and so Dunn was all the more annoyed and embarrassed when Graves quoted from this personal letter in an article he wrote for the *Daily Mail* refuting some of the criticisms of *Goodbye to All That*. Dunn was particularly annoyed to be caught up in a controversy surrounding the alleged cowardice of Scottish soldiers during the battle for High Wood on the Somme in 1916. As he resided in Glasgow he feared that he would be contacted by the local press. Graves felt obliged to answer his critics in, *But It Still Goes On*, published in 1930. When *Goodbye to All That* was republished in 1957, Graves made a number of corrections and amendments, and admitted in the prologue that it was a wonder how his publishers had escaped a libel action in 1929.

Dunn was critical of Graves and what he had written for a number of reasons. Dunn, the literal man, found Graves the literary man, prone to factual inaccuracies, hyperbole and distortion of the truth.[25] Dunn objected to Graves' caricaturing many of the officers of the Royal Welch Fusiliers, 'who fell short of his moral & cultural standards: as a poet he saw all (& himself included) with complete detachment & naturally as sportsmen who would not understand him. O Lord! O Lord!! The best of us deceive themselves, but a man more wrong-headed—arrogantly wrong-headed.'[26] Dunn did not understand that *Goodbye to All That* was a mixture of autobiography and literary fiction. He dismissed it as a work of literature, 'It is not that RG's writing has any literary quality. The structure is good, but the text is just good average journalism.'[27] He believed that *Goodbye to All That* gave a distorted and exaggerated view of the war, the life of the infantry, and in particular, the 2/R. Welch Fusiliers. To Dunn, Graves had shown himself by writing *Goodbye to All That*, 'insincere, catchpenny & deplorably wanting in taste.'[28] Although Graves gave Dunn permission to use *Goodbye to All That* as a source for his own work and offered additional material, this was not taken up. As Dunn wrote to Sassoon after *The War the Infantry Knew* had been published, 'There was nothing I *could* use; I did not add that I feared the tone of anything he might send, & the unpleasantness of rejecting anything from him.'[29]

Thus it was a combination of motives and influences, including his own disappointment with the regimental history and the encouragement of Sassoon and Blunden, that persuaded Dunn to prepare his manuscript for publication. Dunn was provoked also by what he regarded as the sensational and 'catchpenny nature of so much of contemporary output [about the war] & the one sidedness of nearly all—the lurid side that gives a delicious shudder or excites a sexual reflex no less deliciously.'[30] Graves stand admonished. 'I don't want the moods of the officers & men of the front-line dished up second hand in the manner of Phillip Gibb & Beach Thomas: nor distorted by facts and notions acquired after the war, there is that in Mottram: nor ridiculed & caricatured by savage disillusion & revolt: nor mellowed to a form of art.'[31]

Through his correspondence with Sassoon and Blunden between 1928 and 1938 it is possible to see how Dunn edited the chronicle, to understand his concern about style and to follow his motivation in writing a book about 'the war the infantry knew.' Although Dunn was to consult over fifty former officers, N.C.Os. and other ranks of the 2/R. Welch Fusiliers and other regiments, 'From Laventie in Aug 1915 to May 23rd 1918 the great bulk of the stuff is mine.'[32] Dunn was determined to capture the mood and atmosphere of the war years as experienced at the time, and not written up long after the event. He was critical even of Blunden, who had acknowledged in the preface to *Undertones of War*, that, 'a fragmentary account of his experience, written nearer the date of the events, was different in tone from his published account. Events of the war years described more in the mood of the war years is what I wo[d] like to read. I wo[d] like to see that fragment. The "forced gaiety" which today Blunden thinks "depressing" was the atmosphere of the events he writes about.'[33]

Dunn was aware of how difficult it was to 'get a correct account of an action from one man's observation. My opportunities of knowing the facts of many events were exceptional. I was often an actor witness & usually had HQ information. My habit was to make notes within hours of occurrences & later on to correct & expand them from other witness-actors' recollections & notes.'[34] Responding to comments from Sassoon and Blunden, and prompted by his own intense desire to accurately represent the real attitudes and feelings expressed during the war, Dunn continued to re-draft his manuscript. 'As I disliked many passages into which I had expanded my diary telegraphese I looked up the letters my old Aunt's death had restored to me, & found in them fuller, better versions & written in billets & dugouts in the mood of the time. The years between seem to blur outline & deepen shadow.'[35] In the original draft manuscript, Dunn had written up all the contributions based on letters, diaries and reminiscences as a narrative, but he decided to restore it to the form of a diary, supplemented by memoir, 'to preserve the book as far as possible, as an expression of the personal experiences & feelings of the number of men writing at first hand from the battalion point of view—the view of the time, with a minimum of afterthought if any at all.'[36]

Dunn asked Blunden to 'ruthlessly blue-pencil' the manuscript draft he forwarded in 1933. He was conscious that he had included too much material, and was doubtful about his own contribution. But then, 'It all interested me or I co[d] not have made a jotting, wo[d] not have written home about the scenery, political points & little bits of economics that had a very close bearing on the war, & that affected us collectively & individually at the front; the scenes in which we fought & rested; our food; bits of play; types of men; characters among them; the sort of C.O. we had; historic ground we trod—if we knew it—were all bits of the "war we knew": our collective & personal reactions *at the time* were very big bits of it.'[37] Dunn wanted to correct the popular notion of war and the experience of the infantry, 'I do not hunger after authorship or editorship. I do want to publish the work because it is the most complete & dispassionate biography of a battalion throughout the war I know. It gives relaxation & jollity & mere boredom their place alongside hardship & bloodshed, it shows the condition & the mind of the Battalion at different times & it gives glimpses— some of my own mostly—of the many interests there were for such as looked around with open eyes. Think of a man like Stockwell noting in his diary how poplars seen by moonlight impressed him.'[38]

As he was to write in the preface of *The War the Infantry Knew*, 'war in the battle zone between antagonists of equal tenacity and resource is prolonged drudgery—that is what many people say about life in general—but drudgery with fearful moments: and, as in everyday life, there is very much that is trivial, or seems so. War is neither a glitter of high lights nor a slough of baseness, it calls forth the best that is in the human spirit: its worst aspects are found far from the battle-line.' Dunn attempted to put actual battle into the total experience of the 'war the infantry knew.' 'I have found that even intelligent people have the strangest idea of a battle as a battalion wages battle: to them it is hours of physical exertion & of maiming. 5, 10, 15, 30 minutes of activity & 23 hours & 30, 45, 50, 55 minutes of idleness during which there are noises on or off & there may be accidents, are scarcely credited.'[39]

As the years passed and Dunn continued to tinker with his manuscript he was under no illusion about the difficulty of getting it published, writing to Sassoon in January 1936, 'I am very doubtful if the book could be published to sell; the interested public is too small; the book can't be cheap, for the length must be around 250,000 words & a number of maps are necessary.'[40] Sassoon continued to try and interest publishers, but, as Dunn feared, although it was thought that the manuscript was interesting and should be preserved, perhaps at the British Museum or War Office, no commercial publication was possible.[41] So it was to the credit of Dunn's perseverance and Sassoon's steadfastness that the lengthy manuscript was published finally in 1938, even if it was a limited edition and by a small publisher.

Dunn had no literary pretensions, and *The War the Infantry Knew* was not subjected to the usual process which writers used, to such good effect, to dramatize, polish and in many instances re-arrange and highlight the events which they describe in order to increase the dramatic effect. If there is a break in style, then it reflects the fact that the period from August 1915 to May 1918 is largely based on Dunn's diaries, letters and personal recollections, whilst the earlier and later periods of the war draw upon other men's material. Dunn's very low key approach to the narrative explained in the preface as, 'plain has been preferred to coloured in the telling of an incident,' does tend to put everyday events and great moments of action and horror into perspective, although his restraint over certain incidents is more than understatement. For instance, the entry for 20 August 1916, 'In the morning Dolling and his C.S.M. were killed by a shell: a great loss,' covers Dunn's own personal distress at the loss of two men he greatly admired.

Dunn had been very concerned to maintain the language and style of each contributor, and it is to his credit that he used a number of N.C.Os. and other ranks, usually conspicious by their absence from regimental histories. Dunn's own interest in people, the countryside, the weather and little incidents is reflected throughout the chronicle. *The War the Infantry Knew* has a magnificently detailed index with entries that will delight the reader—anecdotes, birds, canteens, chilblains, the names of estaminets, games, landscape, newspapers, restaurants and cafés, rumour, scrounging and trench names. Dunn succeeded in bringing to life the atmosphere and the mood of any particular period of the war, which is often at variance with either contemporary official accounts or later reminiscences. *The War the Infantry Knew* is not a long monologue of battle and suffering; it reflects the total breadth of experiences of an infantry battalion over four years of active service in Belgium and France. It shows how the war changed and how the 2/R. Welch Fusiliers adapted to different circumstances. Certain incidents, not important in the total context of the British military effort on the Western Front, were quite momentous at the time for those serving with the battalion. The blowing of the Red Dragon Crater and the ensuing counterattack in June 1916 is one example.

Of course, *The War the Infantry Knew* does reflect Dunn's own prejudices, however hard he tried to conceal them through understatement. Dunn had a great admiration and affection for the professionalism of 'the Old Army,' the pre-war Regulars, and a corresponding low opinion of the Territorials and the Kitchener volunteers. He associated himself with the judgement and prejudices of 'the Old Army,' with comments about 'indifferently officered Territorials' and the nickname, "Chocolate Fusiliers," given to the 20/R. Fusiliers on account of the size of their food parcels sent from home and their liking for sweet things. Like many men who served with the infantry, Dunn was extremely critical of the operational and administrative incompetence of divisional and corps commanders and their staffs, and he waxed lyrical against the support and service branches of the army behind the lines, along with "shirkers," politicians and the home front.

But Dunn was sensitive to the effects of stress on the infantry, and although he had no sympathy for malingerers and "shirkers," he attempted to give aid and comfort to those who were temporarily unable to stand the strain. Dunn's own loss of confidence and depression can be documented from even before the traumatic events of 26 September 1917. As he wrote to Blunden after reading through the completed draft of the chronicle in 1934, 'I thought that some of the heavy going in the winter of 1916/17 reflected the depressing effect of recurring influenza attacks & a throat that did not clear up.'[42] That combined with his dislike of the then Commanding Officer is strikingly obvious. In fact by 1917/18 Dunn was worn out through physical and mental stress. Another R.M.O. who had a similar experience to Dunn's of lengthy service with an infantry battalion later wrote, 'But the revolt that grew in my heart against the killing business—the constant fret of casualties—was another story. The battalion kept changing, seven Colonels came and went and I could never school myself to grow indifferent to these gaps. They left wounds which even now are hardly healed and my own decline in morale in the last months of the winter of 1916–17—obvious enough to me though not, I think, to others—was probably the outcome of those wounds.'[43]

The War the Infantry Knew chronicles the experiences of 2/R. Welch Fusiliers from mobilization in 1914 to demobilization in 1919. It was not written for a wide commercial market, and Dunn assumed that his readers were familiar with the organization and history of the regiment, the broad details of the war on the Western Front, and would be able to identify the personalities briefly mentioned in the text or relegated to the index. For contemporary readers it is necessary to provide this background information to *The War the Infantry Knew*.

When Dunn became R.M.O. of the 2/R. Welch Fusiliers in November 1915, he joined one of the few Regular battalions of infantry still retaining a high proportion of its pre-war personnel. The Royal Welch Fusiliers had been in continuous existence since the Regiment was first raised in 1689 by William III to oppose James II. During the War of the Spanish Succession the Regiment was specially selected to be one of 'Welch' Fusiliers. Until then the Regiment had been known either by the name of its Commanding Officers or by its number, The 23rd of Foot. Eventually the Regiment became officially known as The Royal Welch Fusiliers, The 23rd of Foot. Initially only consisting of one battalion, the Regiment formed a Second Battalion during four periods of its history—1756–1758; 1804–1814; 1858–1948 and 1952–1957. Before 1914 the two battalions of the Regiment had participated in nearly every major British land engagement and colonial war since 1689.

Like other Regiments of the British Army, by 1914 the Royal Welch Fusiliers had acquired important customs and traditions important for ésprit de corps and frequently referred to in *The War the Infantry Knew*. All ranks wore 'The Flash' which easily identified any soldier as a Royal Welch Fusilier. It consisted of five black ribbons worn on the back of the collar and were a link with the days when soldiers wore pigtails which were enclosed in what was known as a "queue bag." When the "queue" was abolished in 1808 the Regiment was serving abroad and on returning to Britain in 1834 retained the ribbons of the "queue" or Flash on their uniform. Despite attempts by the military authorities to get the Flash removed, William IV granted permission for it to be worn. The Royal Welch Fusiliers were noted also for having a Goat paraded for ceremonial occasions. The Goat, never referred to as a mascot, was provided usually from the Royal Goat Herd. The Regular battalions and most of the Territorial battalions each had a Goat looked after by an N.C.O., and the Goat sometimes accompanied the battalion on active service. St. David's Day has been celebrated in the Regiment since its foundation, in peace and war, with all ranks wearing the leek. The Regimental ceremonial of eating the leek remained unchanged over the years. In the officers' mess, the sergeants' mess and the soldiers' canteens, the latest joined officer, N.C.O. or soldier eats a leek and then toasts St. David. The Regiment tenaciously clung to the old English way of spelling "Welsh" with a "c," which finally received official confirmation by an Army Order in 1920.

In August 1914, the Royal Welch Fusiliers consisted of two Regular battalions, the First in Malta and the Second in Portland. The Third or Reserve Battalion was in Wrexham, but from May 1915 until November 1917 it was at Litherland, Liverpool, before being sent to Limerick in Ireland. There were also four battalions of the Territorial Force based in Wales. Before 1914 the two Regular battalions alternated between service at home and abroad, with the battalion at home under-strength. So on 4 August 1914, the 2/R. Welch Fusiliers had a strength of 20 officers and 580 other ranks, which after mobilization and the recalling of Reservists brought it up to 29 officers and 1066 other ranks.

Although the Third Battalion acted as a cadre, effectively during the war it became a recruit training depot for officers and other ranks who were then drafted to battalions of the Regiment at home or abroad depending upon requirements. During the First World War additional Territorial battalions were raised, and the "Service" battalions were formed from the Kitchener volunteers. As a result of casualties and the introduction of conscription, by 1917 there was little difference between the Regular, Territorial and Service battalions on active service.

Despite the Regimental connection between the two Regular battalions, each led a quite separate existence before 1914, and only rarely did officers and others ranks serve in a battalion other than their own. This encouraged very narrow loyalties and interests but sustained morale in battle. The Second Battalion had served for just over eleven years in India and Burma before the war. Life as experienced by a private soldier during that period can be seen in Frank Richards' *Old Soldier Sahib*.

Although ostensibly a Welsh Regiment, before 1914, it was nicknamed the "Birmingham Fusiliers" on account of the very high proportion of recruits from that city. Dunn calculated that in 1914 only ten per cent of the Second Battalion were Welsh, although this was to change during the war, so that by 1917, after conscription, the Welsh made up fifty per cent of the other ranks.[44] Before the war, the officers were middle class professional or landed gentry by background, many of them living in North Wales. Casualties and the expansion of the Regiment was to see an influx of temporary officers from a social and educational background quite at variance with this tradition. The relationship between officers and other ranks was strictly formal before the war. Frank Richards noted that the officers, 'were strict disciplinarians, in the sense that if they gave orders they expected unquestioning service, but they were far from treating us with contempt. The case was one of mutual trust in military matters and matters of sport, but no social contact.'[45]

When the 2/R. Welch Fusiliers was fully mobilized it consisted of a HQs company and four rifle companies, each having a fighting strength of about 200 soldiers. Attached to HQs company was a machine gun section. But the firepower of an infantry battalion depended upon the proficiency of its riflemen. The 2/R.

Welch Fusiliers landed at Rouen on 11 August and were deployed as Lines of Communication troops of the B.E.F. On 22 August, along with three other battalions, it was formed into the 19th Brigade, which acted as an independent unit throughout the retreat from Mons and the advance to the Aisne, being attached to first one and then another division. From 12 October 1914 until 31 May 1915, the 19th Brigade was attached to the 6th Division, and was then transferred to the 27th Division. It was attached to the 2nd Division from 19 August 1915 until 25 November 1915 when it became an integral part of the 33rd Division.

By the spring of 1916, with its manpower still largely consist-ing of Regulars or Reservists, the 2/R. Welch Fusiliers was regarded as "lucky" and quite unique. Unlike the First Battalion which had suffered heavy casualties during the First Battle of Ypres in October 1914—only 90 ranks left on 30 October—and at the Battles of Festubert—only 253 ranks left on 16 May 1915—the Second Battalion had suffered comparatively few. As late as 21 March 1916, General Haking, the Corps Commander, could be heard contratulating the C.O. of the Second Battalion on having such a high proportion of Regulars in the ranks. Graves was convinced that this lack of heavy casualties combined with the fact that the battalion had so recently returned from nearly eight-een years' service overseas meant that peacetime standards, social prejudices and draconian discipline were maintained long after they had disappeared in other Regular battalions.[46] Both Graves and Sassoon were unhappy serving with the Second in contrast to the First Battalion.[47] But their opinion should be treated with caution, as neither served with the Second Battalion for any length of time. Graves served with the Battalion from September to November 1915, when the C.O. had him transferred to the First Battalion. He then served with the Battalion from the 5th to 20 July 1916, when he was severely wounded. Finally, he served with the Second Battalion from 17 January to 22 February 1917, when he was invalided home with bronchitis. Sassoon's service was even briefer, from 11 March to 16 April 1917, when he was wounded. More than Sassoon, Graves was very arrogant and unconventional, and was calculated to appear abrasive and incon-siderate. Sassoon has left a vivid picture of Graves at this time, referring to him as "David Cromlech." 'At his best I'd always found him an ideal companion, although his opinions were often disconcerting. But no one was worse than he at hitting it off with officers who distrusted cleverness and disliked unreserved utterances. He was with our Second Battalion for a few months before they transferred him to "the First," and during that period the Colonel was heard to remark that young Cromlech threw his tongue a hell of a lot too much, and that it was about time he gave up reading Shakespeare and took to using soap and water. He had, however, added, 'I'm agreeably surprised to find that he isn't windy in trenches.'[48] In fact neither Graves nor Sassoon were typical representatives of the kind of temporary officers in the Royal Welch Fusiliers.

The Second Battalion's "luck" was soon destroyed during the Somme battles in 1916. The 19th Brigade frequently was held back and then used to press home attacks following failure by other brigades. The brigade was usually split up with its battalions being deployed piecemeal. The movements and engagements of the 2/R. Welch Fusiliers reveal the varied routine of an infantry battalion. Between December 1915 and July 1916 the battalion was engaged in trench warfare around Givenchy, Cuinchy and Cambrin; in July and August 1916 it fought at High Wood on the Somme before resting at Condé-Picquiqny in October. Between November and December the battalion was back on the Somme at Les Boefs, Guinchy and Clery. In March 1917, after a period of trench warfare, the battalion moved to Amiens, where between April and June it took part in the Arras offensive. In July there was a period of rest at Condé-Picquiqny on the Somme river, before a move north to Nieuport until September, when it fought at Polygon Wood and around Passchendaele during the Third Battle of Ypres. At the end of the year the battalion moved to the Messines-Neuve Eglise sector.[49]

Dunn was critical of both the commanders and staffs of the 19th Brigade and the 33rd Division. From June 1915 the commander of the 19th Brigade was Brigadier-General P. R. Robertson, who was promoted to command a division in July 1916, and was succeeded by Brigadier-General C. R. G. Mayne. Dunn's comment about the succession was, ' "dud to dud!!" '[50] He had very little time for Major-General H. J. S. Landon who commanded the 33rd Division until he was sacked on 23 September 1916.

Landon was succeeded by Major-General R. J. Pinney who failed also to impress Dunn. Pinney was an unfortunate divisional general in that he became a caricature thanks to Sassoon, who was inspired by him to write the poem, 'The General,' and thus he became the 'cheery old card' whose plan of attack did for Harry and Jack. Pinney was regarded as a crank by many of the soldiers under his command because of his dislike of the rum ration. In lieu of the rum ration he substituted tea which did not greatly impress cold and wet soldiers. Frank Richards, not noted as a tee-totaller, referred to him as, 'a bun-punching crank and more fitted to be in command of a Church Mission hut at the Base than a division of troops.'[51]

Due to manpower shortages G.H.Q. decided in January 1918 to reduce each brigade from four to three battalions. Many battalions were disbanded or amalgamated, and in the ensuing reshuffle, the 2/R. Welch Fusiliers were transferred from the 19th Brigade to the 115th Brigade in the 38th (Welsh) Division. Pinney had regarded the battalion as the most effective in the 19th Brigade, and the transfer was not a reflection on its fighting qualities, but rather the need to strengthen a weak brigade in another division. The 2/R. Welch Fusiliers had always been regarded as a very effective and aggressive battalion, although Dunn believed that its fighting qualities had declined by 1917.

Like other infantry battalions, the 2/R. Welch Fusiliers changed in organization and personnel during the war. The size of the battalion was reduced progressively during the war reflecting both the level of casualties and the introduction of new weapons. After the Somme in 1916 the battalion left behind out of the line a certain number of troops, known collectively as the Battle Surplus or the Minimum Reserve. It consisted of either the C.O. or the Second-in-Command, the Company Commanders or their Seconds-in-Command, and a proportion of N.C.Os. and specialist soldiers. The aim was to preserve a third of the battalion's specialists and to work on a platoon strength of twenty-eight. Thus in the event of the all too recurring heavy casualties there was a substantial cadre around which to re-build the battalion with new drafts. In 1915 the infantry acquired a variety of trench mortars, but these were removed eventually by March 1916 to brigade and division. An infantry battalion's heavy machine guns were gradually removed and replaced by sixteen Lewis guns.

Dunn was very critical of the fighting ability of the battalion during the last eighteen months of the war. He blamed the poor quality of the drafts, their lack of training, low morale and the absence of fighting spirit. Nevertheless, it was largely a conscript battalion which fought the successful battles of the summer and autumn of 1918, suffering proportionally high casualties. During the First World War the 2/R. Welch Fusiliers lost 39 officers and 1106 other ranks killed in action, more than the fully mobilized strength of the battalion in 1914. In contrast the First Battalion lost 43 officers and 1343 other ranks killed in action.[52] The regimental records do not include wounded and missing, but a fair estimate would be double those killed.

It is difficult for someone without military experience to realize just how important the personality, character, physical courage, professionalism and sheer leadership of a Commanding Officer is for an infantry battalion in war. Dunn was thoroughly convinced of this, noting on 31 January 1916, 'To a detached onlooker at close quarters the supreme importance of the character of a commanding officer to the efficiency of a battlion was strikingly shown. Time was to show the grave misfortune of a slackness in any command.' Apart from temporary appointments, the Second Battalion had seven commanding officers during the First World War. The pre-war C.O., Delmé-Radcliffe, was sent home after suffering a mental collapse on 26 October 1914, and was suc-ceeded by his Second-in-Command, O. de L. Williams, who held command until 7 May 1916 when he was promoted to command the 92nd Brigade. O. de L. Williams has had a bad press thanks to Graves who thought him rude and reactionary when he first met him in September 1915. But Dunn approved of Williams, 'there is none of the RWF regulars I like & respect so much tho' he was never popular. He is a man of good capacity—but little imagin-ation whose faculties atrophied in the Army—& he acknowledges it.'[53] The regimental obituary described him as, 'Normally grim, withdrawn, almost forbidding, this fighting soldier could, on occasions, display a quizzical humour and a charm which turned the lasting admiration of his officers and men into something close akin to real affection. He was indeed a fine wartime C.O.' It was during his period of command that the battalion enhanced its reputation for being aggressive trench fighters.

O. de L. Williams was succeeded by C. H. R. "Tibs" Crawshay until he was wounded whilst out on patrol with Dunn on 25 January 1917. "Tibs" Crawshay was a great horseman, and he was adjutant of the 3rd Battalion in 1914 when Graves met him. He was a very effective and popular C.O., and Frank Richards observed that, 'he was universally liked by everyone, a stickler for displine, and when in the line, no matter what the conditions were, was always visiting the front-line trenches and seeing things for himself. He had a cheery word for everyone and was as brave as they make them.'[54] In 1919 he retired on half-pay on account of his wounds, and after over fifty operations died in 1937. Crawshay was succeeded by W. B. Garnett on 19 February 1917 who commanded the battalion until 4 May 1918 when he was promoted to command the 121st Brigade. Garnett had begun the war on the staff of the 3rd Battalion before commanding the 20/R. Fusiliers. Dunn disliked him intensely, 'So incompetent & brazenly callous a C.O. had to be seen & heard speak to be believed possible.'[55] But Richards, comparing him with Crawshay, wrote, 'he was a decent old stick, but not to be compared with the colonel we had just lost.'[56] Sassoon who called him, "Easby," thought him, 'indulgent and conciliatory.'[57]

Major de Miremont was acting C.O. from 4 May to 5 July 1918, but was not confirmed in command. The new C.O. was J. B. "Cockie" Cockburn who only commanded until 26 August when he was wounded capturing a German machine gun post. "Cockie" Cockburn was a great character, who had spent most of his pre-war service in West Africa. From 1914 to 1916 he had commanded a battalion of the West African Frontier Force in the German Cameroons. Returning to Britain, he was posted to France and was severely wounded by shell fire in September 1916, which smashed his face and nearly blinded him in one eye. In 1919 he commanded the First Battalion but was forced to retire due to his wounds in 1923. From August 1918 until April 1919 the Second Battalion was intermittently commanded by Major de Miremont. In September and October he was replaced by C. C. Norman, who had been an adjutant of a Territorial battalion of the Royal Welch Fusiliers in 1914, before commanding the Seventeenth Battalion in 1916. A popular, efficient and zealous C.O., effectively he commanded the brigade, and was confirmed in this appointment at the end of October. Major de Miremont was neither efficient nor popular, and the extent of his competence can be judged by the fact that he never had his acting command confirmed. Dunn refers to de Miremont as "the Count," and Richards calls him "The Peer." Before the war he was on detached service with the Colonial Office in West Africa. When he joined the Second Battalion in 1916 he was put in charge of the signallers who disliked him because he tried to re-impose pre-war discipline and "bull." But Richards found that after de Miremont had done a tour in the front line under shell-fire, 'he dropped his pre-war ways and started to act like a sensible human being.'[58] Dunn had little time for de Miremont, 'one correspondent summed him up for all—"A first class coward in the line, & a bully out of it." '[59] It was the appointment of de Miremont as acting C.O. in May 1918 that persuaded Dunn after he had been gassed to apply to be R.M.O. to another battalion. Dunn blamed both Garnett and de Miremont for poor leadership, writing after the war that, 'Except for one unpointed remark I made no reference to what every thoughtful officer & NCO said, each in his own way: that the undoubted serious deterioration of the battalion from March 1917 to July/Aug 1918 was due in a very large measure to the incompetence and indifference of the C.O.'[60]

Few of the pre-war Regular officers stayed with the Second Battalion for any length of time, either being killed, wounded, sacked or promoted. Rowland "Sloper" Clegg-Hill, called "Buzz-Off" by Graves, had retired from the army in 1912, but was recalled from the Reserve to serve with the battalion until he was wounded in September 1915. After a period of convalescence he served on the staff from March 1916 until the Armistice. G. J. P. Geiger commanded 'A' Company in 1914 until he was sent home with an appendicitis in October, then served on the staff in France from October 1915 until the end of the war. C. S. "Bingo" Owen was adjutant of the Second Battalion until he was promoted to command the 6/Royal West Kents in the autumn of 1915. He then commanded the 37th Brigade from 1917 to 1919, reverting in rank to command 1/R. Welch Fusiliers in 1921. Owen was well known for his colourful and foul language which both amazed and delighted onlookers. Richards wrote, 'we all admired the adjutant very much, he could give us all chalks on at swearing, and beat the lot of us easily.'[61] This is confirmed by Alan Thomas, a temporary officer in the 6/R. West Kents who observed that Owen, 'was known as "The Fireater" . . . [with] a tongue as sharp as a razor and a command of language that a sailor would have envied.'[62]

A formidable regular officer who commanded 'A' Company from September 1914 until March 1915 was C. I. Stockwell. At the outbreak of war he was on the staff of the 3rd Battalion before being posted to the Second Battalion. His soldiers nicknamed him "Buffalo Bill," and Richards who served in his company in September 1914 observed that Stockwell was, 'agreed to be a first-class bully. Bullies as a rule are bad soldiers, but he was an exception to the rule.'[63] Later he wrote, 'I never remember him having any favourites: he treated all the men in the same way—like dirt.'[64] Richards' extreme views may have been coloured by the passage of time and Graves' rewriting. In *Memoirs of a Fox-Hunting Man*, Sassoon called Stockwell, "Kinjack," and remembered Joe Cotterill, the Quartermaster of the First Battalion telling him that Stockwell, whom he had known since he was a subaltern, was, 'a bloody fine soldier but an absolute pig if you got the wrong side of him.'[65] In March 1915 Stockwell was transferred to command a company in the First Battalion, before serving as Brigade Major of the 59th Brigade from August 1915. In February 1916 he took command of 1/R. Welch Fusiliers, and Sassoon served under him as a junior officer, observing, 'He was the personification of military efficiency. Personal charm was not his strong point, and he made no pretension to it. He was aggressive and blatant, but he knew his job and for that we respected him and were grateful.'[66] In September 1916 he was promoted to command the 164th Brigade which he commanded until the Armistice. He commanded the Second Battalion from 1924 to 1927. Stockwell's image as a rude, abrasive, aggressive and uncaring officer contrasts sharply with his private diaries which show him to be a sensitive, perceptive, intelligent man.

Other pre-war Regular officers included Reggie Kearsley, who served with the Second Battalion from July to September 1917 and then from December 1917 to January 1918; he was wounded several times and injured in two accidents. In September 1918 he was posted as Second-in-Command of the depot at Wrexham, and eventually retired on half-pay in 1922 due to the effect of his multiple wounds. Pyers Mostyn was a subaltern in the battalion in 1914, and soon distinguished himself as an aggressive patroller in no-man's land during the early months of trench warfare. Wounded in August 1915 he was sent home, and then posted to the Eighth Battalion in the Middle East where he was twice wounded in 1916. In 1920 he retired on account of ill-health contracted during the war, and was killed in a riding accident in Kenya. W. W. Kirkby, known as "Uncle," was a Special Reserve Officer before the war joining the Second Battalion on mobilization. He served with the battalion throughout the war, and was called "Leake" by Sassoon, who noted that, 'Kirkby is short, red and round, thirty-three and good-humoured (except early in the morning) with a slight weakness for standing on his dignity as a senior captain. A Welsh land-owner (owns part of Harlech Golf Course, which is to his credit).'[67] Kirkby was very seriously wounded in October 1918, but survived the war.

The one pre-war Regular officer who had unbroken service with the Second Battalion was H. Yates, the Quartermaster. According to Richards, "Papa" Yates had been a very popular N.C.O. before the war, and had received accelerated promotion to the rank of Lieutenant-Quartermaster. Sassoon referred to him as "Bates," and confirmed his popularity and efficiency. Like so many infantry Quartermasters, Yates was a rock-like figure, and by experience and "scrounging" made certain that the battalion rarely went short of vital supplies and comforts. He survived the war to retire on a pension as a major.

During the war the Second Battalion received a number of attached and temporary officers. R. A. Poore was a forty-six year old major in the Royal Wiltshire Yeomanry (not the Hants. Yeomanry as Dunn states) when he volunteered to serve overseas and was attached to the 2/R. Welch Fusiliers. He had won the D.S.O. serving with the Yeomanry during the South African War, and although noted for his stutter and old fashioned ways was a brave officer who was killed in action commanding the battalion on 26 September 1917. One of the first temporary officers to be attached to the battalion was P. Moody, who had served in the ranks of the Artists Rifles before the war. He was given a temporary commission in 1915 and sent "on approval" to the Second Battalion. He proved a resourceful and gallant officer who Sassoon met at a Guest Night at Litherland in January 1916, describing him as, 'A little nonentity with a pudding face and black hair, but a stout soldier and worthy of his laurels.'[68] N. H. Radford was a temporary officer in the North Lancashire Regiment who was one of an officer draft sent to the battalion in September 1915. He served with the Second Battalion for nearly three years, as platoon commander, adjutant and then company commander. Llewelyn Evans, another temporary officer, served with the battalion from 1917, and was adjutant in 1918–1919. An important contributor to the chronicle, he was to write Dunn's regimental obituary in 1955.

The majority of the contributors to The War the Infantry Knew were officers, and in many respects it is their view of the war that dominates the chronicle. But Dunn did make every effort to include contributions from N.C.Os. and other ranks. Both C.S.M. Boreham and C.Q.M.S. Powell survived the war, although neither saw continuous service with the Second Battalion. After the Armistice they soldiered on as R.S.M. and R.Q.M.S. respectively. Two magnificent pre-war N.C.Os. were Stanway and Fox, who, according to Richards, were the, 'only two sergeant-majors of our company who never pinched our rum.'[69] At Ypres in October 1914 Richards was in Colour-Sergeant Fox's platoon with Stanway as C.S.M., 'They were the two best non-commissioned officers I ever served under.'[70] Stanway was commissioned as a second-lieutenant in the battalion on 31 October 1915, and by June 1916 was a captain with a D.S.O. and M.C. On 2 July 1916 he was promoted to the temporary rank of lieutenant-colonel and given command of the 6/Cheshires, in Dunn's words of understatement, 'an achievement for one who was a Company Sergeant-Major only twenty months ago.' Stanway won a bar to his D.S.O. whilst commanding his battalion, and served on after the Armistice as a captain in the South Wales Borderers. Fox was commissioned in August 1916 and served with the Second Battalion for the rest of the war, and was a captain in the Labour Corps in 1920.

A number of private soldiers, including Dunn's orderlies,

appear fleetingly in the pages of *The War the Infantry Knew*. For the majority, few details concerning their background and military service survive, and so inevitably one turns to the well documented figure of Private Frank Richards. Born in 1883, "Big Dick," was an orphan brought up by his uncle and aunt in Monmouthshire where he worked as a coal miner in the 1890s. Attracted to army life during the South African War he enlisted with the Royal Welch Fusiliers in April 1901 and qualified as an army signaller. Richards was sent with a draft to the Second Battalion in India in 1902, and served there and in Burma until he completed his seven years with the colours in 1909. He then worked as a timber-man's assistant in the South Wales coalfields, extending his service with the Reserve for another four years in 1912. Recalled to the colours in 1914, Richards served continuously with the Second Battalion throughout the war, as a rifleman until June 1915 and then as a signaller. A physical injury aggravated by the war kept him out of the pits after demobilization, and he relied on a variety of temporary jobs at the Labour Exchange. In 1930 he began writing his story because the few books he had read about the war were by officers, and it seemed a different war to what he knew, being in the ranks. Graves described him as, 'Tall, resourceful, very Welsh, the company humourist.'[71] Dunn thought Richards' *Old Soldiers Never Die* had, 'Far too much of the Graves flavour for my liking. But the portraits of old sweats of our Old Army by one of them is worth having: he and I have a number of them in common.'[72]

The War the Infantry Knew is a unique chronicle of an infantry battalion during the First World War. The 2/R. Welch Fusiliers lives through its pages, and the chronicle complements, and in certain areas corrects and puts into perspective the powerful autobiographies of Siegfried Sassoon, Robert Graves and Frank Richards. Read together they provide a wonderful insight into the life of the Second Battalion. But Dunn certainly would never have claimed that *The War the Infantry Knew* represented the history and experience of a typical 'everyman' infantry battalion. It would be too easy to draw upon *The War the Infantry Knew* to make generalizations about other Regular, Territorial and Service battalions during the First World War.[73]

The War the Infantry Knew is a fine testament to the courage, imagination, literary skill and perseverance of Captain James Churchill Dunn R.A.M.C., 'perhaps the greatest "Royal Welchman" who never wore a Flash.'[74]

NOTES

1. Robert Graves *Goodbye to All That* Jonathan Cape, First Edition, First Impression, 1929, p. 260. Graves was to make some amendments in the 1957 reprint
2. Frank Richards *Old Soldiers Never Die* Faber & Faber, 1954, p. 154. In this edition there is a very useful preface by Robert Graves
3. Siegfried Sassoon *Memoirs of an Infantry Officer* Faber & Faber, 1930, p. 192
4. Dunn–Sassoon Correspondence L/2652/2 15 November 1928, Archives, Royal Welch Fusiliers
5. Lieutenant-Colonel R. W. Williams Wynn and Benson Freeman *The Historical Records of the Yeomanry and Volunteers of Montgomeryshire 1803–1908* Oswestry, 1909, p. 127
6. Dunn–Blunden Correspondence 19 September 1939, Harry Ransom Humanities Research Center, The University of Texas at Austin
7. Dunn–Sassoon *ibid*
8. Dunn's obituary in *Y Ddraig Goch* The Journal of the Royal Welch Fusiliers, Summer 1955
9. *The War the Infantry Knew* p. 323
10. Richards *ibid* p. 238
11. Dunn–Graves Correspondence 16 November 1929, Archives, Royal Welch Fusiliers
12. Dunn–Sassoon L/2652/6 1 March 1929 and Dudley Ward *Regimental Records of The Royal Welch Fusiliers* Vol. III 1914–1918 France and Flanders, Forster Groom, 1928, p. 343
13. Richards *ibid* p. 218
14. In his own copy of the First Edition, First Impression of *Goodbye to All That*, Dunn pencilled "balls" against this sentence. Archives, Royal Welch Fusiliers
15. Dunn–Graves, 9 December 1942
16. *Suggested Syllabus for 2nd Battalion Section* L/2653/49
17. *ibid*
18. Dunn–Graves, 8 October 1925
19. Siegfried Sassoon *The War Poems* Faber and Faber, 1983, pp. 147–150
20. Dunn–Sassoon L/2652/1 14 October 1928
21. *ibid* L/2652/5 4 December 1928

22. Blunden–Dunn Correspondence, 21 December 1929, Archives Royal Welch Fusiliers
23. For the background details see Martin Seymour-Smith *Robert Graves His Life and Works* Hutchinson, 1982, pp. 191–200
24. Blunden–Dunn *ibid*
25. Dunn's pencilled comments in his copy of *Goodbye to All That*
26. Dunn–Blunden, 19 March 1930
27. Dunn–Sassoon L/2652/9 12 December 1929
28. *ibid* L/2652/11, 13 October 1930
29. *ibid* L/2652/29, 18 April 1939. Dunn and Graves continued to correspond until 1943, exchanging news, and with Graves forwarding to Dunn copies of his latest books. Graves valued Dunn's judgement and sought his good opinion, and according to his widow, 'always spoke very affectionately' of him—letter from Beryl Graves to the author, 19 April 1986
30. Dunn–Blunden, 19 March 1930
31. Dunn–Sassoon, L/2652/6, 1 March 1929
32. Dunn–Blunden, Undated, but probably 1933
33. Dunn–Sassoon *ibid*
34. Dunn–Graves, 16 November 1929
35. Dunn–Sassoon, L/2652/11, 13 October 1930
36. Dunn–Blunden, 27 March 1931
37. *ibid*, Undated, but probably 1933
38. Dunn–Sassoon, L/2652/16, 24 January 1936
39. Dunn–Blunden *ibid*
40. Dunn–Sassoon *ibid*
41. F. V. Morley, Faber & Faber Ltd., to Sassoon L/2652/40, 31 July 1936
42. Dunn–Blunden, 27 July 1934
43. Lord Moran *The Anatomy of Courage* Constable, 1966, p. 59. As Charles McMoran Wilson he served for thirty months as R.M.O. with the 1/R. Fusiliers 1914–1917
44. Dudley Ward *ibid* p. 305
45. Frank Richards *Old Soldier Sahib* Faber & Faber, 1955, p. 155
46. Graves *Goodbye to All That* Penguin, 1960. See in particular Chapter 14 for his reception by the officers of the Second Battalion in September 1915
47. For Sassoon's reaction in March 1917 see Graves *ibid* p. 209
48. Sassoon *Memoirs of an Infantry Officer* p. 108. Like Sassoon, Graves was a very brave officer and slowly came to admire the Royal Welch Fusiliers.
49. These movements can be followed in *The War the Infantry Knew*. The Second Battalion was in thirty-nine sectors between November 1914 and December 1916, fourteen of which were considered "quiet."
50. Dunn–Graves, 27 October 1925
51. Richards *Old Soldiers Never Die* p. 217
52. Dudley Ward *Regimental Records of The Royal Welch Fusiliers* Vol IV

1915–1918, Turkey, Bulgaria, Austria Forster Groom, 1929, Appendix VIII

53. Dunn–Sassoon L/2652/4, 30 November 1928
54. Richards *ibid* p. 180
55. Dunn–Blunden *ibid*
56. Richards *ibid* p. 221
57. Sassoon *ibid* p. 186
58. Richards *ibid* p. 208
59. Dunn–Blunden, Undated, but probably 1933
60. *ibid* 19 March 1930
61. Richards *ibid* p. 31
62. Alan Thomas *A Life Apart* Gollancz, 1968, p. 56
63. Richards *ibid* p. 328
64. *ibid* p. 50
65. Sassoon *Memoirs of a Fox-Hunting Man* Faber and Gwyer Ltd. 1928, p. 372
66. *ibid* p. 374
67. Rupert Hart-Davis (ed.) *Siegfried Sassoon Diaries 1915–1918* Faber & Faber, 1983, p. 148
68. *ibid* p. 117
69. Richards *ibid* p. 180
70. *ibid* p. 32
71. *ibid* p. 3
72. Dunn–Sassoon L/2652/14, 9 March 1933
73. Over the past twenty years a number of battalions have been studied by authors using archival material and interviews with veterans. Although I suspect Dunn would be very sceptical about the value of such work, nevertheless, John Baynes' *Morale* A Study of Men and Courage Cassell, 1967, was a brilliant study of the 2/Scottish Rifles in 1914–1915; Ian Beckett has examined several Territorial battalions in his chapter, 'The Territorial Force,' in Ian F. W. Beckett and Keith Simpson (eds.) *A Nation in Arms* A Social Study of the British Army in the First World War Manchester University Press, 1985; and G. D. Sheffield studied a Kitchener battalion in his unpublished M.A. Thesis, University of Leeds, 1984, 'The Effects of War Service on the 22nd Royal Fusiliers (Kensington) 1914–1918, with Special Reference to Morale, Discipline and the Officer/Man Relationship.'
74. Dunn's obituary, *Y Ddraig Goch* Summer 1955

CHAPTER I

" The suddenness of a thunderbolt"—Mobilizing—Crossing the Channel—Rouen—Amiens

Contributors:—BOREHAM; GEIGER; HOLMES; OWEN; POWELL; RICHARDS; RODERICK; WILLIAMS; YATES

Sketch:—1

'At [1] the outbreak of the Great War I was Company Sergeant-Major of B Company, 2nd Battalion The Royal Welch Fusiliers. I have often thought how, in April and May 1914 when we were engaged in platoon and company training, Captain Douglas Powell, in his lectures, would picture us with Germans as our opponents. Few of us dreamed at the time that in a few short months we should have them as such in reality. Even when events on the Continent were reaching a climax I do not think that we discussed our chances of having to take any part in them. To me personally the War came with the suddenness of a thunderbolt, and it was in this way.

July 30th, Thursday.—The Battalion was in Bovington Camp, at Wool in Dorsetshire, engaged in training and musketry. We were to return to Portland, our station, towards the end of July, stay there about a week, and then go to Salisbury Plain for manœuvres. We Company Sergeant-Majors had just received the detail for the moves from the Adjutant, Captain C. S. Owen: I had not got back to my tent when the bugler sounded "Company sergeant-majors, at the double." Back we went to the Orderly Room. This time the Orders were very brief: "Pack up, we march back to Portland to-night." Then the thought flashed through my mind—War. The men were jubilant, as is usual in such circumstances. I'm not afraid to place it on record that I was not; the South African War had taught me that there was nothing at all to get jubilant about. It is strange what thoughts pass through one's mind in times of crisis. The very first thing that came to

---

[1] Boreham.

A

mine was the recollection of being verminous in South Africa, and the intense horror of being so again. Then I began to think of other things. It would be about 7 in the evening when the order was issued, and we got to work at once.'

Pickets were sent out to round up the men who were out of camp, but of course there were the usual few absentees at tattoo: greatly surprised they were on returning to find only the party detailed to tidy up, and hand over the camp to Ordnance. (A correspondence about the equipment was to occupy Orderly Room for a good part of the winter.)

Yates, the Quartermaster, took the first train to Portland to prepare for the Battalion's return, and to ration the expected Coast Defence troops. The local butcher and baker were surprised at the amount of the orders given them. The recruits and boys at the Verne had a heavy night's work to get the barracks ready at such short notice. It was an all-night job for everyone concerned.

The Goat,[1] which had been unwell, died. "He must have known something."

'Williams [2] and I had gone to Bournemouth for dinner. On our return to Wool we noticed flames. My first idea was that the Canteen was on fire. However, on our pulling up, Knox Gore rushed to us and, in a voice quivering with emotion, informed us that we were ordered back to our peace stations, and were starting in ten minutes. My Company's peace station was Dorchester, the other three Companies were in the Verne Fort at Portland.'

The march began at 11 o'clock. Fortunately the night was *July* 31*st*—fine. The Dorchester Company arrived at its quarters at 3 a.m. in great spirits. For the main body the march was long and dreary. The Band and Drums were unable to play the whole night without their music, but they put up a wonderful show. Day was breaking as we came down the hills to Weymouth, and, as daylight increased, the awful sleepiness always associated with night-marching wore off and the march became less irksome. When we sighted the harbour we had our first forecast of war. It was full of warships when last we saw it; now there were none. The Navy had been mobilized on July 15th as a long prearranged test of administration; it was being kept in commission pending the development of a recent and unexpected political crisis abroad. The

---

[1] The Regimental Goat is borne officially on the Strength.   [2] Geiger.

Band and Drums had started to play again, and the good folks of Weymouth were roused about 6 o'clock by the Drums playing, "I do like to be beside the seaside." The next sign of war was a guard that had been mounted at the bridge over an arm of the sea, beside the Whitehead Torpedo Factory, near Portland. A "state of war" was not yet in being, but because of "strained relations" the Coast Defences had been manned. It was strange what an impression of the very unusual these various signs made. Portland rises so abruptly from sea-level that the final climb of nearly 600 feet was not a very nice finish to a march of about 22 miles in marching order. Needless to say we were all very pleased when we reached the top. There those of us who had wives found them waiting wide-eyed and apprehensive of the reason of our returning so suddenly.

Preparation for the expected mobilization followed. Although the order had not been received, our regimental authorities anticipated it, so that when it did come there was less to do than otherwise would have been the case. Indeed, owing to an Orderly Room blunder anticipation went too fast: mobilization telegrams were sent out. The incident had to be explained away in Parliament when the Houses met the following week, and the Orderly Room telephone nearly fused with the questions that came in—and other official and semi-official remarks. Mobilization stores were got out, and the wagons were loaded in case of a sudden move. Our equipment was indifferent: the men had dixies instead of field-kitchens, better known as "cookers"; our machine-guns were on heavy antique gun-carriages instead of the tripod mounting. All this was because, having just arrived from India, we did not belong to any brigade or division, did not—on paper—belong to the Expeditionary Force of six divisions. The Battalion had been fitted-out with home-service clothing and equipment after our home-coming in March, the Band and Drums completed with their respective types of tunic: everything had to be packed away or handed back to Stores. Pay-books and identity-discs were checked up to date, and nominal rolls for everything were prepared. 'Fortunately [1] for me, I had finished my tour of duty as Sergeants Mess President the previous quarter; Bill Barling had the job of packing up the Mess in addition to all his other work.

[1] Boreham.

I've often reflected since then on how many things came true. When first we got the pay-books and identity-discs, about two years before the War, we smiled at the idea of ever having to use them. Behind the Commanding Officer's table in the Orderly Room was a mobilization chart—another smile. What an awful bore it was to have to listen to the King's Rules and Regulations relating to Active Service being read out each quarter! And when we had to make out family allotment forms the smile changed to a broad grin.

As the days passed the situation became more critical and the work of preparation more strenuous. I had just time to rush home, snatch a bit of food, then back to business. It was usual to be roused in the middle of the night and told by an orderly that I was wanted in the Orderly Room. I don't think Jimmy Caldwell, the Orderly Room Sergeant, got much sleep at this time.' We were getting orders continually, mostly over the telephone and rarely confirmed. A few officers' private cars were invaluable. The Quartermaster could not have overtaken his work without someone to drive him about: 'O. de L. was my friend these days.' Because we were a spare unit our mobilization scheme was only in the rough, it had not been vetted.

'If [1] there was any discussion on the prospects of war it was done chiefly by the women-folk—I generally found a group of them busy at it; I'm afraid I was rather rude to one good lady who was taking things badly and upsetting others.'

For the detached Company at Dorchester, once all transport and other arrangements had been made to set out for Portland as soon as the mobilization signal came through, these few days were a time of anxious waiting and rumour. Otherwise, the only excitement was the Assizes, presided over by Mr. Justice Darling, the wit of the Bench.

August 4th, Tuesday.—'In [2] the evening Owen sent for me and showed me a telegram, and told me to take it to the Colonel. The C.O. was at Walwyn's, where there was a dinner-party. They had not finished dinner when I was shown in. I think those few minutes, talking about nothing till the ladies had retired, were the most strained I have ever been through.'

'About [3] 9 p.m. "Company sergeant-majors" sounded as I was

---

[1] Boreham.   [2] Holmes.   [3] Powell.

having a drink with "Pip" Parsons, who remarked, "That's it": drank his beer, and requested the production of a dozen Germans. Then to work copying out Orders. When we had finished the Mess was closed, sad to relate.'

August 5th.—'The [1] signal arrived at Dorchester at about 2.30 a.m., and we were under way by 3.15. We started in pouring rain, the men in the best of spirits, singing at the top of their voices. I have forgotten what they sang, but it certainly was not "Tipperary," which was already out of date in Quetta the previous year.' ("It's a long way to Tipperary" was, however, soon associated in the public mind and in the journalism of the time with the marching of our Old Army.) 'The rain eventually ceased. As we climbed the hill to the Verne, at about 8 a.m., I noticed a Red Cross flag flying from the Naval Hospital flagstaff at Portland, and so knew that war had been declared. The next hours were passed in a whirl of mobilization.'

Thomas, the Transport Officer, went off early in the morning with a party to Wareham, to take over horses as they were collected there by Remounts.

'In [1] the afternoon we got Orders to start next day. The excitement became even more intense. As we seemed to be under the direct orders of the War Office there was no one we could possibly sound as to our destination. My wife was on a bed of sickness and unable to join me; my mother was, so far as I knew, held up in Switzerland; consequently it looked as if I should have to depart without seeing any of my small family.

In the evening the Garrison Gunners at the Verne took some of us to a sort of conning-tower where a good view out to sea was obtainable, and where, by some fire-direction system that seemed too good to be true in those days, they could put a shot into any square yard of sea within range. I am sure most of us expected a German cruiser to appear suddenly and be sunk; I know I did—and I don't think anybody thought about submarines.'

August 6th.—When the day for departure arrived there were not many of the administrative staff who were at all sorry. After an early breakfast we paraded to leave the Verne Citadel: 20 officers and 580 rank and file. The Transport wagons were being left ready so that when the horses arrived they had only to hook in.

[1] Geiger.

'Just [1] as we turned out the first draft of Reservists from Wrexham marched in. They were allotted to Companies, and because a roll had to be rendered to Orderly Room at once, I sat down just as I was, in marching-order, and wrote it out. Several Reserve officers joined us on parade. A second party of Reservists, making about 300 altogether, arrived later in the morning.'

'We [2] got off at last, at 7 o'clock, and marched down to the station. I have a vivid recollection of Norah Walwyn at the main gate with a kodak in her hands, but much too overcome with emotion to manipulate it. Our departure from Portland created little excitement among the local population, of whom few were about; I did, however, hear one humorist call out, "Bring us back some sausages, Bill." ' We hung about for a considerable time before entraining. Nothing showed us where we were going. Excitement ran high. Once in the train, rumours and guesses at our destination circulated rapidly; consequently, when we arrived at Dorchester and were told to get out, it was rather an anti-climax. Room had to be found at the Verne for its scheduled garrison, a South Lancs Territorial battalion, so Dorchester was our actual mobilization point.

We were told that our stay was indefinite, and that we were all to go into billets, which was a new experience for us. It was not real billeting, however, because the officers went into one or other of the hotels, H.Q. was in the King's Arms, and the men were in various public buildings. 'A. Company's first billet—Infant School, block floor with pack for a pillow.' B Company, in the Corn Exchange, were also able to test the discomfort of sleeping on the hard wooden floor. 'I [1] had the opportunity of a bed in a house but preferred to be close at hand; besides, it would be easier to get up off the floor than to turn out of a comfortable bed if I were wanted.'

August 7th.—The first fatigue was wiring-in the old Artillery Barracks which were to house enemy internees of military age; otherwise there was not much to do except take a route-march or two to accustom the men to their new boots, and do a little musketry drill.

August 8th.—The Reservists and the Transport, having marched from Portland, joined us. There were many stragglers, which was

---

[1] Boreham.   [2] Geiger.

not to be wondered at because some of the men had been several years on the Reserve and were consequently soft, and some had the wrong size of boot. It was not possible to get boots from Store for these men, 'so I [1] suggested to Captain Powell that, as there was a war on, we could commandeer boots for them. B Company did this, giving the shopkeeper a requisition.' There was no need to ask who was a Reservist, his white skin distinguished him from the tanned, fit serving man; and many were at sea in the new organization of a battalion, for the number of companies had been halved and the number of sections doubled since they were with the Colours.

The boys under age had been replaced from the Reserve. A party of N.C.Os. had been sent to the Depot; the 8th (Service or "Kitchener") Battalion was formed later from this nucleus. The Establishment of N.C.Os. had to be made up to strength, so the Adjutant convened a board consisting of himself, the Regimental Sergeant-Major, Company Sergeant-Majors and Quartermaster-Sergeants, and went through the rolls of the Reserve N.C.Os. One or other of us knew something about each of them and was able to guide Captain Owen in his selection of those to be promoted. Mobilization was then complete: the strength was 29 officers, 1 warrant officer, and 1065 other ranks. 'I [2] remember two absentees returning. One was a man who had deserted to the Channel Islands from our 1st Battalion, our predecessors at Portland, two years before; he returned at his own expense. The other was one of the bad hats of my own Company who had cleared off nine days previously, and was making his way to the South Wales coalfield; this man, on reading the mobilization posters, turned round and walked back again.'

A rigid censorship on troop movements, which was new in England on the outbreak of war, was being enforced. Its object was loyally observed by those who knew anything, and was fostered by the fancy of those who knew nothing. Sergeant Roderick had been rushed off to the Records Office at Shrewsbury for the Reservists' documents. On coming back to Portland he 'found that the Battalion had vanished. The married folk said it must be well in Germany by now, so I hurried back to the station. A merry little porter said it had gone to Germany, and

---

[1] Boreham.   [2] Geiger.

I began to think so too. The station-master said he did not know where it was, but very tactfully he put me in a train and told me to get out at Dorchester, and from there, he said, I would probably get to Germany.'

August 9th.—The Psalms at Matins were extraordinarily truculent, and appropriate to the first Sunday after War had been declared. Our wives and friends came to see us. Saying good-bye over again was rather trying to the nerves.

We were told we would start again to-morrow; again no one had the faintest idea of our destination.

August 10th.—'I [1] was called about 3.15 a.m. No one could have slept much. We started about 6.30, A and B Companies with the senior Major, Williams, in one train, H.Q. with C and D in a second train. We all began guessing where we were off to. Southampton was voted as most likely. Williams went so far as to offer odds that we should be lunching on a sumptuous Cunarder, with unlimited champagne at the Government's expense.' About 10 o'clock we ran straight into Southampton Dock, arriving there five months to the day since our arrival from India. No one was allowed to leave the shed, but Boy Scouts did "good deeds" running for fags, etc. 'A [1] and B Companies marched to our ship, the *Glengariff*, a wretched pig boat on which I made the voyage to Cork with recruits from the Depot some years previously. She was not very clean, and, since there was no food whatever on board, we subsisted on the ration we had with us—bully-beef, biscuits, and water. The Embarkation Officer wished to prevent us going on board since we were not the H.Q. half of the Battalion. Williams bluffed him all right, but when the C.O. arrived he took command of us, so Williams had to remain ashore in the Rest Camp with C and D Companies and part of the Transport. In the afternoon I spotted an old friend in the senior Embarkation Officer, who told me, under an oath of secrecy, that we were the first Regular troops to embark, that we were going to Rouen, and were to be employed with three other battalions in passing the Expeditionary Force up-country.'

The senior N.C.Os. were given a long narrow cabin on the upper deck. 'I [2] was one of the first in, and had a berth at the forward end; there was only one door, and it was at the end

---
[1] Geiger.   [2] Boreham.

farthest from where I was. When I awoke we were out at sea:
August 11th—the vessel had sailed at 2 a.m. I studied the port-
hole that was opposite me, wondering if I could get through it
were we attacked by a submarine. However, our trip across the
Channel was quite uneventful.' About 10 o'clock, with no land
in sight, we fell in with a large French tug. It hailed us, and our
Captain, who had opened his sealed orders by now, replied:
thereupon the Frenchmen started cheering, and kept on shouting,
"Vive l'Angleterre," "Vivent les Anglais." Our fellows, who
were swarming all over the rigging, shouted most uncomplimentary
remarks in answer in the way peculiar to British soldiers. Our
French friends would have been disgusted had they understood.
A pilot boarded us from the tug. Soon we sighted land, then
Havre, which we passed on the left. Next was the little town of
Quillebœuf; when we approached it not a soul was to be seen,
but no sooner did the pilot sound the siren than, as if by magic,
someone appeared at nearly every window, most of them with
a tricolour. The enthusiasm was terrific, a foretaste of what was
to come. At every town and village the inhabitants turned out
and yelled greetings. The trip up the Seine was very fine, though
very hot; the only drawback was that a couple of our subaltern
officers did not give the ship's siren a rest the whole of the way.

'We [1] got to Rouen at 4.30 p.m. It was very evident that we
were in for a reception of some sort, because a French battalion
was drawn up on the quay, and a lot of French Brass Hats were
there too. As soon as we tied up a French General came on board,
and I, as the reputed French scholar, was pushed forward to
welcome him. I conducted him to the C.O., whereupon he at
once launched into one of these graceful and charming little speeches
which the French are so good at. With an agonized expression
the C.O. turned to me and said, "For goodness sake, say something
in reply, my French won't run to it." I made a few halting
remarks; then, there being nothing to offer in the drink line, we
conducted the General over the side again.'

We must have begun to disembark about 5.30. It is of historic
interest that we were the first of many thousand troops to disembark
at Rouen, and, with The Cameronians and 1st Middlesex who
landed at Havre, and the 2nd Argyll and Sutherland Highlanders

[1] Geiger.

who landed at Boulogne, all on August 11th, the first combatant British troops to land in France for the Great War. 'The [1] first man of the Regiment to land in France was R.S.M. Murphy. I am quite certain of that, because I was standing by the gangway trying to be first myself, but of course I had to give way to my superior officer.'

'I [2] had gathered from a French officer that one company was to be billeted on the right bank, and the other, with Battalion H.Q., on the left. I decided to try for the right bank, since, quite apart from the pleasure of being away from the Big Drum, I knew that the town proper is on the right bank, the other side of the river consisting of rather squalid suburbs. Accordingly A Company's marker was sent ashore with instructions to stand on the far side of B Company's marker if possible : we were disembarking on the right bank. It worked all right.' After disembarking B Company crossed the river by the Transporter Bridge and marched, loaded with offerings of fruit, vegetables, and flowers, to billets in the École Pape Carpentier.

August 13th.—C and D Companies arrived at 7 a.m., and billeted in other schools. The rest of the Transport arrived at 7 p.m. 'I [3] spent the two days we were at Southampton badgering the Embarkation Officer for a passage, fearing that the War would be over before we could be in it.'

Our rôle was to have been that of Lines of Commiuncation troops, and for a few days we carried out our duties as such, preparing camps for the arrival of other troops. These camps were pitched on the hill beyond the Racecourse, where the Base Depots were afterwards built. Most things seemed quite strange to us : marching on the right of the road took a bit of getting used to ; and to see opposite our billet two policemen on duty leaning against a post, smoking, looked funny. 'One [1] day as we were marching to the Racecourse a young lady ran out of a house and placed a large bunch of flowers in the arms of the officer who was in charge of the party before he was aware of what was happening ; when he recovered himself he pushed them into my hands, and I passed them back one by one to the men.' We also found various guards. A guard was on a quayside store containing great vats of wine. It has been said that one can do many things with bayonets. A man

---

[1] Boreham.   [2] Geiger.   [3] Williams.

who was always thirsty got to the wine with his bayonet, and he was generous to his comrades. The resource of an indulgent sergeant, the timely arrival of the blanket wagon, and "the luck of the British Army" spelt escape from the Guard-room for everyone.

There was no leave from the billet for the first day or two, but it was besieged by all the children of the neighbourhood, and they ran errands for the men. It was funny to hear the attempts to make the children understand what was required; even Hindustani was used; one fellow was overheard saying to a native—"Here, malaam, 'bacca." 'When [1] we were permitted to go into the city the first thing my C.Q.M.S., Albert Miners, and I thought of was to get something decent to eat. We were fortunate in meeting an English-speaking French corporal, who took us to a restaurant where we got a several-course dinner for one and a half francs (1s. 3d.) each. We went afterwards to one of the cafés on the quay for a drink; there our French friend expressed his wonder that our men could afford to drink bottled beer. He did not know, until we told him, that the English soldier's pay was quite sufficient for him to do so; it was a great contrast to the sou a day the French soldier got then.'

The officers were in separate billets, messing in various restaurants of their own choice except for dinner, when they met at the Restaurant de la Poste. A disturbing duty that fell to the sub-altern's lot was Curfew Picket, seeing that all ranks were out of town by a certain hour, 'but one did see life.'

Major Geiger's narrative of A Company detachment.—We marched off to the upper part of the town accompanied by an admiring crowd, and on arrival at our quarters (the École Théologique, rue des Champs du Quiseau) found ourselves on velvet. The men were in the dormitories of the students, most of whom were mobilized already, and had beautiful clean straw to sleep on, and the nuns insisted on cooking for them; not taking long views, they one and all were of opinion that a European war was excellent business. On inspecting my own *billet de logement*, with which we were provided in those early days, I saw that Samson and I were to be the guests of the Archbishop of Rouen at the *Archevêché*. We were shown into bedrooms that were like private chapels, and the major-domo told me impressively that, up to that night,

---

[1] Boreham.

no one under the rank of bishop had occupied my bedroom. The
bed, however, did not give way under the weight of my sins.
His Grace was unable to entertain us that evening, but bade us to
déjeuner next day.

August 12th.—I went over to H.Q. first thing, and was told that
at 5 p.m. I was to go on to Amiens with my Company, which was
good news as it meant being on one's own. On getting back to
my billet I asked if we could be given a guide to see the Cathedral
and the Church of St. Ouen. The Archbishop's Domestic Chaplain
volunteered, so Samson and I spent a most instructive morning,
and ended it with a most excellent lunch with the Archbishop
who, on our taking leave, gave us his blessing.

We entrained very comfortably, the officers being in two first-
class carriages—everything was done luxuriously in those early
days. (We were 4 officers, 120 other ranks, and one horse. One
officer, 104 other ranks, 2 vehicles and horses followed on the 14th.)
As our journey progressed it became more and more hilarious.
Crowds seemed to be waiting for us at every station, we stopped
at every one, and a good deal of osculation went on. I personally
was handed out nothing better than numerous children of tender
years, most of them grubby, to kiss, but the subalterns next door
seemed more lucky as far as I could see out of the corner of my eye.
The climax of the ludicrous was reached at some station or other
where the town band met us and played the "Marseillaise," to
which A Company responded by intoning "God save the King"
with much solemnity. We were met by a French corporal-inter-
preter who, I discovered next day, was the Duc de Luynes. He
led us to our billet in the Saint Acheul district, a poor quarter
of the town. Our quarters were in what we would call a Council
school (in the rue Sadi Carnot). Although the straw was clean,
the premises were not, particularly the sanitary portion. Succeeding
incoming French Reservists had been quartered there before us,
and had not troubled about cleaning-up before leaving : it is not
the French way. There were some admirable, if somewhat
offensive, drawings of the Kaiser and other German personages
on the blackboards. The officers bedded down on straw in a class-
room : hardly as luxurious as the bishop's bedroom.

August 13th.—We got to work and thoroughly cleaned our
billet ; and I set about finding what we were wanted for and

how the land lay. H.Q. Lines of Communication were in a hotel opposite the station. The O.C. Troops had my Company, and various Service, Ordnance, and Medical Corps Details under his orders. These Details were a bit of a trial; being nearly all Reservists just recalled, and having very few officers to look after them, they were all over the shop. Our duties were to furnish orderlies to L. of C. H.Q., sentries and escorts to guard ammunition lorries, and parties to be ready at the station with rations and water for the Expeditionary Force troop-trains on their way through Amiens. The trains began coming through that day or the next. Having got cleaning materials and disinfectant, seen about daily rations, etc., I looked up Luynes, and with his help the officers were soon installed in decent billets. Where I was lodged the wife had spent many years as a lady's-maid in England. The house had a bath!

'First [1] pay-day in France! As Acting C.Q.M.S. of the detachment I went to the Goods Station to draw rations, and was asked, none too kindly, how I expected to take away the rations—they had "no . . . transport." So I commandeered an old cart, probably the first act of the kind by the British Army in France. It was curious to see that when the French peasant Reservists reported for duty they were accompanied by their women-folk.'

August 14th.—Warned that Sir John French was coming for a night to the Hôtel du Rhin, and that we must furnish a Guard, we were mildly agitated because all the officers were wearing the Flash with Service Dress. Sir John had ordered it off the 1st Battalion at Aldershot when he was in command there seven years ago. The 2nd Battalion, then in India, naturally took no notice of that order. We had landed from abroad in March wearing ours and hoping for the best. Up to date we had got away with it, but this was the first time Sir John had seen us. If we had thought twice we need not have worried; the C.-in-C. was occupied with matters of rather more import than the dress distinction of His Majesty's 23rd Foot. He ran into the Orderly Officer turning out the Guard, but all the O.O. got was a benign smile. Once, in France, I was asked if I was an *aumonier* (chaplain), an explanation of the Flash that was new to me.

The next occurrence was the arrival of the King's Message,

[1] Powell.

which was read on parade. The cheers I was instructed to call for were given very heartily, bringing heads to the windows of houses adjacent to the yard of the school.

Then H.Q. and four squadrons of the Royal Flying Corps arrived by air. We supplied the firing party at the burial of a pilot-officer and mechanic whose machine crashed when they resumed their journey. They were given an impressive funeral, attended by the Prefect of the Department, the Mayor, and a battalion of French Territorials (the ancients who were the local garrison).

August 17th.—I was summoned early to L. of C. H.Q. and told that General Grierson, commanding II Corps, had died suddenly in the train, and that his body would be taken out at Amiens. A. Company was detailed for Guard of Honour and any other relevant duty. There were a lot of stupid rumours about General Grierson's death. I have the best of reasons for knowing that he died from the bursting of a blood-vessel, probably brought on by the heat and a heavy meal. He was a man of full habit, the weather was torrid, and the Staffs of higher formations were at that time living exclusively on hampers supplied by Fortnum and Mason— purveyors of edible and potable delicacies.

During A Company's stay in Amiens the officers took their meals at various restaurants. The more or less luxurious establishments familiar to the B.E.F. when Amiens was the chief centre of relaxation behind the Somme Front did not exist then, except the famous Fish Shop, which, being in a side street, the rue des Corps nues sans Testes [old French=têtes], we never discovered. Samson and I took all our meals at the Café Mollard, a modest establishment, which I saw again in April 1918 with a shell through the front of it. We used to wind up the evening in a café in the Place Gambetta, where an orchestra played. The performance always concluded with all the Allied National Anthems, when everyone stood up and solemnly saluted during the ten minutes it took to play them. The show ended at 9 p.m., so we were never kept up late.

All this time the Expeditionary Force was passing through Amiens. The other officers of the Company were waxing very impatient, and confiding to me their impression that we were doomed to remain there for the whole of the War. As I had from the first openly expressed my opinion that the War would last about two years—how wrong I was!—I was not particularly disturbed by

these outbursts.   All doubts were set at rest when I was summoned
August 20th—to O.C. Troops Office in the rue des Trois-Cailloux,
and told that we were about to become a unit of the 19th Infantry
Brigade, and would be off in a couple of days.   The O.C. then
said a lot of kind things about the conduct of the men which
was not flattery, they had certainly earned his good opinion.   Right
from the first they were perfectly wonderful.   They were exposed
to every sort of temptation, in very truth the town of Amiens was
at their feet ; yet during the ten days we were there not a single
man was drunk, and only one came in late (only ten minutes)
for tattoo at 9.15.   A few gave away their cap-badges as souvenirs,
but on an intimation that no one would go out without one this
ceased at once.   The fact that the school was surrounded by a high
iron fence helped to keep everyone together.   A Staff Officer told
me that he had congratulated one of our men on the Company's
good behaviour, and got the reply, "Well, the Captain told us that
the better we behaved ourselves, the sooner we should go to the
Front."   If I had spun that yarn a year later I wonder what the
effect would have been ?   All ranks were, of course, now full of
excitement.

On my way back to our billets I saw a long column of motor
vans with such well-known names as Harrods, Maple, Whiteley,
etc., etc.   They belonged to the supply columns, and looked very
incongruous in Amiens.   ('Apropos, a tribute is due to the old
London bus-driver who was presumed to be devoid of all discipline.   One night a fire broke out in a lorry.   Very calmly the
drivers started up and got all lorries not affected clear, then proceeded to deal with the burning ones.')

Our billet was invaded by about 150 youthful enthusiasts with
motor bicycles, a large percentage of whom had no idea how to
manage their mounts.   They were, for the most part, University
students and young schoolmasters, with a sprinkling of young
business men, who had been collected speedily and sent over as
despatch-riders.   I imagine that all who did not become casualties
eventually got commissions.

August 20th.—The Battalion had orders to stand-by to move :
Guards and other Duties in Rouen were called in.

August 21st.—Our Brigadier, the Hon. L. G. Drummond, arrived
at the Hôtel du Rhin, Amiens, with a Brigade-Major, Johnson of

the K.R.R.C., and looked round to complete his Staff. I was sent for and, after some desultory conversation, asked if I would like the job of Staff Captain. Given an hour to think it over, I decided to stick to my Company for the present. As events turned out, my decision did not make much difference to me, except that I should probably have drifted to the Q. side of the Staff, which I am glad I avoided.'

CHAPTER II

*" To the War in Earnest"—"Mons," A Rumour: Retreat—
"Le Cateau" — Sleep-walking—St. Quentin — Wayside
Comedies—"Still on, on"—A Rose Garden*

Contributors:—BOREHAM; DELMÉ RADCLIFFE; GEIGER; HOLMES;
MOSTYN; OWEN; POWELL; RODERICK; WILLIAMS; YATES

Sketches:—2, 3, 26

August 22nd.—At 10.25 a.m. the Battalion left Rouen by train—
H.Q., B, C, and D Companies: 23 officers, 2 interpreters, 752
other ranks—7 other ranks remained in hospital—58 horses, 17
vehicles. 'At[1] Amiens a good deal of badinage was exchanged,
but I was able to tell them that they were bound for Valenciennes,
and that the other battalions in the Brigade were The Cameronians,
the 1st Middlesex, and 2nd Argyll and Sutherland Highlanders.
They went on; A Company was to follow later with Brigade H.Q.
We left our billets—incidentally, a good deal cleaner than the
French had—about 8.30 p.m., and pushed off to the War in earnest
at 11.' Two other ranks remained in hospital.

August 23rd.—At 2 a.m. the Battalion arrived at Valenciennes,
and detrained just outside the station. It had been in Valenciennes
before, having marched through three days after Waterloo.
Rations and ammunition were issued. Some boxes, which had
been objects of speculation, were opened; they contained Ordnance
Maps of sections of Northern France and Belgium, and handbooks
for dealing with the authorities of these countries; 'my[2] share
was eight, not a welcome addition to the already weighty contents
of a pack.' There was a report that a man, dressed as a woman,
was caught about this time on the station platform with pigeons
under his skirt. 'Somewhere[1] about 6.30 A Company rolled
into the station. I had time for coffee and a roll at the buffet
with the other officers before the Battalion fell in on the Place
de la Gare. We got under way in rear of the Brigade,' D Company

---

[1] Geiger.   [2] Boreham.

at the tail of the Battalion, and marched on a pavé road in a north-easterly direction. 'A [1] number of lorries returning to the town passed us. Although we had been away from home for but a few days, the familiar names on them—one, I remember, was Maple—made me feel quite home-sick.'

After a couple of miles B Company left the main road and went to a village named Rombies. There we put out one or two posts and then proceeded to get some breakfast. The villagers were very interested in the making of tea; they were horrified at the way the milk, which the cooks got from a farm, was added. (The Army method of making tea is to boil the water, stir in the tea, then the sugar and the milk before taking the kettle off the fire. If the water has been chlorinated the flavour is unimaginable; a taste for the decoction is never acquired, it has to be endured.) As already mentioned, the Battalion was engaged in training when war broke out, and, since we had not yet become acquainted with real shells and so on, it seemed that we were still going on with the training, for when Captain Powell read out the situation, according to which the enemy's cyclists had been seen at So-and-so, there was nothing strange about it. In the afternoon we rejoined the Battalion. It, meanwhile, had gone a few kilometres farther, then it bore off left-handed to a position between the village of Vicq and the river Escaut (Schelde).

We were about two miles south of the Condé Canal, on which the 1st Middlesex and The Cameronians were finding the outposts; the Argylls were in support. The Brigade formed, with the possible exception of a few cavalry vedettes, the extreme left of the Allied Line. Here we got orders to dig trenches. No one seemed to have a very clear idea of how they were to be sited or of what pattern they were to be, so A Company dug a length of wretched one-hour shelter-trench with our small entrenching tools. Others scraped out rifle-pits in the banks of dykes. It was a lovely Sunday afternoon; B Company were in a field where the corn had been cut recently. It was still difficult to realize that there was a war on. The local people strolled round, dressed in their Sunday clothes, and the men fraternized with them. They were, of course, very interested in our proceedings; they were in excellent spirits, and totally oblivious of any possibly impending

[1] Boreham.

cataclysm. They spoke Flemish among themselves, not French. To requests for cigarettes or matches from the men they replied, "N'y a pus," the local dialect for "Il n'y en a plus," from which "na'poo," soon an expressive word in the Army's daily speech, is easily evolved. D Company had dug outpost trenches near a little farm. Some cap-badges were parted with, and some rendezvous for next day were given that evening. So far things were not bad, and few of the men took the War seriously; none knew what was happening although there was any amount of wild rumour.

We were instructed next to watch all roads coming from a northerly direction. We carried out this order to the best of our ability, but it was difficult because our maps were on a smallish scale, and the whole place was a criss-cross of roads and paths, and of dykes coming from the Canal and the river. While we were sitting peacefully around at about 8 p.m. we began to hear gun-fire, field-guns. For us, this was the first sound of war; it denoted the opening of the Battle of Mons–Charleroi in our part of the Field. An hour or so later we heard that the Middlesex outposts had been engaged with the enemy across the Canal, and that they had at least one officer wounded. Our Company officers got a little sleep in the intervals of visiting their sentries, and most of us were badly bitten by the insects that abounded in the sluggish dykes.

August 24th.—About 2.30 we got orders to fall in at once. It was pitch-dark. Without details of any kind being vouchsafed we pushed off along the road into the blue. The Brigade was, in fact, concentrating near Elouges. For two days it was to be the Infantry Support in the running fight in which Allenby's Cavalry Division foiled the efforts of the First German Army to envelop the left of the B.E.F. To the Army the German General von Klück was "Old One O'clock." Gun-fire, of which there had not been much, had ceased for some time, and for the first couple of hours we marched without incident. 'My pocket-compass informed me' that we were going first of all south and then a little north of east. The first event of interest was our arrival in the small town of Quiévrain, just over the Belgian Frontier. Here the inhabitants were very agitated. Firing could be heard again, and all arms were, or had been, in evidence. We marched straight

on, the noise of gun-fire getting nearer. On our left we could
see the puffs of exploding shells on the other side of the nearest
crest-line, about half a mile away. Just as we got to the village
of Elouges we were given the order to "About turn," and thus
unknowingly began our long trek south. (General Allenby had
ordered the withdrawal of his troops before he knew that the
3rd Division was being pressed by the pursuing Germans; a sharp
little action occurred before it shook them off.)

'We [1] soon reached Quiévrain again, and halted. I suppose it
was about 8 o'clock. After about ten minutes the Brigade-Major
came and told me to picket the entrance to the town at one road
and at the railway station, and to fire at once on any German
cavalry patrol that might approach. Nothing happened. After
about half an hour I was ordered to collect my Company and
fall in with the rest. There was a report later that a platoon of
the Argylls, similarly engaged, never got its order to retire, was
left behind, and was badly cut up shortly afterwards.

After marching about one mile, and nearly in Baisieux, I observed
a large body of cavalry, like a brigade, manœuvring about 900
yards east of us. Some of them, the 9th Lancers I suppose, trotted
forward in two lines about 150 yards apart, and eventually broke
into a charge. No enemy was visible to us, but as soon as the
cavalry began to gallop gun-fire was opened on them, and one
could see through glasses a few empty saddles and horses down.
After charging about half a mile the cavalry wheeled and returned,
and when I lost sight of them they were re-forming. Meanwhile
I had remarked a long sausage-like balloon which I assumed to
be a Zeppelin but, according to subsequent experience, it was
merely an observation-balloon.'

The next halt was after midday in a field near Rombies, where
we started to dig-in with our entrenching tools, for the few proper
picks and shovels in the company tool-cart were not nearly enough
to go round. We started to dig several times, because Brigade
sent order after order each amending the previous one, so Major
Williams went to Brigade to find out what was really wanted.
While he was there General Allenby, wearing slacks, drove up
in a car. The sequel to that incident was that Holmes was asked
to exchange a pair of slacks for a pair of breeches, and for his

[1] Geiger.

acquiescence was detailed temporarily as Brigadier's Galloper. It was here that we saw the first German aeroplane; it flew quite low. We had hardly scratched the soil, and eaten some bully-beef and biscuit, when we moved off again. The day was very hot. Before long we began to see signs that a retreat was in progress; packs which had been cast off were lying by the roadside. We arrived finally at Jenlain, where we were to halt for the night, about 6 p.m. In spite of the heat the men had marched well, but it was becoming apparent that the Reservists' boots were going to give trouble; there had been a little straggling from that cause, and 17 men were missing at Roll-call. During the march, and on later marches, wine was offered to the men so liberally that a check had to be kept on its consumption, sometimes by breaking the bottles.

French Territorial soldiers were digging trenches. The long-handled French shovels looked very awkward. We were soon engaged in the same form of exercise, for the Battalion was ordered to entrench between the road [from Sebourg] we had been marching on and 'the [1] small Fort of Curgies which, I fancy, dated from Vauban's day, and was part of the defences of Valenciennes, of which we were now south-east. The Fort was the left of the line. This time, with the Brigade-Major's assistance, I got an idea of the whole scheme, and since it looked as if we might really have to fight I set about getting more suitable implements than our entrenching tools. Luckily I fell in with a small party of French Territorials [2] who were wheeling home a large number of picks and shovels, which they let me have on my promise to return them without fail to Monsieur Dupont in the village. We dug some real trenches, and, as far as I remember, returned the tools to Monsieur Dupont.' Packs were used instead of sand-bags, of which we had none, and some ammunition that was rather in the way was buried. Captain Walwyn, shot in the foot when he was walking in a corner of a harvest field at dusk, was our first casualty. 'As [1] soon as it was dark we lay down in our trenches, and I for one felt certain that we were in for a battle next day.

[1] Geiger.
[2] Territorials were almost the only French troops seen during the Retreat. They would not have felt complimented by the men's opinion of them; 'when they were not just sitting down they were singing the "Marseillaise."'

August 25th.—Everything remained peaceful till about 3.30 a.m., when orders were received to stand-to. In pitch darkness we marched off, still heading south. The Brigade was all together; I think we were leading. Soon after it was light a German aeroplane passed right over us as we were marching along a very zigzag bit of road near Sepmeries. It could not have been more than 300 feet up, since the two men in it, who waved their hands derisively, were plainly visible without glasses. The order for rapid fire was given. I should say that, owing to the shape of the road, every man in the Brigade was able to fire at least five rounds at it—without the slightest result. It went on its way, the pilot and observer still waving their hands. Like nearly everyone else, I suppose, I had yelled to aim well in front, but I doubt if anyone had taken the least notice. About a week later, when I was censoring some of the men's letters, I came upon an account of this incident in which the writer described how he had brought the aeroplane down, and was going to be decorated with the V.C.

Again the day was very hot. At 10.30, or soon after, we arrived at the village of Haussy. The whole Brigade halted and drew up in mass-formation on some grassland near the railway station. We remained there for a couple of hours at least. We were in a hollow surrounded by low hills on the tops of which our cavalry patrols could be seen retiring, and being shelled while doing so. If we had been spotted by an enemy aeroplane or cavalry patrol we could have been made very uncomfortable by any enterprising German horse-battery, so crowded were we. Nothing untoward happened, and about 1.30 we were off again.'

As we were marching through St. Python word was passed that the enemy were near, and shortly after we cleared the village a few shells fell in it. Thereupon we extended and lay down in a field of roots, facing north. We could see the enemy in the distance advancing in artillery formation. They started to shell the ground on our right. The first shell burst about 400 yards from us, near a troop of our cavalry, who soon moved out of sight. Shells then burst ever nearer where we were. Suddenly there was a bang and a noise like tearing calico as a couple of shells in close succession burst over us. This was the first time we had been under fire, and, since no one was hit, the men began to make merry with one another on the subject. 'I [1] was thinking we would soon be for it when a sharp rainstorm came down, and we moved away under its cover. I think that was about the only time I was glad to be out in the rain.' It was then after 5 o'clock. This time we retired in extended order, and by half-companies alternately, covering the withdrawal of the 1st Middlesex.

We got on to the road again later and resumed columns of fours. Soon, near a cross-road in Solesmes, we began to get mixed up with other troops, mainly artillery, and there was considerable congestion for a time. 'We [2] were in the shallow valley of the Selle. Looking through my glasses while the jumble was sorting itself, I saw a German cavalry patrol of four or five Uhlans on the western side of the valley, not more than a mile off. Seemingly blissfully unconscious of our presence, they advanced in the same direction as ourselves and were soon lost to view.' Our march continued. Towards dusk we were all pretty leg-weary in spite of the frequent halts we had made. The men had been without sleep for a couple of nights, so it was difficult to keep them going. As we passed guns on the road we saw drivers asleep on their horses' backs. Belfield, our Armourer-Sergeant, told how, during one of the halts of the Transport, he waited so long for the wagons to move on that he walked up the line to see what was the reason for the stoppage, and found the driver of the leading wagon asleep. 'At [2] a road-corner I met an officer I knew, who told me that he belonged to the 4th Division which had detrained only that day. He said they were now all at hand, and that "with such a large reinforcement" we could "give the Germans hell." He also told me what none of us knew, that the 6th Division was still in England.' [3]

By the time we got near Le Cateau the roadside estaminets were lighted, and we could see that they were filled with stragglers of other units. When, at last, we tumbled into the Grande Place about 9 o'clock we were pretty well done-in. Holmes's platoon of B Company was the rear-party. 'We entered Le Cateau by

---

[1] Boreham.   [2] Geiger.
[3] A factor in the delay to complete the B.E.F. was the possibility of conflict in Ireland. A dangerous state of affairs had arisen there before the outbreak of war, caused by the factiousness of English politicians siding in an old Irish quarrel. Perhaps as great a factor was the fear of invasion that obsessed successive Ministries until near the end of the War, in spite of our greatly stronger Navy.

a long straggling street. I could see the Battalion incline right-handed into what was obviously the Market Place. Suddenly there was a clatter of horses' feet behind. Looking round, I saw some Uhlans coming up the road. I believe the following is the command I gave: "Right wheel; double march; halt; right turn; front rank kneeling, rear rank standing, three rounds rapid, fire." I know the last part of it is correct. Odd word of command in modern war.' In Le Cateau the Sergeant-Major formed our first-line transport into what he called a zareba. Perhaps it was as well that we did not have to test its efficiency as a form of defence.

We managed to cook some tea for the men, but they had only bully, biscuit, and "mousetrap" to eat. One sergeant 'went into a jeweller's shop in the Square and had some jam and biscuit, with the show-case for a table. What a haul for Gerry! Then on to the pavement, there to snatch a couple of winks: very hard, and the rain for a blanket.' 'We [1] A Company officers now began to look around for a meal ourselves, and found a sort of table d'hôte going on in a third-rate restaurant within three yards of where the Company were seated on the kerb. We were a motley crowd. There was a young officer of the Dorsets who, as was usual with young officers who lost their units in those days (and everyone else in the circumstances, or after any unsuccessful action), said he was the sole survivor of his battalion which had been cut to pieces, according to him, on the previous day. Another individual, in plain clothes, proclaimed himself to be an American drummer (commercial traveller). He was much interested in the young officer. He spoke with a strong Yankee accent, but I have often wondered if he were not a German spy. I think I was a fool to have left him alone. The interpreters had pinched the bed in a room upstairs which the landlady told me about. I would probably have avoided it anyhow in those squeamish days; so, having had my valise spread on the floor, and having told my servant, Preston, to call me at 3 a.m., I sought sleep.

August 26th.—By 3.30 I was up and in the street to see that the men were getting something hot. We were all in the dark as to what was likely to happen. The events of the past two days made it obvious that things were not going according to plan. Except,

[1] Geiger.

however, for the fact that we were going the wrong way, and the young Dorset officer's account of the annihilation of his battalion, we knew of nothing untoward having happened. Nobody had been killed in the Battalion, everyone was being fed. (But the missing were now 18, and there were 16 sick.) It was becoming obvious that what with the heat, the boot trouble, the long marches, and the want of sleep, the men could not go on carrying the weight they had at present; it was fully 56 pounds. Samson, my excellent Sergeant-Major Stanway, and I held a council of war, and decided it was better the men should abandon their packs by order than throw them away themselves, as some others had done. ('Told to stack packs, Transport would pick them up. But whose transport ?') At least one other Company did the same thing when I told their Captain what I had done. Doubtless the Germans found them inside the *porte cochère* where they were stacked.

The men had finished their tea and eaten some food, and were seated among their grounded arms. The whole Brigade must have been in or close to the Market Square, and every unit in the B.E.F. represented in it during the night. Suddenly I heard a Frenchwoman calling out, "Les Allemands arrivent." Getting up, I saw a number of women pointing down a street on the other side of the Square. They did not seem in the least alarmed, rather were they amused, probably—poor creatures—looking on the affair as affecting only the Germans and the English, and no concern of theirs, little thinking that they were about to entertain the Germans for over four years. I have only a confused recollection of what occurred on this alarm being uttered.' When, at last about 5.30, orders arrived we marched with bayonets fixed, not along the street down which the enemy's approach had been signalled, but uphill in a north-westerly direction, and expecting to see Uhlans up every street. We had an impression of marching round the place a few times before getting away, so much so that one humorist started singing, "It's a long way to Tipperary." But we were soon out of the town without anything having happened.

Turning left-handed, we were at once cheered by the sight of a large number of British troops, the 5th Division, digging trenches, and sitting about just as if it was any other old field-day that was going on. 'It [1] was obvious from the trench digging, the number

[1] Geiger.

of troops, and the proximity of the enemy that we were going to
have a battle of sorts, but I have no recollection of being told
anything of what was in the air. It was difficult then to think out
what was happening, and it is difficult now (1920) to give a
coherent account of events from a purely regimental point of view.'

The Brigade had been transferred to General Smith-Dorrien's
Command. His hard-pressed Corps had reached Le Cateau and
was preparing to stand and fight its pursuers: with its right on
the town it extended westwards. 'The [1] Brigade passed through
to Reserve just south of a small wood one mile north of Reumont.
A field artillery brigade was deployed all round us, so I anticipated
a rather warm time if we stayed there long. It was then about
8 o'clock. There was a little gun-fire going on to our right, but
the batteries round us did not open; and a few aeroplanes made
their appearance. Upwards of an hour later, probably rather
after 9, we were ordered to fall in. We were told we were to
move into the line to support the 5th Division. The Middlesex
and Argylls abreast led the way in artillery formation, followed by
The Cameronians and us similarly deployed. After going east
for about half a mile The Cameronians and we were halted by the
Brigadier. In another half-minute both had about-turned and
were moving in the same formation westwards into Reserve
again. That was our last contact with our Brigade Staff.

We swung left-handed after a bit, got on to a road, turned left
and were soon passing II Corps H.Q. in Bertry. Until then none
of us knew that a Corps Commander was in the vicinity.' Clear
of the village, we sat down by the roadside for a bit with a big
wood behind us, where we saw some fine work by the gunners,
and there was quite a lot of noise all round. After about half an
hour we went on again and halted in Montigny. Here we sat
down again. 'As [2] we were moving forward my Platoon Officer
told me there was "a slight skirmish," but I thought what a
prodigious lot of stretcher-cases there were.' 'A [1] field hospital
was established in the Mairie, otherwise all was peace except for
the banging going on all round. The inhabitants were strangely
unmoved, probably for the same reason as those in Le Cateau.
I remember buying chocolate, and exchanging badinage with the
old lady who sold it. As we were eating it General Hamilton,

[1] Geiger.   [2] Powell.

G.O.C. 3rd Division, appeared. We learned that there were quite a lot of Germans about, that his Division was giving them as good as they gave, and he wanted just us and The Cameronians to clinch matters. He was about to ask Corps to let him have us. Another wait.' At this time B Company were in a sunken road where the artillery ammunition wagons were. After some wagons had returned from delivering their load, the lead-driver of the first one told a group of our officers, "The —— can't shoot for —— ——." The officers were highly amused, and did not seem to mind that it was not the usual way to speak to them.

About 2 o'clock, as Owen recollects, he was told to go for orders to II Corps H.Q. at Bertry. There he 'was interviewed in a cellar by a rather windy Staff Officer who had been left as liaison since Corps had withdrawn to Maretz. When I asked him for orders he commiserated with us on the job we were going to be given, and said I would get orders from 3rd Division, whom I would find near Maurois. So off I went along the road till I got to the Le Cateau–St. Quentin road (the Roman Road), which was being shelled heavily all about Maurois. Next I was told that a Staff Officer was off a road at the north-west end of the village, so I went full split up that road and eventually found him. The Orders were that the whole B.E.F. was retiring; The Cameronians and ourselves would cover the retirement, Colonel Delmé Radcliffe to be in charge of the two battalions. Then I went as quick as my mare could go back down the Roman Road, which was still being heavily shelled. There was a conglomeration of broken-down lorries and other transport, wounded, etc., all over the place. I got safely to the turning to Bertry with my mare in a sweat. Soon afterwards I found the Battalion, and gave D. R. his Orders.'

About 3 o'clock we fell in again, but we were not to be at General Hamilton's disposal as we expected. It had become apparent that all was not as it should be. Hostile shelling was appreciably closer. The line had given way somewhere on the right. The Battalion, with The Cameronians, was hurried away.[1] General Smith-Dorrien met it, seized Major Williams, 'and said, "Tell your Colonel to form a rear-guard to cover the retirement." I got out my map and made the General mark it at the exact place.' (The mark follows the course of a stream which runs

[1] Williams.

west from Maurois to the railway.) As we got on to a road near a railway we could see shells falling in Bertry and Maurois. We continued our march south along the railway, crossed the St. Quentin (Roman) road, and spent some time looking for positions, south of Honnechy and Maurois, which offered fields of fire. There we extended in two lines facing north-east. D and A Companies were in front, distributed in platoons. C and B were on and in front of the Busigny–Bertry road. The Cameronians, deployed north-west of the Roman Road, were on our left.[1]

The afternoon was drawing in : firing seemed to have died down : only parties of stragglers and some refugees kept coming along the Roman Road. There was no sign of the enemy. With the reported fate of the Argylls' platoon at Quiévrain in mind, Geiger had 'arranged with Williams, who was in command of the two rear Companies, to give me a signal when it was time to retire through his half-battalion. At last, at twilight, we were withdrawn through it. I stopped to talk to Williams, when suddenly a cavalry officer appeared, and, coming up to him, asked in great excitement if he did not "see that enemy patrol," and why he did not fire at it. The patrol was about 500 yards away on our right front ; it looked uncommonly like our own people as I saw them through my glasses, and I said as much.' 'The [2] rain and the bad light made it difficult to be sure, the water-proof sheets or capes they wore made it more difficult, but Solly-Flood (afterwards Major-General) was sure they were Germans ; "It's the chance of a life-time," he said.' So an order for rapid independent fire was given. There was a clatter of hoofs, and at least a troop galloped across our front amid a hail of bullets. The men were excited and the estimation of the range was as bad as the light, but we certainly knocked over several horses. They were our own people right enough, 19th Hussars, although we didn't know it for certain for an hour or more. 'This [3] mishap produced the inevitable humorous incident. Two men, Reservists, near me, who were masked by a cottage and could see nothing at all, elected to obtain indirect-fire results by firing in a *feu de joie* attitude until somewhat rudely checked.

[1] The *Official History*, vol. i., map ii, which places the rear-guard north of Maurois, is erroneous : it is, however, as General Smith-Dorrien marked the map, and probably noted in his Diary.

[2] Williams.   [3] Geiger.

It was now nearly dark. As we had no orders from anyone the C.O. sent me to Maretz, which could be seen quite close behind, to try to find out what was going on. I stupidly went off across country instead of round by the road, and soon got bogged in some very marshy ground from which my horse could hardly extricate himself, for he was nearly dead-beat. There was no one in the village but The Cameronians' rear-party, preparing to follow their battalion, and the Corps H.Q. Guard of Cameron Highlanders. We soon joined The Cameronian party, who waited for us, and started off down the Roman Road at 9.30. The Cameronians' experience had been much the same as ours. They had little news, but could tell us that the Brigade-Major had been seriously wounded. He had to be left in a field hospital, where he died soon after the Germans captured it.' At Maretz we saw some of our "enemy patrol" walking down the road without horses, and found out what we had done. We waited for them to get on.

As rear-guard we marched in file with fixed bayonets; our orders were to form outwards in the event of attack. When we looked back we could see the glare in the sky of places that had been set on fire by the shelling and otherwise. 'The [1] march was a painful business. Mercifully the night was cool, but we were all pretty beat. The marches had not been excessive, about 20 miles on each of the first two days and about 16 miles already this day; but no one had had more than a couple of hours sleep a night since Friday and it was now Wednesday, consequently after leaving Beaurevoir, where we made a slight detour seeking Brigade H.Q., many of us were reeling all over the road with fatigue. I remember Owen falling into me several times, and I suppose I was doing the same sort of thing.' 'We [2] managed to keep the men fairly well together, though it was a bit of a job to prevent some of them falling out to lie down and sleep. I saw a man leave the ranks and wander towards the gate of a farm we were passing. Taking hold of his arm I asked him where he was going; he looked at me with a fixed stare, and mumbled that he was going to have a sleep. I pushed him back into the ranks, and the movements of the other men kept him going. I am quite sure he had no idea what he was doing, his senses were numbed by want of sleep for so long.'

[1] Geiger.   [2] Boreham.

August 27th.—'Having [1] struggled into Estrées, we turned into
a field on the left, full of stooks; it looked deserted, and we
decided to halt and get some sleep under the sheaves. I sat down
on an attractive-looking heap, whereupon it gave a volcanic
heave and, to my consternation, a General Officer—Lord Edward
Gleichen, 15th Brigade—and his Brigade-Major emerged, but
were quite affable. The whole of his H.Q. were hidden beneath
sheaves of which there were plenty for every one of us also. I
found a comfortable place and fell asleep about 3 a.m. About an
hour later I was wakened by the Brigade H.Q. stirring. The
Brigade-Major came across and told us it would be wise for us
to be off too. The night was cold, the field was large, and the men
had scattered; some escaped notice under the sheaves, others were
too dog-tired to be wakened. When we moved off at 4.30
about 50 of the Battalion were left behind—my servant, Preston,
among them; when next I got news of him he was a prisoner
in Germany.' There would have been more left but for Stanway,
who knocked up a lot and pushed them along in rear of the
Battalion.

We marched off in a south-westerly direction. When it became
light we saw more signs that we were part of a retreating army,
for we began to pass lorries that had broken down or run out
of petrol, and had been abandoned. At one place rations had
been laid at the side of the road for the men to help themselves
as they went along, but in view of General Gleichen's warning
we did not stop for them. 'Before [2] long we turned left. I said to
myself, "Now we are for it," because I thought we were going
to take up a defensive position. We had, however, turned off
to avoid the congestion on the main road. It was full of small
bodies of troops and of single men who had lost their units,
but our men still kept very well together. During a halt that
followed the men were discussing the situation. One of them
said, "Well, there's one thing, we are advancing," and he appealed
to me for confirmation. "Oh yes," I said, "we shall be in Germany
in a couple of weeks." I did not mean quite what he thought
I did. On starting again, the Medical Officer was marching at
the head of my Company, and was telling Captain Powell how,
having to attend to someone during the night, he gave his horse

¹ Geiger.   ² Boreham.

to a man to hold, and when he had finished with his patient both horse and holder had disappeared. Almost as he finished his story a man of The Cameronians came past riding the very horse: he was most loath to give it up.'

Soon we came to St. Quentin by the St. Quentin–Cambrai Route Nationale, and halted in the street 200 yards short of the central Square. It was about breakfast-time, but there was no breakfast. We had not seen anything of the Transport since we left Le Cateau—in fact we thought it had fallen into the enemy's hands. 'We [1] were feeling pretty hungry, and I was sitting opposite a grocer's shop; that led to a suggestion to the C.O. that he ration the Battalion, and so he bought up the shop. The *épicier* protested, but he accepted our requisition. Potted meats, jam, biscuits, chocolate, and anything that could be eaten,' made a welcome change from the meals we had been having. 'During [2] the short halt I was sitting on a doorstep when the door opened and a large jug of beer was passed out.' People gave us chocolate, bread, and other food; 'they must have thought we were winning.' A man to whom a bottle of wine was offered was told by Major Williams that it would make him drunk; he replied, "It would take ten bottles of that to make me drunk, sir." While we rested some officers' grooms, who had been "missing" since the previous afternoon, turned up with their horses.

'Resuming [1] our march, a big black-board, erected in the Square by the Staff, directed us to take the left fork of the road in front. (From Le Cateau the 5th and 3rd Divisions had used the same roads so far; their march was continued on parallel roads.) Clear of the town, the G.O.C. 5th Division, Sir Charles Ferguson, and his Staff stood in a field. The Brigade was attached temporarily to his Division. While the C.O. talked to the Staff we halted, and I was accosted by a Sandhurst contemporary, now at G.H.Q. Obviously very agitated, he began at once, "Isn't it awful! The French on our right have been heavily defeated, and we got a bad knock yesterday, etc., etc.," and declared that we should have to retreat behind the Seine. Having concluded this doleful story, he clasped both my hands, shook them warmly, and exclaiming, "God bless you, old chap!" he entered a particularly luxurious Rolls-Royce, which disappeared displaying two large cases of Fortnum and Mason on the luggage grid. Then we continued our march. Whether it was the effect of Z's words on my morale, joined to the fatigue I was suffering from, I know not, but after another mile or so everything suddenly whirled round and became black, and my next recollection is of lying on my back in a horsed ambulance during a halt about the middle of the night.'

On and on the Battalion went the whole day until we reached Ollezy about 4 p.m. 'Mullens,[1] my batman, got me some water and I bathed my feet, but before I could put my boots and puttees on we were off again.' Some men could not get their boots on after taking them off. This time we did not go far, and the men had a chance to make tea in their canteens. We had marched 33 miles. Late in the evening we made another move, this time to form outposts on a line Tugny, Dury, Pithon.

August 28th.—Outposts were withdrawn about 9.30. We returned through Ollezy and continued to march south. The Brigade was rear-guard to the 5th Division. We marched all day, passing through Cugny, Villeselve, Berlancourt, Guiscard and Noyon. At Noyon the French were getting their rolling-stock away, and we were checked at the level-crossing for a long time before we could continue what had become a crawl, the road was so congested with transport. At one place our pompous R.S.M. appeared on horseback. With little control of his mount he careered down the densely packed road, shouting, "Make way there; I'm galloping; I'll run you down." 'One [1] of the heroes of the Retreat up to this stage was Captain Powell's horse; I don't think he had known what it was not to have someone on his back. At 9 p.m. we came to Pontoise, a few miles beyond Noyon, having marched 16 miles. Here we met the Transport. We were greatly pleased to see each other, for each had heard that the other had been taken prisoner. The Quartermaster had some stew and tea ready, and we had an issue of rum, and, what was still better, some letters from home.'

'Yates [2] gave the company officers news of a catastrophe. A panicky Staff Officer, or A.S.C. officer of sorts, had ordered the second-line transport of the Brigade to lighten the carts by throwing out all the blankets and officers' kits. The kits in the H.Q. wagon—

¹ Boreham.   ² Geiger.

the C.O.'s, Williams's, Owen's and his own—were saved! With the faith born of many years manœuvres, in which one's kit always turned up sooner or later, I had packed nearly everything in my valise—burberry, razor, even a miniature of my wife. A year later (27.8.15) I got a letter from an acquaintance saying he had the miniature. Our kits had been looted by a battery of our own artillery. A Bombardier Johnson took the miniature, pocket-book, and doubtless some useful articles. A year later it struck him that the miniature might be useful to its owner, so he got in touch with my friend whose card was in the pocket-book.' Holmes got his "flea-bag" months afterwards from a military policeman; 'my dogs sleep on it now' (1930).

The Quartermaster's narrative of the first days of the Retreat.—'When the Battalion marched out of Valenciennes the Brigade Transport followed it. We filled up at Onnaing in the afternoon, then went on to Quiévrain and halted. Monday morning's start was made in the dark. Soon we had trouble with the 18th Hussars, who chased us off the main road, saying that in daylight we would be giving the show away. One of their officers showed us a round-about way to Elouges, which we got to at dawn. At Elouges we turned south and marched through Roisin to Jenlain. A Staff Officer met us there, at a cross-road that runs west to Valenciennes, and called all Transport Officers and Quartermasters into an estaminet. He told us to detail parties to go into Valenciennes and take delivery of the travelling cookers that had been sent out to us. Very few were keen on the job, and when some talk was going on a French officer and a civilian came and told us that the Germans were in the town. After that the order cancelled itself. There is a bit of higher ground near the cross-roads that I went up, and could see a lot of German cavalry in a wood between us and Valenciennes.

On Tuesday afternoon, just beyond Solesmes where the railway crosses the road, we saw General Snow, who had come up with the 4th Division. One of his Staff stopped us and said that all men who could be spared were to go and line the railway embankment until relieved, so I took command of a mixed lot from all the Brigade Transport. From our position we saw strong German cavalry patrols away over on the left; in front were only our own troops coming down. We were relieved by a battalion of the Rifle

Brigade, and my party rejoined the Transport in Le Cateau. Sir John French was in the Square talking to an English-speaking French General. Sir John was gesticulating and talking loud enough for fifty of us to hear him. He was complaining that he had been promised the support of two French divisions, that he hadn't got it, and was in a bad situation. I understood the General to say to Sir John that the two divisions had been lost at Valenciennes.[1]

During the night, as we lay parked up a side street of Le Cateau, I was warned by a note from the O.C. Train that we were to march to Estrées–Maretz at 4 a.m., so I went at once to find the way out of the town. I think it would be about 3 o'clock on the 26th when the alarm went that the Allemand was in the town, and we had to move. Knowing the road out I was able to get away quick once we got the order, which would be about 5 o'clock. Our horses had not been unhooked, and the drivers slept on the seat. When about half-way up the main street I found that I was a G.S. wagon deficient, though I had wakened every driver myself. As I galloped back and passed our Battalion going out, Jones Vaughan called to me that he had left his burberry, would I bring it along. "To hell with you and your burberry!" I replied. The driver was fast asleep on his box, so I hit him with my whip. Two A.S.C. drivers for the supply wagons had been posted to us on the Tuesday; it was one of these men who had gone to sleep again. I got the wagon away all right, managed to get up to the others, and eventually we arrived at Estrées where we took on rations. We were then ordered to push on as quick as possible to St. Quentin. On the way, about 2 p.m., we were blocked for quite a long time by motor transport that passed us taking up ammunition. They had not gone very far before they turned back, dashing in among us. We stopped them as soon as we could, and asked why they had turned back. They said that someone had given the order, but they did not know who. We turned them about, and told them to go where they were ordered, and not to listen to any rumours.

On arriving at St. Quentin, between 3 and 4 in the afternoon,

---

[1] The expression is summary : the facts are set out tactfully in the *Official History*, vol. i., p. 109 (p. 116, 3rd edition). These " divisions " are referred to again by a French cavalry officer in St. Quentin.

I parked the Transport in the Square.   Everything was chaos.
I asked various Staff Officers for orders, but they did not know
anything, or were too busy and excited to have any time to answer.
A French officer told me, in English, that our H.Q. Staff was at
the Mairie, so I went there.   At the door I met another French
officer who spoke English.   He was very tall, about 6 feet 4 inches,
resplendent in brass helmet and mane of horsehair, his accoutrements glittering in the sun.   The picture he gave me was appalling.
He told me to get out of St. Quentin as quick as possible, or I
would see some of the most atrocious things ever seen on this
earth.   He said that the French divisions arriving at some station
quite close were detraining right into the Boches' hands, that he
was going to tell the Mayor, and then ride out to some place I
forget and cut the wires to save any more trains going up.   The
Mayor came out, and this French officer repeated to him what he
had told me—at least, that is what I made out from the way the
Mayor started throwing his arms about and shouting.   When the
Mayor went inside I followed him and asked where the Staff
were, as I had been told they were here.   He said they had all
cleared out that morning and gone to Compiègne [Noyon].

As I was going out General Smith-Dorrien came up in his
car.   He called me to him and asked if Sir John French was in.
I told him what the French officer and the Mayor had told me.
He said that things were bad, but he could not understand Sir John
French not being there as he had an appointment with him.   I
called the Mayor out to him.   The French officer had disappeared,
gone to cut the wires likely.   General Smith-Dorrien said the
officer was probably a spy, but the Mayor said that he knew him.
Then the Mayor repeated his story, and told Sir Horace of the
annihilation of his own Corps.   When I had told the General
who I was and what I wanted he took me with him to the railway
station where he had a long talk with the railway authorities.
They told him that they would be able to get a few ambulances
away by train, but nothing more.   The General then told me to
get away to Noyon as quick as possible.   After I had explained the
state the horses were in he said, "Take what you can, if the horses
cannot take their loads dump them anywhere and get along with
the empty wagons; if they cannot pull them along, leave them
behind, but get as many horses and men to Noyon as you can."

I explained to him that I must get rations up to the Battalion. Just then the O.C. Train came up and had a talk with the General; he said that he had got some motor lorries to take up rations to all the battalions in the Brigade, and an armed escort for each lorry. Then the General told me not to worry about rations, but go and carry out his instructions and do the best I could. I went with Clifton Sheldon, O.C. Train, 19th Brigade, and saw the rations start up with him in charge, armed with a rifle and lying down at the ready on the leading wagon; there were 4 men on each of 4 lorries. While we were talking to the General at the station a French covered wagon drove up with about a dozen French cavalry soldiers, shouting and throwing their arms about. To a Staff Officer who questioned them they said they were the only survivors of their regiment, that the British Army was annihilated, and the Boche was close behind them.

When I got back to my lot I explained to them what General Smith-Dorrien had said, put a N.C.O. in charge of each wagon, and started for Noyon. During the journey to Ham we got frightfully mixed up with all sorts of transport and troops. Halting at dawn, August 27th, at Ham, I collected my lot together and found that R.Q.M.S. Welton had dumped all the officers' kits from his wagon. He said a Staff Officer had ordered them all to dump everything and take on the refugees. I tried to get his wagon back but got only a few yards, the whole road was blocked with transport; then a Staff Officer came and said I had no right to halt, and ordered me to get on to Noyon quick, as the troops were just behind us. At Noyon we halted by the cavalry barracks, and I went in to see if there was anyone who could give me some information. On coming out I met our Brigadier, looking very ill; he said he was glad to see me as he had not expected to see any of the Brigade Transport again. While we were talking a Staff Officer came up and ordered me to push on to Pontoise, as the troops were immediately behind us and all transport must be got out of the way. From Ham to Pontoise there were dumps of rations on the roadside, placed there by the different divisional trains for all to help themselves, but I still had the rations I had picked up at Estrées. When we arrived at Pontoise a Staff Officer, the first with any decency that I had spoken to since leaving Le Cateau, told me to draw into a field and do what I could for the men and horses, that the Battalion would be arriving shortly. The cooks were set to work, and prepared for them. While we were at work R.S.M. Murphy arrived on a pony. He said the C.O. understood I had been captured in Le Cateau, and had sent him to see what Transport there was and to take charge.

When the Battalion arrived the C.O. was more than delighted to see us, for they had heard all sorts of rumours. He was very pleased when he heard I was complete, except for the kits, especially when Colonel Ward told him the state the other battalions were in. I had Welton up before him over the kits; he told the same story as he had told me, so the C.O. said that Welton could do no other than obey orders. I don't think Welton would have done it if he had been in his sober senses.' Colonel Ward, 1st Middlesex, was Acting Brigadier, for the Brigadier had gone home; for a couple of weeks the Brigade Staff was a very scratch affair.

August 29th.—'We[1] were let sleep undisturbed, and woke up feeling very refreshed. We found ourselves on the bank of the river Oise, just by the Suspension Bridge. Transport was coming over the bridge and was being regulated. As each heavy lorry came across the bridge bent under the weight; I could see it distinctly sag down, and my heart bumped when I thought that we had had to thread our way through a mass of transport which was stationary on it the previous night. Apart from reorganizing the day was passed in a lazy manner, but at 7 p.m. we found outposts on the river bank. B Company and one platoon of A were the bridge guard. I spent the night trotting round with Captain Powell.'

August 30th.—'At[2] dawn the Sapper officer responsible for blowing up the bridge remarked that his Orders were "to blow it up at dawn, and he didn't care if the rest of the Army was on the other side." So he fired the charge, but the effect was only partial. Soon afterwards a cyclist pushed his machine across and up the bank. While we were still hanging about my platoon officer said he was hungry, and asked if I had anything to eat. I had only a tin of jam—(Yates says, "Powell was always hanging round the Store after strawberry jam")—but I pointed out a likely-looking house across the river; so my officer went over and returned with a loaf which, with my jam, several of us, including the Sapper officer, shared.' Later we heard that two Sapper officers had gone back and completed the job of the bridge almost in face of the enemy.

The day was spent in marching through wooded, hilly country. Tracy le Mont lay on our route. We found the rear-guard. 'The [1] incidents that stand out in my memory are that we got our first issue of tobacco on the road and, in the afternoon, we were rationed by lorries. Once during a halt I fell asleep, and woke up to see everybody, from the C.O. downwards, fast asleep. In the afternoon we crossed the Aisne at Attichy. A number of troops were bathing in the river; they were enjoying themselves, and we envied them very much. And we saw a trainful of troops, invalids we supposed, and these also we envied. Couloisy is the name of the place where we halted.' 19 miles.

'On [2] the morning of the 30th I got out of the ambulance as it was passing through Couloisy on the off-chance of catching my Unit should it pass through. I have always kicked myself for the next occurrence. As I was standing in the road a car passed going towards Compiègne. It was of unusual shape, painted a filthy orange-yellow colour, and contained four men in plain clothes who were certainly not French. If my mind had worked quickly enough I should have recognized them for Germans and taken steps to stop the car; that would have been easy as there were lots of our men about. I let the opportunity slip. At that period German Staff Officers in plain clothes were working ahead, spreading false news and trying to create panics. Shortly afterwards I heard myself hailed: turning round, I recognized in a chauffeur driving a 15 h.p. ambulance an old friend who had landed the previous week as a motor cyclist, and had already promoted himself to something bigger. He told me the Battalion was in the Jaulzy direction. On going east I found them halted for the day. Our bivouac was on the high ground south of the road. The country hereabout and from now on was very pretty; many of the roads were lined with apple and pear trees, the fruit of which was a pleasant variant to bully, biscuit, and "mousetrap." While strolling about in the evening I approached the village Calvaire and saw two other officers approaching it from different directions.

¹ Boreham.   ² Geiger.

We found we were school contemporaries; this was our first
meeting since leaving school over twenty years previously.'

August 31st.—Before marching off we were told of the victorious
action of our light cruisers in the North Sea—Heligoland Bight.
Someone remarked that it was a good job we had a Navy. We
started later than usual. After going for a mile or so towards
Compiègne we turned south through Guise Lamotte; on coming
within view of the magnificent Château of Pierrefonds we turned
west again into Compiègne Forest. The turf of the rides was
pleasanter than the hard dusty roads, though it made trying
work for the transport animals, especially at first owing to the
hilliness, but that soon flattened out; and the shade of the trees
was most grateful, for the day was very hot. In other circumstances the Forest would have been very nice. It was full of
troops, and German cavalry were reported to be about. With
everyone having flanking parties out we should have looked rather
a rabble to anyone in an aeroplane; there was, in fact, no real
confusion. We emerged on the Compiègne–Senlis road, turned
south and marched to Verberie station and level-crossing where
we halted for the night and, as usual, threw out outposts.

'A.[1] Company's sector was from the Compiègne–Senlis road
to the railway bridge over the Oise. After posting my people—
we had to do it without a map these days, but it always panned out
—I took an hour off for some food and rest, and then set out
along the railway line to look at my pickets. It was pitch dark.
On approaching the bridge I was met by a very excited French
officer, who explained rapidly that he was not a Regular, that he
had been ordered to prepare the bridge for demolition, that the
Germans were close up on the other side, "faut-il faire sauter
le pont?" Only five weeks previously I had been peacefully
engaged in company training, in the course of which had any
of my men damaged so much as a cabbage I should have been
held strictly to account. Consequently, with the fear of being held
accountable for a sum of half a million francs or so, I sternly replied
that if he blew up the bridge he did so on his own responsibility.
At that moment an engine arrived from the direction of the station,
and the C.O. descended from it. I reported my conversation with
the Frenchman, and he cordially approved my action. We then

[1] Geiger.

proceeded back down the line after looking at the picket. We had not gone many yards when we heard a terrific explosion. My French friend's nerves had settled the matter: the bridge had "sauté-d." I then set about seeing my remaining pickets. I was talking to a "group" at a small level-crossing when the sentry challenged. To our unspeakable astonishment, out of the night came the following words, "For Gawd's sake don't shoot, gents; I ain't no spy." And from the darkness emerged a small, fat man in plain clothes, carrying a bundle, and so pale he positively illuminated the darkness. He added hastily, "I'm a stable-'and in these parts, gents. They told me the woods was full of Germans and that I'd better be off, so I 'opped it—but I ain't no spy, gents." This district is full of training stables. I sent him back to the reserve Company under escort, and saw him no more. An Englishman wandering about the Forest in plain clothes would not have had much chance that night if he had fallen in with a German patrol.

The next incident was not entirely comedy. On my return journey there was suddenly an explosion of fire, beginning on my left—I was walking east—it continued almost in front of me. I hurried towards the level-crossing and there found Williams. Apparently some cavalry had come dashing down the road and had been fired on by the pickets; they had gone over the level-crossing—which, stupidly, was open—and disappeared into the night. Williams and I went up the road to investigate, and soon came upon a dead horse with undoubted English saddlery and equipment. This was not very cheerful, particularly with the incident of the evening of the 26th in mind. There was no sign of a man; he might have bolted into the Forest which came down to the road on both sides. Going on for another 500 yards, we came across the A Company picket watching the road. I was beginning a few honeyed words to the sergeant in charge when I saw another dead horse. Going up to it and putting my hand down, I picked up something furry which, on inspection, proved to be a Hussar's busby of unusual pattern and very obviously not English. We then began to look carefully, and at once discovered a man lying full length by the horse. His hair was shaved close to his head and he looked a typical Hun; he was, also, obviously shamming dead. Ordering a party to bring him along, we turned back towards Company H.Q. to interrogate him there. We had not gone far when groans made us turn round, and we found the wretched German being frog-marched behind us. It was then discovered that, though far from dead, he had a bullet through his leg; so a stretcher was substituted for the previous mode of progression. At Company H.Q. I started in on my prisoner and discovered that he belonged to the 8th Hussars, and that, patrolling along the road from Compiègne, they had suddenly come upon a patrol of our cavalry just as these were mounting. The Germans had gone for them, and the whole mob had come tearing down the road, fighting as they went, their horses by this time unmanageable. Arrived abreast of our outposts, they had, not unnaturally, been fired on, as the whole lot had been taken to be enemy troops. He did not know what had happened to his pals except that they had careered on down the road after he was hit. It was obvious that they were somewhere behind our lines by this time. Not, at this date, being an expert at eliciting the last crumb of information out of a German prisoner, I did not press for anything further but sent him on to H.Q. We had been watched by at least half the Company, who contemplated their first prisoner with open-eyed and open-mouthed curiosity. The rest of the night passed quietly.'

September 1st.—'As[1] usual in retreat, the brigaded Transport started ahead of the infantry. The morning was misty. Between 5 and 6 o'clock we were passing the village of Néry. The road there bends to the right, and is at the foot of ground that rises on the left. There was a battery of ours in a field on the right, we heard afterwards that it was L Battery, Royal Horse Artillery. A lot of the gunners were washing, some had on only their shirts. Suddenly some German machine-guns opened on them from the height on our left. They ran, everyone ran: all our Brigade Transport ran along the road to get clear of the action, and we ran with the rest. I heard afterwards that German artillery came up too. After we had gone some distance a Staff Officer halted us, and ordered every man who was not needed to drive the wagons to get on to a ridge on the left that faced east, and watch more German guns farther out. We stayed there for a while, taking no part in the little action out on our front. After it was all over,

[1] Yates.

Colonel Delmé Radcliffe came up with the Battalion and relieved us. When we got back to the road about 40 German prisoners were brought in, in 5 or 6 wagons. We saw the same lot again in the next village we passed through, still being carried in wagons. One of them waved his hand and called out in English, "We're in for a good time now." When I got back to where I had left my horse it was gone; the groom had too many to hold. I was looking about to see if I could pick up one when some cavalry came past, so I spoke to them. They said they had a mare they had dragged along from Mons. She was in wretched condition, she had a sabre cut on the near shoulder and was lame, but I took her. That's how I got "Girlie."'

'At [1] 3 a.m. the if-anything-over-cleanly Samson roused me to have a wash in the Ladies Waiting-room at Verberie Station. We got comparatively clean, and he lent me his razor. At dawn we were relieved. We had not gone many yards on our way south when rifle-fire was added suddenly to the gun-fire we had heard to the east for some time. This, though we did not know it then, was the doing-in of a German battery and some cavalry by the 1st Middlesex, the Germans having just previously scuppered L Horse Battery and some of our cavalry. Both incidents happened at Néry. We had not gone many yards farther when we were astonished by an outburst of musketry very close to us. Down an embankment to the left were two dismounted German troopers in a field, dodging about like rabbits, while a few aged French Territorials took pot-shots at them from every direction; bullets were whizzing over us. They were doubtless a couple of our 8th Hussar friends of the previous night. We left them to it and went on.

While we were climbing a hill we met the Composite Household Cavalry and other cavalry coming down. They were evidently going to try to take part in the Néry affair we could still hear going on. At the top of the hill we came upon General Snow and the Staff of the 4th Division. Our appearance was unexpected and pleasant. Divisional Generals at that time did not seem to have heard of the 19th Infantry Brigade. The materialization of a "perfectly good" battalion at an unexpected moment, apparently at no one's orders, and at the disposal of the first General Officer

[1] Geiger.

who could lay hands on it, had given much satisfaction, if only momentary, to the G.O.C. 3rd Division on the 26th, 5th Division on the 27th and subsequent days, and now the 4th Division was to be similarly blessed. Perhaps the General knew we belonged to the same Formation as he did—the 4th Division and the 19th Infantry Brigade had constituted the III Corps since August 30th— for we were sent off in a south-easterly direction, and told to watch the eastern flank of the retirement. We soon spread ourselves out in some roots, and lay down for what turned out to be a nice long, well-earned rest. The Battalion was in reserve to the outposts. The horizon was empty. The men, when not sleeping, munched raw beets, seemingly a welcome change of diet. After an hour or so some half-dozen German guns from Néry, the first captured in the War, passed down. Unlike the field-guns taken at the end of the War, they were highly finished weapons. Each had the Imperial Crown and Cypher engraved over the breech, with the appropriate motto, "Ultima ratio regis." After lying for another hour or so gazing into vacancy we resumed our march. We had another long halt at Raray, where there was a small château with a pleasant garden; there were various other units and a few Staff Officers, but no rumours, though obviously the German cavalry were not far off. In the late afternoon we moved on again, and after crossing a lot of fields, a railway, and climbing a steep hill, we halted on the high ground south-west of Fresnoy, and about 6 miles east of Senlis of sinister memory. A 15-mile march. With evening came the usual outpost duties, my Company being in reserve this time.'

'That [1] night Miners and I were sitting rather fed-up. We had tried to make a fire for some tea, but had been unsuccessful, when a form loomed up in the darkness and held out to me something which I found to be a canteen with stewed rabbit in it. It was good. It was a present from a group of men who were the best foragers in the Regiment. This accomplishment was afterwards known as "scrounging."' Just as night was falling there was a sudden outburst of gun-fire, concluding with a rocket display on our immediate front, but nothing further occurred.

September 2nd.—We fell in about 4 a.m. and resumed our march south, moving for a long time in extended formation with scout-

[1] Boreham.

parties in the woods, and taking up positions. After about 2 miles
we came upon an abandoned German field-gun and limber, which
was astonishing to say the least of it. It was obvious that some
German troops had got past our line in the night, and it looked
as if we should have a fight shortly. That, however, was the end
of the incident.[1] After passing through Montlognon Wood and
Montagny we found ourselves in the middle of our own extended
cavalry, so we closed on to the road again. 'The[2] whole Brigade
was together, and I remarked how few our stragglers were compared with our other units. We had plenty of lame ducks, but
they kept up in the most heroic manner; we had no men riding
on the First Line Transport, although all the officers' chargers were
giving joy-rides to those in need. The tight-boot difficulty had
been solved so far by cutting vertical gashes in the uppers; some
men had cut the front part—except the sole—completely off.

We were rather hampered by refugees on the road, having to
thread our way between the farm wagons laden with household
goods, and the cows that were being driven along. This was the
first time we saw that the War had affected the whole population
to the extent of making them try to get away from it. So far
the townspeople and villagers had stood at the doors of their
houses and seen us march by as if such a sight was quite normal,
although we had been passing farmers, and probably others living
in isolation, for eight days. When we were marching through
Dammartin, which is quite a town, in the late afternoon I pulled
up at a shop to satisfy a perpetual craving for chocolate. The poor
woman who sold it to me was in great distress, and kept asking
me if the Germans were coming. I could only reply that if they
did it would not be for long, they would soon be chased out
again, a statement I was far from believing but which proved
correct. I left the poor soul in tears.' Longperrier was our next
halting place. Again the day had been scorching, and quite
uneventful. There was a rumour that we would go by train to
Paris, and a dear old gentleman told the laggards, very few in
truth, that there would be no leave for them when we got there.
A rumour it remained. We started cooking dinners, concluding

---

[1] A portion of the 4th German Cavalry Division had worked round the flank,
been scared, and had retired, abandoning some arms and equipment. (*Official
History*.)

[2] Geiger.

that we should stay where we were for the night; at 11.30, however, outposts were withdrawn. 'It was still "on, on."'

September 3rd.—'About [1] 1 o'clock we hit the road again. The hours that followed were, I think, the most exhausting I have ever experienced. We had already had a fairly tiring day, and marching by night is always the more tiring, there is no change in the landscape to keep one interested. All I can remember of this night is a seemingly endless ribbon of straight white road with an occasional village, and passing the usual crowd of fleeing villagers who were to be met at any hour of the day or night. When the whistle blew for each halt officers and men fell down in the road and slept like logs until it sounded again. Whoever was keeping the time must have had an iron will to keep himself awake. My poor horse too was so done that I had to refuse anyone a ride.' Days and miles became confused on the Retreat, for no one seemed to know when it was or what he was doing. On the roadside just short of the Marne Bridge were some big French guns, apparently intended to be destroyed and abandoned; and as we passed over it we saw the holes which had been dug in the roadway for the charges to destroy the bridge.

'We [1] finally struggled into Lagny about 9 a.m., having covered 26 miles in 26 hours. Ordinarily speaking, that was not a great feat, but quite an achievement if our previous exertions are taken into account. When we were half-way through the town a halt was called in a pleasant, wide road shaded by trees: substantial houses lay back from it. A bold explorer soon discovered a convent opposite, and, having an ingratiating manner, persuaded the nuns to let us go into their garden. In it we discovered several fruit trees, and, best of all, a fountain playing in a basin. Soon relays of us, all ranks, were having the first real wash we had had for eleven days. It is to be hoped that the Sisters were not scandalized. They were more than kind, providing us with towels and soap, and racing off to buy tooth-brushes, hair-brushes, tooth-powder, and the like for those who had lost their all on August 26th. We contributed to the upkeep of the orphan school of which they were in charge, and parted with mutual expressions of esteem. After a halt which must have lasted about three hours, we pushed on to some meadows on high ground. Word filtered through

[1] Geiger.

that we could take a long rest. Blankets and waterproof sheets
had been replaced; they were got out, and, as soon as I was able,
I lay down for a sleep which lasted about eighteen hours.'

September 4th.—We all had a jolly good night's sleep. It was
a treat to wake up naturally instead of being dragged out in the
middle of the night. The day was spent eating and sleeping. A
mail was received and our first newspapers, the latter telling us
much more than we knew ourselves. The first Orderly Room
since leaving Rouen was held, and one or two offenders realized
that discipline was not quite dead.

Lagny was the end of the Retreat. It was also the nearest
point to Paris reached by the Germans. Although we made one
more march south it was not in presence of the enemy; it was,
though we knew it not, a concentration. (The German right had
swung eastwards, the mistake which led to their defeat on the
Marne.) We had retreated daily for eleven days. The weather
throughout was unpleasantly hot. According to our own com-
putation we had covered 174 miles, an average of 16 miles a day;
this does not include a good deal of counter-marching—notably
on the 26th, inspecting outposts by night, and other minor detours.

'I [1] don't think we lost to the enemy a single man in the Battalion
through straggling, I know I did not in my Company. The
unfortunate overlooking of the men in the corn at Estrées was
not their fault. Upwards of a score straggled and rejoined via the
Base. Boots had given trouble; that in origin was the fault of
the wearers, for it was owing primarily to the lax fashion in which
they had been, so to speak, fitted. The system was for a paper
tracing of the man's foot to be taken when he fired his annual
musketry course under the superintendence of the Permanent
Staff-Sergeant of Territorials nearest his home. Actually the
Sergeant asked the Reservist what size in boots he took, and he
gave the first number that came into his head. Atkins has
notoriously little imagination, and it never dawned on him that
he might have to wear the boots some day. If we had not scrapped
our packs when we did, I am positive we would have lost some
men from that cause.' Tudor Jones, commonly called "Buffalo,"
almost alone if not alone, carried his pack all through the Retreat.
In those days, and until July 1916, subalterns carried pack and

[1] Geiger.

rifle when the Battalion was in full marching order. It came to be not unknown for a subaltern's pack to contain nothing heavier than an inflated air-cushion, but that was a few months later.

The Supply Columns, at any rate our own, worked without a hitch. On no day did we fail to draw our rations, except the 27th when we might have had them. It is notoriously easier to supply troops retreating than troops advancing, but, as we were conforming to the German plans instead of our own, and the roads were congested—crowded with refugees and their carts,—it was a very fine performance. The Quartermaster has explained his system. 'We received orders to go to different Dumps to get rations. I never took any notice of orders, but as soon as I had delivered one lot of rations to the Battalion I filled up from the first Dump I came to. The officer would say, "Are you such and such a division?"—answer was always "Yes," and away I went loaded. We came through with our draught horses complete, but shoes were the trouble all the time, the mobilization supply was soon used up. It was awful to see the number of horses that had gone lame for want of shoes, and had to be left on the road.'

'The [1] fact that we were kept without news of any sort made the days more trying, particularly as the men were longing to know what was happening. It was exceedingly difficult to invent any news to keep them cheerful, having regard to the fact that we were obviously marching in the wrong direction. For all that, they were in excellent spirits up to the last. By far their chief grouse was the lack of cigarettes, of which they ran out early; the few packets of "Caporal" I had been able to get for my own people were not an efficient substitute for "Woodbines"— "fags." We had not been seriously engaged; for all that we had been in the thick of all that had taken place. Such things as hot food, rest, and the minor stimulant of tobacco had been unobtainable; and no one could have removed his boots for more than a few minutes at a time. When these facts are considered, the morale of the men was really extraordinary.

September 5th.—We started about 2 a.m., still going south. While halted at some park gates Williams insisted on me waking up the concierge to ask to whom the château belonged and, on hearing that the owner was one of the Rothschilds, that he should

[1] Geiger.

produce a case of champagne. We were told that "Monsieur
le Baron est absent," and before the argument could proceed the
march was resumed.' Our route took us through Ferrières, Pontcarré, Ozoir la Ferrière, and Chevry. The road was entrenched
and picketed when we came to the environs of Paris, and trees
had been felled for barriers. It was 9 a.m. when we arrived at
the small village of Grisy, having covered 16 miles. Our bivouac
was in a rose garden. We were told we might billet, but the C.O.
preferred to have us concentrated; as it was still warm and fine,
and we were surrounded by rose trees, it was pleasanter. 'The [1]
Transport started three hours ahead of the Battalion. Most of the
march was made in the dark, pitch darkness in the Forest of
Armainvilliers. The column was held up often by the passage
in the opposite direction of motor lorries and buses, and vehicles
of all sorts, filled to overflowing with French troops brought up
from round Paris, for the garrison was being cleared out to strike
at the open flank of the First German Army as it swung eastwards.
The Frenchmen were cheering wildly. Other French troops in
the roadside trenches threw out some sort of challenge. At the
level-crossing south of Pontcarré we had to wait while two
long French troop-trains passed westwards. "Girlie" looked so
like crocking altogether by then that I gave her to the old gate-
woman, but after we had gone on a mile I repented and went back
for her. The Transport got into Brie Comte Robert, about 4.30
a.m. I think, and parked in the Square. After we had rested and
had breakfast we joined the Battalion at Grisy.' The Medical
Officer and five men who had been missing rejoined.

[1] Yates.

CHAPTER III

Recoil: "Marne"—La Ferté-sous-Jouarre: "Aisne"—
Septmonts

Contributors:—BOREHAM; PICTON DAVIES; FLETCHER; GEIGER; HILL; OWEN; POWELL; DELMÉ RADCLIFFE; RICHARDS; RODERICK; STOCKWELL; WILLIAMS; YATES

Sketch:—3

September 6th.—'We [1] started in the afternoon, retracing our steps for some distance. It was not until we had marched for half an hour in a north-easterly direction that I dropped back to comment on this with Powell at the head of B Company. We had, as usual, been given no inkling of any development, had not been told a word of any change of direction of the enemy.' After passing through Pontcarré we branched off to Jossigny, where there was a halt, and two platoons were on outpost. Finally we arrived after dark at Villeneuve St. Denis, having marched 16 miles. We had to bivouac without blankets because the Transport failed to arrive. Our first reinforcement, an officer and 98 other ranks, joined here.

September 7th, Monday.—'It [1] was obvious that something was going on. There were a lot of troops on the move. Unlike preceding days, there was an undoubted feeling of exhilaration, although very few can have known what was happening; presumably it was simply due to the knowledge that we were going forward and not back. We pushed off at 9 a.m., halted at Romainvilliers, then on to Villiers sur Morin. I cannot remember crossing the Grand Morin, it must be an insignificant stream, certainly the bridges were not destroyed. The day's march was uneventful; I can only remember the Germans shelling another column, about 500 yards ahead of us on the same road, shortly before the end of the march. We bivouacked at La Haute Maison, having marched

[1] Geiger.

15 miles. As there was no outpost duty there must have been other of our troops out in front of us. My junior subaltern, who had shown signs of a breakdown for a few days, crocked and was sent home.' The third reinforcement, an officer and 23 other ranks, joined during the day.

September 8th.—'An eventful day. We stood to arms at 3 o'clock, moved at 4, and got near to the fighting,' 'in fact, we got mixed up in it when we reached the banks of the Marne. All up the valley could be seen the dust raised by the retreating Germans.' 'A welcome sight. The tables were turned. Right throughout our retirement all that could be got out of our troops was, "Let's turn round and fight the bastards." The Spirit was wonderful.'

'A[1] and B Companies were left flank-guard to the Brigade, C and D were reserve. We began operations by searching a wood for possible Germans. We were part of a column, I was told, under the Brigadier of the 11th Infantry Brigade—A. Hunter-Weston. (Colonel Delmé Radcliffe says the early morning orders were issued by the 19th Brigade; Major Williams thinks that, later on certainly, the III Corps operated in two columns of two brigades each, commanded by Brigadier-Generals H. F. M. Wilson and Hunter-Weston : less senior officers were sure that H.-W. lost his own brigade in the morning and just wandered round giving orders to anyone who would listen to him.) I have a vivid recollection of this distinguished officer early in the day's proceedings careering past me on the flapper's perch of a motor bicycle, and of thinking how such a means of progression was possible only for a British General ; it would, even in the last days of the War, have been inconceivable for a Frenchman, or for a German— even in defeat, to get about in such an unseemly manner.

We were marching on the Crécy–Sameron road. About three-quarters of a mile short of Signy-Signets the ground falls away, and we could see right across the Marne Valley although the river, about two miles off, was invisible. Our leading battalion, the 57th (1st Middlesex) moved off the road to the left and assumed artillery formation. The Cameronians were out in front on their left. We watched the 57th feeling their way towards the river. Something flashed in the sun's rays on the high ground on the other side. With glasses a German battery could be seen coming

[1] Geiger.

towards us with the obvious intention of engaging our advance-guard. This promised to be very interesting, so we all lay down to watch the performance. It was not long before the Germans opened on the 57th, whereupon they all lay down and, where possible, took cover and the advance ceased. After an interval a few slightly wounded men approached, each attended by two or three solicitous friends, one carrying his rifle, another his water-bottle, and so on. These willing helpers were gently pushed back into the fray.' One of our batteries drove up not long after noon and took position to engage the German artillery, but it came under such heavy fire that it had to change position in order to continue in action.

Our next move was to side-step to the right, and go downhill towards the hamlet of Signy-Signets. A batch of our recovered stragglers rejoined here, they had been collected at Le Mans and sent up. 'We [1] were resting by the roadside when General Hunter-Weston came along on the carrier of a motor cycle. The driver of the cycle was an officer, I think; (none of the General's Staff was with him either then or at his subsequent appearances.) He came to me and told me to open my map as he had orders to give me, Orders I wrote down. We were to march to a château which he pointed out on the map; he said he would see me there and give me further orders. Then he went up the road again on the motor cycle.'

'I [2] was sent for by the C.O., and ordered to take my Company, A, and drive out anyone who might be in the wood on the top of a rise at right angles to our previous line of march. Off we started : scouts in front, then one half-company in artillery formation under Samson, then myself with the Company bugler as orderly, then Stanway with the other half-company in artillery formation 100 yards behind us. We were advancing with great caution when my scout corporal, who had topped the rise, doubled back, with a grin a yard long, to tell me that a lot of our own troops were crossing our front. A battalion of the 11th Brigade was marching parallel to our original route towards the river. Orders being Orders, we performed a *chassé-croisé* with our comrades-in-arms and dived into the wood. It was a mere belt of trees surrounding a small park, in the middle of which lay the rather attractive

---

[1] Delmé Radcliffe. [2] Geiger.

Château de Perrouse. In a broad grass-ride in front of the house
we found a litter of boxes with German markings, that had once
contained rations. The house was shuttered, and had not apparently
been entered by the enemy. After sending back a message to H.Q.
I pushed on with the Company past a lake, and came to a lodge at
the northern exit of the park, where we were acclaimed as deliverers
by the fat and aged lodge-keeper. While the Company lined the
northern wall the old lady told me that a German cavalry regiment
occupied the grounds the previous night, and that they had only
just left. When we took our departure she presented me with an
enormous doyenne de comice pear.'

'The [1] Battalion had barely reached the château when General
Hunter-Weston arrived again on the motor cycle, and again told
me to open my map. He then gave me as my objective the high
ground above La Ferté-sous-Jouarre, which he indicated, overlooking the Marne. His further orders were that from that position
I was to check any movements from the opposite side, and to co-
operate when possible with the troops marching direct on La
Ferté and other points on the low ground by the river : the Argyll
and Sutherland Highlanders would be under my command to carry
out these duties. His last remark was to the effect that he would
visit me again when I got into position and give me yet further
orders. I do not remember how long we were in getting into
position.' [2] The 57th and The Cameronians were operating against
villages lower down the river.

'A. Company [3] continued its north-easterly advance, quite in
the air and by itself. Moving across country through orchards
with the help of wire-cutters, in columns of platoons two abreast,
we came to the crest of the heights south of the river, and could
see across. There was a good deal of gun-fire by this time, most of
it, if not all, our own. [4] There was no enemy in sight, but we
recognized his machine-guns by their slower rate of fire. We
stopped to examine the situation. Only the river could be
identified, we had not the faintest idea where we were, for
we were without maps. Within minutes—I think it would be

[1] Delmé Radcliffe.
[2] A III Corps order, issued about 2 p.m., directed the 11th and 19th Brigades on
to La Ferté-sous-Jouarre. (*Official History*.)
[3] Geiger.
[4] The German artillery on this front ceased fire at 1 p.m. (*Official History*.)

about 4 o'clock—a gorgeous General Officer, he of the flapper's perch, burst on our vision. He asked who we were. On my respectfully informing him, he waved his stick and, pointing downhill, exclaimed in the theatrical manner which later made him so celebrated, "Follow me." He then strode off so rapidly that before one platoon had fallen in he had disappeared—for two years as far as I was concerned. However, we had got some sort of orders, for the rest of the Battalion was nowhere to be seen. We continued to advance in the same direction as before. After descending for about 200 yards we were brought up sharp by a precipice. With no possible line of advance near, we climbed the hill again and lay down near the skyline with an excellent view across the river. Nothing could be seen yet of the enemy till a well-placed shell over a wood two miles off drove a party of them out ; they started running down a road where a couple more shells fell nicely in the middle of them. Encouraged by this distant view of the foe, Wynne-Edwards asked permission to open fire ; although nothing more could be seen I acquiesced as it seemed good for morale. The platoon on the left then fired bursts of independent into the blue. Its effect was to draw the invisible enemy's attention to us. Within a couple of minutes we came under traversing machine-gun fire. A cry, "Oh, Christ! I got one" was from '600 Griffiths, the Goat-Major, one of my most ancient warriors. He came along to be dressed ; he had a bullet through his forearm, and a very aggrieved look. As news was passed down of three or four more casualties, I decided to withdraw the Company over the skyline. We soon came on Powell ensconced in a long deep ditch. He told me that C and D Companies had gone down into La Ferté-sous-Jouarre by the main road, somewhere on our right, and that our Companies were in reserve. We accordingly sat tight in our ditch listening to occasional outbursts of musketry and occasional shells, for firing had nearly ceased.' So little were the sounds of bullets known to the Company that when it was being withdrawn up the slope their zip-zip was thought to be caused by bent twigs striking on groundsheets. There was some rain about then.

'I [1] was in rear of the column, and had no notion that anything out of the ordinary was in prospect, yet when we halted I got

[1] Williams.

uneasy and went forward. I found D. R. and the O.C. Argylls (they, I think, were in front of us) contemplating the cliff that fell away at their feet; it was precipitous and much overgrown with trees and bushes. I left them discussing the situation. When I was back in my place a runner from General Hunter-Weston came along with a message for D. R. to whom I took him. D. R. was asked if he was in the town or had sent patrols into it.'

'I [1] had a short consultation with Major Williams. It was clear that it would not do to send a small party down, and I said so. Williams then said something to this effect: as it must be a large party, will you let me take C and D Companies down?—with that strength I shall be able to get through, and report to you what is the situation about La Ferté. I thought his proposal was sound and ordered him to act accordingly. (That was about 4 o'clock.) After Williams moved off I went forward with Owen, and came on Wynne-Edwards's platoon of A Company and Stanway. They were extended and lying down, firing, and being fired at mostly by machine-guns. As we were going forward we were spotted, and drew some rather brisk fire from across the river. This annoyed Owen, who borrowed a rifle and fired a few shots to relieve his feelings; he also treated the Germans as a whole to some of his best expletives. Very little movement could be seen across the river, the enemy had such good cover from houses, trees, etc. Later, while it was still daylight, General Hunter-Weston arrived. He asked me about my dispositions, and gave me some Orders for the night; as he went away he said he might have to send me further orders during the night.'

'Taking [2] C and D Companies, I dropped down the cliff to a road; it was fairly steep, the last drop into the road was about 20 feet. We went on until we came under machine-gun fire. I then left the Companies under cover and took on a platoon of D. We saw a few odd men about, probably 4th King's Own, who told me yarns about a redoubt, a house farther along the street, and that we would be shot if we went towards it. I had no idea what it was all about, and I had no map, so I went through the gardens behind a row of houses on the right of the street The King's Own spoke of. Some way down I went into a house to observe from the windows. There was a large house nearly opposite, and to its

---

[1] Delmé Radcliffe.　　　　　[2] Williams.

left a small open space or public garden running down to the river, which was only a short distance away. I could not see a soul, so I went out by the front door into the street. Someone from a house farther along shouted, "Come in, you bloody fool, or you'll be shot." I shouted back, "There's no one here." Two of my men came out and joined me. The Germans had evidently been waiting for a bag, for they opened a heavy fire at what seemed very close range. I thought at the time it was from the big house nearly opposite. We rushed back into the house we had come through. Both the men were wounded, but I was not hit. This shook us up a bit, and we returned with the wounded to where we had left the Companies. On the way I met General Seely, the Official "Eyewitness," coming down the road in his car : I stopped him and persuaded him to continue his journey on foot. By this time it was getting late. Generals Wilson, G.O.C. 12th Brigade (from to-day G.O.C. 4th Division) and Hunter-Weston appeared next, and asked who was senior officer in the town. I had seen no other officer, although I have no doubt there were many about in the houses, so I said I was senior as far as I knew. They then told me to take charge of the town for the night, to erect barricades in the streets, and to establish posts. All that was seen to as far as it could be in daylight. I sent word to D. R., and occupied the château [1] as a billet. Some bodies were seen on the road in front of the open space, but they could not be got at until dark. One was that of a subaltern, revolver in hand, evidently shot when charging, and there were two or three other dead ; and there was Major Parker, wounded : all were of The King's Own. Parker was brought into H.Q.'

'At [2] dusk, about 7.30 p.m., I got a message from Williams saying he had been appointed Town Major by the G.O.C. I think the same patrol that brought his message brought one from the General directing me to take my other two Companies into La Ferté. Going down through the woods on the steep hillside took a long time. The men were in the best of good spirits despite the fact that they had been on the move since a very early hour, though the actual distance covered was only 9 miles. When,

---

[1] The French invariably call the largest house in the vicinity a château, usually a misnomer ; here it was merely a moderate-sized villa in a couple of acres of ground.
[2] Delmé Radcliffe.

as sometimes happened, a man missed his footing and slid a good way down on his back he was the butt of much chaff by the others. (The last drop into the road was made by candle-light. A. Company missed all that fun by marching down the road.) At the château Williams told me of the steps he had taken with regard to night pickets, etc. We purposed searching the houses, but decided to do no more until everyone had had a meal. He showed me German cavalry cuirasses, with holes in them, lying about, and said "We seem to have made it warm for some of the German Tin-bellies."' There had been a press of German troops waiting to cross the river when our guns came up and shelled the bridge and its approaches.

'After [1] dining I took Clegg-Hill and one platoon and went to see that the dispositions for the night were complete, and to search the house from which I thought we had been fired at. A burst of fire from across the river, which is 70 to 80 yards wide there, was opened on us. I realized then that it was from the other bank I had been fired at in the afternoon. After another talk with D. R. at the end of my round, I went out again to post extra parties and bring up our machine-guns.' 'At the house we heard movements inside, but the door was not opened to us, so we broke it open and found the wounded Germans Geiger, who came in later, tells about in his own way.'

'Williams,[2] Clegg-Hill and Co. had caused a comparatively sumptuous repast to be prepared. The sole remaining occupant of the château, a servant who proclaimed himself openly to be an Austrian, adding that he only desired to lead a quiet life, and had no use for the War, provided sundry bottles of quite respectable Burgundy from the wood-stack under which they had been hidden to avoid seizure. Dinner, under the influence of Chambertin, Hermitage, or whatever it was, became decidedly animated. Some-one asserted that the Rifle Brigade, a battalion of the 11th Brigade, was going to clear the town in the middle of the night. This was taken as a reflection on our capabilities; so, the meal over, parties from each Company were fallen in—without authority, as far as I knew,—to go out and comb the town on our side of the river. Much the greater part of the town lay on the other side, from which we were cut off by the Germans having blown up the

---

[1] Williams.   [2] Geiger.

road and railway bridges in the afternoon. Before starting off I ran in to see Parker. He told me that there were no Germans in houses on our side, and that our fellows who got him in had behaved very gallantly. The parties proceeded slowly down a broad street that led straight from the château gates, breaking into each house. There was not a German, not even a peaceful inhabitant, in any. About 100 yards down on the left we came on an open space of which Williams knew. Making little noise, we got across without incident. It was pitch-dark. The first house on the left was a large one. Here we struck oil. Upstairs was a large room with about 50 wounded Germans, all in bed, being tenderly nursed by French Red Cross Sisters. The Germans had their arms and ammunition, which so enraged one officer already in the house that he insisted they should be taken out and shot forthwith, although the Sisters were most emphatic that these men had not fired a shot while in the house. The Germans were badly wounded; all the rifles I had time to examine were clean; so, as senior officer present, I left a guard with the prisoners and stacked all arms downstairs. On going outside again I was told that a half-platoon of mine had been installed with Wynne-Edwards in a house at the extreme north-west corner of the open space, where they could see the other bank on which, very obviously, a German machine-gun lay close at hand—about 100 yards from the road. After proceeding round all the posts we went home, and I found a bed—the first for many days.'

Meanwhile Tudor Jones's platoon searched houses, back-yards and estaminets by candle-light. At one well-lit-up house the men were halted in the road while Jones, finger on trigger, circled round the garden to get to the back door, having Sergeant Roderick and a man close behind him. Suddenly "Buffalo" plunged into a pond. The disturbance, as he spat foul slime and fouler language, brought out the occupants of the house: an old man, carrying a lamp, an old woman and a youth. They administered coffee, by urgent request.

'The [1] Battalion spent the night in the grounds of the château. A small lodge inside the gates had been turned into a hospital from which some wounded cried out in pain. I dozed very fitfully, and my sleep was disturbed by the most horrible visions.'

[1] Boreham.

September 9th.—With the first streak of light the C.O. was out examining the position, and establishing more observation posts which were found by B Company. 'I [1] got up as soon as it was light and sought out Wynne-Edwards's half-platoon. Using houses as a screen, I got in without incident. My people were in two first-floor rooms; they had piled furniture against windows, leaving loopholes for observation and firing. Next I was sent by the C.O. with a message to Williams, who was on the top of a rise east of the house, where an excellent view was obtainable. While we were there German machine-gun fire started again. We were scarcely back at the château when young Thomson was brought in seriously wounded; he had been standing at the corner of the open space calling to Wynne-Edwards.' He died next day. A man of his platoon of B, which he was taking out, was wounded too, and another man of the Company was killed. Soon afterwards we were ordered to rejoin our Brigade at Signy-Signets on relief by the 1st East Lancashires of the 11th Infantry Brigade, as were The King's Own. They arrived about 7 a.m. under Colonel Le Marchant, Williams's cousin. We related all we knew of the lie of the ground and the situation, drawing his attention specially to the open space and the German machine-gun on the opposite bank. For all that, he got himself killed by it before the day was out. The Battalion casualties were 1 killed and 12 wounded.[2] The important bridge-head at La Ferté was relatively strongly held by the Germans behind broken bridges. The Battalion achieved nothing, but it did all it could and more than it was asked to do. The circumstances did not offer an opportunity for a few determined men; a deliberate plan had to be followed. In those days orders were few and sketchy, and we were never told the purpose or the plan of the moves we were pushed into from point to point.

'The [1] rest of the day was passed lying and sleeping in a field of corn-stooks. The new Brigadier, the Hon. F. Gordon, had arrived. The new Brigade-Major, Heywood of the Coldstream, came along and made himself very popular, as far as I was concerned, by producing a map and appreciating the situation; it was the first

---

[1] Geiger.
[2] The total B.E.F. casualties during the same time were under 600. (*Official History.*)

time I had had any really authoritative information since the War started. We moved off as soon as it was dark, 7.30 p.m., to cross the Marne by a pontoon bridge that was expected to be ready soon after daylight. No smoking or striking matches was allowed, and we marched in silence. Suddenly a glare in the sky was seen in front of us, and a large Staff car with an enormous headlight appeared over the rise, coming toward us. One of my front section of fours observed to his neighbour, "''ere's a bloke what's lit a cigarette.'" When we got to La Corbière, close to La Ferté, we turned into a field and bivouacked.

September 10th.—On the move at 4.30 a.m., it was about 6 before we crossed the river. The whole of the 4th Division preceded us, so we were very much in reserve. Befouled furniture on the lawns, and empty bottles, bore witness to German ways. The inhabitants turned out in large numbers, very jubilant and enthusiastic. One woman pointed derisively to the corpse of a German soldier by the roadside, a victim of shell-fire. A small boy of the mischievous type eagerly showed another, pointing out that he had "la tête fondue." Signs multiplied that the Germans were retreating. Wagons, a gun, pieces of equipment, lay about. Among the last was a German officer's cuirass, a gorgeous affair, with holes in front and back-plates. And their cavalry evidently found that they could ride better without their lances. For three miles beyond the town bottles were practically touching on both sides of the road, and for ten miles one was never out of sight of at least one bottle.

'At [1] one halt I heard a couple of shots behind me. I thought no more about it until the next halt, when the A.S.C. subaltern following A Company, which was at the tail of the Battalion, showed me a bullet-hole through his cap. One of the many German stragglers who were lurking in the woods and copses had emerged from some cover, and crawled forward for 50 yards while a crowd of our people watched him with interest. Suddenly he aimed and fired, whereupon the A.S.C. Sergeant-Major shot him dead before he could get off another round. A brave man, he understood that it is the duty of a soldier to go on trying to kill as many of his enemies as he can until he is killed or put *hors de combat*: a counsel of perfection not realized by many.'

[1] Geiger.

Tancrou, Cocherel, and all the other villages we passed through had been looted by the Germans. Things not carried off had been thrown out of the windows, making a fearful litter in the midst of which stood the inhabitants acclaiming us and vituperating the departed foe. Finally, after a march of 13 miles, and making one halt of two hours at a farm one mile north of Limon, we brought up at Certigny [? Germigny], where it began to rain.

September 11th.—At 7 o'clock we moved off, again in rear of the 4th Division. It poured all day, but we kept ourselves fairly dry with waterproof sheets. We had an hour's halt at a cross-roads while another column crossed our front. 'I[1] had an old oat-sack on my back, and the rain was running into the seat of my trousers. I didn't feel happy. But a passing Seaforth Highlander had on an old silk hat, he had lost his cap, and he was carrying an old umbrella of which the cover had departed. I thought if he could be happy so could I, and I dropped the oat-sack.' The march was by Cerfroid and Chezy to Marizy Ste. Geneviève, 12 miles, where we spent an uncomfortable night in the open. It was here that Stable picked up the Mess-cart which served the officers so well for about three years. It was the travelling shop that is so common in France, a light four-wheeled cart having trays inside and shutters on each side that let down as counters.

September 12th.—To-day's march began at 6 o'clock, still in rear of the 4th Division. We moved along very slowly through Chouy, Louâtre, and Villers-Helon; our destination was Buzancy, 17 miles. The day was as wet and uneventful as yesterday, but there was heavy firing ahead on the Aisne. Our billet was in one of the smaller stately houses of France that dated from the Middle Ages; it had armour in the hall and ancestors on the walls. The Staff Captain cannot have seen it, or he would have taken it for Brigade. It was deserted; there had been a little looting, but no damage done. 'There[2] were vast caverns in the hill behind, used as cellars and store-rooms, which were occupied by the Companies. We Company Sergeant-Majors were accommodated in the Hall; the room in which the Officers dined opened off it. After dinner we went into the room to receive orders from the Adjutant, and I noticed some bottles of wine on a sideboard. When all was dark I went back in my stockinged feet to annex a bottle. Just as I

[1] Powell.   [2] Boreham.

reached the door someone with a lighted candle approached a door on the far side: I hopped back. When all was quiet I tried again; this time as I stepped into the room a board creaked loudly enough to awaken everybody in the house: again I hopped back. Then I started again, but on hands and knees this time, and was at last successful. One bottle was not much among four or five, but it was stolen. (The nimble forager is 6 feet tall, but only those who know the punctilious Regimental Sergeant-Major can relish the scene.)

Next day Sergeant Dealing told me a queer story. He and his platoon were billeted in an outhouse. While he lay still awake he heard in the distance the sound of mounted men approaching; he could hear distinctly the tramping of hooves and the rattle of armour and weapons. The unseen cavalcade came nearer, and, passing over where he and his men lay, the sounds died away in the distance. He maintained that he was wide awake the whole time. We had not heard then of "the Angels of Mons," or I should have suggested that it was a mounted section of them.' (Versions of Divine intervention in aid of the II Corps at Mons were reported in the home papers, and much talked about.)

September 13th, Sunday.—Moved at 2 p.m. To-day's march of 4 miles brought us through Rosières to La Carrière l'Évecque Farm, near Ecuiry, where we bivouacked in a field. We were told we were only waiting for the engineers to put bridges over the Aisne to continue the pursuit of the enemy. On the high ground above the château some of us spent a pleasant evening, in spite of the rain, on top of a haystack watching the sixty-pounders firing, and thinking that before such enormous weapons the enemy would be forced to retire soon. We could not visualize the fifteen-inch howitzers, and twelve-inch naval guns on railway mountings, we were to become familiar with.

September 14th.—'At [1] 12.45 a.m. we moved to another field behind a large wood a mile south-east of Venizel. It was raining again. I dug myself a hole in a haystack where I kept quite dry. To me Williams remarked casually that he had seen a dead German grasping a lance on which was a pennon with the skull and cross-bones device. I dashed out to get this interesting souvenir, only to realize before I had gone ten yards that I had been sold, and

[1] Geiger.

Williams was sitting snugly in my hole. Later in the morning, at 11.15, we moved into a hollow road north and north-west of the village. In the afternoon we came in for fifty high-explosive howitzer shells; they did no damage except to some transport mules and one of our horses. It was our first experience of high-explosive. At the time we thought it less frightening than eighteen-pounder shrapnel-fire, but these must have been small hows., and the fuses less efficient than those of the 5·9 hows. of later on.' Towards evening we returned to the wood and bivouacked in it, making rustic dwellings of branches and waterproof sheets.

September 15th.—At 2.15 a.m. the Battalion changed position again, to the south-east of Venizel. There was heavy rain all night and day. Stockwell arrived; 'everyone surprised.' Released from the Depot, he had crossed to St. Nazaire, to which the Base had been moved from Havre when the Germans were sweeping south. From the Rest Camp at St. Nazaire, where he found the second draft kicking its heels, the journey was by a crawling train round the south-east of Paris; railhead was at Neuilly St. Front; the journey thence was by casual lorry. His arrival raised problems of seniority such as continued to cause heart-burning and hardship throughout the War.

September 16th.—Yesterday's artillery duel continued all day. The Battalion was not being shelled, but shorts, intended for the howitzers behind us, came fairly close, and one man was wounded. Everyone, however, got in some arrears of sleep.

September 17th.—A. Company cleaned up the mess left in Venizel by the Germans. 'A rotten wet day.'

September 18th.—A fine day. 'This place is getting very smelly. Doing nothing. Got a bucket and had a wash all over.' In billets a wash all over was to be the infantry officer's luxury to the end of the War.

September 19th.—About 1 p.m. we moved on short notice back to Septmonts. One hundred paces was kept between platoons—four hundred paces between Companies, Colonel Delmé Radcliffe says—the first time we did this. It was an idea of the C.O.'s as we had to be within view and range of the German guns at parts of the road. At one exposed place an intervening wall protected the tail of the last Company from the bursts of half a dozen shells which fell near it. This incident is alluded to in a rhymed alphabet of that date in which all the officers were named, and a nickname or characteristic was mentioned; unfortunately it cannot be recovered. The Transport followed after dark. 'A beastly cold night,' which most of us passed in the open.

September 20th.—At 2 a.m. the second reinforcement arrived, bringing with it 17 convalescents and stragglers from the Base. It was two weeks after the third reinforcement in reporting. It had arrived at Havre; had been fed on rumour, and put to frantic digging; then it was marched to the railway station. While the very junior officer in command was dreaming dreams of leading it in battle and triumph it was countermarched to a ship and taken to St. Nazaire, to which the Base was being moved, away from the German onrush. There it was received with the enthusiasm affrighted people feel for defenders. And there it was, at the Rest Camp, when Stockwell passed through a week ago. (After ten years Picton Davies was only winding up a correspondence with the Pay Department about a sum for his command which he had drawn from an accommodating field cashier. The Department had run him down and reclaimed about £28 for which there was no acquittance-roll. A long search brought to light one pay-book in which was an entry that could be taken as proof of the disbursement.) The arrival of this party brought the strength up to 27 officers and 1115 rank and file. Another dozen stragglers rejoined during the following week.

The Battalion was out all day entrenching north-east of La Carrière l'Évecque.

Two weeks were spent at Septmonts, where the Battalion was got into comfortable billets. The Battle of the Aisne had become trench-warfare. The Brigade was held in reserve, with detachments on sundry duties. The Battalion was engaged almost daily in digging a supplementary line, under some shelling. On the whole the routine was peaceful in spite of plentiful alarms. We were little disturbed in the billets, for the front line was 8000 yards away and there were no night-bombing aeroplanes in those days. Every evening the French, who were on our immediate left, fired off their seventy-fives at an almost incredible rate, and the Chemin des Dames was lit up with exploding shells. Our deficiencies were made up; field kitchens, modern machine-gun mountings, and other proper mobilization stores were issued. Rum became a daily and welcome ration. Discipline had become slack in the stress of the campaign; the Battalion had to be got back into shape. At the end of the first week Stockwell notes a 'direct order from the C.O. to "Buffalo" to take off his face moss: very sick—he is a nasty sight.' One battalion 'looked like apes, neither officers nor men shaved'; that was part of an all-round slackness for which their C.O. was heavily dropped on. For us there was drill and some route-marches, and special route-marches for the returning stragglers, although one or two had been in action with battalions to which they had attached themselves. Near the end of the fortnight there was a general anti-enteric inoculation.

A large room in the village inn accommodated a Battalion Mess. From Soissons, and once from Paris by a brigade officer sent for the purpose, stores were brought. The woods round Ecuiry contained pheasants, and there were lots of partridge and rabbits about. A search unearthed an old pin-fire twelve-bore with a twenty pound pull-off, and about two dozen cartridges. As the shooting was to be for the pot, and a serious matter, only really good shots were allowed to use the gun and its slender store of ammunition. The C.O. provided most of the stew.

Letters and newspapers arriving regularly gave everyone a good idea of what was going on. Some quite senior officers were taken in by the story of Russian troops crossing England. The Russian "steam-roller" had many staunch votaries. For two weeks at the end of September and beginning of October the Russian Armies, from East Prussia to the Roumanian Border, made an impressive advance that inspired delusive hopes. But while the advance lasted the optimists, who had prophesied originally that the War would last only six weeks, and had become discouraged, got their tails up again and announced that it would be over by Christmas. One night a solitary horsemen galloped through the village yelling, "Peace is declared," and disappeared into the darkness, to be seen no more.

'A[1] few days after we went into Septmonts, my friend B. turned up to see me again. Since my last seeing him, on August 30th, he had scrapped the 15-Sunbeam and got a 50-Mercedes, apparently looted in Paris from the Mercedes shop; the owners, being German, had fled. I next saw B. a year later when he had blossomed into

[1] Geiger.

Major on the Staff at G.H.Q. In 1916 he became a Brigadier-General of Tanks: an excellent fellow who had thoroughly mastered the art of getting on in the world.'

The home papers, particularly the Local Press, were full of lurid letters containing astonishing accounts of the writers' personal prowess. This was the consequence of £5 or more being given for good "Letters from the Front." Naturally the most highly coloured letters were selected, so the men sat down with their tongues in their cheeks to try to make a fortune in literature. The officers censored the men's correspondence, but as these adventures were untrue and of no value to enemy agents most of us did not trouble to erase them. 'The C.O. enjoys reading all our letters'— for at that date the letters of company officers were censored too.

'The [1] time at Septmonts was a godsend to the Transport animals. The Advance was harder on them than the Retreat, for they were going from rear to front and then back again the whole day and night. I made it easier for ours by belonging to the Division or Brigade of the nearest Refilling Dump I could hear of; that saved miles of travelling, though it caused rows with the O.C. Train. And I pinched horse-shoes out of every smithy we passed on the road. I wished I had thought of that on the Retreat, although we came through it complete.'

September 21st.—Entrenching all morning: in future only half-day shifts are to be worked. When the Battalion went into billets at Septmonts two platoons of D Company, under Stockwell's command, were sent as escort to Corps H.Q. at Ecuiry. 'Men in nice dry barns: fresh meat, bread, and tobacco—doing ourselves proud.' There were few men whose ambition it was not to get that sort of "staff job," for it meant good quarters and living, an easy existence and dignified. It was to be of short duration for the two platoons, but they depended on a route-march or two to pass the time. To-day a party went 'Uhlan-hunting in the woods: they're full of game. Spies everywhere, we've sent sixteen to the French; they'll be shot.' But while German prisoners were in our fellows' custody they were made pets of. If the news of the sinking of the three Cruisers, *Aboukir*, *Cressy*, and *Hogue,* cast a gloom over the detachment, a few of its O.C.'s usual explosions kept it from moping.

[1] Yates.

September 24th.—The Battalion rested from digging. 'The [1] part we are playing in the great Battle is an absurdly tranquil one. We drove the woods here with beaters for straggling Germans, of whom a few are often reported. We stood along the drives and round the edges of the woods like men waiting for pheasants. The woods contained exactly three rabbits.' There was a false alarm in the evening, and another at daybreak. In future we are to *September 26th*—stand to arms for one hour before dawn. A first attempt at anti-aircraft action was made to-day. One or two Maxim-Nordenfelt guns, our old friend the "pom-pom" of South African days, fired at an enemy plane with no apparent result.

September 27th.—There was an alarm at 3.30 a.m., and an order, soon cancelled, to move to Serches. The dropping of a bomb by a German airman on the adjoining French Army H.Q. caused so much alarm at our Corps H.Q. that 'all wagons and other impedimenta cleared off.'

September 28th.—After another false alarm the Battalion was put to barricade all the surrounding roads against motor-spies.

September 30th.—Orders to move were countermanded. Madame, on whom Stockwell and his subaltern were billeted, 'cut up rough, so we turned on our own cook—three soldiers in the house!

October 1st.—Madame has thought better of it, she is feeding us again.' Soissons was put out of bounds owing to a great increase in the amount of shelling. It had remained full of people so far, although shelled, and was the almost daily resort of any of the Battalion who could get leave.

October 3rd.—Yet another alarm, and orders to move—cancelled. 'We are fed-up with Septmonts, a dreary wait that has got on our nerves ; nothing but suspense, orders and counter-orders, stand-tos and digging.'

October 4th.—'4.30 a.m. stand to arms, fairly warm. Church parade, lots of watercart.'

October 5th.—'4.30 a.m. stand to arms, damned cold.'—The Brigade-Major told us of an overlapping movement that is going on to the north-west. Our part of the front is to be handed over to the French. We are off to fresh woods and pastures new,

[1] Fletcher.

having played a very inactive part here in the fighting which can be heard going on all day and every day. The explanation is that belonging to an independent brigade, and not forming part of any division, we remain in reserve. 'Orders to move at 7.30 p.m., baggage cut down. We are going we don't know where, but——'

CHAPTER IV

*The Race for the Sea—To St. Omer by Night—Outpost
Affairs—A Hair-cut in Ypres—A Forced March—"La
Bassée": Fromelles; La Cordonnerie, "We are not moving
back"*

Contributors :—BOREHAM ; PICTON DAVIES ; FLETCHER ; HILL ;
HOLMES ; R. MORGAN ; OWEN ; POWELL ; RICHARDS ;
RICHARDSON ; RODERICK ; STOCKWELL ; WILLIAMS ;
YATES

Sketches :—1, 3, 4, 5, 6

The Battalion began its part in what is called "The Race for the
Sea," in which the massed armies tried by extending to the north
to turn each other's flank. We left Septmonts at 7 p.m. : 'beastly
cold march.' During the night some French troops passed us in
lorries ; most of us were seeing that means of moving troops for
the first time. After marching 14 miles and being about 16 miles
October 6th—southward of Soissons, we bivouacked in a wood
near St. Remy at 1 a.m. At 7.10 another night march began.
Going westwards, we had done 17 miles when we got to 'a very
October 7th—good bivouac' at Vez, beyond Villers-Cotterets. Our
route was through the Forest of Villers-Cotterets ; 'poplars look
extraordinary by moonlight.' We left again at 5 p.m. and marched
to Bethisy St. Pierre, 11 miles. So far 'we had to get off by night,
march till morning and then get into the wet and frosty woods
before daybreak, and sleep in the woods till about 8, hang about
all day, and go on the next night. Secrecy, of course, aeroplanes.
The men carry rolled greatcoats, waterproof sheets, spare boots,
socks, towel and washing things, three days emergency rations,
rifle, 150 rounds of ammunition.' Secrecy ! but fires were lighted,
in secret, and the culprits escaped in the wood.

October 8th.—Being well behind the line we marched in daylight
through Santines and Verberie to the station at Longueil Ste. Marie,

8 miles. We expected to entrain, but bivouacked. Geiger was sent home with appendicitis, so Stockwell was given A Company.

October 9th.—At 8.30 a.m. we resumed the march by Rucourt, Canly, Arsy, and Moyvillers to Estrées St. Denis. All this time no one had any idea where we were going; the Adjutant, when he gave us the orders, said he himself did not know.

October 10th.—H.Q. and A and B Companies entrained, and left at 6 a.m.; C and D followed in a second train at 10. We passed through Montdidier, Amiens ("Aemeens"), Abbeville, and then Étaples ("Eatapples"), and next Boulogne. Where were we going? All sorts of conjectures were made; the best one was that as we were the first troops out we were going home first. But no such luck. On we went into the night, and arrived at St. Omer at 10. We detrained at the Goods Station at midnight. The London Scottish had come in just before us. Their C.O. and all of them were greatly indignant at being sent out to the

October 11th—War "too late to have a look in." The Companies went into a French barracks. B was allotted some rooms at the top; by the time we had got the men settled down it was time to reverse the process and get them all out again. These barracks were infested with millions of fleas, no one had any comfort, everyone did more scratching than sleeping. We moved off about 7.30 a.m., and marched via Arques and Fort Rouge to Renescure, 9 miles. C and D Companies, who had detrained at Arques at 6 a.m., joined us there. The officers were billeted in the château; the building is partly eleventh century, very interesting, and very well appointed.

October 12th.—4 o'clock réveillé. The Battalion marched at 5 as left flank guard to Brigade and 6th Division, one of whose brigades was still on the Aisne. The morning was cold, but marching soon warmed us up. We passed through Staple, from which an enemy detachment had been chased by our cavalry not long before. At a farm on the cross-roads the Germans had concealed a machine-gun in the roof very cunningly; there was a small hole in the thatch, just sufficient to fire through. The enemy being so near, A and B found outposts with supports in two farms, while C and D dug trenches. Our cavalry were out in front.

October 13th.—Wet. We moved at 7 a.m., halted at La Bréarde and put out outposts. At 3 o'clock we moved again, and found the rest of the Brigade in Rouge Croix; then we marched via Caestre to Strazeele, 5 miles. It was rather a nasty march, and seemingly we were lucky. Guns were popping off alongside us. Bullets were passing from various directions, sometimes quite uncomfortably close. Two Maxims and some prisoners were captured just on our left, and the enemy was pushed back. He was not in strength on our front; we had to be content with rumours and conjectures and standing-by for immediate action. The Brigade had been in reserve while a brisk little action was fought at Meteren by 6th Division units. The people of Strazeele were found in tears; they said their priest had been shot on the steps of his church an hour ago for refusing to allow horses to be stabled in it. That night the Battalion bivouacked in a field.

October 14th.—It was 11 o'clock when we moved on Bailleul as advance-guard, A and B Companies leading. As we neared the town two German cavalrymen were seen riding along about 500 yards on the right flank. The vanguard opened on them, but shot so badly that they trotted away calmly and disappeared in a small wood. Some opposition was expected, but the Germans had gone. The people of Bailleul were very pleased to see us, and gave us bread and chocolate as we passed through. Beyond the town more German patrols were seen and fired on. As Steenwerck was approached our cyclist scouts exchanged shots with the Uhlan garrison of a barricade of torn-up pavé across the road, other Germans fired from trees. Sections of A Company extended, at 600 yards, on each side of the road; they tried to fix the garrison and keep down its fire while dispositions were made to envelop and then rush the barricade. By now darkness was drawing on. Soon the flashes of the German rifles in the dark were the only target. Before our movement had developed orders came from Brigade to stand fast, and to resume operations in the early morning. On the left, on the railway, No. 4 Platoon had two men wounded. In some desultory firing on the Armentières road B Company had one man badly wounded. Meanwhile H.Q., C and D Companies were at Le Lenthe. At 9 p.m., on further orders, the outposts and A Company were withdrawn through B. A. was crowded into a barn just outside Bailleul. B Company also was withdrawn to a farm on the outskirts of the town. It was a good job Fritz did not come to visit B that night, for the men were put into a loft reached only through a small trap-door; it took about an hour to get them out next morning. C and D Companies found outposts on the Bailleul–Nieppe road.

October 15th.—In the early morning mist a German cavalry patrol ran into one of D Company's pickets. An officer and 2 men were killed, and 3 prisoners taken. D Company had 2 killed and 3 wounded. At 5.30 another advance was made on Steenwerck, with orders to push through this time. C and D Companies led, commanded by Major Williams. The enemy retreated as we advanced and entered the village. There were enemy graves on both sides of the road, and it was strewn with dead horses. A trap for our cavalry to tumble into had been made by digging up the road and putting harrows, with the spikes uppermost, into the holes. An examination of the barricade, and of some of the houses in rear which had been prepared hastily for defence, and to cover the holders of the barricade and their withdrawal, was instructive. The village was a litter. Clothing, furniture, half the contents of the houses, had been thrown into the street. Only one house remained untouched, owing presumably to the fact that it had been the German Staff's billet. But the inhabitants were convinced that the woman occupier was a spy, and a riot was going on outside it; to prevent violence it was necessary to put a guard on it. A woman of resource, she could be all things to all men; two years later she was running the B.E.F. Officers Club at Steenwerck.—One or two of us met with the only instance of personal molestation to come under our notice during the War. Two girls, living in an estaminet, described their experience with a vivacity that astonished their hearers, and showed proof in a way that would have left innocence with nothing unlearned.—As at La Ferté, there was fouling of furniture by numerous individuals among the retreating Germans. Possibly students of ethnology in the ranks suggested this primitive sacramental use of excrement.

'During [1] this operation by C and D Companies, B Company advanced only to the cross-roads short of Steenwerck and made some rough defences. While we were there Captain Powell told me that Captain Knox-Gore wanted C.Q.M.S. Miners and me at

[1] Boreham.

an estaminet on the corner. We had a plate of ham with bread and butter, and a bottle of Bass each. We did not know the song then, or we should certainly have agreed that it was "a lovely war." The Germans could not have stopped long to have missed that lot.' This incident is one of the happy memories of those days of another senior N.C.O. 'A.[1] Company, the Machine-Gun Section and H.Q. were resting on the side of the road. Captain Powell had found some BASS! The C.S.M. was first asked if he could drink one. I have no recollection of him refusing at any time. He was not to tell anyone else, but to send the platoon sergeants along as if they were being called to be given orders. As I was Platoon Sergeant of No. 3 my turn came fifth; by that time the game had been seen, so I was like a young school-girl going for her prize. But it was good!' A and B Companies moved on Steenwerck at noon. Half an hour later Brigade ordered the Battalion to return to billets at Bailleul. Before being withdrawn D Company scouts beyond the village saw and fired on a German horse-artillery gun. At 7 o'clock we were ordered back to Steenwerck, to a bivouac in front of the village.

October 16th.—The Battalion stood to arms at dawn as usual. During the morning there was much amusement when the Brigade Chaplain brought in a fully armed Uhlan he had "captured." The Chaplain had gone out to collect eggs for the Field Ambulance, and found this man in one of the farms; he gave him the basket to carry and, flourishing a swagger-cane, shoo'd him along. For the rest of the morning the Battalion stood fast. The 16th Brigade had rejoined its division, and the 19th had been taken out of the III Corps and returned to G.H.Q. Reserve. By 12.45, as a mail was arriving, we were on the move again, this time crossing the Belgian Frontier. The first village we passed through was Neuve Eglise, at 2 o'clock. There was a shop with MARGARINE in large letters right across the window. Now, before the War R.S.M. Murphy took on the job of looking after the messing of the Battalion. One of his economies, which did not meet with the approval of the men, was the substitution of margarine for butter. As each Company passed that shop a loud cheer went up from those who had perforce eaten the delicacy. It was quite a breath from the homeland. The march proved long and dreary, and 'it [1] was

[1] Powell.

rotten going on the pavé. On the way I overheard an argument between two officers about the possibility of a bullet going through two men. My mental observation was that I should not like to be behind the first man.' Dranoutre, Lindenhoek and Kemmel were villages we passed through. 'At [1] one place was a park-like enclosure; it had a notice on which "labyrinth" was written. I guessed it to mean a maze, like that at Hampton Court: there was not much of it left when we passed that way in 1917.'

It was late when we got to Vlamertinghe, 14 miles, and billeted; B Company was in a school. Sentries were posted at the doors of estaminets, which doubtless saved a few men from making asses of themselves. A baker worked all night making bread which was *October 17th*—eagerly bought. The people were very good to the troops so long as no question of the use of well-water arose; they made a lot of trouble over that, some padlocked their wells. That sort of thing was done sometimes elsewhere in later years. The local people were very sick with their Generals—"mostly spies," according to them. The Germans had been through the place, but, except for some looting, had done no damage. Motor cars rigged up as armoured cars, manned by naval ratings, were all over the place—'owned the blessed place.' The 1st Battalion was about six miles away, somewhere north of Zillebeke, so there were hopes of meeting them. Thomas and Yates 'rode into Ypres,[2] and, after having our hair cut, we were enquiring how we could get to the 1st when a Staff Officer told us to go back at once. We found the Battalion parading to move.' Orders to move at once to a position just behind the 1st had come in at 3 o'clock, but they were cancelled. On the Sunday we were *October 18th*—confined to barracks, ready to move at a half-hour's notice. The Cameronians experimented with buses, of which 40 had been allotted to the Brigade to quicken movement. The event of the day was the issue of two French awards, the Médaille Militaire; they were given to men of C Company for good work at La Ferté. At 4 o'clock A Company found outposts.

October 19th.—Orders for a forced march came in in the morning, again the move was cancelled; but at 1.30 a further order caused us to start at once on the Kemmel–Estaires road. At Neuve Eglise we were delayed a lot by the cavalry; they were barging about

---

[1] Boreham.   [2] " Yeeps " or " Wypers " in Army Speech.

and talking excitedly of affairs in the Messines area. The Cameronians and Argylls made the journey in the motor buses. 'We were rather envious of them as they passed us on the road; they were in our thoughts a good deal in the later stages of the march.' One stout footman, however, 'thought the buses were top-heavy, and was glad we marched.' At Steenwerck, at 7.15, there was a one and a half hour's halt for tea. When we got into *October 20th*—Laventie at 1 a.m. we had marched 24 miles. 'A. Company [1] were so fed up, and so crowded in their billet, that a man commented there was "no room," but our hasty Company Commander said, "If you move that mess-tin there will be room for another man." In the darkness another sergeant and I selected a place which we thought was rather soft and warm, and got down to it; at dawn we found we had been sleeping on the dung-heap. Woolman slept in a dog kennel.' 'Miners [2] and I had a few hours sleep in a fowl-shed, which was quite comfortable.' The Germans had been in Laventie. In the house the C.O. occupied their officers had amused themselves by using mirrors and ornaments as targets for revolver practice.

A big battle was being fought all along the Flanders Front. The Brigade had been put in between the II and III Corps to fill a hole in which detachments of French cavalry and cyclists were acting as stop-gaps. Brought in to support the flank of the II Corps, it was again attached to the 6th Division, III Corps. Geographically the Battalion had a part in the II Corps "Battle of La Bassée," and it was given a Battle-Honour for it; its action has been referred to officially, it is not described, under the "Battle of Armentières," which was fought by the III Corps.

At 8.30 the Battalion moved off and dug trenches north of Fauquissart. At 1.30 we advanced to Fromelles and occupied French-made trenches in front of the village. Those taken over by A Company looked, at first sight, all right, though the parapet seemed inordinately high and the trench disproportionately shallow. Poking a stick into the parapet proved that it was made of hay revetted with ladders and covered with earth. 'Williams [3] came up about then, and, while the improvement of the trench and tools for the work was under discussion, the Brigadier appeared and pooh-poohed the notion; he declared we were "shortly

---

[1] Powell.   [2] Boreham.   [3] Stockwell.

advancing"—presumably in accordance with the G.H.Q. Order for a march to Berlin.

Fournes, which was being heavily shelled, was about 1½ miles in front of our left flank. "The Quail" and I walked out to get in touch with the French to whom we were in reserve, and got up to their reserve trenches some distance short of Fournes. There we found a battalion of Chasseurs Alpins, who wear a dark blue beret and jacket. They were not over-polite; they wanted to know when we were coming to do a job of work, as they had been having a dirty time and had had very heavy losses. (A lot of wounded passed through our line during the day.) I think we talked glibly about a general advance, at which they scoffed, saying the Germans were in great strength, while they were holding on only by the skin of their teeth. Our return walk was most unpleasant as we seemed to be pursued by "woolly bears." [1] The question is, will the Boche attack? A trench relief by our Ally's cavalry was a most interesting sight. As the French had no field-service uniform until "horizon blue" was issued in 1915, they were in their full Cuirassier dress: enormous white metal helmet with horsehair hangings; breastplate, covered with cloth, over a dark blue tunic; red breeches and black leggings. They advanced to the line in single file carrying a carbine, like a popgun, in the left hand, and a lance in the right, and an enormous sabre was hooked up on the left hip. When asked why they carried lances, they said that their popguns were no use, and, having no bayonets, they wanted something to deal with the enemy if he came to close quarters.'

The Brigade had a quiet day except for some dispersed artillery fire by field-guns and 5·9 howitzers. 'I [2] was superintending the issue of entrenching tools to one of the platoons when a salvo of these Jack Johnsons came over. It was my first experience of them. I am sure I was too surprised to be scared. One of the shells hit the railway shed in which was a section of B Company. Only one man was hit, but the explosion drove the coal-dust into the pores of the men's skin; and, because they had no chance

---

[1] " Woolly bear " was a big shell exploding with a lot of black smoke; " Jack Johnson," after a nigger pugilist and world-champion of the time, " Willie," after the Kaiser or Crown Prince, " Black Maria " and " coal box," were other names the Army gave them.

[2] Boreham.

of washing for nearly a month, it was easy to identify the members of that section all that time. During the afternoon a French battery came into a field close to where we were, and prepared to open fire. Captain Powell strolled over in his leisurely way, and drew the attention of the artillery officers to several shell-holes in a long garden-wall which bounded the rear of the field. The Frenchmen then had a discussion, during which it looked as if they would come to blows; after that they led their battery out of the field, and we saw no more of them. Practically all the inhabitants had left Fromelles, I saw one old woman in the place. There was any quantity of abandoned live stock; stewed fowl was a treat for the catching and cooking. It is strange how one takes everything very casually on Active Service. There we were in a deserted village; although the houses looked as if the occupants had just gone out for a few minutes, and although plenty of them had been damaged by shell-fire, somehow or other it did not seem —how shall I say?—unusual.'

October 21st.—D Company, which had been in reserve west of the church, was brought up on the left, for the Middlesex had side-stepped to the left. On the right, a squadron of the 15th Hussars kept up liaison between us and the Royal Irish, the nearest II Corps unit, who were between Herlies and Le Pilly, nearly two miles south of us. The morning was quiet: the line was improved: observation was made from the top of hayricks, and nothing hostile was seen. At 2 o'clock there was some shelling by German field-guns, "whizz-bangs"; and a battery of French seventy-fives put over a tremendous quantity of stuff. At night the Battalion was withdrawn into Fromelles where it bivouacked in fighting formation. There had been no enemy infantry in sight, so the French, who remained in position in front of the Brigade, were very sick when we were ordered to retire. The weight and success of a German attack on the left was not appreciated where we were. A serious gap had been made in the III Corps line at Radinghem, and the Brigade's left was in the air. Unaware of this, the C.O. sent to Brigade to ask if it was necessary to retire since we were well entrenched. He got a snorter in reply from the Brigadier. Meanwhile we had started to dig fresh trenches. 'Captain [1] Powell had told Miners and me to make ourselves

---

[1] Boreham.

comfortable in a cottage. Since we were going to lie down fully dressed and equipped we took the sheets off the bed so as *October 22nd*—not to dirty them—as if it mattered! We were roused from sleep by someone who whispered to us to come out quietly. We did so, and the Company moved off down the road in silence at 2 a.m. The move was made on ten minutes notice, just when rations were being delivered. The Battalion and the Brigade were concentrated at La Boutillerie. Two companies of Argylls at Maisnil, who did not get the order to withdraw, stood fast. They got away in the morning without trouble, but there was a to-do about it.

At 6 o'clock we marched off to La Cordonnerie Farm, about 1000 yards south of Là Boutillerie. Brigade gave the flanks of a new line, which was about 1000 yards long, and the C.O. divided it among C, D, and A Companies. It was roughly parallel to the Cordonnerie–Boutillerie road, Cordonnerie being behind the left centre, where the ground falls slightly from the right to the level of the Flanders Plain. Rouges Bancs and Ver Touquet are hamlets on the right front and front. The roads and many of the fields are bordered by deep ditches, which were dry at that time, and by trees. Hedges, which were fairly numerous, and ditches cut up the front. The soil is clay, mostly, and sand. The fields were then grass or plough, or still under their root crop.

The company commanders set their men to dig behind covering parties. Company officers had a great deal to say about the site. A withdrawal and straightening of the B.E.F. line was an accepted necessity; but it was agreed that a worse position could hardly have been chosen, whatever the Higher Command responsible for choosing it may have thought. The Germans could look right down into it and see our every movement from the dominating Fromelles Ridge which had perforce been abandoned to them: the Ridge rises about 90 feet above the position. Higher Commands in these days didn't leave their offices to go and look at the ground over which they drew lines on maps. The local view was that a withdrawal of another mile would obviate the serious disadvantage of the new line without endangering the railway communications or Channel Ports! And the local view was as strongly expressed about the nearness of the houses along the tree-lined Ver Touquet road. To get as far as practicable from

the houses was to contravene a G.H.Q. Order banning the making
of trenches within 200 yards of a road, the Boutillerie road in this
instance ; to observe the Order was to increase the risks from snipers
and observers in the houses.   C and D Companies had to take the
risks of their position.   A. Company disregarded the G.R.O., and
heard a good deal about it from the C.O. when he came round,
but since 18 inches had been dug the work was gone on with :
thus A was echeloned behind D, which had, as a consequence, to
bend back its left.   C and D dug regulation traversed trenches
by sections.   A. dug by platoons : Stockwell argued that that
would give easier command and better control ; and he made
no parapet, arguing that the occupants would be less visible.
Digging went on all day and next day.   In the time to come the
front Companies were to be troubled by snipers in isolated barns
and buildings ; C was also under inescapable enfilade from Rouges
Bancs, which was only some 350 yards away ; A. was farthest
from Ver Touquet, about 650 yards.   A. was to suffer least from
snipers, shell-fire, and infantry assaults.   B Company dug a support
trench on the right rear of Cordonnerie, and left one platoon to
man it.   The other three platoons went to a willow-lined dry ditch
behind Cellar Farm, the next in rear, and improved it with their
trenching tools.   H.Q. was in Cellar Farm.   Its kitchen walls
were decorated with landscapes, seascapes, and pictures of still life,
the work of artists who had stayed in it as lodgers.

'We were told that there was to be no going back, we were
to hold on at all costs.'

The Transport was at Fleurbaix.   The first echelon was about
midway between.   There the R.S.M. was supreme.   "What
have you got here ?" he asked once of the Water Orderly, and
tapped the cart.   "Water, sir," said the Orderly, an Irishman like
himself.   "Water ! you (obscenity) !   Don't I know that ?"   And,
thumping the cart with his stick, he bellowed, "How much ?"
Then he turned away, demanding, "Does the (obscenity) think
anyone can pull my leg ?"   Second echelon handled rum.   "Good
morning, sir," said the Q.M.S. to the Quartermaster of another
battalion.   "Morning, W."   "Got a drop of rum to go ?" the
Q.M.S. asked, lowering his voice.   He was told to "send round."
Back in his lines, the Q.M.S. called to the Sergeant-Cook, "Here,
Bobajee, take this round and see 'Old Tubby,' he'll give you a

drop of the stuff"; and he handed over a jar. "Tubby" was rarely known to be without "a drop of rum to go." Back in the lines, Bobajee was the first to taste. He spat. "Bli' me, Quarter, it's tarry"; and he spat again. "Tarry! you bloody ass," said the Q.M.S., "give it to me." He tasted, and spat. "God bli' me! Creosote!" Being a man of resource, he took a large basin from an officer's kit, poured the liquor into it, and skimmed it. After some not entirely commendatory resampling, the Staff was invited to "have a drink." They had been losing sleep watching the comedy and stifling their laughter, and, the only time within memory, they said they were "too tired" to turn out.

The French were still out in front, although they had fallen back on their breastwork of hay in front of Fromelles. Later on, Hughes, the Orderly Room Clerk, related a conversation he overheard between our H.Q. officers and some French officers who came to discuss the situation. One of the Frenchmen asked the C.O. what he would do when their troops moved back. Major Williams said, "We are not moving back." "Oh, but you will probably have to do so," answered the French officer. Again Major Williams said, "We are not moving back." The Frenchman saw his meaning, he then saluted very gravely, and did not carry that part of the discussion any further.—There was a good deal of firing in front after dark.

October 23rd.—The French cavalry was unable to hold on at Fromelles; it came in on, and slightly in rear of, C Company's right, having our II Corps on its right. The German vanguard followed up, and German guns were brought forward. 'A certain amount of sniping and shelling' made it risky to show oneself above ground now. A good deal of the artillery-fire was at the guns behind us. Suddenly fire was opened on H.Q., setting it ablaze. The inhabitants bolted, but, in spite of the shelling, some of our men got the horses and cattle out. The horses were given a spank, and they made off to Fleurbaix where their owners recovered them. One of the cows, a Friesian, calved in the middle of it all. The calf got killed, but the cow wouldn't leave; she was a fine cow and full of milk, so when it was dark a bay of A Company's trench was enlarged and she was installed. She gave milk till November 8th, when she met a full toss from a shell. When H.Q. was burned out of its house it went to the ditch in rear, on B Company's left. The front trenches were already fairly deep. At night 'our dear old friends the Sappers came to help us. They put up three strands of wire—to keep the cows from coming into the trench!—still, it proved an obstacle.' The ditches, with which the district abounded, were most useful as communications between front and rear; there was no other cover. Our Allies used their ditches as latrines also, as Holmes learned when he was sent to them to get back a borrowed stretcher, and had to take to the ditch to escape being fired on by them as well as by the Germans.

Although the position of the support Company was covered by the front line there was no lack of incident in it. B Company was the first to have anyone killed; there were two casualties, the total for the day. The C.S.M. 'superintended[1] their burial, and the job of doing so for the other Companies kind of devolved on me. The bodies were brought down after dark, and I had the melancholy duty of burying several of my old friends: there were "Pip" Parsons, Tommy Maunton, and others. But there were things, too, one could not help laughing at. This night I had just finished the burial when heavy rifle-fire started. I and the couple of men with me dashed across the road and jumped into the ditch—on top of R.S.M. Murphy and Jimmy Caldwell. They had come up from the first echelon transport "to see if there was anything going on"—and there was! The front was under fire, more or less, all night. Another, and very unpleasant, incident was when we had, I think, 19 men to bury. A large grave had been dug, and the first few poor chaps put into it when the usual nightly attacks started. There was no cover where we were except the grave, so in we went—the quick and the dead together. ("If you're not quick you'll be dead," was an often quoted war-witticism.) Far the most of the deaths were from rifle-fire, shells caused comparatively few, and trenches caving-in caused fewer. Strangely enough, no one of the burial party was ever hit.'

The day proved to be the prologue to an epic fortnight during which shelling and sniping went on all day, and never quite stopped at night; there were occasional attacks by day, and repeated attacks every night: about which the Battalion has contributed

[1] Boreham.

only meagre scraps of news, and few of these refer to the two
Companies that endured most, C and D.

October 24th began fine and cold. 'Changed [1] socks, very glad,
feet were sore. Quail did a shave, I didn't.' Awaiting attack,
C and D Companies had four platoons each in line. A. had three,
and one in support on the Boutillerie road. The enterprising had
the present comfort of some straw in the trench. A sheer want
of study in digging led to platoons and sections being able to
support each other, an advantage which increased as segments of
trench were joined up; A. was well covered by D. On A Company's left were the 57th, a stretch of whose trench ran under the
walls of a bygone Carthusian Abbey. The Cameronians were
beyond them, and the Argylls were in brigade support. Eight
guns were said to have come in behind the Brigade.

Enemy shelling and sniping were much heavier than yesterday,
and never ceased all day. In the morning, when we were all
digging, the Germans were seen coming over Fromelles Ridge
and down its slope. 'I [1] counted eleven lines in open order. We
lost them when they got to the bottom of the Ridge because of
the high hedges.' We were digging again when, suddenly, at
1.30, they appeared from behind the hedge lining the Ver Touquet
road. They deployed smartly and came on across the beet-fields.
At once our men began to fire rapid, and our machine-guns
opened. Failing to advance in line, they tried to come on by
short rushes of sections. Our fire stopped them. Where a platoon
of A downed two or three they swung off. Everywhere they fell
back and started to dig in, with snipers in all the houses to cover
them. 'This [2] then was not the real effort, so we got on with our
own digging. At 3.30 they shrapnelled our line, my man wounded
rather badly. Men tired. It's cold and wet, and my burberry
is bust.' No. 3 Platoon had its first man killed. The sergeant 'had
warned them against looking over the top, but there seemed to
be no fear in them. This man was looking through a pair of
German field-glasses he had picked up in Steenwerck, and inviting
the "—— bastards to come out and fight."' At 6.30, when it
was becoming dark, something like "the real effort" was made,
without achieving anything. '8 p.m. attacked, attack beaten off.
We send out patrol. 11 p.m. Hun again. Seven got through on

---

[1] Stockwell   [2] Davies.

our immediate left: promptly done in.' The brunt of the day's action was borne by the right of the Battalion, but no details can be given. The casualty return is 2 killed, 1 officer and 14 men wounded.

October 25th.—The French on our right have been relieved by an Indian brigade, two battalions each of British and Native troops. Vaughan's Rifles, the first to be in touch with us, were old friends from Quetta. At 1.15 a.m. and at 4 attacks were made on the Battalion line and driven off. One platoon on the left fired 780 rounds, officially, during the night; the actual number was probably greater. At dawn a heavy attack was made on C Company and the Indians: the latter had a lot of casualties, and lost some locally important ground on their right. The night and morning were misty. Half an hour after dawn our machine-guns searched the ground in front. All morning our position was heavily shelled, but work had to be got on with. 'Stockwell [1] urging on digging, I try to get the men to dig like hell, for the Hun sniping is very severe.' During the night the Germans had entered a line of ditch and hedge about 300 yards in front of A; nearer than that the only cover was shallow folds in the ground. They were at work improving the cover of the ditch. We employed our best shots to pick off any who showed themselves. '90 Davies (he became R.S.M.), 'who is a beautiful shot,' was got to snipe at thirty or forty in a part of their line: 'Saw a few drop.' In the afternoon 'our shrapnel was bursting well and doing damage.' At 8.30 the 'Hun again. Looks nasty on the left. We O.K.' 'The enemy opened that attack with very heavy rifle-fire, and used what we thought were star-shells, which lit up everything as bright as day. Don't think they won much.' This was the only time the Germans used artificial light at that period. When the attack began B Company had made a good start on a trench behind the ditch it was in, but was preparing to quit. Earlier in the day, when our guns were being shelled, it looked as if the enemy's shells were just missing the willows bordering the ditch, and that a "short" would burst in one of them. That had happened, killing a sergeant and two or three men, and wounding others. During this night attack the new, partly dug position was found to be too exposed, so the Company was withdrawn another 200

[1] Davies.

yards into the seven-foot-deep dry bed of the rivière des Layes. Battalion H.Q. had gone there already, and was living under a wooden culvert at the side of the Fleurbaix road. 'The day was fine. The men very tired.' Casualties: 1 officer and 10 men killed, 23 men wounded: A. Company had none.

October 26th.—The night was awful, pouring rain, and so muddy one could hardly move. A succession of attacks, beginning in the dark at 2.30, was made on D and A Companies without gaining anything. That was the night when Captain Clegg-Hill told D Company to think of our mothers, wives, and sweethearts if the Germans got through. Some of Gerry's dead were on D's wire, but that was as far as any of them got, or ever got. 'After [1] one of these attacks, "I'm wounded," was said in English on No. 3 Platoon's front, but there was nothing doing. In the morning we saw he really was wounded, so two of us got the poor blighter in, and the man who helped me carried him back to H.Q.; and I will say in justice to Gerry that they did not fire.' During the day Willies were coming over thick, and the German snipers were watchful. After dark there was another attack. Casualties: 2 officers and 12 men killed, 10 officers and 28 men wounded; and the C.O. was one of the sick who were sent away. Major O. de L. Williams took over the command.

The German snipers observed and fired from under the eaves of houses, so it was most difficult to locate them. When a parapet was blown in by a shell, or when a trench caved in with the rain where the men had undercut it for shelter, the sniper looked out for the repair or rescue party. The want of communication trenches, which there had not been time to get on with, and the places where sections had not yet dug out far enough to join up, were the causes of many casualties. Snipers covered their working parties; worse still, they covered attacks, preventing our men lining the parapet until the attackers were close up. Only in the dark could food and ammunition be brought up, and the wounded and dead be taken down, and the ground was being traversed by machine-guns when attacks were not being made. A lot of the sniping from houses had to be put up with, so had the shelling, for our guns had not enough ammunition to cope with them. But the circumstances in which some men had been shot led to the

[1] Powell.

belief that there was a sniper behind us, so Stanway, who had
several snipers to his credit, took out a few men to make a search.
While they were halted beside a large strawrick one of the men
noticed some empty German cartridge-cases at his feet. On
thrusting their bayonets into the rick the party was rewarded by
a yell and a German coming out headlong. Inside was a comfortable hide, having openings cleverly blocked with straw, and
a week's supply of food. The sniper could come out at night
for exercise and water. Only his carelessness with his used
cartridges cost him his life, for he was finished there and then.

The chief damage to C Company about this time was caused
by two 6-inch guns of ours; 'they shelled its trench with the
greatest accuracy at frequent intervals, and blew one of the
platoons to bits.' Our guns, however, destroyed Fromelles
Church tower, to the pained surprise of the French civilians behind
us, and denied the Germans that observation post.

The technique of night defence had been learned quickly.
Besides having patrols and listening-posts, trip-wires, which fired
a set rifle or rattled tins, were laid out. It wasn't altogether
unknown for a bullet-riddled farm animal to be seen beside a
trip-wire by daylight. In time the carcasses of slain animals, and
of unmilked cows that died of udder trouble, came to be a nuisance.
To aim for the most effective fire at night two strips of white tape
were stretched between upright sticks, and rifles were levelled to
fire between the tapes. Once at least a burning strawrick lighted
up the attackers. From now onwards, while the strain lasted,
50 men of B Company went to the front each night as a reinforcement, and returned at dawn; this was additional to the platoon
entrenched in front of Cellar Farm.

October 27th.—It poured again last night. The Germans had
withdrawn a little during the night, and were going to ground
again. Once when, as now, they were digging some of our
fellows fired at their shovels appearing above the parapet; Gerry
entered into the fun, signalling our hits and misses. And the old
shelling and sniping game went on all day, 'but they do no damage
to A.' Rain and mud were by now causing a lot of trouble with
rifles; and the supply of oil had given out. There was nowhere
to lay or lean a rifle without its getting clogged with mud, or a
plug into the muzzle, which caused the barrel to bulge or burst

when a shot was fired. D Company had two ramrods to clear jammed barrels. "Pass it along, 'the ramrod's wanted'" was constantly being called from right or left of the company. Often it became "Mr. Ormrod's wanted," and the wretched subaltern was kept dashing about the trench. The serviceable rifles of the support Company had to be sent up to the front, leaving their owners practically unarmed. Once when things were rather threatening, the C.O. ordered those who had no rifles to arm themselves with picks and shovels; a few lucky ones had German rifles and bayonets which had been brought in. Some of our bayonets too were broken owing to the various uses to which they were put. In those hastily dug narrow trenches the fixed bayonet was an encumbrance. There was the usual Hun attack in the evening, again D Company got most of it: 4 men killed, 1 officer and 8 men wounded to-day; 52 reinforcements joined.

October 28th.—During the night the Battalion searched the enemy dead on its near front, and collected 438 identity discs, 58 of them between C Company's trenches and wire. The number, and there would be more farther out, contrasts sharply with our 34 dead to date; our wounded were 77, theirs must have been a big number.—'A Hun shell killed a chicken just behind our trench. Chicken for lunch.' One of A Company was 'shot by a Maxim trained on the road, carried off under fire . . . good work.' There were intervals in the day's sniping and shelling, but in the end we had 2 killed and 20 wounded. The day was 'wet and beastly.'

'We [1] are buried deep in the ground, and spend our time digging deeper and joining up our trenches. The Germans snipe us most of the days from trees and houses about, but—unberufen! —as far as my Company is concerned, without much success, as we were lucky and got into the ground pretty early. Every day they shell us, and at night make about three attacks which keep us awake. Some of the other Companies have suffered, and there have been some losses among officers. Can't say I have noticed any loss of morale amongst the Germans, and their shooting is damned good. The most awful twaddle is written in the papers. These cocks in front of us are as bold as anything, and don't give a damn; they push through the line at night, and snipe us during

[1] Stockwell.

the day from all sorts of places. One loses count of the days of
the week here, I can't tell what day this is though I know the
date. "Quail" is invaluable and most sound; he has, however,
a mania for shaving. I've lost my shaving kit for the time being,
as it was in my holsters, and my horse had to be sent back as the
farm he was in was shelled. I've now developed a most damnable
beard of seven days growth. I don't know what it looks like, but
it feels beastly. Send out chocolate in tin boxes; everything in
one's haversack gets soaked with rain, and musty: and cocoa—
one gets so sick of tea with rum and without milk, though I raised
some milk the other day from a deserted farm by getting one of
the men to milk the cows. Our cooking-place is a culvert under
a road near the trenches. I believe the people at home are at last
realizing what this war means, and what fools they've been.'

'It [1] has been most awfully cold in these clay-soil trenches as
I have nothing but my burberry and waterproof sheet with me,
all the kits being three miles away. I was taken unprepared. I am
in the most awful state of filth, not having been able to get a wash
for ten days. It poured the other night when we were attacked,
everybody and everything became covered with slimy mud
which is just beginning to rub off. All the officers and men are
in the same box, and have long beards—looking awful ruffians.
I have to sleep in a trench with all my men, and no officer within
250 yards. I shall be very grateful for an air-pillow when it arrives.'

An artillery officer came and asked Davies to suggest a good
target on which to try a few rounds of a new explosive just issued,
probably T.N.T. 'With glee I point out a barn from which much
sniping has taken place.' It was always a danger because the
trench could be enfiladed from it. The Platoon Sergeant gives
the current story of the shoot which he watched. 'He asked for
a round: it was over. He made his correction: the next round
was short. When he asked for a third round he was told that was
all he was allowed for one day, but he got it, and, good luck to
him, scored a bull—which put "paid" to that barn, for it caught
fire and we heard the explosions of ammunition caused by the
heat.' And everyone there breathed easier that there was one
sniper's lair the less.

C Company had only two officers left. They were "Tiger"

[1] Richardson.

Phillips, the Company Commander, (who owed his nickname to a craving for jam in his callow youth), and Holmes, the whimsical, the wit of the unit. The exposed position of the Company, and the gruelling time it had had, made another officer a necessity, so Davies was transferred from A. Going round in the dark he found that A and C were 'quite a bit away from each other'; he arrived just before 10 o'clock. 'Phillips, considering an attack is impending, hastily takes me round the position,' the weakness of which was evident. There were nasty little gullies, or depressions, running up to the Company's trenches. They contained many German dead; but they had advantages as assembly positions, and they gave cover to approach uncomfortably near and prepare to rush our trenches.

'11.30 p.m.[1] The Hun attacks: the hardest I have yet encountered, it was all we could do to beat it off. My servant badly wounded. There were dead Germans on our parapet and in our trench.' The weight of this attack was greater on the right and centre. Of the left there is only Stockwell's laconic note, 'night attack, Sloper most of it.' ('C. is Clegg-Hill, whom Sloper we call,' in the words of the Septmonts alphabet; he commanded D Company.)

October 29th.—Fresh attacks were made, and met with equal grit, at 2 o'clock and at 4. Every man was standing-to in the wet trench throughout the night. A story of one of these attacks is told among the men of that time of Fletcher, a recently joined officer from the Despatch Riders. He was patrolling a decent way along a willow-lined ditch, up which one of our machine-guns fired, when he saw an attack coming. He shouted an order in German to the attackers to halt, and make their way by the line of the ditch. Having seen that they were doing so, he hurried back and got our machine-gunners and the riflemen near them to open fire, with what good effect the morning showed. C Company buried its Germans in the parapet. A revolver was taken off one of their dead officers; he was one of several Germans who jumped into our trench before they could be dealt with; it was a French weapon dated 1875. A great many German dead were seen in front of D Company. On its extreme right an officer was killed on the last strand of the wire: in spite of the incessant fire some souvenir-hunter had taken his revolver and other small articles

[1] Davies.

before daylight. A patrol of A Company, sent out in the early
morning, found German trenches about 600 yards off, and two
dead. Another patrol of volunteers went out to search for snipers;
they brought back two of their number wounded, after locating
two machine-guns. 'During [1] the morning Gerry kept sending
Jack Johnsons over, and our artillery made matters worse by
dropping a few shorts on the left of D Company. In the afternoon
Gerry began shelling again; some shrapnel found me and delivered
me from the firing-line. I found sanctuary in Bailleul, and was
away for a few weeks.'

An isolated barn which Fritz used constantly as a sniper's lair
was a source of casualties to C Company. Phillips told his new
subaltern to look if it could be burned, and to see the Sikhs, on
the right, and ask if they would burn a barn on their front. After
examination, and a conference with the Sikh O.C., it was arranged
to try to do the jobs at the same time, 4 in the afternoon. Our
raiders crept out at dusk; the barn was kept under heavy rifle-fire
until they got to it. The slope of a road and the cover of some
bits of hedge let them get up fairly easily. A bundle of paper,
rags, and twigs, heavily soused with petrol, was put against the
side of the barn, and more petrol was thrown over the woodwork.
When that was lighted the wind did the rest. A lot of cartridges
exploded inside during the burning. Our barn was not so difficult
to tackle as the other. The Sikhs had casualties, but they stuck
to their job till it was done.

There was more shelling than usual throughout the day. At
' 9 p.m., another bad show. Holmes is wounded. Some Huns
are captured. D Company made a counter-attack, C assisted
with cross-fire. The Hun attack continued all night, their last
October 30th—effort was made at dawn. The number of their dead
has increased.'—' Sloper has 150 dead in front of him '—' forty
of them were within 10 yards of D's front, not one had reached
the parapet. D had two officers by then, Childe Freeman and
myself'—' Richardson, left platoon, got into mess a bit '—' charged,
got 6 German dead and 2 wounded '—' As the whole of B Company
went up to reinforce the front line there would have been no one
to stop the Germans if they had pushed through '—' Prisoners say
that twelve regiments are opposite our front, and that their losses
are heavy.'   [1] Roderick.

These few terse phrases are all that five [1] men who took part wrote at the time or have to say 15 years afterwards about the third, the climactic, day of the greatest of the German attacks on the Brigade front; it was part of a much wider attack. The Middlesex line was broken, and not restored until the support battalion, the Argylls, was sent up. Our left platoon, Richardson's, was compromised by the break and took part in the counter-attack. One of the prisoners was a truculent person; H.Q. gave him rum to appease him. He complained at Brigade that his watch had been taken from him, so we got a chit about it. As we could get plenty of watches off the German dead we sent down two dozen for him to choose from. Stanway was the culprit. 6 killed, 1 officer and 48 men wounded, is the total for three days.

R.S.M. Murphy, R.Q.M.S. Welton, and C.S.M. Stanway were promoted Second Lieutenants. Welton was posted to D, the others to C. The day was strangely quiet. At 8 p.m. our machine-guns traversed the front. Two Argyll machine-guns were a welcome reinforcement of our thin line. The position was shelled at night; it was wet, and an attack was expected. To our right attacks of a desultory nature were made from midnight until *October* 31*st*—daylight, but we were left at peace and got some sleep. ' Sloper [2] came in and had breakfast, he is relieved for twenty-four hours, he looks done. Got a chicken boiled for lunch. Shelled all lunch, some wounded, fire enfilade.' There was some rather bad shelling of C in the afternoon. 'The Hun is trying to get in his dead near his trenches. We try to prevent him, it's good for him to see how many there are.' Our casualties : 1 killed, 15 wounded.

November 1*st*.—The night was unrestful, except on the left. An attempt was made to cut C Company's wire, so the whole company front was patrolled. The day was quiet, but there was more shelling than usual just before dark. ' Got some cigarettes.' 1 killed, and 4 wounded.

November 2*nd*.—The front was quiet, but first echelon and the cooks were shelled and had to move. 1 killed, and 3 wounded : 21 reinforcements reported.

November 3*rd*.—A patrol from A surprised the enemy digging, accounted for a few, and got back safely. Another time a venture-

---

[1] Stockwell, Hill, Richardson, Boreham, P. Davies.   [2] Stockwell.

some German patrol was scuppered by a section of No. 3 Platoon.
'Hearing [1] a commotion round a traverse, I looked and saw a
few of my bold lads standing in the open, taking pot-shots at
four Germans who were crawling on their stomachs to get into
a ditch about 50 yards from our trench. They had left it a bit
too late, they did not get their leave, and I had the satisfaction of
knowingly getting my first Gerry.' '9.10 a.m. [Davies] hit in
the right elbow by a sniper, painful.' While he was waiting in
the bottom of the trench for darkness word was passed along
that Phillips had been hit in the head, also by a sniper, and was
dying. The profuse apology which Davies made at H.Q. for
having been wounded was being told as a Battalion joke eighteen
months later; and when he turned up at Limerick in 1919 he was
remembered for it by those who had not seen him since the
happening. Shelling was intermittent during the day. 2 men
were killed, 1 officer and 10 others were wounded, besides Phillips.

November 4th.—After a strangely quiet night there was more
sniping than usual during the day. 4 men were killed, 1 officer,
and 3 men wounded: 38 reinforcements reported.

November 5th.—But for some heavy shelling in the evening the
day was moderately quiet.

'I [2] have had 8 men wounded in my trench, 7 from shrapnel
and 1 from a bullet. Shells are going over our heads all day;
one has to keep one's head pretty low in the trench or one gets
picked off by one of those beastly snipers who are all over the
place. I have got some sacks which I get into at night and keep
fairly warm, the nights being awfully cold. . . . I wish to goodness
they would send out the Canadian people [Canadian troops arrived
in England in mid-October for training]; let us get a move on
these Germans and have done with it, as it has got to come to an
end; personally I think the War will last another two or three
months at least. The Russians seem to be making mincemeat
of them. It is pitiful to see houses and villages destroyed by
shell-fire, and poor people trudging along the roads, dozens of
fine cattle lying in the fields round—killed by the bullets and
shrapnel. I am getting awfully bored by the trenches and am
feeling fearfully tired. I hope we won't be in them much longer.
I wish they would order the advance.'

[1] Powell.   [2] Richardson.

November 6th.—There was a thick fog in the morning: when it cleared our guns concentrated on Fromelles. The Germans retaliated by shelling us heavily in the afternoon, killing 2 men and wounding 11. The fog came down again at night, and did not lift until after dawn.

November 7th.—Our position was shelled heavily all day; 4 men were killed and 9 wounded.

November 8th.—The heavy shelling was resumed, but only one man was wounded. Stockwell's cow was killed—'damned nuisance.'

For several nights the enemy infantry had been quite inactive, and there was other evidence that their ability to attack with hope of success had ended for the time being. The shelling, too, soon died down. With a dominating position, superior artillery and an incomparably greater volume of fire, more machine-guns, and ample reliefs of infantry launched in attacks which were made with great doggedness and gallantry, the enemy had looked, time after time, like getting through. The attacks were deceptive because the men came on at a jog-trot; there was no dash about them, but they were insistent. The line against which that fine endeavour was broken began as isolated segments of trench into which none but highly trained, trustworthy men could have been put: men who were masters of the infantry weapon, and had complete confidence in each other. In time, as opportunity offered, the sections dug out to each other and back to Company H.Q., with numbers dwindling and weariness growing: for there was no relief for anyone, and little sleep, yet all had to be alert to meet assault upon assault. This drawn-out battle was, for the most part on our side, an affair of the rifle, and there were tense moments with the bayonet.

'It [1] seemed strange at the time that the Support Company in the river-bed escaped having casualties; one man only appears to have been wounded. We used to hear the shells coming closer and closer, and to expect that each following one would land among us, but suddenly the guns would lift and the shells go right over. Afterwards, when looking at the map, it occurred to me that the enemy thought we would not be silly enough to sit in the middle of what was shown as a river; so, since air recon-

[1] Boreham.

naissance had not reached the standard it did later on, our presence there was not suspected. The Quartermaster used to bring the rations up to the bank of our river each night after dark; they were laid out, and parties came from the front line to fetch them. I suppose the enemy were occupied in the same way; so things were quiet at that hour for a couple of nights, and the ration-parties became careless because of it, and laughed and talked on the way back to their Companies. One night when that was going on Gerry opened up with rifle-fire, whereat everybody hopped into the river-bed for shelter. Next night the same thing happened. I thought that everyone was under cover when, on looking up, I saw a figure moving about on top of the bank. I somehow guessed who it was, and called, "Is that you, Albert?" "Yes." It was Miners. I told him to come down out of it, and he replied, "I lost the tin of jam last night." Then there was a morning when a figure on horseback suddenly appeared on top of the bank, he was a fellow called Twyman, one of the Battalion Transport. "Go back," everybody shouted, not so much on his account as their own—they were not wanting the enemy's fire to be drawn. Anyhow, Fritz saw him, and he did go back—all out: luckily he got away without being hit.

With the end of the battle a start could be made to give the men some relief from the life they had been living. One platoon per company was withdrawn each morning and marched to Fleurbaix, to the farm where the Transport was. The Quartermaster arranged for them to have a bath, 'badly needed,' and an undisturbed sleep; then they returned to the line in the evening after dark. And a small amount of charcoal was issued. We had been so long without anything but cold food that I shall never forget how delicious a Maconochie ration, made hot, tasted.'

November 10th.—There was a good deal of traversing fire after dark, and 2 men were killed. Two pigs roamed about A Company's area. To-day one of them got stung by a bullet, dashed over the reserve trench and dropped dead. One of the Company H.Q. men crawled out and cut its throat. It was sent back to the Company's cooks after dark, and we looked forward to pork for the Company's dinner next day. But a two-hundred-pound pig produced only two dixiefuls. The cooks heard about it, and were ordered up to the front trenches, being relieved by men who had got no pork. Two days later the other pig met its fate, and produced enough for the whole Company. C.S.M. Boreham tells of one of these pigs. He had the duty, since the R.S.M.'s promotion, to report to the Adjutant when platoons going to rest were clear of the line. A passing man called back to another, "Come on, Jimmy, that'll break your caste." When the laggard, who was seen to be carrying pig, came along he was recognized as a Jew. "That's not quite orthodox," said Boreham. "No," he replied, "but if I don't carry it they'll give me none." A. Company, these days and for some months to come, practised the belief that God helps those who help themselves. With the aid of a find of potatoes in a field close by, and of eggs and chickens while they lasted, A did fairly well at Cordonnerie.

November 11th.—Second echelon was shelled, there were no casualties but it was thought prudent to go back another thousand yards.

A Belgian settler in the back area had come under suspicion. He was tried by the French, and convicted of trafficking with the enemy. The Mayors of Fleurbaix and the surrounding communes were ordered to be present at the execution. The Belgian owned a white horse, and was commonly said to have used it according to a code. From now, for months to come, the coincidence of a white horse in a plough and the shelling of a near-by battery, or a relief, was apt to be thought significant along this front. The white or light-grey horse is, in fact, very common in the Flemish lands. Puffs of smoke from a chimney, and the manipulation of the hands of a church clock which faced east, were other alleged signals, with or without grounds.

November 12th.—' "Last [1] night I was on watch from 9 p.m. till midnight. At about 11.30 an awful hailstorm came on, with stones nearly as large as marbles, that fairly stung our faces. After that the wet loosened the parapet, it fell on top of two men who were sleeping and buried them from their waists down. I had to dig them out, which took about half an hour; luckily they weren't hurt. The Germans are scared stiff to attack us with any vigour, and we are just waiting for the order to advance and give them a hiding such as they have never had yet, to pay them out for their underhand sniping way of fighting, and their shells to which

[1] Richardson.

infantry cannot reply. Twelve hundred Germans were found in front of the Brigade trenches after a scrap the other night; they won't face us by day. We are being quite well fed, and are in good condition, considering the wet and other troubles.'"

November 14th.—Except for one access of sniping and the shelling of the Transport, the everyday note for a week is "quiet"; and in seven days the total casualties were 3 killed and 3 wounded. 'My [1] platoon was out when the welcome news came along that we were being relieved. Incidentally, I pinched a blanket.' The [2] 2nd Scots Guards, 7th Division, 'came at 8 p.m. We got out all safe,' *November 15th*—and reached billets at Sailly-sur-la-Lys, about three miles off, at 1 a.m. 'Eat, and slept, on the floor, in the same room as Sloper, who snored.'

Men who lived through these days and the Battalion's later service on other fronts, look back on La Cordonnerie with a pride and awe no other name calls up.

Military Operations, France and Belgium, 1914, vol ii. p. 227 (footnote) states of the 6th Division: "One of the *four* brigades was always out of the line in rest." That gives a wrong impression. The 19th Brigade was never relieved between October 19th, when it was attached to the 6th Division, and November 14th.—Map 13, Operations of the III Corps, Battle of Armentières, issued with that volume, shows the part of the line occupied by the 2nd Royal Welch Fusiliers on November 2nd somewhat in rear of their line on October 22nd. That is an error. The Battalion handed over to its relief the trenches it dug on October 22nd; not even one of its sections had been dislodged or withdrawn in the interval.

At the end of "The Race for the Sea" the Germans held the advantage of ground all along the line, not only as a tactical position but as habitable ground. Both sides were physically exhausted, and they had scarcely a shot left in their artillery limbers. For a few months there was fairly general quiet while they recuperated, made up their depleted supplies, and laboured to make trenches habitable.

---

[1] Powell.   [2] Stockwell.

CHAPTER V

Stalemate: Houplines, flood—Christmas 1914—Bois Grenier, mud—Armentières estaminets, and other Amusements— Patrolling—Echoes of Neuve Chapelle—A Chinese Raid— Echoes of Festubert—Ypres, "Even for an egg-shell!"— Summer on a quiet Front—Laventie—Intelligence

Contributors:—ATTWATER; BOREHAM; COLTART; KIRKBY; MCKAY; MOODY; R. MORGAN; MOSTYN; POWELL; RICHARDS; RODERICK; STOCKWELL; WILLIAMS

Sketches:—5, 6, 7, 20

At Sailly there was a welcome seventy-two hours rest and a scrub; then, reclothed and straightened up, for it again—whatever it was to be. Brigade and Battalion officers inspected some 'rotten trenches' which they were to take over about a mile east of Houplines, a suburban district north-east of Armentières.

November 18th.—The Battalion marched at 2 p.m. and relieved Dublin and Royal Irish Fusiliers—A. Company [1] the latter. 'On being shown round by one of the R.I.F. officers, I asked where the men were; he replied that they had gone out half an hour ago, that there was nothing doing, since the Germans were 800 yards away. What a change these trenches were, so quiet!' They turned out to be quite comfortable for the men, but, being unconnected, they were dangerous for officers and orderlies, so digging-out was started at once. A. Company H.Q had a room in a moated farm, but slept in a dry hole in the side of the moat. 'Brigade H.Q. took to the cellars of the château, and was jumpy there.' Six very quiet working days were spent in the line. But for a little sniping on both sides 'nothing doing' describes the War during them. An officer could get away for a few hours to go into Armentières, to which the people were returning, have a bath, and an excellent lunch at the Café Comte d'Egmont or tea at a first-class confec-

[1] Powell.

tioners; and the men could get liquor into the trenches, too much
for some. A platoon was withdrawn from each Company daily
to rest, a practice which continued for the next eight months.
The provision of comfort had become urgent, for the weather had
turned wintry. There had been rain and mud; on the second
November 20th—day in the line there was 'heavy snow, one and
November 22nd—a half inches, and frost.' Two days later it was
'fine, freezing all day.' Next day there is a wail—'freezing,
November 23rd—damned stove won't work': then came thaw. A
man shot himself through the arm, 'probably on purpose.' He
was not the first of whom that is said, or by any means the last.
This man took ingenious precautions to conceal the evidence of a
point-blank shot. He died of haemorrhage.

November 25th.—The Battalion was relieved by the Middlesex,
and withdrawn to billets in Houplines.

One of the greatest luxuries was 'to have clothes off, especially
boots.' Ideas and irons were passed round for getting lice out of
clothing. Personal cleanliness and the contrivance of comfort are
two of the outward signs of an efficient soldier. Individual resource apart, the provision of creature comforts was organized
officially and semi-officially as siege-warfare was entered on.
Relatives and Comforts Committees posted parcels—'got a A1
cake from Mother, had a proper burst on it.' News Offices sent
their papers. Anything the Post Office or Shipping Agencies
accepted was sent. French tradesmen, soon to be partly superseded by Army Canteens, stocked the articles that were in demand.
Home leave was arranged for: it was only five days in all to begin
with. The departure and arrival of the Leave-bus was one of the
vivid pictures of life at the front, the novelty of which did not
wear off for many weeks; and there was no more poignant war
scene than the departure of the Leave-train from Victoria Station
in these days.

Armentières is described as 'a dirty town,' but leave to visit it
was greatly sought and taken. In estaminets and billets the men
discovered omelette; they called chips "pompadour fritz" (*pomme
de terre frite*); and they learned what a lot a French woman can cook
on the peculiar-looking stove, *poêle*, that projects into her kitchen.
Difference of language was bridged with an ease that would have
been surprising, since the language of each party was quite unknown

to the other with very few exceptions on either side, had not intercourse been limited at first to the dealings of an eager buyer and a very willing seller. For few of the men did intercourse ever go much further. Ignorance of the coinages and of exchange was the chief cause of trouble. That phase soon passed, but until it did the civilians were seldom the losers. To these early days belongs the classic case of the draft who, feeling that he had been swindled, sought counsel and help of an older hand. "Do you know the lingo?" he asked. "Aw, yes," was the assured reply; and they went to have it out with the *patronne*. "Heh, madame, parlez-vous français?" the older hand demanded. "Mais—oui!" "Then why the hell don't you give the man his right money?"

December 1st.—The 1st Battalion was near enough for visits to be exchanged. It found a Guard for the King, when "H.M. complimented the Regiment."

December 2nd.—The 2nd was likewise honoured. Stockwell commanded a picked Guard of 4 officers and 200 men whom the King inspected. 'Rather a unique occasion, guns firing half a mile away.' The Prince of Wales, who was with the King, was observed to have grown. The parade was spick-and-span without, but most verminous underneath.

December 3rd.—The Battalion returned to the line, in the left half-sector this time, relieving The Cameronians. The approach over the top, which looked so dangerous in bright moonlight, was made in safety. Again all four Companies were in line. A. was on the left between the Houplines–Frélinghien road and the river Lys, where Nomansland narrowed down to about 80 yards. The Seaforths were the original occupants of the position on the left. They had been trench-mortared out of Frélinghien brewery, whereon they sat down close behind it in what was a dry ditch. It was 'wet and muddy' when the Battalion took it over.

December 4th—Within twenty-four hours there was 'rain, rain, rain.' The winter floods had come, the ditch turned out to be a stream which opened into the river; it was one of the main drains in this much-drained low country. The parapet fell in right and left; the ditch-trench ran with a rapid current, and had to be abandoned by day. On the fourth night the Sappers came to help. Ordinary shoring-up had failed when 'a gallant young Sapper informed us that there was unlimited timber available, as the saw-mills were running on electric power from Lille—a leakage the Germans did not discover for several months.' It was decided to make a box-revetment of 2-by-5-inch timber. The baulks had to be carried 1000 yards; each one had to be driven into a moving mass of mud, and nails, hammers, and sledges had to be handled in the dark by men working in two feet of mud and water, within shouting distance of the enemy. A few days later the Company did without the Sappers, whose officer had been changed—most unfortunately. Two weeks of hard labour produced a dry trench with a floor above the ordinary flood-water level. But for some difficulty in moving about, caused by the top cross-pieces needed to keep the revetment splayed, it was a good trench. (In 1917 it was still the driest in the sector.) Less elaborate contrivance served the other Companies.

The one enemy activity with which the Battalion had to contend was sniping; the amount of work that was so plainly going on encouraged it. Not all of it was in deadly earnest. On the left the Germans amused themselves by aiming at spots on the walls of cottages, and firing until they had cut a hole. Our men said, ' Fritz had to be chummy, he had a brewery working just behind him.' It was a towering building to have so close, about 50 feet high. 'The [1] Saxons opposite were quite human. One, who spoke excellent English, used to climb up into some eyrie in the brewery and spend his time asking "how London was going on," " how was Gertie Millar and the Gaiety," and so on. Lots of our men had blind shots at him in the dark, at which he laughed. One night I came out and called, " Who the hell are you ? " At once came back the answer, " Ah, the officer—I expect I know you, sir—I used to be the head-waiter at the Great Central Hotel." ' One of A Company's duties, about which higher authority had issued strict orders, was to stop all communication between Armentières and the enemy by bottles floated down the river. Sentries were posted, who, much to the amusement of the Germans, fired on everything that floated—during daylight !

December 6th.—Our guns shelled Frélinghien, the Germans shelled Houplines, and there were a lot of aeroplanes aloft.

December 8th.—There was more sniping than usual by the

[1] Stockwell.

Germans, probably owing to the amount of work being done on the collapsing trench; only one man was wounded.

December 9th.—The Argylls were attacked, but the Battalion was left in peace.

December 13th.—The front quiet: the day dry after three wet ones. A reinforcement of 95 reported.

December 14th.—The Germans put a thousand shells into Armentières, creating a great commotion among the inhabitants, of whom five were wounded and a woman was killed. Six days ago they bombed it from the air, 'surprising one of the subalterns in the pursuit of an amour.' The town had become a regular place of resort for all the troops around.

December 15th.—As the French in the north are attacking all the B.E.F. guns are active to-day as yesterday.

December 18th.—News that German ships had bombarded Scarborough caused some excitement.—The Battalion was standing-to in case of being attacked, for the 6th Division was attacking.

December 20th.—For three days attacks by the B.E.F. and the French had been going on to north and south; very disjointed they seemed, probably owing to shortage of men and shell. A succession of gains in Ploegsteert (Plug Street) Wood offset fiascos elsewhere. The Battalion's only part in it all was to snipe at anything like movement opposite. Work by all the Companies never ceased. A. Company's wooden case was finished, but, since the Germans *December 21st*—had sapped to within 30 yards, the Company began sapping out, with the notion of bombing. In the afternoon heavy rain set in; the river rose; C Company was flooded out, and its parapet collapsed. 'The shortest day, and a long one at that. Beastly cold. Feel rather down in my luck. Trench work very *December 22nd*—trying, so inactive. We are sniping all day again, it gives the men something to do. We use steel loopholes.' Patrolling by night was another useful pastime.—There was a slight *December 23rd*—snowfall in the morning. The Battalion had verified the notion that work is the only means of mitigating insecurity and discomfort. The constant active efforts to exist in these water-logged trenches were found to be the one practical preventive of "trench-foot." That ischaemic condition was wasting battalions and filling hospitals. Toes, even feet, were being amputated because of gangrene which occurred in the

worst cases. "Trench-foot" is a war-coined term for a condition
that was not new, but had been forgotten; it is described in the
record of a campaign of over two thousand years ago: "shell-
shock" was described about the same time. Medical advice about
trench-foot was not very helpful in December 1914; anyhow,
from its nature prevention depends on the internal economy and
discipline of the unit. The Battalion began by having the cooks
save all grease, and, after stand-to each morning, the men rubbed
each other's feet vigorously with it. To have a change into dry
socks each Company detailed a man to a Battalion Laundry run by
the Quartermaster,[1] who sent up a clean pair for everyone with the
rations. So successful was the Battalion that, although it was for
months on end in the wettest sectors, only one case of trench-foot
occurred during the first Winter. Socks were sent from home in
such quantities for the first two years of the War that men were
throwing them away after only one wearing. The Laundry was
closed by Divisional Order at the end of 1916. Conditions had
changed, and made difficulty in carrying it on, but Divisional
arrangements fell short of what they replaced. For body warmth
goatskin coats were issued; they were greatly prized by the
handful of men who managed to keep theirs for wear the following Winter, when there was no issue; a flannel-lined leather jerkin
was more serviceable.

Most people learn in time that war changes many values,
material and moral. The Army was quick to discover a number of
the moral changes. In one of the Companies was a Corporal "Z,"
once champion boxer of his weight in the Battalion; he was
a smart-looking man but a poor non-commissioned officer. In
his platoon was an undersized man, "X," who had been looked
on as a dirty and unhopeful recruit. He was still a poor soldier on
parade and in billets. In the line he showed he had a great heart
in his small body. He was always on patrol at night, sometimes
by himself. Corporal "Z" would not go a yard beyond Company
H.Q., a cottage about 20 yards behind the front line, unless when
ordered on duty. One morning there was a commotion, and he
reported, whining, that the Q.M.S. had struck him. The Q.M.S.,
a former gymnastic instructor, explained that he had found the
boxer knocking "X" about, told him to stop it, got some "lip"

[1] He ran a bakery at Béthune.

from him, so he laid him out. Under Military Law, as ordinarily administered, the Q.M.S. could not well escape a court-martial. It was decided, however, that if he knocked Corporal "Z" down again, round the corner, justice would be done—and was.

December 24th was very quiet on the front. A pheasant in Nomansland was shot through the head, and brought in. It was probably a refugee from Plug Street Wood, and raised by Hennessy of brandy fame.

December 25th.—'Our [1] Pioneer sergeant, "Nobby" Hall, made a screen, and painted on it, "A Merry Christmas," which we hoisted on Christmas morning. No shots were fired. On the left we could see that our fellows were carrying the breakfast in the open, and everything was quiet. Both sides got a bit venturous and looked over the top; then a German started to walk down the tow-path toward our lines and Ike Sawyer went to meet him. The German handed over a box of cigars. Later the Germans came boldly out of their trenches, but our men were forbidden to leave theirs, so they threw out tins of bully, and plum and apple jam, etc., with plenty of sympathy in the shape of, "Here you are, you poor hungry bastards," and other such-like endearments. When Fritz rolled over two barrels of beer Captain Stockwell went and spoke to two German officers; it was agreed to recall all men to the trenches and have no more fraternizing. But there was no more shooting,' and the Germans were allowed to bury their dead.

Captain Stockwell's account.—'I think I and my Company have just spent one of the most curious Christmas Days we are ever likely to see. It froze hard on Christmas Eve, and in the morning there was a thick ground-fog. I believe I told you the Saxons opposite had been shouting across in English. Strict orders had been issued that there was to be no fraternizing on Christmas Day. About 1 p.m., having seen our men get their Christmas dinners, we went into our shelter to get a meal. The sergeant on duty suddenly ran in and said the fog had lifted and that half a dozen Saxons were standing on their parapet without arms. I ran out into the trench and found that all the men were holding their rifles at the ready on the parapet, and that the Saxons were shouting, "Don't shoot. We don't want to fight to-day. We will send you some beer." A cask was hoisted on to the parapet and three men started to roll it into the middle of Nomansland. A lot more Saxons then appeared

[1] Powell.

without arms. Things were getting a bit thick. My men were getting a bit excited, and the Saxons kept shouting to them to come out. We did not like to fire as they were all unarmed, but we had strict orders and someone might have fired, so I climbed over the parapet and shouted, in my best German, for the opposing Captain to appear. Our men were all chattering and saying, "The Captain's going to speak to them." A German officer appeared and walked out into the middle of Nomansland, so I moved out to meet him amidst the cheers of both sides. We met and formally saluted. He introduced himself as Count Something-or-other, and seemed a very decent fellow. He could not talk a word of English. He then called out to his subalterns and formally introduced them with much clicking of heels and saluting. They were all very well turned out, while I was in a goatskin coat. One of the subalterns could talk a few words of English, but not enough to carry on a conversation. I said to the German Captain, "My orders are to keep my men in the trench and allow no armistice. Don't you think it is dangerous, all your men running about in the open like this? Someone may open fire." He called out an order and all his men went back to their parapet, leaving me and the five German officers and a barrel of beer in the middle of Nomansland. He then said, "My orders are the same as yours, but could we not have a truce from shooting to-day? We don't want to shoot, do you?" I said, "No, we certainly don't want to shoot, but I have my orders to obey." So then we agreed not to shoot until the following morning when I was to signal that we were going to begin. He said, "You had better take the beer. We have lots." So I called up two men to take the barrel to our side. As we had lots of plum-puddings I sent for one and formally presented it to him in exchange for the beer. He then called out, "Waiter," and a German private whipped out six glasses and two bottles of beer, and with much bowing and saluting we solemnly drank it amid cheers from both sides. We then all formally saluted and returned to our lines. Our men had sing-songs, ditto the enemy.

December 26th.—He played the game, not a shot all night, and never tried to touch his wire or anything. There was a hard frost. At 8.30 I fired three shots in the air and put up a flag with "Merry Christmas" on it, and I climbed on the parapet. He put up a sheet with "Thank you" on it, and the German Captain appeared on the parapet. We both bowed and saluted and got down into our respective trenches, and he fired two shots in the air, and the War was on again.'

We were relieved at 5 in the evening, and went out unmolested, in perfect quietness. During these twenty-four days the casualties were 2 killed and 8 wounded.

Six days were spent in the drying-sheds of a factory with green blinds at Erquinghem. The first two days were wet, and there *December 28th*—was a gale the second night.

With the coming into the Mess of officers, promotions from the ranks, and others with no income but their pay, Colonel Williams imposed a maximum subscription for extras of 1½ francs a day, and he limited the liquor bill for junior officers by barring spirits except the rum issue.

The germ of specialism began to sprout vigorously at this time as new means of offence and defence were introduced, and old weapons belonging to siege warfare were brought out. There was no lack of volunteers for these duties, for they were adventures and departures from routine. Army and Corps Schools sprang up to teach battalion instructors. Barbed wire had taken the place of the chevaux-de-frise of earlier wars as an obstacle and entanglement, so each company formed a section who practised devices for putting out wire. The Germans used hand-grenades or bombs in October. The earliest British bomb was an improvisation which the Engineers made by charging empty jam-tins with cordite and scraps of metal; a short length of fuse had to be lighted by a match or the glowing end of a cigarette. The minenwerfer, anglicised as minnie, or trench-mortar, was introduced by the Germans at Ypres, also in October, and before long their Army was equipped with it. The first British mortars were as crude as the bombs. They were called "drainpipes." They were, in fact, sections of drain or water-pipe closed at one end by a fused-on breech; the barrel, supported by two feet swivelled to a ring, rested on the breech. The shell and fuse matched the weapon. Only the most adventurous cared to handle these contraptions. After loading with great care, the team took cover behind a traverse and used a long lanyard to fire. Our Army probably lost more men from accidents with its drainpipes than from the enemy's mortars during the same time. They were not superseded until Spring of 1916, when the very efficient, but greedy, Stokes mortar was issued. Catapults and other types of propulsion which antedated the invention of gunpowder were also used. Then there was the rifle-grenade. As time passed the training of yet other specialists out of the rawest of drafts, both officers and men, had to be undertaken by active battalions. To the last days of the War blind chance alone decided at what stage of knowledge or ignorance anyone was when called on for action.

January 1st.—A draft of 99 other ranks joined. Dinner in Mess was signalized by the cook sending in the brandy-butter with the turkey, and the bread-sauce with the plum-pudding. "Joe" Powell, the Mess President, heard most about it.

January 2nd.—A short move was made to Gris Pot ("Grease Pot"). The billets were scattered, inhabited farms, pronounced summarily to be 'rotten.' They were to be the Battalion's home when out of the line till after midsummer, except for a short time in March. H.Q. and a Battalion Mess were in "Streaky Bacon" Farm, so called because the white freestone of which it is built is varied by courses of red brick ; it is on the left of the rue de Lettrée, the Fleurbaix–L'Armée road. The line was just under two miles distant, so the area was within shelling range. The Companies (A and B shared a billet), the Transport, and that of The Cameronians, were in a group of farms at La Rolanderie, half a mile in rear on the rue de Biez, the Erquinghem road. The village of Bois Grenier and Moat Farm were midway to the front. Bois Grenier housed a dressing-station, wash-house and other conveniences. Moat Farm was H.Q. of the right battalion in the line. On the left, and across the rivière des Layes, are La Guernerie and La Vesée, the area of the left battalion. Behind La Vesée is L'Armée, and 2 miles farther north is Armentières.

January 3rd.—The Padre turned up half an hour late for Church Parade, to find that it had been dismissed. Brigade and Battalion officers visited the new front of about 3000 yards. It ran east of north in front of the Touquet–rue du Bois road, from the Bois Grenier–Touquet road to the Armentières–La Bassée railway. Water Farm is at the first rectangular bend of the rue du Bois road, and Grande Flamengrie is 300 yards to its left ; both are in rear of the road. The left of the line could not be reached in daylight because the communications and other parts held 5 feet of water: 'the trench on the right was awful.' Nomansland was cut up by a number of small streams, ditches, and drains; its width, rather less on the right, was from 200 to 400 yards.

The 22nd Brigade, in which was the 1st Battalion, was on the right. The two Battalions had spent a few hours together at Malta on March 2nd, 1914, when St. David's Day was celebrated, for the 1st was Sunday. The sailing of the 2nd Battalion's transport was delayed a few hours to allow the Feast to be held. It was their first meeting since 1880. At the Sergeants' Dinner R.S.M. "Shem" Williams, of the 1st, said he did not think they would meet again in our time. There they were, about to be side by side in the trenches; and there was a barrier, some 500 yards behind the line, across the Touquet road which both Brigades used, where the reliefs and ration-parties of the two Battalions often met, and old regimental acquaintance would be accidentally renewed.

January 4th.—Another awful day of rain.

January 5th.—A trench-mortar demonstration which officers attended was given at Divisional H.Q. in Croix du Bac. 'A rotten show, very inaccurate.'

January 6th.—Raining all day.

January 7th.—After lunch the officers went out into a field near Streaky Bacon Farm to see Murphy demonstrate with a bomb. A man of ingenious devices, he had just returned from a course of instruction in a weapon with which most of the officers were still unfamiliar. Instead of the jam-tin, the bomb was a Hale's long-handled stick-grenade. Murphy explained it with characteristic gravity and precision to a somewhat impatient, if not frivolous, audience. He showed us the use of the tail of tape to make it fall on its detonator, withdrew the safety-pin with due solemnity, and then, informing us that the proper action of throwing was that of bowling a cricket-ball, with a good round-arm action he bowled it across into the plough on the other side of the road. The explosion was not very startling, nor the displacement of soil considerable. We trooped across to look at its effect. Someone did say that it might be useful in trench-to-trench fighting.

January 8th.—While we were preparing to go up to relieve The Cameronians a rumour went round billets that a corporal of the 1st Battalion had been found dead some way behind the line, black in the face, and apparently strangled. This was said to be the work of enemy spies or patrols, and with so many undefended gaps in the line it was easy enough for them to get through. It was learned afterwards that the corporal's death was due to an immoderate draught of the company's rum ration, of which he had been in charge.

The route to the trenches was through Bois Grenier to Culvert Farm, where the Touquet road crosses the rivière des Layes, and thence by communication trench. But the going in the communication trench was impossible, it was up to the knees in mud. Although we were told that it was dangerous to get into and out of the line unless the trench was used Samson soon took his Company into the open, and told the guide to take us overland to Water Farm. For several months we never tried to use the communication trench again, reliefs being always henceforth over the top in spite of a Brigade Order to the contrary. D, C, B, and A Companies were in line. 'The Cameronians had just lived in water.' For the first night the Battalion could do nothing else. In Winter the ground-water level is only about one foot below the surface of the reclaimed Flanders marsh, and the making of military tracks and other works had disorganized the drainage. These trenches had been made before the rains. They were very deep, and were paved throughout with bricks from damaged walls, or with bully-beef tins: unopened tins make the better pavement, so they were used largely in those open-handed days. C Company was in the worst bit of the line; there was only cover enough for one platoon during the day, so it was arranged that three would go out to Bois Grenier at dawn. 'The only consoling fact about this front was that Brother Boche was in the same pickle.'

January 9th.—In daylight the means of remedying the position was studied. Our first orders were to make a new parapet with the help of the Sappers. The work proceeded for two weeks in mud and more or less water underfoot; overhead, there was as much rain, sleet, or snow as fair weather; the fair was oftener damp than frosty. Then another plan was adopted, and two months were to be spent almost entirely in remaking a habitable line, tenable against attack.

The hours of darkness were, as always, the most strenuous. Everything entailing movement or disturbance of the surface that could be seen by day was done at night: carrying rations and stores; making, improving, and repairing trenches; putting in loopholes; wiring; patrolling. Every morning a platoon was sent from each Company to rest. The brewery at Bois Grenier, which was not working, was fitted as a doss-house. There were other mitigations to the life in front. At first there was an estaminet near enough the trenches to tempt the venturesome. They could slip out to have a swill of beer, to have a jar filled to take back with them, or they might sit down to a plate of chips. No one knocked in vain on the back door of the "Cheval" at L'Armée after hours. In those days, too, a girl came to the trenches to sell chocolate.

January 12th.—Our covering battery shelled what they believed to be a searchlight in the enemy trenches. Whatever it was, if it was knocked-out—as claimed—it was not the searchlight which was to prove a particular nuisance. Its beam was kept on Water Farm for a long time the following night; it was never located or put out of action.

January 13th.—Now, and for several months, sniping was the most active form of infantry action. Seven Germans were claimed during the day. 'Captain [1] Joe Powell was "honourably pingoed" in the foot by a spent bullet, about 1200 yards behind the line. Occasional bullets fell as far back as the Bois Grenier cross-roads. Later on, when the ground was frozen, I remember walking out from the line in the early morning with Stanway, to the curious music of birds singing and ricochets humming and purring.' At night the 1st Battalion took over trenches on our right. The Germans opposite C Company were heard singing and playing a piccolo. Late at night H.Q. was damaged by shells, and A Company's cook-house was smashed.

January 14th.—A dull night. In the morning 20 Willies were aimed at Water Farm. The Gunner Observation Officer sat up in the rafters trying to spot the guns firing; but the support platoon of one of our Companies cleared out without their arms, and were chased by a few whizz-bangs. The C.O. was very wrath, and changed the command of the Company. One of our machine-guns spotted and fired on a trench-mortar. The art of concealment had yet to be learned, and our enemy was the first to learn. 'The men sang all the afternoon. When a Welshman sings there's not much wrong with him.'

[1] Attwater.

January 16th.—Again yesterday, and to-day the day billets were shelled. Two field-guns, which D Company spotted, were made to move by our covering battery.

'Found a new wart from the Artists called Owen, seems inoffensive' : thus Stockwell's note this day. The new "wart" came to be known affectionately to everyone as "Binge." He was one of a draft of three. A Territorial corporal and two privates, and a fellow-private sent to the 1st Battalion, were the first Temporary officers posted to the Regiment in its long history. Temporary officers were "sent on approval" in those days. That batch made good. They arrived in ranker kit, but were given a week's leave to fit out. There was much that they and other fledgeling officers had to learn, and it was no infant-school system they had entered on. A. Company's subalterns more than the others, except perhaps the D's, were chased by their Company Commander, as later he chased his subordinates when he commanded a battalion and a brigade ; and he chased away to something else any who failed to attain a reasonable measure of his own undoubted, if blusterous, efficiency in war. Binge did his tutor credit from the first, but that never saved him, or his fellows, from a blistering when found at fault. On a remembered occasion a party of warts, enjoying themselves in Armentières, had lunched well. One of the party withdrew for a necessary purpose. After a very long absence, and a search, he was found where he had gone—asleep. The consequent lateness in returning to billets mattered nothing to the others, but the sleeper had been warned for duty. There was a short-cut, a cross-country route over ditches into which revellers had fallen. It was risked this time : then while the sleeper scrambled into equipment the others tried to decoy Stockwell from discovering that a wart of his was late on parade. No record was made of Binge's playful wit telling about the unique emotion that apprenticeship was, and unhappily he has not lived to recall it.

January 17th.—There was neither shelling nor sniping to speak of, but it snowed at night and was very cold. Quail returned off leave in the middle of the night with the news from home that *January 18th*—all will be over by May. He had been given no sympathy at home because he was so fat. To the end of the War that was the common condition throughout the B.E.F.—There was snow and sleet all day, and a great quiet.

January 19th.—On relief by The Cameronians the Battalion returned to the Gris Pot billets. This was the beginning of a routine of duty which, except during the second half of March, lasted until the end of May. The Battalion worked the right of the line with The Cameronians; the Middlesex and Argylls worked the left; the 5th Scottish Rifles, Territorials, were in between on an alternating two-company front. The tours were mostly five days in the trenches and five in billets. The Scottish battalions of the Brigade did not work well together; whereas, subject to the usual bickerings when individuals or societies hold things in common or alternately, these mixed unions proved happy. The only antipathy was between two Commanding Officers. That deplorable state of affairs cannot be set down to national antagonism; it arose from a physiological or aesthetic difference, probably the latter, it was so bitter. The contention was all about a sanitary utensil. At alternate reliefs the servant of the one knew to take the tin abomination out of his officer's sleeping-quarters and fling it away, and the servant of the other knew he must search around until he found the enamelled convenience and put it beside the bed. The principals became involved in their deputies' quarrels. An official correspondence on the subject was said to have been brought to an end by the Commanding Officer who objected to the utensil requesting the one who needed it to indent on Providence— or Ordnance through his Quartermaster—for ' physiological equipment (officer's) of a greater capacity.' Ten years after these events the affair still rankled.

Murphy was detailed to run the day billets at Bois Grenier when the Battalion was in the trenches. The appointment gave him more scope than he had as a platoon commander, and won for him the nickname of " Mayor of Bois Grenier." He was very funny sometimes, and the hero of his own melodrama always. Bemoaning the come-down from Regimental Sergeant-Major to Second Lieutenant, he would exclaim, " There was I, a thousand men at my control, the Commanding Officer was my personal friend, the Adjutant consulted me, the Subalterns feared me, and now I am only a bum-wart and have to hold my tongue in Mess." Some time later, when told that he was to be invalided with gout, he said, " Me, go home sick ! No ! I will go up to the trenches, put my breast to a loop-hole, and take it like a man."

January 20th.—Stockwell, who had succeeded Powell as Mess President, 'sacked Parks,' who had not been able to live down the confusion between brandy-butter and bread-sauce on New Year's Day: 'got Smith instead, a great improvement.' Smith was said to own an eating-house in the East End of London. In the evening an experiment with searchlights was made. Several Divisional Brass Hats attended. Except for a drizzle all the time, it went off without a hitch; but it is difficult to see men at all clearly, even at 300 yards, with one of these lights. 'Mess was again quite delightful. Instead of port, rum goes round in a decanter looted from some ruined estaminet. The conversation turned on looting. The C.O.'s method of sending the Regimental Police to pick up trifles is Gilbertian.' As C Company officers were 'coming home after dinner, Cuthbert looted a sack of coal from the Jocks. He stood outside their billet and said at the top of his voice, " Shall we take a sack ? " The Jocks' Quartermaster slept on, and Cuthbert lifted a sack.' That was not the only time "Tubby's" bing was raided. The next loss was a whole dump of coal, to A Company. That taught him to put a sentry on his Store. Even then Cuthbert once got a couple of sacks when the sentry's back was turned—he was sent to the Quartermaster with a chaffing message envying him his stertorous slumber.

January 21st.—'Very wet, but C Company had a short route-march through Erquinghem, H.Q. of the Divisional Artillery, Sappers, etc. Mud and dirt were everywhere. All the horses had staring coats, and legs caked with mud. Every man was untidy, though personally clean; none had a cap-badge.' The night was frosty. There was a battalion route-march in the morning to *January 22nd*—Erquinghem. 'Passed some Leicesters with bearded officers.' The day was fine.

Recreations in the area were few, but they were encouraged and enjoyed. Officers played polo who could; all ranks played Association football, although games were liable to interruption by bursts of shrapnel. There were frequent sing-songs in the billets. And there was Armentières, and Riding School: for a Young Officers Riding School opened to-day, and was held daily when the Battalion was out of the trenches. It served the double purpose of the education of those junior officers who could not ride, and the amusement of their seniors and all the idlers of the Battalion. In a field near Streaky Bacon four sticks were put in the ground for corners, outside which the School had to keep, and senior officers stood at each with whips and sticks to ensure the ordered pace being kept. The first parade started sensationally. Immediately the class mounted three of the pack or draught horses took charge of their riders, Moody, Owen, and Attwater, and dashed out of the field, determined to return to their stables at Rolanderie. Owen's succeeded in its purpose, but was shoo'd back by an unsympathetic groom; Moody's came to a stand outside Brigade H.Q.; Attwater's jumped a ditch on the rue de Biez, unseated him in a ploughed field, and was recaptured by a peasant. The C.O. re-collected the deserters and conducted them back to the field where the Quail officiated as Riding-master. Another time a pony finished in the middle of a pond; on yet another, in a ploughed field exhausted, its rider still aboard, reins and stirrups lost, clutching his saddle. ' The [1] riding class was not popular with the warts, chiefly because it seemed a terrible waste of time during the short period out of the line, and Armentières so near.

January 23rd.—A very pleasant day except for riding class. I had a very lazy ammunition beast, very tall and heavy. Feeling to-night rather like having been " tubbed" as a fresher.'

January 24th.—Sunday Service, a new Padre—not W. P.; the men liked him and sang well. Relieved The Cameronians.

January 25th.—An officer and 50 other ranks joined.—News was coming in every day that the Lys was still rising, so it was decided to let the trenches go and build a breastwork. Work began to-day. The siting of the new line was not easy owing to the falling in of so much of the old trench, and to the fighting over the ground during the Autumn; C Company, at their first attempt, after digging for a short time began to turn up dead bodies. On land where water lay so near the surface it was often difficult to find earth solid enough to fill sand-bags, so during the following weeks the battalions toiled building breastworks out of liquid mud. The wooden frame for the parapet was made in sections by the Engineers. These sections, large brushwood hurdles, sheets of corrugated iron, and innumerable sand-bags, formed the load of nightly carrying-parties which were usually found by the battalion out in billets. On the left of the Battalion front a gap was found

[1] Attwater.

through which much of the trench there could be drained for occupation. A shack was run up for the Company Commander, and a fire fitted in. There the work on the line could progress faster than elsewhere, 'and it was pushed on with the Company Commander's characteristic energy, and vituperation of The Cameronian carrying-parties' slackness, actual or alleged, in bringing up material.' Battalions in the line always complained that stores for which they depended on their opposite number, or on the R.E., were late. At one stage the Sappers undertook to bridge a stream that ran through C Company's line. When, after a long delay, the parts of the bridge arrived the Sappers were not to be found. The following evening two of the Company's subalterns had succeeded in putting the bridge together, and were finishing the work when the C.R.E. appeared and began to tell them off, 'they were sure to have made a mess of it, and then they would blame the Engineers.' While this reproof was being administered the Quail came up on the other side of the stream, and called through the darkness, "Who's there?" "C.R.E.," said the R.E. subaltern who was accompanying the Brass Hat. "About time too," said the Quail, having caught only the last two letters, "you ought to have been here last night." "It's the C.R.E.," said the Sapper subaltern with shocked emphasis. Followed apologies and explanations; but at any rate the bridge was built, and it stood. While breastwork and trench were in the making the company wiring sections worked in rivalry. Often more wire was wanted than could be got; but in time belts of barbed wire, several yards across, fixed on stakes, extended along the entire front. Until the line was completed, and that was not for weeks, it remained disconnected. To get along a company front, parts had to be taken at the double or by flying leap, running the gauntlet of German snipers, who accounted for most of the casualties during the first months of the year. On this, as on the entire British front, the reconstructed line differed from the earlier one in being as straight as it could be made. The Germans, having observed the marvellously effective siting of the B.E.F.'s almost haphazard October line, issued a pamphlet on the subject of enfilade fire, and remade their line with planned salients and re-entrants.

After the B.E.F. had spent several weeks labouring on these Flanders trenches a large-scale map, obtained from Armentières, showed that the fall of the ground is only about 5 feet in 3 miles. Small as it is, the Law of Gravity held; efforts to make water run uphill had met with indifferent success, though G.H.Q. had pulled its weight all the time. A pumping station had been erected near Estaires. Unfortunately the natives had not been consulted about the site; it had always become a pond in the wet season. Before the pumps were installed the station disappeared below the waters, in a manner of speaking. It was reported credibly that Sir William Willcocks, the Engineer of great irrigations in India and the Sudan, was then consulted; he estimated the time needed to drain the area of the trenches at five years, and the cost at £8,000,000—over and above the ruin of French Flanders.

The approach of the Kaiser's birthday had roused suspicion. Rumours of a German concentration at Lille put the wind up the Staff. Precautionary measures were to be taken. The O.C. A Company looked on his green and indifferently officered Territorial neighbours as the main weakness he had to deal with; so he wired his left communication trench and formed a defensive flank. Shortly afterwards the Brigadier, making one of his infrequent inspections, demanded to know what this wire was for, and declared that it was a deliberate insult to his nation. As a punishment A Company was ordered to wire its neighbour's front—'it badly needed it ' : but the Company felt justifiably hurt at its Brigadier's attitude to its soldierly thoroughness.

January 27th.—The Kaiser's birthday. There was sharp frost in the night. The Germans fired hardly a shot. Our artillery bombarded 100 yards of the German line for three-quarters of an hour : 'a fair hell, knocked everything to blazes.' We followed with two bursts of rapid small-arms fire just before, and after, 2 o'clock. The German infantry replied, firing high, and their artillery fired on H.Q. We had 1 man killed and 2 wounded : our Gunners had 10 wounded. Two good stories of the shoot came round to us after relief. While our guns were giving the Prussians opposite us hell, the Saxons opposite the Middlesex applauded the hits. Later, they shouted across, "We are being relieved by Bavarians to-night. Give us time to get out and then shoot the ——s."

January 28th.—The night was bitterly cold, with bright moon-light. Even with the naked eye the Germans could be seen working on their trench. There was frost all day, and an attempt to snow. A new French communiqué about sudden night attacks is circulated.

January 29th.—'Back [1] in the farms. The Cameronians left one drunk, and piles of filth in ours. We are rather particular about cleaning, and so I think we overestimate the filthiness of the Scotchmen. Dinner at Streaky Bacon Farm, as jolly as dinners always are during the out period, and then the hell of a sleep.'

January 30th.—A bathing parade 5 kilos away. Rumour has it that the massing of German troops in our area has put the wind up our Brigade H.Q. so that they have everything packed ready to move back, as Welton puts it, 'like pen and ink.' We stood *January 31st*—to arms in billets by companies at 7 a.m., but everything was quiet as night. Church Parade later.

February 1st.—Mostyn rejoined with 50 reinforcements.

February 3rd.—Returned to the trenches.

The Germans did not begin to be really troublesome for another couple of months, so a few cheery spirits played mouth-organs when going up to the line. The platoon commander of No. 8 organized his mouth-organists; 16 were trained and led by a corporal; on route-marches these led their comrades in full song, and kept good march discipline.—A Brigade Order that the communication trench was to be used near the front was honoured for the first few yards at most. Platoons marched straight over the top, and the take-over was simply a jump into one's usual place. One night when the C.O. was in the communication trench he saw a man on top, and felt bound to ask him why he did not obey the Brigade Order. In reply, something was said about "cauld feet." Allowing for his Glasgow accent, there were signs of the man having had more than the regulation tot of rum, so he was reported to his Orderly Room. His C.O. replied that he was not "drunk" as the term is used in Scotland, and that no action was being taken. Possibly judgment was warped by the affair of the sanitary utensil.

February 4th.—At night for forty minutes, besides shelling and a burst of rapid rifle-fire, the Germans threw over enormous shells, causing a terrific explosion, from two trench-mortars. Our guns replied. We had 2 killed and 6 wounded, only one less than our total casualties on this front so far.

---

[1] Attwater.

February 6th.—Yesterday quiet, lovely this morning. The enemy used his minenwerfer against the Scottish H.Q. At night the German searchlight caused a lot of annoyance. It had been seen first from the Houplines front when experiments with it were being made, and it seemed to be behind Wez Macquart. It was most disturbing to parties working on the wire, or on the new breast-work, or to reliefs going in over the top. If it was turned on to a patrol in Nomansland it did not really show up anyone who lay flat and still, but it made one feel rather naked and exposed, like the common dream of walking down Bond Street without any trousers. The men called it Willy's Eye.

February 7th.—More sniping : a devilish dark night, and rained all the time.

February 8th.—Back in billets. 'There [1] were rumours at Mess of an advance, of a return to St. Omer on the 13th, of relief ultimately on the 23rd., and the usual lying tales culled from credulous Scotchmen. Everyone very pleased with life, but I depressed, for between Bois Grenier and Gris Pot I lost my pipe.'

February 13th.—A woman and child were wounded when a few "coal-boxes" were flung into L'Armée. Back to the trenches. The evening, like yesterday, was very wet.

February 14th.—A quiet day of heavy rain, so heavy that at night all work became impossible. 'Murphy and I were fugging in a dug-out when we heard, in a neighbouring shelter, a machine-gunner yarning with my servant, "What's your officer's name ?" says the machine-gunner ; "Attwater," says Wakelin. "Gawd! I should think we'd all been (obscene) well 'at water' these three (obscene) months."'

February 15th.—As wet and quiet as yesterday. News came in of an expected German attack along the whole line on the 15th or 16th. Although it snowed and rained all night everybody had the wind up.

February 16th.—Fine. One of our aeroplanes came to have a look at the German trenches and was fired on, so our guns shelled them into silence. Sniping increased. A minnie flung behind C Company's right made a hell of a noise : James Cuthbert's subsequent Casualty Report, "one spade."

February 17th.—As wet as ever again. Two platoons of Canadians

[1] Attwater.

had been attached overnight to A Company. They took into
the trench bagpipes which they played in the afternoon, much
to the disturbance of the siesta of A Company's officers and to the
mystification of the Germans, who kept shouting across at night:
"Are you the Jocks?" "Are you the bloody Welch?"

February 18*th*.—Out to billets. Stockwell detailed to instruct
the Canadians.

February 20*th*.—An officer reported for duty, bringing 29 rank
and file, mostly returned sick and wounded. The C.O. got the
D.S.O.—'our only medal.'

February 23*rd*.—Back in the line. There was snow and sleet next
day, the other days of the tour were fine.

February 27*th*.—'The enemy fired rifle-grenades: no result.
We shelled their trenches in return.' This is one of the earliest
occasions on which the artillery hit back when the infantry had
been catching it. The Brigade front was covered by two batteries
of field-guns, the Battalion by the 72nd Battery. Their allowance
of shell, to begin with, was one round per gun per day except in
emergencies or by leave of higher authority. Compared with
that the enemy's allowance was lavish. After the infantry had
chafed long at having to endure a strafing without any protection
from its guns permission was given to ask for retaliation. 'It
might have been got sooner but for the Brigadier's fear of doing
anything to rouse the enemy or aggravate his activity.' One of
the early applications provided a story that was current during the
following months. Our covering battery fired four rounds
somewhat as follows: into Nomansland, into our parapet,
behind our line, on to a Company H.Q.; and then telephoned,
"Is that enough?" The shells at that time—in fairness to our
Gunners be it said—were largely the produce of makers, at home
and in America, who were only learning the processes. With
the artillery so much in abeyance, for even the Germans did not
resume shelling to any extent until May, ordinary activity by both
sides consisted in sniping, patrolling, and an occasional "hate."
A hate was a short intensive shoot by all the infantry weapons
that could be got into action: rifle and machine-gun, fixed rifle,
rifle-grenade, and trench-mortar. It was usually directed on some
object, or a place where movement was seen. Often it was in
revenge for some local incident; it might celebrate an incident

elsewhere. Our machine-gun equipment was still only two guns per battalion. The Germans had more machine-guns, and relied more on them; their tactical use was more developed. Our only advantage was with the rifle, for our men at this time knew the rifle and maintained their supremacy with it, although sniping was not systematized as it was by the Germans—it never was in the B.E.F.

February 28th.—The 7th Division is being relieved by the Canadians; our 1st Battalion is already off to Laventie. This move parted the two Battalions of the Regiment after their two months neighbouring in the line, and prevented their being together, as last year, on St. David's Day. D Company saw the 1st go with tempered regret. The "drainpipes" of the 7th Division were under the charge of "Tracker" Richardson, of the 1st Battalion, who would come into the line on D's right from time to time to demonstrate with one of them. D Company's opinion of "Tracker" and his frightfulness was probably shared by the 1st Battalion, but no one could have expressed it as forcibly as O.C. D Company. The shells from the mortars scarcely ever reached the enemy's line, they only served to annoy him, and he had considerable artillery superiority. To-day the Germans shelled the farms behind our line, our guns shelled their trenches. Relieved at night.

March 1st, St. David's Day.—A really lazy day with no parades, fatigues, or riding class. A few shells dropped rather close in the afternoon. The St. David's Day Dinner was at Streaky Bacon Farm. Eighteen officers ate their leek; the Brigadier, the only guest, was the eighteenth. It was eaten to the roll of the Drum, but there was no Goat. The reported speech of the Junior Subaltern in replying to "The Ladies," proposed by the Senior Subaltern, was a model of brevity and point. Turning at once to the General, he said, "Talking of the ladies, what about a spot of leave, sir?"—and sat down hurriedly.

Armentières was already the chief attraction during the periods in billets when the arrival of the Canadians stirred it to fuller life. The Café d'Egmont and an underground tea-shop, lighted by electric current which was said to come still from Lille, were favourite resorts of officers. Subalterns could get drinks in the Café that a provident sumptuary Order denied them in Mess. For the Battalion the most valuable institution was probably a furnished house it rented as a Rest-house for officers. During January and February there was a great deal of mild sickness among the officers, influenza, or what was afterwards called trench fever; a few days at No. 37 rue Nationale often worked a rapid and comfortable cure. Armentières was a real relief after the drab monotony of trench and billet, and every time the Battalion came out of the line some new story of somebody's adventures there would be added to the Mess repertory.

The 4th Division had taken over the Theatre and staffed it from its own personnel, assisted by two Parisian *ingénues* whom the B.E.F. called "Vascline" and "Lanoline": after a few weeks their parts were taken by female impersonators. "The Follies" were the model on which all other divisions formed a troupe of entertainers.

From the earliest days there were restaurants and estaminets for all ranks and purses. A few estaminets which had a piano got a running start in the Army's favour. The piano attracted men with parlour tricks. In amusing themselves they drew so much custom that men waited outside to get in, or just to listen. The performers were inspirited and repaid by the house with free drinks; they were also bidden to wait within hail of the back door until the Police had made their rounds, and were then given supper. Everything was free-and-easy; there was no programme, but there were few intervals. A song with a chorus was most thought of; the words, the voice, might matter little. Topical improvisations of four or eight lines, with a climax often repeatable only in convivial company, passed into circulation. One of the earliest jingled two phrases the men soon learned from hearing them often from civilians:

> Après la guerre fini,
> Anglais soldats parti,
> Mademoiselle can go to hell [or a variation]
> Après la guerre fini.

Another very early one ran:

> Mademoiselle from Armenteers—parley vous!
> Mademoiselle from Armenteers—parley vous!!
> Mademoiselle from Armenteers—
> She hasn't been [to taste] for forty years—
> What you pensez—parley vous.[1]

[1] See also p. 427.

Fellowship gave these cabarets a favour the organized entertainments never drew. No one went dry though his pocket were empty, he would be asked to drink with one of the pools. A regular customer might run up a score against pay-day or a postal order from home: the latter was apt to be somewhat heavily discounted. Admission was free, whatever the cost of the evening in the long run. Returning to the Brigade billets after tattoo, it was easy to slip round the Police post at the level-crossing if the red wine, laced with the house's wrongfully got rum, had not been lapped too freely. Another cup that could be deadly was champagne and stout, both of a sort; it was for high days or those who were flush of cash. The dark barns in which the men were billeted screened the absent reveller at roll-call, unless there was no clear understanding that one only of his friends would answer for him. At the worst, No. One Field Punishment had real compensations for those who courted it. Many a man would rather be tied for a couple of hours to a post or limber than go on a route-march, especially if the place of punishment was within sight of an estaminet or billet and he was on ordinary good terms with the women; the burying of a horse might be made to last over most of the days his company was in the trenches; and there was always shelter and regular hours in the Guard-room.

March 4th.—A Brigadier's inspection in billets, and a bomb-throwing fireworks display by Murphy. Bombs are really a form of frightfulness, and the damage they do is little compared to the noise they make. Murphy's demonstration was against rows of rum-jars set upon sticks along the far side of the field behind Streaky Bacon, where riding class is held. Most of the jars remained undamaged, but a stray fragment of bomb went through the window of the Mess-room and much disturbed one of the senior officers who, sceptical of the value of the bomb, was quietly reading a paper.

March 5th.—To the trenches. 'Oakley (of The Cameronians) complained that they could not stop their men burning everything, bridges and all.' Perhaps the superior discipline of the Royal Welch is explained by the following note from a subaltern's diary of this date: 'Had an amusing visit from the Adjutant, whose language warmed a chilly dug-out.' ("A.'s our Adjootant of courtly address.")

All through the winter, whenever the weather was at all possible, the C.O. had kept alive the fighting spirit in the Battalion by means of patrols whose duty was, in official terms, "to deny Nomansland to the enemy." Patrolling was done by an officer who was rarely accompanied by more than four to six men, often by only one. Knowledge of the enemy's wire, reliefs, troops in the line, and so on, was sought. The capture of an enemy patrol, a dead man's identification marks, overhearing talk and recognizing dialect, aided Intelligence. Pyers Mostyn and Fletcher were the most indefatigable and adventurous of patrollers. Either singly, or with a N.C.O. and a couple of men, they would be out almost every night that the Battalion was in the line if the weather was not quite impossible. Mostyn was always aggressive; the policy of "crossing to the other side of the road" on sighting someone whose looks were not liked was not his. He was so much at home against the German wire that on a cold night he took a blanket with him to be quite comfortable. Fletcher's knowledge of German led him to spend much time listening under the German parapet. "Sol" Salisbury was his frequent companion. If any news of an Allied success came in which Fletcher felt it would be kind to impart to the Germans, he would write it in German on a blackboard and display it over B Company's parapet.

Sergeant Roderick, Mostyn's frequent companion, tells of a patrol that set out this night. 'We crept through the barbed wire and made for the bank of a stream which ran across from Gerry's trenches to ours, and was bordered by willow trees. Then we crawled along the edge of the stream, taking cover behind the willows. After going about 20 paces we noticed a hurdle, or something like a hurdle, about 5 yards from the bank. As we watched it carefully we saw a Gerry crawling from one of the trees back to it. Without waiting for any order from Mr. Mostyn I fired at the crawling man. No sooner had I done so than up sprang three Gerries from behind the hurdle. We took potshots at each other, with the result that we drew fire from both sides. Mr. Mostyn and I rolled down the side of the water again, and had to run the gauntlet to get back to our line. The hurdle could only be used at night; it looked like a bush, and in the shadow of the tree-hedge it was well camouflaged. It was a listening-post that had been established quite recently, only about 20 yards from our wire.'

March 6th.—'Another beastly wet day : striving hard to keep the water down in the trenches. The C.O. came round in the afternoon, and he and I went all down the line. Pretty risky in C Company—had to scuttle across gaps : Quail's parapets very low.' 'The [1] day was relieved by a visit from the C.O. and Stockwell, whom the rain kept in our dug-out for quite a long time. The C.O. wanted to know if Samson's warts "argued about altruism." As he had come from B he must have been referring to Fletcher. The Quail acquitted us.'

March 7th.—'Another [2] soaking day : still at the water, which we are getting under. C. S. came along in the afternoon, full of cheer, and we had an A1 tea.'

March 8th.—Snowed all morning : quiet day : night frost.

In spite of the continuance of wet weather, steady work had made what was little more than a series of isolated posts into a continuous line along which it was possible, with due caution, to pay visits by day to neighbouring companies. It had been not the least of the benefits of the common Mess at Streaky Bacon that it brought the officers together at a time when the separation of billets and the isolation of company sectors of the line militated against their meeting sufficiently. Work on the trenches became easier as time went on. The new breastwork—though, having no parados, it seemed likely enough to be unhealthy in the event of shelling—did provide dry and roomy sleeping accommodation for officers and men. "Cubby-holes" were made by the Engineers in sections, and dug into the side of the trench or breastwork. A cubby-hole was not, however, always as safe as it appeared. Craig conducted a Gunner Officer, who had come up overnight to C Company's trench for a shoot, to sleeping-quarters in the breastwork, and lodged him in what seemed a dry and pleasant hole. The Gunner awoke in the morning with somewhat too clear *March 9th*—observation of the German line, there being only a brushwood hurdle lightly covered with earth, between him and the enemy. Craig thought it more of a joke than the Gunner did.

The day was fine, the enemy's trenches were shelled lightly. About 10 o'clock at night Pyers Mostyn, Sergeant Roderick, and 4 men of D Company started through our wire. 'The [3] listening-post at the hurdle of a few nights ago did not exist now. We

---

[1] Attwater.   [2] Stockwell.   [3] Mostyn and Roderick.

crawled along and made for Gerry's wire. We were not far from it
when we came on a German patrol of 20 or more men. As we were
getting into a shell-hole they opened fire: Private F. Powell was
wounded in the back. Roderick, "helped by luck," got him into
the shell-hole. Our party had replied to their fire, and they did not
come for us. The three men were told to make their way back to
our line, Roderick was to help Powell while Mostyn covered
them. Supporting fire was opened from behind, so the party was
between two fires. After Roderick had dragged Powell 20 or
30 yards he returned and told Mostyn he could not get him
any farther single-handed. Eventually they got him in between
them.'

March 10th.—The First Army attacked at Neuve Chapelle,
beginning with some local success. The German trenches opposite
us were bombarded, there wasn't much reply. A man of D
Company was killed by a bullet which came through the breastwork, another was wounded. At night the Battalion went out
in the hoped-for peace.

March 11th.—The German line opposite was again bombarded.
Because of that and the battle just south of us everyone was confined to billets. 'No news through yet, though rumour says we
are doing well.'

March 12th.—Still confined to billets: 'I want a bath, and cannot
get one.' The day was hazy. As a minor diversion to the battle
'we were [1] told to stage a Chinese attack of sorts, so Mostyn
was selected for the principal part. I took him round to the
Brigadier, who studied him carefully and, afterwards, said to me,
"He doesn't look very fierce."' Roderick was Acting Provost-
Sergeant in place of Butcher, on leave. 'R.S.M.[2] '90 Davies, in
giving me instructions, impressed on me that no one was allowed
in Armentières. However, I found myself there in a café where
some of the Brigade people in the rear usually rendezvoused.
I remained there in secluded bliss until one of our Signallers smelt
me out and told me that the Regimental was looking for me.
Back I flew to billets where he waited me. He was foaming to
think that I had violated his instructions, and, with a few threats,
he ushered me into a room where Colonel Williams was lecturing
to Captain Clegg-Hill, Lieutenant Mostyn, Lieutenant Fletcher,

---

[1] Williams.   [2] Roderick.

and 21 men of B and D Companies, who were to take part in an impromptu raid. I expected Colonel Williams would give me a dressing-down, but, to my relief, he seemed pleased to see me, and said, "Oh, here is Sergeant Roderick." Having been given a few instructions we went into the trenches.' Clegg-Hill directed the operation from behind, Mostyn commanded the raiders: he, Fletcher, and Roderick carried whistles. 'After [1] the word had been passed down The Cameronian companies that a party of R.W.F. was going out, we crept over at 10 o'clock in two parties; Lieutenant Mostyn, myself, and 10 men of D Company made one party, Lieutenant Fletcher and 11 other ranks of B were the other, 10 yards on our left. Approaching the German line we ran into a known listening-post. The two, perhaps three, occupants fired, but when we made a rush for them they hopped it and got away. We pushed on to their line. Fletcher spoke in German to try to put the garrison off, telling them we were Germans, but they were ready for us when we started bombing. There was nothing for it but to get back as best we could. A blast of Mostyn's whistle broke off the action, and a flash of his torch let Hill know. Again we were between two fires, and our guns were barraging our flanks at 50 yards distance— as Mostyn insisted, for the gunners wanted it to be 100 yards.' 'Getting [2] back was an adventure I don't think any of us will ever forget. It was everyone for himself, and the one who could lie flattest on the ground stood the best chance. I did not carry much meat on me in those days, and my previous experiences helped me through, for I found a hole and remained close to Gerry's wire till the fire died down. While trying to transform myself into a worm a bullet parted my hair, and a Verey light fell and burned itself out a few inches from my head. When the fire died down I skimused back.' 'A [1] couple of orilux lamps, separated by 100 yards or so, were flashed from our line to guide us. To create confusion the Germans flashed lamps too.' 'The [2] effort ended in the loss of one of our men, about 5 were wounded, and some of us left pieces of clothing and flesh on wire. In the morning Brigade H.Q. sent a message commending us for the night's work. Instead of getting the expected court-martial I found myself in the Dressing Station; two days later I was at the Base;

[1] Mostyn and Roderick.   [2] Roderick.

and two days after that in England.' 'The [1] Show didn't amount
to much for nothing much was intended.'

March 13th.—A very jolly day, with the feel of Spring in the air ;
everybody full of expectation, and plenty of movement. A
sudden change was made to the 57th's billets in L'Armée. 'Things
reported to be going on well' at Neuve Chapelle ; but when the
facts came to be known the affair was pronounced 'rather a fiasco :
lack of co-operation between guns and infantry.'

March 14th.—A telegram to the 6th Division states that the First
Army's losses were 300 officers and 11,000 men : estimates German
losses as at least 22,000—and they were defending !—Church
Parade was in an upper hall of a school at L'Armée. The Padre
preached about his "terrible experience" in having to talk to some
men who had been condemned to be shot. Corporal Hughes,
of C Company, a stout little fellow on patrol, remarked to a friend
as he was leaving the hall, "And indeed, it must have been a terrible
experience for those poor men to be talked to by a Padre like that."

March 15th.—Murphy gave another demonstration with a new
kind of bomb, a tin canister said to contain an almost unbelievable
number of shrapnel bullets. The corporal who was to throw the
bomb over a heap of mangolds missed his aim and landed it into
the heap on our side. "Lie down," shouted Murphy in his best
voice, and we all complied, wondering how many of the innumerable shrapnel bullets would be lodged in our anatomies.
The bomb exploded with a kind of metallic sneeze, and one mangold sailed majestically into the air.

The road to the trenches was good, but fire-swept. At 8 o'clock
we relieved the Argylls in front of La Vesée. An infuriated band
of them came back, invading A Company's trench, and explained
in violent and difficult language that the R.W.F. had stolen their
rum.' They would not be flattered into reason by being told that
no one could take spirits from a Highlander. But our fellows were
so quiet about it that they probably had pinched the rum. Anyhow,
a period of embittered relations followed. Possibly it was the same
Argyll company who pinched the Middlesex's rum.

March 16th.—'At lunch, when a shell landed somewhere behind
C Company's Mess dug-out, we all stopped feeding, and then
went on again. The Quail said, "How like rabbits we get in these

[1] Williams.

burrows, munching until we hear a noise and then stopping, and then, after a pause, munching again.'" The *Daily News* has a wonderful effort by "our Military Correspondent" who talks of "awaiting with great expectation the news of the column which is advancing on Lille from L'Epinette." L'Epinette was apparently a little private affair of the South Staffords.

These trenches were as bad as was expected. Only of A Company's part is there any contemporary detail: 'beastly breastwork, no parados, and holes in the line—one 30 yards and one 20.' The men dug all the first night under fire from machine-guns and snipers: very good work. Two were killed and one wounded. The gaps were expected to be closed the second night, and a parados was being made. To-day, however, Stockwell decided to dig a new fire-trench on his Company's front. 'After much havering, "Old Stick-in-the-Mud"' consented.' This opprobrious mention of the Brigadier may be no more than an allusion to his first inspection of his front, when the attendant orderly dutifully pulled each of his legs in turn out of the mud, but according to tradition the active-minded found him slow to move. Miners were put on to dig. Nasty work it proved, for bursts of *March 17th*—fire came across. But the men worked all right, and dug 100 yards of fire-trench.

March 18th.—After a morning's shelling of the German trench there was much less sniping and machine-gun fire than hitherto. An officer and 42 rank and file joined.

March 19th.—Slight snow. 'C. S. came round at night; otherwise all quiet.'

March 20th.—A and B Companies were enfiladed by a machine-gun. Besides 1 man killed and 2 wounded, 'Fletcher [1] was shot through the head by a sniper just after breakfast. During this tour he had gone out and brought in a French tricolour which the Germans had fastened to a tree right over their wire. The flag was afterwards presented to Eton College where he had been a master. He will be a great loss, not only for his gallantry, but for his personality and his conversation at Mess. To return off a cold and sticky digging-party to Streaky Bacon to find him sitting up over a decanter of rum with Wynne-Edwards and chanting in Greek a chorus from Aristophanes, or to hear his gay voice through

[1] Attwater.

a billet window on a bright March morning declaiming Swinburne's "The Hounds of Spring are on Winter's traces," or to watch him blowing smoke-rings after Mess while he parried the C.O.'s chaff about "University education," was an essential part of the amazing mixtures of those days. There was something truly Elizabethan about "the Don." He was buried in the cemetery on the right hand of the road as we go out to Bois Grenier.' As long as O. de L. was in command a party was sent from time to time to tend the Battalion graves there, and Colonel Crawshay had them tidied up before the Battalion left Béthune in 1916.

March 21st.—Relieved by the Middlesex, the Battalion spent the *March 22nd*—night in billets at L'Armée. A and B Companies went to Gris Pot, and were followed by C and D next day. 'Hell of a big new gun came up to-night on its caterpillar feet.' And A Company's moated billet was chosen about this time as a suitable position for an archaic weapon which had been used at Ladysmith fifteen years ago. A. protested violently but uselessly. With intense labour the cannon was propped up on the edge of the moat. No one knew what would happen when it was fired, so all the windows were opened, and the occupants of the billet withdrew to a distance and cover. 'When we returned there was no cannon. It had apparently reared up and leapt backwards into the moat.'

March 23rd.—'Mess to-night very jolly; Pyers Mostyn has the Military Cross'; and Sergeant Roderick had a Distinguished Conduct Medal.

March 24th.—The 46th, North Midland, Territorial Division arrived in the area, and the Battalion supplied its quota of the temporary instructors the Brigade was ordered to send to them.

March 27th.—Back in the La Vesée front since yesterday: the enemy, believed to be Saxons, is much quieter. Cold, but the day being lovely several aeroplanes came over. 'News of the result of the National: "Ally Sloper," by all that's mad.'

'On [1] the last night that we were in the billets at L'Armée, at Mess in the café of Le Gros Tilleul, there was some discussion among the great ones above the salt about the Courau de La Grande Chapelle. Stockwell maintained that "courau" probably meant "track"; where it passed through his front it was a track. Happening to leave the café at the same time as the C.O., I walked

[1] Attwater.

along the moonlit, poplar-lined road with him, and said I thought
Stockwell was wrong, and that in my belief the Germans had two
listening-posts at its bends to cover their working-parties, etc.
The C.O. said, "They've no more right to be there than we have,"
and I cheerfully agreed. In a patrol report I had already described
the Courau as a stream about 4 feet wide and 3 feet deep in places
where I had measured it with the broomstick handle I used to carry
on patrol. (It is one of the main water-courses of the district; its
branches unite and enter the Lys at Houplines.) It came from the
German line to a point about 150 yards from the right of
C Company; there it made a rectangular bend and ran between
the lines for 150 to a point about 200 from C Company's left,
where it bent towards our line, running through it finally in the
middle of A. A ditch ran from C Company's front to this bend.
At both of the bends were willow trees. The German line, which
here ran irregularly, was from 150 to 75 yards beyond the stream.

This afternoon a message came from H.Q.—"Would C Company
like to send out a patrol to bomb German listening-posts?" Quail
and Cuthbert were against it, because there was likely to be a
bright moon; but I felt that O. de L. meant to test whether I was
prepared to back my statement to him, and I thought that by
2 or 3 in the morning the shadows cast by the moon would be
more of a help than a hindrance, so a patrol I had worked with
already was warned. Quail let me off a night-watch, and kept
the first watch himself. I settled down in the Company H.Q. to
Mr. Clutterbuck's Election, which I had bought in Armentières. It
was still amusing me when the Quail came back between 11 and
midnight. He was annoyed that I had not gone to bed to get
some sleep. I appeased him by saying I knew he would not like
to sample by himself the Mess barrel of beer his servant had fetched
in his absence. So we each had a glass before I went to my dug-
out to sleep.

March 28th.—Corporal Hughes called me about 3 o'clock. It
was very cold. My idea was to get behind the post at the right
angle to bomb it, and rush it from the rear. So we went along
our wire to the right and set out across the open from the middle
of D Company's front. An earlier experience, when Hughes and
I were nearly trodden on from behind by a returning German
patrol, suggested our formation: Hughes and I in front, Clewly

just behind, and another man a little way off as rear-guard. We had been allowed two bombs. All was found quiet at the right angle, and we crawled up to it. Some strands of wire, which I cut in places, went to confirm our idea that it had been a post. We then followed the stream along to the bend on our left, and there also we drew a blank; but across the stream was an excavation, unoccupied; and all about us was quiet. In trying to see how we could best cross to search this pit for evidence of occupation I must have moved carelessly, for suddenly fire was opened at us by about a dozen Germans in a trench, which seemed too near for their main line but may have been a sap-head in front of their wire, some 30 yards from us. Corporal Hughes dropped with a groan. Dropping down myself I called up Clewly, a trained bomber. Lying by my side he asked, "Must I stand up to throw?" I, remembering the mangold episode, said "Yes," and we both jumped up. The explosion of his bomb was followed by a cry, and the firing ceased. Unfortunately, just after the bomb left his hand he got a bullet through the right arm, so I told him to follow the ditch back to our trench. The other man was nowhere to be seen, but Hughes was lying on the ground, hit in the leg. I hustled him on to his feet, and pushed him off, limping. In doing so I saw our second bomb sticking from his pocket. I was angry with myself for messing up things; so I took the bomb—although I had never thrown one, Murphy had shown us how to do it— pulled out the pin, and went back to the edge of the stream to have another shot. The Germans, but fewer of them, had started firing again in a desultory manner. As I swung over at the finish of "bowling it like a cricket ball" I felt a sharp punch below the navel, and dropped. Again there was a cry from the German line after the explosion, and the firing ceased. As my left leg crumpled up under me when I tried to rise I became terribly frightened that the Germans would come over after me; so, sitting up, I tried to push myself backwards by my arms and the sound leg. The corporal's rifle, which was in one hand, and my revolver loose from a lanyard round the shoulder, in the other hand, were too much of an impediment. I "shamefully abandoned" both. Even then this method of progress began to be too painful, and I doubted having strength enough to crawl the 200 yards to our line. After a rest I started to move diagonally to the left, where a clump of willows and bushes would give cover if it became light, or my strength failed, before I could reach our trench. I also found a better means of progression; hitching the useless leg on top of the sound one I crawled on "all-threes." I remember thinking I had not much farther to go—I had, in fact, lost direction—when I must have fainted. When my mauled patrol got back some of my platoon set out to look for me. They spotted me by the lucky help of a German Verey light. My next memory is of being carried through the wire on Private Collins's broad back. Daylight came very soon. Investigation in hospital showed that the turn of the body in throwing made the course of the bullet relatively oblique; the hip-joint was shattered, other important structures were intact.'

March 30th.—Stockwell's transfer to the 1st Battalion deprived this Battalion of one of its strongest personalities. A shelling of the left of our line did no damage.

March 31st.—A quiet day: relieved by the Middlesex.

April 4th.—Relieved the Argylls in the Bois Grenier trenches.

After weeks of continuous work, and the drier weather having come, the line was quite habitable. Sump-pits for drainage had to be an early feature; there was now a pavement of brick; there was cover from rifle and machine-gun fire, and revetted fire-steps. The Mess-shacks had become quite 'eligible residences,' and officers' servants vied with one another in making and improving each his officer's shelter. None was so luxurious as Knox Gore's. His own mechanical turn was displayed in a glass window that opened sideways by sliding—to avoid damage by passing carrying-parties, a pull-down wash-stand, folding-table, and other gadgets. Knox Gore was also called in as a consulting sanitary engineer by other Companies. D Company Mess, and his guests, counted themselves fortunate in sharing his parcels of Irish butter and eggs, and salmon now it was in season.

All the time the approaches were being steadily improved. From near Moat Farm to behind Water Farm a road of fascines had been laid down which made easier the journey of reliefs and carrying-parties to the line. About the middle of March, on completion of the breastwork, a new communication trench was begun. This, mainly the work of Stanway and his Sapping Platoon, had a run of about 500 yards and was wide enough for troops to move in column of route. An orange tree in a green-painted tub decorated each side of the entrance. Plainly visible to the enemy, this trench was not made the target of a shoot, it was intact and unique three years later. The Sapping Platoon was the earliest of the new Specialist Details battalions had to form. It began as a purely battalion organization. Miners and tradesmen, preferably, were detailed for duty in it. Ordinarily its personnel had no part in company duty, the men rejoining their Companies only when a battalion was in rest. To be returned to duty was a penalty to be avoided. Rifle-grenadiers and all other such specialists received training when a battalion was out of the line. Later on the Sapping Platoons were brigaded for work.

In those days there was no lack of change of clothing. Everyone was refitted each time a battalion came out of the line. By the end of 1915 this lavishness was checked, by 1918 there was little refitting, single articles were given out with a niggard hand. Rations too were abundant in 1915, and varied. Yates was given credit for the generous tot of rum the Battalion generally had. Ordinarily rations were taken to the communication trench in limbers and thence by hand to the Companies. At Bois Grenier the experiment of sending pack-ponies up to the line was successful. "Touche" saved Thomas's Company many minor fatigues. He was a draught dog of mixed ancestry, such as is seen with its cart in Belgium and Northern France, that Thomas bought for his own purposes.

April 5th.—Mostyn was out on patrol as usual, accompanied by a corporal—Bennett probably. They were about 50 yards from the German wire when they heard someone sloshing through the wet grass, and saw a man in front of them. Taking him for a German, Mostyn fired: he dropped. Flares went up, and there was some commotion in the German line. When it was quiet again the man rose and made for our line in a hurry. He turned out to be Maltby, also of D Company. Mostyn's shot had wounded him, not badly, in the foot. He had gone out to fetch in the patrol, for word had come up that our guns were going to bombard the line opposite us.

April 10th.—Relieved by the Canadians.

The life of a war-story was apt to be short; so frequent were the changes in a battalion's personnel that the topical and personal interest was soon lost. Thanks to an artilleryman, Major G. A. L.

Green, R.F.A., this one has been recovered. 'At the beginning of
1915 my Battery happened to be in the neighbourhood of Bois
Grenier, covering the 2nd Battalion Welch Fusiliers. We were on
the best of terms with our Infantry, the officers frequently meeting
at scratch games of polo, and the men at quoits, etc. The entente
was not marred even when one of their enthusiasts mistook our
observer on a haystack for an enemy sniper. The village had been
badly shaken by the enemy artillery, and hardly a house remained
undamaged. Some of us, thinking it a pity that a good piano in
the Mairie should be ruined by shell-fire and the weather, had
taken the liberty of hoisting it on to a hand-cart and installing it in
the Battery billet; and round it our talent would gather of an
evening. One day, when the Fusiliers were out at rest, their
Colonel begged the loan of our piano for a sing-song that evening.
My Major agreed on condition they treated it with care and
returned it before they went back to the line. Pianos are apt to
be mistaken for platforms, and beer has a knack of getting inside
them during the extra turns that may follow a sing-song. When
we had to send and fetch our piano a few days later we found that
it had suffered, so a second request for its loan was refused curtly,
and there was no more about it.

A few weeks later my Major was surprised to receive a letter
in a delicate feminine handwriting, signed by a Mademoiselle
Suzanne Delettrée, and written on notepaper bearing the stamp
of "La Mairie de Bois Grenier." It was a pathetic little note in
which Mlle described how she had been compelled to flee before
the advancing Boche, with nothing more than she could carry,
and was now on the verge of privation. Having, however, heard
that M. le Commandant had rescued her piano from the ruins of
her home, she had hit upon the plan, if Monsieur would have the
kindness to let her send for it, of making a little money by giving
piano lessons in Hazebrouck, where she was living on the charity
of friends. She was "desolée" to deprive Monsieur's "braves
soldats" of their recreation, but she was sure that Monsieur,
being a gallant gentleman, would have compassion for a daughter
of the stricken land for which he was so nobly fighting. One of
our subalterns was nearly reduced to tears when the letter was
translated to him. Of course the Major, who was a finished
French scholar, wrote back to say that Mlle Delettrée could have

her piano whenever she cared to send for it, and thanked her for
the enjoyment his men had had from it. A few days later four
rather villainous-looking men in civilian clothes appeared with
a hand-cart, and a note full of heartfelt thanks from Mlle, and
removed the piano. About a week later, when, as it happened,
the Welch Fusiliers returned to the line, our Major had a note
from their Colonel thanking him for the piano and hoping his
sleep had not been spoiled by thoughts of the destitute condition
of poor Suzanne.'

April 15th.—Returned to the line. This tour was quieter than
some had been—once a German patrol came close up and threw
bombs,—but from now for a month the guns in the north were
seldom long silent. The Second Battle of Ypres was being fought ;
the Salient was being contracted round the town, which, for
sentimental and political reasons, had to be held. When the
Battalion was again in billets the Germans introduced drift-gas,
April 24th—chlorine, to aid their attack up north. Owing to a
bombardment of our front the Battalion was confined to billets.
Next day an officer and 25 reinforcements arrived ; and we
April 25th—returned to the front. The German artillery fired
occasional short bursts on the trench or immediate rear at some
April 27th—time of each day, and the appearance of some of our
April 30th—aeroplanes roused great activity. But the day of relief
to billets was again quiet.

As the nights became shorter so did the working hours, and
reliefs were later. There was more time for recreation and for
jollity in Armentières. A pony Stanway rode was accustomed to
go up the steps and into the bar of a café for the snack of sugar-
biscuits which the divinity there gave it. One evening Murphy was
returning from the town, where he had been introducing to its
amenities a recently joined promotion from the Coldstream,
when the C.O. was seen overtaking them. Eager to impress his
Guardee junior, Murphy called him to 'Attention !—while I salute
my Commanding Officer.' The salute would have been irre-
proachable if it had not dislodged a bottle which crashed on the
road.

Another accident to a bottle occurred in the line. The earliest
anti-gas device was a respirator—a pad of cotton-wool wrapped
in gauze, which had to be made wet with a solution of a soda

compound carried by everyone in a "split" bottle. One of the men complained of feeling ill after drinking his solution "by mistake." A. Company's practical C.S.M. pointed to an idle spade and a job to be done, which was quite an efficacious cure.

May 5th.—Back in the Bois Grenier trenches. A warning order, *May 7th*—which gave promise of an active move, came in, but was soon cancelled.

May 8th.—Although there was quiet on the Battalion front the battle in the north flared up again as the Germans attacked the last ridge overlooking Ypres. There were signs of continuous activity there for several days.

May 9th.—Our covering guns bombarded the German trench and rear in the early morning. Although the rest of the day was quiet here there was heavy firing in the south where the French were attacking, and two B.E.F. Corps on their left were preparing to attack. For an hour and a half after dark the movement of a great deal of German transport going south could be heard. *May 10th*—In the morning our left was shelled. A later shelling of our communications ended before the relief began.

The time in support was humdrum. For two days before our *May 15th*—return to the line the 1st and Indian Corps were bombarding the German line from Givenchy to Festubert, preparatory *May 16th*—to an attack. Our 1st Battalion was in it. It lost nearly three-fourths of its strength, and the command devolved on Captain Stockwell.

May 17th.—Just before dawn a Zeppelin passed east almost ten miles to the north. For an hour before midnight our own guns were extra active on the German rear positions. Their S O S went up, and our front was kept lighted with their flares.

May 18th.—The day, like yesterday, was very quiet.

May 19th.—More officers of a newly arrived Kitchener Division were attached for twenty-four hours to learn the art and practice of war.

May 20th.—Relieved. The only incident during the five days in support was the interruption of football, not for the first time, *May 22nd*—by German shells about the field of play.

The last five days of the month, which were spent in the line, were very quiet. Owing to the incoming of a new Yorkshire *May 27th*—Territorial Division on the right some strengthening of that flank was effected without incurring rebuke or penalty this time. Although the month finished so quietly there had been a greatly increased amount of shelling by both sides, and the Germans made much use of rifle-grenades. There was a great increase in the number of casualties; our dead were two and a half times as many as during any of the previous five months, when the incidence was so small and spread-over as scarcely to cause remark.

A tale of this time is told of "Dai" and "Evan," both Welsh of the Welsh, who were overheard talking during the breakfast interval after stand-down. "Dai, which would you rather be killed in—a railway accident or an explosion?" Dai munched for so long that the question was repeated, and he continued to weigh the choice before answering: "Well—I think I would rather be killed in a railway accident than in an explosion." There was a pause before he was asked, "Why would you rather be killed in a railway accident than in an explosion?" A tin was opened, and jam spread on bread. "Well, Evan, I think I would rather be killed in a railway accident because there you are, but if you are killed in an explosion where the hell are you?" In time every battalion in the Welsh Division claimed the story as its own.

May 28th.—The 6th Division went out, the 27th came in in *May 31st*—its stead, and the Brigade was attached to it. During the past six very active weeks on the Flanders Front, and sporadic outbursts for other two weeks, both north and south, Indian, Canadian, Territorial, and New Army Divisions had been used, but the 19th Brigade was left in the stable centre.

June 2nd.—The routine of reliefs was broken again; the Battalion relieved the Argylls in the rue du Bois trenches on the left, the *June 3rd*—reserve platoons being at La Vesée. On the second night women's voices were reported to have been heard in the German *June 4th*—trenches. On the third night Mostyn was patrolling with three men when they bumped into a large patrol of two dozen men crossing their front at about 30 yards' distance. They did a lot of damage to so good a target with a volley of Hale's bombs. On being driven off they hurried home, got more bombs, went out again and bombed the salvage party. There was a good deal of shelling and a great deal of sniping during the tour of six days, *June 8th*—after which the Middlesex came in.

June 10th.—Having been only two days in support the Battalion again relieved the Argylls, but in the Bois Grenier trenches. Both sniping and shelling increased during this tour. The only *June 15th*—exceptional occurrence was the coming of an officer from Corps, one night, to try to identify the occupants of the trench opposite. Mostyn took him over to the German wire. His guest was not rash enough to come again.

June 16th.—Relieved by the Middlesex, the Battalion had again *June 18th*—only two days out before going in on the left in relief of the Argylls. One day of this tour was 'quiet on the whole,' otherwise rifle-grenades and shells caused losses. The German artillery-fire and sniping were co-ordinated; the snipers, firing from behind steel loopholes, laid their rifles on the gaps which artillery or rain made in our breastwork. One night a field-gun, its wheels muffled with rubber, was brought up the L'Armée road to a prepared position in the front line, from which our men were withdrawn. About twenty rounds were fired over open sights at the snipers posts. The German artillery plastered our line, but the gun was got away and no one had been hit. For no obvious reason *June 22nd*—there was a great deal of cheering at night in the trenches opposite. The Battalion had been in the line for eighteen *June 24th*—days of the month when it was relieved. Next day an officer and 50 other ranks joined.

Three familiar inhabitants were removed from the district, arrested for espionage. An officer's billet at Gris Pot was the cottage of a clergyman, a sour-tempered man. He was charged with signalling from his church tower, which could be seen from the German position. And there were two girls in Armentières whose shop was known to the men of all the brigades in that region. Besides cards of the boulevard type, they sold others with patriotic devices and sentiments worked in coloured silks, which were very popular. They were convicted of having relations with German agents. Newly arrived troops had a keen scent for spies. At an earlier date than this a guard of the 5th Scottish Rifles held up Colonel Williams and the then Medical Officer when they were riding into Armentières, not improbably to include in their afternoon's programme some practical joke on an unwary sojourner in the Rest-house. They were let pass reluctantly. Perhaps they were let pass at all because of the gravity with which the C.O. commended the guard's vigilance, and told them that there were suspicious characters at large who might call themselves Royal Welch officers. He knew his Company Commanders were behind. They and the Adjutant were arrested, and detained in the guard-room until a Scottish officer could be found to identify them. Charles Owen shrewdly declared "That —— Guillaume is at the bottom of this."

June 29th.—In the Bois Grenier trenches, in relief of The Cameronians, the Battalion side-stepped slightly to the right in front of Touquet. The tour began with two days of rain, and a lot of explosive flying about, which did remarkably little damage. *July 2nd*—When we fired on an aeroplane the German retaliation with shells and rifle-grenades wounded only one man. The next *July 3rd*—two days were quiet. At night, on the right, the Germans introduced us to coloured signal rockets. The Cameronians *July 4th*—came in on relief.

July 6th.—A third sweltering day was followed by a heavy thunderstorm at night.

In the summer of 1915 life in the line had not been made miserable by the wearing of steel helmets, and respirators hanging on the chest. The Battalion wore slacks cut short, a shirt, puttees, and boots—the officers stockings and sand-shoes. The prudent wore sock legs as knee-caps when patrolling. The life was pleasant in fine weather; hostile action at its worst was occasional and of short duration. The land was cultivated close to the trenches, fruit could be picked, Messes and cubby-holes were decorated with flowers.

July 8th.—There was a harmless shelling of the billets in the afternoon.

July 9th.—Back in the line. Tampering with the fuse of an *July 11th*—unexploded shell caused the death of 3 men and the wounding of 2. A salient in the German line opposite was *July 12th*—apparently a tender spot, because shelling it was generally followed by a cessation of German activity.

July 14th.—Relieved. Twenty other ranks reported for duty.

July 19th.—The Battalion marched to billets near Steenwerck: 7 men fell out. The Brigade was being moved to another part of the line. Its next attachment was to the 8th Division, on whose *July 23rd*—right it went in. The Battalion took over a front

extending from Fauquissart, where the Indians joined on, to Red
Lamp Salient. The angle of a stretch of breastwork, which turned
back at that point, was marked at night by a red lamp that troops
in rear might know to fire to the right. All four Companies were
in line, each with a platoon in support. Things were quiet on the
right, where we were 400 yards from the Germans, but at Red
Lamp Corner only 80 to 100 yards separated us, so it became lively
there. A wooden frame and screw on which stout elastic bands
were wound stood at the Corner; it was an early bomb-thrower,
now it was used mainly for hurling abusive messages wrapped in
clay. Our Territorial predecessors and the enemy had been on
friendly terms.

Both sides were burning or cutting the grass in front of their
wire to prevent hostile patrols coming too close unseen. On
July 25th—the second night our grass-cutters were fired on, one
man being killed. True to the C.O.'s doctrine of an eye, or two,
for an eye, retaliation was called for. In the morning a German
shouted across, "You dirty (obscenities)." For the next two
nights German working-parties were fired on. The Brigadier was
now Robertson, lately commanding The Cameronians. During a
visit to the trenches he met the C.O. and told him that his Defence
Scheme had not been sent in yet. Taking a used envelope from
his pocket, the C.O. wrote, in effect: "I will hold my line to the
last. If the enemy penetrate it he will be driven out. If the troops
to right or left give way I will form a flank." For a year to come
that was the Battalion's Defence Scheme each time it went into the
line.

July 29th.—On relief by the 5th Scottish Rifles we went into
billets at Laventie, about 2 miles behind the front. The little town
was not badly damaged excepting the church and the houses
round it; they were destroyed. There was room for a Battalion
Mess in the château, and there were comfortable billets for all. A
fair restaurant and hotel was open. An Asylum for Aged and
Infirm Persons had not been cleared although struck by shells
several times; the Sisters and their charges remained when the
Advanced Dressing-station, which it housed, was withdrawn about
this date. The district was well wooded, so games and training
could go on unseen and unshelled. The orchards, of which there
were many in the area, were the setting of casualties; behind the

line men were seen and hit when climbing trees after fruit. To save further loss, one battalion at least detailed company fatigues to pick fruit after dark. Five miles behind the line was Estaires, just too far off for convenience, where all ranks could get many of the things they sought when in rest. The Indian and 8th Divisions had cinema-music halls there. The charge was from one to three francs a seat. Each division advertised its programme on walls and in shop-windows, just like the Halls at home. The Meerut Division had the whole town billed; their prices were half ours. The Divisional Hall belongs to sedentary warfare, it has nothing to say to the billet or camp sing-song any unit may get up anywhere.

Although the French Government had forbidden the sale of spirits, an illicit traffic, being tolerated, prospered wherever our troops were. Whisky, so-called, was sold as "vin blanc écossais" or "white wine" with a nod. English beer had a very limited sale owing to the price, a small Bass cost a shilling. The men's usual drinks were French beer, and *vin ordinaire*—sour acid stuff. The brewer at Estaires admitted that his output had trebled since the B.E.F. came here. A Tommy had written that "French beer costs only a penny a glass, but it would cost Uncle George a sovereign to get drunk on it." In the following Spring a sergeant spoke to me informally, "I think I'm a bit liverish, sir." "How much beer do you drink in the day, Sergeant?" was my first question. "Oh, a couple of dozen glasses, sir." "What!" "It's only that French beer, sir." Another stalwart beer-drinker, promoted to a commission, would not allow that any beer could be "bad," but he counted the days between the weekly post which brought a bottle of his favourite English brew.

July 31*st.*—Three Companies took over the subsidiary line. Next *August* 1*st*—day A Company changed into billets in front of Laventie. 20 other ranks joined.

August 4th.—The Middlesex were relieved, very peacefully, in front of rue Tilleloy, less than midway between Fauquissart and La Cordonnerie. This part of the line, like the right, had not been kept in repair. In lifting the tiles of an abandoned house, to floor a trench-dwelling, a cache of several excellent liquors was found, and Madame's best china. Finds of buried valuables were rarely *August 5th*—made. Another draft of 25 came in. There had been

a noticeable increase of air observation of late. The amount of
rifle-fire it drew from one or other line gave the artillery on both
sides chances of strafing.

August 7th.—Hitting and hitting back went on all to-day : guns,
trench-mortars, and rifle-grenades were in action frequently. Two
New Army officers, attached for instruction, and one of our men
were wounded.

At night Mostyn and his corporal companion went to search
for a German listening-post which had been reported. The idea
was to go out with a party next night and rush it. They approached
its whereabouts in file, Mostyn leading, and hoping the post would
fire or do something to show just where it was. They had crawled
quite close to it, probably they had been spotted and allowed to
get closer, when a shot was fired which wounded Mostyn in the
left arm. He sank into the long grass and lay doggo while the
firing continued. Only when the post got up to come out for
him did he and Bennett open fire. That sent their assailants
scurrying back to their line, from which flares were sent up. The
lair was examined at leisure, and then the patrol went home ; and
Mostyn was lost to the Battalion.

August 10th.—Relieved to billets at Laventie. The Divisional
August 12th—Train ran an Athletic Meeting at Calonne for prizes
given by the Canteen Fund. It was a very dull affair.

August 14th.—Two to three francs from all divisional officers
made up the prize fund for a Horse Show. Of the performance
of the Battalion leapers, an onlooker at the back of the crowd,
ignorant then of their identity, cannot say too little. A succession
of officers, of whom only James Ormrod is remembered, made
conspicuous by their wearing fluttering black ribbons between
the shoulders—it was the Flash come into the onlooker's ken,—
appeared and promptly disappeared, each between his horse's ears.
A time came when the onlooker would have given a good deal
to have been within earshot of the Young Officers who agonized
at Riding School, as their tormentors sprawled.

After our arrival in the area there was talk of the arrest of a local
horse-dealer and his wife, who would be missed at the Show.
They were said to have a wide acquaintance in our Army, and to
be allowed great freedom of movement about the countryside.
A decorative custom of ours, which was enjoined by Superior

Order, would give them all needed information. Every unit, every little section such as a battalion tailor's shop, had a conspicuous name-plate on the field or billet it occupied. The lettering of some plates was very ornate; many had also finely drawn and blazoned badges. A few days after the arrest there was a G.H.Q. warning in Orders that statements in officers' letters of the position of batteries and billets had "frequently" led to these being located and shelled. It was, in fact, rare for anyone seeking the way to a billet to be told where it was with any such accuracy as the warning implied. The further implication that German agents permeated our family circles was staggering. The warning issued from a Superior "Intelligence," who can never have heard of the other superior intelligence in an adjoining office who ordered the name-plates.

Two rumours circulated at the Show. One, said to come from G.H.Q., that the War will soon be over, was heard by the infantry with cynical unbelief. The likely rumour was that the Brigade would take the place of the 4th (Guards) Brigade in the 2nd Division: the occasion was the assembling of a Guards Division.

August 15th.—The Battalion marched in the evening to billets at Doulieu, two miles north of Estaires. An elderly inhabitant worked all summer building a brick addition to his house: a sad miscalculation on his part, for it was razed to the foundations in less than three years.

August 17th.—The Brigade came out of the line. It shed its supply train, ammunition column, General Officer's motor car, and other appurtenances of G.H.Q. Troops. Next day the Battalion route-marched to the Forest of Nieppe, had dinner, and returned.

CHAPTER VI

Béthune—The Front in 1915—"Loos"—Discords

Contributors:—BLAIR; DOCHERTY; KENNEDY; MOODY; OWEN;
RADFORD; RODERICK; WILLIAMS

Sketches:—5, 8, 9, 10

August 19th.—The Brigade went south to the 2nd Division's area at Béthune. On the road it marched past Lord Kitchener, who was damned by the men for having posted himself at the top of a hill. Nevertheless, the Battalion's appearance won unusually complimentary remarks from him. Of course, everything that would detract from the turnout of the Brigade had been sent, as was the Field Ambulance, by another road. The billets were on the west side of the town and in adjacent hamlets. Many of the troops, Welsh and Scottish, were within hearing of the chuff-chuff of winding engines and other pit-head sounds familiar to them. The French miners, like our own, had made short-cuts across fields. A shirt or singlet of blue and white material in finger-breadth stripes is their working wear, where our miners' is dark blue. Their sports were boxing, and cock-fighting, which the older of us remember our miners indulging in on the quiet.

August 21st.—The Brigade was inspected by the new G.O.C., Major-General H. S. Horne.

August 22nd.—After Church Parade in the Theatre we marched past the Corps Commander, Lieutenant-General H. Gough. The Battalion's billets were in the town. Our wearing shorts caused a mild sensation among the sophisticated inhabitants. Béthune, though of very moderate size, had some good shops, and it offered a variety of amenities that the villages in which the earlier months had been spent were without. The men had more scope for the happy estaminet life to which they had become used. The billets were in the midst of it, or round about it, whereas at Armentières there was a walk of three miles—and return. Altogether, it was a pleasant place then.

Béthune was the centre of active preparations for the attack which, as was soon an open secret, was to be made on its front, 6 miles to the east. The front was of tactical importance when Marlborough threatened France in 1710. The Regiment passed the lines of La Bassée, and took part in the capture of Béthune, after a very short siege, in August of that year. The La Bassée position was again so important that neither side had spared labour to make it defensible after both had failed to pierce it. The 2nd Division straddled the Béthune–La Bassée road and canal. The Cambrin or Auchy sector, 1300 yards long, was south of the road : the Cuinchy sector included the road and extended for 900 yards northwards to the canal : the Givenchy sector ran north of the canal for about 1500 yards. Two battalions held the front of each sector, having one in support and one in reserve. The La Bassée trenches were to be the Battalion's alfresco home for so long, and the scene of so many of war's comedies and tragedies, that it will help the story along to describe their main outlines as they were in August 1915.

The *Cambrin trenches* were very deep, and so narrow that two men could pass only with a squeeze. Stretchers could not be carried naturally except in parts ; they had to be raised at arm's length above the berm. Leave was begged in vain to make the worst corners more passable ; when the battle and the greatest need had passed another division did the work. The communication trenches kept their original French name, boyau—gut : some were partly traversed, fire-stepped, loopholed, and wired to form a defensive flank. Nowhere else did I see such an organized flank. Someone had distrusted his neighbour. Nomansland had an average width of fully 250 yards on the right, it narrowed to about 100 yards on the left where were "Etna," "Vesuvius," and other mine-craters. Between the support and reserve lines on the left was a small brickfield ; a pump in it was a boon. In a dip among trees, 1500 yards in rear, were Cambrin Church, a school, and a few houses ; these were south of and separate from the double row of houses bordering the main road that made up the greater part of the village. From the line of the brickfield level unfenced fields of rank grass and self-sown corn stretched to the mining village of La Bassée. The front trenches were cut in these fields. La Bassée, the German stronghold, was nearly all single-storey, red brick cottages in rows, damaged by shell-fire, and occupied only, if at all, by enemy detachments. Its broken roofs, stripped doorways, and gaping windows were as sad to look on as a face with scarred, sightless eyes.

The *Cuinchy sector* was just east of Cuinchy, a straggling and now shattered hamlet. Its right rested on two partly ruined, fortified houses standing apart in front of Burbure ("Burberry"), one on each side of the tree-lined, grass-grown pavé road : thence the line ran through a brickfield ; it had an easy fall to a spongy area on the left of "The Cabbage Patch," which was unoccupiable in the wet season but was covered by bits of breastwork called "The Grouse Butts" : thence the front line rose quickly to "The Bluff" and ended in the canal bank. Mine-craters gave No-mansland an irregular shape and width ; in general it was 200 yards wide on the right, about 100 yards in the middle, over 300 at The Grouse Butts, and 250 at the canal bank. The Germans had what benefit of contour there was, and they held three-fifths of the brickstacks from which the sector took its best-known name. These large, compact piles, roughly 35 feet square by 18 feet in height, were adapted as observation, sniper, and machine-gun posts. In and beneath them were dug-outs giving perfect cover, but many men on the surface were injured by flying fragments of brick. To the stacks the area owed at all times a grandeur I never saw on any other part of the organized front. It was a witching grandeur under the moon's cold light, or when a falling rocket's ghostly glare glided over their deep shadows, but terrible in the red, smoking fury of a strafe in the dark. Trenches were named mostly after London streets. The whole sector was lively. The intervals were not very long in which some missile was not in flight : the enemy used aerial darts at times. The canal bank-railway embankment was a tender spot. The O.C. Company in garrison there, who lived in a frowsty, sand-bagged culvert, learned to be wary. Fatigues were heavy in this sector, so constant was the need to repair dilapidations owing to shelling. An attempt to lighten fatigues had been made by erecting a hanging mono-rail over Herts communication trench, but it was too often in disrepair to be serviceable. To the end of the War the mechanical and automatic substitutes for porterage and man-handling used by the French, and still more by the Germans, were the envy of the

B.E.F. Our men's rest, and their strength and spirits often, were broken by long carrying fatigues.

The *Givenchy sector* was in front of the village of that name. It had a dry but sticky trench system running northwards to "The Warren," where the ground fell sharply; thence the line ran west of north to Festubert since a small gain in June. Here, too, the Germans had the advantage of elevation. Nomansland was more than 300 yards wide on the right: at The Warren a rectangular projection in the German system narrowed it to 100 yards, and mine-craters nearly filled the space, reducing the distance between the opposed bombing posts to 25 yards. Craters along much of the front were mostly German-blown; they were of great tactical value in defence. Nowhere on the Western Front was mining so active as here. Yet, for all the underground devilry that comes at once to the mind of those who knew Givenchy, there was a strange charm about the northern shoulder of its gentle rise; the elements were a broken shrine, the broken fabrics of a church and of some cottages, each mean in itself, and a few maimed elms.

The defensive strength of the entire divisional area was increased by scattered keeps, either earthwork or fortified houses: one was "The Tower," but they were mostly called after the sapper who designed them or the battalion that first sweated on their making.

Running northwards from the Béthune road, some 1200 yards behind the front line, is a parish road the Army called Harley Street. It crosses the canal at Pont Fixe and runs to Festubert, but "Windy Corner," where a road runs east to Givenchy, was the northern limit of the divisional area. Harley Street housed, in its shelled buildings, two battalions in support, Engineers workshops, advanced dressing-stations, and, in 1914, two Brigade H.Q. These H.Q. had moved, one to Cambrin, 300 yards farther back, the other to the canal bank at Le Quesnoy, but they came forward again during the battle. Our nearest guns were dug-in in the orchard of a small farm bordered by the street. A familiar semi-ruin in the street was the Bath-house. In 1915 the number of tubs became too small. Some coffins, found in an abandoned workshop, made excellent baths when puttied. Until mid-September 1915 a few civilians remained; ostensibly agriculturists, they lived well by ministering to the troops.

For two hours each evening the street was thronged with work-parties, reliefs, runners, and vehicles with rations and stores. At dusk the rattle and clatter of the enemy's limbers was plainly audible, but the artillery on both sides had a nice regard for the other's ration limbers.

Battalions in reserve had billets in the mining villages of Annequin south and north (Tourbières), and in the scattered hamlets of Le Préol and Le Quesnoy. Brigade in reserve had billets in Annezin, Béthune, and Beuvry. French mining villages are very like our own, neither better nor worse.

August 24th.—The Battalion went into the line at Cuinchy at 3 p.m. in relief of the 1st Berks. Life in the trenches on the La Bassée front was quite different from what it had been at Bois Grenier and Laventie. The sense of war was always present. The visible difference was the slightly elevated site on a ridge. Deep trenches could be dug because there was natural drainage in its medium loam or clay, sand, and chalk. In the absence of rock it was easy to mine and counter-mine. Mining was the primary activity, and the only novelty in trench warfare the Battalion found in its new area. Where a mine was sunk the infantry in garrison had to find a carrying-fatigue for the spoil sent up by the miners. The tactical advantages of a mine successfully blown caused daily activity in sapping and wiring; and small arms, bomb, trench-mortar, and artillery covered or hindered the work. The knowledge that dirty work was going on underground gave a new meaning to sounds. The tread of an unseen man pacing up and down for warmth on the bricked or duck-boarded trench, the tap of a foot beating time to a tune running in someone's head, the drip of water, any repeated sound of that sort, was apt to be hair-raising—especially in the small hours when vitality is low and we are alive to fancy's prompting—until familiarity with a mined area bred disregard.

August 27th—Relieved by the 1st Middlesex, the Battalion went to billets in Annequin. The usual hour for reliefs on this front at the time was 3 to 4 in the afternoon. A return to the same trenches *August 30th*—dispelled any doubt about this being a more active front than the Battalion had been used to, but the deadly competition of wits was entered into with zest.

September 2nd.—The new Colonel of the Regiment, Sir Francis

Lloyd, visited the trenches. After the relief he saw the men in their billets in Annequin. He was called, familiarly, "Frankie": less familiarly, "The Yellow Peril." Other visitors in these trenches were two old Regimental Officers, appointed to command New Army battalions, who had been sent out for a couple of days to learn all about the War. They expected to have to live in their haversacks, but so well were they catered for that, on returning to their units, their gratitude flowed back in a case of Chartreuse for the Mess. Some can recall a yet earlier visitor. According to legend, it may be scandal, he fired one shot over the parapet, then, exclaiming "Thank God, I've done my bit," he tottered down the trench. Anyhow, he went home "for the duration."

September 3rd.—Rained all day, the one wet day in a long dry spell.

September 4th.—The Battalion, in reserve and now in Béthune, had to find large working-parties daily. No one got much rest during September. There were fatigues for everyone, whether in or out of the trenches. A new front line was dug in Nomansland in the Cambrin sector. Everywhere assembly trenches were dug behind the support line, and gun-emplacements were dug in it. Stores for bridging trenches, ladders for getting out of them, had to be carried. Large and heavy metal cylinders, slung from a pole, that weighed on the shoulders of two men, were carried from Annequin cross-roads to be dug into the front line. The official name for the content of these cylinders was "accessory." It was a crime to call it "gas." No printable vocabulary could repeat what the men called it as they struggled and sweated up the narrow angular trenches, which were festooned with loose telephone wires that gripped sometimes the throat, sometimes the feet.—New batteries rolled in behind us, flung up emplacements in the chalky soil, and registered: all with the barest pretence of secrecy. Troop, train, and wagon movements were unconcealed. There was so much to be seen and sought for by both sides that observers excitedly poked their telescopes through the slits of the most cunningly contrived observation posts, "O-pips," so that they flashed in the sun like heliographs. And air activity increased greatly on both sides.

In these full days Roderick was once Fire-picket Sergeant, Pattison was Company Sergeant-Major-in-Waiting, and Graves was Orderly Officer. Roderick went out into town, 'Pattison shut his eye; he said I was ill when the Orderly Officer asked for me. Next morning into Orderly Room went a document vociferously worded, volumes of it. If it had been to the point Pattison and I would have been for it. But Colonel Williams was a soldier and a sport, and I don't think he had much time to waste on literature, so the matter dropped.'

September 8th.—Blair, 'on joining the Battalion, was struck by the strict observance of orders not to discuss movements of troops, guns, or anything to do with the coming offensive. At the Base, where I had spent five weeks, everything was open and public; for weeks beforehand the offensive was the general topic among all ranks. It was a dog's life for the men, and rather irritating for junior officers, at Havre. Subalterns were either in charge of fatigues or listening to windy lectures. Hundreds of men paraded early every morning, marched some miles for a fatigue and marched back, arriving about 7 in the evening. One man said he'd been on fatigue for nineteen consecutive days including Sundays, hadn't had his shirt off and was covered with lice. If he had washed his shirt and hung it up to dry it would have been pinched for a certainty while he was away. Off-loading stores at the Docks and loading trains for the front were the chief jobs. Because the R.E. indented for too many men, parties of 150 to 200 were often detailed when 75 would have been more than enough, the glut got in each other's way and delayed the work. To load 20 trucks with stores I worked in three shifts; one off-loaded the boat, one loaded the trucks, and one rested. We finished before lunch-time; two-thirds of my men had done the job in half the time allowed. Having then been dismissed by the R.E. officer in charge, I marched the party back to camp, and was reported the same evening for "allowing my men to idle."

At Béthune we were a very cheery lot of subalterns, and life there had plenty of attractions. There was "The Globe" in the Square, with its billiard-table and inexhaustible supply of beer. I remember one of our number, a youngster but a big fellow, backing himself to drink six long glasses with one breath between each, and winning easily. There was a *pâtisserie* where one could get an excellent tea with an infinite variety of cakes, candied fruit, etc. And there was the Theatre in the evening.

September 13*th*.—(Back to the line in a new sector.) My first and last experiences in trenches were similar. I began and ended with a mine at Givenchy. C.S.M. Lawrie took me round the saps in our part of the line. They were never places in which to stop and talk. Fritz was very close and generally chipped in on any conversation. But it was my first day, and I was interested and inquisitive. "Sergeant-Major, what——" The Sergeant-Major and Fritz interrupted simultaneously; the former, "Ssh, sir"; the latter—— fortunately the bomb did not land in the sap. *September* 14*th*—Robertson and I were on the fire-step at Stand-to, it was 4.45, when a shower of earth and stones fell all round us. Fritz had blown a small mine. It failed to wreck the sap, but the walls caved in and partly buried a man, without injuring him or doing any other harm. During the morning the German trench-mortars were very active on our right, and his howitzers on our left. The sand-bagged, 9-by-2-inch timber roof of a dug-out was blown on to a man's skull. There were no deep dug-outs in which one could not be hurt, and no wire beds, only the very hard, perhaps moist, earth floor, at Givenchy in September 1915.'

We had 5 killed and 14 wounded during the day. Next day there were two outbursts of trench-mortar activity; and there was *September* 16*th*—a real hate by both sides the following afternoon.

The wounds on this front are mostly multiple and often horrible, being nearly all caused by shell or mortar-bomb or grenade. One wonders how the Germans fare with their bombs, so many of our wounded are the victims of our own bomb accidents. (This was before the day of the Mills hand-grenade and the Stokes mortar-bomb, not but that there were accidents with them.)

September 17*th*.—The Germans blew a small mine at The Warren soon after 9 o'clock, and another in the afternoon. Twenty yards of parapet had to be rebuilt, but that was the sum of the damage. Relieved by the 2nd Worcesters, we marched to Béthune. The École des Jeunes Filles ("June Fillies") was a billet at that time; soon to be an Ambulance H.Q., it became the Area Bath-house.

Day after day of glorious September weather was passing, and "the Day" seemed no nearer. There was no limit to the fanciful tales that ran riot, gaining currency and prompt discredit, to account for the delay. Superstition preyed upon many; it was among the youngest that I remarked it. Men sat in gloom rather than have a third candle or carbide lamp in a room; matches and candles were put out violently to prevent a third man lighting a cigarette or pipe from the same flame.

September 18th.—Yesterday hot, to-day sweltering; the evenings *September 19th*—are cool to cold. Our 9·2s are registering; it sounds as if the shell left the muzzle wobbling and steadied itself *September 20th*—in flight. Heavy and continuous gun-fire in the south is in its second day. The Battle of Loos in the British Army Calendar is the northern extension of a French attack eastwards from the northern end of Vimy Ridge, made in conjunction with an attack northwards in Champagne. In the dressing-station we were told to cotton-wool our ears to-morrow. The Battalion relieved the 57th in Cambrin Right, which is to be its battle-front.

September 21st.—At 7.30 in the morning every gun from 3-inch to "Grandma," the 15-inch, opened fire. Later in the day there was of a sudden a flash in the sunlight on Auchy, the walls of a cottage quivered, and were at once hidden by a huge broad-based mushroom of smoke and brick-dust which hung about for a few minutes, for there was very little wind. When the smoke cleared there was no wall, no house. A 15-inch shell had hit it. We thought a lot of the bombardment at the time, but it was nothing to what we were used to in later years. The Germans replied with only a few salvos. A hint as often as a guess was conveyed in the question, Is the real thrust to be at Vermelles?—on our right.

Blair's story of a patrol.—'Samson, who was always relieved to know that anyone in his command was not married, sent me with a corporal and a bomber to examine the German wire. We started at 9.30. We were in shorts, so I soon felt I was well over the age-limit for patrolling by night with bare knees; I was a subaltern, but the C.O. was the only officer older than myself. We had been out a long time, and I was straddling a disused trench in Nomansland when a German flare fell close to us; in that posture, and holding my breath, I stood stock-still until it burned out. Beyond the trenches were patches of self-sown standing corn, which made progress easier. Suddenly we came out of the corn with the moon at its brightest shining on us and on a party of Germans working on their parapet, and there were only 30 unpleasant yards of burned grass between. We lay low hoping they would go to bed and let us get on, for we had been out two and a half hours already. We had strayed from our course and were well inside a re-entrant in the German line, as I discovered next day. As the Germans did not go we started a snail-crawl at a yard a minute—myself, then the bomber, then the corporal. Arrived at their wire, I signed to the bomber to stop while I crawled in and tested it. The Germans were busy and not throwing flares; the officer or N.C.O. in charge was quite close to me, *September 22nd*—standing in a gap smoking. Rejoining my men, we crawled back at the same break-neck speed to the friendly cover of the corn. It was an hour since we left it, an hour of strain, so we sat down for a breather before making for "home." Nearing our wire, I changed places with the corporal, he was leading and I was in rear, for I wanted to warn the listening-post, who might not be expecting us after nearly six hours absence. Not a minute after our change of places two shots were fired from the post. The corporal was hit in the chest and stomach; he died, poor fellow, soon after being got back to the trench. The sentry told me he had been warned that only two had gone on patrol; spotting a third man, he inferred that we were being stalked, and fired. It was a tragic mischance that two snap-shots at 40 yards, by moon-light, at a crawling figure took effect. We got back at 3.15.'

At 4.30 I awoke having just swatted the Archbishop of Canterbury. He was joy-riding at the front, borne along on billowing lawn. When quite near, and making straight for me, he became a bee, dodged a stroke of my stick, darted on to the back of my neck and stung me. Perhaps some small pest did sting me, but the bee's loud buzzing of my absurd dream was from guns which had come in the night close to where I lay, and were in action. The vibration of a gun-barrel after firing has tones that, to my ear, can be heard in the night air but not by day: so has the flight of a shell. Our heavies are less active to-day, but the Germans are shelling our rear with 4·2 and 5·9 to some purpose. In the afternoon I dropped into an artillery observation post to see the shoot. Our field batteries fire 1000 to 1200 rounds of shrapnel daily, wire-cutting. The shooting is remarkably good, but I did not like to hurt the gunner's feelings by saying how little sign there was of cut wire. Casualties are few as yesterday; not 10 from the Brigade came through the dressing-station, deaths are fewer.

September 23rd.—To-day's gun-fire is the heaviest there has been. For a moment of palsied suspense I thought that an unexploded shell was coming down on me. A marauding orderly was tumbling from the attic of our already damaged quarters. The look on his face as he came through the ceiling made me too helpless with laughter to help him. Luckily he was unhurt although he fell on a tile floor. In the afternoon I watched our shoot from the front line at Cuinchy. Our men rest their elbows on the parapet with impunity, but during lulls the German machine-guns sweep our lines. Most of our casualties are owing to premature bursts and loose driving bands of our own shell. Altogether the Battalion casualties these days are 5 killed and 16 wounded; Captain the Hon. C. R. Clegg-Hill, Acting Second in Command, wounded in the head, is one of the two officers. One of the dead was a N.C.O. whose neck was only grazed by a bullet, back at Cambrin Church; the skin was not broken. The 9th Division, on the right, demonstrated as if they were going to attack, and the Battalion fired some bursts. After 7 p.m. it rained and thundered, and continued to rain, our first rain for three weeks; soon the trenches were muddy. The Battalion was relieved, and was drenched to the skin marching to Montmorency Barracks. Operation orders came out late at night.

September 24th.—The morning sky grey. There was more rain; after breakfast it became only a drizzle. Later in the day there was a beautiful and complete rainbow against a louring sky behind the Germans. There has been more din all day, and the enemy has been retaliating. The wind, what there is of it, is unfavourable to us; very disquieting. The evening was still dry but, after dark, black and ragged clouds from the south drifted low across the waxing moon. The Argylls M.O. was eloquent with exuberant optimism, the Middlesex M.O. just quietly hopeful, when we met at night to discuss arrangements. According to the official forecast and programme the gas is to lay out all the Germans, the leading battalions have just to walk over, the supports do any needed mopping-up: there will likely be some resistance at Les Briques farm and walled orchard, 1000 yards distant: then the advance will continue through Auchy to Haisnes, nearly two miles off. Both these villages are trenched, wired, and loopholed. Where will my dressing-station be? "Where it is to-night,"

I said, "unless the wind change, and I see no promise of a change."
Then we had words, but parted on an understanding. The happy-
go-lucky tone of our infantry programme jarred on me in the
circumstances.

Brigade Orders gave the Battalion its assembly position and
required it to support the Middlesex, but gave no time for its
advance or other detail. In Battalion Orders it was calculated that
our leading Companies would be forming in the front line as the
last of the Middlesex went over. The morning had been spent
fitting and preparing: Orders were issued and explained. After
the final inspection of the awful gas-masks of that period the men
were dismissed until evening. There was a Battalion dinner with
the G.O.C. and Staff of the 24th Division, who were taking
over the billet, as unexpected guests. It was a cheery affair at the
start, but there was a shadow on it, and the diners were too pre-
occupied to keep up the cheeriness to the end. At 10.45 we left
Béthune and marched the 9 kilometres to Cambrin, where R.E.
stores were collected. The night was very dark, it poured with
rain all the way. The march was a depressing affair, which C
Company tried to enliven by a constant repetition of "China,
China, Chinatown," but without great success.

September 25th.—B Company reached its assembly trench, some
200 yards behind the front line, about 1 o'clock, and lay down to
await zero. The assembly trenches were deep and cramped.
Everyone was inconvenienced by his kit and equipment. Besides
rifle, bayonet, 200 rounds of ammunition, and extra ration, every
man had to carry a pick or shovel or other tool, and several new
and unwieldy bombs known as "cricket balls." The match-
striker on which the bomb fuse had to be lighted had become so
wet as to be useless until it might dry. All had to wear a rolled
P.H. helmet on the head, ready to be pulled down at a moment's
notice; a cap was balanced on top of it, and the whole was tied
on with a piece of string passed under the chin. Things might
have been worse, for although the night was cold the pouring rain
had become lighter showers. A rum issue was to be served out
an hour before the attack. Freeman countermanded his Company's
issue, to the dismay of his men and more than dismay of those
who saw it poured over the ground. A. Company lost theirs.

Heavy gun-fire awakened me in No. 1 Harley Street. No notice of zero hour had reached me, so I ran upstairs to a paneless attic window that was out of bounds. A grey watery sky: shells bursting on the German front line, and a line of smoke forming on our front: the air was raw, it was nearly windless; there was some crackling of small arms, a bit like sticks kindling. I ran down and called the men, pulled on some clothes, and rushed round to Wimpole Street, a shallow communication trench in which we had made a dressing-station of a sort by digging into the side and sand-bagging a rafter roof. We were overwhelmed at once by a score or two of slightly wounded, who said, "All's going well," and breathless men who said they were "gassed," though few looked like it.

Zero, 5.45, had found the Battalion ready to move up to support the 1st Middlesex, C and B Companies leading. The whir-r-r of shell splinters mingled with the zipp and whip-lash crack of rifle and machine-gun bullets over its assembly trenches. What followed can be understood only in the light of what happened in front. Our artillery treated the German front line with rapid fire; the shooting was good—but the garrison had been withdrawn to the support line. At the same time the Special Gas Company opened the cocks of the cylinders. The unfavourable wind had been reported early to the Brigadier, and he applied to have the gas countermanded—without avail. What wind there was caused it to drift along the line from right to left and to fall back into the trench. Men in the front line got mouthfuls of it, and some became panicky. Gas helmets were adjusted. While the wearers were being stifled in them, the German artillery opened on the crowded trench with well-aimed fire which caused casualties. The first rearward stream of walking wounded began, and the scared, including many of the gas merchants, went with them. Some disorder had been caused, but the Old Line steadied itself. Scaling-ladders were put in position, and other final preparations were made.

The infantry assault was not to start until 6.30—"to let the gas act." During the time of waiting to go over German shells were bursting on the front line and communication trenches. A portion of the Middlesex climbed out of their trench ahead of the time-table to escape the gas, and began a forward movement. The Argylls climbed out on time from both front and support trenches; the cover given by craters let some of the first wave get to the German wire; the second wave dashed forward and was checked by their own front line and wire. "Forty officers and 800 men shot down in 5 minutes" summarizes the Brigade's attack.[1]

The main items of this scene were reproduced on the rest of the front of the 2nd Division. The 6th Brigade at Cuinchy was more affected by the gas, which put most of its machine-guns out of action. Elements of only one 2nd Division unit got a footing in the German position: one machine-gun prevented the replenishment of its ammunition, and it was bombed out. On the right of the Division, gas, and the direction of the wind relative to the trenches, was a great factor in a considerable and promising initial success.

The C.O. had left the soil-covered shelter dug into the side of a trench, in which H.Q. was temporarily housed, to meet his Companies in the front line. When he arrived there it was not yet clear of the Middlesex, apart from casualties. What he saw of the attack was "forlorn little groups" that assembled in front of the wire and dissolved in trying to go forward, and the Germans standing shoulder to shoulder on their fire-steps, visible from the breast upwards, firing deliberately. The attack was failing, it had already failed, and his Companies were not yet in the trench: 'I[2] thought we were eternally disgraced.' He climbed on the parapet to try to see them, but a Middlesex officer pulled him down. After ordering everyone still in the trench to advance he went in search of his own men. While he and Owen were in the communication trench near the front a shell burst overhead, wounding him in the forehead and arm.

When C and B, the leading Companies, began to move forward at 6.30 the support line and communication trenches were being fairly heavily shelled. They could see nothing; and they knew nothing of the state of affairs in front. 'With[3] Freeman were Pattison—the Company Sergeant-Major—a few bombers, and me. We had gone only a short distance when the trenches were found blocked with debris, walking wounded, runners and stretcher-bearers, so progress was terribly slow. When we arrived at what

[1] The Argylls' casualties that day were 330, early estimates were 500. The Middlesex lost over 450.
[2] Williams.   [3] Moody.

was expected to be the front line, but proved to be the support line, Freeman found that only 20 of his men had got through the jam and kept up with him. As his Company was due in the front line in twenty minutes, he sent Pattison and me over the top to find and bring on the others. During the search, in which we failed, Pattison—hearing a shell coming—dropped on his face. When the dust and smoke had cleared he was in the fresh shell-hole of a 5·9 in a sitting posture. Collecting himself, he remarked, "That one nearly had me," and carried on. Just as we two returned to Freeman to report our failure Colonel Williams ran forward with a wound over an eye, from which the blood ran down his face. He was very concerned; he had seen that the Middlesex attack was failing, so he ordered the troops in the vicinity to advance at once over the top to support it. At that moment Freeman collapsed—it was proved afterwards that he had died of acute heart failure. I led the small party forward. Six had become casualties by the time the front line was reached. Most of the party thought, in the excitement and confusion, that it was the German trench. ('The sight of the trench was horrible, it was literally packed with wounded, dying, and dead men; one had the greatest difficulty in avoiding treading on them.') And the scene beyond was the same. The ground was strewn with dead and wounded in numbers diminishing with the distance; many of the wounded were crawling back through the grass. Gas was still rising from cylinders in our trench; and, drifting up from the right, it came back over our line and fell into the trench for lack of a breeze to disperse it: thus many of the helpless wounded were gassed. Again I made search for the main body of my Company and, having found it, reported to H.Q. for orders. Owen, who was commanding now, because the C.O. had gone to hospital, told me in characteristically picturesque language to advance. I thought of the tactical situation as it had appeared to me, but went and got the Company into line.' C Company were in position; they too had been held up by wounded Middlesex working their way down, though their move had been through a less busy traffic route.

'The [1] Battalion attack was a forlorn hope. About 8 o'clock the officers blew their whistles and over we went, B Company on

[1] Blair.

our left. I saw no shells bursting over the German trenches, so, the morning being bright and sunny, the German riflemen and machine-gunners took their toll of us undisturbed. C Company may have gone 40 yards and then the line just fell down. Samson was very badly hit, and died later in the day; Goldsmith and I were badly wounded; the casualties among the men were heavy.'

'Half [1] of B Company fell in 30 yards. Since there was no prospect of the remaining 200 yards being covered by more than a handful, I ordered the remainder of the Company to halt and scratch themselves in. This was done with remarkable rapidity. The prearranged plan of advancing by rushes of alternate platoons never had a chance to function. At 9 o'clock a runner was given a message to H.Q. As there was no reply by 10.30 another message was sent. Then we were ordered to stand fast, ready to take part in another attack that was to be made at 11 o'clock, the appearance above the parapet of the bayonets of the fresh wave would inform us when to move.'

A and D Companies had assembled in Maison Rouge Alley, in front of Cambrin Church; their progress to the support and front lines was somewhat similar to that of C and B. Their further advance was countermanded by Owen, who had watched the useless sacrifice of C and B. They waited expecting anything, but the impossibility of infantry action on this front was represented by Owen and the other Officers Commanding. At noon they relieved the Middlesex, and The Cameronians relieved the Argylls. They helped to tidy up and to fan the gas out of the trenches. Stanway was given command of C Company. The break-through by the divisions on the right had become known, infantry movements could be seen; the artillery behind us had switched to the right. By 4 o'clock Moody, 'tired of looking for these bayonets, returned for orders—no earthworm ever crawled closer. At H.Q. I was greeted by the Acting C.O. with the exclamation "Hullo! I thought you were dead," and told to go and bring the men back. Having had no food for about twenty-two hours, I was grateful for a square inch of chocolate from Rugg, the Intelligence Officer, who appeared to have nothing in particular to do. The Companies were withdrawn with difficulty. Men were sent back singly through the long autumn grass of No-

[1] Moody.

mansland to leap quickly into the trench on reaching the parapet, where ready hands helped them in.'

During these hours the wounded were being helped, and helping each other, and more wounds were being incurred in the helping. Blair 'was out of the picture with a fractured pelvis. A less wounded man near me wanted to carry me in, but I told him we would both be shot; however, he started to get up and was wounded again immediately. I crawled back slowly and was laid in the bottom of the trench, where I was nearly suffocated with gas before the doctor came and had me moved to a narrow communication trench; I lay there for 5 hours. No stretcher could be used even if one had been available. Eventually I was carried down slung on my puttees between two rifles. It was an exceedingly painful journey. Once clear of the trenches the medical arrangements were very good.'

As soon as it was dark parties went out and did excellent work bringing in the wounded and the dead. Work in the Dressing-station went on into the night, for twenty-one hours in all without food or pause. One of our batteries, about 200 yards in rear, had sprayed the ground beside us with shrapnel from muzzle-bursts now and then; twice one of us was well peppered with ricochets, but the bullets had no penetration. Of some scores of men of the Brigade and flank Brigades who came complaining of gas, few were affected to any appreciable extent; lots of men who had nausea and intense headache remained at duty. There was a period of watery sunshine in the morning, the rest of the day was overcast and there were hours of drizzle or more.

The night was dry. There was quiet on the Brigade front except *September 26th*—for occasional shells, some of them tear-gas. During the morning, while Thomas, O.C. A Company, was watching the action still going on in front of Vermelles, he was shot by a sniper. A man also was killed and 8 were wounded. The day, otherwise, was uneventful for us, since the expected diversion on the Brigade front was not called for. Two dead Middlesex officers having been found in Nomansland during the night stripped of their uniform, a warning was issued, so everyone in the uniform became suspect. Empty gas cylinders were removed and replaced by full ones, whereat Owen excelled himself in speaking his mind to the Gas Officer. Our dead were buried in

Cambrin Cemetery. The action had cost the Battalion 7 officers and 113 other ranks killed and wounded, nearly all in two Companies.

September 27th.—The expected order for a diversion came in the late afternoon. The direction, at least, of the wind was perfect for gas. The infantry were not to move unless the Brigadier approved. I watched the affair from an observation post in Burbure. Visibility was poor, the evening light very poor under a low leaden sky. Gas was turned on at 5 o'clock. It didn't amount to much, and a stiff breeze swept it over the German line in no time. Apart from the Germans' prompt lighting of fires in braziers to cause an up-current, it looked as if our shells bursting on the trench broke up the cloud, which rose quickly into the air and, being swept on, soon dispersed. The braziers were not less than 50 to 60 yards apart; they were thought to be beside machine-guns. I stayed long enough to see the German fire-steps stiff with men, and the flashes of small-arms fire. What a target for our guns but for the sections of Cameronian bombers in between, who could not be seen from the O.P. It was said that they were "wiped out." Only a couple passed through the dressing-station. Their Medical Officer was hit when bringing in one of them: "a nice cushy one" he called it excitedly, for shock made him as if happily tipsy. By then it was nearly dark, and rain had come on. Chaplin of The Cameronians and Owen had told Brigade of the hopelessness and waste of sending their Battalions over, so the infantry attack was not made.

September 28th.—The Brigade side-stepped to the right, the Battalion remaining in its position. This move brought the Brigade close to the Hohenzollern Redoubt, an area of ceaseless activity, but it was not called on for any operation. Until we were relieved there was quiet except for occasional moderate bombardments, and sudden intense bursts of machine-gun fire at night. Since the 25th the weather had been wet and cold. As the men were still in shorts they felt the change acutely, so they supplemented their insufficient clothing with sand-bags; some made for themselves complete suits.

For two nights covetous eyes had been cast on a luminous wristwatch. Two of the Battalion characters, "Fizzer" and his friend Seth of A Company, offered to go out and collect the identification-

SEPTEMBER—OCTOBER 1915   159

discs and valuables of the dead if they might have that watch.
They were noted gleaners; at La Cordonnerie they cut off a dead
German officer's finger to get his ring. To approve their proposal
would have been to condone a felony, but they were not ordered
to remain in the trench. They returned from an expedition with
a pocketful of discs each, and they handed in valuables to a total
of one half-franc and two pence. The watch wasn't seen again.

September 29th.—Battalion casualties, 3.

September 30th.—The C.O. rejoined, bandaged. After the
fragments of metal had been removed at a Base Hospital he took
his leave and lorry-jumped his way back. The hospital accounted
for his unauthorized absence by returning him "died of wounds."
A second officer-draft consisted of four subalterns of the Loyal
North Lancashire Regiment. They were so ingenuous that, when
ordered to report to the Battalion as soon as possible, they asked
Divisional H.Q. for the use of a motor car, but made most of the
9 kilometres journey on foot. One of them reached his Company
in a beautifully new British warm, another his in his lightest and
thinnest Sunday boots, to find themselves among men who were
wet, cold, grubby, and weary; so they were not made much of.
As one of them was being shown round by his Company Sergeant-
Major he plunged headlong into a flooded cubby-hole; he got
out unaided except for an apostrophe in the pure dialect of
Birmingham.

October 1st.—The Battalion was relieved at 5 p.m. by the remains
of the Warwicks and South Staffords of the 7th Division, and
marched to Sailly-Labourse. Our new-comers were further
impressed by the annihilating possibilities of a French field battery
which drove down a congested road in pitch darkness at a hand-
gallop. Their feelings at their reception by the front were mixed;
they were murmurous when two or three of them were gathered
together, for the Battalion did not take intruders to its heart
at once.

That the position in front at the time was "mysterious" was all
Brigade could say about it, before demonstrating on a map of
Europe, 12 inches by 18, how Roumania would come into the
War and mop up Austria-Hungary.

October 2nd.—The Germans put some 11-inch shell into Béthune
Railway Station.

October 3rd.—The Battalion, on Church Parade, was warned to stand-by. The Guards had just marched through, going to the Hohenzollern; we were told we might have to follow them at any moment. Instead, we moved at 1 o'clock to billets in the mining village of Annezin. A general clean-up began with an issue of clothing. The Young Officers Riding School reopened. It is a painful memory for some. Drafts were absorbed in a routine of platoon and battalion drill, and route-marching.

"Drum now to drum did groan"—for the band or pipes of two or three battalions on route-march, heard at once, and asserting themselves in different airs and tempo, made pandemonium round Béthune. Battalions marched through it well-nigh annihilated, or rejuvenated. Some that had the worst mauling were to be seen spick-and-span again; cheerful and singing, they put aside the trench-crawl for the time being. The amount of new blood in them made the difference. On the move newly-come units were easy to tell from those that have been out some months. The older lot crawl, the new march; the old plod along, mostly quietly and seriously, the new sing and whistle, and cock an eye at any responsive woman.

Béthune never was so thronged or so gay. Everyone in the area who could get a horse or jump a lorry went into it. Heavy batteries changing position moved alongside milk-carts drawn by dogs. Peasants, townspeople, and workpeople of many sorts, officers and men of most of the regiments, and every arm of the Service, crowded its streets. Men from the ends of a county or of the earth, who had not seen each other for twenty years, met in the Square, "The Globe," the "Hôtel de France," the "Paon d'or," the barber's. Tables at restaurants and cafés had to be booked or waited for. To wait an hour or two for a chair at the barber's was usual. Nurses had come up to the hospitals in the town; others gave merry At Homes on the deck of the hospital transport barges; cress was the staple sandwich. Every officers gathering was liable to be broken up by a Brass Hat ordering everyone of such-and-such a Formation to return at once to his unit which might be going into action. These rounds-up might be made several times a day: all arrangements seemed to be improvised. Thousands of men were having their first glimpses of a society other than that into which they had been born. The

Gallic outlook on one subject in particular shocked the un-
sophisticated Islander. It was alien to his upbringing to hear the
decent materfamilias of his billet recommend as a respectable
resort a house with discreetly curtained windows, in a side street:
it held "billet stores" the French troops had left behind. The
recommendation might well awaken concupiscence in the simple-
minded. The anonymous Army wit who first called "red lamp"
for "number three," the sign and street number, when playing
"House" and in other connotations, set up a memorial of the
Great War that may outlast some solemn observances. . . .

'. . . We get the London papers regularly and promptly as a
rule. Delay is rare, but there were delays recently. Any explanation will pass, but at the back of our minds was the notion that
the powers that be thought it unhealthy for the infantry to see the
papers when the pain was sharpest; the discrepancy between what
the survivors saw or told each other and the official account might
have caused them to die of laughter. Gallipoli, as you say, is a
muddle, a fateful muddle because it is at a vital spot, and means
so much to us. Loos is not vital, our defeat here is only waste.
We have entertained the Germans again, at their strongest point
too, at the bidding of the French. One may acquiesce reasonably,
or generously, or weakly. There is a muddled head here; one
not able to say "no" with good reason given, or, having said "yes,"
to carry the undertaking through competently. Gas was the one
weapon that gave us a chance. On the 2nd Division's front it
was let loose, according to plan, although the wind was adverse.
What a plan! And the artillery had a programme that did not
fit the infantry movements. Where the boasted success was
achieved the troops were too few, some were ill-chosen and not
on the ground when needed [3/10/15].' Although some of the
Territorial and Kitchener Divisions that have been out for a time
did very well, I'd rather have a brigade of the Old Army, for all
the wastage and replacement of fourteen months, than a division
of the New. Raw enthusiasts are ideal for a dashing attack, but
when they've got to the limit they don't know what to do next;
seasoned troops do. The observation isn't original, Napoleon said
something of the sort.

October 9th.—The Battalion has been standing-to since yesterday
owing to a German attack on the Loos–Hohenzollern line.—At a

Conference, the C.O. was asked by the Corps Commander about his new officers, what were they like. He said that he had not had time yet to learn much about them, but one had been the hind-legs of a hippopotamus in a revue. Dewhurst, an actor, one of our Loyal North Lancs, had spoken of some of his professional engagements.

'In "carping at our victory" in a letter of a week ago, for which you scold me, I share and expressed a general feeling out here. An angrier lot of men never was than the infantry I had been speaking to for a week before writing. They cursed our "Cavalry Generals" from their hearts. Still, if the Censor at the Base had opened my letter . . . Since then there have been questions in Parliament about Hill 70. It is only an item in what has been lost; in fact, most of the gain has been undone. A good thing too, in a way, for the "great advance" that set London mafficking, and sundry bigwigs wiring congratulations to each other, would have left us with just such another running sore as our sentimental Salient [10/10/15].'

October 11th.—The Battalion did a route-march, and a practice attack on a line of trenches on the way back.

October 13th.—From 2 p.m. the Battalion stood-to at two hours notice—for the last time at this period; again there was no move. Six 11-inch shells fell in the north-eastern district of Béthune during the afternoon. As a consequence it was decided not to employ nurses in the town's hospitals. There was ample opportunity to see that though windows close to a shell-burst are blown in, other windows in the concussed area fall out. This shelling took place during the last biggish effort that was made to improve the positions to which our gains of September 25th had shrunk under eighteen days of daily, and almost nightly, attack and counter-attack.

Yesterday's newspaper has an "intriguing" article under the name of one of the troupe of journalists kept at G.H.Q. to tell the public at home what G.H.Q. thinks it may be told. Kitchener saw to that when Official "Eyewitness" was objected to. A well-informed soldier could not write with more technical knowledge, or a jury advocate with more plausibility. When the good people have swallowed it we should get the official Despatch. The first paragraph chides the public for entertaining extravagant expectations: as if expectations had not been inflated by the official pæans of victory, which, by the way, the journalists "despatches" echoed. Then there is a dissertation on the use of reserves. One may guess that there has been a searching of the text-books at G.H.Q. The reference to the magnitude of the success attainable if calculations had been fulfilled is the lollipop. (The Medical Department had pegged sites for hospitals 30 miles east of here.) To-day's papers give the appointment of another Cavalry General to a high command in this war in earth burrows [26/10/15].

Well, you'll have read the Despatch. Can you make out anything thro' the smokescreen? If you haven't read the article you needn't now; the Despatch repeats its substance and elaborates it. The same topics similarly treated. Sheer coincidence. Two minds with but one shade of thought: the Fleet Street scribe and the War Office high-brow on his own recondite subject. Happy scribe. "It's just sublime" [5/11/15].' The battle which was to have restored the war of movement failed completely of its purpose. It was just a vast upheaval in the deadlock. Here it is in epitome as quoted to me—"mismanagement at the top, inefficiency in the middle, want of training at the bottom."

CHAPTER VII

Béthune: Winter—Navvying—New Army—Christmas 1915
*—Bickering—"R.W.F. Crater"—A Sing-Song, by "Punch,"
and other Play*

Contributors :—McKay ; Moody ; Powell ; Radford ; Roderick

Sketches :—4, 5, 8, 9, 10

The 2nd Division was one of the last to come out of reserve. Its
last days of "rest and readiness" were filled with a rumour that it
would repair its old trenches, hand them over to a New Army
division, and go to Serbia. For the Battalion the reality was to be
some dreary months of trench routine on familiar ground, miti-
gated by quite amusing breaks behind the line. We marched
October 16th—to Beuvry : finding all billets occupied, we went back
October 19th—to Béthune and billeted near the station. For one
October 20th—night we were in the rue d'Aire, before relieving the
Middlesex at 3 p.m. in our battle-front of September 25th, and
taking over a programme of trench repairs. German comments
October 23rd—on Loos, reported in to-day's papers, are cruelly true.
Last night, at 11 o'clock, we fired a two-minutes burst on working-
parties. This morning being misty, a few of us went out on top
to see if any of our September dead had been overlooked. The
mist cleared suddenly, the searchers were spotted, and Cuthbert
was wounded through and through the lung. Moody, a Territorial
corporal commissioned ten months ago, was given command of D.
At 9 p.m. the Battalion joined the artillery in another two-minutes
October 25th—jolly on working-parties. It poured all night, and
has poured all day.

On relief we went to support between Cambrin and Annequin.
Steel shrapnel helmets, for use by bombers in sap-heads, were
first issued now. The first wearers we saw were Argylls. To the
Adjutant a kilt was the limit of the ludicrous. The sight of one
always excited his mirth, which he expressed in Army slang

implying that these Jocks wear no under-garment. When he espied one of the objects of his derision in a tin-hat his thoughts found vent in terms of Rabelaisian ribaldry that made new-comers gasp.

October 28th.—Pouring all day. Casualties in the Cambrin and Cuinchy brigades: 6 wounded, none badly.

October 29th.—Casualties in the above: 4 wounded—all slight.

October 30th.   ,,   ,,   ,,   none.

October 31st.   ,,   ,,   ,,   7: 2 of them killed and 5 wounded, owing to a dud exploding in a dug-out when a K.R.R.C. draft, who wanted the nose-cap as a souvenir, was trying to prise it off.

The Battalion's only relaxation from fatigues these days was marching by platoons to the baths at the Girls School.

November 1st.—On relief it went to billets at Busnettes. Two Lewis automatic guns were issued. After sections had undergone an intensive training the guns were withdrawn, to equip a Guards battalion it was said. There was training in the use of a new gas helmet. It was not so bad as the P.H. which it replaced, although the nose-clip was an affliction. The Army called the Tube helmet, which soon followed, the "Googly (obscenity) with the teat."

November 3rd.—The Loos Official Despatch is published: a plausible screed: the 2nd Division, and what was expected of it, is not named; only the quasi-success is set forth.

November 6th.—The Battalion, having spent one night in billets in the rue d'Aire, Béthune, took over Cuinchy support: H.Q. in *November 7th*—Harley Street. Harbison, who had been Medical Officer for over a year, returned to the Ambulance. He was a sociable Irishman with sporting tastes, and a general favourite. The assembler of this Chronicle succeeded him.

November 8th.—A fairly familiar sound in Harley Street these evenings is the cry, "Pypers, pypers"—as if a Cockney Tommy were amusing himself. A little French boy comes to sell the morning's London papers, "Eengleesh pypers," 500 yards inside the range at which men get bullet-wounds.

November 10th.—A 5·9 blew in C and D Companies Mess in the brewery at Pont Fixe during lunch. A slightly wounded Mess-servant was my first Battalion casualty as their M.O. The members of the Mess remember the affair best because of the grab one new-comer made at a milk-pudding and sped with it, at a

hitherto unsuspected pace, to a place of temporary safety a good
way along Harley Street. This day and the next, five hundred
5·9s were dropped about Pont Fixe, mostly on the brewery. In
these parts of late the amount of shelling by both sides far exceeds
the daily ordinary for months before Loos.—A. Company H.Q.
was the cellar of a house near Braddel Point. Among the occupants
were two much-made-of kittens, and Graves. Graves had reputedly
the largest feet in the Army, and a genius for putting both of them
in everything. He put one on a kitten: it was enough. Not long
afterwards he and "Dirty" were transferred to the 1st Battalion.

November 13th.—Having worked for six days on communication
trenches, and come to look forward to the front line as a place of
rest, we took over the front on a wet day following a wet night.

Repairs had not kept pace with dilapidations, partly because
of a shortage of materials, partly because the drafts, officers and
men, with which battalions had been made up, had to learn
the job; and the Staff was in a fluid state everywhere. Officers
who had gained some experience of Staff routine were bidden
go up higher, and favourites of fortune took their places.
Directors of business concerns, given the chance, made good
Staff Captains. The routine of trench life was never so
systematized as in the winter of 1915–16. The line was stable.
The antagonists were marking time. The large civil population
that war had brought into the field partly trained had to be inured
to campaigning. There was the experience and, soon, the material
that were lacking in 1914–15. The trench system was a year old:
much labour was needed to repair and remake trenches that
collapsed with time and weather as well as from damage by
shell-fire. New trenches and keeps were made. There was an
unlimited supply of sand-bags for revetting. Sand-bags cost
fourpence each; a year later the price was ninepence, and it rose
until in 1918 it was said to be half a crown—but they were little
used by that time. Hundreds of miles of duckboard were laid to
mitigate the mud and the consequent wastage by trench-foot.
The Cambrin–Cuinchy–Givenchy front was not a wet part. The
consistence of the mud varied with the wetness of the weather from
that of pea-soup to that of dough; it was rarely more than 6 inches
deep in an unfloored trench, although it might be knee-deep until
a bit that had collapsed in rain or thaw had been repaired. Only

in the hollow covered by The Grouse Butts did water lie for any length of time, there it might be 2 feet deep.

To live in trenches in the winter months some stoicism, a little experience, and a good deal of individual resource are needed. Those with the resource can make for themselves comforts, shelter, and additional hot meals, for instance, out of the slenderest means. The Navy hasn't all the handymen, the Army has them too. Territorial and Kitchener battalions haven't the tradition of handiness of the Old Army battalions; trenches they have just left show it. . . . The life is sociable, and there's always occupation, there are some visitors, there's shop and gossip, and rumour unending; but it's a succession of interruptions, and too communal not to be irksome. There's interest at first for the intelligently interested, but interest flags in that atmosphere; the deprivation of individual preoccupations is the worst of it, and so the life becomes monotonous to the active-minded. . . . The rats and the lice are always with us. It's rough when a man is badly hit; a "blighty one" is a matter for congratulation. An immense amount of metal can, in fact, be flung about trenches without doing much harm. In the front of a lively sector our casualties for three *November* 17th—days have been 1 killed by a rifle-bullet and 2 wounded by shell-splinters.

November 19th.—A self-indulgent company commander had taken his valise and bedding into these trenches. It made a large unwieldy burden for some fatigue-man to carry through narrow, greasy communications. In the afternoon I turned out of a side-trench and looked on that part of a man which is made to receive stripes in early years. He rested on hands and feet across this fallen bundle. While I waited his convenience, and to give him a hand to shoulder his load, he straightened himself, raised his cap, drew a sleeve along his sweating brow, and, in fervent prayerful tone, muttered : "God strike me, and (obscene) the (obscenity) what's got this kit." I brawled inwardly with approval. This little scene happened on the afternoon of our relief. The move to Beuvry proved to be the first step in breaking up the Division and Brigade.

November 21st.—Marched to Gonnehem. H.Q. is in a picturesque moated, red-brick farm with a corbelled and pierced parapet, and a walled yard : not unlike our Border peels. A tall tree or two perfects the picture. There are other similar farms around.

Freestone, or brick laid in Flemish bond, is the building material about here and to the north.

November 24th.—The 2nd and 33rd Divisions have been shuffled. As the junior brigade we have gone to the 33rd, although the G.O.C. is said to have wanted to send the 6th Brigade; the Middlesex and Argylls have gone to another of its brigades, we are to have new Royal Fusiliers instead. 'Without [1] disparaging the New Armies, the 33rd Division was, as material, the best that could be found in Great Britain but the most impossible as soldiers; in fact, about four battalions were sent back to make officers of.'

'About a month ago I wrote of my unexpected meeting with Bob H., and of the likelihood of our seeing a good deal of each other. Now I can tell of a change that had loomed up and was then upon us. Higher circles had taken alarm at the poor quality of the New divisions, of some anyhow, or else at the consequences of using New divisions, hungry and weary, that had never heard a shot fired in earnest, against seasoned troops in a first-class engagement. So each Old Army division has been shuffled with a New one. . . . Of all the crazy crowds to be shuffled with is our crowd. No other people on the face of the earth would have tolerated the enlistment of the units of this division; only senti-mentalists like ourselves could, for it's done to the hurt of everyone and every interest concerned. South Africa should have taught that "select" companies, or battalions, are of doubtful use in war.[2] This is mostly a division of that sort. A whole brigade is University and Public School men, Bob's lot, men accustomed from infancy to be waited on, with not a soul to show them an active soldier's chief job—rough casual labour. Two battalions are "Sportsmen": but not sportsmen enough to join up with the ruck of their fellows. Of all these what-nots I've most hope of the Church Lads Brigade, 16th K.R.R.C., because they're a mixed lot. Kitchener and the War Office have learned nothing, or forgotten everything, that the raising, training, and service of the Yeomanry and C.I.V. in South Africa proved. Those lessons entered into my marrow. Every blunder of that small-scale rehearsal has been repeated in this war, and they're all repeated in this absurd division. We're in with the pick of it and know what we have to live with.

---

[1] Powell.
[2] There is more loss than gain in any sectional or narrowly drawn recruitment.

Lord pity the 2nd Division who have the rest. The whole boiling should have been distributed throughout the Army; the men on the whole are all right individually [13/12/15].'

November 26th.—A visit from the new G.O.C., Major-General H. J. S. Landon: he was not ingratiating, for he crabbed some well-proved details of our organization—about which his own regiment will just have another way.

The week at Gonnehem was enjoyed by all, though there were no estaminets near. There was some work every morning, inter-something football every afternoon, and a sing-song nearly every night, at which some Flying officers and two Glasgow Highlanders were star turns. The weather was fine and frosty throughout; *November 27th*—one night brought the first sprinkling of snow.

November 29th.—A two-hours march in rain to Oblinghem: its filthy billets were used until recently by our Allies.

December 1st.—To Le Quesnoy. The 33rd Division is taking over the Cambrin–Cuinchy–Givenchy sectors. We are being inundated with commissariat queries, but none on recent operations: the views of Staff and Regimental officers on the Loos operations can't *December 5th*—be learned through any official channel.—The fourth very wet day. Helped Ma'mselle Seline to write in English to the 7th Division subaltern to whom she has given her heart. Poor heart!

December 6th.—Going into the Givenchy trenches, at their worst, we had our first meeting with our Royal Fusiliers. The dainty way they tiptoed about the road to avoid puddles when in column of route, but flattened themselves on it in unison when a shell came over, tickled us to much quaint comment. This obsolete safety-first drill, brought in after the South African War of 1899–1902, is thoroughly bad for discipline in all but highly trained troops, and is of doubtful use in lessening losses.—'Gum-boots, thigh,' were issued under Divisional arrangements at Windy Corner. When we were drawing them one of the R.Fs. went to the C.O., who was talking to the Second-in-Command of The Cameronians, and complained that someone had taken his greatcoat. His jaw fell and his knees sagged when Darling said, "Then why don't you take someone else's?"—After dark The Cameronian R.S.M. was accosted by two figures, and asked for a direction in tones so genteel that he went out of his way to escort them, thinking they were officers. His discovery that they were company cooks was never mentioned in his hearing by anyone with chaste ears. So averse were the R.Fs. from any fatigue that our men were tipped to carry their rations, even their rum, for them—until one or two hungry and rumless experiences taught them the worth of self-help and watchfulness.—New-comers to the front are either rash or over-cautious. A R.F. platoon sergeant next to us saw smoke. Stooping low, he stepped lightly along the trench to where some of our men sat by a brazier, and, with lowered voice, ordered the fire to be put out. "It's all right, Sergeant," one said ; "they haven't got the range yet." Surprisingly cautious they always were.

With men of the uncommon culture of not a few of our R.Fs. the look-out for spies, which affects all new troops, took unusual forms. Dolling came to us a month ago. A native of Ireland who has knocked about Canada, his speech savours of both countries. Already he finds nap and poker in the dug-out insufficient change from the tedium of ordinary trench warfare. *December 9th*—In the afternoon he came to H.Q. to discuss with the C.O. one of the bombing stunts with which he afflicts the Germans. Returning to his Company in the dusk, and new to the sector, he asked the way of some men he met. He did not recognize them as our R.Fs. until they detained him with questions. Impatiently muttering an obscenity he turned away, soon stumbled into a brimming shell-hole, let out the same obscene word, and disappeared up the road. The C.O. was in the Orderly Room when a R.F. lance-corporal and a stout, unsoldierly private came and asked to see the Adjutant : Mann was Acting. The lance-corporal described a tall dark man, wearing spectacles and the uniform of a R.W.F. officer, who had excited their suspicion by his questions and his speech. The C.O. has the gift of expressionless silence, and he always enjoys such a situation as this, so he left the corporal to go on with his story. A bit embarrassed, the corporal asked if a R.W.F. officer would swear. The C.O. thought that might happen under great provocation. The stout private then spoke up. He said that he was a Lecturer on Phonetics at Oxford, who had studied his subject for three years at Heidelberg. In his opinion the terminal "er" of a word the suspect addressed to them and to the shell-hole was pronounced as in the Silesian dialect of

German; therefrom he deduced that the man was a spy. He was thanked and dismissed before the Orderly Room allowed itself to explode. A dirty day.

December 10th.—When we were marching to the Tobacco Factory C. S. Owen, who was lately given command of a Royal West Kent battalion, rode up and joined the C.O. Because his "language" has become legendary in and beyond the Regiment an authentic specimen is worth preserving. The C.O. saw another battalion down a side-street and asked, "Who are these?" in an uncommunicably supercilious tone—for he suspected what it was. C. S. scrutinized it, and him, and said, "That's my bloody push"— A pause,—"What do you think of the lousy (obscenities)?" he asked with a nervous little habit laugh. No less characteristic was the C.O.'s half grim, half quizzical smile, and silence. Another: he copied some lines he found at one of his battalion sentry-posts, and sent them to his superiors as a model of a concise Order that men could understand and remember.

> If a whiff of gas you smell,
> Bang your gong like bloody hell,
> On with your googly, up with your gun—
> Ready to meet the bloody Hun.

The don is quite touchy, sticks to it that Dolling's "'er' is undoubtedly Silesian." So little was learning valued by the alumni of Manchester Grammar School that he was transferred to a Labour Battalion soon after this, and was seen at Lillers sweeping the highway.

December 11th.—With others I spent a second afternoon at the pastrycook's.

December 12th.—Le Cornet Bourdois, between Lillers and St. Venant, is our place of Corps Rest. Our seven doubtful-to-negligible foot cases all marched. Billets were good if small and scattered, but an estaminet was far to seek. The land was so water-logged, where not actually under water, that a bombing practice-ground was the largest dry area to be found. There could be next to no active training, no outdoor games, and no organized sing-song. Officers who could get into Lillers found a remarkably good oyster-bar in a wine-shop; and an attractive young woman barber was the cause of some needless hair-cutting.

December 17*th*.—The C.O.'s sickness and removal to hospital was a misfortune. The Commander-in-Chief's quite-looked-for super-session stirred no outward sign of regret. Cavalryman to cavalryman succeeds: Haig to French.

At 10.30 at night the arrival of a Brigade Runner added a momentary interest at one vingt-et-un [1] table. His message required an "immediate" answer to the query, "Did you get Maconochie ration on the 14th?"—typical of much with which units in the line were pestered, often at midnight. The gunners say that the loss of the Cuinchy railway triangle, in early days, was owing to an insistent priority query from Ordnance, about curry-combs, blocking their line and preventing an observer getting through his message to have a German concentration smashed before it could deploy.

Reporting on gum-boots: they are no good for front-line troops; they are good for troops returning each night to billets where they can be taken off and dried inside. They were not issued in subsequent winters except for a few pairs as trench stores.

December 19*th*.—Heavy gun-fire beyond Béthune and an order to be "on the shortest notice" gave a brief prospect of relief from this boredom in which even a Brigade route-march is welcomed. A Staff ride for Commanding Officers of the 19th Brigade is the only exercise of the kind I know of while we remained in it.

December 20*th*.—Our 17th Battalion passed through.

'You propose to send out reading matter. Don't. The *London Mail*, and such like stuff, has readers, and there are men who get their local paper. That suffices them. Remember how few people read, really read. Out here men sit over braziers and gossip, play strange card games, write a letter, lie down and snooze, but read they don't. An estaminet is a great boon to them, as is the rare entry to a farm kitchen, for there is a chair to sit on instead of the ground, or floor, or straw of a barn, and there is a table for dishes, mugs, and elbows. The only sort of writing you would care to send will be burned or cast aside, as were parcels of *The Times* Broadsheets. (Passages from our classics selected by a popular Oxford Professor of Literature.) Every refuse-pit, every in-cinerator, is full of the unread secular and other matter which the

---

[1] Vingt-et-un, became "pontoon" in Atkins' speech, was a popular game in the ranks.

Chaplains hand round. Reading is difficult enough for an officer, it must be far more difficult among the men. I remember how it was in South Africa: I remember too that one man read Shakespeare through and through again. In this life there is neither privacy nor quiet.'

Preparations for Christmas had been going on. Every turkey within twenty miles had been bought before we arrived, but there was no lack of geese and other fare. To buy some extras for my *December 22nd*—own little lot I rode into St. Venant. The day was dull, but the town, even at its best, must look down-at-heel. Red brick ramparts that the Regiment looked on during the siege of 1710 have the charm of weathered age and not unkind neglect. The little town is shrunken within them. There isn't an architectural feature to detain one, but the pathos of the seventeenth and eighteenth centuries in comely decay made me loiter.

December 24th.—H.Q. and B Company, who mess together, had a Christmas Eve dinner, a breezy affair. I went to bed at 2 in the *December 25th*—morning nearly 300 francs to the good.

Saturday, Christmas: anyhow it didn't rain. There was Church Parade at 11 o'clock: then James Ormrod, who is Acting O.C.—officiously prompted by two of the Company Commanders—set out on the customary round of billets with Robertson, Adjutant since C. S. Owen's promotion. At eleven Messes they were offered, and had to drain, 5 glasses of port, neat whisky 3, rum, claret and champagne 1 of each. A "glass" is a conventional term for a quantity served in a tumbler, mug, or mess-tin. Each would drink about three pints of the mixture. At the last dyke they had to cross the Transport Sergeant fell in, embracing the plank he meant to place for their crossing. They got over without mishap. It was the last effort that nobility required of them. Lunch had been served before they got back. After leering for a few minutes at a plate of tepid mince they went to bed. Robertson, a rising hope of the Admiralty Bar, looked very quaint. I got off lightly with only one obligatory lot to visit. My Corporal dashed out half a tumblerful of what I assumed was white wine; my nose warned me in time that it was whisky—barbed-wire blend. But it went over without cough or splutter. There's something in race! My total for three or four years can't be more than I drank then.

A. Company nearly lost their dinner. Some of their own choice spirits made off with the dixies when the cooks' backs were turned; but for carelessness in neglecting cover at the corner of a field they would have got away with it. C Company's cooks had their eyes about them. When the Orderly Officer came round Pugh—"Pug"—an Old Soldier, called the squad to "attention," and said in an audible aside, "I think I see an Officer coming who will give us 10 francs to drink his health." The plum-pudding sent by the Comforts Committee divided up at three-quarters of a pound a man. There were sing-songs in the billets, and some minor casualties, such as black eyes among the Drums.

The officers' dinner was an affair of Companies, because the largest billet held only two Messes. Our menu was in the French of near Bowe: "Hors d'œuvre; consomme a la Royal; Rognons sauts; Dinde Rotie; Pudding Noel; Sardines en Papier; Orange, Noix, etc.; Café." To Ormrod and Robertson dinner was as naught, and no wonder. Ormrod went off to bed again half-way through, leaving Fletcher's father [1]—one of our two guests—to me. He was pathetically interested in his dead son's Battalion, and in the youths effervescing at the table. We found common ground in Sussex until the Staff car came for him. For the younger members the festivities were just beginning when *le patron* looked in, said it was past midnight, and asked us to remember the Sabbath Day, to keep it holy. So the party broke up. This is a pious district. There is a Calvary, if not a Shrine, at most of the cross-roads. Every evening one hears in each dimly lighted Shrine the low gabble of peasant voices reciting the prayers.

December 27th.—This wearisome rest has come to an end. We marched on partly flooded roads to the Tobacco Factory in the rue Michelet, Béthune; next day we went out to Lower Beuvry.

December 29th.—A and C Companies went into Cambrin Right; B and D remained at Beuvry to find working-parties.

December 31st.—At 11 p.m.—midnight in Germany—for five minutes, and again at midnight for two minutes, the German artillery fired a New Year Greeting: we had one man wounded. On our left the second shoot was preceded by a shout from a German, "Keep down, you bastards, we're going to strafe you."

---

[1] Historian, joint author with Kipling of *A Child's History of England*.

We retaliated on their front line with rifles and Lewis guns, and the artillery fired twenty-four rounds of high explosive. The Acting *January 1st*—Adjutant of the half battalion at Beuvry was wakened at 1 a.m. to cope with this urgent message from Brigade : "Does your Battalion recommend nails or heelplates for the men's boots ?"

January 2nd.—The Germans blew two small mines a few days ago, to the usual accompaniment of a short, intense bombardment. A strafe started to-day when H.Q. was at lunch. As the shells hurtled overhead Robertson remarked, "I like to hear that, the people behind are getting it." By mischance 3 dead and 2 wounded of "the people behind" belonged to one of D Company's working-parties, sand-bagging the gable of Brigade H.Q. Brigade asked for what our fellows got, for the house can be seen from Auchy. But the strafe was incidental to a much bigger operation. Just north of the La Bassée road, while a relief was taking place, the Germans had blown what was then their largest mine. One man was blown on to the top of a near-by brickstack. The total casualties were put at three-score or more. A few civilian casualties included the Mayor of Cambrin, who was visiting his Commune ; he lost a leg. He and his wife had opened a wine parlour in Beuvry, which was frequented by many of us because of its homely, sociable atmosphere. Madame was a motherly soul who delighted to bake a cake for someone's birthday, or do any kindly service for a customer.

January 3rd.—It is curious how death, the death of an acquaintance or of their nearest, is dramatized by very many people. In the morning I was making up a sick-return in a trench shelter when the exceptional monotony of a voice caught and held my attention. One of two Engineers on a job within earshot was describing an incident of yesterday to his mate. ". . . 'e was killed, 'e was. Bes' pal I ever 'ad. They was shellin' like 'ell. My pal was Brigade Despatch-rider, 'e was, an' 'e comes up the —— road on 'is —— motor-bike, an' comes into th' estaminet w'ere I was. You know th' estaminet, just this side Brigade 'eadquarters, w'ere th' Orderlies lives. The —— Fusiliers was comin' out, them new ones. A —— shell 'it one of them, 'it 'im on the —— leg an' smashed it ; 'e was lying on the —— road, and they was shellin' it like 'ell. My pal 'e goes out to 'elp the poor ——. Just as 'e gets to 'im over comes another —— shell, an' blew 'is —— 'ead clean off. 'E was my bes' pal, bes' pal a man ever 'ad." That lament was spoken on one tuneless note. I felt sure that the speaker had told the story of his bereavement already, and that he will tell it many times yet, always with the same senseless obscene garnishing.

January 4th.—For the future, movement near the front in daylight is forbidden. Hitherto reliefs on this front had taken place by day although the two approaches were under observation, and Bands must have been heard often by the Germans from the point to which they accompanied battalions. Even during Loos the main road through Cambrin was scarcely shelled, there was not a hole in 50 yards. Of late the German artillery had been more active on roads and tracks. Our artillery took to that some time ago; and when it wanted to be annoying it fired on the German billets with high explosive instead of, as formerly, with shrapnel on the support line. B and D Companies relieved A and C.

January 7th.—Two platoons of A and C came up to Sims's and Arthur's Keeps. What's feared?

January 8th.—Captain Denison of the K.R.R.C. arrived to command.

January 9th.—The first night relief: it was breakfast-time when the last of us got to our billets at Beuvry: the old system would have let us into them yesterday afternoon. No Order caused so much grousing as that ordaining night-reliefs; but henceforth they were taken as a matter of course, so easily do we fall in with what we must.

Another innovation about this time was soup for issue during the night, sent up in thermos containers. It suited the New Armies, but the Old Soldiers and the Drafts who had adopted their ways and prejudices denounced it blasphemously. The Old Soldier liked to cook and eat what he saved of his ration in his own way and time; he resented the diversion of any of it to this communal cooking, and he feared that broth might be substituted for rum; besides, to fetch it was another fatigue. (Soup was not issued during the next two winters.) Other innovations were felt more in the Orderly Room and Quartermaster's department, and by the old N.C.Os. To New Army units Divisional Orders detailing routine and administrative procedure were necessary at the beginning, but when they were addressed to Regular battalions they generally conflicted with accumulated experience and established custom, so they were ridiculed as spoon-feeding, resented and evaded.—A mechanistic theory of the conduct of war was being developed which bade fair to make cyphers of the individual and the unit. The foundation of a bureaucratic means of handling operations was well and truly laid during this winter lull. And the tide was in flood that carried the great part of the personnel borne on the War Office vote into what were colloquially called "Staff jobs"; the suction of it was already draining the combatant units. Battalions were also being combed, by specially appointed officers, for munition workers. A gibe among us was that the War would end when a Staff job had been found for everyone and there was no one left to man the fire-step.

January 15th.—To Annequin North: working-parties in the Brickstacks found life so strenuous that respite was hoped for in the front line, even there.

January 20th.—There was quiet as we were taking over Cuinchy Left, but the changes in the line since September, most of them recent, boded ill. The ordinary activities of trench warfare increased on both sides during January, and during the last ten days of the month bombardment and counter-bombardment reached an intensity that had not been known since Loos at its intensest. The front line in the Brickstacks was enfiladed by a battery of howitzers on the left; stretches of it had to be vacated again and again. For the centre company there was no rest; the shelling and scarcity of cover kept them wakeful and moving by day, the constant work repairing dilapidations occupied their nights; there was bright moonlight to help the work. Less destructive on the whole than the howitzers, but more upsetting, was a large minenwerfer, well covered from our artillery by a brickstack, which threw a bomb $2\frac{1}{2}$ to 3 feet long: "flying pig" was one name it got. Sentries indicated by whistle-blasts the line of leisurely, wobbling flight of this demoralizing charge of high explosive; the platoon concerned barged to the right or left accordingly, sometimes in dire peril, sometimes with linked arms in the mood of a jovial Bank Holiday party. The sector cherished the story of a young Gunner who was spotting from the front line while his battery tried to knock out the hitherto well-shielded minnie. After his gun had put three 9·2s into our own lines in Back Street, just behind him, he telephoned that the minnie was

"silenced." The chance bursting of a derelict gas cylinder by a
German shell caused us two casualties; one of them died. The
chance bursting of a smoke-bomb, another relic of Loos, when
the wind blew from us, caused a scare among the Germans, who
thought we were letting off gas on them. During one of our
bombardments a German shouted across in exasperation, "You
(obscene) John Bulls!"

January 25th.—Dolling, always watchful of the doings of enemy
working-parties, had reported some new stakes. Expecting that
wirers would be at work on them he and five bravoes stole across
after dark. A party was seen and bombed—very successfully,
judging by the cries of woe. Our guns co-operated, all but
knocking our fellows' heads off. Stanway was giving occasional
but deadly aid to the snipers. Once he snapped an officer where
the German parapet was low. Another day he got a pheasant for
the pot. He had a disconcerting habit at one time of keeping his
revolver on the table when playing cards, to shoot rats as they ran
along the cornice beam of the dug-out.

January 26th.—Robertson was killed when our line was being
strafed with everything. Of six inside C Company's tin-roofed
sand-bag shack he only was hit. The minnie burst just outside
without touching any of the half-dozen men standing near. Before
starting to go round the Companies he had telegraphed to C. S.
Owen wishing him "many happy returns of the Kaiser's birthday."
C. S.'s reply, "Can do without any ruddy return.—Owen," was
intercepted. Binge Owen had been asked by Brigade for a
machine-gun return; he was suspected of having sent this frivolous
and impertinent message, and was called on for an explanation.
A cabal has been formed already to bar Mann from the Adjutancy.

January 27th.—The Kaiser's birthday. White flags, at regular
intervals, were flown on the parapet opposite: they were taken in
after dark. There is more air activity than usual, for the weather
has not been so fine for two months—there have been several
hours of sunshine on recent days. Extra movement is reported
on the German-run railways. German guns are more active even
than yesterday, when we had 14 casualties. Corps is interesting
itself in these portents. The Archie guns on both sides were
blazing away at aeroplanes, and their shell-splinters rained on us
this morning. One whir-r-r ended in a thud and a cry, "Oh,"

from a seated man. His wrist was broken. He had barely exclaimed when half a dozen men scrimmaged for the nose-cap that hit him, and two grovelled between his feet to get it. There were those who collected nose-caps and driving-bands as connoisseurs collect. Most men in their early days were interested in souvenirs; some were easily satisfied, not a few lost their lives souvenir-hunting.

Relieved at night: B, C, and D Companies to Annequin North; A. remained in Harley Street to support the 20th R.F. This has been an uncommonly active tour, our casualties greatly exceed the weekly average. Dewhurst, returning off leave, met his Company stretcher-bearers carrying down one of the dead; following them was a man with something in a sand-bag. As money, letters, and other personal possessions were taken off the dead and sent home, Dewhurst asked, "Are these his effects?" "No, sir, it's his pal"; for of a second victim of the same shell only parts of two limbs could be found.

January 29th.—By ignoring a shrew of a landlady H.Q. had a peaceful morning after 36 hours of alarms, of orders to return to the trenches, to stand fast, to be on the shortest notice. After dark the Battalion marched to Fouquereuil, which Atkins pronounces according to a transliteration of his own. A dull little village. The aged *patronne* of one billet expected her guests, who usually played cards till all hours, to be in bed by 10 o'clock.

January 30th.—Going on contract leave: our boat was held up in Boulogne till the Channel was cleared of mines; our Destroyer escort was said to have run on one. Returning twelve days later: a tramp blew up off Folkestone shortly before the Leave-boat was due to start.

January 31st.—Colonel O. de L. Williams returned. During the two months of his absence the Battalion suffered from an uncertain command, which was the more unfortunate that the transition from Old Army to New Army administration was taking place. After Major Owen's departure in November Colonel Williams and the Quartermaster were, with one very junior exception, the only pre-War Regular officers remaining. The other officers were Temporary, with a sprinkling of recent Special Reserve, and young Regulars who were not commissioned until after mobilization. (The Battalion officers were, in the main, of that order and in that

proportion till the end of the War.)   Although the N.C.Os. were
all experienced soldiers a palpable slackness had come to pervade
the Battalion.   The C.O. set about rooting this out.   To a detached
onlooker at close quarters the supreme importance of the character
of a commanding officer to the efficiency of a battalion was
strikingly shown.   Time was to show the grave misfortune of a
slackness in any command.   The C.O.'s first act was to appoint
J. C. Mann to the vacant Adjutancy.   He himself was then detailed
to the Temporary Command of the 100th Brigade.

As Acting Brigadier the C.O. took over a state of affairs just
south of the La Bassée road that caused displeasure in the Upper
Regions of command.   The Germans had recently blown and
occupied the third of three small overlapping craters; from the
latest, and largest, middle one they dominated part of our line.
The troops on the spot had failed in a couple of attempts to turn
them out, and they were shy of trying again.   When Division told
the C.O. what was wanted of him he asked for leave to use his
own Battalion, and got it.   So we were called out of rest and sent to
February 5th—Annequin South in the forenoon.   In the afternoon
the operation, which Stanway was detailed to command, was
rehearsed on marked ground.   Tin-hats were issued for it.   After
dark the Sapping Platoon, now under Moldsworth Williams,
improved an old sap and listening-post that approached the large,
and near, crater.   At 9.45, under cover of a slight artillery bombardment, sections of bombers rushed the near lip and bombed
the occupants out.   At the same time Dolling's and Dewhurst's
platoons of C Company went into Nomansland and protected
the flanks.   The old sap was extended into a new trench which
was dug in a segment of the side of the crater below the rim by
a party of A Company under Binge Owen and Radford.   At
February 6th—4 a.m. B Company parties under Barrett and Morris
relieved Owen's party.   These again were relieved at 8 o'clock
by D Company parties under Smith and Williams.   Williams was
killed and Smith wounded almost at once, so Radford was recalled.
By dawn the position had been consolidated.   Casualties were light
at first, but consolidation had to be done under artillery and
machine-gun fire, bombs, rifle-grenades and trench-mortars: in
the end they numbered about 40, including 5 officers.   The position
was shelled all afternoon, but there were no further casualties.

Radford commanded the garrison of bombers until the relieving battalion came in at night. We found loopholes from which the Germans had fired into our front at a range of 35 yards. The Corps Commander was very complimentary about the whole affair. "R.W.F." was the name given to the triple crater.

At night, on relief from this minor operation, the Battalion took over the Cambrin Right front for six days. The Germans opposite *February 7th*—specialize in rifle-grenades, so they are being countered with their own weapon. McKay, just off leave, and reckless, and sent on patrol by his Company Commander, was badly wounded on the German wire; he was brought back with difficulty by Sergeant Bale, and Radford who went out to help. McKay was a fire-eating Scot promoted from the East Yorks. He would ring a good target impetuously, and remark, "That'll put the wind up him," but he had not the patience to take, like Stanway, his chance of a timely shot that got home. Morris was *February 9th*—grazed doing a piece of good work on patrol of Mad Point.

February 12th.—Out to Annequin. The supposedly easier days there were remarkable for the numbers reporting sick. They had variations of "pain in me back"; the striking departure from type was unique for its candour, "Fed up with the fatigues, sir." Wet weather made matters worse.

February 18th.—We returned to Cambrin Left in a downpour. The Germans had narrowed Nomansland by connecting-up their saps. A party from the Fleet went in with us as guests. The weather was dirty all the time of their stay. The sailors entered boisterously into the life and activity of the trenches, bar the fatigues, but they went away saying they would much rather have the North Sea in spite of its submerged mines and submarines.

February 19th.—Bright moonlight: five bombs were dropped in the back area; there is much dispute if signal lights were thrown out by the bombers or thrown up for them.

February 20th.—One of our Air-observers was brought down behind the support line: fired on and shelled, he escaped unhurt.

February 21st.—The mystery of a fireworks display has been solved. Fritz soused with oil a body on his wire and set fire to it, exploding the cartridges in the pouches. We moved into Montmorency Barracks, the favourite billet in the area.

This was the beginning of six weeks of which the interest was elsewhere than in the trenches. The Battalion was in the Brickstacks for five days and for three days—both were quiet tours for the Brickstacks—and in Cambrin Left for four days, all of them quiet. During eight days in support, divided between Le Quesnoy and Annequin North, we were not overworked. Two turns of eight days each in the Barracks, and two of four days each at Beuvry, were very agreeably spent. The weather was the chief snag these weeks. The winter of 1915–16 was open. It was the least severe of the five winters the Battalion spent in France. The one continuously trying spell was the fortnight at the end of February and beginning of March; it was wintry with snowshowers. Throughout March quick changes through frost, thaw, rain, snow, and sunshine with keen wind, continued. Troops, when in the line, had to work day and night trying to keep pace with the ravages of the weather, for the trenches fell in in anything from ounces to tons. The problem of keeping warm was partly solved by work, of which a maximum was required even at a sacrifice of rest and sleep. It was taxing, but the hardest-working units are the healthiest in bad-weather conditions. It is odd that a shell which bursts does only local damage to a trench, whereas a dud may cause extensive collapse: once a big one filled in 20 yards. Weather and fatigue apart, life in the line was greatly affected by what lay around. There is an eerie fascination, whatever the night or season, when in the cold, quivering glare of a falling Verey light the shadow of a skeleton roof shudders and moves. On a sunless March day the grey of last year's tangled grass, the darker grey of new barbed wire, the bleached sand-bags of old parapets, and the desolation of human homes—roofless, windowless, doorless—among which not a being stirs, make a scene that chills the heart. A curl of wood-smoke from a pit where some German or Briton cooked, or the sinister report of a sniper's rifle, might be the only sign of living man. An owl or two flew about the ruined houses; no other birds were seen; last summer's kestrels had gone from the Cambrin elms, not to return. On neither side of Nomansland was there any interest in the War. The gunners shared the lack of interest. Respites from this winter discontent were too short to reawaken action. But the respites were real. "Like a May morning," is a note on March 14th. And Winter was passing. In a garden at "Kingsclere," the Brickstacks H.Q., about that date anemones, primulas, and violets raised their heads above a veil of snow ; and two weeks later one avoided treading on little frogs in Cambrin trenches.

At the beginning of this period the command of Small-Arms was divided. The Machine-Gun Corps came into being as Brigade, later as Divisional units. This insane act was not reversed until the War was over, although from August 1918 onwards a Machine-Gun Section was attached to each infantry battalion and acted under the orders of its O.C. About this time, too, "drainpipes" were withdrawn, the Stokes mortar was issued and brigaded— another sub-division of command in front.

March 1st, St. David's Day.—We awoke to St. David's Day 1916 in Montmorency Barracks, Béthune. The Bugles sounded Long Réveillé, the Drums played "Old Mother Riley" and, after Salute, marched round the Barrack Square, and through the adjoining streets where the officers were billeted, to the air of "The Staffordshire Knot." Yates had a leek for everyone's cap, and the Drums had gilded each officer's leek—a compliment and an investment. As a move had to be made in the early afternoon the customary celebrations could not be held, but estaminets were the meeting-places of many informal gatherings, and the officers all found themselves at The Globe. The inhabitants of the town saw that there was something unusual in the day, so rows of civilians and others lined the streets when we marched out to Le Quesnoy, headed by the Drums as far as Beuvry. At night B Company, which had the best Mess—its O.C. was Billeting Officer —entertained an invited company. No coherent account of the night was obtainable, but there was evidence that one celebrant reached his billet, a quarter-mile distant, on all fours. So the Saint had not much to grumble about although there was no Goat to take part in the ritual.

Our route that day, and at other times, was through a part of Beuvry in which there was an estaminet that caught the eye for no reason except, perhaps, its air of incongruity. It was a shabby place in a slum. The slattern who conducted it, a familiar sight at the door, was suckling one unwashed child, and scolding another who cried because she had fallen in the dirty road. Beside her was an unshaved A.S.C. man in an unbuttoned coat, wearing his cap on the back of an unkempt head ; over them hung the signboard, inscribed in paint that simulated gilding, "La Gaieté" : possibly not the misnomer it seems. A St. David's Day rumour that we were booked to capture the Hohenzollern never came to anything. My last note under this date is, "a louse." Lucky in my circumstances, I rarely had to contend with that pest in the plural.

March 5th.—A splinter of a 5·9 shell fired at our 6-inch battery killed a lark on the wing. German planes came over in the morning to see what yesterday's tell-tale snow and frost would reveal, and saw the guns that have been in one position for fifteen months. Now they are moving, and our billets will be the quieter.

March 6th.—A bitter night, a bright cold morning. After dark we went into the Brickstacks. The weather changed. Soon we were living in mud and icy water, and the trenches were falling in.

March 9th.—Steel helmets issued. Many did not know them by any other name than "tin-hat." "Battle-bowler" strove for a few days for recognition. When we wore cloth caps I never knew a man seek to shield his head from flying metal although he were bare-headed, but when we wore tin-hats and metal was flying about I never knew of a bare-headed man who did not bolt for cover; even in a deep dug-out there were few who did not reach for their helmet if shells burst outside.

March 11th.—Much milder, some rain : relieved. There is a rumour that the Division is to have three weeks rest, and, being "fattened," to be for it anywhere.

March 12th.—Warm and sunny.

March 15th.—On the second of three days in the Brickstacks a Battalion Canteen faltered into being. The C.O. had spoken once or twice of the benefit of a canteen. As time generally hung heavy on my hands I offered to start and run one. It took a week to settle down to steady business. The first outlay was 250 francs instead of the 40 francs which a Chaplain told the C.O. would be enough, but the amount was increased to 1250 francs within the week. (The rate of exchange was about 28 francs to the £ sterling throughout the War.)

March 16th.—A. Company has been rained on this tour by minnies and rifle-grenades : relieved.

March 18th.—We stood-to in Montmorency Barracks when a more than usually violent eruption, started by the Germans, took

place at Hohenzollern. The easterly wind filled the town with
the acrid fumes of high explosive bursting six miles off. Ever
since Loos battalions on both sides had been bled white in the few
yards of the Chord and the Hairpin. C. S.'s battalion lost 300
men in two weeks, most of them in five days, during a tour of the
Hohenzollern and its support.

March 21st.—Inspected by the new Corps Commander, Lieut.-
General Haking. The C.O. gave the order, "Royal Welch,
slope arms"; and reported, "Royal Welch present, sir." "But
are you not going to give me a General Salute?" asked the Corps
Commander. "I had not thought of doing so, but I will if
you like," the C.O. answered. In this informal atmosphere the
Inspection proceeded. The General found that many of the men
came out in August 1914. He was at home with these—he had
just come from inspecting the 20th R.F. He chatted and chaffed,
pinched their arms and ears, asked how many children they had,
and if they could be doing with leave to get another. As he passed
from one 1914 man to another he dug his elbow into the C.O.'s
ribs and exclaimed, "You're a lucky fellow." When it was over
he said to the G.O.C., "That's been a treat. That's the sort we've
known for thirty years." Orderly Room estimated that the
Battalion still had 250 originals, mostly in the Transport, Drums,
and Signals, and among the N.C.Os. Of the other originals, some
500 had been killed or wounded; some were detached; the
balance had gone home sick and become scattered. With comparatively few exceptions the men are Regulars, Reservists, and
Special Reserves.

Béthune during Spring and early Summer of 1916 was still the
most cheerful town near enough the British front to be accessible
to numbers of front-line troops. It was rail-head for two or three
divisions. It was not thronged as during Loos, but it had the
attractions of those days. The Expeditionary Force Canteen had
its then largest Store in the town, and several other organizations
had opened Recreation-rooms. The Theatre, quite a large
building, had been taken over by the B.E.F. Many boxing
tournaments and matches took place in it. Once, at least, a
Frenchman on leave was the best draw on the bill. The Battalion
had sufficient boxers of all ordinary weights to uphold its Indian
reputation. The 33rd Divisional Troupe of squabbling actors,

"The Shrapnels," and other divisional troupes gave performances.
A threat to return the whole troupe to duty was needed to compose
one jealous quarrel. The Battalion's interest in The Shrapnels
was stimulated by a few appearances Dewhurst made. He thought
the dialogue needed brightening. Certainly the audiences were not
March 22nd—large or pleasantly demonstrative until his second day
on the stage. His gags, hoary chestnuts though they were, filled
the house. Then the Chaplains intervened, and he was absent
from two performances of "What a Night!" After a reappearance,
March 26th—for which he rode in from Beuvry, the Theatre was
closed. It did not reopen till he was back in the Cambrin trenches.
Receipts fell to their former level after that. A violinist was our
one constant contribution to The Shrapnels. They included
a Concert Party. One of its entertainments is described on
the programme as "refined." Since it was "presented" in a
Church Army Hut it is sure to have been well chlorined for the
occasion.

During the long occupation of Béthune many irregularities had
grown up. Clothing and other stores in large quantities were
being got by civilians. One cache was found in a garden under
rows of hastily planted vegetables. Army stores were sought by all
sorts of civilians. Two of our rascals once raised a few francs by
selling two or three tins of foot-grease to which they had fixed
jam labels. They were frowned on by their fellows; that sort
of thing was not done—it spoiled the market. On a like scale
beauty, or complaisance, took stores as tribute. North of the town
a woman was asked how she came by the Army boots she was
wearing. "A Jock gave me them." "Who is the Jock?" "Ah!
la, la! le pauvre! Jock mort. Poor (English obscene) Jock."

It was thought, too, that the town had become a centre of the
German Intelligence Service. There were stories of dogs and
pigeons carrying messages across Nomansland, and there was
colour for the pigeon post. For ten days about this time the town
was held by a police cordon; no one was admitted without a pass
while a comb-out of evil-doers of all sorts took place.

Beuvry came next to Béthune in the men's favour as a billet.
Besides being near Béthune it was large enough to have a choice
of estaminets, from the quiet to "cabaret." At one of the latter
the Battalion Conjurer used to bill himself in the window. He

could do a few tricks, and he sang unprintable songs with indescribable pantomime. His worth as a draw was said to be rated
by the owner at free drinks and 10 francs. The one hall in the
place had to be shared with other units, but the C.O. arranged as
many sing-songs as was possible. Unable to distinguish one note
from another, he insisted on Welsh Glees being one of the items.
The men without exception treated that item as the interval,
though the unaccompanied singing was really good. At Beuvry
there was more opportunity for football than elsewhere. Inter-
platoon and inter-company games were always encouraged; here
inter-battalion matches were arranged. Our Royal Fusiliers kept
its team in training, and kept it intact by exempting the players
from duty in the trenches, so it was unbeatable.

An upper room in Beuvry was the only billet in the whole area
in which there could be a Battalion Mess—it seated all but one
company. The cost of foodstuffs had risen since the subscription
for extras was limited to 1·50 francs, so 2·25 francs a head a day
was allowed. I, who had been in charge of H.Q. messing since
Robertson's death, had no friends at these times, because all five
Messes did themselves better than was possible on the allowance.
The most vocal grousers were, as ever in such conditions, some
of those on account of whose slender purses and narrow home
circumstances the limit was imposed.

March 28th.—Officers attended a demonstration of a captured
flame-thrower. Its premature operation scorched some of the
Staff, to the unconcealed delight of the infantry. After that the
demonstration was a dull affair. Meanwhile the once khaki
collar, now nearly bleached by many washings, of one of the
Battalion subalterns had caught the eye of the G.O.C. He sent
his A.D.C. to ask the C.O. where his subaltern bought his collars,
and was given the reply, "At the same shop as your A.D.C. buys
his breeches."

March 29th.—Back in Cambrin Left since last night. The sector
is now known as Z1 or Auchy Left: here the original names of
sectors is kept. Larks sing in bright sunshine, and buds are opening.
In the parapet of Old Boots Trench a German has been buried, it
must have been in the autumn of 1914. The weather has exposed
a pulpy arm; there was a wrist-watch on it. Some whimsical
passer wound the watch, it went, it was a repeater; passers-by

would give the winding a turn, but soon a souvenir-hunter took the watch.

April 2nd.—Brigade is moving back another mile, the Brigadier's barber having been wounded while he was cutting the Brigadier's hair at Annequin Fosse. Coster, a very recent acquisition from the Honourable Artillery Company, went out with 8 others and bombed a sap east of Midnight Crater, to some effect.

April 4th.—Beuvry: "Happy" Holden, who has just joined, took a toss at the Young Officers Riding School and was carried to hospital, his sunny nature shining through his bruises.

April 5th.—A Battalion concert, with two 5th Scottish Rifles "obliging" us, was a great success. The following article from *Punch* of August 16th is founded on this concert: it is reproduced by permission of the Proprietors of *Punch*.

A RECITATION IN REST BILLETS

In a way the C.O. was to blame. His constant desire to amuse the men while in rest billets greatly taxed the resources of the officer whose duty it was to arrange the concerts. Briggs, being the Intelligence Officer, and erroneously credited with a certain allowance of this quality, had been entrusted with the re-shuffling of the items we all knew so well. As in the trenches, the men bore the attack bravely. They would let their pent-up feelings burst forth in joining in the choruses, and then applaud their own efforts vigorously; further, should the Chaplain not be present, a Scottish Sergeant would amuse them considerably, while the officers looked up at the ceiling. It happened that Briggs's difficulty over the lack of fresh talent reached the ears of our latest arrival, one Captain Knibb, who was small and had trouble with his eyeglass. Approaching our little group before luncheon on the day of the Concert, he casually observed to Briggs that if he were short of turns he wouldn't mind reciting something. For a moment Briggs looked dubious; but, after all, a cadaverous subaltern named Byson had recited "Gunga Din" at every concert held, and it was quite good fun to prompt him from the "stalls" when he broke down. "What will you recite?" asked Briggs cautiously. "Oh! I've written a little topical thing for the men," replied Knibb modestly, and we all looked grave. On reflection I hold the opinion that Briggs should have put his foot down then and there, but, failing to realize the possibilities of the situation, he weakly said, "Good," and was led away to hear "the little topical thing." When Briggs returned we knew by his face that the worst could be anticipated.

"It's simply ghastly!" he muttered when the Mess-waiter had tended him into a state of coherence. "The men will never stand it. It begins like an election address, something about—

> Colonel Blankney and the boys he leads,
> Ye who have fought because Belgium bleeds,

and yards of similar piffle." We shuddered, knowing the men's sense of humour. Still, you can't tell a Captain he's going to make an ass of himself, so with dismal forebodings Briggs wrote, "Captain Knibb—recitation—selected," on the programme, and hardly touched his food.

The concert began at six. It was, as usual, packed, being held on a pay-day, which may have accounted for the Battalion conjurer's total incompetence and the officers' lack of enthusiasm when he wanted to borrow a watch; however, since we knew that he could do the tricks when he was all right, his exit was triumphant. When "Gunga Din" had been duly rendered according to custom, and B Company's Sergeant-Major had illustrated with a cornet that "Where my caravan has rested" was a place to be avoided, and the Scottish Sergeant had been dragged off the stage owing to the presence of the Chaplain— when, in fact, everything was proceeding with customary smoothness, the audience received the pleasant shock of Briggs's announcement that a new item would be given: "Captain Knibb—recitation—selected." For a moment the C.O. seemed pleased that one of his Captains should help in the entertainment, but when Captain Knibb strolled dramatically on to the four-by-two stage and bowed unctuously to his Colonel, the latter stiffened visibly. You could have heard the habitual pin drop, the men seemed so determined to give him a respectful and sporting chance. Slowly and heavily he began:

> "Colonel Blankney and the boys he leads,
> Ye who have fought because Belgium bleeds."

This was followed by a slight pause, during which the Captain's servant hastily applauded, the Q.M.S. shouted, "Order, please!" and several subs. turned their profiles on the C.O. The Chaplain seemed to scent competition.

> I speak of the Battling Seventh's name!
> Men of imperishable fame!

At this point "Defaulters" sounded jarringly outside, and several "men of imperishable fame" left the building hurriedly; and amidst the general disorder the "Battling Seventh" choked audibly. Growing more and more impressive, our White Hope and Kipling's Despair unburdened himself still further of the result of a late supper, and louder and louder grew the gurgling, until, as he ended the first stanza with the terrific climax—

> Men of the Battling Seventh, Charge!

a thin voice cried, "As you were!" and even the C.O. swung on his moustache with both hands and rocked helplessly.

What would have happened then, Heaven and the Staff alone know, but in the midst of the unrestrained emotion which now pervaded the audience an orderly flew in and whispered, "Test gas alarm, sir!" to the C.O., who turned purple and in a choked voice repeated the order to the assembly. Never have I seen the men so reluctant to get into their gas helmets, and it was with strangled splutterings of protest that they hurried away to "stand-to."

Indisposition has robbed us of Captain Knibb for a while, but we are all hoping that he is busy in his leisure moments.

The foregoing article is exempted from the assurance of the substantial historical accuracy of this Chronicle, but to analyse it and assess each statement would be ungracious. Captain "Knibb's" stay with us was very short. He joined only on April 1st. His professional qualifications fitted him for a technical position on the Staff for which the Battalion, probably among others, was asked to nominate an officer. For once the C.O. could make a nomination without just getting rid of an encumbrance, but not without falling under suspicion. The G.S.O.1 met him in the afternoon and asked, "What's wrong with that fellow you sent me this morning?" "Nothing, why do you ask?" "I've been asking you for an officer for one thing or another for months, and you've always replied, 'None suitable.' My signature was hardly dry on the chit this morning before this one appeared on my doorstep."

The time since November may be divided into three periods of six weeks each; first, navvying and boredom: second, navvying and bickering with the enemy; third, strenuous navvying and having rather a good time which was scarcely affected by an epidemic of influenza. Thirty cases were ill enough, or ill when they could not be treated in billets, to go to hospital.

April 6th.—In Cambrin Left again, and no port to be had. What are things coming to? Not so long ago a subaltern sent out of the trenches for whisky had to go 15 miles for the nearest supply.

April 8th.—A small mine of ours, blown at 8 a.m., cost us 4 wounded.

CHAPTER VIII

Béthune: Spring and Summer—Cambrin Raid—Cuinchy Raid—A Battalion Canteen—The Duck's Bill goes up— Red Dragon Crater—The Warren Raid

Contributors:—BLAIR; FOX; HIGGINSON; MOODY; RADFORD; RODERICK; STANWAY

Sketches:—8, 9, 10

For some little time past it had looked as if we were at war again. A new notion of a raid had been practised by the Canadians. It is the mode. Every self-respecting battalion will want to raid, the others will be ordered. The immemorial notion of a raid is to enter the enemy's lines by stealth or surprise, to kill or capture, plunder or destroy, and get away with no fighting or little. The new notion is a battle in miniature with all the preliminaries and accompaniments magnified, often manyfold. Since last we were here a new-model raid had been planned by the C.O. and Lieut.-Colonel Rochford Boyd of the Divisional Artillery, a pious fire-eater, and a most acceptable referee at the boxing-matches at Béthune. There was a great regard between him and the Battalion. (He died of wounds at Cambrai in October 1917, to the regret of all of us who had known him.) The idea is to close on a sap and capture or scupper the garrison. Parties of volunteers of A, B, and D Companies take part. While B carries out the object, A and D are to engage the occupants of the trench to right and left. The artillery, firing high explosive instead of the shrapnel of Loos and earlier, is to make a passage through the wire for A. Division wants to test the practicability of a bangalore torpedo, a pipe filled with ammonal, for destroying wire. The Ds.' job is to take it out and make themselves small when it blows a *April 9th*—gap for them. At 1.30 a.m. the three parties went away well, covered by the artillery. The As. found themselves against impassable wire, except at two places of the kind made for egress or to lure patrols to destruction, so they bombed the trench from outside the wire. The Ds. did their part with the torpedo, but, the sappers' detonating gadget having failed to explode it, they too could only bomb the trench from outside. The Bs. lost no time in rushing the sap, but before they could get in the garrison was heard bolting out. And so a well-arranged little operation miscarried.

At 8 a.m. the Germans blew yet another small mine on our part of this much-mined area. Five miners were caught underground; and four or five of our men were more or less buried in the collapse of part of our trench; a broken leg was the worst injury. It has been an exciting affair for the miners. They could hear the German miners only 10 estimated feet off, so there was a race against time to get a charge tamped and fired. The camouflet that was blown yesterday morning obviously failed to wreck the German work: Division was peeved because it had not been consulted.

April 10*th*.—A week of glorious days and very cold nights. When we went out to Annezin Coster and a few of the D Company raiders stayed behind to salve the dud torpedo. Made in two pieces, it broke and the distal part was so far in under the wire that it could not be got away. Coster found the salvage operation much more exciting than the raid.

The passing of "Fizzer" took place at Cambrin. He was one of the oldest of our Old Soldiers who rolled up on mobilization. He respected a soldier's loyalties; he and Seth were inseparables, but he had no respect for anything or anyone else, alive or dead. He was a skilled and fearless member of A Company's Wiring Section from the start of it. In all else he was a good bit of a nuisance. At Christmas, when his Company Officer was rather like the morning after the night before, Fizzer and Seth were sent for and given a stripe. From that moment the nuisance in both was abated. (Seth, become lance-sergeant, died of wounds in July.) After dinner I was sent for to the Aid Post to see a wounded man who said there were more to come. He was followed by two stretcher-cases who were too shocked to speak. When they had gone the drumming of feet on duckboards, and semi-articulate unprintable language in which "pipe" was distinguishable, preceded Fizzer's entry with a baddish wound in an arm. He talked only of his lost pipe, a bit of cherished clay. A machine-gun burst had laid out the Wiring Section. Perhaps the glow of Fizzer's pipe gave the gunner his target. Anyhow, Fizzer refused blasphemously to go into the trench until the men of his command had been got in; then he had to be stopped going out again to look for the pipe he had just missed. When I fixed his tag on a button and said, "I'm not issuing any return tickets to-night," Fizzer smiled, the only time I ever saw a smile on his grim visage. He went away fumbling in the empty pocket of an old waistcoat where he carried his pipe. The etymology of his nickname was given me thus: visage or physiognomy, phiz, fizzer.

April 13th.—This is the first day for two months without a rumour of impending action somewhere on the front. To occupy its typists Division circulated a leg-pull on fly-catching, after Heath Robinson: he was a caricaturist whose burlesques of war-time mechanical contrivances and proposals were sometimes grimly to the point.

April 15th.—A route-march.—German fliers have dropped notes saying they will be in Béthune on the 22nd. Their visits are few, but well timed; our fliers are much more over their territory.—A Brass Band of 14 instruments, trained by C.Q.M.S. Dealing, *April 16th*—made a first, and quite good, appearance on Church Parade. Three months later circumstances had brought this Band *April 17th*—to an end.—The Battalion found a Company to keep the Square at Béthune when the French Territorial General presented decorations to his countrymen. At the finish he was so complimentary that Higginson, tall, fair, and blue-eyed, blushed at the thought of being kissed.—A Territorial battalion which came *April 19th*—over in November 1914 is said to have had its first officer casualty.—New divisions are still arriving in France. It would be worth knowing how many of their G.O.Cs., Brigadiers, and O.Cs., battalion and company, are sent home within a month of going into the line—many of the old gentlemen being very glad to go.

April 20th.—Annequin North. It looks as if we had extra troops about here; but the recalling of all officers on leave two days ago was because of the want, or misplacing, of a comma in a G.H.Q. message. (Later on we heard that the stopping of B.E.F. leave was to let the stay-at-homes have their Easter travel in comfort.) A tale of the time told by Moody. 'Barling brought papers for signature into the Mess after dinner. Before reading them I said, "Have some whisky, Sergeant-Major, help yourself." Whether he took up the nearest bottle or the uncommon-looking one I don't know; I heard that he had helped himself and, with a "Good health, sir," he tossed over his drink. Then he coughed, spluttered, choked, and was in real distress. So was I on finding that he had nearly finished the remaining half of a bottle of DOM, sent me as a present. DOM was almost unprocurable, and correspondingly expensive. For twenty-fours hours he was ill. When he recovered speech his first words were, "These officers are able to get damned strong whisky." The gravity of whisky had been lowered, and the tax greatly raised, as a war measure.

April 22nd.—We took over Cuinchy Right which has been held for six months, and much neglected, by Territorial and New Army units.

April 23rd.—A beautiful Easter Day. A parcel of de Bry's marrons glacés from E. is a good egg. Sergeant "Billy" Townsend is wounded; on his Indian performances he was always our middle-weight hope.

April 25th.—Another raid has been planned by the C.O. and Rochford Boyd. Fifty-five of B and C Companies are to go for the re-entrants of a small salient on the left of the road. Stanway was in charge in front. The night was dark, the air clear and still: the surface was dry: the whole front was quiet. Suddenly, at 10 o'clock, many guns opened on the salient. They pounded it for 15 minutes; then they boxed it, pounding its surroundings until all was over. Things went wrong from the start. "Uncle" sent his contingent up tail first, and so late that they barely got out in time. Then most of them followed Sergeant Joe Williams, who made off half-right, shouting, "Lead on, B Company: lead on, B Company." They ran on to uncut wire, were enfiladed by a machine-gun and Joe was killed. That gun was to have been kept quiet by the two new trench-mortars, the Stokes, detailed to protect the right flank, but both broke down when they began to fire. The few of B who followed their officers got into the enemy's trench, but found it empty. C Company's 2 officers and 25 men also got in, but all they could bring away was an anti-gas apparatus. Both parties were heavily strafed from behind. No identification was found, but a second sergeant was left behind dead. Another of the dead was Earnshaw, an ambitious lance-corporal, whose application for a Commission awaited considera-tion. All four officers were wounded, one of them was able to remain at duty. Our other casualties are 21, so Fritz had the better of the exchange unless our bombardment caught him. It was agreed afterwards that the previous day's and the morning's wire-cutting had made him wise, and he was ready—in his second line.

Watching the raid from the fire-step was a hair-raising affair at the start, for our field-guns had so little clearance that the draught of their shells could be felt on the back of one's neck. What was to be seen was like nothing else. Against the night there was a wild dance of red fan-shaped spurts of fire seen through a thickening haze. Soon, so it seemed, Stanway said quietly, "The boys will be over now, they'll want some light," and he fired a Verey cartridge. It fizzled up and flared. Myriads of drifting specks of smoke and dust distorted its light. Through the translucent mist there loomed a figure running hoppetty-kick, he was a sergeant wounded in the foot. Then the light went out. In the brilliance of a second rocket two men crouched and shuffled, supporting a third. Two or three other men dashed over, one of them holding an arm. The strangely refracted radiance made them look un-earthly. And all the time the unchecked machine-gun on the right stuttered in fits and sparked viciously. This weird, fascinating scene was played to the crashing notes of guns and of bursting shells and bombs. After the briefest diminuendo there was quiet, and only the dark in front. Stepping down, I asked, "What's happened?" Someone said, "They're all back."

Joe Williams was a first-class fighting-man. He had been a sailor before he became a soldier. 'As observer, Joe could see more of Fritz's doings in one dark night than the rest of us could see in a week.' He was the sort of man who is a sergeant to-day, and to-morrow a private doing a court-martial sentence for being drunk and spoiling someone's features, a policeman's for choice. A few days earlier, in Béthune, he laid out an interfering Red-cap who called him a "Welsh bastard." He was released from detention for the raid. Apparently a sympathizer had passed liquor in to him during the day.

Another man, of much the same type, earned the remission of the remainder of a court-martial sentence for a piece of insubordination at which everyone had laughed. When he was not spending his pay riotously he was forfeiting it in field-punishment sentences, so his account was seldom in credit. Craig, a tall fair youth who looked younger than his nineteen or twenty years, was paying his Company two of the then customary 5-franc instalments. "Can I have 10 francs, sir?" asked the reprobate, whose credit was strained to pay 5. When refused, he said, "5 francs are no use to me, sir." Told he was not in credit, he persisted, "Can't I have 10 francs, sir?" Then the C.Q.M.S. pointed firmly to the acquittance sheet and told him to sign. Slowly and with much show of unwillingness he took the pencil, turned it round and round, and signed: took the 5-franc note, fingered it, then threw it down in front of Craig, saying as he walked away, "You can keep it, sir, and buy yourself a (obscene) rocking-horse."

One comes to see that the older men, not the younger, volunteer for the bigger risks, and wonders at it. The last to speak to me on the subject is a nineteen-year-old subaltern with a flair for making others think his geese are swans. His theory is that the young ones feel that life is before them, and they want it; the older men are mostly married and disillusioned about life. (The same observation has been made, and opinion expressed in the letters of Germans.)

April 27th.—At Annequin North: gas drifted through the village at 5 and again at 7.30 this morning. The Germans put it over at Hulluch, a couple of miles to our right, and entered 300 yards of front and support trenches. They were "rejected," as *Comic Cuts* (the official Bulletin) put it. Here, the gas crept along the ground in thin dilution, at a fair pace, well below the height of a man standing. It didn't inconvenience any of us except Moody, who was having a bath when the alarm sounded. He pulled on his gas helmet and stood waiting for the "all-clear," forgetting that he was defenceless because he had not a garment on into which to tuck the free end of the helmet. From that ridiculous attitude he was released by the entry of his servant. Horses and tethered cattle were startled, and tugged at their head-ropes. A little dog on a heavy chain, unable to scramble on to his kennel, ran about frantically; hens flew on to walls and outhouses, clucking loudly; little chickens stood on tiptoe, craning to raise their gaping beaks above the vapour; mice came out of their holes, one climbed the gable of a barn only to fall back when near the top. Seedling peas and other vegetables were bleached, and wilted. Béthune buzzed with excitement, we were told, and pealed every bell. There was more gas at night. It should thin out the rats, filthy pests. Two of them once woke Ormrod, mating on his bed; his vigorous kick threw them on to Robertson, who mumbled, "Yes, what is it ?"— thinking that Brigade Orderly's familiar midnight hand had been laid on him. Other rats gnawed away Ormrod's Flash to swaddle their young.

April 28th.—More gas this evening: quite harmless here.

April 29th.—A cuckoo. In the afternoon No. 1 Harley Street was knocked about. An attic window, that was out of bounds in my time, has become too popular with sightseers; it was an O.P. in earlier days. My regret is the smashing of one of the two magnificent Lombardy poplars at the gate. Genial weather has made bathing in the canal a popular pastime. What a canal to bathe in !

April 30th.—Back again to Cuinchy Right.

May 1st.—A perfect May day. Our first news of the surrender of Kut came on a sheet of paper which a German had wrapped round a stone, and thrown into one of our saps after dark. Townshend's name is spelt correctly. How many of us could have done it ?

May 4th.—This is another uncommonly lively tour. The Bavarian Jaegers who kept us warm last tour have been relieved by as hot a lot. Shells, minnies, and rifle-grenades fly about in profusion; trenches on both sides are blown in daily; no one has been killed on this side. Moody tells of a day of the kind in Cuinchy Left. The C.S.M. shared the servants' half of the sand-bag-partitioned culvert. 'Just as dinner was beginning Barling appeared, looking calamitous; there had been casualties that day. "What's the worst, Sergeant-Major ?" I asked. "Well, sir, I don't want to interfere with your staff, but I think you ought to know that I saw Jenkins stirring the soup with his finger." '

May 5th.—Glad to be relieved and go to Montmorency Barracks. We had turned our backs for the last time on the Brickstacks, scene of much jollity and much that was tragic, and of my earliest impressions of day-to-day trench warfare as an efficient, and efficiently commanded, body of men practised it. Two recent incidents are as deeply graven in memory as any. One morning

I joined a little group of A Company who were watching a German try to hit a periscope which one of them held up interruptedly in place of one he had hit already. Each time he fired he stepped clear of his fascine hide opposite The Grouse Butts. It was much too likely that he was covered by one or two other snipers for one of our men to expose himself to fire on him. He was played with rude signals after each miss, to egg him on, but he prudently stopped before the arrangements in hand to get him could be carried out. From his position it was likely that he was the sniper who shot two of our sentries upwards of a week earlier : anyhow, he was a good man. That time, when on a sanitary round, I stood in a trench junction looking on the scene. Its position was raised enough to give a bird's-eye view of our trenches. An extension of the straight run of trench which fell away from there would have joined the German line obliquely at a point about 500 yards distant. I don't know how long the panorama had held my interest before it occurred to me that the spot could be mighty unhealthy, so I side-stepped one pace to cover. When H.Q. was beginning lunch there came a report that a sentry had been killed. The C.O. had been round, and had him posted beside that junction to prevent loitering and the use of so dangerous a route. Before lunch was finished we heard that the dead man's relief had been hit. After dark some overhead traverses were put up to deny the sniper any more such heedless victims, and let the trench be used.

May 6th.—Blair rejoined.—At Battalion boxing in the afternoon there was hard clean hitting, but no one was in training.—On a *May 10th*—Brigade route-march the Battalion looked mighty fine, swelled by its draft, a good one of 120 New Army men, but we are still below strength. At Brigade boxing in the afternoon Lane was all over an A.S.C. pro. Lane is an excellent boxer (he won the 2nd Army Championship in 1917) : he is commonly called "Hammer," the sobriquet of his grandfather, a former Birmingham celebrity of the Ring.

May 13th.—The country has become solacing to go about in. Looking westwards there is much that is reminiscent of Norfolk in the landscape. There is the same general flatness with a few knolls which redeem, while they accentuate, the flat : there are more dykes and still fewer hedges here : but Norfolk fields and verges are richer far in poppies, cornflowers, and other wild blooms.

Every green of Spring is showing in the fields, and on the scattered trees and clumps, from the pale lime through the rich elm to the dark stately poplar. The farms and villages are generally of red brick, often whitewashed, with roofs of red tile or thatch : set amid trees they have a homely charm. The lark is the only songster I have heard yet ; likely all the others, because they alight on trees, go into the French pot. So the next common birds are the shy magpie and another crow. (A couple of weeks later, when rambling in by-ways near Hesdigneul, I thought I heard a nightingale.)

Prices seem to be mounting very fast both here and at home. In buying for the Mess and the Canteen I remarked a sudden jump in a lot of articles at the beginning of this month. It looks as if we would soon have at home the German ticket system.

May 15th.—At a Brigade Tattoo in Béthune the Battalion had the smartest turn-out, but fifes are a squeak beside bugles.

May 16th.—As we were going up to Cambrin Right a winsome little girl said plaintively, "Officeers plentee smile," when no one fell out to buy her oranges. The little minx beside her who cut in with "Officeers beaucoup swank," will likely go further.—Since last we were here the pugnacious regiment opposite has got the upper hand so completely that our predecessors have been denied observation of Nomansland, every periscope being shot down as soon as it was put up. Our first morning confirmed the report. The enemy's use of rifle-grenades and minnies made this the hottest tour of the line the Battalion experienced since January. The C.O.'s policy is found everywhere in the instinct that activity, and the spirit behind activity, is the means to win, though sometimes it may be more costly to be active than to be inert. Rifle-grenade retaliation was organized at once. So effectual was it, and the sniping it covered, that soon the close array of German periscopes was thinned, and we had observation of his parapet. For four days the contest went on. Although we had to quit a stretch of trench sometimes, casualties were remarkably few. Counting periscopes as points, the Battalion was easily the winner. The experience was a severe test for the new draft, but it came through well. Its only casualties were owing to the epidemic of German measles it brought from the Base. One of the draft was carrying some freshly made tea when three whizz-bangs burst in a bunch and apparently on him. When the smoke and dust cleared away, his C.S.M., Fox, was astonished to see him uninjured though blackened. "I thought you were napoo," he said. "Yes indeed," Morgan answered, "and, look you, they nearly upset my canteen." A man in the front line with an obvious physical defect was a novelty at that date, so there was a lot of talk when it was discovered that one of the draft could not hear rifle bullets or machine-gun bullets. "They are sniping heavy to-night, Corporal," he said to the N.C.O. of his sentry-post as whizz-bangs flew over him.—Throughout the turmoil a pair of swallows tried persistently to build under an overhead traverse in the strafed front line, and a lark nested among the wire.

The daily visit to H.Q. of a Machine-Gun officer was one of the minor comedies of the time and place. We soon knew his step when he approached the splinter-proof. He was redolent of the warehouse. Having saluted the C.O. and said, "Good morning, sir," he stood in an easy respectful attitude, removed and held his tin-hat as if it were a silk hat, and asked, "Do you mind, sir, if we fire indirectly on (such and such) to-night?"—all with the air of a salesman soliciting from some esteemed customer a trial of a new line in soft goods. He always got the same smiling assent, "Not in the least, and I'm sure the Germans don't mind either." The last vestige of control of the machine-guns by battalion commanders had been withdrawn in January.[1] The command and position of these weapons had been removed yet farther from the front; less and less were they available for direct and opportune fire, and more were they practised on hypothetical targets on the map; it was not unknown those days for hundredweights of lead to be buried in some intervening bank or elevation.

May 21st, Sunday.—For four months from to-day watches at home are to be kept an hour fast: a German economy idea. (The B.E.F. changed over on June 14/15th.)

May 22nd.—Back to Beuvry, the frogs serenading. There were 16 casualties that tour. A detachment of K.R.R.C. from the 39th Division, attached for instruction, gave some good items at our sing-songs. As we were out of the line the C.O. could not send the officers on patrol, but the Young Officers Riding School, which a Gunner Rough-rider was borrowed to conduct, was put at their disposal. One of the party was saved from probable serious

---

[1] Lewis guns were issued to battalions.

injury by his horse; it had bolted with him to its stable, but before going through the door the intelligent animal dropped him on the dung-heap.

May 28th.—Our return to the line is cancelled at the last moment. We're for the Somme to await events; we're for Vimy for immediate action; what are we not for? H.Q. dinner was ordered for 7.30 as usual.

May 29th.—Cambrin Right: a slight rearrangement of the line, that is all; spreading us out a bit to increase the balance in hand for the coming Show down south. In fine weather the trenches can be a picnic, with tragic incidents. Luckily this was a pretty quiet tour, for we had a large detachment of a newly-come division in for instruction, the 66th—"Clickety-Clicks." Some of the poor devils had never fired a rifle, others were awaiting discharge when their battalion was ordered overseas. A lackadaisical youth, when shown the German wire, drawled, "But have not we a similar obstacle in front of our trench?" One of our sergeants, stupidly showing off before the novices, was shot through the head.

In the afternoon we were brushed by the fringe of a deluge on our right, begun by our artillery. It looked like the Hairpin again. The Germans poured 30,000 shells on it two weeks ago, and captured the debris from what had been a Scots battalion when the shelling began. Anyhow, to-day's colour effects were a sheer joy to watch. According as a shell burst in coal, chalk, or soil, there was a dust fountain of black, white, or terra-cotta, or a mixture of two of these; and there were woolly air-bursts that rolled out in whorls—grey-black, pure white, and lemon. Sometimes there was a hint of the human soil on which shells were falling when a largish, flaccid thing rose in the spout, and one was sorry for the men there, whichever side they were on.

One day the C.O. came in thoroughly enjoying having been told off by one of our recent draft. The man was digging when asked what he was doing. His answer, "I don't know, sir," always annoys the C.O. "You must be a damned fool not to know what you are doing." "I do what I am told and ask no questions, sir; after I have done a bit more of this I may find out what I am doing, sir." No Old Soldier would make such a speech; something would be chanced, however far-fetched.

Our guests' Second-in-Command, a most worthy provincial

solicitor, has driven more than the C.O. nearly frantic, amidst the
splutters of the juniors in the Mess. Every time he is spoken to
he looks up, raising his eyebrows, and his eyeglasses fall off. At
table they have to be retrieved from whatever dish is before him,
wiped, and replaced on his bony nose, then the remark has to be
repeated—if one have patience enough. And he means so well.
Some three months later I met him again. He was more happily
placed in a Staff job at the Base. "We had a dreadful time after
you left," he told me, "it was raid, raid, raid." In mischief I
asked, "Who did the raiding?" "Oh! they did, they did"—
and his head shook. Not long after this a Brigadier, appointed to
a New Army division, told me that his brigade was "At Home to
the Germans on Tuesdays and Fridays"—a state of affairs he soon
mended.

June 2nd.—When the Canteen accounts were made up at the end
of May there was enough cash in hand to repay advances. Since
yesterday the Canteen has been a Battalion concern with 450 francs
(about £16) worth of stock at cost price: cash for £35 worth
of goods on order has been set aside, and there remains about the
same amount wherewith to open an account at Cox's. The
Canteen was begun as a convenience for the men, and run at my
risk. For two days things went wrong, partly from want of
stock: then the R.S.M. brought along Lance-Corporal Mills,
one of the Old Lot. An engineer by trade, he seemed to have
nothing to learn of the small shopkeeper's craft. The stock was
checked daily. My chief fear was when shells were going its
way, because a battalion next to us had its canteen blown to
smithereens. There were other risks. The day after the Cuinchy
raid we had in an extra large stock. A man looked at it and said,
"I know where the next raid will be." Only the week before
that the Canteen had to be moved out of the too broken-down
house it was in. A few of the Old Sweats who frequent Orderly
Room were found behind it, they had already removed some
bricks; "Sapping in," Mills called it. It may have been the same
lot who "made" a quantity of "comforts" a week earlier. Some
of our Royal Fusiliers were overheard grousing that a parcel post
had come when they were getting ready to go into the line; they
would have the bore of carrying in their parcels themselves. Soon
the stinking smoke of a seemingly fortuitous fire among rags and

refuse to windward of their billet drove them out. When they returned there were no parcels. Besides their large parcel-mails the R.Fs. of that date had so much money to spend, and spent so much on the costlier foodstuffs, sauces, and confectionery, that they were commonly known as "The Chocolate Soldiers." Our Canteen owed much of its good start to their custom and full purses. It always owed much to Yates's generous transport arrangements.

Most of the goods—we stocked quite 60 kinds, often many more—were bought at the Expeditionary Force Canteen. Ours was the cheapest canteen of its kind I heard of. The only profit on penny articles, and these had the largest sale, was the 5 per cent. discount given by the E.F.C. A halfpenny was added to the cost of articles up to one franc, with remissions on the lower-priced ones, over a franc a penny was added. Slices of cake, a cup of tea or coffee, and "coolers," were very profitable at a penny. In starting these sales the foundation of Lyons' Tea-shops was in mind —"Thammy, my boy, I've jutht found out that you can make five cupth of tea for a penny." Thanks to the interest of Mann's father, tobacco, biscuits, sausages, chocolate, and some other articles in large demand were bought from the makers, and sold at shop prices. Other goods with a steady sale were sauces, meat and fish pastes, and milk in tins, sardines, writing-paper and note-books, soap and candles, brushes, tooth-powder, button and boot polishes, and laces. Sales showed queer vagaries of taste or fashion. Thus, a quite popular brand of cigarette became an occasional ration, from the time of the first issue that brand was unsaleable in the Canteen. The "fag" always had a large sale, although it was the common ration. About the beginning of 1918 direct buying was forbidden. The E.F.C., which had a Government nominee on its Board, withdrew the 5 per cent. discount on being given a virtual monopoly; only the French shops remained. Once a few men, one of them a schoolmaster, who had wanted meat paste, paté, and made a purchase in a French shop, asked me if it was "all right," and showed me a large tin of a pink metal polish, pâte, half-eaten. Exchanging postal orders was as great a convenience as the Canteen offered. One- and two-shilling orders were common, five-shilling orders were exceptional, and incoming orders greatly outnumbered the outgoing. No avoid-

able profit was made on the exchange; with what trifle there
was, the Canteen was credited—to Mills's amazement. "Well,
I thought that would be a little bit for yourself anyway, sir," he
said in an undertone. Again, he disapproved of a refusal to raise
the price of a stock that had gone up since it was bought. His
big eyes grew bigger as he looked at me, then he sighed—"As you
wish, sir," and turned away with another sigh.

June 3rd.—News of a North Sea fight: it looks as if we had
come off second. Some lost vessels were known to the Battalion
at Portland.

June 8th.—At Annequin South: Colonel Williams left to command the 92nd Brigade; an overdue promotion, but he was just
a bit affected at leaving his Battalion. Stanway is acting O.C.

Jnue 9th.—To Fouquereuil; a delightful march in the evening
and early dark, no gun fired within hearing. There I found
myself doing a civilian practice among miners' families. In a
house are three women refugees from La Bassée: one's husband
is killed, another's is insane, the third's is lamed and has lost an
arm.

June 11th.—Whitsun Day: the children are all dressed for
Confirmation.

June 13th.—A Memorial Service for Lord Kitchener at the
Béthune Theatre. All the French notables around attended.
Chaplains of every variety took part, very commonplace all of
them. Handel's March was well played by the Band of the
12th Division. Our Bugles sounded "The Last Post" at the
somewhat quick time of the Regiment. Later, I came on this
panegyric by one of our men, written on the door of his billet—

> Boney was a great man, a soldier good and true;
> But Wellington he beat him at the Battle of Waterloo;
> But greater far and truer still, and tougher than shoe-leather
> Is Kitchener, the man who could have beaten them together.

Atkins does not appraise his leaders as tacticians or strategists. A
General is "lucky" or "unlucky." Roberts and Kitchener were
lucky, and esteemed for it: the Gods smiled on them. One
other means to win Atkins's esteem is attention to his rations. In
South Africa Buller saw that his men were well fed, so Colenso
and Spion Kop were condoned; he never lost the favour of the
rank and file.

June 14th.—Captain C. H. R. Crawshay, R.W.F., from the Welsh Division, the new C.O., arrived with the biggest kit any of us has ever seen; when it had been unloaded a friend who came with him was found in the car.

June 16th.—To Béthune, the rue d'Aire. The new C.O.'s paternal heart was wrung when a demure figure, draped in weeds, tripped across the street towards him. Poor little war widow! She shot him a wink as she passed: a compliment to his youthful appearance, or "Number Thirteen" has taken to flying at higher game than callow subalterns.—Inspecting the Transport, the C.O. bowled Rugg over by asking if he dressed by the horses' heads or the wheels of the limbers.

The disbanding of another of our Chocolate Soldier battalions has given us a draft of an officer and one other rank. Pryce Edwards was to be buried in his dug-out within a week. Parry, a Paris-trained chef from a first-class London restaurant, was a great gain. H.Q. had been in a bad way since Colonel Williams took with him his servant who was our cook. We were more than satisfied now.

A procession of "Cook's tourists" was passing through the town these days: among others, Conan Doyle getting local colour for his new pot-boiler, and a Russian Prince, whose A.D.C., General Itchas, supplied the facetious with a topic.

June 17th.—A gas alarm at 5 caused a commotion that awakened me. As the cloud was below the level of my first-floor window and did not look lethal, I went back to bed and to sleep. The Battalion stood-to in gas helmets, as I should have guessed. There were no casualties.

We marched to Gorre in the afternoon to billet in the château and its out-buildings. The furniture has been taken away, the building is scarcely damaged. Some fine Spanish chestnuts grow in the spacious courtyard, and ripe geans can be plucked from windows. Most of the rooms are shared with swallows which fly through the broken window-panes to their nests on the cornices.

June 18th.—The Argylls' C.O. is dead—sniped: he was married a week ago.

June 19th.—At the Divisional Horse Show yesterday the C.O.'s insinuating asides perhaps helped the judges to see excellences in our entries such as, in his absence to-day, escaped them when they gave the prizes to other units. We have no officer now, except him, to uphold the Battalion's Indian reputation for horsemanship; the others are products of the Young Officers Riding School. There is nothing professorial about the Army Commander, Monro, of the family of former Edinburgh anatomists.

The O.C. Mining Company dined at H.Q.; he was invited to explain the underground situation to the C.O. Spreading his plans, he showed how a recent camouflet and two small mines had done such damage to the German galleries that six to eight weeks must elapse before anything to endanger our front line could be completed. I was not present when the Miner made a further explanation to the C.O. in three days time.

June 20th.—At to-day's reconnaissance Company Commanders who were on this front when last we were here, in January, scarcely recognized it, so many new craters have been blown, and new saps have quite changed the front line. Dead Man's Trench had been given up. The old saps at The Warren had been joined, and thence a breastwork re-entrant ran westwards for some 500 yards, made a sweep in front of Le Plantin, and so north again to Festubert.

These were pleasant days. There was specialist practice in the morning—the Lewis gun, making concertina wire, bombing. The Mills was still new; lobbing blind bombs was a game, a good average throw was 20 yards. "House" had its devotees in the afternoon.

Blair's Narrative.—'B Company, both officers and men, had a real good time. We were billeted in a farmhouse with big out-buildings, surrounded by a large fruit and vegetable garden; there were several well-built Army huts in the orchard, there were beds for all and to spare. We took over from Heaven-knows-who-or-what they were, a Corporal and one weary sentry were all I and my Sergeant-Major ever saw. The taking-over was note-worthy for two things: the disgustingly filthy state of the latrines, and the casual way in which a Dump of R.E. stores, clothing, and other equipment, was handed over. After the Corporal had been well damned for the state of the latrines he explained that he had been left in charge of the R.E. Dump, and that a fatigue party under another N.C.O. had been detailed to clean up the latrines. Apparently they had not fancied the job and had faded away before our arrival. Of the stores, the Corporal said he had never been given an inventory nor had he made one. Nobody seemed to know anything about the stores or to take the slightest interest in them. Excellent news for B Company! Permission having been given to the Corporal to retire, he and the sentry faded away. I fancy they had visions of spending half the night cleaning up the latrines. Sentries were placed over the Dump, partly as a precaution against a Staff Officer happening around and seeing it without a guard, but more particularly in case somebody else in the Battalion came "shopping"—a not unlikely contingency when one could take what one liked, pay nothing nor sign for anything. All dirt and rubbish was quickly cleaned up, new duckboards were laid in front of every hut; inside the huts was almost everything that the heart of man-at-the-front could desire. Our billets were a model. The Company was a delight to the eye in new uniform and equipment. Indeed, Gorre was a nice place!

The day before taking over the trenches at Givenchy the C.O. and Company Commanders had a look round. My opposite number was quite reassuring regarding the underground position in the Duck's Bill. At night we had a dinner-party in our billet. Besides my Company officers—Pryce Edwards, Barrett, Banks, and Crosland—there were Moody, Higginson, and Heastey: a very cheery crew. Full of good food and bonhomie, we afterwards played follow-my-leader across country with me as leader. I think that was one of the best rags I have ever had. It was practically dark when we started, but we got along safely till I tried to jump a brook too wide for my powers; I landed on the far side in the mud, my cap fell off and I sat on it. I am glad to say there were at least two other casualties. Obstacle number two was a haystack which the farmer was cutting up into trusses. The steps were high, but we all got to the top safely—it was quite dark now—we lined up on the ridge of the stack, and on the word "Go" we all tobogganed down the side and off into space. This part of the show was repeated thrice. By the mercy of Heaven no limbs were broken. Then someone had a brain spasm and suggested that we raid D Company's Mess, which we promptly did. They were playing cards, so we were vastly unpopular. We withdrew. Thereupon some cheerful lunatic suggested climbing through the barbed wire where it was high and thick and many yards in depth—this in

pitch darkness. We got through; but, in spite of the able assistance
of two of my subalterns, the seat of my trousers was torn clean out.
And so to bed after a real jolly evening.'

June 21st.—Late in the evening we moved off to take over
Givenchy Left, with B, C, D, and A Companies in line. That
march in the waning of the long twilight will linger in memory:
we seemed to linger in step, so soothing was the beauty and
tranquillity of the midsummer night. The sky was flawless but
for a deep flounce of fleecy, dove-coloured cloud, edged with
bronze, on all the horizon ahead. The whole front was unwontedly
restful, not even a distant gun broke the stillness.

Blair's Narrative continued.—'I marched with young Crosland
and his platoon most of the way. He was thrilled. It was the
first time he had ever been in the trenches. Poor boy! three
hours later he was dead. We took over from the 4th Suffolks
shortly before midnight. The company commander I relieved
assured me that the German mines had been "knocked to bits,"
not a sound had been heard since we blew camouflets the previous
day. This was comforting, but——

About half an hour after midnight I began a round with my
June 22nd—Sergeant-Major, Pattison. The trenches had been
knocked about in places by shelling during the day. A perfect
network of saps ran out for a considerable distance between deep
mine-craters. In one of the saps I met Conning, the Bombing
Officer. He told me he could not spare more than two-thirds of
the complement of bombers, but I insisted on having the full
number. I had an uncomfortable foreboding of impending
trouble. I cannot say why, I was neither worried nor depressed,
but the feeling grew as time went on. It was a lovely peaceful
night. Perhaps it was the almost uncanny stillness, too quiet to
be natural in that unpleasant part of the line. Anyhow, I was
filled with a haunting unrest. I sent my Sergeant-Major to have
boxes of bombs placed on the fire-steps and the pins pinched
ready for use, boxes of reserve S.A.A. too were to be ready to
hand. It was nearly 1.30 a.m. when my Sergeant-Major reported
again. Conning had made up the complement of bombers; we
all went for a last look round. Everything was quite in order, so
we strolled towards the company dug-out to have a drink before
turning in. A few yards from the dug-out somebody, Conning

I think, looked at his watch; it was twenty minutes to two. He said he was dead-beat and, if I did not mind, he would prefer to turn in at once, so we postponed the drink. He and another, whose name I forget, went off in the direction of C Company. Conning's change of mind saved his life, at the time, and mine.

After they left us I went back with Pattison to the far end of one of the saps and spoke to the sentry and Lance-Corporal Morris. There was stillness everywhere. I had just stepped off the fire-step into the sap—Pattison was about 5 yards from me—when I felt my feet lifted up beneath me and the trench walls seemed to move upwards. There was a terrific blast of air which blew my steel helmet Heaven knows where. I think that something must have struck me then on the head—it was said in hospital that my skull was fractured—anyhow, I remember nothing more until I woke to find myself buried up to the neck and quite unable to move hand or foot. I do not know how long I had been unconscious. I was told afterwards that there was a heavy bombardment of our trenches lasting nearly an hour after the explosion of the mine, but I was quite unaware of all that. I awoke to an appalling shindy going on, and gradually realized that heavy rifle and machine-gun fire was taking place and that bullets were whistling all round. Several men passed within a few feet of me. I saw them distinctly by the light of the flares. I remember hoping they would not trip over my head. The men were shouting to each other, but I was too dazed to appreciate that the language was German. When I heard a hunting-horn I was certain I was having the nightmare of my life—pegged down and unable to move, with a hailstorm of bullets all round, and men rushing about perilously near kicking my head. The firing died down, and I realized it was no nightmare but that I was very much awake.

Soon day began to dawn. I was extremely uncomfortable with violent cramp in my left leg; also, I was in a very exposed position. It was then for the first time that I noticed Corporal Morris; he was wedged up against me and was evidently in great pain—both his legs were broken. The dead body of Private Bayliss was lying close to us and partly under my left side. After some struggling I got my right arm loose, pulled out my big pocket-knife and started busily to make a "dug-out" as far as my cramped quarters would allow. I managed during the next two hours to excavate a good-sized hole, and carefully piled the earth handful by handful between us and the Germans. Thanks partly to my parapet and to the unevenness of the ground Morris and I were able to hide from the German snipers. Later in the morning we must have been seen by some of our men. A rescue-party [of Cameronians] tried very gallantly to come to us, but it was shelled immediately by the Germans, so any further attempt at rescue had to be abandoned during daylight. Foolishly I waved my arm to them. Whether the Germans saw the movement or not I cannot say, but they had discovered or suspected our where-abouts and turned a machine-gun on to the spot. The bullets kept hitting the top of our little parapet or passing some inches above us, but we were able to crouch down in the hole I had dug.

The weary hours dragged on. I continued to dig, it was some-thing to do. Every handful of earth was disposed of carefully lest the Germans detect the movement and intensify their fire, or bomb us. After several hours I freed my right leg, but my left leg was fixed down firmly under me and felt quite dead. The sun was very hot and beat upon my bare head, which ached badly; but my eyes were very much worse, they were full of grit and dirt; they were running in streams and were excessively painful. By the early afternoon we were in rather a bad way. Morris was in great pain and was becoming light-headed. He begged for water. He said he would put his head over the top of our little parapet and "finish things off." For a time I was able to persuade him to carry on. At length the poor fellow, who was half-crazy with pain and thirst, raised himself right up. There seemed only one thing to do; I hit him with my fist in his wind and he collapsed. Personally I felt less discomfort as the sun declined; though my eyes and head throbbed there was no pain in my leg or body and I did not feel so thirsty, so I tried to take an intelligent interest in our surroundings and prospects. My appreciation of the position was that if we kept quiet the Huns would not trouble us, they probably thought we were dead by now. As soon after dark as possible the rescue-party would come for us, therefore all was well—provided our party found us, and provided the Germans did not send a party to investigate. For I felt qualms: our rescuers might fail and the Huns might gather us. Morris was quiet during the later afternoon, partly numbed, so I think, by the pain of his legs, about which he was extremely plucky. We talked in whispers of the certainty of rescue at dark. Again and again he could not help asking me to give him a few drops of water.

Very slowly the long summer evening closed in. It seemed ages before the darkness of night began to fall. Our one topic, our one thought, was how soon the rescue-party would come for us. The last two hours of our imprisonment were far the worst of that long day. 9.30: No, too light. . . . 10 o'clock: still too light. . . . 10.30: they ought to come now, if they let it get too dark they may not be able to find us. . . . 11 o'clock: the worst time of all—had our rescue-party been unable to find us and given up the search? We were parched with thirst and had visions of lying out another twenty-four hours without water. We were getting depressed and losing hope when—it must have been nearly 11.30—I heard footsteps and a muttered whisper: English, thank Heaven. I called softly, and the rescue-party came up to us; our doctor and a covering party of Cameronians. We were given water. I think we should have drunk gallons if we had not been stopped. Owing to Morris's position it was necessary to get me out first. It took about three-quarters of an hour to release me, and it was over two hours more before Morris was carried back to our lines.'

The drama in which Fate had given Blair a part and let him live was the blowing under his Company of the largest mine the Germans put up on the Western Front. Even on the broken ground of the Givenchy sector the new crater dominated the landscape. It was estimated to be some 120 yards long by 70 or 80 yards broad, its walls were upwards of 30 feet high. Figures vary according as internal or external estimates are given; the actual cup was some 40 yards across and about 60 yards from front to rear. The mine went up at 2 o'clock. The shock was felt over the divisional area. Within minutes Division telegraphed from Béthune to know where it was. Battalion H.Q. was among the few places where no one felt it. The site and extent of the damage were not known till daylight, when it was found that B Company's H.Q. and its two centre platoons were buried out of sight in the ruins of their trenches. Loose earth was showered on the two flank platoons of B, and the door of C Company's gimcrack H.Q. was twisted. An intense bombardment of the front line followed. After 15 minutes the guns lifted, and an area including C Company's right was boxed; the reserve line and communications were shelled; Battalion H.Q., in front of Windy Corner, was under field-gun and 4·2-howitzer fire for about an hour; Brigade H.Q. on the canal bank, 2 miles in rear, was plastered with 5·9s.

Sergeant Roderick, 'on the Company's left, had reported, "No. 8 Platoon all correct." Peter Pattison and I shared the fatigues of the Retreat. After that we took it in turns to carry some comforts into the trenches, and I had the run of his dug-out. I do not remember ever missing taking advantage of the privilege until that fateful night. I hallooed to the C.S.M.'s batman as I passed, and he called back, "Come down," but I passed on to my platoon only a few yards away. As I reached the first man there was a rumble, a tremble, an explosion. Up flew dust and soil and everything behind me, and then it fell about us; the C.S.M.'s dug-out was filled in, and young Roberts was never seen again. We were dazed a bit by that, but it was nothing to the bombardment of the trench which followed. Jack Johnsons and all were dropping like manna. There were only eleven of us, in three bays of the Company's trench, not buried by the explosion. Lieutenant Banks, who had never been in a trench before, was on the flank. He sent me a message by Bandsman Walsh. I advised him to stay on his flank and I would stay on mine. When Gerry's guns lifted we could see his men coming over in three lines; there was enough light, especially when flares went up on someone's front on our left or right. They made a lot of noise talking, and the white armlets they were wearing showed them up. We opened with all our rifles and our Lewis gun. We could see them being knocked over and being carried away by their pals. They got confused, and hesitated, and made to come on in groups by the side of the crater. We fired whenever we could see anyone. One man came right round behind us; he was spotted by his armlet and was shot before he could heave a bomb. He said, "Oh, Mutter," when he was hit. Some of our lads climbed out at once and stripped him of his revolver and souvenirs, though I told them they were damned fools. While this sort of thing was going on Mr. Banks suddenly ran across our front. I shouted to him, but he went for three Germans on the crater slope. One of them lifted his hand and struck Mr. Banks before I could fire. Mr. Banks's last effort was to jump into the trench. I ran up and finished with my bayonet the Gerry I had wounded. The other two ran away, letting go one of our men they had seized. When I got back to Mr. Banks he was dead, stabbed in the abdomen. We had the measure of Gerry, and were not shooting all the time; when it was quiet the men talked and made jokes and laughed.

After a time I thought of getting in touch with someone on the right, so I left Lance-Corporal Davies in charge. I ran at once into four Gerries on the crater. I fired among them and downed one with my entrenching tool, then I tripped over my rifle and bayonet. How I escaped being stabbed is still a mystery to me. They were between me and my platoon, so I had to follow the crater backwards. It brought me among some Labour Battalion men. They didn't think it was their job to go up to the front trench. Before I had left them the Show was over and it was getting lighter, so I rejoined my platoon. When I got back our Lewis gun had been smashed by a minnie; two of the team were killed and there were two dead Gerries beside it. The young fellow in charge had done very good work with his gun. Davies and Lane, and Walsh in particular, did well. Lane was full of fight and temper. Walsh was full of humour; he did a lot to keep us going, and he carried ammunition, and later attended to the wounded. We dug one man out of the side of the crater, but unfortunately he died. We might have captured some Gerries who got lost in the crater, but we had all got a good shaking-up, and let ourselves be put off going for them. If there had been an officer about it would have been all right, someone to give an order and take no back-chat.'

Stanway, during his round, 'had been in touch with some of the Tunnelling people. They said they were getting water in their galleries, but everything was O.K. and they were not anticipating trouble.' He left the men getting the trenches ship-shape, and went to C Company's H.Q., a shanty not far from B and C Companies' junction. He was 'chatting there when there was a most colossal bang, and the whole area just rocked from one end to the other. Out went every candle; there was pitch blackness, but not for more than a couple of seconds, for it was turned almost to daylight by the flashes of a hell of a bombardment, and the trenches began to go up all over the place. Then I realized what had happened, and said to the other three lads that the Duck's Bill had gone up. (Outside help was needed to let the inmates of the shanty out when), after the lift of the guns, over came the Germans. The men were ordered up on to the parapet, where they knelt to fire. The raiders were held on the little bit of C Company's front, but with no opposition on the right they just went through. Craig was sent out between the support and front lines with a few men, and got mixed up with some Germans on C Company's right rear.' Meanwhile, Stanway was collecting men as he could and 'pushing them out to the right, forming a flank that kept moving forward. While this was being done Craig was found, captured, sitting in a shell-hole with a large German standing over him—he did not stand long. Going on, they joined up on the crater slope with a few of our men and of the Divisional Labour Battalion. (Conning had collected that party in the support line and brought it up over the top.) The raid had now pretty well fizzled out, there was only some shelling in rear.'

Moody had finished inspecting his area, and had just returned to D Company's H.Q. with his Sergeant-Major when the mine went up. They felt the shock, and came in for the bombardment. So rapid and accurate was the fire that there was no getting out until it lifted. Every man about H.Q. was then collected, and the party went forward. All was found quiet in the Company's area, but the shelling had killed or wounded 5 men. The strafe continued on their right. A. Company H.Q., except the signaller on duty, felt nothing; and knew nothing of what was happening on their right.

With the coming of light Stanway 'got some idea of the havoc. It was a pretty ghastly sight. Six more or less buried men were seen and dug out of the crater slope; one of them died in the Aid Post. There were a good few dead raiders lying about. From one under-officer a map was taken which showed the whole scheme of the operation. Meanwhile Conning had been sent round the crater to find out the state of affairs on the other side.' He learned that No. 5 Platoon had a somewhat similar experience to No. 8. The Lewis gun and two of the team were missing, and were believed to have been carried off; about midday, however, the lance-corporal of the gun and a German were seen dead beside it in the long grass between the parapet and the wire, but the other man was missing. 'On both flanks the survivors of B Company were found cheerful, for all they had been through, and still game to do anything required of them.'

Having made his own observations and heard Conning's report, Stanway went to H.Q. Until then the C.O. had no news of the front; all wires had been cut early, and casualties were taking an alternative route; there had been only unpleasant good guessing. H.Q. had sat through the bombardment somewhat precariously while more and more fragments of its tumble-down dwelling were being strewn about, but there were no casualties. The C.O. went with Stanway back through communications which were evidence of the excellence of the German Intelligence and gunnery. Conning was sent to relieve a 20th R.F. officer whom Sergeant Rush had called in during the early morning when he found his platoon cut off from the Company. A comprehensive scheme to repair the damaged trenches, restore the line, and prevent the enemy turning the new crater to his advantage, was arranged; and the work was put in hand under Stanway's direction.

After breakfast a Cameronian company relieved the remnant of B, there were about 40, who were sent to the Transport lines to rest. As they were going down the O.C. 5th Scottish Rifles halted them to compliment them, and pointed to them as models for his own battalion. He was shot by a sniper a few days later when inspecting the crater.

Shortly before noon a Cameronian sentry saw Blair and his companions. Signs were exchanged, but rescue was not possible in daylight. A Cameronian had been killed already when trying to crawl to one of three dead German officers or cadets lying on the side of the crater, whose wrist-watch he was after. As soon as it was dark "Moldy" Williams's Sapping Platoon began connecting up with the crater lip. Seeing "Moldy," a thin-limbed man, skip from footing to footing on the uneven surface as he struck off in the dusk to mark the line of his sap, brought to mind childhood's pictures of Will o' the Wisp or Puck. At the same time I went with a small party to bring in Blair and his men: a section of Cameronians covered us. Morris was becoming exhausted; his restlessness and moaning increased the irritability which shock and exposure to hours of a hot midsummer sun had induced in Blair. To get to Morris, Blair, who was nearer the surface, had to be got away. With him joining in the work like a terrier, it took the better part of an hour to free his imprisoned leg from the grip of the damp, compressed earth and trench debris. The freeing of Morris from that tangle of barbed wire, torn sand-bags, pickets, angle irons, and one of Bayliss's legs, amidst *June 23rd*—which he was half-buried upright, was a long and difficult business. He was helpless, and it was found early that his right thigh-bone was broken. Tools were of little use, the work had to be done with the hands, and done in the dark until the digging was deep enough to shade a light. The enemy fired often, shot after shot just clearing, or stopping in, a billow of the ground that gave partial cover; one of the covering party was wounded. It was so near daylight when Morris was taken out that Bayliss's body had to be left. By daylight the line had been cleaned up, and the crater lip made tenable.

B Company lost just under two-thirds of its strength, including two very recently joined young officers and its fine sergeant-major, in the upheaval of the mine. The Battalion was wreathed in compliments, and "Red Dragon," after the Regimental Badge, was the official name given to the crater. A wounded Jaeger left in our lines told us that the raiders numbered 150, being 50 from each Battalion of the Regiment, and that 25 per cent. were volunteers. The German wireless account of their exploit was given in quite moderate terms. *The Times* published on June 27th a journalist's version let loose from G.H.Q.

In 1926 a farmer ploughing on the site had to clear his plough-share of an obstruction, a piece of timber; its removal led to the discovery of a cavity containing the remains of two bodies identifiable as those of Pryce Edwards and Crosland in B Company H.Q. Other remains bearing a R.W.F. identity-disc have been found from time to time.

June 24th.—At 9.45 in the morning our artillery opened on the German line. It was the Somme overture: of little account on this front, but thunderous and unbroken down south.

June 27th.—Relieved to Le Préol on the branch canal. Our total casualties are 113, 93 of them in the mine.

June 29th.—A grey day with very little rain after five wet ones. This has been a wet June. All ranks are fishing in the canal with any procurable tackle. One man fished from 4 in the morning till 9.30 at night for one five-inch roach; another fished contentedly for hours without knowing that someone had put a carrot on his hook when his back was turned.

July 1st.—The Somme Show has started in a great racket. Every prisoner taken in raids on this front knew where we would attack. The French people about here are quite sure the War will be over in a few weeks, and our Staff is full of confidence in itself this time.

July 2nd.—Stanway has been given command of a battalion of Cheshires: an achievement for one who was Company Sergeant-Major only twenty months ago.

July 3rd.—The last of six really restful days. Their sunsets have been wonderfully fine. The foreground is the canal, the flowering herbage of the marsh where reeds nod and whisper, and willows and poplars aslant the dykes sway and ripple in the breeze. When night comes the rising and falling of Verey lights and star-shells along the Vimy Ridge, against a sky all shimmering with gun-flashes, makes a scarcely less splendid picture. In the dusk we returned to Givenchy, and found that the Germans had greatly improved their hold on the big crater and had placed a machine-gun to annoy much of our line. They had also blown another mine, a small one at The Warren, which did little damage.

July 4th.—The artillery and infantry at one are at cross-purposes with our divisionally controlled machine-guns.

July 5th.—A second day of thunder and some rain.

The disaster to B Company aroused a general wish for a return blow. The German salient at The Warren was the likeliest spot, or it would have been suggested by the map taken off the dead raider because every dug-out and feature there is marked. Brigade and Division approved; for a time Division thought of seizing the ground, not just raiding it. During the days at Le Préol the C.O. busied himself with his scheme with Rochford Boyd's enthusiastic help. Moody and Higginson, whose Companies were to have the chief task, added their local knowledge. Aerial photography was a great help by this time. The idea is that D and A Companies, 200 in all, assault from the west and north-west respectively; that A push through to the reserve line and hold it, while D mops up and helps the Engineers of the 11th Field Company to destroy all tactical details: B Company, in two parties of 20 each attached to A and D, is to carry explosives and bombs: C Company holds our own line. The time since the Battalion came in has been spent in observing and preparing. The C.O.'s order impresses 'on all ranks that success depends on keeping a clear head, and working at concert pitch during the operation.'

At dusk the assaulting Companies were ready to move into position under the barrage. At 10.30 the bombardment opened with field-guns and 4·5 howitzers, 6-inch howitzers fired on known machine-gun positions; Stokes mortars and the Battalion rifle-grenades also took part. D and A left their assembly positions when the guns began. "They went away like a pack of hounds," said the C.O., who was up to see D Company start. Using the cover given by the craters, D got as far forward in the very broken and wire-entangled ground as was possible and waited. A. Company moved into Nomansland in single file. The ground scout who preceded the Company Commander and C.S.M. was shot through the head when he had gone only 10 yards. Without further casualty or incident the Company went eastwards for about 600 yards over soggy, marshy ground, through long grasses and bits of barbed wire, across abandoned trenches, and lay down, in close column of platoons, fronting the steep northern face of the German re-entrant, about 120 yards away, having Mackensen Trench on its left. A white tape had been paid out to guide individuals and parties returning. 'The men were very happy and soon had their cigarettes going. They were cracking jokes and calling Fritz a few choice names while the guns carried on the good work.' To give the Companies time to cross the intricate or long way from their assembly grounds the guns hopped to and fro on the German front, support, and reserve lines in irregular rotation and at irregular intervals of from 3 to 8 minutes. At 11.15, when a box-barrage, much denser than for our earlier raids, was formed round the area to be raided, the Companies rushed forward, each platoon making for its allotted place.

A. Company's Sergeant-Major 'began [1] badly: when standing on the parapet it gave way and I fell in a heap at the entrance to a dug-out, unable to help myself, having a Verey pistol in one

[1] Fox.

hand and a rifle and bayonet in the other. "Are you hit, Sergeant-Major?" Higginson asked. "Yes, sir, with my own rifle." Next moment I was calling the Boches from the dug-out. The reply was a bullet, so Mills bombs were thrown in. When the dug-out was searched four dead were found in it. Later an ammonal charge was placed in the mouth of it, and so they were buried.

The next dug-out also contained four men. They came out with their hands up—"Kamerad." Their belts and bayonets having been taken off them, they were told to get on the top and sit in a shell-hole. One of them, speaking good English, said, "Not for you or your officer." He got a wallop on the chin—and was hoisted up by his pals. Soon after, a man of ours came along with a wound of the left arm. He was given a revolver, and told to take the four prisoners back to the Company's trench and hand them over to the C.Q.M.S., who was waiting in a deep dug-out to receive prisoners. The Q.M.S. had brought up rations, and wanted to go on the raid, but he was given the job of collecting prisoners. Those four never got to him. The escort wrote from hospital to a pal in the Company that he thought they were going to slip him, so he shot them, but he was "sorry at losing the Sergeant-Major's revolver." '

A dozen half-stupefied occupants of the front line had surrendered at once to D Company. In the support and reserve lines a stout resistance was met; the conduct of one German officer was spoken of with special admiration. A. Company did most of the fighting, D, the bombing and destruction. ' It [1] was a Mark I success, and went absolutely without a hitch. Our fellows fought like demons.'

When resistance was overcome looting and destruction followed. After D Company's C.Q.M.S. had dumped the rations he waited for news, got impatient, and joined the raiders. So did men of B Company after carrying the extra stores. The German dug-outs excited envy by reason of their solidity and comfort. As many as could be found were wrecked with explosive, so were the mine shafts, saps, trenches, and a mortar too large to carry away. Everyone had personal souvenirs. Among the captured weapons was a machine-gun of British make. It was carried down by Private Buckley. His affable handshake with the Chaplain reflected the supreme satisfaction of all the raiders as well as his own. The

---

[1] Higginson.

weapon of Buckley's choice was a bill-hook: one of the wounded
prisoners appeared to have been chased by him. Little Heastey
too carried a bill-hook; two other officers carried a cosh. 43
prisoners were sent back, some of them wounded, and 15 identity-
discs were taken off the dead. The first batch of 25 prisoners
came down under the sole escort of Moody's servant. They were
Saxons of the 241st Regiment, a well-set-up lot of men. Our
bombardment caught them when rations and a mail were being
July 6th—distributed. After the strafe had lasted two hours in all
the recall signal was made. The expenditure of shells, mortar-
bombs, and rifle-grenades ran into thousands. The Battalion
never had anything remotely approaching the artillery cover given
for this raid in any of its battle-pieces.

The long preliminary bombardment, and the frequent raids by
the Division during the two previous weeks, let the enemy know
what was afoot. From the start of the operation his guns retaliated
on our front and rear positions, inflicting losses. Fox recalls, 'when
I got back to our trench I went to the dug-out to see how Powell,
the C.Q.M.S. was getting on. He was in a fine stew. A German
shell had hit the parados opposite, nearly filling the entrance. I think
he had had a worse time than we had in the raid. Now comes the
most awful part of the Show. A man of A Company had a
brother in C Company. When he got back after the raid he said,
"Pass the word to my brother, 'I am all right.'" A few minutes
later he was sitting with two others in the trench when a German
shell landed plumb among them, killing them all. Shortly after
daybreak I met his brother coming to see him; he asked me if I
knew where his brother was. His body had been taken to Cambrin
for burial, but I couldn't tell him. When he did find out he
nearly went out of his mind.' Pathetic too was the killing by
a German shell of two of our men who were attending to a young
German with seventeen wounds. Our casualties were 1 officer
and 6 other ranks dead, 1 officer and upwards of 40 other ranks
wounded. The dead included Lloyd, one of the men who made
off with A Company's Christmas dinner. Most of the wounds
were from shell and bomb splinters, and occurred in A Company,
whereas bayonet-wounds were commonest among the German-
prisoner wounded. During the day the Germans shouted across
that they had captured a corporal of A Company.

CHAPTER IX

Somme–Ancre—Facing Bazentin Ridge—High Wood—
Amiens—Old Army into New—Moles

Contributors:—ARMOUR ; BOREHAM ; COLTART ; CRAWSHAY ;
CROCKETT ; CROMBIE ; FOX ; FYSON ; HYDE SMITH ;
C. JONES ('200) ; MODERA ; MOODY ; POWELL ; RADFORD ;
ROBERTS ; RODERICK ; SMITH ; T. SPENS ; STOCKWELL

Sketches:—1, 11, 12, 13, 14

July 7th.—The Division goes south : a battalion at Gorre had
20 minutes notice to be clear of its billets. We were relieved
July 9th—at 2 o'clock, and marched through Béthune, in the quiet
and freshness of the morning, to Fouquières. In the forenoon
I rode in again, to the Bank. With few troops in it Béthune
looked rather tawdry, even on this perfect summer day. It is
a small, rather drab provincial town, surrounded on three sides
by a coalfield ; its streets and buildings, even its Gothic remains,
are without distinction, the newer part is formal. The Battles
of La Bassée and of Loos, and the coming and going of resting
brigades, cast on it—for the B.E.F.—a passing glamour ; and the
eleven months we had spent in its area were to be looked back to
with longing by those who lived them and were to know camps
and billets elsewhere.

In the afternoon our late C.O. rode over to see us. His division,
after sharing in the disaster at Serre, has come to convalesce on a
quiet front to the north. He looked as if he would gladly be
back with us.

We entrained at midnight, the last unit of the Division to go.
July 10th—At 7 we arrived at Longueau : 20 officers and 686 other
ranks, a magnificent battalion for its strength, not more than a
dozen unreliables in it. At 8.15 we moved off. The route was
through Amiens, so I slipped away to have a glimpse of the
Cathedral. Little of the detail of the lower storey can be seen

because it is protected by sand-bags. Our march was by Poulainville through rich, boldly rolling country, a delightful chequer
of cultivated, hedgeless fields. The people of Cardonnette, where
we billeted, were shrilly insistent on their "rights." The rapacious
French peasantry is battening on the War, doubly so in the British
zone, and their labourers can't buy sugar or coal on the paltry
two francs paid for a long day. Might one know if the blood of
the Ancre smells sweetest to a French farmer, or a British tradesman,
or an American manufacturer.

July 11th.—Yesterday's march was 6½ miles: to-day's 4 miles
to Daours, through the same charming country still seen in
sunshine. On entering the village I heard, added to the crunch
of many feet on a gritty surface, the sound of running water, and
presently a stream tumbled towards us, broken over a stony bed.
A vision of a Highland glen appeared in the clear brown water.
It was gone in a moment—like the snowflake in the river, for,
raising my eyes to mind my step they rested on an unplaned,
weathered board on which an unskilled hand had painted, "rue
napoo." The pleasing illusion had vanished, but I looked at the
water, and listened, because it was said to be the Ancre. Actually
it was a mill-lade; the river was farther over, and the Ancre farther
up the valley. Other village paths had been named as sardonically
—"verité," "grand mari"—by the French troops from whom
our Fouth Army had taken over. We were packed for the night
into the top floor of a mill, dear knows how.

July 12th—At the beginning of an afternoon march of 8 miles
up the right bank of the Ancre we saw Corbie across the Somme.
It cold-shouldered Henry V when he marched along its ridge,
to turn at Agincourt on the host that beset him. Its church looked
as if it would repay a visit. But from what unnamed church
near-by did Bardolph take the deceptive pyx ?—and for the theft
be broken on Fortune's furious fickle wheel. On the road we
passed the transport of the Welsh Division coming out after the
mauling at Mametz Wood. Arrived at Buire, we settled into
tents in an orchard. The battle-front is only 7½ miles away, but
not a sound can be heard although the gun-flashes play brightly
on the sky after dark and a big gun must be fairly close. Having
come through the II Corps, we are now in the XV Corps for
business; Horne, our G.O.C. of Loos days, commands it. We

are the reserve battalion of the reserve brigade of its present reserve division.

July 13th.—A body of cavalry passed up when we were at breakfast. Afterwards the C.O. and Company Commanders went to prospect the forward area, so we should be "for it" soon. On their return Higginson wrote to Blair: "You can guess where all good troops are now. I am enjoying it immensely. This is real war; no burrowing, no wind,[1] no boredom, plenty of marching and changing of scene, and I am splendidly fit."[2] And Moody wrote: "the whole outfit is splendid." Mann was ecstatic.

At night the guns became increasingly audible: an atmospheric change.

July 14th.—An early morning drizzle was followed by an hour of heavy rain beginning at 8 o'clock. "The situation is satisfactory" is the best that *Comic Cuts* can say of it. Then why was a cavalry division sent up yesterday? If only we had no cavalry the operations might not be spoiled. This is an infantry and artillery war. From all one hears it is plain that the infantry, "the Queen of Battles," is being subordinated to the artillery. Fritz has two new well-wired lines on this front, and it is the conviction of those who have tried him that he is full of fight.

At 11 o'clock we moved to Méaulte, a squalid, only slightly damaged village, where we had a haversack lunch: then the whole Brigade bivouacked on a forward slope one kilometre farther on. On that bit of the way we passed 900 prisoners, then a smaller party, being marched down; a major who looked very haughty and resentful was mocked by the men. At 10, in the dusk, three 5·9 duds fell in the bivouac and one woolly burst above it. Since the Brigade had been in full view of two observation balloons, which were still up, no one need have felt surprise. A new Brigadier had come to us at Buire in place

---

[1] In trench warfare much of an officer's time was taken up with making returns and reports, and reading and noting orders and circulars. During the later months at Béthune the company commander had to make these daily returns to Brigade: a.m.—3.30, one; 8.30, one; 11.30 one. p.m.—3, one; 3.30, one; 7, three; 10, two indents. Besides daily Battalion returns, occasional returns and reports were called for by both Brigade and Battalion. Incoming orders and circulars, which had to be digested for observance, might run to several foolscap sheets of type.

[2] Two months later he was sent to hospital with early lung disease of which he died in a few years.

of Robertson, who had been promoted. He came from his quarters and, running along the lines, himself told the men to get to the cover of the reverse slope; so the less disciplined elements of his Command swarmed over anyhow, and the unsteady ran devil-take-the-hindmost. Comment on the incident was that the Brigadier deserved better of the change. As the air rarefied, and the noisy bivouac fell asleep, there arose from the Fricourt road below us the steady grind of heavy traffic. At midnight it became intermittent, then it stopped, for the enemy was putting a barrage of large shell *July 15th*—about the road—2, 3, and 4 to the minute. Between the bursts the neighing and snorting of horses and the raised voices of men came from the valley with singular clearness. This lasted for an hour, then the shelling ceased and the halted traffic rolled along again.

Brigade réveillé was at 2.30. Kit is reduced to groundsheet and haversack. At 4 o'clock the Battalion moved down to the Fricourt road through a thick mist. A few broken wagons, dead horses and drivers—casualties of the midnight shelling—were passed soon after the road was reached. The soil gave off tear-gas, making eyes and noses run, and spoiling the taste of tobacco. Ambulances, stragglers, detachments, messengers, broken guns passed down. A dead German lay on a stretcher by the roadside. Where the front line of July 1st was crossed we came to ground all pitted with old and new shell-holes; rifles, equipment, clothing, and the litter of a recent and an older battle-field strewed it. The villages of Bécordel, excepting the church tower—strangely, and Fricourt were flattened. Beyond Fricourt a detour to the right was made because of a barrage of 5·9 shell on the road. The march had been interrupted many times, but at 8 o'clock a halt was ordered and we fell out. Suddenly the mist cleared, the sun shone down, and we saw that we were among the dead of the Welsh Division. Friends were recognized, and buried in haste lest we had to move on. "The cavalry are in Martinpuich," so said report. The truth, when we got it, was that a squadron had been sent up to the Bois des Foureaux, "High Wood," hope-fully; it was driven back by heavy fire. The 2nd Queen's, 7th Division, had occupied a corner of High Wood on the 13th, had failed to advance, and had been withdrawn. Whether their report was misleading or thoughtlessly misread, infantry operations were stopped that cavalry might come up and push through : as if the Germans would not use the respite to mend any weakness of their position. Now the task of the Division is the capture of a Switch trench which runs from High Wood to Martinpuich ("Martin's push"). The village is expected to be the Brigade's morsel.

The attack began at 9 o'clock. Again easy progress was seemingly looked for. The 100th and 98th Brigades, the latter in echelon on the left, were sent forward. The first reports were all smiles. Then there was an uneasy blank. Another short move took us across the road to the south-east corner of Mametz Wood. The gossip and grouse of time that hangs heavy began again. A runner going down was asked, "Any news ?" "They've got it in the neck." An understanding look and an unspontaneous smile passed round, "We'll be for it now." Meanwhile there was nothing to do but loaf about and seek diversion in small things. Large letters in white paint on a German gun proclaimed it a trophy of our 1st Battalion, also in the XV Corps. Our 17th Battalion had claimed it already in chalk. Two lively Irishmen in our Field Ambulance sent their Pioneer to claim it in yet larger lettering than Colonel Stockwell's. In the afternoon Stockwell and others from the 1st Battalion visited us, and told the bare outline of their doings here, and at Bazentin Cemetery two days ago : both good Shows. Some of us went exploring in Mametz Wood, where the Welsh Division was so mishandled, and there were nasty sights. A little spasmodic shelling of our area was going on, harmlessly. Scraps of talk filtered through from 100th Brigade H.Q., and from the front. There was angry complaint that our artillery support was poor and misdirected, and that messages to Division were unheeded. As the scraps were put together a local disaster took form. The German guns were splendidly served, the machine-guns were sufficient and artfully placed. Hidden by the long grass and covering the Switch were new wire and unreported posts which stopped all progress. Smitten in front and enfiladed, the two broken brigades ended the day where they began it.

After sunset flights of 0·77 shell twittered over and burst about us with a quiet plop. My first notion was that the German ammunition was strangely defective. It was noxious gas-shell, and we were encountering it for the first time although some

had been in use for several months. Drift gas was no longer used.
These shells gave off bromine fumes which were choking only
to anyone who was close to a burst. A few casualties occurred, so
a move forward of 100 yards was made, and we bivouacked by
July 16th—the roadside. At 1.30 the Argylls, withdrawn from
the front, passed through to bivouac in rear. We became support
brigade. We are assured that "the G.O.C. has the situation well
in hand," and we are promised that officers of the Staff will come
up—from Fricourt—to view the scene in daylight. We are duly
impressed on observing how seriously Division takes itself—at
Fricourt.

The night was spent close behind our main artillery position.
The noise was more nearly "ear-splitting" than anything I have
known. A battery of French seventy-fives had taken station at
dusk just in rear. Their high-pitched bark repelled sleep, and
attracted the German artillery, whose overs reached the Indian
Cavalry picketed close behind the French guns. The fine physique
of the French gunners was a revelation. To the noise of their
guns and ours had to be added that of ammunition limbers, an
occasional squealing mule, constant shouting, and a frequent
German shell-burst. The where no less than the how of sleep
baffled me quite, although most of my neighbours solved it. Any
shell-hole or scraping in a bank was a couch, whatever attitude of
recumbancy it imposed. I tried one such scrape for a time; it
was too short and narrow to give even relaxation of muscles:
I lay wondering whether a shell, a limber, a mule or man—dead
or alive—would fall on me. Some men seeking "a better 'ole"
in the dark, and not seeing that mine was fully occupied, tried it.
Two men dodging a startled mule team stepped, one on my wind
and one just not on my face. After that I sat down in the open
and longed for day. One of our Sapper officers slept beside a
several-days-old corpse without noticing any unpleasantness. All
about us the air was heavy with the reek of the dead in Mametz
Wood.

In the morning the Brigade transport, which had followed us,
was sent away, but Yates chose to keep ours where it was. Throughout the day batteries rolled into the Happy Valley, the prosaic
called it the Valley of Death, east of Mametz Wood, and on to the
slight rise of Caterpillar Wood until these sites were stiff not

with guns but with batteries. "The shelling on both sides is tremendous," Higginson wrote to Blair, "but nobody worries. Whole brigades sit down *en masse* in a field, and we bivouac in close order every night. The whole show is in the open, guns and all. Think of us, in your nice white bed with beautiful Sisters floating round. I sleep in my burberry, and we are down to bully, biscuits, etc." Rain came on in the afternoon.

July 17*th*.—The rain and the noise lasted all night. H.Q., which alone had any shelter, occupied a warren of joined-up shell-holes roofed with shell-punctured iron sheets, through which the rain dripped or streamed to the sodden ground on which we sat or lay. The sun came with day. Ground and wet clothing dried. Orders and counter-orders arrived. There was nothing to do but watch the guns beside us in action and the enemy's counter-battery. Again and again the gunners were driven to cover, and guns were disabled; once the tyre of a wheel went spinning 20 or 30 feet into the air. The German gunners could not have shot better over open sights. There was a story next day of an observer with signalling gear having been found up a tree in Bazentin Wood. The overs were few, but they caused us some casualties. Our total so far was 5 killed and 21 wounded; 2 or 3 of the latter were bromine gas cases. In the afternoon G.1 came among us, charged with another official platitude, "The morale of the Division is unimpaired": a sure index of failure and loss.

The Division was relieving the 21st Division north of Bazentin-le-Petit; it had already relieved the 7th in the village Cemetery. At midnight the Battalion moved through a light barrage of explosive and bromine shells to relieve the 4th King's between the Cemetery and the Martinpuich road. A corporal had been sent to guide D Company to the Cemetery. "The blighter lost his way," says the C.S.M., "and my language quite shocked such a hardened sinner as von R. Graves." There were a few casualties *July* 18*th*—going up. The night was noisy and wet, the morning quiet and fine. An appalling lot of our dead strewed the easy rise of the High Wood–Martinpuich glacis. Towards midday a gunner subaltern galloped up a gun-team, hooked in an abandoned German gun which no infantry seemed to lay claim to, and galloped away with it. His men, who had never been so near the front, looked as if they thought the earth would open and

swallow them. For four hours of the afternoon our position was
under a bombardment that caused losses in which H.Q. Details
shared largely. One of the first to be wounded was a sergeant.
I turned at the sound of a coming shell and saw it burst. Almost
at the same moment he shouted, "I'm hit," in a joyful tone, flung
off his equipment, and, grinning, came to me for his "ticket to
Blighty, sir." It didn't occur to him to have the wound in his
back looked at. We had 5 killed and 32 wounded during the day.
Dinner was prepared for the C.O. in a deep cemented "dug-out"
the servants discovered. Our stomachs turned at food which had
been left unfinished before search showed that the floor was
removable ; it was the lid of a cesspool. After dark the Battalion
side-stepped to the right. 'Hordes of rats came over D Company's
ground. They made a noise like wind through corn. It was
uncanny.'

July 19th.—There was rain most of the night. For the first time
since the night of the 13th I slept for more than an occasional
snatch of a few minutes : had a real good sleep, swathed in silk
brocade curtains. Two large and very substantially built dug-outs
had been found in an Engineers yard. They were furnished with
the spoil of some opulent house. All the work in this German
yard was thorough, it had the solidity and finish of permanent
work. There was reinforced glass in the workshop windows, and
in the frames and hot-house of a well-cultivated kitchen garden
the like of which I never saw anywhere else in France. The day
was fine. There was more activity in the air than usual. We
watched the superiority of our airmen with much satisfaction, for
the Germans had been having the best of it of late. The Battalion
had a quiet, easeful day after several days of physical discomfort
and broken sleep, of the exhaustion of mere drawn-out waiting,
of being amid almost incessant noise, and of suffering appreciable
losses. In all, 10 had been killed and 53 wounded so far.

An early morning operation to-morrow is substituted for
yesterday's cancelled night operation against High Wood. It
looks like "the goods" this time. High Wood is about a mile
east and north of Bazentin-le-Petit, at the waist of a tactically
important ridge which it would be good to bestride. The Wood
is roughly diamond-shaped with the angles to the cardinal points.
Its western angle and the adjoining westerly, and slightly higher,

ground was organized as a strong-point to which the partly sunken road to Flers, bounding the north-west side of the Wood, gave the Germans their simplest access. An incomplete trench ran through the Wood from the middle of the north-east side to the Point; it was part of the Delville ("Devil's") Wood–High Wood–Martinpuich Switch. The 800-yard south-west face of the Wood was to be attacked by the 5th Scottish Rifles and The Cameronians, the latter taking on the strong-point. The 20th Royal Fusiliers were to support the attack, follow the 5th S.R., and, pivoting on their own left, mop up the Wood from east to west. The 11th Field Company R.E. was to be at hand for the making of strong-points at the east, north, and west angles. Our approaches are over open ground that rises, in two long shallow billows, to about 60 feet above the Longueval–Contalmaison road. The 7th Division, on the right, and the 5th beyond it, would attack Black Road and Wood Lane at the same time. These were entrenched cart-tracks running from the southern and eastern corners of High Wood to Longueval. The 2nd Worcesters were to cover the left of the Brigade's assembly, but once the advance began the left flank would be open. Such in barest outline was the problem, and the scheme of a Corps operation.

By midnight the units of the Brigade were moving to their assembly *July 20th*—positions. The Battalion was relieved amid confusion, and held in reserve among the shell-holes between the Longueval–Contalmaison road and Flat Iron Copse. Any exit from the Happy Valley was usually a busy traffic route, so our position was an obvious barrage area. All night the Germans dropped krumps about it. Our massed artillery was behind us; H.Q. and its Details were under the muzzles of two batteries. In the dark hours guns fired. Not even youth could sleep; from zero, 3.30, for what seemed a long time we had to shout to be heard. For hour after hour of daylight guns fired. The krumping of the area increased, but the Companies suffered little. That was largely because so many men were detached for Brigade carrying-duty between the dumps at Montauban and the front. Traffic, perhaps fortunately, was nearly all through Montauban. During these hours little happened to interest the rest of us. A man was walking along the Contalmaison road when a 5·9 burst beside him; out of the smoke and dust he was flung in a series of somersaults, just like a rabbit shot when at full stretch : like the shot rabbit he lay all of a limp heap. Another 5·9 tossed D Company's officers, sending Nigel Parry to hospital to lose an eye. They moved. About 10 o'clock there was more commotion among them after a fresh burst. When Barkie detached himself Mann said, "He's coming for you, Doctor." We laughed quietly at the quaintness of his stooping gait, straddling as he ran ; it was the agile man's usual run over shell-pocked ground under fire. Graves had a bad chest wound of the kind that few recover from. And so, while we just waited on events and orders, the hours sped.

The events on which our orders would depend were taking place about a mile, as the crow flies, to our right front, on top of the slope that rose before us. We could not see anything of them, and no news or rumour came our way ; but without a knowledge of these events an account of our later concerns would be meaningless. When the attacking troops were moving in artillery formation from their assembly position to their line of deployment the German barrage fell on the middle of the column. The casualties were mostly among the 20th R.F.—two score or so of whom thereupon fell back to the cover of the roadside ditch—and the Sappers. On the right : as the Wood was approached the German barrage was nasty but there was no rifle or machine-gun fire. Proceedings, however, became confused, the assault troops and their supports got all mixed up, and thus 5th S.R and 20th R.F. pushed through to the other side of the Wood ; any who went beyond it were fired on from farther forward, where there was a strip of trees. About a dozen Germans had been captured in an abandoned gun-emplacement : others had been seen bolting back to a trench, the Switch, outside the Wood. Parties of both battalions began to dig along the boundary hedge on the far side. There was scarcely any firing then : the Gordons, on the right, were moving about in the open. After it became light, however, a lot of rifle and machine-gun fire developed, inflicting loss. On the left : The Cameronians right half-battalion came under small-arms fire, but it pushed through to its objective, the far side, without much loss. The left half-battalion was held up by heavy small-arms fire from the edge of the Wood, some riflemen were up trees, and by machine-guns farther to the left. Trench-mortars were sent for to cope with the machine-guns, and they did good work in knocking them out. Upwards of two hours elapsed before The Cameronians, with R.F. co-operation, drove the Germans from their strong-point. Dead and wounded of both these battalions lay in the Flers road. It is doubtful if the strong-point was actually occupied, owing to the fire poured into it from farther west, but The Cameronians and the Germans denied it to each other. The north of the Wood was still in enemy possession, so the Acting O.C. Cameronians asked for reinforcements. By that time men of all three battalions were mixed in the middle of the Wood. German shelling, which had been on its approaches, had shortened on to it; and our guns were firing a lot of shorts into it. As the morning advanced German small-arms fire from three directions became more active. There was a wide drive the Germans had used for vehicles, that ran from side to side east of the middle of the Wood; it was littered with bodies; some of them were from an earlier attack (that by the 2nd Queen's). Anyone entering that drive was fired on. Casualties mounted up everywhere: officers became fewer; men fell back singly and in small parties to the lee side. 'From quite early the unfortunate R.F. men seemed to be getting killed all over the place to no purpose. The whole operation had been conducted in confusion almost from the start, and for want of superior direction it became a shambles.' (The foregoing paragraph has been written from statements by Royal Fusiliers, Cameronians, and Scottish Riflemen.)

The C.O. became impatient in the absence of news, so he sent Conning and Sergeant Roderick forward to learn what had happened. Soon afterwards, getting on for 9 o'clock, he had a message from Brigade saying that nothing [recent] of the situation was known there, asking if he knew anything, and suggesting that he send to find out. About an hour later the O.C. 20th R.F. was seen coming along the road, wounded. He was intercepted. After summarizing the situation he added, in a torrent of ejaculations, that nothing was being done; everything was chaotic; no one was in command; not a reply to a message, not an order, had been received from Brigade. When the C.O. had recovered his breath he suggested to Colonel Bennett to call at Brigade before going to the Dressing-station: but this he did not do.

The passing of messages, assuming they were sent, between

front and rear was always a difficulty, and a vexation at both ends.
Before the action Radford had been asked for by Brigade to be
employed as Forward Liaison Officer. He was detailed with some
signallers to use Bazentin-le-Petit Windmill, 200 yards east of the
Cemetery, as the forward post of a relay system. The Windmill
had been the target of our artillery, then of the enemy's, according
as the Germans and then we occupied it. It had been mostly
destroyed during the week. Being near the village and the
Longueval–Bazentin road it was bombarded at every period of
enemy activity. 'At [1] the beginning of the morning attack the
enemy barrage cut the wires. The barrage smoke made lamp
signalling impossible, even if adequate preparations had been made
for it. The wireless set provided was for transmission only, so it
was not known if messages were being received. The supply of
runners was soon exhausted and was not replaced. At noon I
went to Brigade to report the futility of it all.' Brigade was in
poor quarters, a thinly roofed trench in the south-east bight of
Mametz Wood, nearly two miles from High Wood, although
deep and roomy dug-outs made for a German division were in
Bazentin-le-Petit within a few yards of screened view-points from
which the face of High Wood and the Flers road could be seen.
Advanced Brigade, so-called, in the quarry by the Cemetery
roadside, was a mere relay post. This remoteness was laid down
in a General Routine Order issued because of casualties earlier in
the War. The Order was circumvented by Brigadiers who knew
when and how to do it, but times without number it warranted the
utter negation of Command when prompt and authoritative
decision was needed, especially if more than one unit was concerned.
Prompt decision and action were essential this day, 'yet none of
our Brigade Staff came within hundreds of yards of its dissolving
units.' The cost in all the lower ranks of preserving some Generals
of brigade and division, and some members of their Staffs, is
beyond reckoning, but must be stupendous.

About 11 o'clock the situation in front changed suddenly. A
confused mob of all units fell back on the southern side and made
for the open. The Second-in-Command of the 5th S.R. was one
of the officers and N.C.Os. who rallied them; he met them as he
was coming over from Advanced Brigade, having been sent for

[1] Radford.

when his C.O. was wounded early in the morning. A line was
re-formed upwards of 200 yards from the southern corner. The
Germans had counter-attacked and recovered their western strong-
point, but they did not penetrate the Wood elsewhere, or to any
depth there. Nothing was known about it half an hour later to
a R.F. party whom one of their officers found on the north-east
side, to the left of the fatal drive, and recalled. The newly-come
O.C. 5th S.R. was killed when he was reconnoitring with a view
to recovering abandoned ground. (This paragraph is from R.F.
and Scottish sources.)

An Order to complete the capture of High Wood was delivered
at H.Q., also about 11 o'clock. Said to have been issued by
Division at 8 o'clock, it was seemingly a compliance with the
Cameronian early morning call for reinforcement. Company
Commanders were summoned to H.Q. for orders and instructions.
Conning and Sergeant Roderick arrived with them to help at
the talk; they had little to tell except of confusion, and that no
one could say much about the situation. The Wood was to be
mopped up from east to west. Dispositions were simple: the
C.O. added that no obstacle was to cause delay.

A large part of the Battalion was still on fatigue. Little time was
needed to fall-in the small body that remained. The perfect
steadiness with which the weak Companies formed up on the
shelled road was a stirring sight. They marched off in column of
platoons in fours, later in file, at 100 yards interval. Moody led
D Company, followed by B, C, and A. 'The [1] day was bright,
the sun was high, and I was pleased to be moving. Colonel
Crawshay and Mr. Mann stood on the left of the road (near the
Blasted Tree) and cheered our happy band of about eight men,
which comprised the whole of No. 8 Platoon.' Of the full mile
to be covered more than half was in a howitzer barrage line.
Good though the shooting was it caused neither check nor disorder. Two or three shocked men dropped out: a shell bursting
on a section ended it: casualties, however, still were remarkably
few. Near Crucifix Corner, before we turned left off the
Longueval–Bazentin road, the jovial R.C. Chaplain, McShane,
chaffed and cheered us. He had assumed virtual command of the
R.F. fainéants there. As the Wood was approached the Intelligence

---

[1] Roderick.

Officer of the 5th S.R., being carried down wounded, was met and questioned, but still the enemy's dispositions remained a mystery to us. Elements of the entire Brigade were seen lying mingled half-way along the south-west side. Part of A and B Companies' carrying-parties were there; they rejoined their Companies. A feeble 5th S.R. company in the eastern angle was the only organized body any of us saw. Moody and two of his subalterns went into the Wood at once to reconnoitre. They had gone beyond where some 20th R.Fs. were, upwards of 200 yards, and learned very little, when Moody was hit in the foot and Barkworth through the cheek. Meanwhile D Company, waiting for the others to come up, was sheltering from machine-gun fire from its near front, and long-range fire from its right or right rear. D, B, and C were deploying along the south-east side of the Wood, with two platoons of A in close support. They were in three columns of three lines each. 'Waiting [1] to attack is like what waiting for the hangman to come and do his job must be. Everyone is eager to get going, one way or the other, for the uncertainty of being launched into eternity or of coming back in pieces is not comforting in these tense moments, but once the button is pressed and the machinery set working all such thoughts are dispelled.' By 2 o'clock all were ready. Few of us can credit the flight of three hours since the first stirring of this adventure.

'It [2] was the quietest part of the day in my corner of the Wood when I heard movement behind me, and saw Moody forming up his Company. These Welch Fusiliers were a magnificent sight. They were very weak, their platoons were only the size of sections, but they were out for business. This small controlled force was a most effective contrast to the large loose mass that had been herded into the Wood in the morning, when one attacking battalion and one in support, not mixed with it, would have been ample. Immediately after the Welch Fusiliers had all formed up (their C.O. ordered the advance). They were obviously out for blood, and were most heartening. The platoon sergeant [3] of their right platoon was shepherding his men like a mother, picking up spades, ammunition and anything likely to be useful.'

The going was not bad just at the start; but the luxuriant July

[1] Roderick.   [2] Coltart.
[3] Sergeant '200 J. Jones: he became Quartermaster in after-years.

foliage on the low-hanging and broken branches, and fallen beech trees,—the result of ten days' shelling—made keeping any sort of alignment or direction more and more difficult.

'Beyond [1] the 20th R.F. Details was Sergeant Hinder and his Vickers gun. He was one of ours who, along with his team, had been transferred to the Machine Gun Corps. I was going on by myself when I came on him. He said, "For God's sake, don't go on, the place is full of Gerries."' Roderick, however, went on ahead of his Company, B, until he arrived on a road outside the Wood without seeing a German. 'After looking north I turned south and saw a machine-gun in a T-sap across the road. It let me have a burst, two bullets in the forearm and pieces in the thigh: I found afterwards that a bullet had broken up on the Verey pistol in my pocket. Naturally I made back for the Wood. The Battalion had been held up and was advancing again, but my chapter of the War in France was ended.'

A machine-gun which D Company had been feeling since their arrival gave a lot of trouble. They lost another officer, Crockett, and were held up. The gun was spotted near the middle of the north side, in a trench without the Wood. Sergeant '200 Jones turned Corporal Shearsby's section of his platoon half-right. 'They silenced it'—is all I have been able to learn of the incident. The Company barged forward again in rushes from cover to cover such as tree-trunks and shell-holes. In the middle of the Wood the artillery of both sides had to be faced, for the Germans were putting shells into it and our guns were still firing short. Small-arms fire was more and more met as the Companies advanced. A's platoons had closed up on B. C Company, on the left, had passed parties of the other battalions. All were converging on the western corner whence a deadly fire came, but they thrust forward without counting the cost. D Company's last officer fell wounded in a bit of trench near the far side of the Wood. He [2] saw his men 'pass on in a hopeless mix-up, bombing and firing at very close range.' The C.O., standing near H.Q. at the southern corner, saw a lot of Germans bolt from the Wood to the open beyond the Flers road. Not long afterwards a message informed him that the Wood had been captured. '200 Jones, however, reported that the right of D Company was held up 80 yards short of their objective,

[1] Roderick.   [2] Roberts.

and that they were too few to push forward farther against the
volume of fire coming from their front. He was told to dig-in:
that was as far as his platoon got. The C.O. made a short tour
of inspection, and sent Higginson up to order the Companies to
make the western corner secure. The shelling had ceased by then.

Soon after the C.O. launched the attack a Brigade Order
arrived appointing him "O.C. High Wood." The other units
were thereupon told of the attack in progress, and the Trench
Mortar Battery was called on to co-operate—it did not, however,
fire during the operation, or any more that day; the subsequent
co-operation of all units in consolidating was detailed: "everybody
must work at high pressure." Until the arrival of an amending
Order the 20th R.F. were not included in his authority. In the
interval the officer on whom their command had devolved entrenched himself in the Army List. "I am sainior to Major
Cra'shay," he reiterated, and sat tight; and he let his men at
Crucifix Corner sit tight.

When approximate casualty reports were made up it was
found that 150 of all ranks of the small number in action had been
killed or wounded. Every officer who took part in the attack
was a casualty. Heastey, the last of the likeable gallant trio of
youngsters who joined from Sandhurst in June, was killed: at
night his platoon carried him back two miles for burial. Bowles,
who came home from Argentina to serve, was brought out smiling,
dying. As O.C. High Wood the C.O. was dismayed on learning
that the other units were in no better case than we. The
Cameronians had lost their Adjutant, all four company commanders and eight other officers, and a great many rank and file.
The 5th S.R. had only one officer left. The R.F. were disorganized; their losses were nearly two-thirds of the strength with
which they began the day. Few Engineers were left; they had
no wire and scarcely any other stores. The bulk of the men were
enlisted "for the duration," or were Territorials; being without
leaders they were a difficult lot to get started on work. In these
circumstances Brigade was advised that fresh troops should relieve
those on the ground if the holding of the Wood was to be reasonably
assured.

Roberts mentions 'a flare-up like a counter-attack by the
Germans' on their lost strong-point about 3 o'clock. Some

Cameronians joined in the affray, during which a small party of Germans ran from among the trees on the left and escaped into the Flers road. Of the 5 he saw, one, in passing, had a shot at him as he lay. Nothing of the affair was seen by the right of his Company. It is not unlikely that it arose from Germans who had been cut off making a dash for their own side. Apart from that the Wood was a peaceful spot for a couple of hours, cool to walk in on a rather airless afternoon. One could step clear of its north-eastern side with impunity, and at the north end of the beech hedge bounding the Flers road one could stand in gaps apparently unseen, certainly not fired at. But from Delville Wood the enemy kept up a dropping long-range machine-gun fire on the south-east side and southern corner. Exposure near the western corner was apt to draw fire from across the Flers road : perhaps because there was no officer among them earlier our men were not dug into effective possession there. Meanwhile all our working-parties and the Sapping Platoon had rejoined, providing a much-needed reinforcement, and an officer became available for each Company. Chaos had been lessened, and a start was being made with work.

Some time about 5 o'clock the original defence scheme was superseded by an Order to dig and wire a trench running diagonally across the Wood to face the German Switch. The Order to the Battalion to complete the capture of the Wood had been issued by Division, or higher authority, before the successful German counter-attack was made. We never heard what was known behind of the situation when this latest Order was issued. The new line simplified the work to be done, but we on the spot were concerned at handing back to the enemy his strong-point at the western angle and the Flers road that gave entry to it, the only parts of the Wood by which he seemed to set much store. An hour or more later the G.S.O.2 came to H.Q. and explained that the reduction of the ground to be held was because of the machine-guns across the Flers road. To us it seemed that an extravagance of effort had been asked for in ordering, twice, the assault and capture of a position it was imprudent to hold or deny to the enemy. Had not the whereabout and strength of that armament been known since the disaster to the 100th and 98th Brigades a week earlier? Yet an effectual means of dealing with these machine-guns had no place in the scheme of either of the day's attacks.

Nothing, however, was so maddening as his parting remark, " the General has the situation in hand"—spoken with a straight face. The situation never was grasped. Fumbling fingers far away had trifled with opportunity for hours ; and days ago a hopeful infantry advance was stopped that cavalry might be brought up. Now, before our Companies were withdrawn, all was quiet across the Flers road. A R.F. sergeant-major, Armour (of The Cameronians), entered the road, although our men protested that he would draw fire, and walked leisurely round the corner without being fired at.

A fresh start was made. The digging and manning of the new line was divided between D Company, to which Conning was transferred, and B, Coster's—about 70 all told, on the right, and two R.F. companies, actually elements of all their companies, on the left. Sergeant '10 Jones's attenuated platoon occupied a bit of the Switch as our covering-party. There was a machine-gun where the two battalions joined and one on each flank. A. Company, Higginson's, and C, having Moulsdale Williams in temporary command, were withdrawn to support; H.Q. and they occupied and improved 150 yards of Black Road. The 2nd Gordons continued this line to the right. Elements of the rest of the Brigade still lay mingled along the south-west of the Wood; the 5th S.R. company was in the eastern corner; and there were overlooked oddments inside, but that detail was learned later.

The day had been warm and still with a slight haze, the evening was serene. The escorts of our Air observers and the German fliers met over the Wood and regaled us with some great art as they manœuvred and fought. The trees masked much of it from us, but our 1st Battalion at Bazentin-le-Grand saw it all. About 8 of our slow planes were patrolling, or spotting for guns, when two Fokkers appeared. One of them marked down a spotter, and had driven it almost to the ground when one of the escort came to its help, and the Fokker fled. A few minutes later a Fokker pounced on another of ours, like a hawk on a bird ; the bird, turning and twisting to escape, was being forced always farther down. Our plane was down to about 300 feet when one of the escort rushed to its rescue in a swoop of about 3000 feet. The Fokker gave up its quarry—which went off groggily,—swerved and tried to mount, but our fighter was too quick for it. A Lewis gun rapped out short, sharp bursts. Then the Fokker came evenly over us, at only 300 feet, with seemingly splendid bravado, but it was out of control: the pilot had been hit. Our fighter left it to its fate. As it glided slowly over Bazentin Cemetery the troops there fired at it: when above Bazentin-le-Petit Wood it crashed and burst into flames, and a great cheer went up behind. It was a splendid fight, both sides. Guns and all stopped while everyone stood agape.

Shelling by the Germans had begun again before this; intermittent for a time, it became continuous although not at all heavy, and our answering guns fired short so often. A good deal of movement was seen on the right front beyond the Flers road; if the information about it that was sent back reached the artillery no action was taken. Between 7 and 8 o'clock the Sapper officer inspected the new line. He reported to the C.O. that D and B Companies had dug a good trench, but that the R.F. had made very uneven progress; in parts they were down only 6 inches and there was barely cover anywhere. Manual labour was distasteful to them, and was not seriously enforced, for they were officered from their own ranks. The trench did not then follow the line of one dug later at more leisure; it began on the north-east side and ran diagonally across the Wood; near its middle a short piece of earlier, probably German, trench was used.

That the enemy had taken heart of grace, and was closing on the dearly bought ground that had been handed back to him, was apparent after sunset. What looked like a ration-party came up in the direction of the strong-point. Soon afterwards a solitary German strolled across the open towards D Company's right flank. Someone shot him, unaware that others hoped to take him for what he might tell. By this time any detected movement by our covering-party drew such accurate small-arms fire from the west that they were glued to the ground. Since that fire increased until it became continuous the party rejoined its Company when the light faded among the trees. The small-arms fire ceased after that, and there was a short time of quiet. Next, the Germans started a heavy creeping barrage eastwards through the Wood. It stopped short of the trench and lifted on to the communications.[1] The R.F. were feeling comforted at the lifting of the guns when a mixed

[1] Our 1st Battalion, who were about to be relieved when the German guns opened, stood fast until things were quiet again.

party of their men, Cameronians and 5th S.R., about 20 altogether, drifted in from the front, past the centre machine-gun, shouting excitedly, "He's coming over." They were not demoralized, just leaderless. A R.F. officer had no difficulty in stopping them and bringing them back. He was shot just after doing so. The R.Fs. belonged to some posts which had been overlooked. Their H.Q. promptly informed the C.O. that their line, or outpost line, had been rushed and that an attack was developing. It was then about 9 o'clock.

No connected account of the bush-mêlée in which D and B Companies became involved was ever given me, or any real detail of what happened to B, by those who could have told most. Statements made then, and much later, agree that not a few of them failed to connect the sudden coming of loose bodies of Germans on to their front with an intended attack, consequently it had much of the advantage of surprise. 'A [1] strong body of Germans appeared advancing without formation or apparent leadership towards D Company's right. (They came through the Wood from the direction of the Flers road.) It looked as if they were going to give themselves up when they started firing, and we replied. Sergeant Hinder, who was on the Company's flank, ran forward, clear of the Wood, with his machine-gun to try to enfilade them; the wonder is he wasn't killed or captured. Feeling we were outnumbered I ordered the men with me to retire to the edge of the Wood. I had exhausted my own bombs, to good effect I think, when I had to jump quick and beat it as a German aimed at me point-blank and fired.' One of our wounded, whether of B or D cannot be learned, told a R.F. stretcher-bearer who dressed him that a party of Germans came over with the seeming intention of surrendering, but on getting within bombing distance they began to sling bombs which they had been carrying hung behind them. 'The Welch quickly stopped them' can refer only to a temporary check. No one knew what was happening beyond a very limited circle of himself. Some men lost their heads and fell back, and could not be recalled by their N.C.Os. That night Conning told how he had tried to pivot his broken Company and maintain a fighting front. Of B Company, it was said at the time that rifle-fire at close range was opened on them, and the attackers closed

[1] Powell.

Q

quickly to bombing range, and that they had to fight on front
and rear. C.S.M. Miners, a most dutiful soldier, and half the
remnant of the Company became casualties. Coster, a stout,
level-headed officer, got away with the residue when they were
being rolled up. The right of the R.Fs. 'heard the Germans
coming through the Wood from a north-westerly direction, but
none were seen.' 'The men were ordered to fire in the direction
of the sounds, and fire was opened among the trees.' 'The Vickers
gun in the centre was trained on the direction of the sounds, but
it did not fire, it could not do so for fear of hitting the Welch.'
Singly and in twos and threes men of ours came back, clear of the
Wood behind the strong-point at the eastern angle, and a machine-
gun took position there. In the dim light that blurred their forms
they were looked on with suspicion when first they were seen,
and were not being fired on from Wood Lane or the Switch, but
the support Companies were steady enough not to fire. There
came to be such a jumble at the edge of the Wood that it was not
easy to sort out the two Companies again. Nothing was heard by
the C.O. from Conning or Coster, or of them, until they had time
to report in person at the end of the affair.

The Germans had reoccupied the Wood up to the Switch;
then they made a left-hand drive of the ground in front of it, and
attacked our part of the Brigade line. By 10 o'clock they had
mopped up a dozen unwounded prisoners of the Brigade. The
last to be taken, the witness to these details, was a 5th S.R. lance-
corporal who had spent the whole day lying among dead and
severely wounded men in a 'gun-pit' beside the traffic gap on
the north-east side. His companions were mostly victims of the
machine-gun that fired through the gap. From daylight, for hours,
men and groups who entered the ride along which it fired had
been shot down.

Very soon after all was over a fresh Engineer company arrived
with wire and other stores that had been wanting since morning;
and the Divisional Labour Battalion came to dig a communication
trench. But an inept Command had let the unforgiving hours go
by, bearing opportunity with them. When O.C. Labour heard
of the altered situation he marched his battalion down again,
although the need for a communication trench was greater than
when he was sent up. The only fresh troops who might have

been used for action were our ration-party under R.Q.M.S. Boreham, and 98 drafts he had brought up; they were all kept as a reinforcement. It was not understood when renewed action was under consideration that the R.F. part of the line was intact until a subordinate officer withdrew his men on hearing that the Labour lot had arrived. Anyhow, a night attack on an unlocated enemy in a wood was not undertaken. And at 10 o'clock the Germans began a bombardment so merciless that any attempted operation would have been vain. 'They plastered the Wood with heavies, machine-guns, and what appeared to be most of the guns on the Somme. This lasted for an hour or more.'

The hours of darkness were a time of strained suspense. The experiences of seven such days and nights as had been ours, and the chagrin at the end of them, made nerves susceptible to trivial impressions. A large shell coming from the right rear at intervals and bursting beside the right of the Battalion was, in fact, the only disturbance, but it caused intense exasperation because it looked as if one of our own guns was firing short. We learned two days later that it came from a German enfilade gun at Combles. At *July 21st*—1.30 two companies of the 1st Queen's and one of the 16th K.R.R.C. appeared unexpectedly and announced our relief. To change over was an affair of minutes. The difficulty of communicating with Brigade continued to the end. Battalion runners had been very unlucky in the barrage: as we went out the last of them to be sent, a corporal of the Signals, was found at the side of a track, wounded in both legs. When we passed through the Happy Valley it was quite silent for the first time since our coming a week ago.

Arrived at our bivouac on the south-east of Mametz Wood, some, even of the hard-bitten, showed signs of the strain through which they had passed now there was no more need to key themselves up. Everyone lay down where he found himself and slept, though the imaginative shouted, cried horrors, and gesticulated in their sleep.

The morning and early afternoon were spent in peace and quiet, cleaning up, and resting in the warm sunshine. Our casualties yesterday were 2 officers and 29 other ranks killed, 9 officers and 180 other ranks wounded, 29 other ranks missing. Many of the missing were of B Company, the result of the German counter-

attack at dark. D Company began the day with 4 officers and
101 other ranks, there were 43 other ranks on relief. One of
those wounded at night escaped capture, and crawled out two days
later; he wrote from hospital that the Germans behaved well in
collecting the wounded. A German N.C.O. was in charge of the
left-hand mop-up. He marched the unwounded prisoners of the
Brigade to the rear. About two miles back he halted them at a
canteen, went in and bought a box of cigarettes and a bottle of
brandy; each prisoner was given six or seven cigarettes and a
pull at the bottle.

Our disappointment was great that what had been gained so
dearly had been lost so supinely. Weakness behind us had ruled
the day, but our Companies ought not to have been deceived by the
appearance of the oncoming Germans at dusk. Many of us had
never seen Germans attacking; those who had seen them had
forgotten that they ambled forward in a purposeless-like way, in
a very loose line however open the ground; and it was not known,
or forgotten, that the German stick-bomb was carried hooked to
the back of the belt. The surprise apart, "duration" men felt
themselves helpless without bombs to reply to bombs; even the
Old Army's ready dependence on the rifle had yielded to the cult
of the bomb, and few of our men had one left since the afternoon.

About 3 o'clock the Battalion and its Transport marched to
Buire. We passed the 51st Division going up: they were a fine
body of men, although the kilt is a costume that flatters. Our
Division was coming out. By holding the south-east of the Wood
the nett gain of its costly operations was the High Wood approach,
from which Corps or Army withdrew the 7th Division eight days
ago to give the cavalry a run.

July 23rd.—A Divisional Order pats its own back enthusiastically.
The full flavour of it is only for those who know that an acrimonious
quarrel rages between Division and Corps. Each blames the other
for the recent mismanagement. The affair has gone to Army.

July 24th.—Corps, now the 5th, 51st, and 19th Divisions, is said
to have failed again dismally against the Delville–High Wood
Switch.—Our camp is a pleasant, restful place by a musical stream
with the tones of a rocky bottom, and birches overhanging its
steep verdure-clad banks. The excitable have ceased to call out
in their sleep.

July 25th.—At Corbie : a large party of newly captured Germans, a fine body of men, marched by in sullen pride. The church is *July 27th*—heavy, cold, uninspiring. Albert, the Encre of Agincourt days, is a very ordinary little industrial town : if the Cathedral had been destroyed nothing of value would have been lost.

July 28th.—Inspected by the Brigadier. We looked quite passable : if only we were so in fact. How superficial and farcical such inspections are !

This was the hardest-worked rest I remember. The quality of the drafts made those of us who were used to a different personnel fearful of the immediate future, so every working hour was given to trying to get them into some sort of shape. We made up with 540 of all ranks. Whether Volunteers, Derbyites or Conscripts, the average physique was good enough, but the total included an astonishing number of men whose narrow or misshapen chests, and other deformities or defects, unfitted them to stay the more exacting requirements of service in the field. Permission to send back a very few was accompanied by a peremptory intimation that a complaint of any future draft passed by the Base would not be listened to. Route-marching, not routine tours of trench duty, made recurring temporary casualties of these men. The truly disquieting fact about the drafts was that a large number had been attested only six weeks before they came to us, so unready had the War Office been to replace losses properly. What was called training hardly amounted to a "lick and a promise," it did not fit the men to take part in any operation. They had fired only five rounds of ball cartridge ; many of them did not know how to load and unload a rifle, to fix and unfix a bayonet. Hitherto training in the Battalion had been the pursuit of specialists or a formality, now it was a matter of H.Q. anxiety and arduous company detail. Men recruited and trained for the Cheshires, Shropshires, and South Wales Borderers arrived resentful of their transfer and unwanted by us. There was a like mix-up in the other battalions of the Brigade. At the time we thought it was owing to confusion at the Base, and incompetence beyond understanding. A rumour, which time proved to be true, was dismissed as a silly joke. Some hairy-eared theorist, in whom the new War Lord trusted, had told him that the way to win was to destroy the Regiment, the immemorial foundation of armies, and nationalize the Army. Roger Poore, who came to us the following year, was commanding a second-line draft-finding unit at home. He told how, in answer to questions at an inspection, he gave his reasons for certain of his methods of training. At a point of his tour the inspector said, "I suppose this is another piece of your esprit de corps. Well, there's to be no more of it." When a chance offered the Shropshires were bartered for half their number of R.W.F. from a neighbouring division. As drafts came in we became less English and more Welsh. One draft was purely Welsh from North Wales, ordinarily the leanest recruiting district in the country; the men were mostly clerks, small tradesmen and assistants, farmhands, schoolmasters and such like. The worst element of all had been combed out of our Garrison Battalion in Egypt. These men paraded protesting, one after another, their unfitness for anything but garrison duty. In general fitness they were well up to the average of the other drafts. Throughout the War it was characteristic of men transferred from category units and subsidiary services to resent re-posting to front-line service, and to scheme to get away from it. I noted only two such re-postings who showed enough keenness to earn promotion. An indication of the Home organization was that the drafts said the food was better than in the camps at home. Yet we had been having tinned food almost entirely since they joined us, and only travelling cookers in which to prepare it.

July 29th.—Something of the French was to be seen at Bray. Their transport is a mixed lot of Army and civilian vehicles. It looks simple compared with ours, but very practical—down to the bits of string with which harness is held together. They work their German prisoners mighty close to the shells. The German artillery shooting at the observation post in the church steeple was good enough to flush the French observers. Just behind the village the corn harvest was being hastened in.

July 31st.—On a route-march of 6 miles no one fell out!—When the death of Bowles and of Graves was reported through the Field Ambulance, nine days ago, the customary letters were written to their kin. Now Graves writes to the C.O. that the shock of learning how much he is esteemed has recalled him from the grave, and that he has decided to live for the sake of those whose warm feelings he has misunderstood.

August 1st.—In Amiens: a dusty drive with a merry party: a day off for the C.O., who has got whiter about the gills with the coming of each draft. Amiens must be the cheeriest provincial town in France: it is stiff with Lines of Communication limpets, with officers who have been in the soup and are for it again, with French troops, and with perfumed "refugees" robed with disarming modesty. It is good to see that the ancient rue des Corps nues sans Testes and the rue des Trois-Cailloux have not been renamed after some modern politician or writer of a day. We lunched at the Hôtel du Rhin, where Gibbs, Thomas, and Co., the official journalists attached to G.H.Q., live in state. It was diverting to contrast the supercilious indifference with which they jostled past the mere front-line officer, and frowned on his unwitting approach to their reserved tables, with their alert deference when a Red-tab entered the room. After Drinkwater had led the way into every bar in or off the rue des Trois-Cailloux, and I had bought some things for the Mess, he said there would "be no damned shopping next time" he came to Amiens. I did not know until later that "Drinkwater" was a nickname, I thought it a coincidence. Dinner at "The Godbert" was good, even at the money, and decorous, although Colonel P., lamenting, after the sweet, that he had not had any dressed lobster, did get down on all-fours to stalk an unwatched dish on another table; and he devoured it with help.

We must have owed the day's outing to some legerdemain by Yates's staff. The O.C. Field Ambulance had to refuse the use of a car unless we found the petrol. The time is supposedly past when a motor-transport man scoops a hole in the ground and fills it with petrol every time he wants to cook a stew, or wash a shirt, or heat shaving water. Petrol is rationed, and car journeys are logged. Since there is no aerodrome near to spare a few tins, Yates was consulted; as usual he said, "It can't be done." Next morning, however, he mentioned, in the course of his official talk after returning from Refilling Point, that "there are two tins of petrol round at my place." In time, as scraps of talk were pieced together, it was learned that the Field Ambulance Quartermaster counted on the roadside the twenty tins of petrol he had indented for; turning about to check his count he made the number eighteen, and no subsequent recount made it more, nor could he or Supplies explain the discrepancy. His C.O. always said he had a "very simple Quartermaster."

August 2nd.—Dolling rejoined from hospital : one good draft anyhow.

August 4th.—Thanks to Division and the C.O. I am one of 5 battalion officers sent by car for a few hours at the sea. We started at 5 in the morning and ran through Amiens, Picquigny, Abbeville, the lower Somme valley and St. Valery to Cayeux, a fourth-rate holiday resort. The sun beamed on us all the time. *August 5th*—The night air is getting nippy. The Somme at Cayeux has not the scenic interest of the Canche at Etaples. Returning, we broke the journey at Abbeville to have a look at St. Wolfram's.

From time to time stories get about of somebody's darling being kept in cotton-wool when a unit is in action. Of one in whom a Higher Command had been induced to take an interest, and convey it to his C.O., is this note : his C.O. got a telegram—"Has my poor nephew come through all right ?" It wasn't for *his* safety that her "poor nephew" had been left out on kit-guard.

A remark by one of our artillery subalterns explains some erratic shooting : "If we fire over you, God help you ; we've only one trained gunner per gun left." Of one group in Caterpillar Wood 75 per cent. became casualties. In our recent operations the 19th Brigade had heavier losses than the 98th or 100th. (The 51st Division came out of High Wood with only two-fifths of the 33rd Division's losses.)

Some of our Old Sweats have been returned by the 10th Battalion to which they had been posted. They were such a nuisance, there being neither company officers nor N.C.Os. who could handle them, that they were gifted to us. The Old Lot in the area have been doing well ; between the fleecing of drafts at "Crown and Anchor," and the gleanings of the battle-field, they have lined their pockets.

Army's verdict is for Division : Corps has been strafed for the High Wood mess. It is just : the fault began at Corps. But the feeling in every H.Q. in the Division is of remand on probation, not acquittal, and that Corps will have the G.O.C. fired yet. The Division is returning to the line with every Brigadier and O.C. on tenterhooks lest he be made the scapegoat of the man above him.

August 6th.—We marched at 10 in the morning to the hillside

behind Bécordel, and bivouacked. Report says that 9000 horses
and mules water at Bécordel, and 17,000 at Méaulte : immense, if
true. For most of a week we were there the weather was broiling.
August 10th—One wet night was followed by a dull day, and an
inactive front : fortunate, for the King was about. On most days
a time of drum-fire suggested a local attack on this unstable front.

The Staff Captain, a near relative of the Army Member of the
Canteen Board, was with the G.O.C. when our prices were asked
about. We sell "Gaspers" at 30 centimes, taking the full trading
profit ; the Expeditionary Force Canteen charge is half a franc,
and the Church Army Huts one franc, for the same packet ; their
prices up here for other articles are likewise extortionate. There
had been questions in Parliament because of an outcry at E.F.C.
prices, which were thereupon reduced.

Training continued, and recreational training was added to
supple unused muscles. It was surprising how few of the drafts,
whether townsmen or country-bred, even the young, could
clear a series of 20-inch hurdles : more surprising that some of the
young officers failed, one a Sandhurst boy. Our awkwardest
recruits were coming on, but some of our number had taken an
active dislike to the outlook. A stalwart, self-assured boy, proud
of the full rank he was given at home, pleaded his youth, and sulked
until his mother's proof that he is only seventeen arrived. Another
model of robust health, who had tried hard to get away, paraded
before the C.O. "It's no use reporting sick," he protested, "you
know what the doctor is." "We have a cheerful time in store,"
Higginson wrote to Blair, "we are going in with about 40 of the
Béthune men per company" [B had less than 20], "the others are
recruits, and the proportion of officer recruits is much the same."

August 13th.—In the dark of morning a short move was made to
Fricourt Wood. We reported the outgoing unit for leaving filthy
lines. At the close of the ensuing correspondence the two C.Os.
were not on speaking terms. The German gunners have made
our last month's bivouac unoccupiable ; they have many more
guns : their infantry is well wired in.—Summoned to attend the
Brigadier : found him a self-willed patient. The German dug-out
in the village, which Brigade occupies, is a three-storeyed, many-
roomed dwelling underground, with heating and sanitary
arrangements ; its electric lighting has ceased to work.

August 16th.—Moody is back: another asset. A German airman he met in hospital at Rouen said their game is up, Austria has let them down, but they will fight to the end: he was quite ignorant of our side of things, thought our Navy was scuppered at Jutland.

August 17th.—A German plane, coming out of a cloud, found one of ours on top of him; about a dozen shots had been fired when the German turned on his side and planed down behind us ablaze, like a comet. It was a fine sight against a deep blue sky and great cumulus cloud, but terrible to think about if the pilot wasn't shot dead.

For six days we found large working-parties to dig a communication trench to High Wood, and to carry from the Bazentin Dumps. They came in for enough shelling to light up the picture of "shell-shocked," and "gassed," for which two years of lurid journalese in the home papers had prepared the minds of the drafts; so the Dressing Station near-by had many importunate applicants for admission. After three weeks of ideal camping conditions the weather had broken, and the drafts were having to make their first crude attempts to get themselves some shelter and comfort.

August 18th.—Another chilly night, and noisy. A grey morning broke fine. More noise from 11 till noon. 2.45 was zero for a push through Wood Lane and High Wood by the 100th and 98th Brigades while demonstrations were made on the right and left. The gun-fire was over in little more than an hour. Through it all the Band of the 6th Welsh Pioneers practised: it's a good Band, and plays good music of the "popular" kind: a great din of guns made the strangest of obbligatos. We had rumours of success everywhere. There appeared to be a local counter-attack, or renewed attack, of short duration about 6 o'clock. At 7.30 we heard that "nothing has been gained," that "the situation is obscure." A warning order for us followed. We moved forward and, after many wearisome halts, arrived in the dark on the Longueval–Bazentin road below High Wood, and hung about. *August 19th*—When day was breaking we resumed movement, still more wearisome, through a communication trench near Crucifix Corner. We were foodless and sleepless. A few widely dispersed shells came over at intervals, as from one howitzer firing at random. Drafts filtered to the tail of the Battalion, persuaded they were "shell-shocked," and formed a little party who would not be convinced by gentle suasion alone that the burst of a shell 100 yards off would not be taken as proof of shell-shock. At last they rejoined their Companies, reluctantly but with heads fairly erect. We relieved the 2nd Argylls. Yesterday they lost 180 men out of 400. High Wood had broken another of several attacks since July 20th.

B, C, and D Companies hold a trench about 100 yards from the Germans, A is again in support. In the autumn heat the air is fouled with the smell of innumerable dead so lightly covered that in unsuspected, though extensive, places one's tread disturbing the surface uncovers them, or swarms of maggots show what one is seated near. An added smell was from charred wood, for an attempt had been made to burn the enemy out by projecting wads of ignited oily rag from old oil-drums converted into mortars. Most of these had been smashed by the bad shooting of our own heavies. And an attempt to sap across Nomansland by a mole, driven by a water-ram, had resulted in the blowing of a gap in our own line, which gave the German snipers targets until we repaired it. In the morning a shell killed the R.A.M.C. Orderly attached to infantry aid-posts in those days. The day was quiet on the whole. In the late evening the German field-guns and 4·2 howitzers plastered the support and H.Q. position along the south-west border of the Wood. An enemy attack seemed the likeliest explanation, so the support line wondered whether our drafts from the front or the Germans would be the first to leap through the beech hedge on to it. After the strafe ended the German gunners continued to be offensive spasmodically. They frustrated two attempts at H.Q. to cook a dinner, by putting shells into the cookhouse and upsetting the pots; they swept our rustic Mess of its contents a moment after we had gone out of it; a shell burst on a Sapper who took a seat from which I had just risen to attend to the trench-mortar team, of whom a shell had killed 5 and wounded 2. When it became dark Radford took out a small patrol from D Company; he found the German trench stiff with men, and Nomansland a tangle of fallen branches and trees that made movement both difficult and noisy.

The C.O. had no news from the front until routine reports came in, so there was nothing after all to be anxious about. There were 6 casualties in the three front Companies in the twenty-four hours, and two dozen in H.Q. and A Company in that lively hour. Two Companies mentioned the shelling in rear, and quiet where they were. One Company's report that 'an enemy bombing attack had been broken up' was received with unquestioning thankfulness and passed on to Brigade. Since only Orderly Room knew the contents of these reports the rest of us suspected Brigade or Division of some invention when G.H.Q.'s daily summary was published: "quiet on the British Front except in High Wood where an attack by the enemy was driven off," it said in effect. Most of us knew by morning what the C.O. learned weeks later. It was a phantom attack. The Company Commander saw it in the smoke-wreaths of a guttering candle in his shelter. The reality may be described in two scenes. The Company Subaltern on Duty was feeling none too sure of himself as the stream of shells swished overhead and burst behind, for it was his first hours in a trench, so he was immensely heartened by the sight of his C.S.M., Dealing, leaning at ease over the parapet and looking round. "See anything, Sergeant-Major?" he asked with what unconcern he could put into his voice. "It appears to me, sir, that there's sweet damn-all." And Dealing found a well-meaning young draft sitting on the floor of the trench, zealously firing his rifle skywards. "Indirect fire on Bapaume! Indirect fire on Bapaume!" was Dealing's rebuke, for sergeants rule by sarcasm. Never can there have been an Army without its Falstaffs and its Pistols. During the War some were hit, many were "invalided with rheumatism," others were sent to jobs by a tactful C.O. Some breathed life enough into their men in buckram to get away with a decoration, and some did earn one; not a few got promotion, which might be repeated, at home or in some eddy overseas.

August 20th.—In the morning Dolling and his C.S.M. were killed by a shell: a great loss. In the afternoon a few of us watched a 1st Division battalion scrambling up the slope beyond the Flers road; the Germans, after failing to outflank them, bolted over the crest. It was a good little surprise rush, though checked by our guns firing short.

Since our Division has not yet made any progress this tour the G.O.C. is pressing, and the Brigadier very pressing, to "do something." D Company is for it to-night. All arrangements have been made behind by some person or persons unknown to us.

Sketchy is not the word for the Order. There is no word one dare utter of the prospects. I went with the C.O. to see our 4·5s register. We thought their observer uncommonly easily satisfied. At zero his battery fired without attracting much attention from those most interested, and no one heard anything of the trench-mortar fire. It was possible that the sounds were drowned by the clatter of arms and equipment in tremulous hands, which someone likened to "a runaway tinker's cart." Anyhow, the senseless scheme of an attack in a thicket after dark by tyros was a washout from the start; the men didn't follow their officers out of the trench.

August 21st.—Wilson, Dolling's successor as O.C. B Company, has been killed at the same place. Our 13-pounders persistently fire short on our right, in contrast to the German guns which we see fire with great accuracy close in front of their own line.—The creeping barrage has been revised; the lifts are to be 50 yards per minute. The where and length of pauses matter more.—An Engineer specialist came to prospect the use of a smoke-screen: the prevailing wind is contrary.—Division and Brigade are calling for skilled patrolling and exact observation. The fun of it is that the trained Scouts of Brigade's original battalions have been kept at Brigade, doing only menial jobs for close on two years, and "can't be spared." No one from the Staff has come to examine the position in our time. Once the Brigadier did come—and go after a hasty look at it.

'"Sunny [1] Jim" was the name by which the troops best knew Private Edge of B Company. He was a bit on the weak side, although he had stuck all the marching of the Retreat, and ordinary duty afterwards until the M.O. gave him a job on the Canteen Staff. High Wood and the ground in rear was an unhealthy place in August 1916. One morning Sunny Jim appeared. He had no equipment but a pack slung by the supporting straps. "What do you want?" I asked. Edge had a slight impediment in his speech. "I fort the boys would want some cigawettes, so I've bwought some up." He had come about 7 miles because he "fort the boys wanted cigawettes." He went round the Companies, sold his stock, and went off again as if it were nothing out of the ordinary.'

All the Companies are rattled. The Old Lot show it too, although there are some splendid stoics. This morning three of B, all good

[1] Boreham.

men, came and begged to be sent to the Transport for a rest : they said that they could not stand being in with the drafts any longer. One fell on his knees and wept when told that they must stick it and show a good example, but they were taken for a few hours rest to a trench where I had slept. Going later to see how they were I found them gone : found too that the trench was floored with very lightly covered dead. I had said it was warm and soft to lie in. When next we met their smile of greeting was sickly.

At midnight the Germans had the wind up. They put up flares all round, threw out their defensive screen of bombers, and dropped *August 22nd*—all their barrages. At 5 a.m. we were relieved, and went into support at Crucifix Corner. Ever afterwards these three days were spoken of by the experienced officers, N.C.Os. and others as "a nightmare." Our casualties for the tour were upwards of 70. The German is master of the air here at present, he flies all over us, scatters our scouts, and slips away from our fighters. These were the days of the supremacy of the Fokker monoplane.

August 24th.—There was a tremendous din for two hours in the early morning. The 100th Brigade made some progress between Delville and High Woods : we got the overspill of the shelling. We were often under dispersed shelling during four days of finding day and night working-parties. A dud made a trench cave in on two men ; although dug out ever so quickly they were dead.—Some of our Old Lot were offered an extra tot of rum to bury a more than commonly unburied body. After dark they had a funeral, and got the rum. In daylight next morning another squad earned the rum.

August 26th.—At 4 a.m. we returned to High Wood through a barrage, slight but unpleasant enough ; there was one casualty ; only two of the drafts jibbed. A suggestion by the C.O. to make a dash at the flanks and bomb in was vetoed by Brigade, where he is not persona grata. Anyhow, our Division is marking time ; High Wood is to give lustre to another. Untaught by what happened eight days ago when the propulsion of end-to-end tubes charged with ammonal, the leading tube shod with a mole, was tried as a means of blowing communications to the German line, Someone has six moles at work. Our G.S.O.1 came and asked to see them, giving a long technical name in which "hydraulic" was the clue ; he looked more dangerous than peeved at a scoffing response, "Oh, you mean the Heath Robinson stunt." None of us pedestrians understands how a mole can be expected to keep direction among the roots of even such shallow-rooted trees as beeches. Sure enough it was not long before a sentry was seen standing spell-bound by an object in front of his post; like a fabulous monster it rose out of the earth jerking and waggling. It was a dislocated mole. (I never heard of the mole being used at the front in soil where it might have been practicable.) Flame projectors and other gadgets are on the ground to ensure a spectacular capture of the Wood by the 1st Division. A current view among those who knew the G.O.C. 1st Division as Brigadier in the 33rd is that if hot air be the further means to success he has a never-failing supply in himself. (The attack was made a week later. Again the "pipe-pushers" tore gaps only in our own line; and again the Germans had the laugh at the oil-rags; this time a Stokes mortar fired short, lighting them too soon. The rest was tragedy. High Wood was never captured by assault except on July 20th. In the second half of September an attack on a wide front, led by caterpillar tanks armed with guns, making their first appearance, carried the line beyond Flers on both sides of the Wood; the German garrison was cut off from support or escape, and surrendered to the Civil Service Rifles.)

August 27th.—Relieved by the 1st Black Watch, we withdrew to Fricourt Wood in rain. The mud is inches deep in what was a pleasant sylvan retreat nine days ago.

August 28th.—The Gazette with the Givenchy decorations is out. That sort of list always has surprises for those who saw most of the Show; not infrequently the most deserving and the undeserving are rewarded equally. Some details of a shelling of Béthune have reached us. Favourite haunts are said to be holed and tenantless, and some familiar inhabitants are casualties; the proprietor of The Globe is one of them.

August 29th.—At 6 a.m. we moved to a trench in front of Montauban; the trench, in its first state, was a ditch. We are lent to the 98th Brigade who nibble at Wood Lane. A bit for C Company has been cancelled owing to the heavy rain. Operations are at a standstill; our working-parties come back through the mud at one mile an hour. Some of the drafts are singing, others have had to be sent to the Transport for shelter and rest.

CHAPTER X

Somme — Interval — Agincourt billets — a torpid front — a pleasant vale : A wet autumn — Quick moving by omnibus — Just moving on foot : With the French at Morval — "Not to-day" : Lesbœufs — "toot sweet" [1] : Two patrols

Contributors :—CRAWSHAY; FOX; POWELL; RADFORD

Sketches :—11, 12, 13, 15, 16

August 30th.—At 3 p.m. we marched in a downpour on busy roads to our former bivouac at Bécordel. That sun-baked slope is now a slough up which two horses can't drag our Mess-cart. We are on quarter-rations owing to difficulties in bringing up supplies. Enough shell-boxes were on the ground to make shelters for all, and a Battalion Mess. Some good building was done for us by our Battle Surplus. Surplus is a new notion, a reserve which must be left out every time a unit is in action to ensure it against *August 31st*—extinction. The weather cleared in the night. The drafts generally have faced the vile weather conditions with exemplary fortitude, and kept in good health. The Division is withdrawn from the active front. At 8 o'clock, after an early breakfast, we were on the road for Ribemont, via Méaulte and Buire : 5 fell out on the way, 1 straggled in late.

September 1st.—We marched at 8.30 over pleasing, undulating country to Rainneville, a good village ; 20 men finished with raw sores on their feet, and many more had minor chafing. H.Q. billet was the house of a brewer, evidently well to do. Mrs. Bung, stately of manner, and her elegant daughter rolled barrels to help load a dray. From time to time one sees Frenchwomen doing work of a kind one cannot conceive being done by women of similar social pretensions at home. The familiar names of Tennent and McEwan were on other barrels in the yard.

September 2nd.—Starting at 9, we did 16 miles with packs in the

---

[1] tout de suite, at once.

heat of a sultry, sunny day. We heard that the rest of the Brigade had lorries to carry packs. Dinner and a rest at Candas, which stands high and open, and gets a breeze, reduced the heavy casualties of the march; count of the number was lost because ambulances ran to and fro relaying the men. Coaxing and prodding up the weedy, the weary and the heavy-laden, "for the credit of your Company," I felt rather a brute: as the Highland woman may have felt who encouraged her man's faltering steps to the gallows— Come away and be hanged quietly, Donald, just to oblige the Duke. In June Division issued an Order enjoining disciplinary action on men falling out. Orderly Room circulated it with the note, "As cases never occur in this Battalion this notice is given as a guide." What was true then looks silly now. We finished at Bernaville, another good village, in the XIII Corps area. My billet is the teacher's house; all the walls are cob. My landlady seems an agreeable woman—but her horrid little girl has droned *September 3rd*—lessons all this dull and drizzly Sunday.

September 4th.—Rested: we started at 10. A wet night has been followed by a fine marching day. There was a fresh breeze except in the sheltered valley of the Authie. The country hilly and of great beauty: the crops in the stook: liquid sunshine and masses of white cloud: good to be alive. I never saw so many pigs, or farms with such huge muck-heaps. Having a slow-moving squad got all but two along the 9 or 10 miles to Beauvoir and Bonnières, two groups of farms. I did not know then that these were Agincourt billets, or how near Agincourt we would pass.

September 5th.—Dull, with times of drizzle. We marched at 9, passed through Vacquerie, crossed the Canche at Moncel, and halted at Blangermont, another group of farms: 7 miles. No troops had been there since the French left in March, so billeting needed more thinking out anew than the Staff Captain and Interpreter could be bothered with until the C.O. strafed, and then they sulked.

September 6th.—Resting. Strange the silences of these parts, so near a very active front. The guns are audible, only as a distant rumble, for the first time since we left Méaulte. I had a run into St. Pol through the harvest-fields of this pleasant land of ridges and woods: a mercy it is that we don't have to fight over them, they're worse than those we have on hand. St. Pol is a straggling little town with a late seventeenth-century church, which has a finely weathered red brick façade. I have not seen a parish church anywhere we have been in France to set alongside our rural English parish church. Much interior detail of French churches looks well enough from the door, but is meretricious on a near *September 7th*—view. We are still resting, although the G.O.C. wants us to have a daily route-march when we are standing-by : as if a goodly number had not been marched into hospital already. One of his little ways is to lurk at corners, popping out and back, to observe our march discipline.

September 8th.—It was 8 o'clock, and a fine fresh morning, when we started for Moncheaux, 8 miles : well-trimmed hedges make it homely. Our rhymster, the Divisional Gas Officer, dined at H.Q. and handed out some verses.

September 9th.—We started in the morning mist of a perfect September day, and marched by Liencourt to Ivergny, 6½ miles. From Moncheaux, and all round here, the country is liker England than anything we have seen in France. There are hedges round the houses, well-tended strips of garden—flowers in front, fruit and vegetables behind, and here there are window-boxes. For a second night my billet is tastefully furnished and has modern beds. These brass beds have their advantages, but the old French wooden bed is a dream of comfort. Except among the wealthy French sitting-room furnishing is tasteless ; it is never comfortable. Only once before, at Gonnehem, have I been in a farm where one did not step from the house to the midden.

September 10th.—A fine day for a 12-mile march to Humber-camps, our new back area, VII Corps. A Corps Commander is a rare bird to see. This one guffawed at our windy Brigade Order for tin-hats, companies at intervals, no music, 7 miles behind the line. Bands are usual at little over a mile from this torpid front where Brigade casualties average one a week. From Ribemont to Humbercamps is 18 miles ; our perambulation on by-roads was 66 miles in eleven days. Our casualties to hospital must be about 50, mostly with sore feet ; the 16-mile march weeded out the men of poorest stamina. The trouble with the drafts is neglect of cleanliness, and want of self-dependence and of resource in the small things that make for comfort.

September 11th.—Along with Walter Fox, recently commissioned, and a party of 34 other ranks, I was sent to the Third Army Rest Camp on the Downs above Hardelot. Hunting up friends and sight-seeing at places as far off as Calais made me think what a rest my return to the Battalion would be. The most interesting sight was the ammunition dump at Audrecque. One German flier, with one bomb, put up 18,000 tons of shells, etc., worth five to six millions sterling: a local Railway Transport Officer's figures.[1] The practice trenches at Etaples, revetted with sand-filled biscuit tins and other material quite unsuitable at the front, will have got some Base indispensable a decoration and promotion. The men had enjoyed themselves thoroughly, *September 18th*—and had empty pockets when we paraded to return.

We found the Battalion in the line at Hannescamps, to the left of Foncquevillers ("Funky Villas"). Rumour had not belied the repose of the spot we were in, but some pessimists pointed to Pigeon Wood in front. The width of Nomansland diminishes from 1400 yards on the right, where one can sit on the parapet in shirt-sleeves, to 250 yards on the left. There are rats everywhere in numbers hitherto unknown. The C.O. had won an Open Race at a 46th Divisional Horse Show, on Yates's mare, and then gone on leave. He had seen the arrival of another draft of 95, 'awful sights, enough to break one's heart. The others were getting quite good and smart, now this crowd will put us back.' de Miremont is Acting O.C. He joined from West Africa in time to make his only acquaintance with a trench during twenty-four wet hours in reserve at Montauban Alley. He then declared that "trench warfare is a sort of drill." To the bewilderment of those who have lived through a year or two of it he is trying to square the facts to that idea (an idea he never gave up).

September 21st.—Relieved to billets in Bienvillers: the inhabitants have gone, the louse and the rat swarm in it. Houses and out-buildings are alike of brick, and all look much of an age, walls and roof-tiles are the same faded terra-cotta; mingled with the dark green of shading elms they make a picture it is always pleasant to turn to. A long barn covers much of the front of the village; its roof-beams become more gaunt every day, for at each shot of a big gun in rear tiles cascade to the rone or spout on to the road

---

[1] The true cash figure was about one-third of that sum.

and are shivered ; and sometimes in quiet a loosened tile, shaken by the wind, tinkles down tunefully.

September 22nd.—The G.O.C. is exchanging with the G.O.C. 35th (Bantam) Division, Reginald Pinney. As Harries puts it, "He has been given light duty," for at that date the Bantams were not being used on an active front. Soon afterwards they filled up with drafts from the Pool and, ceasing to be pedigree birds, were put to use, not kept for show.

September 24th.—Excess kit called in : warned to move : where ?

September 25th.—We had no luck at a Corps Race Meeting : "Girlie" unfit, our other entries were outclassed.—Our oldest man has gone, he is 53. A shell-blast blew open the door of his billet when he was going through ; his face was cut, so he was sent to hospital. He was decent and willing but a nuisance, he needed too much coddling to keep him going.

September 26th.—The G.S.O.1 transfers to the XI Corps as B.G.G.S. He and the late G.O.C. were complementary ; the one prone to be fussy and exacting, the other pedagogic. Their schemes were perfect on paper but inelastic, unadaptable. "What is your arc ?" G.1 asked a machine-gunner fettered to one of a series of loopholed emplacements. The man's bewilderment was not resolved when the question was reshaped, "What is your arc of fire ?" A correct and intelligent answer was given when the Brigade-Major prompted audibly, "Ask him where his bloody gun fires."

The indigenous building material of the rural parts of Picardy and Artois, that we have seen, is a timber frame and unrammed earth mixed with chopped straw, so a few shells make havoc of farms and cottages. Behind us are white stone single-storey-and-attic farmhouses with pilastered façade and grey-blue slates, somebody's scheme of about 1860 ; they have orchards enclosed in hedges of beech or elm : all just a bit formal.

September 29th.—After being for two nights in the same front as before we have been dribbling out all day, to avoid a night relief, to dirty, crowded billets at Souastre, 3½ miles in rear.

September 30th.—Marching to Lucheux in the morning the men went well. We saw everywhere preparations for wintering troops. In the afternoon I found a woodland path and jogged into Doullens seeking a Field Cashier. Who can have been here ? Instead of being given money as hitherto, whether by cashiers or banks, for the asking I was cross-questioned rigorously and required to prove my identity. Doullens is a sleepy little town at the foot of a cliff crowned by an old-time citadel; it is clean and pretty, and sweetened by the Authie. The name, "Quatre fils d'Aymon," of its large hotel, which looks like an old posting-house, belongs to the Charlemagne legends. The church, nondescript and unattractive without, has fine early twelfth-century details within.

Our stay at Lucheux lasted eighteen days. The billets were quite good. Officers had beds that were comfortable after the occupants had served as bait and caught the lice that infested them. We had a Battalion Mess in an estaminet at a gusset, owned by a cross-grained woman. The C.O. required the cost of extras to be moderate, but did not lay down any figure. (This was the last Battalion Mess for a couple of years or more, unfortunately.) One of the few incidents recalled about it is "Teg" Davies's hearty voice bridging a silence that fell upon the generally talkative company at dinner, to say, "I'm a bastard Saxon myself." The C.O. was shocked; but Teg was an unconscious droll. Shortly before this he poured out the whole of Higginson's last pint of champagne, drank it off, drew his hand along his lips and said, "I don't like these light French wines; I prefer roodge veen (vin rouge) and grenadine to that."

The weather was very unsettled, but the place was the most delightful I stayed in during over three years in France. It straggles like a Cotswold village about a lovely little vale on the left of the Grouche, a rippling stream that hugs, on its right, slopes clad then in early autumn tints. On a spur that rises from the stream is a much-ruined castle with some finely preserved mid-Gothic arcading. Whether under the slanting beams of the October sun or drifts of rain, for there was not much sunshine, the vale is a picturesque spot. We were told that Lucheux water is famous; unfortunately the Australians, who had been here, infected it with dysentery brought from Gallipoli; consequently we had a few cases. The country for miles round is a delight to ramble in. My first ramble—no one else had the time and freedom of movement—was in search of a goat to give H.Q. Mess fresh milk. The *patronne* of one farm wrung her hands and regretted we wanted a nanny in milk, not a billy: then she remembered vivaciously that she had eaten the billy: grief was her note when she spoke

of his youth, his whiteness, his smallness, though he was an *idiot*.
I had to hear how good the *gigôt* was before pursuing an eventually
successful search. Our goat cost 30 francs. It is doubtful if she
had paid for herself when she went dry. In time she cried with
feminine importunity to fulfil the end of her creation, until the
servants complained that her crying kept them awake. We were
far from farms at the time. At a hint that Wynnstay Billy might
step into the breech, so to say, our Old Soldiers, keepers of the
Regimental Tradition, looked down their noses, scandalized. So
imbued were they with the idea of the celibacy of the King's Goat
that they required his substitute to be chaste. Like the little white
idiot, the milkless one ended as *gigôt* and stock, but some she had
robbed of sleep abstained from her flesh. (An enlightened generation has grown up since then, to whom the inhibition of a goat's
proverbial virility is revolting and uneconomical. During the
later service of the 1st Battalion on the Indian Frontier, under the
command of an Englishman able to speak fluent Welsh, the King's
Goat sired a son on a native Kashmiri dam.)

No sooner had the Battalion arrived in rural France than we
became familiar with the farmyard dog, large or small, that was
never taken off the chain except to trot dutifully to the treadmill
which worked the churn, and resignedly return to its chain when
its task was finished. There were rows over the Army's habit of
setting the dogs free, and bitter complaints when the dogs followed
their deliverers out of the area. At Lucheux threshing was done
by an ailing horse which stumbled on a treadmill.

A programme of instruction was entered on at once; it occupied
every morning, most afternoons and one night. Because the C.O.
made training his care everyone worked well. Hygiene was my
subject; my afternoon lectures did not disturb the nap many of
the audience were used to take when in billets. The wet weather
allowed few opportunities for games. There was no suitable place
for sing-songs, but an A.S.C. major of another division's train gave
several open-air cinema shows in the hotel yard—for a considera-
tion. A Dickens character was painted on each of his cars.

Trouble was caused by a potent nondescript liquor sold in some
estaminets. Its abuse by some of the Old Lot who had been
"putting it across" the drafts, gave the drafts chances of getting
their own back. Once the Battalion conjurer was beaten nearly

sober, sober enough to seek the shelter of the Guard-room which he found safer than being under a lorry—and not oily. He had been released from it only that morning; he returned to it officially next morning in spite of a fine forensic effort. Another of our uncommonly thirsty ones was suspected of having found 500 francs, the loss of which was reported by a villager as a theft.

The C.O. spent three days at Flixecourt as one of the Division's representatives to the Fourth Army School's end-of-the-term Show. The other representative was the C.O. with whom he was not on speaking terms. Both declined to go in the divisional car, each thinking that the other would be in it. They rode. At cross-roads six miles from their journey's end they met face to face. Subordinates who heard of the misadventure enjoyed it much more than the principals.

October 1st.—The officers assembled in the school to meet the new G.O.C. 'Seems a pleasant, human man: not too old.' After compliments, he told us that we will be "for it" in a week. Another wood awaits attack. The subalterns adapted the refrain of a popular music-hall song, and sang, "And another little wood *October 3rd*—won't do us any harm." A guest night, the Drums playing: this was the only event of the kind in my time. And *October 4th*—they played Welsh airs in Doullens Grande Place. The French audience increased at each subsequent performance.

October 5th.—At a Brigade Conference Rossignol Wood, near Gommecourt, was named as the Division's quarry. The new G.S.O.1, Forster, a Sapper, put questions to each C.O., the Brigade-Major, Brigadier, and G.O.C. The answers, except from three C.Os., were revealing, but neither helpful nor hope-inspiring. The G.O.C. "hadn't considered the problem." When will he? It's on us. As a rehearsal, Brigade treated us to a tactical exercise *October 8th*—set by G.1. It should have been instructive, in spite of the rain, but seemingly tactical problems are not the Brigade Staff's strong suit. The practice trenches had been dug on the wrong slope and sited the wrong way, so the whole show collapsed *October 12th*—in confusion. The C.O. and others are again at Hebuterne prospecting the approach to Rossignol Wood.

October 14th.—Rossignol Wood is off. Things are not going well farther south. At a divisional lecture on "Tanks and their

October 16th—Tactical Use," we were told that the Rossignol
Wood affair was just to have been a feint : as things are Fritz is
having to shorten his line.

The C.O. has overhauled our administration. H.Q. details are
now organized as a fifth company, except for pay. (The scheme
lapsed with Colonel Crawshay's command. It was set up throughout the Army after the War.) Part of the scheme was the reappoint-
ment of a sergeant-cook. For over a year we have had no such
sergeant ; Companies looked after their own cooking, and great
inequality resulted. The most competent of the Company cooks
was paraded, told that a levelling-up of the cooking was wanted,
and asked, "Do you think you can do it ?" "Yes, sir, and shall
I be entitled to wear the Flash ?"—presto, in a breath. Half an hour
later he was going round the cookers wearing sergeant's stripes
and a Flash. Such is the Regiment's pride in its Flash, and Atkins's
pride in any distinguishing mark. (Since the end of the War all
ranks wear the Flash.)

October 17th.—After a night exercise the men came swinging in
finely ; they are not recognizable as the timid drafts of six weeks
ago. With the fall to a small number of the Old Army men the
snatches of song on the march have disappeared. The snatch rarely
was of more than four lines, and these might be a medley, or
contain a line of burlesque. The challenging call towards the end
of a stage of a march, "Are we down-hearted ?" and the defiant
response had disappeared too. The Army now kept its breath to
cool its ardour, not to fan it. But the old ardour still burned in
one junior N.C.O. of the old stock ; these lines and the tribute to
Lord Kitchener (p. 205) were written on the door of his billet at
Lucheux :

> Bravo ! Brave Fusiliers !
> You're soldiers tried and true ;
> Neither Kaiser's Huns nor giant guns
> Can daunt such men as you.
> And yet again in the dear Homeland
> The Plain will ring with cheers
> For the men who claim Givenchy fame—
> The Second Royal Welch Fusiliers.

Battalion Sports in the afternoon were quite good fun in spite
of some rain and cancellations.

October 18th.—The Transport went off by road to the XIV Corps area, Lord Cavan's, next the French. The roads are sloppy after three nights of rain, the air is saturated, the trees drip.

October 19th.—We're "all dressed up," and feeling as lugubrious as the song. After twenty-four hours of the emptiness of just waiting with no inducement to be doing, we moved off in the late afternoon. The sight of the Brigadier busy and happy in the performance of something he can do was a temporary fillip. The Company officers stood aside while he told their men off in bus-loads and packed them into buses. The drivers were French, the conductors mostly Megalassy. If we had been driven through the dark with less seeming recklessness we might have felt the cold more, for the uplands between Authie and Ancre, though of modest height, are bleak at this season. We arrived at Méricourt-l'Abbé, without mishap, at midnight.

October 20th.—Méricourt hears the guns; at Ribemont, across the river, 1000 yards nearer them, there is silence.

October 21st.—A cannonade at dawn rattled every window and door in the village: the front is about 15 miles off. In the afternoon we marched to the Citadel, on the hillside east of the Bray–Fricourt road: greasy going. Glad to be in tents, it's cold, cold.

October 22nd.—German bombing-planes came over in the early morning. The milk-goat bleated piteously just before they came. By her bleating we learned to expect bombers before we could hear them. Two bombs were dropped on the Transport; providentially they did not explode. It was a bitter night, there was more than an inch of ice on water inside the tents.

The march was resumed by cross-country tracks that thawed, making the going very heavy for the men; and the Transport skidded on the muddy slopes, and strung out as wagons stuck. We left it to collect in its allotted park in a vast expanse of mud at Carnoy, and marched by road to Trônes Wood, a ruin of branchless, riven trunks standing, or fallen, amid shell-holes and crumbling trenches. With little overhead shelter we huddled for warmth for a few hours round green-wood fires, blinking and choking. Binge Owen, who was wounded at the taking of the R.W.F. Crater, rejoined after having been posted to a South Wales Borderers battalion. Mann's judicious neglect of a sick-parade reduced the number reporting almost to the really sick.

After midnight we fell in. In pitch darkness, and with many
October 23rd—stoppages, we made our way on narrow roads
carrying an immensity of French and British traffic. Nothing less
than a dead-stop prevented the returning French transport trying
to trot. A merciful General Routine Order forbids our transport
to trot even when empty. The route was by Guillemont, through
which we passed in the dark, and Ginchy. Attack and counter-
attack under bombardment had made them mere names of sites;
few of us noticed them, for our faculties were numbed. And time
was unnoticed. Night shaded into day. There was no dawn, no
quickening, no radiance. A sullen sky, a flattened vault of ashen
grey, pressed upon folds the like of which we have been used to
see a diaper of sunny harvest-fields, with cottages and trees. There
is no cottage standing, no chance tree or clump. Over on the
right Leuze ("Lousy") Wood, tailing into Bouleaux Wood, is
less mutilated than the woods in rear. It is the main feature in a
wide and bare winter landscape of grey-green stubble stippled
here and there with chrome-grey shell-holes, and scarred with
trenches. Desolation reigns undisputed now, whatever revolution
Spring may bring. Beyond Ginchy Corner the road became less
crowded, we could march in fours and get along, until we had it
to ourselves. The distance we had come was short, but the morning
was drawing on when we came to Serpentine Trench, a part of the
captured Flers Line, in a fold between Ginchy and Morval, and
settled down astride the road. The day was misty and chilly, the
ground was soggy. Any tolerable shelter had been occupied
already by the artillery, whose field-guns were in line of batteries
50 or 60 yards in rear. Four H.Q. officers could get nothing better
than a shack of shell-boxes, some 6 feet by 5, open on one side:
what could any other rank hope for?

The Battalion is lent to the 4th Division, which is in action on
the Morval–Lesbœufs front. The idea is to improve the line
preparatory to a larger-scale attack on Le Transloy, an important
tactical point on the Péronne–Bapaume road. We are to be in
that. There had been two postponements, for the French were
taking part. The 4th Division attacked at 2.30. The ground
shook as the gunners loosed off their rapidest fire, and our ear-
drums were jangled by the clangour. Few of us had seen the guns
during a hurricane bombardment, and a barrage. It was grand.

The rapture of the gunners was catching. But the wondering infantry, who knew the other end of a barrage, missed the gun-layer among the racing loaders and leaping guns, and saw—amazed —why keeping close up under the shell-bursts is so unhealthy. A wonder it is that there are not more shorts.

First accounts of the attack were good. The early walking-wounded are always optimists. Later accounts were not so good. Then there was that awesome word of a situation—obscure : in short, the attack, like earlier attacks on the same ground, had failed. Still later we heard that the French had not jigged. Rain had October 24th—come on. It rained all night. The only relief for anyone was by changing the posture of discomfort. And it rained most of the day, which the men spent "making themselves com-fortable." Nerves were a bit frayed all round. The gunners objected that our modest fires would give them away, but they had blazing fires of their own. There were minor altercations, yet from time to time someone laughed aloud, a merry laugh.

The 33rd Division is relieving the 4th. Since last it was in action the line had been carried forward 3 miles, mostly on a mid-September day when tanks, used for the first time, rolled over everything that did not get out of the way. Since then the German concentration, our lengthening communications, the bad weather conditions and the heavy surface, had all but stopped progress ; but there was no end to attempts to attain small objectives by just hurling shells and men pell-mell at them.

Before nightfall we were on the road again for a short distance ; then our route was over fields by a track that was entered on about half a mile behind Morval. Goldsmith, who was leading, picked up the only guide and raced on, his Company streaming behind him, the others behind it. Touch was lost in the dusk among men and detachments going in and coming out, and no one knew the way. The men were overladen for the going ; on parts of the ill-defined track they sank over their boots at every step. In the sunken road that was our reserve position several exhausted men of the outgoing units had stuck fast ; they had to be dug out of the tenacious clay soil. A shell bursting there cost us Roberts, the Aid Post Orderly, and one or two others. Not a few of our weaker brethren were benighted ; some were struggling in until noon next day, others were taken into the

Ambulance Relay Post and sent to hospital; but before morning
most of the men had got in somehow, weary, mud-caked, wet.

The Battalion was disposed on a two-company front in relief
of the remains of the 11th Brigade. B Company was on the
right, in Slush. They were in touch with the French 125th
Regiment, who were in Antelope. The French were extended
from behind Sailly-Saillisel. C Company was on B's left, in
Frosty; its left was in the air, for there was a considerable gap
between it and the 20th R.F. who were in Snow, facing left.
A. Company was in Ox Support; and D, in reserve, was in
the sunken road in rear. The front Companies were hampered
in getting in, and in working, by dead and wounded of the 11th
Brigade; these were everywhere, some two dozen stretcher-cases
having been left behind. For the three days we were in the position
our bearers worked tirelessly to get these men out; they were
helped towards the end by squads of the 5th S.R. The absence of
communication trenches restricted the work to the dark hours:
nearly half of the men died.

October 25th.—By daylight the rudimentary trenches had been
deepened enough to give fair cover. The position was seen to be
a hollow overlooked by the enemy, to whom situation maps
allotted Hazy Trench, Misty Trench, and other apt names.
The "trenches" were figments of the Staff imagination, but the
names had a colloquial use in pointing the whereabouts of the
groups of shell-holes that served the Germans well for concealment
and defence. So undefined was the position that at dawn the C.O.
and Sapper Officer were just saved from walking over to the
enemy round C Company's open flank. Only less adventurous
was the C.O.'s visit to the French company on his right. He was
looked at with suspicion, and escorted back to his own trench for
informal identification.

Our predecessors, who were not well dug-in, and the Germans
had indulged each other a good deal except during an attack, or if
a patrol blundered into its enemy's lines. Our fellows, having
been made to keep warm by digging, fired on anyone who looked
out of a shell-hole in daylight. Goldsmith was claiming six
Germans in one hole to his own rifle when again a head, the same
head, was raised, and a tired voice pleaded, "Don't shoot at me,
sir, I'm a wounded Hants" (of the 11th Brigade). The day passed in

ever-deferred expectation of doing something. We were to attack with the French, who fixed an hour, postponed it, and then cancelled it. In the afternoon word was sent from behind that a German attack was imminent: nothing happened. Then C Company was warned to do a night stunt: it heard no more about it.

October 26th.—Half of B Company and all C were withdrawn at 7 o'clock to the support line to let our 6-inch howitzers bombard the nebulous German position at Boritzka and Hazy. This was in preparation for an attack by the French and ourselves later in the day. C had casualties from the bombardment, and found their trench pretty well flattened out on returning to it at dusk. The attack was cancelled.

October 27th.—Half B and C were again withdrawn to oblige the French: again our trench was flattened out: and again nothing followed. Late in the day the Brigadier came to H.Q. and wished us "good luck" in a partnership with the French to-morrow. Our liaison officers, seated on velvet, may be complaisant to seventy times seven with unreadiness and whims, but our "Poor Bloody Infantry" is kept on tenterhooks by Gallic ways. Meanwhile the Brigadier wants us to use up our sagging energy digging a trench in dead ground. One cause of the 11th Brigade's failures (and later failure) is that the German front is in dead ground to our field-guns, and they have a clearance of only 6 feet 6 inches of the bank into which H.Q. is dug. Local tradition says that a tall French officer, who stood on one of the little heaps of stones that are raked up before ploughing, had his head knocked off. "The Count,"[1] who retired to the top of the bank, and descended in haste and deshabille, says the clearance is nothing like 6 feet; but he is not a judge of range or direction.—In one respect we are fortunate: our Gunner observer is knowledgeable and helpful, unlike the general run of forward observers these days who disclaim being in any sense liaison.—The Ambulance-bearer work has improved; hitherto it has not taken account of the surface on which stretchers have to be carried. A wounded officer, not of ours, weighing 16 stone, was carried into the Advanced Dressing-station. He told the M.O. that his men were toppers, he would like to kiss them all because they had dropped him only four times. —At last we had a fine morning, it promised well for the day, but

[1] de Miremont.

the end was a downpour. A late warning of relief was very cheering news; the physical conditions were a trial of endurance.

Anything I have seen out here yet was picnicking compared with these four days. Until to-day's downpour it has been horribly raw, with mist or occasional drizzle. The Companies have not been in action or strafed, but food can neither be cooked nor sent up warm; H.Q. has to live on sandwiches made up behind. Taking up rations at night, the Transport found that things were 'simply bloody. Woe betide the wagon or team that got off the beaten track. Everyone had to be challenged. A single man who loomed up in the darkness replied, "A Doblin Fus'lier, and a bluidy poor spicimin at that."' Moldy Williams supplied the daily tonic. Although movement by day was unhealthy he strolled, smiling, over the top each morning to ask the Companies in front if his Sapping Platoon could do anything for them. My part has been one of rather ignominious inactivity. Three of the last four days at Lucheux in bed with influenza, rising only to see the sick, was no preparation for this ordeal. At H.Q., an earthen vault recently cleared of German dead, in a sunken road between Morval and Lesbœufs I shivered in two suits of summer and one suit of winter underclothing; and three pairs of socks in easy boots did not save me from chilblains that made the wearing of boots impossible for two days. How the men, the undeveloped youths, have stood these trenches is beyond my understanding. Contrary to what is usual, H.Q. gets all the shells that are going. The sunken road is a natural target; it has had a fair dose, but the krump on our roof that would bury us has not happened so far. The smoke of our attempts to have a fire may have drawn shelling, besides choking us. The Companies have been almost exempt from shells but for our artillery's shorts.

Relief arrangements, which worked well, had been made with The Cams. before a less simple Brigade scheme arrived. Trouble began after we got out. The lighter-laden officers and the robust carried rifles, Lewis guns, and such of the magazines as had not been "lost." Exhausted men were pulled out of mud from which they could not lift their feet, and hauled over anything they could not jump—however narrow. One spent youth prayed "Only leave me to die": another, when asked how long he had been mired, said with a wan smile, "Since the beginning of the War."

October 28th—We were all back at Guillemont by 6 a.m., most of the men stone-cold. Our "rest billets" were recognized as having been a village by the household fragments turned up on digging, and there was the human evidence of battle. Wood for cover and firing was most sought. By evening the men had made for themselves shacks, and some were singing. Rum is a great reviver; it was no longer an issue in the Division; it had to be wrung out of the new G.O.C. for to-day only. His own habits are not ascetic. An occasional shell still falls on the site. If Fritz is better off for quarters behind his front he is having a poorer time under long-range fire, we are sending over so many more shells than we get.

October 29th.—Rain and bitter cold. Some men who can stand no more have been sent to hospital. The others are wonderfully cheery. A few short-time working-parties are being found. Our losses for the week are about 60 from all causes, two dozen are gunshot wounds; and we have "done nothing." I was feeling that Roberts was irreplaceable. He was the most deft and knowing dresser I met in the Army in four years. He taught me much that a regimental medical officer must know. There was no spoon-feeding in his method, if method there was; all my resource was drawn out. In all he did he was unruffled and dogged, never more so than when reciting "Gunga Din": during his boy-service these qualities were called "obstinacy"—so I was told.

The C.O.'s birthday. A cake arrived, and Company Commanders squeezed into H.Q. for dinner. Near the end a Brigade Order required us to detail a Company to reinforce The Cameronians, so Ralph Greaves took A back to Morval. The Cams. and 5th S.R. had been given the part for which B and C Companies were cast, the capture of Hazy. We had reckoned that a surprise rush by one Company might succeed. The battle-piece, a pretentious night scheme handed out by Brigade or Division to a company from each of two battalions, was foredoomed to failure. Men wandering behind the German position were captured in daylight. It was said that each battalion lost nearly the strength of its company—for nothing. Their enemies helped them to clear some of their wounded—and saved themselves the heavy carry.

October 30th.—Withdrawn to reserve between Trônes and Bernafay Woods: wretched conditions for all: some tents, leaking like sieves, were issued. During heavy showers it looked as if the bellying tarpaulin roof of H.Q.'s crazy shack would release a flood on us. It was more from prudence than sacrifice that *October* 31st—I sat up stoking a brazier and drying clothes while the wearers got some broken sleep. The day was fine and sunny but for one hour of downpour. A. Company rejoined. We made a short move to whole tents in another sea of mud at La Briqueterie, south-west of Bernafay Wood, and had blankets for the men. The conjurer, doing field punishment, was given a small case to carry for the C.O. It was no sleight of hand that opened a locked box of cigars. After dark a German plane came over and machine-gunned : there were no hits. A new interest is going to be watching these night craft play hide-and-seek with our searchlights. I lay, but could not sleep, on a duckboard; the alternative was a ground-*November* 1st—sheet on mud. Riding into Méaulte for a primus stove an army of pioneers, working on ruinous roads crawling with traffic, was passed. Why is railhead so far back? Why have not we such tramways close to the front as the French have? Some of our officers who borrowed blankets from a Coldstream battalion last night have been scratching all day.

November 2nd.—We are still supplying working-parties, not very arduous. A wet morning has been followed by sunshine; we have not seen the sun but once for two weeks. The moon too has been for long a stranger, to-night she walks in beauty. Thanks *November* 3rd—to the warmth and fumes of a coke brazier in a closed tent I had a real good sleep.

What the French do with their weaklings is a mystery. Their gunners may be picked, but here are infantry and supply all as big as our average; they have no such little men in this part of their line as a great many of ours. Their A.S.C. and ours differ also in age; their men are in early middle age, ours are lusty youths.

We were on the move again between 2 and 2.30. There was some half-clouded sunshine just after we started. For much of the way we were on a road that, forking at each end, had to carry a double load of traffic. We could only edge along in single file, and so slowly that when we were no farther than Ginchy there was just light enough to let us see the shells of our big howitzers on the roadside soaring in flight against a gleam in the overcast sky. The road surface was worn to its foundation, broken by shells, and beyond putting in repair as things were. Lines of Labour men at the sides made shift to keep the route passable. They plied their brushes among our feet, and shovelled any rubbish into pot-holes between the closely ranked moving wagons, horsed and motor. Men and animals tripped and stumbled, and wheels skidded, on bits of loose timber and untrimmed branches which were flung into shell-holes for want of other filling. A couple of hundred yards of German corduroy in a dip was the only stretch near there on which the going was fairly good. In all that moving mass little was spoken. There was the monotonous grind of feet and wheels on the crumbling macadam, or the swish-swish where water lay inches deep, the clank of arms and harness, the scrunch of gears and brakes, the burst of a shell, but there was next to no talk. Mechanically a subaltern or sergeant ordered his men to "close up" or "lead on": wearily a driver muttered a curse when his horse stumbled, or his wagon stuck in a hole or skidded; sombrely, stolidly, thousands of men plodded forward or rearward.

Through Ginchy progress became slower when we were moving, stoppages became longer. One long stoppage took place when H.Q. was where a road on the left rose towards the Hog's-back. A long column which was turning into it stood up to view. It was a fine sight; the rhythmic sway of marching files has a rippling flow that's never seen in any city traffic stream. The tiny triangle of turf so often found at a fork had not perished quite. An officer of the Road Control stood on it exchanging short occasional remarks with two who looked as if they loitered for gossip. A wiry Engineer sergeant waited near them; his eyes, head, feet moved restlessly as he scanned the down stream on the right with a set, angry look. He was the most human of the many interests there. My roving eye turned ever to him. Suddenly the tautness of his pose yielded, but his look hardened. "Where the 'ell 'ave you been ?—an' me waitin' 'ere for the last two hours like a (horribly obscene)," he asked in a tuneless, steely voice of a flushed, good-natured-looking private who came out of the throng. Heads were turned towards the voice. I caught the C.O.'s eye; the Road Control group, and other neighbours, looked at each other. We all smiled. The foulness of that metaphor bespoke a mood of time and place and state we could all share. The wiry sergeant was already threading his way to the rear with purposeful mien and shoulders, and the good-natured private was panting behind him. There was a shuffling of feet ahead; "close up," someone said, and the unspeaking column trudged on in the darkening of a dull, raw day. All wheeled traffic ended between one and two miles from the front. Rations and stores, before being manhandled, and shells were taken on pack-animals by tracks which, winding about a contour, had some cover. On a track beside the road a string of mules, their heads bent, their shoulders heaving, laboured to keep their feet in greasy mud more than fetlock deep. The guns of both sides searched the other's approaches to catch reliefs, working-parties, and stores; from evening therefore until after midnight was always noisy; and the forward tracks were marked by more and more shell-holes every night, and by more killed and foundered animals. On the last three-quarter mile of our way, past the left of Lesbœufs, the track was on heavy plough in which one's feet slithered and slid, or sank and had to be dragged out, sometimes with help. We were all in by 8 o'clock, a mean rate of a mile an hour, and there were no communication trenches to lose time in. The German guns had kept up the usual dropping fire nearly all the way. A shell bursting beside a H.Q. group, which had just left the road for the track, wounded R.S.M. Boreham and the Provost Sergeant. Butcher looked his part; and he was the poacher turned game-keeper. To his eye for useful things, and to his skill in fixing-in a window or building-in a good-drawing grate, H.Q. officers had owed much comfort. His personality, rather than character, made him eminent in the Battalion, apart from his office. He never had to officiate at an execution, or it is easy to think of him reporting, as did another Provost Sergeant, "It went off champion, sir."

The Companies took over a narrow front from the Middlesex, under a desultory strafe of the position that went on all night. They were commanded by their second strings. B Company (W. H. Fox) was in front; it was in Summer, under a crest line, and was covered by outposts; its left was on the Le Transloy road, its right was in the air, separated by 500 yards of German ground from what was C Company's left at Morval. D Company (Coster) was in Dewdrop Trench, in close support of B's right. A. (Ralph Greaves) was battalion support in Windy; and C (Radford) was reserve in John Bull, its right being on the edge of the vestiges of Lesbœufs Wood. H.Q. was in a German dug-out, so it faced the wrong way, cut in the chalk bank of a sunken road about 800 yards north-west of the church. The Count was left out, to his own content, but for our peace. Conditions in general were trying enough; in the cramped space of a make-shift dug-out his snoring was unbearable. Conscientiously he gave the signallers written orders so voluminous that they wondered who was barmy—he or they.

B Company sent out patrols at once. One of them found a machine-gun post about 300 yards off on the right flank. Another, an officer's patrol of 30 other ranks, had orders to search the gap on the right where it was said that a very active enemy sniped by day and roved about by night. The patrol was barely clear of its trench when a shell burst close at hand. A consequent general swerve downhill brought the party on to D Company. From there a fresh start was made. The main features of its further pilgrimage were not known for thirty-six hours. The slope of the ground, the greasy surface, and many shell-holes were the physical determinants of direction. A near or farther shell-burst was the only light. The patrol crossed a segment of the gap, and blundered on the 16th K.R.R.C., the left battalion of the 100th Brigade. In the surprise shots were fired. Before the mistake was realized, and the patrol learned where it was, the K.R.R.C. had one casualty, or more. After that a return was decided on. The men bunched to keep touch in the inky blackness. A shell burst among them causing casualties, confusion and scattering. Any sense of direction was lost, so the officer collected in shell-holes such of his men as he could, to await day and knowledge. He had then to wait for darkness again before rejoining. One of the patrol was known to have been killed and 6 wounded, 16 were missing. Later, the Brigadier said that the officer had behaved very commendably, he disapproved of the C.O.'s contrary opinion, and wanted him to apologize to his subaltern for having expressed it.

November 4th.—Daylight is revealing. Any way one goes to Dewdrop is through a shambles. Nowhere have I seen the dead in such numbers on so little space or of so many units. The

Middlesex had pushed forward 200 yards where previous attempts —seven, it is said—had failed. We are warned for a three, or more, division attack to-morrow. Le Transloy Cemetery is our appropriate objective. It is nearly a mile away, in front of the village which is perched on the highest ridge hereabout. We will have to cross and descend an intervening high ridge before tackling a long glacis that is the approach to the Cemetery, all bare, even ground—the terrain of the machine-gunner's dream. Some dilettante at a seaside resort, fresh from a gay time in Paris, is supposed to have devised the scheme. The facetiae of H.Q. had been taken up and embroidered by the Companies when an amended, less wanton, scheme came in; yet no one is optimist enough to think that any consecrated acre will enfold him. What little study of the ground was possible was made. It has been a grey day with glints of sunshine, and no rain. One misses the rain. The guns have been active, especially in the dwindling daylight. The moon is hazy.

November 5th.—Guy Fawkes Day. Another noisy night, and a short drizzle. During the night C Company was ordered up into Dewdrop on D's right. The going was bad. The Company arrived just before dawn : fortunately it was a grey damp morning with a low-lying mist and bad visibility.—Yet another version of the operation gives us a compassable objective. We are to dig-in about 200 very unhealthy yards beyond the crest of the ridge over against Le Transloy. The new line will be some 250 to 300 yards in front of where B Company is now. The French fix the time. They and the 17th Division attack on the right and left respectively of our division. The 20th R.F. on our left, across the Le Transloy road, are to move with us.

'I[1] had forgathered with Coster in his German dug-out for what breakfast was procurable, when the latest Operation Order arrived. Zero hour has not been fixed, but will, if possible, be notified later : if time does not permit of notification Company Commanders will take the opening of the French seventy-fives bombardment as zero : the attack will be carried out by pushing strong patrols over the forward slope, these will hold the ground, the main body of the Companies will advance at dusk and consolidate the ground so occupied. Coster read these orders and

---

[1] Radford.

passed them to me as I was enjoying a cup of hot tea. I was half-way through them when the French barrage-fire commenced. (It was then 11.10.) We looked at each other, roared with laughter, and shouted "The Show's begun." Neither of us had had time to grasp the details. We just bundled our men out, and our Companies surged up the slope *en masse*. There was luck for us in this pell-mell evacuation of Dewdrop. The men were barely out when the German counter-bombardment fell on it, and on A Company, whose orders were to occupy it when we advanced.' It was, however, a less unhealthy spot for A than that which they quitted: there the Germans put down a most perilous and prolonged barrage-belt of rapid whizz-bangs some 70 yards deep.

In the meantime B Company also was on the move. They were soon held up by an unharassed machine-gun on their right. A Lewis gun was played on it effectually. One of the team tried to get away, but Fox dropped him with a rifle shot: he was found later hit in the stomach. The silencing of that machine-gun helped C and D Companies to come into line and get forward. On crossing the ridge to where the ground sloped towards the main German position the Companies came under direct small-arms fire, so a line of shell-holes was occupied temporarily. Patrols were organized to work their way forward; they did so, and established themselves about 15 yards short of the objective line. The three Company Commanders then met and agreed that the most practical procedure for the time being was to consolidate on the crest behind these outposts. Their reasons were the very exposed position of the objective, the difficulty of digging—for the sodden clay would not leave the shovel—and the fatigue of the men. When some senior artillery officers came up later to check the new line there was an inclination to cavil at these 15 yards and our provisional disposition, but the C.O. upheld it.

On the right the 100th Brigade, who had been held up three days before when the French took Boritza, were able to advance. When the Germans in the gap saw the progress that was being made on their flanks they left their shell-holes and hurried back. Except to a few of our men they were in dead ground, but the 100th people should have had a bag. The French, it was said, hardly gained their objectives at Sailly-Saillisel. On our left, a

section of the 20th R.F. on the roadside advanced perhaps 50 yards
and dug itself in; otherwise the 20th made no progress, although
B Company tried to help them with flank fire. Beyond them the
17th Division at Gueudecourt was held from the start.

The men were very well pleased with themselves. As soon as
there was a modicum of cover the work of digging a trench
dragged. Rain came on at noon, and weather conditions became
more and more depressing as the afternoon wore on. Our conjurer
alone rose above adversity; he sang with the raucous vibrato of
outside-the-public-bar door, and with voluntary encores, although
without hope of reward, "Somewhere the sun is shining." Then
he chanced to find a mislaid book of signed blank hospital tallies.
Along the line he went offering to sell "free passes to Blighty."
A form was missing when the book was recovered. One of the
slightly wounded of D Company was a half-baked fellow for
whom a good deal of allowance was always made. After
screaming loudly for the stretcher-bearers to attend to him, he
mulishly refused to act on advice and orders to go to hospital;
but when rations came up and he had drawn his portion he went
away rejoicing. At dusk digging was begun in front.

After dark, Radford 'detailed Mair to seek touch with the 100th
Brigade, our right flank being still in the air. Mair chose three
stalwarts and set off. The patrol had gone only about 50 yards
when a shot fired under the leader's nose caused them to
hustle back discomfited for further instructions. C.S.M. Dealing
suggested that "anyone on the flank should be mopped up"; so
the patrol was reinforced and he went with it. He was enveloped
in the flowing mackintosh cape affected, in khaki, by quartermaster sergeants and, in blue, by maternity nurses in rural parts.
In the fresh breeze that blew from the right Dealing's cloak flapped
like the flaps of a tent in a gale, and every note of his deep bass
was audible in my shell-hole as he asked or gave directions.
"Where are they, sir?" . . . "Form a horse-shoe round them."
. . . "Heave one among them, sir." . . . There was the crash
of a Mills bomb, and in no time four scared Germans were flung
in on me. Dealing had spotted "another likely lair, sir," and
suggested "that we collect them too." So the party went out
again, and formed a horse-shoe round the "likely lair." "Come
out, Allemand," boomed the C.S.M. . . . "Heave one among

them, sir." After the crash.—"Come out, Allemand, come out—
I say." . . . "Heave another, sir." . . . Crash. . . . "Apparently
there is nothing doing, sir": and the patrol came in disappointed.
Later on Mair went out again and found the 100th Brigade about
250 yards away.' The four Germans extracted from their lair so
summarily were provided with five days rations. Along with
them, wounded, was one of the missing of B's fighting patrol.
He said he had "been treated properly," his wounds had been
dressed, and he had been given food and drink. The prisoners
belonged to the 24th Regiment, and the 81st Frankfort-on-Main.
They were 19, 19, 22, and 26 years old. One English speaker was
a pleasant, talkative youth. When one of our fellows said how
"awful" a German bombardment was, he retorted: "You don't
know what a bombardment is, you haven't been under one of
your own."

The weather had cleared as day closed. Away in rear a big
howitzer coughed huskily from time to time, and high overhead
its shell sizzled and soughed eerily beneath the stillness in the starry
sky, to burst so far beyond Le Transloy that the report was muffled
and there was no echo although sounds carried far: else, for the
first time in two weeks, only a rare shot ruffled the calm of
night.

November 6th.—By daylight the three front Companies were
linked up in a trench of sorts, and C and D were covered by strong
advanced posts in T-heads. Owing to the failure of the troops on
the left B Company had to form a flank on the Le Transloy road.
Mist allowed a lot of work to be done unseen by the German
infantry, and, although an aeroplane came and had a good look
at the position, the German artillery was comparatively quiet
during the day. The night too was quiet, only an occasional
field-gun fired. Moonlight favoured work on the outpost line;
it was fairly well connected up, and a serviceable, if shallow,
November 7th—communication trench was dug. In the forenoon
there was much strafing; and rain flooded our new trenches.

At dusk the 2nd Devons, 8th Division, arrived. Relief was a
laborious affair, and the trouble of two days in getting down
stretcher-cases came to a head. A notion that our wounded should
be left as the 11th Brigade had left theirs at Morval was intolerable,
but firmness had to be used to overcome it. Triple squads carrying

on short relays were needed to get the stretchers over the ground, so exhausting was the work. A clear sky and moonlight saved *November 8th*—bearers and wounded from shell-hole hazards. It was well on in the morning before anyone reached the untented part of La Briqueterie in which we had to bivouac. There was a shack for the C.O. and me. Lying on a trench-board was, after the last experience, too suggestive of the rack, so I sat up drying clothes and cursing. Why are tired men given no better resting-place than this half-flooded claypit? Why does our Army now leave its dead lying about anyhow? Why does it now leave its wounded in its midst behind, or bring them out only under lethal threats? Why are men still being flung against an enemy in these appalling weather conditions?—and with far less method than our shells are flung. Were we not told a month ago of the German line having been driven in so far that its flanks must be pulled back? —it doesn't look like breaking. Our total casualties these six days are 150.

At 11 o'clock our withdrawal was continued, via Montauban and Fricourt, to billets at Méaulte. I had a luxurious hot bath at Corps H.Q. They do themselves well. No mud there, duck-boards are laid two-deep; the huts are windproofed, and there are stoves everywhere, yet the poor devils "find it cold sometimes." The yarn that they all ran out of their camp when the German bomber was over it, "to see what he had done over the ridge," is listened to with the politeness due to Corps.

November 10th.—Another fine day, blue sky and sunshine, but wet under foot. In the early hours a hot strafe a few miles off shook the houses. About noon the Prince of Wales had a look at us informally; Geiger had brought him over from Corps. He returned in the afternoon and, after listening to the Drums, had tea at H.Q. A clean-run youth, very fair, looks well in uniform, talks gaily and easily. The Guards passed through, going up to attack Le Transloy. Their beat is slower than ours.—When the Welsh Division was attached to them for instruction a Guards battalion, having its packs carried in lorries, passed a Welsh battalion in full marching order: a little Welshman, sweating and puffing, looked at them and said, "Thank God, I've got my health and strength."

November 11th.—Yesterday morning's strafe is dwarfed by this morning's; there is said to be a German attack at Beaumont-Hamel. For a third night of clear moonlight bombers have been round here. A French dump and one of ours have been blown up; a tentful of men at Buire and a line of horses elsewhere are said to have gone west; four houses in Amiens are wrecked. Our billets are machine-gunned from the air each night, with no more loss than of some roof-tiles so far.

CHAPTER XI

Somme—Winter, a hard one—A chilly rest—Live and let live: Abbeville: The downs above Clery—The thermometer below zero—Les Bouffes!—" Thank God—and the Brigadier:"—Implications and Interactions

Contributors:—KENT; MORGAN JONES; MOODY; RADFORD

Sketches:—1, 11, 12

At 11.15 forenoon we marched to Buire, and entrained at 2. The train took 11 hours to do the first 15 miles. At the end of an hour of one of the halts a wag at the rear called, "Pass it along, *November 12th*—'steady in front.'" We arrived at Airaines at 3.30, then we marched 7 miles more alongside the same railway line to Forceville, where there is a station: C and D Companies went on to adjoining Neuville. Since the Transport left us three days ago to travel by road the men had to carry a lot of gear, but they came along well. Those near me had breath to spare to speak of the scenery, a rare topic of outspoken remark. What charmed them to speech was a wooded knoll rising from pasture, with horses and cattle and more trees, in a Corotesque mist. On beech and chestnut the deeper yellows, amber, graded brown, russet and red of leaves ripe to fall were beautiful even in a sunless dawn. A little snow, our first this winter, fell as we neared our billets. H.Q. is in the château of the Comte de Forceville. It may be seventeenth century. Trees grow close to it; the ground floor is the ground paved with flags of freestone, our room has coco-matting, it smells musty and is raw-cold. A bit of English park is unkept, but pleasing, nothing else is. The pall of neglect is on everything. The comfortless barns, that are the Companies billets, struck everyone with a chill, but our conjurer again raised his voice to the tune, more or less, of "Somewhere the sun is shining." Then he found an estaminet where café cognac, so called, was on sale. Next morning he was charged with being "drunk and resisting his escort." D'Arcy Fox, the Acting C.O., suggested that the second charge be dropped since the prisoner had to be wheeled to the Guard-room in a barrow. Bracey, Butcher's mild-mannered successor, had, in fact, given him a belting before carting him. I left Mann putting into shape a scheme of training the C.O. drew up before going on leave, and went on leave myself. In London I made a note of driving from the station in a hansom; the scarcity of taxis caused many of these famed, obsolete carriages to be brought back to the streets.

November 24th.—Returning through Etaples these lines painted in bold letters on a board at the station confronted us:

> A wise old owl lived in an oak;
> The more he saw the less he spoke,
> The less he spoke the more he heard.
> Soldiers should imitate that old bird.

During my twelve days absence the scene has changed. The exquisite wood is now colourless, leafless; and under the plough the country is becoming an even drab.

November 25th.—Forceville is mainly a group of farms. The village pond takes the surface drainage, and that consists in no small measure of the outflow of the farm middens. The Mayor has just been along to ask us not to wash our limbers in the pond for a few days; the villagers would like the water to settle because they are going to make their cider.

December 1st.—Practising with the new box respirator. Gaspirator soon put out exaspirator as its common name. There was nothing but training to be done at Forceville. The days were raw and misty, and often wet; the nights very cold, sometimes freezing. The Company cooks, having burned swill tubs to eke out the skimp issue of coal, pretended to be scandalized, and helped the farmer to look for them; and the treads of granary stairs went into the men's billet fire when other fuel failed. A lot of the men had chilblains on hands and feet; and a mild influenza was epidemic, it lasted until spring.

December 7th.—The Transport gone by road, we're waiting to go. The Mayor dined at H.Q. He is the most genial official of his kind we have had to do with. He has done all in his power to be helpful; he has tolerated in his house one of our number who lapses into rowdiness. He seems to own the village: has a jute and sail-cloth factory: has visited England repeatedly, and knows Germany better. He did not like unfavourable comparisons of the local climate with ours, but he was most appreciative of Parry's cooking. The district is ultra-clerical.

December 8th.—6.45 a.m.—marched to Airaines, thence by train via Amiens to Méricourt, thence again marched to Vaux-sur-Somme. What a contrast between this country now—leafless, muddy, grey—and its greenery, dust and bright sunshine in July and August. The Division is taking over from the 30th French Division in the line.

December 9th.—At noon we marched to Bray, where we stayed for five days just sheltering from damp and rain, cold and frost. Officers and men, milk-goat and Christmas poultry, were all together in a hut built by the French; it was too large to heat, and its sanitation too French for us.

There has been a lot of agitation among our Regular rank and file over a proposal, that is being pressed, to admit "duration" men to membership of the Regimental Comrades Association. The Old Army won't have it; the 1st and 2nd Battalions are firm in their opposition.

During a reminiscent talk a regimental field-day in this Battalion twelve years ago was described. The attack-formation was two paces interval between each man. After an advance of 100 yards the C.O. and the R.S.M. paced the intervals; if they were ragged the movement was repeated. It seems ridiculous. But if the fatal gregarious instinct can be overcome, and men prevented from closing where the going looks easier or for company, it will be only by insistent training.

Division holds a terrible threat over us: "If this Order is not complied with it will be cancelled." The dear Q. man means that if the privilege of extra baths he has offered is not used it will be withdrawn.

No more will be heard of the German peace offer. The French are regaining lost ground at Verdun, capturing guns by the hundred and Germans by the thousand; and a political General has been made Commander-in-Chief. It was told of Joffre that he consoled Generals he dismissed by saying that he too would be dismissed.

December 14th.—We marched 8½ miles to Maurepas, on a dull

afternoon, and bivouacked in the Ravine where all the divisional transport is, and the mud is many inches deep. Our route was through the valley in which are the remains of Combles : a surprising amount of it is standing—but dumb and mournful walls. Our new Corps is the XV, now du Cane's.

December 16th.—The C.O. is back after a week in hospital.

December 17th.—This is the second day without a potato issue, those supplied being uneatable. The troops think the deprivation is an outrageous wrong. It was our first experience of the shortage which was being felt at home ; the whole food supply of our civil population had become a serious problem.

December 18th.—We relieved the 5th S.R. at Bouchavesnes, near the southern edge of St. Pierre Vaast Wood. Contrary to an invariable habit of footing it when the Battalion marches I had to ride. It is thirty-five years since I had such chilblains, the year most of a Christmas holiday was spent in bed. H.Q. is a louse-infested French excavation in the chalk by the side of the Péronne–Bapaume road : a whizz-bang will be enough to stave in the roof. We all live and cook in it. The Companies were in rudely dug trenches on the crest of a steep-sided down, which were so exposed that there could be no movement in them by day, or access to them, for there were no communos. The only wire was a single strand of barb and an occasional coil of French concertina. But the sector was quiet. We took over a tacit live-and-let-live arrangement, and Division did not require any work to be done. At Rancourt, just left of us, it was quite different ; attack and counter-attack was of daily happening, and shelling was limited only by the difficulty of getting up shells.

Two weeks of continuously bad weather extended over this time. There was snow and rain, frost and thaw by turns—the conditions which cause trench-foot. A four days tour cost us 30 to hospital with broken chilblains and a few trench-foot cases. This was quite a new experience for the Battalion, but the number was said to be the smallest in the Division ; one battalion was debited—by report—with 200 cases. Inactivity chilled the two front Companies, fatigues on steep gradients and heavy going tired the support Companies. Just behind the front men struggled with loads, and pack-horses foundered in mud taking up ammunition of which the guns could not get enough, yet a Decauville railway the French had made and used, was abandoned. On the dejection of that existence one of the C.O.'s orderlies broke, one day, with the news that Péronne had been captured by the French. He replied to the C.O.'s scepticism, "It's official, sir." "What do you mean by 'official'?" "Bob Owens, the cook, told me, sir, and Bob had it from Sergeant Morgan of the Divisional Water Point, sir." The story is typical of the channels through which rumour runs and of the belief rumour gains, but the source of rumours is one of the mysteries of this life. A few days later a report of French origin credited the B.E.F. with the capture of Bapaume. This orderly is one of our minor characters. At Buire, after our first dip in the Somme, it amused and surprised a few chance spectators to see the C.O. greet, like a long-lost child, a little, stocky, newly joined private. H. is a prosperous little Welshman, a haberdasher in the Midlands. I suspect that his wife runs the business. He shares the C.O.'s fancy for Sealyham terriers; the two are friends and rivals in the show-ring. To be C.O.'s orderly is quite a good job these days. H. preens himself in the reflected glory of his office, exaggerates its importance, and has the men believe that he is "a power."

December 22nd.—Relieved, and taken in buses to a comfortable English hutted camp, No. 111, near Bray. Our Army huts hereabout, of plain creosoted deal, made to hold a company, are said to cost £1000 each by the time they have been erected.—G.S.W. casualties are 2 killed and 3 or 4 wounded during these four days.

December 23rd.—D Company's cooker has been troublesome for a long time, and once or twice at Ordnance Repair Shops. The cooks' attempt yesterday to get away with one belonging to the Labour Battalion failed from neglect to obliterate completely the identification marks of the one they left in its stead. We are ashamed of them. They have been admonished. And Yates is complaining that Meredith, who succeeded Gittens as Transport Sergeant, "is no good. He's so honest and truthful that you can't trust him." He had butted in with a higher figure than Yates had declared when a Remounts Officer came to comb out horses surplus to establishment.

December 24th.—A most untimely draft has arrived; it unbalances our numbers and our provision for the men's Christmas dinner. The new men are dismounted Yeomanry, the best physically we have had since Spring. The evidence that they had had a year's training was far to seek.

December 25th.—Conning was suspected of being Father Christmas when I found a tin of vermin paste in a sock, but it was Mann. These two youths are our most popular officers with the men of the Battalion. Radford is the most popular Company Commander, as was made plain to-day; he shares his men's esteem with "Snookie," one of his bad hats. Before the C.O. went down with influenza he decreed a merry Christmas if we were out of the line. The officers and the Canteen subscribed a fund for extras for the men. There were no duties to-day. In the morning there was a distribution of writing-pads and cigarettes from home. One o'clock dinner was soup; roast meat with potato, carrot, turnip, and onion; plum-pudding; an apple, or orange, and nuts. The sergeants had whisky, port and cigars. The afternoon was left free for digestion. Few walked out in two inches of thawing snow. At 5 o'clock there was tea with cake, candied fruit, and sweets. That was followed by a sing-song in each company hut, when every man had a canteenful of beer. Plum-pudding from the Comforts Committee at home had divided up at less than a half-pound per man; a half-pound per man from a private donor arrived later. This year H.Q. made sure of its goose and turkey; we've been fattening them for a month. We had pâté de foie gras, julienne, curried prawns, roast goose, potato and cauliflower, plum-pudding, anchovy on toast, dessert; Veuve Cliquot, port, cognac, benedictine; coffee. Each Company dined alone; after dinner we all forgathered and had a jolly.

December 26th.—We marched 8½ miles to Camp 13. It is in a muddy hollow in the Sailly-Laurette neighbourhood: very uncomfortable, no coal or firewood. A sergeant died in his sleep, from natural causes. It was always a treat to me to see him walk, he had such a fine carriage.

December 27th.—To Buire, 4½ miles, and entrained at "Edge Hill." A cold, otherwise good, railway journey to Pont Remy, west of our recent quarters at Forceville, was followed by a 4-mile march to Vauchelles-les-Quesnoy on the higher ground east of Abbeville. The Transport made a two-days march of it from Bray.

January 1st, 1917.—H.Q. had haggis for lunch. The Southerners can't get enough of that mysterious Scotch dish.—Mrs. "Tiger" Phillips and one of her Y.M.C.A. Canteen companions came to tea.—With facilities for cooking Parry sent up an uncommonly good dinner. Vermouth; hors d'œuvres variées; clear soup; sole and a perfect sauce; roast turkey and sausage, celery; plum-pudding; savoury—enigmatic, but delicious; Veuve Cliquot, port, benedictine; coffee. Present: the C.O., D'Arcy Fox, Mann, Harries, Robertson—all of H.Q.; Binge Owen, Cuthbert, de Miremont, Coster—commanding companies; Barkworth—bombs; Conning—Lewis guns; Yates and Radford. Only one of the party was a nuisance. Our servants must have enjoyed *January 2nd*—themselves afterwards. Harries, whose intake of alcohol is never other or more than a half-glass of port in twenty-four hours, was called by his man at 1.30 a.m.; when he cursed Lewis mumbled in answer, "I'm not quite right myself, sir": and a quiet little hill-farm boy has laughed and wept all day.

The Somme Despatch is enlightening as an expression of the views of G.H.Q., which differ from those of the infantry—notably on the fighting quality and morale of our and the enemy's formations. The German is not what he was, but his falling off seems, on contact, to be no greater than ours. Without our superiority in guns where would we be? The French seem to be far ahead of us in recent attack technique, formation, and the co-ordination of rifle-grenade and automatic rifle-fire.

Three dull weeks were spent at Vauchelles. The highly paid Australians had just gone, so the price of everything in the village was appalling. The Companies were in the out-buildings of farms which were quite good but so cold that the men were rarely warm. H.Q. was well housed in the château of a frigidly pious couple with 15 children: surely a record for France. Monsieur had made money in Boulogne and bought this pretentious mansion; its staircase is oak-grained deal, the walls are marmoreal to the eye but varnished paper to touch. A programme of training, which the C.O. put on a platoon basis, and games went on under his supervision as continuously as bad weather would allow. There was frost, or rain, or snow all the time. 'Sunshine, a welcome sight, after a morning of drizzle,' is my note on January 4th: 'fine moonlight, followed by our first fine day,' on the 5th: 'our second fine day,' on the 15th.—The daily sick parade had become a serious affair by this date in the War. A year ago it was very exceptional to see a dozen "sick"; now nothing was too trivial to be a pretext for "going sick," and 60 was the daily average. Cleanly habits kept the Old Army men remarkably free from minor ailments. Neglect of cleanliness caused most of the foot sores, and the vast amount of itch, lousiness, and consequent debilitating maladies that ravaged the Territorial and "duration" troops, and taxed the capacity of the hospitals. One day a youth reported with a local, and not common, form of parasite. "Where do you think you got this?" I asked. He said that he had "noticed it after sleeping with a Scotsman."—One evening the Mess-waiter made a mystery of telling me that a civilian wanted to see me. A sickly, misshapen youth had a live fowl under his arm, which he offered, with rare natural courtesy, as an honorarium for attendance on his wife.

Abbeville is within walking distance. It is a sleepy town to be on highways. It clings to its age-long sail-making industry although it has ceased for so long to be a port. Its only cab, a four-wheeler, was in much demand for the uphill return journey: a cold journey by cab, because the prudent old cabby took out the windows and stowed them in safety when frolicsome youths bespoke him.

January 7th, Sunday.—A great to-do was made of a Drumhead Service on our lawn, conducted by a bishop. Troops from the surroundings were brought over. Division and Brigade turned up in panoply and in force. It is said that a bishop once preached to a mere half-dozen voluntaries. He made such a fuss about the indignity, and the waste of spiritual unction, that an Order from High Up required the attendance of "the greatest possible number" on these solemn occasions: hence this crush. One can almost pardon the bishops their banalities since audiences were ordered for them. By special request of Division we have a Chaplain at H.Q. We, for our part, are complaining that Division's arrangements for the delousing of the men's clothing are inefficient, that the refusal of blankets for sterilization at the same time as clothing stultifies its treatment.

January 8th.—A very young officer on the Divisional Staff, much disliked for his airs by front-line subalterns, has returned from a Special Course. Mann asked him if the pass-out exam. was stiff.

"No," he said, "it wasn't only for the Staff, there were regimental officers there too." Swelled-headed youth apart, the gap between the Staff and the Front Line widens. Recently, at the Army School, a strong-minded C.O. asked if Staff Officers could not be attached to infantry battalions during the quiet winter months to learn something of their job from the business end; it is the French system. The reply was as expected—half the Staff is on leave these months and the other half "is too busy to be spared."

The Chaplain, who crossed recently, described a scene, typical of the new regime, which he witnessed. Lord Northcliffe was embarking at Boulogne for England; he had visited France to testify in his many papers to the excellence of everything under the Government which he thinks, with some reason, he has in his pocket. Several General Officers, among others, were ordered off a part of the deck on to which a special gangway was run for him and his numerous ink-slinging retinue of serviceable indispensables. The Generals swore roundly. Before we left Vauchelles some officers were overdue off leave. They and many others were hung up for a week at Havre; owing to a shortage of coal, under the new regime, trains could not be run.

January 13th.—The Drums played in the Place de l'Amiral at Abbeville. Our little Drum-Sergeant's bow to the French audience was worth going to see. The price of chocolates has gone up to 6 and 8 francs the pound.

January 17th.—4.30 a.m., réveillé and snow: 6 a.m., marched in snow to Pont Remy: arrived at 7.30 for a train at 9, and did not start until 1.30 p.m. While we hung about the name of an estaminet across the road caught my eye: "C'est mieux ici qu'en face." I was leaning against the railing of the local gaol. Its like is unthinkable at home. Arrived at Bray 11.30 p.m.; back to the cosy huts of Camp 111. Measles, probably brought from Vauchelles, is among us.

January 18th.—A Paris bus, to appearance stranded here, is the loft of the French pigeon post in this area. Our pigeons are hired locally by the month.

January 19th.—The B.E.F. is being extended to the Somme; the Division is relieving the French 17th Division in the Clery Sector. Marching at 2 p.m. on very good French-repaired roads, we passed their artillery coming out. They were mightily in-

terested in our Drums. It seems that the French have 1 officer
to 8 guns; we have a captain and 3 subalterns to 6 guns. Our
billets at Suzanne cramped; we were packed like herrings.

January 21st.—At 9.45 we marched via Curlu and Hem, again
on excellent roads remade by the French. The night was quiet,
and snow on the ground made it light. A communication trench,
in part an old German trench, two kilometres long seemed ten;
everyone was laden, and weary at the end of it. No one talked;
the only sounds were the drumming of many feet on frozen
ground and the clink of accoutrements. Coming again into the
desolation felt eerie, and the eeriness grew each time a rocket
glowing above the ridge in front gave us our spectral selves for
company, and in falling snatched them away, scurrying backwards,
behind us.

The C.O. was in nominal command of the Brigade during the
relief, because the Brigadier would be senior to the French Colonel.
We took over from a battalion of the 90th Regiment. Our H.Q.
January 22nd—was regaled with sausage, *paté*, and sweet champagne at 5 o'clock. Later, the Frenchmen ate with gusto an
English breakfast of quaker oats, and egg and bacon, but they
didn't like our bread: their bread is excellent. The Colonel told
us of a visit he paid to the Russian Brigade in France. Invited to
"coffee," he was given a slice of melon and then kept drinking
champagne for two unbroken hours, which he seemed little likely
to forget. The Battalion Commander, a cavalry officer, admits
that the German is top dog here.

French rations are abundant. Every regiment, three battalions,
has a canteen which sells all we do and such live stock as poultry.
Their medical organization does not necessitate such early clearance
to the ambulance as ours. Their dug-outs are roomy, but they
live too much over or alongside their latrines for our liking.
French construction is as much superior to ours as German work
is to theirs. The construction and upkeep of communications is
the work of a permanent local staff, not, as with us, of R.E. with
infantry fatigue-parties that come and go with every division and
brigade. Their good communications and use of tramways close
to the support line make easy the delivery of material in quantities
that are beyond our manhandling ways of doing. Their telephone
system is good, their trenches free from "festoons"—for our

arrival anyhow, and they have direct communication with the units to right and left. Their system of relief is confusing to us, and original; they do not go out by platoons; the men are given a rendezvous and an hour, and each post buzzes off, collectively or individually, on a relief's arrival.

No one at Division or Brigade has thought of putting ammunition, R.E. stores, or the ingredients of a vaunted trench-foot preventive on order, so we can't get any. This is the eighth day of continuous frost and occasional snow showers. The ground is ice-bound, it rings to one's tread; but there is to be no issue of fuel. What does the G.O.C. think his men are made of?

January 23rd.—Lateral telephoning has been cut out: there are festoons of wire in the trenches. In the morning two French planes attacked three Germans: by their speed and manoeuvre they shot down one in flames and one crippled in a few minutes; the third escaped. Great flying by the Frenchmen. After dark we took over the front of Clery Left.

January 24th.—What a night! I have not been so cold, or for so long, since bivouacking on the Basuto Border. We are on the top of a bare 1200-foot down among downs. Mont St. Quentin, a truncated sugar-loaf peak, is half right; beyond it the steeples of Péronne (seen from our right) are features of a wonderful panorama. The Tortille and the Canal du Nord are in an intervening valley 200 feet below us, and unseen, but on the right the mostly frozen Somme winds between the reedy Clery–Biaches marsh and a high bank on which pine trees grow. A lofty sky is almost cloudless, the air is crystalline, and the dazzling winter sunbeams sparkle on the filmy mantle of frozen snow that drapes everything, as if it were jewelled. But the delight of it doesn't warm chilled bones. During the next four weeks the gunners were reporting temperatures of 15 degrees of frost, and the ground became ice-bound to a depth of 16 inches. The crude untraversed trenches the Division had taken over had no cubby-holes, and no dug-outs except for the various H.Q. These got small quantities of coke. There were cases of coke-fume poisoning—headache on waking, or being roused off the floor, and even to the stage of vomiting; men would not deny themselves warmth who had the chance of it, however unventilated their abode. There was no means of having warmth in the trenches. Cooking was forbidden

in them. Tea and cooked food were sent up in tins wrapped in
hay in sand-bags, but on arrival the contents were tepid at the best.
"Tommy's cooker" of solidified alcohol was not allowed, although
the next division had an issue of a slab a man each day. The surroundings in reach were bare of wood of any kind; a little planting
of saplings had been cut down already, but men hacked at the roots
for chips, and chance graves were robbed of their rude crosses, to
make a miniature fire.

January 25th.—An Anglo-German air duel took place after lunch.
As the other plane was coming down on fire behind H.Q. the pilot
jumped to his death rather than be roasted. His clothing was just
singed. He wore the ribbon of the Iron Cross, 1st Class.—The
G.O.C.'s chauffeur struck a match to see how much petrol there
was in his tank, and burned down part of our Q.M. store containing
Shoey Johnson's watch-mending and engraving tools.—The C.O.
was wounded in the arm and side when inspecting the wire,
fired on by one man of a German patrol who would see our party
against the sky, dark though the night was. Bad luck.

January 26th.—The Battalion was relieved to "P.C. Madame,"
a dirty place at the end of the limb of Road Wood. I remained
behind for one night because my 5th S.R. relief took ill—and this
is the eve of the Kaiser's birthday. But he is fallen, fallen from
January 27th—his high estate; there was no celebration. The
wind has changed, but not the weather so far.

January 29th.—Back in the front of Clery Left, the conditions
are unchanged.

January 30th.—Sergeant Francis, a good man, was killed on the
wire opposite owing to bungling by a patrol. Later, Lindsley was
wounded in the elbow; he was fired on by a sentry group of his
Company whom he forgot to warn that he was going out on patrol
a second time. He died of tetanus, lockjaw, the only death of the
kind to my knowledge in my time; it was common in the early
months of the War, before there was enough serum.

January 31st.—Relieved in bright moonlight, we were brought in
lorries to a tented camp among the trees at Suzanne. The wintry
scene from this camp was most attractive. We looked over snow
and ice on a reed-grown marsh, to pines lining the river and canal,
and climbing the rising bank beyond; everything sparkled,
whether in sunshine or moonlight.

February 1st.—Frise ("Freeze") Bend, where Henry V crossed at Eclusier, is a short walk upstream. The marsh looks much as it is described in Henry's day, although it may be smaller. The river was being shelled to break the ice lest raiders cross on it, and the water was rising into the sunshine in great fountains with rainbow-hued fringes. A poacher's rifle echoes in the valley at long intervals. The starved water-fowl are easy prey, exhausted birds can be walked down.

February 2nd.—Candlemas Day is clear and fair.—When last we were here a Chaplain bombasted : he was new to the forward area. He laid it down, with a jingo air, that "a man's attitude to war service is quite a simple affair : if he's for it he's for it, and vice versa." He has vice versa'd back to the Base already. His predecessor disliked war, even at this range, as much as he, but he had a sense of humour that steadied him. The Chaplain's tent was next a Canteen from which he heard such frequent mention of "(obscene) biscuits," that he asked, and got, his C.O. to make the sergeant post a sentry over the tin, "to see that the biscuits committed no indecency."

February 3rd.—The modern château here is in the debased, bride's-cakey Renaissance style. There is little real damage to the outside, the inside has been stripped and damaged—by whom ? Its owner came to see it to-day. He exclaimed "réclamation" in crescendo as he went from room to room. His last word, spoken with a smile, was "réclamation." He'll try, like the rest of his countrymen, for compensation from his own Government and ours.—Something about a passing French transport driver, a fine-looking man of about my own age, attracted me, so I spoke to him and his fellows. One of them told me that the driver had news of the destruction of his home near Verdun. To my halting words of sympathy he replied, "Mais, j'ai bonne santé, oui. Ça ne fait rien. J'ai bonne santé."

February 6th.—The frost relaxes, a high easterly wind is blowing.

February 8th.—Thaw where the sun strikes. Glad to be away from Camp 17, although we are back to the front in Béthune. The right and left subsectors have been allowed to keep their French names, Girodon and Béthune. Generally the French trench names have been changed, although they were mostly those of dead French officers, thus "Oursel" has become "Wurzel." One was called after Captain Fryatt, one of our splendid merchant skippers. The name Béthune reminds me that last winter my usual trench kit was waders to keep my legs clean and dry, this winter they have not been worn yet. Binge Owen is Acting O.C., Cuthbert having gone to hospital.

February 10th.—A report on the arrangements at the waterpoint, which Division called for, read like a satire. To supply two or three thousand men, two men bail water out of a small tub into petrol-tins and one scoops their spillings out of a hollow in the ice that has formed round the tub. But the conditions are exceptional. To get extra water the men learned what a heap of snow has to be melted to fill a cup. B and C relieved A and D in front.

February 12th.—Relieved : we went out through interminable communication trenches to reserve in Howitzer Wood, an old German artillery position east of Clery, and a fairly comfortable *February 13th*—place as things are. Trench boards are greasy, nearly all the bite is out of the wind.

Since February 3rd, when I noted "we are for it soon," the absorbing preoccupations of H.Q. and the Company Commanders had been a minor operation and the weather conditions, the two interacted. The French had observation of the Tortille Valley ; they were driven from it ; Nomansland was dotted with the dead of their attempts to regain it. At one place close to the parapet a Frenchman and a German lay as they had bayoneted each other, the throat of the one, the chest of the other, pierced. The German withdrawal, which we heard of four months ago, was about due ; that fact increased the Staff's wish to regain observation. It was said that Brigade had toyed, after its manner, with a fancy to "do something" : then Division blew hot and grew cold about it : finally Corps took up the idea in earnest. The seizure and consolidation of Hertzfeldt Trench was ordered. It was a shallow blunt salient on a reverse slope a mile south of Bouchavesnes and 500 yards west of the Péronne–Bapaume road. Its capture would give us a deeper blunt salient on a forward slope. Until our prospective undertaking had been floated it had several "onlie begetters" ; they were all outside the Battalion, which damned it from the first as foolish and wicked. From the 3rd to the 16th there are nine entries in my diary on the progress of the scheme. Assuming that the ground was no longer

white with crackling snow, and not too slippery with thaw for
men to keep their feet and formation in the dark, that our assembly
was not given away by every third man coughing, we held that
there remained the fundamental difficulty of attacking, on a narrow
front, dead ground in which the enemy had an overwhelming
advantage. The most observant of us inferred, from what had been
seen of shoots, that there were no guns behind us which could fire
on the vital part of the German defence, and that the scale and
conditions of the operation denied us any practical means of dealing
with it. Lastly, consolidation was impossible owing to the frozen
state of the ground. The first or second of three or four conferences at Brigade took place on the 6th. It was summarized
thus: the Brigadier exchanged small jokes with the O.C. 20th
R.F., who made puns; the G.S.O.3 and the Acting Brigade-Major
exchanged social gossip; Mann raised the problem of the artillery,
the Brigadier said with pontifical finality, "Ah, that will be all
right, Mann"; Cuthbert and Modera didn't open their mouths.
We arranged that Mann should ask for the attendance of a Gunner
at the next conference, or that the outline of the plan be shown
to the C.R.A. before it went further. When he came back empty-
handed, and was cursed, he exclaimed through tears, "They won't
listen to me, I'm too junior." First Cuthbert, then Binge Owen,
was our senior representative; both were overawed. And so by
conference the data were contributed from which the Brigadier
was to draw up a scheme.

February 16th.—A mild night. A seeming bombardment is the
large Plateau Dump, on the high ground behind us, going up; an
air-raider started a fire in it early in the morning.—Yesterday 105
paraded sick, to-day 80; there were some of the Old Lot among
them. Sore feet, trench-fever, influenza and colds are the chief
real items, but the Battalion is having to carry pickets, wire,
duckboards, bombs, and ammunition through "miles" of trench.
Binge Owen is off to hospital with measles. Mann is Acting
O.C. himself.—An unseen bird twittered. It is long since I heard
the voice of any bird except the water-fowl, but a man tells me he
has heard a lark.

In the evening C Company relieved the 5th S.R.; A, B, and D
Companies are stowed on the left. C is to prepare the line and
assembly position, the other Companies are to side-step into it in

1. Captain James Churchill Dunn, D.S.O., M.C. (and Bar), D.C.M., R.A.M.C.

2. Officers of 1 and 2/RWF taken at Malta on the 2 March 1914 – 2/RWF
officers include – Back Row: Fourth from left, Second-Lieutenant W. G.
Holmes; Fifth from right, Lieutenant Pyers Mostyn; Fourth from right,
Lieutenant and Quartermaster H. Yates; Far right, Lieutenant L. M. Ormrod;
Middle Row: Fifth from left, Lieutenant F. E. Fitzroy; Sixth from left,
Lieutenant G. O. Thomas; Sixth from right, Lieutenant J. A. Childe-Freeman;
Fifth from right, Lieutenant J. C. Wynne-Edwards; Fourth from right,
Lieutenant P. C. Maltby; Second from right, Captain M. J. Phillips ("Tiger");
Front Row: First from left, Captain E. N. Jones-Vaughan; Third from left,
Captain W. M. C. Perry-Knox-Gore; Fourth from right, Major O. de L.
Williams; Far right, Captain and Adjutant C. S. Owen

3. 2/RWF on parade with the Regimental Goat, Agra, India, 1907

Above left: 4. Second-Lieutenant Robert von Ranke Graves, Wrexham, October 1914

Above: 5. Lieutenant-Colonel W. B. Garnett

Left: 6. Captain C. I. Stockwell ('Buffalo Bill')

7. Major R. A. Poore D.S.O (k. in a. 26.9.17)

8. Lieutenant-Colonel 'Cocky' Cockburn

10. Captain Llewelyn Evans

9. Captain N. H. Radford M.C.

12. Private Frank Richards ('Big Dick')

11. Captain J. C. Mann M.C. (k. in a. 26.9.17)

13. 2/RWF in northern France August 1914

14. 2/RWF Billets, Bois Grenier, December 1914

15. 'Old Sweats' 2/RWF early 1915

16. British soldiers wearing a variety of respirators, December 1915

17. 2/RWF at rest after being relieved from the trenches, Somme July 1916

18. A recently captured German trench on the Somme, August 1916

19.   Officers of 2/RWF taken at Buire, on the Somme, early August 1916.
Back Row left to right: Captain Goldsmith (w. 25.9.15); Captain P. S. Wilson
(k. in a. 20.8.16); Captain Moldsworth Williams M.C. (w. 26.9.17); Captain
N. H. Radford; Captain C. R. Dolling M.C. (k. in a. 20.8.16); Captain Woolf;
Captain Loverseed; Captain E. Coster M.C. (k. in a. 26.9.17); Middle Row left
to right: Captain Barrett; Captain J. C. Dunn D.C.M. (gassed 22.5.18);
Lieutenant-Colonel C. H. Crawshay (w. 25.1.17); Captain J. V. Higginson;
Lieutenant and Quartermaster H. Yates; Front Row left to right: Second-
Lieutenants Jagger; A. T. Harries; E. C. Tunnicliffe and Robertson
20.   Battalion field cookers, November 1916

21.   British troops at Victoria Station in transit whilst on leave

22.   Regimental Goat, Fifes and Drums of 2/RWF at 33rd Divisional Horse
Show, 18 July 1917

23.   A group photograph of cheery young 2/RWF officers taken in Amiens
early April 1917. Sitting left to right: Lieutenant R. Greaves (w. 23.4.17);
Captain E. Coster M.C. (k. in a. 26.9.17); Second-Lieutenant S. Sassoon M.C.
(w. 16.4.17); Front: Lieutenant Conning M.C. (k. in a. 27.5.17)

24. Major-General Pinney at 33rd Divisional Horse Show, 18 July 1917

25. 'C' Company N.C.O.'s 2/RWF, taken at Airlaines, July 1917. Standing left to right: Sergeant G. H. Downing, D.C.M.; Sergeant S. Morgan; Armourer Staff Sergeant J. Belfield; Sergeant Drummer W. J. Dyer M.M.; Lance-Sergeant J. Peate; C.Q.M.S. J. Hughes; Sergeant H. Howell; Sergeant F. Webster. Sitting left to right: Sergeant J. Williams D.C.M.; Sergeant N. Rose; Sergeant P. Downs; Lance-Sergeant G. Hedges; Sergeant Shoemaker A. C. Johnson; A/R.S.M. E. Dealing M.M. In front: "Billy" and Lance-Corporal R. Williams

26. German prisoners bringing in the wounded to a Regimental Aid Post, Clapham Junction, 20 September 1917

27. Machine gun post, Stirling Castle, Third Ypres, 26 September 1917

28. The desolation of Chateau Wood, Third Ypres, October 1917

29. Open warfare – British infantry advancing in artillery formation,
September 1918

30. Members of the Sergeants Mess 2/RWF at the Brigade Camp near Blangy-Tronville on the 8 January 1919

31. Members of 2/RWF who landed in Rouen on the 10 August 1914 and served continuously with the battalion until re-embarkation with the cadre in May 1919. From left to right: Captain W. H. Fox M.C.; Armourer Sergeant J. Belfield; Lieutenant D. Roberts-Morgan D.C.M., M.M.; Sergeant Childs; Sergeant Driver Dyer M.M., M.S.M.; Corporal Davies; R.Q.M.S. J. Hughes D.C.M.; Lance-Corporal Wright; Driver Carrol; Captain and Quartermaster H. Yates M.C.

time to go over to the tune of the guns: then, while A, B, and D consolidate the captured position, C is to dig a communication trench out to it. 'Of many absolutely futile ideas given effect to in my three years in France, this operation was one of the worst.'

February 17th.—Greasy mud abounds; communications on the hillside have become water channels, and the French drains are not being kept open. The best way to get about is on top, and it can be used in the morning mist. In these miserable conditions the men are weary and apathetic after several days of long, heavy fatigues carrying R.E. stores and ammunition. Our R.F. comrades in this adventure soon chucked their loads out on top of the communications, a labour-saving device that deprives them of the material needed for their share in the Show. Our patrols say that since last we were in the Germans have been allowed to repair the gaps made in their wire. This front has wakened to activity again. Last night German heavies and bombers were active on the back areas, both very destructively; to-day they have been strafing all along the line here, their machine-guns chiming in.

Late at night the Brigade Operation Order arrived. A first skimming shows that our concentrated artillery is to treat a trench to 15 minutes "intense" when an earlier paragraph has timed us to be consolidating in it. Mann and the Gunner sat down to the Order and found many wrong co-ordinates—experience points to these being Brigade's contribution; the hand of G.1 appears in the outline, and much of Mann's in the detail. We were still conning over this masterpiece, and had counted dozens of manuscript *February* 18th—changes in the typescript, when the G.O.C. blew in to wish us luck. Some things he said made us wonder what operation he was talking about. Was one of his other brigades raiding too? He seemed to have difficulty in understanding that getting through the wire to the assembly tapes while the guns make a distracting noise is not the same as making the assault under their barrage; but we did get a silent, if quizzical, hearing for our complete distrust of the barrage planned for us. The Gunner observer was induced to go away a little earlier than his orders to allow his Group Commander more time to look into some questions we have wanted answered from the first.

The morning was damp and misty. I stood garter-deep in liquid mud retrieving articles from an advanced aid-post. Stores looked like being swamped wherever we put them. Everywhere parapet and parados were sliding in towards each other. There were no duckboards, scoops or pumps. The one pair of gum-boots in the front line was passed by the officer on duty to his relief. Dry socks had come up with the rations as usual, but the men could not change into them; in dumb wretchedness they stood in 6 to 12 inches of ice-cold fluid, unable anywhere to take their boots off. By midday we heard that the Gunners had confirmed our opinion that they had no guns which could carry out the part of the artillery programme needed to cover our advance across the deadly zone. After lunch the Brigadier paid a flying visit. He had left his usual aplomb behind, and we were not inclined to talk. Next, we learned by telephone that there was to be no release yet from the caprice of the abstract tactician who from far-away disposes of us: someone playing fantastic tricks with reality had substituted 30 seconds shooting by two unregistered trench-mortars for the impotent batteries of guns. This was confirmed in an amended Brigade Operation Order, spread over an extra half-sheet of paper. There are times when foolscap is fitting, and ironic mirth is a safety-valve.

5.30 p.m. "Stand fast." At last: thank God—and the Brigadier. Even the soleplate of the 60-pound trench-mortar had risen "in mutiny and rage," and floated into the communication trench. At night the very few who had anything to lie on lay down early. *February 19th.*—The stunt is postponed until the 23rd.—The 20th R.F. Operation Order is a curiosity, although this is their first raid. But for necessarily different map references, and company parts, it is a word-for-word copy of Mann's Order issued, and sent to them, yesterday.

Lieut.-Colonel W. B. Garnett, from the 20th R.F., arrived to be our C.O. He soon had us harassed and embarrassed by his rare accomplishment, spelling. At last Conning inveigled him into "kneading" for "needing" bread, and the subject dropped for the time.

February 20th.—An idle day: conditions worse than ever. After dark we were relieved. The night was black as the pit; tracks and landmarks were washed out; we walked by faith, stumbling down the hillside until we chanced on the road. It was long after

midnight before anyone came on "Madame," that foul spot that was as bad as parts of the trenches. C Company strayed off any practical route; they were eight hours in reaching the support
February 21st—line half-way down the slope, a distance of a few hundred yards. The position had just been quitted by the 20th R.F. Its drainage had been so neglected that water overflowed the entrances to dug-outs; a communication was waist-deep in water, one man disappeared from view in it and was fished out by his equipment. Radford 'lay down on a board at 6.45 a.m. and was woken up about 7.30 by a loud explosion. The cook had started a fire and put on it a French S O S rocket, thinking, in the gloom, that it was a lump of wood. He was rather badly scorched, but I nearly cried with laughing at the funny side of the affair. I then went across country to Battalion H.Q. to report, and found myself under arrest.' The G.O.C. had come up at dawn; he was followed counter-clockwise by the Brigadier, who had got wind that he was about. Passing through C Company's resting-place, the G.O.C. saw rifles and equipment lying on the parapet and parados, muddy—naturally. In the written explanation he required of his prisoner it was pleaded that these were the least wet and dirty places on which the men could justifiably put anything. The affair went no further. Had the old dear expected to see the men scraped clean and shaved? One man had committed suicide, 84 were being sent to hospital, and 18 to rest at the Transport, nearly all victims of the weather conditions.

February 22nd.—50 more go to hospital or Transport; 60 of the total for these two days are from C Company. 1 p.m. Reprieved— the Show is off. Throughout the three weeks run of this farce the O.Cs. The Cameronians and 5th S.R., Lieut.-Colonels Chaplin and Clayton, were unfailing in their support of our views of its tactical side, and they could not be too helpful. Colonel Chaplin, who relieved A, B, and D Companies for the operation, arranged unofficially to send out Lewis guns, whose flank fire would give some cover to our advance and might let us close with the German screen, and to lend a company to try to dig a communication trench. The Pioneer Battalion had been allowed to cry off that job. None knew better than they that the ground was unworkable. Two weeks after this there were still three or four inches of ice-bound soil a foot below the thawed surface. By the 25th it came out that neither Brigade nor Division had any expectation of Hertzfeldt Trench being held, or of any measure of success.

The purpose of relating this projected operation in so much detail will not be "o'ertook unless the deed go with it." The 100th Brigade relieved us: the surface was considered passable by the 28th: raiding for information was wanted; and to wipe the eye of another brigade and battalion is in the game. Our Brigade retold, with amusing naïvety, how the early stages of its operation were borrowed for a small in-and-out raid: all went well until the raiders rose to their feet to make the assault, then they were raked by machine-guns and got no farther. Theirs, on a small scale, was the fate we had foretold all along as ours, because the plan of attack imposed on us ignored or belittled the shell-hole screen the Germans placed at night on the edge of the dead ground.

February 23rd.—No home mail for three days: a rumour that submarine sinkings in the Channel is the cause. Rations are very short: little or no bread, less than a half-ration of bully, no jam. We have not been short yet, but we can't be wasteful as formerly we were. Relieved and well away, for the bivouac is in part the site of a cemetery of which the surface indications have been obliterated or removed, and it smelt like it. The men came along well, and were quite cheery on the march. We got into Suzanne at *February 24th*—1 a.m. Thin stew was to me as nectar, then to bed. Lousy, very.—A fine white goat from the Wynnstay Hills, the *February 25th*—gift of the 3rd Battalion, made his first appearance on a Church Parade: he arrived three days ago. We are being *February 28th*—employed on light work in the camp.

March 1st, St. David' Day.—A genial, almost windless day ending in a crisp, starlit night. With times of rawness the weather was generally fine during this week. Fritz is said to have withdrawn from Gommecourt. When last we were in the line he blew a mine in the road that crossed Nomansland on our left front. As he is expected to withdraw on this front any day now, we, being on an hour's notice, have had little to do since coming here. It was nearing noon before there was any assurance that the officers St. David's Day Dinner could be held. Provisional plans had been made, and leeks had been bought for the Battalion. Yates, Mann, Mess-servants, Pioneers and defaulters, all pulled together. A very scratch kitchen was fitted up in a broken and dismantled shrine, to the scandal of some French details; a hut built on to it, and used as a chapel during the French occupation, was repaired and enlarged. Timber had been got from the Engineers. Tables and benches were run up by the Pioneer Sergeant, "Daisy" Horton. The merit of a plain menu was Parry's excellent cooking: soup, lobster mayonnaise, stew, steam-pudding—the sauce was the thing, Scotch woodcock, dessert; whisky, port, champagne cup; coffee. Roger Poore, transferred from the Hants Yeomanry and recently posted as Second-in-Command, presided; the C.O. was on leave. We had a jolly night. None of the traditional ritual was wanting, and there were many to eat the leek. A German howitzer shell-case, which had been used by the French as a gas-gong, served as loving-cup. It was to have been sent home after being inscribed and decorated by Sergeant-Shoemaker Johnson, a remarkably good artist in metal, but it was lost before Poore could make up his mind about the wording.

March 2nd.—A lot of us watched a clever piece of work by a German flier two or three miles off. He came over at a great speed, made for one of our sausage balloons, manœuvred to keep it between him and our Archie-guns, and set it alight. The observers leapt out. One came down safely; but pieces of the burning balloon fell on the parachute of the other and burned it, so he dropped, and died of his injuries; this was his second leap from a burning balloon.

March 3rd.—There is a coating of ice on still water. To-day's is the second great flight of starlings and of crows since we came here. Do French crows, like Scotch crows, start housekeeping on the first Sunday in March? We have scraped together a trench strength of 450 by taking in the Drums and other details usually left out. We marched by Eclusier. Near Feuillères a whizz-bang had stuck in the stem of a tree, projecting fore and aft. Enough of Clery is standing to make it ghostly. A village razed is not so sad to see as roofless, windowless, sagging walls; they give one creeps at night. On the wreck of one house a cat sat and blinked listlessly as we marched through. The O.C. battalion we are relieving is the kind of ass who can't take a drink without saying his "doctor recommends it." Poore's talk with him was excellent comedy, thus—"You put out your wire at night, what!" P. has not been in a trench in his life. Two of his eccentricities of speech

were timed : in 45 seconds he said "you see" five times, and
punctuated a phrase with "what !" thrice.

March 4th.—Girodon left : we are on about a mile of front.

March 6th.—A sort of raid on one of our saps last night was
easily beaten off. Fritz is spendthrift with his ammunition ; he
checked all his barrages to-day. There are Guards on this front,
very militant they are. At Rancourt, north of us, 6 or 8 Germans
come over every day. Poore, alive to his job and a real strafer, is
waking up everyone from here to Division. But for his zeal the
day was peaceful in front.

March 8th.—Indications of a raid woke me at 5 o'clock. It
turned out to be on our neighbours, two were lifted. Not a sentry
of ours or of the auxiliary company, lent by the relieving battalion,
was to be seen in our rear position. The German line is still held
strongly, but near and far in rear fires glow each night where
houses and stores are being destroyed. Fritz's method of holding
his line now is to have isolated, sheltered posts with easy, foot-
boarded communications, and supports at hand. It's a contrast to
our front line, which exposes the greatest number of men. Our
men have stuck a trying tour well. We have not had so many
killed and wounded—about half and half, and nearly all by shells—
for a long time.

A fine frosty night, and a peaceful relief : our last relief from the
pitiless Somme, where 200 of us have been buried or left unburied.
We got into strongly timbered French dug-outs at Frise Bend
shortly after midnight. There was a powdering of snow when we
March 9th—marched to Suzanne in the morning. This is again
the third day of no home mail ; the cross-Channel service is said
to be suspended. A battalion issue of sardines instead of meat
is odd.

March 10th.—Overcast and raw. Another move, Camp 13 again.
There are elements of comparative comfort that were not here
before, but it's a wat'ry nest indeed that larks leave in this sodden
hollow, they are the only joyous creatures in the camp. There are
other pilgrims of the sky alongside us. The antics of our new Naval
March 12th—triplanes, from an aerodrome close by, are an unfailing
interest, there is none other at Camp 13.

Since the advent of our new Government at Christmas I find
increasingly frequent notes on the interactions of politicians and

soldiers in High Command. Politically minded soldiers, whatever their rank or qualification, were given the ear of the politicians. The Prime Minister was meddling with strategy. Baffled in his attempts to dictate it, he had some success with tactics. Later on by withholding drafts, and by other administrative contrivances, he affected operations until our backs were to the wall. There was a hubbub in Parliament at the end of February over a newspaper interview in which the C.-in-C. defended himself against the implied hostility of the Government, actually of the Prime Minister. Emphasis on a determination to get the cavalry through was the part of the interview which won no sympathy from the infantry, sickened by its Somme experience as battering-ram.

After the extension of the British line to the Somme we heard much about the collecting of a large French Reserve Army. Part of it had a notably successful try-out at Verdun, which made our High Command sit up and think. The organization and training of the French infantry was made the subject of a General Instruction. It is a fighting training. Football and cross-country running, however useful the latter may be in case of a rout, don't appear in the French code, not even disguised as "training, recreational." The letter let the Army into the secret that training on a platoon basis, instead of a company basis, was the solution of our tactical troubles. It is safe to assume that G.H.Q. did not foresee one consequence of making the platoon the unit. In practice it allowed senior officers to cast their burden, if so minded, on the most junior. Planning might be left to the discretion, and arrangement among themselves, of company commanders, and it was not unknown for a company commander to be as uninterested in his subalterns' doings as his superiors were in what he did or left undone. In January, when first the Battalion's training was put on a platoon basis, the C.O. planned the whole scheme; specialists, ground and ranges were allotted, there was daily supervision, and discussion and interchange of ideas. Besides the opening for slackness up and down the middle stratum of command, which emphasis on the platoon and the section in action allowed, the lessening of touch between fighting front and ordering rear increased perceptibly at this period.

We had come into the XVIII Corps. Its commander, Lieut.-General Maxse, ordered "platoon training." In our formation interest seemed to end when Corps' curt order had been passed on. Our strongest platoon, before we filled up with drafts, numbered 22 when the specialists were withdrawn; one platoon numbered 4. Such was the toll the weather, chiefly, had taken of us. One of the lesser factors was a form of fever and digestive disturbance; it seemed to come with a draft in October; the last of it was being seen only now.

Rumour of a return to our recent front, to follow the retreating Germans, came to nothing more than the detachment of the Brigade Field Ambulance to run a Refugee Camp at Péronne, which was entered on the 18th. A sergeant washed the old folk, a corporal ran a crèche. The French civilians were most appreciative of both.

March 14th.—Late at night my leave warrant came in. Dated the 21st, it was an incitement to conduct to the prejudice of discipline. Home leave about this time began and ended with a test of hardiness for divisions on the Somme. The direct route by Boulogne was reserved for senior and privileged officers, everyone else had to make the long round-about by Havre. Three to five days might be spent on the journey owing to traffic interruptions such as mines and submarines in the Channel and, until recently, frozen points and signals on the railway. The trains were unheated, the windows of most compartments were broken, the doors of many were torn off. Moody tells of a night he spent at Havre. The Rest Camp was pitched on the summit of the downs—for air. He could not sleep for cold in spite of heaping about him all the clothing and blankets he had. Three rats, snuggling in next his shirt for warmth, roused him from one of the fitful doses into which he fell. I was in no state to face such a journey; for weeks I had been unfit after a second attack of influenza. Arranging to steal a few extra days occupied my day. In the Camp and Ambulance *March 16th*—accomplices were easily found; at Amiens authority was asleep when I boarded the midnight train for Boulogne, and *March 17th*—there it had a blind eye. We had a fine crossing— to what? On debarking we were ordered to report at once to our local police, and be in readiness for any emergency. This is the only time I know of anything of the kind being required. It was whispered that civil disturbance was feared.

In Russia the Czar Nicholas had been deposed, and the monarchy was in abeyance. A Government of well-meaning men had installed itself under a verbose ideologue. The Revolution was only a week old, but, as is usual, discontent in other countries had been emboldened to be doing. Already parties everywhere threatened trouble. In all the belligerent countries economic and social conditions, which had become the anxious concern of Government, aided these sympathetic reactions. At home the political air was sharpened by the contrasted privation of many and the vastness with which war-wealth had been created for others; by the effect on many minds of the two-months-old German naval policy of sinking every ship at sight; and by the losses, disappointment, and disillusion of the battles of the Somme. The large doctrinaire element among us, for the most part aloof from public affairs, took to political abstraction, and agitated social and economic theories. Men in academic positions, or living on an inheritance, or by their wits—all unfitted for and averse from business affairs and enterprise—became equal to any adventure in an armchair. They found allies in the exponents of political Trade Unionism, and a tool in the organization of the Unions. The alliance aped Russian models later on. It affected the Government's action; and before the year was out the Government was acting to the serious hurt of the Army.

CHAPTER XII

A subaltern's service in camp and in action

Contributor:—SASSOON. An early draft of pages of "Memoirs
of an Infantry Officer"

Sketches:—11, 12, 16, 17, 18

March 12th to April 1st.—I joined the 2nd Battalion at Camp 13.
Posted to B Company I found myself in command of No. 8
Platoon, which contained 8 Private Joneses. Its total strength
numbered 34, including 2 sergeants, 1 corporal and 6 lance-
corporals. Eight of the 34 were Lewis gunners. These being
deducted my compact little unit was unimpressive on parade
and seldom mustered 20 strong. We were in Corps Reserve,
and Battalion H.Q. had issued its order, "carry out platoon
training." A recent draft had added a collection of undersized half-wits to the depleted Battalion. Several men in my
platoon seemed barely capable of carrying the weight of their
equipment: and in one case "platoon training" began with the
platoon commander teaching a man how to load his rifle. (Afterwards I felt that the poor devil would have been a less perilous
ingredient of my command had he been left in his primordial
ignorance.)

Of Camp 13 the less said the better. I cannot believe that
anyone has ever said a good word for it. We remained there until
Palm Sunday, and marched away on Monday, April 2nd. As
we went up the hill to the Bray–Corbie road the smoke of the
incinerators gave the impression that we had fired the camp on
leaving it. Mud and smoke were its chief characteristics. The
long, gloomy, draughty chamber where company officers took
their ease was seldom free from the smoke which drifted in from
the braziers of the adjoining kitchen. Of an evening we sat and
shivered in our British-warms, reading, playing cards, writing
letters by the feeble glimmer of guttering candles. Orderlies would

bring in a clutter of tin plates and mugs; Maconochie stew was consumed in morose discomfort. How peculiar was the taste of tea during the Great War! One sip of that nasty concoction would bring the whole thing back to me more than a hundred war histories by Field-Marshals and Cabinet Ministers! I could hardly have begun my acquaintance with the Battalion under worse conditions. Naturally, no one was feeling over bright. As for myself, I endured my first week minus my valise which had gone astray on the way up from Rouen; my new trench-coat had been pinched off me on the boat, the "Archangel" of cursed memory; and I was inclined to grumble because I had been posted elsewhere than to the 1st Battalion which I regarded as my spiritual home in France; and that well-known M.O., Captain Dunn, greeted me with a double anti-typhoid injection. Kirkby, who commanded B Company, began by regarding my presence with hauteur and aversion. More than once he referred to me as a "bloody wart," too evidently intending me to overhear the epithet. Although he and I got ourselves on better terms as soon as the Battalion got on the move, I never solved the mystery of his inaugural behaviour to me, and I only mention it because no account of Camp 13 would, as far as I was concerned, be complete without it. One expedition to Amiens, with Greaves, Conning and Binge Owen, for a bath and a good dinner at the Godbert Restaurant—that was a cheerful experience, anyhow. We were photographed the next morning, I remember. But otherwise I have no record of what occurred except the following note of beverages consumed:

2 John Collins.   1 Japanese ditto.   1 Oyster Cocktail.
1 Sherry and Bitters.   Pommard Eclatante, trois verres.
1 Benedictine.

Then back to Camp 13 per feet and a lucky lift on a hospital ambulance going to Corbie, passing the only Germans I'd been within 15 miles of since leaving England on February 15th, and these were only a few sullen prisoners working half-heartedly on the road. Aerodromes loom up in the dusk as we approach the Camp, and a brazier glows redly at the cross-roads where the sentry stands. Down in the hollow our Brigade has got through another day of Corps Reserve. News of the "fall" of Péronne and other places fall rather flat. The Germans are withdrawing to

the Hindenburg Line.   And we are told that we shall probably go
to St. Pol "before proceeding to the battle."   "What a hope!"
as the troops used to say.

The Quartermaster asked me to ride his horse in the hurdle race
at the Corps Sports; this cheered me up quite a lot, as the horse
could gallop fairly well.   But the Sports were cancelled.

In spite of hankerings for "the good old 1st Battalion" (which,
at the moment, was being badly knocked about at Bullecourt), I
was now beginning to identify myself with the equally "good old
April 2nd—2nd Battalion."   But it was not until we quitted Camp
13 that I became aware of the identity of the Battalion as a whole.
Hitherto my brain had not gone beyond B Company.   Now,
while the column was trudging and swaying along the main road
to Corbie on that cold, grey Monday morning, the four Companies
knit themselves into a unit.   And I was glad to be going with them
on their journey into a somewhat hazardous future.   As second-
in-command of B Company I toddled along behind it, while
Kirkby ambled in front in full occupation of some patient quadruped
whose face I cannot recall.   To Corbie was a seven-mile march,
and the Battalion was settled in its billets by 1.30.   I can remember
my own billet—an airless cupboard over a greengrocer's shop.
Also I remember that several of us spent a convivial evening
drinking bad champagne in a small room in a wine-merchant's
house, while Ralph Greaves drew pleasant sounds from a piano.
He played as though he were saying good-bye to all music for ever.
Three weeks later he had lost one of his arms.   While I am
putting in all the details I can remember, I may as well mention
that I swore eternal fealty to Kirkby at the door of my billet.
When he had departed I spent several moonlit minutes fumbling
with the key of the greengrocer's door; next morning I awoke
fully dressed and feeling awful.   The room reeked of onions and
made no pretence of having a window.

April 3rd.—We left Corbie at 9 a.m. in brilliant sunshine, and
by the first halt I was feeling splendid, which was just as well, for
we went 21 kilometres, reaching Villers Bocage at 2.   I had some
difficulty in keeping the Company up to strength; several undersized men were beat to the world at the end of the march, and I
covered the last lap trundling two of them in front of me, while
another one struggled along behind, hanging on to my belt.   Not

one of the three stood more than five foot high. Such details seem to me worth recording. Realities are often omitted from records of the War. Foot-inspection after the long march added to my growing sense of responsibility for the welfare of the Company. Blisters were numerous; and I did my best to make the Battalion boot-menders the busiest men in Villers Bocage for the rest of the day. When I revisualize, nine years after, those men showing their sore feet, sitting on the straw in a sun-chinked barn and staring up at me with their stupid, trustful eyes, I can still feel angry with profiteers and "society people" who guzzled their way through the War. But it takes all sorts to make a war; and it wasn't for such disreputable non-combatants as those that the "poor bloody infantry" were wearing out their feet on the road to Arras.

Spent the evening with A Company drinking good Graves. The woman in our billet told us that troops had been passing through for 15 days, never staying more than one night and always going towards Doullens and Arras. The room we slept in was adorned with mouldy, stuffed birds with outspread wings; a jay, a sparrowhawk and a stork; also two squirrels. As I lay awake on the red-tiled floor I watched a seagull suspended from a string in the ceiling; slowly it revolved in the draughts, and while it revolved I fell asleep.

    •   •   •   •   •

Four officers had been left at Corbie, they went to St. Pol to be held in reserve. B Company Mess contained a typical war contrast in Casson and Evans. Casson, aged 23, had been at Winchester and Christ Church; he was a sensitive, refined youth, and an amusing gossip. Evans was about the same age, but had not "enjoyed the same social advantages." He was very noisy and garrulous, always licked his thumb when dealing cards, and invariably answered "Pardon?" when any remark was made to him. That "pardon" became a little trying at times. Equally good when tested, these two merged their social incompatibilities in the end; both were killed on September 26th.

    •   •   •   •   •

April 4th.—Next day we marched 12 kilometres to Beauval. Wet snow was falling all the way. During the march we passed into a new "Army Area." Our new[1] Corps Commander was

[1] The Commander of the Corps the Battalion was leaving.

waiting to welcome us on a long straight stretch of the Amiens–
Doullens road. We eyes-lefted him without enthusiasm. Colonel
Garnett rode up to him and received a volley of abuse in response
to his salute. C.C.: "Are you stuck to that bloody horse?"
Col. G.: "No, sir"—dismounts and salutes again. Apparently the
Corps Commander resented the fact that brooms and other
utilitarian objects were being carried on the "cookers." Or it
may have been some minor detail of march discipline. Anyhow
he probably thought he was doing his duty as a Corps Commander,
though to an amateur soldier like myself such rudeness seemed
irrelevant. And the cookers went lumbering on their way quite
peacefully, emitting smoke and stewing away at the men's dinners.
I can remember nothing about Beauval except that we left it at
April 5th—4 p.m. the next day, and covered another 12 kilometres
to Lucheux, where we billeted in some huts among wooded hills.
Arrived there at 8. It was a calm night, and we dined in the
moonlight, sitting round a brazier with plates on our knees. We
had passed through Doullens on our way; "Arras 32 K," said a
signpost. The wind was from the east; it was only a light breeze,
but it brought us heavy rumours of the huge firing up at Arras.
I can remember going down into Doullens in the pleasant evening
sunshine; I was walking with Major Poore, and we were talking
about cricket and fox-hunting. He was one of the good men
who died on September 26th.

April 6th was Good Friday and I awoke with sunshine streaming
in at the door and broad Scots being shouted by some Scottish
Rifles in the next huts. Someone was practising on the bagpipes
at the edge of the woods, and a mule contributed a short solo
from the transport lines. We remained at Lucheux that night,
April 7th—and went on to Saulty, 15 kilometres, in cold wind and
sunshine. When the Company had been safely bestowed and
I'd stuffed myself with coffee and eggs, I sat on a tree stump in
the peaceful park of a big white château, with the sun just looking
over the tree tops, and a few small deer grazing, and some black-
birds and thrushes singing from the purple undergrowth. Nothing
was there to remind me of the War except the enormous thudding
of the guns 12 miles away, and an aeroplane humming in the clear
sky overhead. We had been told that we should move into our
final concentration area to-morrow—Easter Sunday! Sitting there

alone I felt happy, contented and confident. And the men, I
thought, have seemed cheery, and almost elated, the last day or two.
But they were always at their best when they knew they were
"for it." There was a chance of a "blighty one" for them, anyhow.
The air turned chilly, and the sun was a glint of scarlet beyond the
strip of woodland. And away on the horizon that infernal banging
continued. . . . "The sausage machine," I think we used to call it.

April 8th.—Easter Sunday. Left Saulty 9 a.m. Reached
Basseux 11.30 (about 11 kilometres south-west of Arras). Until
recently this place was only a mile or two from the front-line
trenches, but doesn't appear to have been heavily shelled.
Walking out to inspect the old trench line I was struck by the
appalling inferiority of our position to that of the Germans.

We are living in a derelict château which must have been very
pleasant in peace time. It is good enough for me now. I am
sitting with my feet out of the window of an attic under the roof,
looking down on the courtyard where some officers are playing
cricket with a stump and a wooden ball, with an old brazier for
a wicket. Cheery voices; glorious sunshine; pigeons flapping
about over red and grey roofs. A small church with pointed
tower a little way down the street. Three balloons visible, and the
usual confused noise of guns from Arras direction. Our conscientious and efficient little adjutant bustles across the foreground
with some papers in his hand. No time for cricket among the
Orderly Room Staff!

April 10th.—Still at Basseux, but under orders to move at the
shortest possible notice. Weather windy and cold with snow
showers and intervals of sunshine. Everyone talking very loud
about successes reported from the line—"our objectives gained,"
"5000 prisoners," and so on. I am chiefly interested in my own
physical condition, which is beastly (sore throat, gastritis, several
festering scratches on my hands, and no clean handkerchiefs or
socks). Have consoled myself with an enormous opium pill to
promote constipation suitable for "open warfare." A mail arrived
to-day. Mine consisted of a little india-paper edition of Keats's
poems, bound in green vellum. Can't say I feel much like reading
Keats. . . .

April 11th.—We were having a (single brazier) cricket match on
the Wednesday afternoon. The sun was shining. Then someone

blew a whistle and the match came to an abrupt end. An hour later (5 p.m.) the Battalion left Basseux. We'd been on the march about half an hour when heavy snow began falling. It seemed damned unfair that there should be a genuine snowstorm on April 11th. We passed through villages that were less than heaps of bricks. A couple of inches of snow concealed them altogether. The most demolished village was Ficheux. "Fish-hooks," the troops called it. Any joke was better than none at that moment. The snow had stopped when, at the end of 8 miles, we bivouacked in the dregs of daylight, by a sunken road near Mercatel. The men of B Company were short of cigarettes, but, by the mercy of God, I had purchased a packful of emergency "Woodbines" at Saulty; the issue of these by my servant was, I should say, about the only bright spot on our proceedings as far as B Company was concerned. Casson and I spent the night in a very small dug-out. How we got in I can't remember, but we considered ourselves lucky to be sitting huddled round a little brazier, talking to the trench-mortar sergeant-major and two signallers who occupied that coke-fumed den. The S.M. regaled us, in omniscient tones, with rumours about what the 30th Division had done at Héninel and Wancourt, but I might as well have been in Mesopotamia for all the difference it made to me.

April 12th.—Daylight found us somewhat bleary-eyed and dejected. I can't remember how we got through the morning. By 4 p.m. we had moved on about 6 kilometres relieving the 17th Manchesters, in reserve at St. Martin-Cojeul, 3 kilometres south-east of Wancourt, where the Germans counter-attacked earlier in the day. The afternoon was wet, and the snow had left its legacy of bad mud. B Company occupied an old German third-line trench. The village was a heap of bricks. A few 5.9s arrived while I went to the underground dressing-station to get my festering fingers attended to. Small discomforts of that kind did much to dissipate heroic attitudes of mind! Company H.Q. was the nearest thing to living in a rabbit-hole that I've ever experienced. There was just enough space for Kirkby and myself to sit, and I kept myself warm by enlarging it with a rusty entrenching tool which I picked up in the trench. The dug-out contained a small stove. Rations were short. Kirkby and I had one small slice of bacon between us. I was frizzling my fragment

when it fell off the fork and disappeared into the stove, whence
my already unfortunate fingers recovered it. I don't think it
tasted bad even then. Casson and I finished our only surviving
orange. The night was bitterly cold, and sleep was unprocurable
since there was nowhere to lie down. Evans, the only other
officer with B Company, supplied a continuous obbligato of
Welsh garrulity. Kirkby showed a capacity for sleeping soundly
in any position and under the most inappropriate conditions.

April 13th (Friday).—There was nothing to do except sit there
until further orders. So there we sat, while the 62nd Division
[Brigade] attacked Fontaine-lez-Croisilles from a hill about
three-quarters of a mile away. There was a serene sunset with
large peaceful clouds; Casson and I walked up the hill; I wanted
to get him accustomed to the unpleasant sights, which seemed to
upset him less than I expected. There were a lot of our yesterday's
dead lying in front of the trench. To-day's attacking troops were
a little way down the far slope. The dead lay there in all their
equipment, most of them shot in the head. When Casson was at
Winchester he did not anticipate that he would ever be walking
about on a fine April evening among a lot of dead men. It struck
me as unnatural at the moment, probably because the stretcher-
bearers had been identifying the bodies and had arranged them
in seemly attitudes, their heads pillowed on their haversacks.
Young Casson was trying to behave as if it were all quite ordinary;
he was having his first look at "the horrors of war." While we
were on the hill there was a huge explosion down by Fontaine
Wood, as though a dump had been blown up. On our way home
we stopped to inspect a tank which had got stuck in the mud while
crossing a wide trench. But I was thinking to myself that sensitive
people like Casson ought not to be taken to battle-fields. I had
grown accustomed to such sights, but I was able to realize the
impact they made on a fresh mind. Detached from the fighting,
we had merely gone for a short walk after tea, so to speak, and I
couldn't help feeling as if I'd been showing Casson something
obscene. (Nine years afterwards the whole business has become
incredible. Unfortunately young Casson is not alive to share my
sense of the incredibility of that little evening walk.)

   .   .   .   .   .

[In reply to a pressing request to continue.] I am unable to formulate "the morning at the Block" as a military operation. My brain would refuse to work if I began to think of the episode in terms of Field Service Regulations. Compass-bearings, map-references, and tactical organization in general always alarmed me more than explosive missiles, and I could never write out a report which looked as if it had been made by an adequately trained officer. All the same, I doubt if the most cut and dried Staff College mind could make much of a story out of "the morning at the Block." The truth is that infantry soldiering in the battle-zone was an overwhelmingly physical experience. Such human elements as food, warmth and sleep were the living realities, and it may not have occurred to many a writer of military histories that the weather was a more effective General than Foch, Haig or Ludendorff. A bad blister on a man's heel might be the only thing he could clearly remember after a week of intense experience which added a battle honour to the colours of his regiment. For those whose active unit was company, platoon or section, physical sensations predominated. Mental activity (detached from feet and belly) was strictly limited by gross physical actualities. Whatever exploits a fighting man might afterwards claim that he had achieved, his achievement could usually be recorded in a few short sentences. But how lifeless, how meagre and incomplete that epitome would seem to one who understood but had not shared the experience, unless it was interwoven with those details of discomfort (so difficult to remember) which constituted the humanity of infantry soldiering. If I were wearing a certain pair of wire-torn puttees and scraping the caked mud off them with a rusty entrenching tool I should be able to remember quite a lot about the War. As it is, the War (in April 1917) emerges from its dug-out in my subconscious memory as a very blurred personal experience; the details which might make my page vivid can only be recovered by guesswork, aided by a few inadequately scribbled notes which I made at a time when I expected every day to be my last (a very ordinary infantry emotion).

April 14th.—At 9 p.m. B Company fell in at the top of the ruined village street called St. Martin-Cojeul. It was a dry, windless evening. Even in that devastated region one could be conscious of the arrival of Spring, and as I took my place in the rear of the column when we moved off (to relieve the 13th

Northumberland Fusiliers in the line) there was something in the twilight which could remind me regretfully of an April evening in England and the village cricket field where a few of us had been having our first knock at the nets. The cricket season had begun again. . . . But the Company had left the road and was going uphill across open ground; and already the two cheerful Northumberland Fusilier guides were making the pace too hot for the rear platoon. Like nearly all guides, they were inconveniently nimble owing to their freedom from heavy equipment, and they were insecurely confident that they knew the way in the dark. The muttered message—"pass it along, 'steady the pace in front'"—was accompanied by the usual muffled clinkings and rattlings of arms and equipment. Unwillingly retarded, the guides led us on (we had less than two miles to go). Gradually the guides became less confident, and the Company Commander's demeanour did not reassure them. At a midnight halt they admitted that they had lost their way completely. Kirkby decided to sit down and wait for daylight, and I went blundering off into the gloom expecting to lose myself independently, but by a lucky accident I stumbled into a sunken road and found myself among a little party of sappers who could tell me where I was. With one of them I returned to the Company, and we were led to the Hindenburg trench. There must have been some hazy moonlight, for I can remember the figures of men propping themselves against the walls of the communication trench. Seeing them in some sort of ghastly half-light (was it, perhaps, the light of a descending flare?) I wondered whether they were dead or asleep, for the attitudes of some of them were like death, uncouth and distorted.

We were arriving at the end of a journey that had begun twelve days before, when we left Camp 13. There were men in my Company who had never seen a front-line trench before. If there had been a Dante, a Milton or a William Blake among them, his mind would have been enriched with material for a new infernal vision. For it was a dreadful place we had come to. But it was our business to make the best of it, and I don't suppose that anyone else in the Company felt its dreadfulness as fully as I did. The fact that it was an experience of a pattern which was shared by millions of men does not make it seem any less strange and awful and inhuman to me as I sit at my desk in the isolation of my thought, and remember it nine years afterwards. Stage by stage we had marched to this monstrous region of death and disaster. From afar it had threatened us with the blink and din of its bombardments. Now we groped and stumbled along a deep ditch to the place appointed for us in that zone of human havoc. The World War had got our insignificant little unit in its mouth ; we were there to be munched, maimed or liberated. And we asked no compensation at that moment except a mug of hot tea. We were thankful also that it wasn't raining. (It didn't rain that night, and we didn't get our hot drink till next morning.)

April 15th.—When we arrived in the Hindenburg support trench my Company Commander told me to post the sentries ; he then vanished to Company H.Q., which were situated somewhere down a shaft with fifty steps. The company we were relieving had already departed, so there was no one to give me any information. I didn't even know for certain that we were in the front line. But our sector was about 900 yards (and the Company about 60 strong). The trench was deep, roomy and unfinished looking. I had never occupied such a trench before. The sentries had to clamber up a bank of loose earth to see over the top. (It seemed unlikely that they would see anything, since the Germans were giving no indication of their presence or whereabouts.) The length of the intervals between our sentry posts made me conscious of our inadequacy in that wilderness of destructive activity. If I had needed to be made vividly aware of my forlorn situation as a living creature I could have done it merely by thinking of a Field Cashier. The words "field cashier" would have epitomized my remoteness from everything safe and comfortable, from all assurance that I should be alive and kicking next week. But such thoughts were not wholesome, and when I had posted the sentries I went along the trench to look for the company on our left. Poor devils—they belonged to an amateur battalion that suffered badly in the dud attack thirty-six hours later. I came round a corner and found a sort of panic party going on at a point where the trench was like a wide nullah. A platoon (which must have been more than half as numerous as my whole Company) had taken alarm ; N.C.Os. and men were jostling one another in their haste to vanish through a narrow doorway which led down to the bowels of the earth. As I stood there in astonishment one of them, panting excitedly, told me that "the Germans were coming over." Two officers who were among this rabble seemed to have no idea except to get everyone downstairs as soon as possible. Unlikely as it may sound they all disappeared and I was left alone. Out in Nomansland there wasn't the slightest indication of an attack. As there seemed nothing to be done I returned to my own sector. As soon as I was in that territory I met a "runner" with a verbal order from Battalion H.Q.: my Company's front was to be patrolled at once. Realizing the futility of sending any of my few spare men out on patrol (they had been walking about for hours and were dead beat) I lost my temper, quietly and internally, went along to our right-flank post and told them to pass it along that "a patrol was going out from right to left." I then started sulkily out by myself for a quiet walk in Nomansland. I counted my steps, 200 steps straight ahead, then began to walk the necessary 900 steps to the left. But it isn't easy to count your steps in the dark among shell-holes, and after a problematic 400 I lost confidence in my automatic pistol, which I was grasping in my right-hand breeches pocket. How could I reassure myself? Apparently there was only one reassuring action which I could perform. Turning in the direction of the Germans I utilized Nomansland as a latrine. This caused me to feel less lonely and afraid, and I completed my task without meeting so much as a star-shell, and regained the trench exactly opposite our left-hand post, after being hoarsely and irresolutely challenged by the sentry, who, as I realized at the moment, was a much more immediate danger to me than the Germans. It was now just beginning to be more daylight than darkness; by the time I went down a shaft to the "underground trench" the sentries were shivering under a red and rainy-looking sky. The earthy chill of that subterranean refuge was in accord with my anticipations of appearing in the extremest section of the casualty list before I was much older. Chilled to the bone I lay on a wire-netting shelf and listened to the dismal snorings of my adjacent companions in misfortune. I had seldom felt more acutely aware of "being at the front." Four hours later (at 10 a.m.) I was above ground again, in charge of a carrying-party. It rained all day and the trenches were like glue. We carried boxes of trench-mortar bombs up from a dump between St. Martin-Cojeul and Croisilles.

I lugged loads myself, since it seemed to my simple mind the only
method of persuading the men that it had to be done. The
unmitigated misery of that carrying-party was a typical infantry
experience of disgusting discomfort without actual danger. We
were among the debris of the intense bombardment of two weeks
before; concrete emplacements were smashed and tilted sideways;
the chalky soil was everywhere pitted with huge shell-holes, and
there were many dead bodies—I can remember looking down,
as I blundered and gasped my way along, and seeing a mask-like
face floating on the surface of the flooded trench. This face had
detached itself from its skull. I can remember two mud-clotted
hands protruding from the wet ashen soil like the roots of a tree
turned upside down; one hand seemed to be pointing at the sky
with an accusing gesture. We were out in the rain till 4.30. It
was a yellowish corpse-like day. As soon as I got "home" to my
mug of tea I was told that I had been detailed to take command
of 100 bombers to act as reserve for the 1st Cameronians next
morning. When it was dark I went with a cheery little guide to
discuss the operation orders with Captain Wright (Cameronians)
in his front-line dug-out. (Was it in the front line? I don't
know. . . . I only know that I felt very incompetent and mis-
informed, and that the officers I talked to seemed full of knowledge
and trench topography which meant nothing to my newly-arrived
mind.) It was regarded as possible that the bombing attack would
function along the underground trench as well as above ground.
There was a barrier in the tunnel. The Germans were on
the other side. We should climb over it. . . . Could anything,
I thought, be less pleasant?—while I tried to adapt myself to the
self-protective cheerfulness of Captain Wright and his colleagues
in their little den. I returned with a feeling that I hadn't the
faintest idea what it was all about or what I could do in the way
of organizing my command. Something had to be put on paper
and sent to Battalion H.Q. By the mercy of God I got hold of
Ralph Greaves; I found him sitting in a little chamber off the
underground trench: to him I confided my incompetence and,
while I sat and ruminated on my chances of extinction next
morning, he drew up some scheme for me and wrote it down.
His little room contained a mirror and a clock. The clock's dumb
face stared at me—an idiot reminder of real rooms and real

domesticity. Greaves, with his eyeglass and his whimsical debonair looks and his gentle stammering voice—was a consoling link with real life, for I had known him before the War. When he had fixed up my immediate future, we shared our common knowledge of a certain part of the county of Kent. While we talked by the light of a guttering candle an assortment of our Brigade was passing our open doorway. I don't know where they were going, but I remember seeing a brigade-major and a party of sappers.

April 16th.—Zero hour was at 3.30 a.m., and by then I was sitting self-consciously in the 1st Cams. H.Q. with a rumbling din going on overhead, and my 100 men sitting on the stairs— there were 50 steps up from the tunnel to the outer world; a bone-chilling draught came down the stairway, and the men must have regretted our 33rd Division General's edict against the rum ration. The Cams.' Colonel and Adjutant conversed in the constrained tones of men who expect nothing but ill news. There was a large cake on the table. I was offered a slice, which I ate with embarrassment. I wasn't feeling at all at home. I couldn't make myself believe that the Cameronian officers expected me to do them any good when I was called upon to take part in the proceedings upstairs. (The underground "attack" had been washed out.) The tapping telephone-orderly in the corner very soon announced that communication with Captain Wright's H.Q. had broken down. After, I think, nearly three hours of suspense, it became obvious that someone was coming down the stairs in a hurry. This messenger finally arrived outside the doorway in a clattering cascade of tin utensils. He entered and proved to be a dishevelled sergeant who blurted out an incoherent statement about "their having been driven back after advancing a little way." I got up stiffly—aware that my moment had arrived. Probably I mumbled something to the Colonel, but I can't remember his giving me any instructions. I was, however, sensitive to the fact that both Colonel and Adjutant were alive to the delicacy of my situation. Their unuttered message was—"Well, old chap, I suppose you're for it!" Helmet on head I went out and told my two under-officers that I was going to take 25 men up to the Show. I can easily remember how I bustled upstairs and emerged into a sunlit but noisy morning. The section of 25 men who were sitting at the top of the stairs bestirred themselves at the instigation

of Sergeant Baldwin, and at once I was hurrying up a trench
with my chilled and flustered little contingent at my heels. "15
bombers (each carrying 10 Mills bombs), 4 Rifle Grenadiers (each
carrying 5 grenades), 5 carriers (also act as bayonet men), 1 full
rank (Sergeant Baldwin)." I hadn't the slightest idea what I was
going to do, and my destination was in the brain of the stooping
Cameronian guide who trotted in front of me. After dodging
and stumbling up a narrow communication trench we arrived at
the wide main trench, and there we met The Cameronians. I must
have picked up a Mills bomb on my way, for I know I had one
in my hand when I began my conversation with Captain Wright.
. . . I had the advantage of Captain Wright, since I was advancing
and he and his men were very obviously retreating. Anyhow they
were out of breath and coming away from their objective. I was
told that the Germans were all round them, and that they had run
out of bombs. Feeling myself to be, for the moment, an epitome
of R.W.F. prestige I became unnaturally jaunty and unconcerned.
"But where *are* the Germans?" I asked, carelessly tossing my bomb
from left hand to right and back again. "Where are they?" I
repeated. "I can't see any Germans." My effrontery had its
effect. The Cameronian officers looked a little embarrassed, but
their composure began to reassert itself. Needless to say there
wasn't a German in sight (though there were several just round
the corner). My behaviour became more and more patronizing
and complacent. "All right," I remarked, "you needn't bother.
We'll see to this," or words to that effect. I led my party past The
Cameronians; told them to wait a bit; and went up the trench
with Sergeant Baldwin—an admirably impassive little man, who
never ceased to behave like a well-trained and confidential man-
servant. . . . Having arrived thus far in my narrative, I should
like to remark that (except for self-protective reasons) I never
pretended to be a professionally efficient soldier. My methods
were always amateurish and unsystematic. I always failed to take
necessary precautions, and, on the occasion I am trying to describe,
my only effective quality consisted in an unreasoning resolve to
rush in where The Cameronians were no longer willing to tread.
Anyhow my ignorance simplified the situation, and was for the
time being an advantage. I knew nothing except that I was in
the Hindenburg front trench, outside Captain Wright's Company

H.Q. dug-out with my 25 men. I also knew that our objective was "to clear the trench for 500 yards." The sun was shining in a sky full of large drifting clouds. A few of our own shells were dropping short. It was half-past six on a fresh mid-April morning. . . . I was excited and mettlesome. The Cameronian crowd had been legging it, and I was out to show them how easy it was to deal with the Germans. On the crest of this wave of adventurous ardour I did not remember that the sun was shining on men who had been mown down by machine-gun fire when they went over the top three hours before. I cannot explain why I felt like that. The fact remains that I was just foolhardy. . . . Sergeant Baldwin and I went about 100 yards up the trench without meeting anyone. I think we climbed over some sort of barrier at the beginning, but I am not sure. Noticing that there were a good many Mills bombs lying in little heaps every twenty yards or so, I told Sergeant Baldwin to go back and arrange for these bombs to be collected and brought up the trench. Then, with a slightly accelerated heart-beat, I went round a corner alone. A small man was standing there, watchful and resolute, with a bag of bombs slung over his left shoulder. He was a Cameronian corporal, whose name (I afterwards learnt) was Smart. Neither of us spoke. I also was carrying a bag of bombs. We advanced and went round the next bay. I experienced a sobering shock then, for a young fair-haired Cameronian private was lying, propped against the wall of the trench, in a pool of his own blood. His open eyes were staring vacantly at the sky. His face was grey and serene. A few yards up the trench was the body of a German officer crumpled up and still. The wounded Cameronian made me feel angry with our invisible enemies. I slung a couple of bombs in their direction, and received a reply in the form of an egg-bomb, which exploded harmlessly behind me. I went on throwing bombs and advancing, while the corporal (who was obviously much more artful and efficient than I was) dodged up the saps at the side—a precaution which I should have forgotten. Between us we created a considerable demonstration of offensiveness. In this manner we reached our objective. I had no idea where our objective was, but the corporal told me we had reached it, and he seemed to know what he was about. This, curiously enough, was the first time he spoke to me. I had caught an occasional glimpse of a retreating

German, but the whole thing had been so absurdly easy that
I felt like going on still further. There was a narrow sap running
out from the place where we halted. "You stay where you are,"
I remarked to Smart, and then I started to explore the sap. What
I expected to find there I can't say. Finding nothing, I paused for
a few minutes to listen. There seemed to be a lull in the proceedings of the attack. Spasmodic machine-guns rattled. High
overhead there was an aeroplane. I thought what a queer business
it all was, and then decided to take a peep at the surrounding
country. No sooner had I popped my head out of the sap than
I received what seemed like a tremendous blow in the back—
between the shoulders. My first notion was that I had been hit
by a bomb from behind. What had really happened was that
I had been sniped from in front. Anyhow my attitude toward
life and the War had been instantaneously and completely altered
for the worse. I leant against the wall and shut my eyes. . . .
When I opened them again Sergeant Baldwin was beside me,
discreet and sympathetic. To my great surprise I discovered that
I wasn't dead. Baldwin assisted me back to the main trench,
investigated my wound, and left me sitting there, while he went
back to bring up some more men. After about a quarter of an
hour I began to feel active and heroic again, but in a different way.
(I was now not only a hero, but a wounded hero.) I can remember
talking excitedly to a laconic Stokes-gun officer who had arrived
from nowhere with his weapon. All my 75 men were now
on the scene. My only idea now was to collect all our available
ammunition, and then "renew the attack" while the Stokes-gun
officer put up an enthusiastic barrage. It did not occur to me
that there was anything else going on on the Western Front
excepting my own little show. My overstrained nerves had stirred
me up to such a pitch of febrile excitement that I felt capable of the
most suicidal exploits. This convulsive energy might have been
of some immediate value if there had been any rational outlet for
it. But there was none. Before I had time to do anything rash,
and irrelevant to the military situation, Conning arrived on the
scene to relieve me. Conning's unruffled behaviour sobered me
a bit; he seemed to have the situation sized up. Nevertheless I
was still boiling over with the offensive spirit, and my activity
was only quelled by a written order from the Cameronian Colonel,

who told me that we must not advance owing to the attack having failed elsewhere. This caused an anti-climax in my ardours, and I returned to the 2nd R.W.F. H.Q. On the way I met the M.O., who was strolling along the trench with the detached air of an amateur botanist. I was back in the tunnel within four hours of leaving it. This is all I can remember about that morning, and I am aware that my account has demonstrated how little there was to remember.

CHAPTER XIII

Arras—"Scarpe"—The Hindenburg Line—St. George's Day on Hénin Hill—Croisilles—Whitsunday in Plum Lane—Footnotes

Contributors:—COLTART; PICTON DAVIES; DOCHERTY; LL. EVANS; R. GREAVES; M. JONES; MOODY; RADFORD

Sketches:—16, 17, 18

April 10th.—Offensive is again in season. The Canadians have made a big push over the Vimy Ridge.

Here ends a leave prolonged by more illness. To-day's cross-Channel service was held up; a German submarine had mined the route off Folkestone. Rumour said that a hospital ship and a destroyer had been sunk. From the pier sweepers could be seen bringing mines to the surface and firing on them.

April 11th.—When we cast off half a gale was blowing up the Channel instead of yesterday's smooth sea: one of many sick, I was good for a hearty dinner ashore. In Boulogne the absence of Frenchmen, except the aged, was most noticeable. In London, Glasgow, and in our railway trains there are crowds of carefree, active civilians in their physical prime, "indispensables," coining money and enjoying life.

I got a seat in the compartment of a King's Messenger bound for Malta and the Levant; a brigadier bound for Athens, and three naval officers had the other seats. At the last moment some French people squeezed into an already full train which left at 9 o'clock.

April 12th.—We reached Amiens at 3.30 a.m., two hours late. After waiting for two hours more in a Y.M.C.A. hut for a French train to Doullens to be made up, I got into a first-class compartment in which three "poilus," French private soldiers, had shaken down. A French lieutenant looked in and grumbled because they were there, but they just stared at him. He sent a gendarme to put them out. Law and order looked at them with raised eyebrows, and they looked round vacancy until he went away. All their talk was battalion and hospital shop. Two were going on leave, one was discharged without a leg. We started at 6 o'clock. The lieutenant travelled in the guard's van.

The journey from Doullens, by a jumped lorry, was good going on the Arras road until we struck off to Gaudiempré, thence it was slow. The country was white with an inch and a half of snow which was melting under a drizzle of cold rain; I left early Spring weather twenty-six days ago. The side road was packed with the coming and going of units, detachments and oddments of men—wounded and unwounded, guns and vehicles of all sorts. Adding to the density of the throng was the cavalry, all over the place: again brought upon the scene by hope disdaining experience, or by the professional pride of the cavalry generals who almost monopolized the high commands. There were dead and dying horses by the roadside. The severity of the Winter, short rations, and the exertions of concentration, had told on the transport animals. Division, housed in huts in a sandpit off the road, directed me to Blairville. All its transport was there, and the surface had been churned into a lake of mud. Yates appeared to have been fortunate with his animals, all horses. Poore commanded Brigade's B Echelon. I shared his quarters. There was rest of a sort, but *April* 13*th*—no sleep, because the telephone buzzed, or orderlies stumbled in and out, all night. The camp was beside the old German line. Its dug-outs were said to be vast galleries 40 to 80 feet deep; each company had its labelled part.

My further route was by Boisleux-au-Mont and B. St. Marc, in long-occupied German territory. A robin, a yellowhammer and, I think, a woodlark made an odd little group on the roadside, sitting on a snow-sprinkled heap of sweepings. There was not a twig or a spar for them to perch on. With heads sunk in their shoulders they looked as in utter dejection on the busy road and the devastation around them. The Germans have razed everything that stood or grew on the strip of country from which they retired. Buildings and walls have been thrown down by explosive; the wall of one cemetery has been spared, it encloses many German graves. Culverts are broken and great craters blown at all cross-roads. Trees, bushes and posts have been felled; rarely a conspicuous tree is standing, perhaps as artillery datum. A leaning

signpost points to "Le Chat Maigre," which has joined the majority.
The mere labour of destruction must have been immense. Booby-
traps of most varied and ingenious contrivance were left in both
likely and unlikely places, causing casualties although the R.E.
sterilized as many as were found. Once Companies were halted
for a long time outside a village until it could be searched. When
they entered Yates was seen sitting on the church steps surrounded
by the Transport; he had been waiting for over an hour to dis-
tribute rations. He was lucky: soon afterwards a large quantity
of explosive was found below the steps, ready for the accident
that would detonate it. My journey led to the escarpment of the
Vimy Ridge, stretching along the whole visible front, and looking
higher than it did in autumn. It rises from flattish ground as if it
were the much weathered cliffs of a primeval shore. H.Q. was at
what had been Hénin, all living in the open on that shelterless
hillside.

The Battle of Arras, and its brood, was the B.E.F. share of the
ambitious scheme which the British and French Governments had
accepted from the new Commander-in-Chief of the French
Armies. Converging Franco-British attacks were to envelop the
German centre. The French attack on their Rheims–Soissons
front was disastrous. It was followed by mutinous agitation and
actual outbreaks in the French Armies, of which few in the B.E.F.
knew anything. (The first reference to it I saw in an English
paper was on February 1st, 1918.) In a few weeks there was a
change of Government in Paris. General Nivelle was deprived of
his command, to which General Pétain was appointed. In the
interval and after it British man-power was spent prodigally to
divert the Germans from an attack on the disheartened and
insubordinate French troops. The B.E.F. attack had pierced the
formidable Hindenburg Line. On the right the VI Corps got a
footing at Bullecourt. On the left the XVII Corps got right
through in front of Monchy-le-Preux. In the centre the VII Corps,
into which we had come, failed at Fontaine-lez-Croisilles in the
Sensée valley.

The Brigade is lent to the 21st Division, which to-day failed to
improve on the 30th Division's initial failure. The Battalion is in
support. Everyone is miserable: no one has any shelter from the
cold and drizzle. We are in fighting kit, without greatcoats:

rations are bully and biscuit, and the nearest shops are at Doullens.
There was talk of slackness in the Battalion. An influence that
encouraged looseness in the Company Messes had reappeared; it
eliminated itself very soon.

April 14th.—Cold and the Count's snoring drove me from a
perishing hole at 1 o'clock; by great luck "another 'ole," made
cosy by a brazier and fuel, was found, and shared with Conning.
At 5.30 The Cameronians and 5th Scottish Rifles attacked on the
crest of Hénin Hill. The former were astride and on the reverse
of the Hindenburg trenches: the latter on their left and quite in
the open, had to cross the northern spur of the Hill and advance
south-eastwards towards Fontaine. Another division on their
left attacked towards Chérisy. We ought to have been ready to
move instantly at zero, but orders did not arrive until 6.30. At
9.30 Brigade asked if we had any news from the line. The first
news to come to us was of an advance of 1000 yards, and hundreds
of casualties: next, both figures were whittled down until they
were small. The happenings to the two battalions had been mixed.
A small Cameronian gain in the trenches was lost; there were not
many casualties. The 5th S.R., in advancing over hundreds of
yards of bare ground behind a paltry barrage, exposed to rifle and
machine-gun fire, lost heavily before getting within striking
distance of any enemy line; some outposts had fallen back before
them, but they failed at the German position on the reverse of the
100-metre contour which linked up with the trench blocks, (see
p. 329). A proposal to renew the attack at night was dropped.
We spent the day inactively, untroubled by the enemy artillery.
A high, cold wind chased gigantic clouds across a bright blue sky
in clear sunshine.

Allenby, the Army Commander, says, "We are pursuing a
beaten enemy." 'Strewth!

The Division relieved the 21st on the line, roughly, of the
Croisilles–Héninel road. Its right was on Croisilles; its left
centre straddled the Hindenburg Line on the east side of the summit
of Hénin Hill; from that point its left bent forward with the
100-metre spur. It was to be spent in attacks to, and across, the
Sensée. At 9 o'clock our Companies at Hénin began to go up
the Hill, led by Brigade guides who were unsure of the way.
For several hours we had a place in a scene of confusion. The

new Brigade-Major had been lavish of wrong map references. At Brigade H.Q. units were a rabble in which Company Officers and N.C.Os. strove in the dusk to keep their men together, and their superiors looked on mutely. It took our leading Company three and a half hours to cover two and a half miles on open ground. *April 15th*—What should have been a simple move was not completed until 4.30. Setting out at dawn to restore my circulation in seeking a route for the wounded, I chanced on our ration-parties. They said that they had been looking for us all night, and that for six hours before they could start they had been boxed about by the Staff Captain's misdirections. In daylight, and in rain at the finish, H.Q. moved again, it was over the scene of Corps' first attack, and entered the Hindenburg Line to the left of where the Fontaine–St. Martin and Croisilles–St. Martin roads meet. The G.O.C. was at the start, beaming benediction on us. In the part of the Tunnel to which the Battalion descended units and detachments of two Brigades jostled amidst new mud and old refuse, improvised and untended latrines, and a few dead of both sides. H.Q. chose a space which was hung with tapestry, and had it swept, cleaned and picketed. We were much alive to booby-traps, but there was nothing behind the arras. The Companies made their own arrangements.

The Hindenburg Line was a truly wonderful piece of engineering. It consisted of two trenches 200 or more yards apart. The Front trench, quite 10 feet deep with splayed sides, was just in front of the crest of a long glacis; in the parapet were timbered fire-steps of solid construction; here and there timbered steps led to front and rear, also to concrete machine-gun emplacements along the parapet at varying intervals of 50 to 100 yards; in front was a belt of stout barbed wire 30 to 60 yards across—this had been flattened in places by tanks during the successful assault. The support, or Tunnel trench was on the reverse slope; it was of the same construction, but the wire and much of the fittings were incomplete. There were communications between the two trenches. All these surface works had been considerably knocked about by our heavy guns. Beneath the support trench, at a depth of 40 feet, was a huge dug-out or tunnel some 6 feet 6 inches high, and said to be 2 miles long in this portion. It was fitted down the middle with tiers of bunks, and small living-rooms and store-rooms opened off it; it was wired throughout for electric lighting, but current had not been laid on. There were entrances of solid joiner-work every 40 to 50 yards, and wide timber-cased stairways alternated with inclined planes for stores. Many men, hastening out of the rain, got on to the inclined planes, which were made slippery by the mud on boots and clothing, and shot to the bottom to the consternation of those among whom they arrived so suddenly, and their own. Above and below ground the opposing garrisons were separated by blocks or barriers; the latter had been made by blowing in the Tunnel. The blocks were just east of the Croisilles–Héninel road.

April 16th.—At 3 a.m. the attack of two days ago was repeated. The Cameronians, again in the trenches, had the 20th R.F. on their left this time. The R.F. had relieved the 5th S.R. in the line they had gained; it ran north-east from the "Fiddler-Friedrich" part of the Hindenburg Line in the 95-100 metre contour. This was another dud show. The Chocolate Soldiers went well, and suffered for it. Two of our Lewis guns and our bombers were in support, attached to The Cameronians. Sassoon, a very stout man, was wounded in Tunnel Trench: his craving to renew the attack was not allowed. Conning repaired the Block and held it until we were relieved. The 100th Brigade on our right was said to have got its objectives, or some of them.—When a wounded officer complained, during the night, of the Count's terrible snoring, '42 Jones pressed in muttering, "I'll stop the (obscenity)," possibly not knowing who the culprit was. The snorer's agonized yell at his handling identified him to his assailant, who fled to cover—not without abettors.

April 17th.—Relief, by the 98th Brigade, was a terrible business for a mob confined in dark places. One battalion began to go out at 7 last night; its H.Q., the last of it, passed at 8.30 this morning. We went across country in hail showers to a wretched bivouac, a sunken road and trench of sorts, at Mercatel. Snow fell for a long time, thawing as it fell.

The Brigade is said to be in disgrace, and the G.O.C. perturbed: he needn't be, the Division is his to make or let rip. The Battalion's part has been that of a hard-worked, useful, inglorious *April 18th*—reserve. The Brigadier blew in: he was complimentary: he has looked upon his work and seen that it was good.

The Royal Fusilier who offered to come to us as Transport Officer turns out to be a scarcely prosperous hairdresser in a South Coast holiday resort. "I do not cut myself," he explains unasked. All day drizzle, and mud.

April 19th.—We marched at 5.30 by Boyelles, Maison Rouge and Judas Farm to St. Leger. The Companies occupy an outpost line; they are detailed for fatigues. H.Q. is in a fairly intact cottage; there are crocuses and other bulbs in pots, left by some German lover of flowers. Destruction here is only partial, but sufficient; the village factories and workshops are completely destroyed.

April 20th.—Sun and sailing cloud trailing shadow, a fresh wind blowing, and a blackbird singing, make a fine April day. One of our airmen gave onlookers a thrill by the skill with which he dodged three fighters who tried to down him. Two of our wrecks lie in a field beside us. The Brigadier warned us that we will be wanted to mop up. The G.O.C. says that we won't be wanted at all.

April 21st.—For two nights the Companies have been on porterage in the Sensée Valley, making advanced dumps. After dark, very dark, we groped our way back to Mercatel. Dawn was not far off when the last of us got in.

April 22nd.—The finest day we have had yet, the wind keen. A German flier set one of our sausages alight and damaged two others: one of the observers jumped out without a parachute and was killed. Later, a German swooped from out a cloud on to one of our spotting planes which crashed near Hénin. All day there was a lot of noise, much of it from heavy stuff.

The Division is to continue operations in two groups under the Brigadiers of the 98th and 100th Brigades, J. D. Heriot Maitland and A. W. F. Baird. We are to come under the 98th. Its plan of attack is an elaborate repetition of that of the 14th and 16th along, and on the reverse of, the trenches; the objective is 800 yards distant, but Fontaine is to be overlooked at all costs. On the right, the 100th Brigade is to advance north-eastwards for 1500 yards, covered by night and two tanks, and assault the Hindenburg Line from a point 300 yards west of the Sensée westwards to the 98th Brigade's objective.

In the late evening A and C Companies moved into the Tunnel.

At 9 o'clock Owen and Radford reported to the O.C. 4th Suffolks, who are to attack down the trenches with two companies in each. A and C are to follow along Tunnel Trench in their wake, picket all entrances to the Tunnel, collect prisoners, and maintain a supply of ammunition. H.Q., B and D Companies went to the Croisilles–Hénin road and squatted there. The guns were just behind; *April 23rd*—their blast at zero should have awakened the dead. At 7 o'clock B and D were ordered to Tunnel Trench to be at 98th Brigade's immediate call.

The 33rd Division, and others on its left, attacked at 4.45—before daylight. An initial success of both of its brigades, although their tanks broke down before being of use, was most promising. The Queen's, of the 100th Brigade, got footings in their objective in Tunnel Trench. They were, however, stayed by machine-guns, and unable to hold on in face of the facilities the enemy had to reinforce and replenish from the parts of Tunnel Trench which he held. In the end the gains of the Queen's and their supports, the 16th K.R.R., were lost. The bombing attack of the Suffolk's right companies went merry as marriage bells; they linked up with the Queen's in the Front trench. Owing to reverses in Tunnel Trench this important link was broken, and a cheaply won success became a costly repulse. These two Suffolk companies were cut off, and had many losses before escaping across country in the afternoon. The Queen's lost many more. The fortune of the day on the Suffolks' left, where the Argylls and Middlesex continued the line to its junction with the 30th Division, will be sketched when B and D Companies' part is told. For the Battalion A and C Companies fill the bill until the late afternoon.

By 3.30 A Company, less one platoon, and C were ready to leave the Tunnel in rear of the Suffolks' left companies. 'The first part of the programme worked to admiration.' At zero the Suffolks pulled down their barricade. A superb trench-mortar bombardment with thermite shell had practically obliterated the German barricade, 30 yards distant. The Suffolks dashed off. 'The Germans scuttled like rabbits without putting up a fight: they left their day's rations in the trench.' But the Suffolks had to pull up when they were about 200 yards short of their objective and of any party of the Queen's. A and C Companies followed them. Three men were posted at each entrance to the Tunnel.

Persuasion, backed by bombs, caused some 200 Germans to come up from its depths. They were sent to the rear, where one of them told how he had been in a listening-post during the night, and inferred from the noise in our trench that we meant to attack, but he said nothing about it because he hoped to be captured. The prisoners disposed of, carrying-parties were organized to bring up supplies of bombs. The work proceeded quietly but for occasional shots from the left. 'By 7.30 all was peace and quiet. About 8 o'clock a German made his appearance in the trench, carrying a tin of soup. He was seized, and his soup was consumed. No one knew just where he had come from, but apparently it was from a communication trench on the left. Because the Argylls were to advance over that ground at zero his emergence was somewhat ominous, especially as a good deal of movement was seen in that direction shortly afterwards.' Owen and Radford tried to find the Stokes-mortar section: having failed they treated the area with rifle-grenades, but with only partial effect. At 8.30 urgent messages came in from the Suffolks that they had run out of bombs. In their elation, as they made their dash along the trench, they had squandered bombs in the Tunnel entrances. They had failed to advance farther and gain touch with the Queen's. Now, the Queen's having been driven out, 'the Suffolks were being counter-attacked. About 9 o'clock a lot of them, and machine-gunners and others, started to swarm back. Soon they had all passed through our Companies, and for the rest of the day not a soul of them was seen by any of us.' In this precipitate flight 4 machine-guns and 2 Stokes mortars were lost, and the enemy recovered his own heavy mortars undamaged. A light mortar and 2 machine-guns of his had been brought in.

A. Company was in advance, strung out over a great part of the trench, carrying bombs. With the Germans coming down the trench a bombing fight began; it was a rear-guard action in which the Germans had an advantage, their stick-grenade—the "potato-masher"—having a much longer range than the Mills bomb, which was rather big and heavy for many to grasp. By 9.30 A Company had fallen back on the barricade which C Company had made haste to rebuild. By the loss of Tunnel Trench the troops in the Front trench were exposed to attack through the communications, for they had not been blocked. (The same had happened to The Cameronians on the 14th and 16th, and for the same reason.) Only a small part of the Front trench gain was held.

For two hours A and C Companies had a bad time at the barricade. There was a good supply of rifle-grenades and bombs; parties were organized to use them, but 'it was the turn of the Germans to be in the ascendant. They manned their trench-mortars and sent over a colossal collection of every kind of aerial torpedo, "pineapple" bomb, and rifle-grenade.' The position became very unhealthy, casualties increased every moment. Owen, with the notion of lessening the pressure, called for volunteers from A and C Companies to go over the top. He and Ralph Greaves took out parties who bombed the enemy back some distance. 'But [1] by that time the enemy had riflemen posted in a cross trench, one of the communications between Front and Tunnel Trenches, so the volunteers were driven off with a good few casualties including two of A Company's subalterns; all of these were, however, brought back to the barricade. Next, a Lewis gun was mounted in a trench flanking the barricade, it kept down the riflemen effectually: our rifle-grenadiers also were making good practice, and the enemy did not seem inclined to press matters. A stray N.C.O. of the 1st Middlesex turned up and did very good work. C Company were in the trench behind A, and we felt fairly happy. We tried to get in touch with our artillery, but they were completely at sea as to the situation. I was attending to a man's rifle, which had jammed with a grenade, when he called to me to "look out," and ducked into the trench. I looked up and saw one of Gerry's grenades in the air right above me. It hit the barricade level with my chest, I got the issue into my arm, and was carried down the trench.' Soon afterwards Owen, who was preparing to lead another party of about a dozen volunteers over the top, was killed by a trench-mortar bomb. Rhys Jones of C Company was wounded about the same time. A Company had now no officer left at the barricade, so Radford brought up his own Company from support and relieved A. He remained in charge of the barricade for the rest of the day. It was noon before things quieted down. By that time his three subalterns had been wounded, and a fine N.C.O., Sergeant Hughes,

[1] R. Greaves.

had been killed. With the ending of the German strafe a guard
was posted at the barricade, and the remainder of C Company
found shelter in the Tunnel immediately below. The afternoon
was generally quiet. A report reached us that Division and Corps
were each congratulating themselves on the first success when the
reverses were taking place, and that the news of them caused a
violent disturbance of temperature and wind in these high altitudes.

So far O.C. Suffolks had been in nominal command: the tough
old man had been seen in child-like sleep somewhere on a fire-step.
Late in the afternoon the O.C. 5th S.R. was put in command.
One of his companies had been holding the Front trench barricade
since about noon. Now one was sent up to Tunnel Trench. The
early morning attack was to be repeated by these two S.R. companies at 6.24: our A and C Companies were to cover their flanks
with a rifle-grenade barrage and Lewis gun-fire, then mop up
Tunnel Trench as in the morning. This attack was part of a
Brigade operation in which B and D Companies were used on the
left. Although the S.R. in Tunnel Trench were splendidly led by
their officer, until lately their R.S.M., their attack failed badly.
They did not know the ground. Very few got beyond the
barricade, those who did were faced by a tangle of barbed wire
which was covered by a machine-gun farther back. The attack up
the Front trench also failed. The only result was that the Germans,
beginning at 7.45, plastered our barricade [both barricades] and
its neighbourhood with shells and trench-mortar bombs, and the
brunt of its defence fell on C Company. The bomb-throwing
competition started all over again. A bomb thrown by one of
the Company hit the top of the trench, fell back into it, and blew
into fragments the feet of a young private of the Company who
had been sitting there for hours imperturbably straightening the
pins of the Mills grenades. Casualties were increasing: the number
of men to call upon was lessening: the Tunnel was near and safe.
The 5th S.R. officer, who tried to get the men remaining with
him to attack again, was mortally wounded. Then C.S.M. Marks
of C Company was hit; he died in the Tunnel. 'We were never
really anxious,' but behind us someone's fancy soared, someone
gave tongue—"the barricade has been forced." Upstairs, in the
trench, madness broke out. Rifles, just fired into space, got hot,
while officers yelled targets and ranges. Order was not restored

until a controlled company of 5th S.R. had taken position between, and supporting, the garrisons of the Front and Tunnel Trench barriers. Some of the frenzied bogy-spotters on the fire-steps had to be brought to their senses by having their feet suddenly jerked from under them. The fury lasted for the better part of an hour : then there fell a dead calm. Downstairs, at 98th Brigade H.Q., papers were burned, and much else incidental to a disaster happened. 'At [1] a Divisional Race Meeting two weeks later I overheard the Staff Captain giving a graphic and detailed account of the "forcing of the barricade." I told him fairly forcibly that he was recounting a pack of lies.' That kind of myth outlives denial ; it has appeared in print as fact.

By 8.30 the garrison at the Tunnel barricade consisted of Radford, Sergeant Jack Williams, Lance-Corporal James and Private Bennett, all of C Company, and one man of the 5th S.R.[2] 'By [1] then the place was a shambles. At 10 o'clock I demanded of the O.C. 5th S.R. to be relieved, for we were worn out. Nothing came of it—the Suffolks were again in command, unseen. By midnight, however, the 19th Brigade had taken over, and we were relieved by a company of The Cameronians. We spent the night in the Tunnel. A. Company's fourth platoon was there ; it had been kept in reserve to advance up the Tunnel if the Suffolks consolidated their gains above ground. In the morning we were astonished, and annoyed, at the news that the Germans had abandoned their barricade and hundreds of yards of trench during the night. When we came out the Tunnel gave up a bigger number of men than I thought were left. Some of them must have hidden themselves well the previous day.'

The early morning attack by the Argylls and Middlesex was held completely near the centre and on the flanks, but in folds where the ground gave less advantage to the defence two of their first-wave companies got through and advanced about 800 yards. Nothing was heard from them, and all attempts to get in touch failed, so it was believed that they had been captured. At 9.30 B and D Companies were sent up to take their place in the Brigade line ; H.Q. was left to while away the time in the sunken road at Hénin. At 2 o'clock we had a warning for a renewed attack, but it lapsed. At 5 o'clock we were ordered to join B

[1] Radford.   [2] They were all decorated.

and D Companies, and be ready for action at short notice. The plan was for B and D to attack the sticky middle part of the German line on the Brigade front, and for the remaining Argyll and Middlesex companies to advance on our right and left respectively. On getting the order the C.O. and Mann hurried to learn what they could at the Argylls' H.Q. Their C.O. and Adjutant had just become casualties, and such was the account given of the state of their companies that the C.O. forwent their co-operation. Apparently the Middlesex had no orders, for we were left to ourselves at zero. H.Q. had to make arrangements while on the move, and to issue orders without knowing anything of the ground. On arriving, the German position was seen to be about 150 yards distant. There was barely time to see that it was on the far side of a spur which dropped steeply to a line of pollard willows, and that there was dead ground on the left.

We were standing beside a former German gun-emplacement close behind the left of the shallow trench. Behind us, to the left, lay an officer of the 5th S.R. The last of the men were shuffling into position when there came from the right a flurry in the air: it ended in a sputter from some 18-pounder shells in front of a few yards of the German line, the vital yards as we were to learn. A fresh breeze from the left swirled the smoke aside. A hen pheasant with a broken wing ran clucking between the lines, and had more of our attention than a second sputter of shell. Officers and N.C.Os. looked at each other—puzzled, looked round at H.Q. Can these few poops be our bombardment, we wondered. It was 6.24. Mann waved, and shouted "Get on." The two right platoons of B did not follow Phillips, owing to a misunderstanding. Hanmer had just been wounded by a shell splinter, so Jackson jumped out to wave on D Company, and C.S.M. Gittens blew his whistle and jumped out after him. The barrage, what there was of it, had lifted already. A third or fourth sputter was in rear of the Germans, who were quick, we found, to mount their machine-guns, two, I think. They had been given a rehearsal in the morning, and two before then. Among shell-holes and the dead and wounded of these failures our men were dashing forward on converging lines. They dropped fast—killed, wounded, or to escape the jets of bullets. The two B Company platoons scarcely got across their parapet, some were hit on it; Phillips was killed before finding his feet. They were on even ground that sloped down to them. D Company was mostly in dead ground for about half the distance it had to go. Where the slope rose to the flat they came upon a nearly solid hurdle about thirty yards long, a swathe of Royal Fusilier and some Middlesex dead, lying where the machine-guns swept the brow of the rise—all shot in the head or chest, as was seen in the morning. Jackson, Gittens—with a leap, and '10 Jones were among the very few who got past it. Close to the wire Jackson was wounded, and the others dropped down. All was over in little more than a minute. In the aweing quiet that then fell on our front the "barrage" could be heard again, fainter and fainter. It was "creeping" into the distance by leaps and bounds, where pillars of smoke and dust took fantastic shapes in the wind, and drew like wraiths into the shade of the fall of Hénin Ridge. The day was dull. The blighted landscape was a dun colour, the clouded sky behind it a flat grey without a rift, deepening the feeling of defeat.

The empty trench was manned by the two inactive platoons of B Company, and the slow-to-start, by H.Q. signallers and servants. On our left were two weakened companies of Middlesex; they were in the air owing to the untimely withdrawal of a 30th Division unit. While twilight lasted there was little to do but watch Monchy-le-Preux being pounded to rubble and dust, and to follow a to-and-fro going of khaki figures where Guémappe had been, and bombs were being hurled. Two Germans made furtive signs of surrender from the left of the willows on D Company's front; more would have come over, but they were fired on by the Middlesex. As they shivered with cold and fear Mann stamped, and cursed them; then he gave them whisky, and to abject expressions of thanks he retorted that he hated them. His only brother was killed a few weeks earlier. None could have been more scared than they were during a bombardment which suggested that a counter-attack might follow, or so relieved when, at last, they were sent away with a stretcher-case. We had a few casualties from the bombardment, it killed Jackson: Gittens and Jones had the luck to come through unhurt. There was no further offence on B and D's front, but we could see and hear that a lot of explosive was being used at the Tunnel Trench barrier, so Mann sent a runner for news. As dark was falling some of the men in shell-holes tried too soon to come in, they were seen and hit. Later on all came back who could.

There had been leisure to survey the position. It looked as if a couple of Lewis guns on the right could keep the enemy off his fire position while use was made of the dead ground on the left to get near enough to rush it in front and in reverse. But by that time the men had been used.

My imperturbable servant relieved a famine at H.Q., and gave hints of the vision of pandemonium he had coming through Tunnel Trench. We heard, after relief, that the peril in which 98th Brigade thought it stood was reported behind. So hopeless was 19th Brigade H.Q. of our situation, and of the Hindenburg Line being held, that the Brigade transport at Boiry Becquerelle was warned to move farther back. It stood-by during the night, hooked-in, and the Staff Captain, girt for battle, and ready for flight, was eager to turn the horses' heads west. Yates chose to misunderstand the order, but he was not allowed to send up any rations.

The night was fairly clear, and fresh. Our immediate front was lighted by frequent enemy parachute-rockets. More frequent were the bursts of a traversing machine-gun that ceased towards *April 24th*—dawn. In the yielding darkness some wounded were seen looking out of shell-holes. While individuals were bringing them in a bandaged Argyll mounted the German fire-position and came through the wire. He was looked at with much surprise and some suspicion, but he came on confidently and shouted something. Someone of B Company ran out to him, and called back, "They're gone." The Companies were ordered forward at once behind patrols. Not far beyond the willows there was a small war-worn copse near which the missing Argylls were met coming in, bringing a few prisoners with them. They had gone to ground twenty-four hours ago, and had not been disturbed. Mann ran on searching the ground from side to side in front of the patrols. They went close to where the Hindenburg Line crossed the Fontaine–St. Martin–Cojeul road before being fired on, and stopping to exchange shots with the Germans. By direction of the G.S.O.2, who turned up very soon, a line of outposts was established there. The ground from which the enemy had withdrawn was honeycombed with shell-holes, and spread about it were a few concrete strong-points—the "pill-boxes" of Passchendaele. A very few wounded and unwounded Germans were found.

The dead of five battalions of the Division lay in front of the abandoned German machine-gun position; they were the relics of four assaults. A survey confirmed last night's impression of its vulnerability to the minor infantry tactics, learned from the Boer rifleman in South Africa, which were routine instruction before the War, and were used to good end in its early phase; and exposed the tragic ineptitude of just going on throwing men against it after such a futile artillery bombardment as must leave its defenders practically unscathed and quite uncowed. Ours was the third bull-at-a-gate attack to be detailed since the 5th S.R. dug-in nine days ago. The occasion was but one of the occasions innumerable when a company or a battalion was squandered on an attack seemingly planned by someone who, lacking either first or second hand knowledge of the ground, just relied on our maps of moderate scale. "Brigade," as we knew it, was remote in action, and ineffectual. Battalion information about local detail was not always taken well. A practical suggestion might be received as if it were a reflection on the higher rank's competence or initiative, hence nothing might be thought of but high-explosive shell, which so often gave warning of an infantry assault and failed to aid it. Except quite often for raids infantry manœuvre in the B.E.F. had come to an end, or fallen into disuse. H.E. was supposed to blast the trail—so often it only blazed it—a unit or formation had but to follow. If the partly trained infantry cast a look to right or left it was because it had learned to fear cross-fire, not to help by cross-fire a flank unit in trouble, and any delay lost it its own artillery cover. It was not unusual, therefore, for a brigade to reach its objective with only 100 casualties, more or less, and have 1000 in falling back because the position was untenable, made so in part by its own failure to help clear its flanks during the advance. As with brigades in larger operations, so has it been with battalions in brigade attacks. In the smaller operations the use of ground is everything, and an intelligent plan can be carried out even by half-taught officers and half-trained men.

We were relieved early in the day, and the Battalion was reunited at Boiry Becquerelle. A draft was waiting there,

and Picton Davies rejoined coming from the 4th Battalion.
April 25th—Cleaning up. Being alongside our heavies, "Coughing
Clara" and her husky sisters, was anything but restful, so we were
April 26th—glad to be away from such an explosive neighbourhood
when we moved to Blairville. Socks, dozens of pairs, are being
thrown out all over the camp, the result of a consignment from the
Welfare Association having been delivered. Those in the packs
of the dead were just thrown out, and shirts too, all good, to rot
or be burned.

Our casualties for the tour are 13 officers, 4 of them killed,
and about 120 other ranks out of a trench strength of 350. The
Division took 730 prisoners all told. What was its loss in prisoners?
In the afternoon the G.O.C. came among us, shook hands everywhere; was rightly complimentary to Radford and Mann: would
have us know that Army, not he, ordered the 6 o'clock attack.
He went away even better pleased with himself than when he
came. Bouquets from G.H.Q. and downwards have been coming
in all day. Division and Corps contend for the credit of having
"pushed the enemy back." Both are interested in making the most
April 27th—of the unexpected. We marched to Basseux, smiled
on by the Corps Commander. The billets are comfortable. What
a treat to have a mattress. The villages are almost undamaged,
and farm work is active.

April 28th.—The night was as restful as the previous night was
wakeful, when Poore was going on his first leave. All afternoon
he had been excited and fidgety, wondering and asking if he was
going the best way, how he should do, how much money he would
need, and so on, and so on. Rising in the middle of the night to
be sure of catching the Staff car four hours later, he packed and
repacked his travelling kit, tramped, tramped in boots about the
uncarpeted room next mine, and sought again a solution of all
his doubts. At last he got away, and the other occupants of the
billet got to sleep. I spent a lazy afternoon lolling in the warm
sunshine, with birds twittering around and aeroplanes droning
overhead. Spring is backward, not a bud is opening on hedge or
tree, but the few birds in these parts are building.

The account of our recent action which G.H.Q. has received
and published makes very entertaining reading. "Our troops
charged down the ridge," "driving the enemy down at a canter":

of aught else—nothing. What artistry! We felt we had been bluffed, for the enemy had walked off at his own time and pace unknown to us and our neighbours, and to those at the Barrier. But orderly as was the withdrawal the German local command must have had the wind up, like our own, to order it. On a different level of imagination was the belief at the Argylls' H.Q. that their missing company got forward, was driven back, fought its way forward again, was surrounded and captured. It had, by its own account on the 24th, gone to ground in comfort from the start and been little troubled. Later it was said, rightly or wrongly, that a detached party had been scuppered. Rumour is never so busy as during a fight. Following the fight comes the legend, and it grows hourly as individuals, often far away, and units gather to themselves credit and garlands, or have these thrust upon them for the credit of someone else. It's all so human and amusing.

April 29th.—Sunday: a church bell never sounded sweeter to my ear; the bell of Bailleulval tolled to me like a melody.

April 30th.—Another of a succession of fine days, the nights clear and starlit. A Brigade Conference was, as usual, a monologue by the G.O.C., and the usual romancing after a Show. He has the haziest notion what his columns did; the "canter" touch in official wind is his very own. He was quite apologetic about B and D Companies attack, "Army ordered it." Temperamentally he and his G.S.O.1 are poles apart: his brigadiers are not a band *May 1st*—of brothers.—The diary of a captured German N.C.O. is published. What use can a man full of such loathing have been! —The quiet in front must portend a push.—Our billets are too comfortable for a battalion; 50th Division H.Q. is turning us out. *May 2nd*—I grudge my bed to some Q. fellow. We marched to a bivouac of leaking tin shanties, at the best, between Adinfer Wood and Monchy-au-Bois, where the old front line runs. Rations were never better than they've been these days, the fresh beef and mutton are excellent.

May 3rd.—There was heavy gun-fire at 3.45 a.m. Formations of the Fifth, Third, and First Armies are said to be attacking all the stickiest spots on this front. Early reports were of very unequal fortune: the afternoon was quite quiet; the evening till 11 o'clock very noisy. Nett gain nil. (Not strictly accurate, according to later reports there were small gains.)

May 4th.—Sweltering. Greenery is appearing everywhere. In a four-furlong race between Yates on "Girlie" and Montgomery, the G.S.O.2, who rode a fine gelding, "François," for the A.S.C., Yates was giving away over four stones and could not do it on the day, so the Battalion dropped a few hundred francs.

May 5th.—Chilly; we got the fringe of the rain of distant thunder. Division has circulated a reminder of the value of rifle fire!

May 6th.—Sunday. A shivering morning. A Battalion shooting competition proves how appallingly bad our shooting is, and how awkward many, if not most, of the men are in handling a rifle.

May 7th.—Sunny and fresh. To-day's Race Meeting at Ayette, near St. Leger, was a really good show and good fun. The G.O.C. can put knowledge into this sort of thing. He is an excellent horseman; a straight line across country, and the misery of his straggling retinue, delight him. Everything was appointed—Tattersall's enclosure, a bar, and all—and run with the precision of a first-class meeting at home. Our infantry chargers weren't in it with the long-tailed artillery lot, although Yates won this time against all comers. A professional jockey in the R.F. Transport won the mule race, the "Prix d'Alphonse," on an unlikely-looking mount. The Shrapnels and others supplied the fun of a country fair and a circus. (An illustrated report of the event was published in *The Sporting and Dramatic News* of June 20th.)

May 8th.—Grey and cold. In heavy rain, as last night, our shacks are quite good shower-baths.—G.H.Q. has made the momentous discovery that it has become habitual in the Army to refer to the 'Drocourt–Quéant' line. It is pointed out that Quéant being on the right, the correct nomenclature is the 'Quéant–Drocourt' line: for compliance—G.H.Q. does not deign to add "please."[1] We humble ranks feel that G.H.Q., having been safely delivered of this G.R.O., may be able to get on with the War. And yet this topographical solecism was on the maps issued by G.H.Q., and was still being printed on its maps of later date.

May 9th.—Scarce a gun fired. Our time here is all but up, and we are in dire need of purposeful training. What a treat it is

---

[1] Throughout this text deployments and descriptions are given from right to left: the few exceptions are obvious from the text.

to awake to hear a cuckoo's call, and the unrest of rooks in Adinfer Wood—the very name fascinates me. It was never part of a battle-field, and was left whole when the Germans withdrew. On its front, hidden in the beech hedge, are machine-gun emplacements of concrete and armourplate, like large letter-boxes. Within it are gun-emplacements and shelters built of large boles, planted over with ferns and grasses for concealment; smaller shelters are woven cleverly of branches, some growing and some partly or wholly cut. Its trees are erect and unbroken. Moss and ivy, violets, bluebells, anemones and wild strawberry carpet it. The relics of its occupation are unobtrusive, they take nothing from the charm of a wood wherein "to lose and neglect the creeping hours."

May 10th.—Brétencourt, the paymaster's abode, is just within our old line. Its fruit trees are coming into blossom. It is not badly damaged, many of the inhabitants never left it. The occupants of one abandoned cottage have just returned and begun to make it habitable—habitable as understood in a district where war has lingered. There is not a window or stick of furniture left, and half of it is filled with the partly blown-in roof; but a man and two women have come to live in it.

May 11th.—A Scotch vendetta, inter-regimental or inter-battalion of the same regiment, is a terrible thing when seen out here. Once in a while something reminds one of the hideous truth underlying the horror of *The House with the Green Shutters.* Three weeks ago the . . . let an officer of the . . . lie in their midst, an offence, rather than bury him. To-day they sneered that their aversions took khaki aprons for their Pipers off dead. . . .

May 12th.—Our horses, again turned loose, revel and roll on the fresh young grass. A tranquil twilight landscape had a distant border of shell-bursts and rockets against a glow of pale lemon and blue, a curiously pleasing scene.

May 13th, day of memory: Sunday. German graveyards are worth a visit, they are the best by far. Many of the memorials are stone, which good craftsmen have ornamented with a robust art. Rarely some French civilian grave has been robbed to furnish a block. The inscription is distinctive. A German is always *tapfer*—brave, or a *held*—hero; an enemy is " a French " or "English soldier," so far I have seen one exception—"a brave

French soldier." Later on I saw one or two of our Air Force who were "brave." I never saw an English or French memorial to a German, although our Air Force marked their fliers' graves.

May 14th.—A fifth broiling day. In the afternoon I rode by Mercatel to Arras, a town of a few cellar-dwellers now, but there was neither occasion nor chance to see anything of its underground life. I took in only its silence and its squalor. Doors are shut, many hang by one hinge; windows are shuttered, much of the glass is broken. There was no one in the vast Square of fine old low-gabled houses; its pavement is pierced by shells, and the holes hold fetid water. No one was to be seen anywhere, once I heard voices within. The Hispano-Flemish Town Hall is nearly a complete ruin; otherwise there is little real destruction in the western half of the town, which was all there was time to see, except the Cathedral and round it. The pity is that such a soulless piece of masonry as the Cathedral was ever built. A sudden plump drenched me to the skin, but I dried on the way back: a pleasant evening ride by Boiry Ste. Rictrude.—We are threatened by rumour with the cutting-off of parcels containing cake, biscuits and the like. It seems that German parcels are pooled as rations.

May 15th.—After lunch we marched to a camp-bivouac in front of Judas Farm, a mile north-west of St. Leger. The Brigadier is again left out; his battalions are divided between the other two brigades.—The creeping barrage, which dissatisfied everyone, has been revised; its rate is to be a mile an hour when the going is bad, and nearly two miles an hour when good: no one is excited, it won't be less futile in volume.

May 16th.—A leaden day, damp when not drizzling.—The only ground the enemy has lost since last we were in the line is the 300 to 400 yards of the Hindenburg system on the left of the Sensée. Some of the 21st Division men, engaged in the operations and taken prisoner, are said to have escaped and rejoined owing to one of our shells cutting the wire of their cage. Rumour and expectation have been rife of a further German withdrawal to the Quéant–Drocourt line. Preparations are said to have been made to follow up, but we're not yet on the bully and biscuit of an 'Army of Pursuit' of the Somme pattern. Confirmation of the rumour by a captured officer is the reason given for Division's battle being postponed for three days. A much more cogent

reason is that the wire is barely cut yet, as 5th S.R. patrols discovered and their C.O. insisted.

May 18th.—Three weeks ago the 1st Battalion's casualties at
Bullecourt were 150, now they are 350, and the situation thereabout
remains obscure. Our Brigade patrols sent to look-see found
plenty of Germans between there and here. A few shells have
barely disturbed our rest, so it is the odder that, for no reason I
can give myself, I rose from the floor of our hut seconds before
a splinter cut through my spread valise and stuck in the wood.
Late in the day we moved for the night to an unfinished German
earthwork, meant to be an outpost to cover the Sensée valley
west of Croisilles; the dug-outs are in great part excavated,
May 19th—the trenches are little more than spitlocked. We
changed round to a sunken road south of Croisilles. Our
cook found spinach and leeks in a garden, and promise of a
crop of strawberries and currants.—The day fine, yesterday was
very oppressive.

May 20th.—At 5.15, in a thick mist, the usual converging attack
began. The 100th Brigade is in action from The Hump to the
river with Fontaine as its objective, the 5th S.R. form its right
flank: the 98th Brigade, beyond the Hindenburg Line, has Chérisy
as objective. There was no making head or tail of the reports
that came in during the morning. We were reduced to listening
to Army chestnuts. "A true story of the Retreat" which has been
current since early days: A man saw that an officer had detected
him killing a sheep, which was contrary to orders, so he stuck it
again with his bayonet, exclaiming loudly to be overheard,
"Would you bite me, you . . . !" It was told in South Africa
as an original incident there, seventeen years ago. It may date
from the Peninsular War—or the Wars of the Roses. The famous
story of the piper, unprintable unless eviscerated, is another restored
antique—very popular among the padres.—Told as a Battalion
tale: "Damn it ! Your thumb's in the soup," an officer exclaimed
to an uncouth mess waiter. "Yes, sir, but it isn't hot."—Colonel
Jones Williams is "Jones Billy" to all the subalterns who have
passed through the 3rd Battalion which he rules with a light touch.
He is evidently a man of few and very ordinary words, but the end,
which never varies, of the patriotic exordium he delivers to all
overseas drafts should not be lost: "May God go with you!

I will go with you as far as the station."—I became interested in a *Morning Post* notice of a book of verse by Sassoon, *The Old Huntsman and other Poems*.

Our guns were remarkably quiet after the morning: a reported shell shortage seems incredible. The Germans strewed the country with 5·9, 4·2, and ·77. By nightfall there came out of the fog of war the broad fact that attack, counter-attack and renewed attack, gains and losses, ended in the 100th Brigade, reinforced by The Cams. and 5th S.R., gaining and holding the Hindenburg Front trench from The Hump to the Sensée. They failed at The Hump itself, and at Tunnel Trench—though it was entered. The 98th Brigade, and 20th R.F., is nearer Chérisy after a very costly flying visit to it. One battalion's losses are given as 500, probably a great exaggeration, for they are all windy on this side, and it is doubtful if any have such a trench strength. A and C Companies had casualties carrying for the 100th Brigade, whose own carriers were absorbed as reinforcements. "Teg" and a party of A were dedicated for patrol into Fontaine; it would have spelt death or captivity for all had they been called on.

May 21st.—The Divisional front was uneasy with wind all night. Again there is early morning mist.—The German machine-gunners are evidently as good as ever. The usual German tactics now are to take a heavy toll, at the cost of a screen, for giving ground, and then counter-attack when we are depleted and disorganized; and the garrison lies out to meet our attack in front of our bombarded objective, instead of withdrawing behind it: sound moves when well judged.—Reports from Division say there's no holding the G.O.C., he's on his toes and his tail is right up over his back: he was out for a gamble with his troops and he had it, putting in every man except B and D Companies. He had a fairish measure of success, but he won't rise to a rum issue. The Army Commander came up to a vantage point near St. Leger to look on. What did he learn of realities back there? Only in the midst of reality can opportunity be seized, and it is rare for anyone who combines authority and nous to be on the spot.—The day was quiet but for desultory shelling by both sides, of which Bullecourt got most. We were warned, quite late, for the line: it was *May 22nd*—raining.—The relief of the 2nd Worcesters last night was a tiring affair. They told us we are dangerously few. B, C,

and D Companies are 300 strong on a 400-yard front, and have
A Company in support. It was wet and miserable all night.

This bit of the Hindenburg Front is far from being as complete
as that at Hénin, only the fire-steps are revetted, there are no
machine-gun emplacements. It has been knocked about so much
by our heavies that we are digging out a narrow trench through
the debris at the bottom. There was a plausible case for the German
official news, that "a demolished trench had been abandoned
according to plan," one of the stock euphemisms of the War.
Our approach is in dead ground except for the last hop. Nomansland, quite 300 yards wide, might be on the Somme, it's so
ploughed up. The day was quiet in front. After midnight we
arrived in the railway cutting south-east of Croisilles, a shelterless
May 23rd—and cold site for a bivouac, but everyone slept until
far into the morning. The published account of achievement up
here seems uncandid, to say the least.

May 24th.—The 1st Battalion is near Achiet-le-Petit, six miles
to the south-west. They invited us to their Sports. Every Regular
Soldier, and all officers who could be spared, went over. With
"Ginger" Owens, our Mess Sergeant, and "Big Dick," Richards—
a signaller, two sterling fellows, as makeweight, we won an inter-
Battalion tug-of-war for officers. Hearing about their system and
practice of training made one rather envious of the 7th Division
in which esprit de corps has real meaning and, therefore, value.
Proud had turned up with a bruise between the eyes. My look
must have touched him, for he volunteered the explanation—
"You know, sir, that Dolly kicks sometimes." About the same
time one of the other grooms was telling his Company Commander why his face was askew: a loose horse had walked over
him in his sleep!

May 25th.—Warm. The German heavies are active on our gun
positions. We and The Cameronians are for it. Eight hundred
yards of Tunnel Trench from Plum Lane to the Croisilles–Fontaine
road, both inclusive, and a hundred yards beyond, south and east,
are to be taken, and trench blocks made and manned. Elements
of several battalions entered parts of the objective on the 20th,
but failed to hold on and make good. Zero will be in the early
afternoon: Fritz has an after-dinner sleep then, and the artillery
and trench-mortar bombardment may not awake him in the

depths of his tunnel—we don't think! When we and The Cams.
go over, a 5th S.R. Company, to be attached to each, will be at
hand to occupy the present line: Engineers will follow to consolidate, and machine-guns to reinforce the defence of the captured
ground, in which a new telephone device is to be installed—on no
account is it to fall into the enemy's hands. Thus the Brigade Order.
In Mann's absence, sick, Conning is deputed to adapt our dispositions to it.

May 26th.—Moody rejoined from an instructorship, via the
1st Battalion: he and Orme are exchanging, (Orme was killed in
next day's affair). He has viséd the draft scheme and shares
Conning's misgivings. During fifteen months with the Battalion
Conning had been a happy-go-lucky fellow; this time he arranged
his affairs as if, for him, the end of everything had come. Because
we had a group of keen company officers and there were good
N.C.Os., I was hopeful until the Companies were ordered to take
in raw drafts they didn't want, distrusted, and a great many
merely trench-shy turned up on a huge sick parade. The day was
oppressive out of the breeze.

A good relief: D, C, A extend from Plum Lane, with B in
support—our order of battle. H.Q., again in the quarry about
a mile north-east of Croisilles, was greeted by numberless bull-
frogs. The dug-outs are safe as houses when one's in, but chancy
to get in and out of, for the quarry is shelled and sharp-edged
flakes of hard stone fly about.

May 27th.—Plum Lane, a communication trench shared by the
enemy, is the Battalion's right. Tunnel Trench is about 300 yards
distant on a reverse slope, and is screened by the crest of the ridge
from a man standing on our parapet (the parados of the trench
as the Germans dug it) although he may be seen from the left
front, opposite The Cams., where the ridge flattens as it falls to
the Sensée farther to the left. Between Tunnel Trench and the
crest the Germans have made an intermediate line of connected-up
shell-holes with a simple wire fence in front; the top of a few
pickets can be seen from part of our fire-step. We are shoulder to
shoulder in the trench, there are so many of us. In a scratch
line within speaking distance our 5th S.R. Company, Engineers
and trench-mortarmen are equally huddled. Movement is not
easy, and it is discouraged, for German spotters, and splinters from

German shell-bursts in Nomansland, have been flying over us ominously all morning. There is the usual random shelling of the country behind us. Our guns are unusually quiet. A beautiful Sunday morning, Whitsun, is keeping its promise of a fine day. The untilled fields around us, that were so forbidding six weeks ago, are now fresh and green, and filled with flowers; the fallow is gay with yellow and gold, and the sheen of one long slope off which the noon sun glances is a delight to look on.

"Messages! Ah, I'll hear all about your success afterwards," said the Brigadier when he looked in at H.Q. and the C.O. asked how many reports he wanted during the operation. After lunch he joined the Divisional Staff and others who rolled up, in cars and on horseback, to a commanding spur about 3000 yards in rear, and made a gallery to see the Show. If they can see, can they not be seen?—we asked. No German would think they were there for the scenery. Allenby and all his retinue had watched a battle from that spur a week ago.

The opening of the guns at 1.55 brought Conning and Picton Davies on to the parapet to call out C and A Companies. Conning chaffed the stiff-limbed and the laggards, and gave some of them a hand to climb out. Again he reminded his men not to hurry, "just stroll over behind our shells as if you were taking a quiet Sunday afternoon walk"; and, in line with Picton Davies, he led them at that pace. Moody was waiting on top to direct D Company up Plum Lane and make good our flank to the right of it. "Cheerio," Conning called to him with a forced little laugh: Moody nodded and said, "Cheerio, Conning." B Company was led by Lawrence Ormrod; he was never without a stick and a cigar. B formed a third wave supporting the two waves each of C and A; it was to mop-up. The Cameronians, acting on their previous experience, had been lying out 50 yards in front of the trench. They went away at once behind the barrage, thus there was a gap between the two battalions. Everything else was going according to plan, with nothing to disturb the advance in the open. In Plum Lane D Company's leading platoon had pulled down our Block, and rushed the German Block. Bombs were flying very soon, and our men advanced well until they were faced by a machine-gun firing down the Lane. An attempt to bomb it had to be organized before any more progress could be made there.

On our left the slight gap between ourselves and The Cameronians
tended to widen. Picton Davies charged C.S.M. Prime to keep
touch with them, and went to his right to ensure touch being
kept with C Company. The line was on the crest by then, and
the following waves were closing up. The 9th H.L.I. were
demonstrating noisily with Lewis guns and rifle-grenades on
"Nellie" Lane, the next communication trench on our right,
400 yards off. Davies had recrossed to his left: seeing that The
Cameronians were sidling off and advancing half-left he sent
to ask the 5th S.R. to close the gap. The German S O S had
gone up quickly and had been answered quickly, but it was behind
B Company that the shells were bursting. Our only casualties,
all slight, were owing to some shorts from our own guns on
C Company's front as it was crossing the ridge: they caused
a check, and the rear wave closed on the second. During the
pause men, with rifles still slung, and hands in pockets, turned to
watch the German barrage. After the check the advance slowed
down as the enemy's shell-hole line was approached. The lifting of
our guns and this lag let its garrison get ready to resist. Conning
was killed, and, not far from him, Teg Davies. The wire
was poor, but it was not just gone for. The many, as if waiting
their turn, shuffled to the places where the few made passages.
Through these the heads of the assault were bursting on to and
over the shell-holes when our guns lifted off Tunnel Trench. Its
garrison promptly manned the parapet and opened fire, which
was not replied to. A. Company's left 'had[1] occupied the intermediate trench, but my right had not. The German fire seemed
to be more concentrated on my right centre, and the men were
having difficulty in getting through the wire. It was so important
to get my line up that, leaving Prime in charge on the left, I ran
along the Tunnel Trench side of the shell-hole line shouting to
the men to "come on." Some of the Germans were leaving the
shell-holes and making for Tunnel Trench, others remained and
were firing. Some of my Company on the right passed through
the wire and were fighting with the enemy in the shell-holes at
close quarters. Farther to the right I could not see. I was about
the centre of my Company urging the men on. The bulk came up
and were approximately in line advancing on Tunnel Trench

[1] Davies.

when I was hit by a machine-gun in it, right opposite, but as yet out of bombing range. I dropped, and remember no more for an unknown period. Then, I recall dimly that I remembered my left was in danger. I think I made off in that direction, and I could not make out where my men had gone. I did not get far before falling again. The next I recall is that two slightly wounded Scotsmen had picked me up, and I was being half-dragged, half-supported along, and shells were falling to left and right. The machine-gun had registered five "bulls" on my person in various places.'

While the drama was hasting to its climax in front the German guns were lifting little by little towards our trench, and our rear wave was moving slowly down the reverse of the ridge. The Sapper officer came along the trench. We agreed that things seemed to be going well. "I'm going to follow up. When do you come on in this?" Without waiting for his reply I turned aside to look at another slightly wounded man. Just then a shell burst behind, throwing earth about us. Looking round I saw the Sapper fall, half on the newly broken parapet, and slide to the fire-step. He was dead. A brisk small-arms fire, mostly from German machine-guns had started up; there had been short bursts from one gun before this. The 5th S.R., followed by other detachments, were scrambling forward to the better cover of our trench. One of them made aloud a very disparaging remark. He and others were looking in The Cameronians direction. Again my hands were on the parapet to climb out when a dribble of our men ran back, from the right at first. The dribble became a surge, on they came, but none sought to go beyond the trench. Cameronians too were back. The collapse was stupefying in its suddenness, the manner of it was sickening. Some men said they "were stopped by wire," others that they "had orders to retire." There were, however, no officers and very few senior N.C.Os. among them. Little groups and individuals followed at short intervals. Moody was among the last, making for Plum Lane into which he hurried. When the attack in the open collapsed his concern was for our Block in Plum Lane. Another violent exchange of bombs had broken out there. The Germans had come over the top on the right to counter-attack. Some of them jumped into the Lane, and were dispatched, but some of D were cut off. Moody took part in the bombing that covered his men's withdrawal and the rebuilding of the Block. Until it was made secure the bombing was fiercer than when our attack in the Lane was launched. A 20th R.F. Lewis gun on the right had helped by firing on Germans who advanced to the crest of the ridge.

Of what happened in front Shelley told most when he came in wounded after dark. The leaders of the assault had been left in a hopeless position. They were ringed in by good Germans who were well led. From the lifting of our guns an officer stood on the Tunnel Trench parados giving orders, and, a revolver in each hand, choosing his targets. From shell-holes, and over the top round A Company's open flank, the enemy came and fought at close quarters. Occupants of the shell-hole line turned and fired to their rear after the danger on their front dissolved. With enemies on all sides, fine men strove to an end that came quickly. Most of our dead lay beyond the shell-hole line. Richards, a young C Company subaltern, fell wounded on the parapet of Tunnel Trench: his leg was amputated in a German hospital. Several men reached Tunnel Trench. Sergeant Parry of A Company died fighting in it. He was a handful of trouble in his earlier, irresponsible days.

The drama had not held the Gallery of Olympians for more than ten minutes. They broke up into little groups, lingering in talk before going away.

Torkington came in wounded in the arm; Cooper followed, wounded in the foot. Ormrod was carried in, and then Picton Davies, both badly hit. German shells were dropping in front of and behind our packed trench, but not into it—thank heaven. The shelling did not last long, and when it ceased C.S.M. Prime made a sudden dash from the left. He was not long back when C.S.M. "Buster" Cumberland unexpectedly started over the crest from the centre. Others must have been as breathless with anxiety as I, but like me they smiled, and some laughed aloud, at the strain and fluster of his filling-out figure during that zig-zag sprint, as of a coursed hare: and he wasn't fired at. A man who had fallen across the wire of the shell-hole line, mortally wounded and helpless, made some convulsive movements for quite a time before becoming still.

Moody was the one officer in action not a casualty. In

reorganizing the line he was helped by McChlery, the only
5th S.R. officer on our part of the ground. After that was done
a German concentration in Fontaine was reported from another
part of the line. Through the official round-about the suspicion
passed of a design to counter-attack us; it reached Brigade, then
H.Q. got it, and a warning was sent to Moody. He asked the
trench-mortar officer to open fire. Our wounded, lying out in
front of Tunnel Trench, had seen no stir there. They said our
trench-mortar bombs were all overs, but they put the wind up
the Germans, causing the same restlessness that a trench-mortar
strafe causes in the B.E.F. These bombs lurching through the
air are peculiarly demoralizing. Anyhow, long before this the
Machine-Gun Corps claimed to have broken up the concentration,
laying out 1500 Germans—with the jawbone of an ass, according to
common opinion. The empty valley in rear was shelled for two
hours after the failure of our attack. Providentially our trench was
left alone, for it was overcrowded until nightfall. Renewal of
the attack was out of the question; but no one appeared to be in
command of the operation, no one to have authority to move
the dangerously superfluous detachments, although they could be
withdrawn unseen into dead ground. Only the Ambulance bearers
were wanted, and they took it upon themselves to go. Late in
the afternoon de Miremont was sent from H.Q. to take command
of the two left Companies. All was quiet by then. Later the C.O.
looked up and expressed himself satisfied, "Moody has the situation
in hand." Quiet continued throughout the night, except that at
9 o'clock our guns bombarded Tunnel Trench and killed some of
our wounded, none of whom had come in yet. Our Germans
had behaved well to the wounded; in the heat of the afternoon
a N.C.O. came out and gave them water. Those who came in,
or could be got in, after dark numbered little more than a dozen.
Shelley, of C Company, was the most informing about events in
general. Sergeants Ibbotson and Onions had most to say about the
collapse. Onions summed it up as 'panic among men without
enough training and discipline'; but he nodded assent when
Ibbotson said that the capture of Tunnel Trench 'only wanted
running forward instead of running away.' Ibbotson added that
the shell-hole wire was so poor that a man had only to put his
foot and his weight on it to make a way through, and that the

loss of time waiting to file through the few gaps made by the resolute let Gerry man his parapet and get up his machine-guns. It was fairly plain that there had been no lack of leadership, but the irresolute mass had not been trained out of the habit of the turnstile, or into the use of the rifle.

Corps called for a report on the failure of the operation, where-upon Colonel Chaplin, with the generosity which distinguished his relations with us, took blame for his battalion. His right company overran the barrage and had casualties, and orders to steady the men gave rise to the cry "retire." His left companies attained their objective, but could not maintain themselves in it. Our Battalion casualties in this calamitous affair of minutes were 10 officers and 155 other ranks, almost half of whom were dead. Not long afterwards another division entered Tunnel Trench by a ruse at a cost of half a dozen. When the wind was favour-able smoke-shell mixed with gas-shell was fired on one or two days; next time, behind smoke-shell only, the infantry walked over and surprised the Germans in their gas-masks.

May 28th.—A day of peace in nature, and in the line. Relieved, and withdrawn to Moyenville.

May 30th.—The G.O.C. presented immediate award ribbons for April 23rd. He said that such action as Sunday's was meant to hold the Germans and let the Messines attack go on. We thought that the explanation did not square with what was given out, in contrast to what was done, a week earlier.

May 31st.—Marched to billets at Bailleulval. The discontent *June 1st*—and short temper of the past few days is mellowing. The senior N.C.Os. are complaining of slackness in the Battalion. *June 2nd*—The C.O. being on leave, Poore called us to attention—"R'—oyal Welch," to be inspected by the Corps Commander, Lieut.-General Snow: the Army calls him "Slush." He asked Poore why the men were not in uniform equipment. Yates had not had a chance to exchange the unwanted leather of our last draft for the unwanted web of a leather-wearing battalion, but Poore's conclusive answer was, "W'—ell, you see, sir, s'—ome have l'—eather and some have w'—eb, sir : w'—hat !"—Training *June 4th*—is most elementary; we have still only six officers all told, and not a specialist among them.

Holmes, now commanding the 1st Battalion, sent over their

Band. A good afternoon ended with a comic extra; half of them
fell in a heap on the road owing, partly, to the tailboard of their
departing lorry giving way as they leaned over it and waved
"Good-bye."

10 o'clock, an exquisite nocturne: our hamlet—its fruit trees
in blossom and the larger trees in leaf shading lichened roofs,
candle-light glimmering through chinks, woodsmoke from cottage
chimneys drifting in still air, and a sweep of hill for background;
all silvered by a full moon floating in a clear sky.

June 5th.—A third grilling day. G.H.Q. enjoins rifle-practice,
and circulates these verses—

> Alf is old as a soldier goes,
> With hair that is rapidly turning grey;
> Ever since Mons he has strafed our foes
> In his own cool, calm, methodical way.
> He learned to shoot on a Surrey range,
> His aim is steady and quick and true.
> "Bombs," says Alf, "are good for a change,
> But it's the rifle will pull you through."
> Lads who have scarcely been out a year,
> These are to Alf but as half-trained boys,
> The name of Mills to their heart is dear,
> And they won't be happy without their toys.
>
> "Not," says Alf, "that they're much to blame,
> Bred in a trench, as one might say,
> But when it comes to the open game
> It's the well-aimed bullet that wins the day."
> With his cheek to the stock he will cuddle down
> While swathes of the Hun as grass are mown;
> At a burst of rapid into the brown
> Alf is a Lewis gun on his own.
> "Clean her and oil her and keep her neat,
> She's a wonder," says Alf, "when she gets her chance;
> She stood by our boys in the Great Retreat,
> She will do the same in the Great Advance."

Hot air! "Intensive training" has no time for the infantry weapon.
It is no secret that the Base Depots pass everyone as a "fair" shot,
although only one bullet in ten hits the target.

One of the officer drafts of this time, who was to see the War
to the end with the Battalion and to gain an insight into its more
intimate affairs, has written of the emotion with which he joined

it and his abiding memory of it.—'My [1] first contact with the
2nd Battalion of the Old 23rd was at Litherland. I reported there
in April 1917, a very fresh and green, newly gazetted Second
Lieutenant, direct from a Cadet School, after having had ranker
service at Home and Overseas. In the 3rd Battalion were con-
gregated officers and men from all the Regular, Territorial and
Service Battalions of the Regiment. They had come from
hospitals, courses, Cadet Schools, and recruiting offices. They
would be sifted and trained, and detailed singly or in batches to
all fronts where Battalions of the Regiment were serving. In the
huge Mess were officers who had served with one or more of all
these battalions. There were "returned heroes," so I thought
them, from the First and Second. Some struck me as being really
heroic. Others were of the talkative sort who wished to impress
on "these Service Battalion fellows" that "of course it was
somewhat different in the Regular Battalions."

The betting was on Egypt when the lists for drafts were nearing
my date, but to my big disappointment it was France again.
Early in May a newly made chum and I found ourselves, via
Southampton and Havre, at the Base Camp, Rouen, there to
await posting to one or other of the umpteen R.W.F. Battalions
at the front. We hoped fervently it wouldn't be the Second,
because "it used up subalterns by the dozen" and had been extra
lavish with that species of King's officer recently. But Fate,
Providence, Luck, call it what you will, elected that it was to the
Second Battalion that both of us should offer the privilege of our
unstained and mythical swords. Deviously through a course or
two thrown in at the Divisional Depot Battalion at St. Pol, but
relentlessly we found ourselves actually reporting to the 2nd
Battalion in rest billets in Bailleulval. On the train journey from
St. Pol—this by the way—I was introduced to the subtleties of
Auction Bridge.

The story of two years will be told mostly by others, but my
earliest impressions insist on forcing themselves in. There was
the detached air of Major Poore; and "our Mr. Harries" with
the tousled hair and immense importance, and his fervently
expressed "Thank God, the battle's over," to Fox and others of
Battle Surplus. Harries was Acting Adjutant at the time; (he

[1] Ll. Evans.

gives dignity to the Indian Bench to-day, 1938). My posting was to D Company; it was debonair Moody's, soon to be kind-hearted Coster's. I never regretted being posted to the Second. I lived to bless the day which led me to it, for there couldn't have been a happier unit, better fellows—officers and men (incidents and exceptions of course), or another Regular battalion where the Temporary Officer had as much fair play if he had anything in him.'

June 6th.—The night very noisy, lights were flashing from air-craft: a Zeppelin at large bombed Arras.

June 7th.—There are wild reports that the French are going to take over this front again, to set more of us free for amphibious *June 10th*—adventures on the Belgian coast—Rode over to call on a R.W.F. Brigadier, but missed him. His staff said he was at Boulogne, courting.

The evening was hot. H.Q. details craved to be diverted, and someone asked our little haberdasher to recite. He was never backward, for he liked the sound of his own voice, an audience, a pedestal, and he had a small repertory of Robert Service's verse. He came from his billet stripped to the waist, stood on the dung-heap, and launched into "The Shooting of Dan McGrew," a favourite of his. He had come to the climax of the ballad, and he was in fine fettle, when the old dame of the farm came out and opened the big door of the barn. The harsh creaks of warped wood, and the shrill rasping of rusted hinges, drowned the voice of the artist. He stopped for a few seconds, then, with a dramatic gesture, he shouted at the pitch of his voice, "damn and blast it!" and retired in a mighty huff. And the old dame went about her work not noticing him or anyone else.

June 11th.—Thunder and rain in the night: hailstones as large *June 12th*—as I have seen. Poore is putting some ginger into the training. The men are in good spirits, working cheerily, and apparently looking forward to the Sports—my preoccupation, that and the heat, and a controversy with Corps about local sanitation. *June 13th*—I revisited Adinfer on going to ask for more gear from Commings, the A.A. and Q.M. at Division. He is always pleasant and helpful, but he can't give us a lorry to fetch beer. The G.O.C. is adamant. Before night, however, arrangements were made elsewhere to get beer from Doullens by a divisional lorry, without

compromising Commings. Preliminary heats and minor events
June 15th—took place from 4.30 to 8 o'clock. The men are the
devil: 50 enter for each event, or their sergeants enter them; after
June 16th—much shouting and hunting up 5 start. Our Gala Day,
4.30 to 7.30, then prize giving by C. S. Owen. Our tug-of-war
team was scratched for delaying to turn out: heard afterwards
that they thought the cash prize too small. The 1st Battalion Band
made sweet music.

June 17th, our last day here: another hot one. At the 5th S.R.
Sports a race for the village boys was keenly enjoyed. To the
girls a footrace was not *convenable*. The older ones suggested
doubtfully that the little ones might run, but the little ones were
equally observant of the national sense of propriety.

The Army Commander, Allenby, has gone to Egypt. He is
not popular—no stories of his little ways are in circulation, and he
is quite unknown to regimental officers and men. The Army
calls him "Tin-hat"; its Upper Circles call him "The Bull."
Byng succeeds him; another cavalryman!

June 18th, a night of thunder and rain. We left at 6 in the
morning for a canvas camp behind Moyenville. In the wasted
area the swallows, missing their ancestral eaves and rafters, set
to building in our lean-tos. A pair has nearly finished a nest in
the small run-up tin hut that houses H.Q. Two strands of wire
belonging to our predecessors' mess-bell support the nest. To
let the bell be taken away we cut 18 inches out of the circuit, after
fixing the wires to the frame of the hut with surgical plaster until
the Pioneers could clamp them securely with screws. These
beautiful creatures, with such plain faces, are most interesting to
watch at close quarters. They made themselves quite at home
among us, went on building, and accepted help in adding daubs
of clay. The cock does all the work, the hen never takes her eye
off him. Someone says that polyandry is not unusual among them.

A draft of one, a boy of 17, reported. He turned out to be
a deserter from Litherland. The Provost Sergeant has him in
charge. Having made his way overseas, he got to the 1st Battalion
by jumping trains and lorries; but he wanted to serve with us,
so he walked along the Hindenburg front to reach us. He was
reconciled to being sent home by being allowed to take his rifle
and equipment. His declared intention is to tell the Drum Major

at Litherland that he has been "over the top." The D.M. hasn't been overseas.

In our last draft was a man who had been "invalided out of the Navy with shock after being torpedoed four times" : conscripted into the Army in Category C 3, he was reclassified A and sent out here. The sanitary man of the 101st Field Ambulance is said to be an Education Office official skilled in languages.

June 19th.—We returned to the line on the left of the Hump, which is said to have changed hands twice since we were here. The trench is now fire-stepped and sand-bagged. We have not seen its like since we left Béthune, and never saw its like again. The surface tracks of three weeks ago are now communication trenches. H.Q., in the quarry, is the most ambitious piece of B.E.F. work of the kind we have seen, it nearly comes up to French work.

Our howitzers fire short persistently, sometimes short of us. The Germans have a new extraordinarily sensitive contact fuse ; a shell makes scarcely any shell-hole, so the horizontal burst is not lost ; a fair-sized splinter, which hit a man beside me below the knee, had carried the better part of 200 yards with a nearly flat trajectory. *June 22nd.*—Relieved to support. The C.O. having stayed out Poore was in his element, active and keen, stirring up machine-gunners, trench-mortarers, everyone ; his Orders were his own and uncommon.

June 23rd, a quiet day, and fresh after rain. The Battle of Arras has fizzled out, but the Division has a programme of mild counter-irritants and blood-lettings. Another bombing of Tunnel Trench is on the bill. First, the G.O.C. said that The Cams. would crack the shell and we would get the yolk, then that they were to make *June 24th*—one bite of it. They didn't. At midnight they bumped on to manned shell-holes in front of uncut wire. Fritz has become an artist in shell-hole defence. An enterprising platoon could walk out and pull up a lot of his wire, but——

Relieved, and moved back to Camp A at Hamelincourt. Division, C Mess, had delicious strawberries for dinner. Eatable fruit can't be got in the gardens near here, it's always picked before *June 25th*—it's ripe. For a week there have been fresh sunny days, chilly evenings and nights.—Bapaume is a town of ravaged homes, there is scarcely a house that won't need to be rebuilt entirely.

French building is flimsy at the best, town houses are shells.—By dinner-time we had gone up to a bivouac behind Croisilles. H.Q. shares dug-outs with the 9th H.L.I., "The Glasgow Highlanders." Official expectation of a German withdrawal has revived.—An unpublished incident at Blackpool is being told. A Yankee said to a wounded Tommy on the pier that they had "come over to finish the War." T.A. threw him into the water, and was given a year for manslaughter. The Yankees are fussed over officially, but few among them endear themselves.

June 26th.—A Corps or Army detective has been put on the front line telephones, secretly—but Ginger Baird has passed the tip to his battalions. A lot of our divisional movement on a sky-*June 28th*—line behind us is seen by the enemy.—There was thunder and rain in the early hours: the day was stifling. We heard that our swallows' hut was damaged by the storm; we never heard what befel the nest.

Three days rumination reduced a battalion battle to a company *June 29th*—dash. The result was tragi-comedy. Twenty minutes before zero Fritz was seen massing in his sap-heads at the objective. At zero the "surprise" party had a score of casualties from fire opened on their parapet, and those of them who did jig were met by bombs from shell-holes covering the objective. It's a postscript to their Brigadier's tip that there was a detective on their telephone. This fiasco was given out officially as "a successful raid." G.1 suggested that the "mistake" was owing to "a clerical error at Corps." Why Corps? It had no motive for sophistication. Fully a year before this, and not far from us, we heard of compliments and rewards being bestowed for "a successful raid." Actually, it was whispered, an old disused trench in Nomansland had been bombed. A couple of weeks afterwards the derring-doers were the amazed victims of an exploit not unlike their own. Their pious comrades, engaged in their prentice operation, lost direction in Nomansland, blundered on their neighbour's wire, and dashed over. Luckily very little hurt was done. *Comic Cuts* called their well-meant deed "a gallant raid which penetrated to the support line." Despatches are very human, be they plain or coloured.

June 30th.—The 2nd Worcesters, who relieved the H.L.I., helped us to pass four idle days. Their C.O. provided one hilarious turn of five minutes to some mixed groups of onlookers by his leaps into a ditch to dodge shells that were just missing the road he was walking on. In the late afternoon we moved to a poor bivouac at Monchy; H.Q. was in an orchard, lately a horse-standing.

This is our adieu to the Arras Front. In the operations of the Division the Battalion had more officer casualties than any other unit. The series of failures here may be fairly divided between units and the Command. The needed purge looks to be no nearer the making. The Staffs planned without essential knowledge of the ground, or else they failed to adapt plans to surface conditions. The Tunnel was a new factor in operations, so it may not have been taken into account by the Higher Commands which chafed from afar at poor or barren results. It was a desirable shelter from the elements, or for reserves, but it was an irresistible lure to troops of indifferent quality when there was "war" abroad; men could fade in driblets or mass into its dim nooks. The German command, according to captured papers, had already experienced the problem. So widely true it is that—

Security
Is mortals' greatest enemy.

CHAPTER XIV

A quiet Summer—Rest and Sport: Echoes of Crécy—of de Vere—of the Ironsides: Nieuport: St. Omer: Slow March on the guns at Ypres

Contributors:—HUGHES; M. JONES; KENT; MOODY; RADFORD

Sketches:—1, 4, 5, 11, 19.

July 1st.—Alas for Paris leave, it's stopped for the present. A comb-out of the disaffected and agents of discontent is said to be in process. A comparison of London and Paris in war-time would have been interesting. We go to prepare for a big push in three weeks, perhaps to be the dog it's tried on.

July 2nd.—Moving west. The country is only partly cultivated, probably because of shortage of labour. Acheux is a drab village, formerly railhead. The petit château, a plain modern building, has a huge walled fruit and kitchen garden jealously guarded by a female Cerberus. She will need all the wits of three heads to cope with the band of lawless Australians who are in possession of the village. The Australians were undesirable predecessors in billets, because the French people didn't like them in spite of the free spending their high pay allowed. The local doctor has been mobilized and is serving somewhere. Another mobilized doctor, who has been with the Army, is living here, appointed to look after this and five other villages. The incumbent seemingly adds to his professional income by the sale of aerated waters, champagne and other wines, as a painted notice alongside his brass plate announces.

July 3rd.—To-day's march was to Talmas, over fine undulating country. It is a pleasing rarity to see French cottages with ramblers on the walls, one, as in a yard at Béthune, had wistaria. The Talmas people removed their pump handles to prevent the men drawing water, this was the more resented that we did the 11 miles in packs in the heat of the sun. Although 70 fell out we compared favourably with other battalions, report said 300 of one. The Brigadier is "axing" : has he been dropped on by Division for not marching in the cool of the morning ?

July 4th.—When we fell in I saw myself being looked at with a curiosity that made me uncomfortable. After a little a junior officer, pulling himself together, asked diffidently if it is true that one of our men was picked off the road yesterday just in time to die in the ambulance. He went on to say that three men of another battalion had died in the same way. Then the C.O. came along to fish for facts ; the Brigadier had been whispering to him. What the seed was from which these myths sprang I never heard. We started three hours earlier than yesterday, in heavy rain, and made a better march ; about 30 fell out. Melbourne Street proclaims Vignacourt an Australian resort. The first trench and street names English troops think of are High Street and Piccadilly : Scots begin with Argyle Street and have a Cowcaddens : the Irish begin with Grafton Street. Towards the end of the march we had pleasing glimpses of the Somme bending between steep wooded banks. A draft of 130 waited, and crowded us, at Belloy, all eager to be posted to Radford's or Coster's Company. H.Q. was in a small Louis XV château ; at home we would call it the manor. There are two storeys and an attic with dormer windows ; it is all length, each room opens off a corridor running along the back. The finish and furnishing are of fine quality and in very good taste throughout, just too French and formal to be quite comfortable— except the beds. Monsieur of that ilk is a quiet, reserved man, Mayor of the village ; his English is much less than my French. Madame is gracious and most comely, scarcely distinguishable in dress and bearing from the best type of Englishwoman. Her English is more than my French. She took me round her flower garden before dinner. Cornflowers are sold to the local chemist, at 4 francs the kilo, to make eye lotion ; the money goes to the Red Cross. There are 8 or 10 acres of grounds, but no labour can be got ; the service of the house is reduced to a *bonne*. A son is in the artillery, a daughter nurses at Amiens. We made our own messing arrangements, otherwise we were received as guests.

July 5th.—We had to disturb our agreeable hosts at 3.30, tramping on their polished floors. The start was too early for the Signallers, they slept in. The Battalion swung along quite well through

Hangest and Soues to Airaines. Ground for training was given unwillingly; every pole is jealously kept, and cropped or grazed.

Three and a half weeks passed very pleasantly at Airaines. The weather was fine. The billets turned out not so frowsty after a thorough cleansing, but they were stuffy. A short acquaintance dispelled the impression of detraining and entraining in Winter conditions, that Airaines is cheerless. It is quite a good little town, built on a slope, near the middle of a shallow basin in a district of delightful fields, woods and streams, for miles around. Duty and pleasure took me into these surroundings. The cottages are very ordinary, but in Summer the setting of any group of them is pleasing. The wood near Forceville that charmed us in the ethereal light and the colours of a late autumn dawn, drew me. In plain day and without an enhancing mist it is but one wood in a richly wooded landscape. On that day's ride I was the interested and amused witness of a case of precocious love. The damsel and her swain would be 12 or 13 at most. Mindless of a companion, of me, of all the world, they loitered along in ecstasy, their faces drawn with passion, sighing, choking, devouring each other with their eyes. The companion was of their age; she lingered behind, a little embarrassed as I passed, beaming with sympathetic, generous envy on their rapture. In rural France adolescent lovers are totally unselfconscious.

There is no better company hereabout than Froissart. In 1346 Edward III was chevied down the left bank of the Somme; in 1415 Henry V was chevied up it; both were seeking a passage to the north bank and Calais. Here is the scene of the prologue to Crécy. An English division levanted from Airaines leaving dinner cooking and the wine untouched. After Crécy Airaines was the Black Prince's H.Q. for quite a long time. The castle, an old possession of the Luynes family, is a ruin. Little of it looks as old as the Black Prince's time; the most recent part, the gateway, looks like sixteenth-century work. The old Church has lost any architectural beauty or interest it may have had. The distances Edward's and Henry's troops marched with the transport, and on the roads, of those days, skirmishing day by day, fills me with wonder when I think of our performances. No doubt an encircling enemy does give wings even to weakness.

Airaines of to-day has a cinema. Our connoisseurs say the local beer is good, for French beer. The inhabitants were glad to have us, and took an interest in our doings: no troops had been among them for many weeks. The rare visits of the Divisional Band, when our turn came round, were a great popular attraction; Gilbert and Sullivan music, "Poet and Peasant" airs and such like, were probably unknown previously to these provincials.

The billeting officer took for his Company, after the way of his kind, the only decent Mess. The lady of the house gave nightly musicales to which she invited her lodgers. The C.O. borrowed these quarters when he commissioned me to arrange a dinner to the officers of the recent tour—Poore, Moody, Radford, Coster, *July 8th*—Yates, Harries, Hywel Evans, Robertson and Fox. It began stiffly and finished well. Parry was at his best. Hors-d'œuvre; soup; sole; cutlet reforme; roast chicken, etc.; strawberries; angels on horseback; whisky and perrier; Veuve Cliquot; port; cognac; coffee. It all came out at 17 francs a head (12s.).

July 9th.—An idyll of the Base, like enough others one hears about, was told us by a Canteen lady, a good sort, who knows the Regiment and looked us up. Her giggling assistant became engaged to a man in the Naval Division, "often wounded: a millionaire—the orphan of parents who went down in the *Lusitania*." The girl's father, an ancient colonel, came out to approve, and fell to the widow of a Chocolate Soldiers sergeant. The brides went home to fit out. The naval hero turned out to be a cold-footed fraud; the widow found someone more to her mind; so father and daughter are left lamenting—more or less.

Poore's host, the local notary, invited him to shoot wild boar. Poore spoke of the day as "an amusing experience" he "would not have missed," and he showed me an account of it he was sending home. Proud, who was deputy for his groom on leave, told me "it was a fair knock-out." The guns and beaters were marshalled by a citizen in a green velvet coat dating from his youth, its St. Hubert buttons had to bear the strain of a portly middle-aged figure. At the edge of a wood hope became feverish when footprints of *le sanglier* were pointed to in dry clay, and "*silence*" was enjoined, finger to lip, in a whisper. The guns moved off, some on tiptoe, but twigs would crackle under foot, and the whispered injunction rose to a shout when a sportsman on the right of the line called "*silence*" to a sportsman on the left of the line, and the sportsman on the left testily called back "*silence*." Proud went with the beaters: they were circumspect. Quite soon the line of guns closed on a loud report. Two of the party had fired together, and almost point-blank, at what the vestiges proved was a rabbit. There was nothing for either sportsman to disclaim and present to the other as "your rabbit." Next, Poore fired. "*Monsieur le Commandant a tué un lapin*," shouted his neighbour and wrung his hand. From gun to gun the message passed in crescendo, "*Monsier le Commandant a tué un lapin*." All wrung his hand and congratulated him. After that rabbit someone shot a squirrel. Dinner time approached. The beaters were called in, and the party returned in excellent spirits. At parting, Poore was again congratulated on his marksmanship. When he was leaving his billet for the Mess Madame la Notaire gracefully handed him a long brown-paper parcel, neatly tied— his trophy of "*la chasse à sanglier*." He prevailed over her reluctance to accept it. Henceforth *Monsieur le Commandant* was a personage in Airaines.

The efforts of the serious-minded G.S.O.1 to give work a real place failed. His stock was low. Before the Division left Croisilles there was a view-halloo after him, led by the mocking japes of one of the Brigadiers; and the G.O.C.'s ribald chaff was repeated widely. Here too the G.O.C. struck the note for his Division. Training was out of mind. A Battalion field day indeed was *July 13th*—appointed. It may have been the oppressive heat that shortened the Divisional Staff visit to a few minutes; and it may have been the heat that caused shade and rest to be sought by the Battalion as soon as the Brass Hats' backs were turned. Guard-mounting in the Square was the event of our day. Next day's guard, and the reserves, were excused all duty to make themselves *July 14th*—pretty. The French National Fête Day, a holiday. A Guard of Honour of our hundred tallest men paraded under Radford, who has the *Croix de Guerre*, to salute the *Tricouleur*. Since the oldest gendarme kept his pipe in his mouth and blew clouds of smoke while he raised the Flag the ceremony lost some-thing, to English eyes, of its intended solemnity. In the afternoon a few of us took a run into Amiens. All the shops were closed, but the restaurants were as full as when the B.E.F. was concentrated

on the Somme. The best dinner behind the British Front was still
to be had at the Godbert.

July 17th and 18th.—A Divisional Horse Show was the G.O.C.'s
own stunt. He meant it to be the success that forethought and
two weeks of painstaking preparation could make it, and he had
his reward, although he could not get his artillery out of the line
to take part. Nothing was wanting that the resources of a division
could achieve. The layout of the site—ring, enclosures, buffets,
bunting and all—was a triumph of organization, design and lime-
wash. It deserved to be enjoyed, and it was; and the G.O.C.'s
own enjoyment of his masterpiece was complete, although he was
limping about in slacks. Our entries might have been more
successful if the C.O. had not entrusted both Poore and Yates
with the arrangements, mischievously telling each that the other
would "just help" him. They are too self-willed not to be at
loggerheads over every detail. Of the prizes, we got a couple of
leavings apart from the Officers Charger Class: there Billy
had a 1st and 2nd, Mugwump a 2nd and 3rd, Jenny was
commended and Rabbit a runner-up. It's a great matter in
these events to be on the right side of the judge. This one recognized Billy as having come from his brother's stable on
mobilization; so the C.O. went off with a cup, and a smile as
expansive as the Chesire Cat's. The Drums took their turn in
providing the music; they played their "Cambria" selection:
"The Men of Harlech," "The Ash Grove," "From dull slumber
Arise," "Poor Mary Ann," "Hunting the Hare," "Jenny Jones,"
"New Year's Eve," "The Bells of Aberdovey," "Welshmen from
where," "Forth to the Battle," "God bless the Prince of Wales";
and later "Rag a Scale" from *Joyland*. A Liverpool daily paper
unkindly published a back view of one of our Company Commanders at the hilarious beginning of an estrangement from his
saddle—about which the Brigadier interviewed him.

July 20th.—For a day or two we have been hearing of a staff
ride for Brigadiers and Commanding Officers, designed by G.1.
The G.O.C. has been aloof, one brigadier has been outspokenly
resentful. It began this morning: by a general tacit understanding
the scheme was being guyed, so G.1 stopped it.

July 21st.—Battalion Sports. In the wilderness we could get all
the structural material required, here scarcely anything can be had.

I've had several pleasant rides in the country around, scrounging. Greatly increased interest and good entries have been got by an unorthodox programme that attracts all sections and ages. Little men have done best at the high jump, older men at the long jump.

July 22nd.—Sunday: Our Gala day, for finals and Brigade events. A general invitation was given to the townspeople, and they came in crowds, were given tea, and were "*bien charmé.*" Poore's hostess presented the prizes with a grace that eclipsed Mlle la Comtesse [1] at the Horse Show. Her invitation was a matter of the gravest concern to the C.O.; he would not allow her to be thought of until the Interpreter had reported that she was eligible, and acceptable to local society. The Canteen made a serious loss. Mills and I miscalculated the beer consumption badly. Too much respect for the C.O.'s deference to the G.O.C.'s addiction to vicarious abstinence caused the beer tent to be out of the way. Five hundred francs were dropped in compensation to the brewer in spite of all efforts to recoup ourselves before leaving Airaines. We had lost double that sum already owing to the shippers misdirecting an order to the 1st Battalion, who acknowledged the "gift" graciously to Mr. Mann. The acknowledgment of such another "gift," costing 1000 francs, delivered to the 8th Battalion in Mesopotamia, was very stilted.

July 23rd.—Kearsley, soon to become a favourite with the men, rolled up three days ago; now Mann is back: two pillars of support. M. has nearly lost his stutter. I have never been able to decide if it was owing to fatigue, or unconscious imitation of the G.S.O.1 for whom, and for whose instruction, he and other keen, capable youths in the Division have a great admiration.

July 24th.—The second day of Brigade Boxing in the Square. The Sports and the Boxing confirm the impression that the last draft, largely young South Wales miners, is much the best that has come to us for two years.

July 25th, 26th, 27th.—The A.D.M.S. offered me a couple of days jolly at Le Tréport, a car to go and return, and the G.O.C.'s leave to take three companions. On my reporting to the C.O. he at once proposed himself, Poore and Harries. Three days of crowded interest: my notes seem fuller than for any other three consecutive days when not in action. Oisemont, to which our

---

[1] Army term: daughter of the local Count.

troops beat it from Airaines in 1346 : Gamaches, which—at a little distance—has the finest parish church exterior I've seen in France these two years : the bend in the airless valley of the Bresle, 4 or 5 miles from the sea, where a breeze met us bringing with it the tang of brine : the first glimpse of blue water, light blue flicked into little crests : the chine at Mers Touquet, remotely reminiscent of Dover's cliffs : the château at Eu, the fine park and forest ; Eu is a Belgian depot : the memorial to a major and an exciseman who, in 1806, manned the coast-defence guns and drove off three English "corsairs" which had chased a merchantman inshore : how a creaking bed and a marble-topped washstand in one's neighbour's room can be more destructive of sleep than drum-fire : first experience of a meatless day under a food-economy order : a visit to the hospital to see the earliest "mustard" gas cases in the wards and post-mortem room ; "mustard" is corrosive, but not so insidious or so deadly as the gas we used at Fontaine, both are cloudless : a drive with Harries to the Field of Crécy, the pleasant village, the memorials, but the old mill is gone : an English Labour Company felling timber and charcoal-burning in Crécy Forest : Annamese labourers at Noyelles : a peaceful river mouth, pure dairying and grazing on its flats, the back-water charm of St. Valery and Novion : a forlorn, appealing little English child who would have me play with him, and kiss "good night," when I would have visited the fine church at Eu : a woman's work— shovelling, carrying and tipping creels of shingle for Liverpool bottle works—very hard : poppy cultivation behind Tréport : scenes of frailty, meanness, decency and nobility from the human comedy as seen on that placid fringe of the War and of the Ocean : and never a sign of a vessel but the blue-sailed, inshore fishing smacks.

July 28th.—Because the C.O. wants the General to be able to depend on him at all times, he was so breathless to be back in Airaines by breakfast, that I tramped over the falaise twice last night in the dark, and ran into barbed wire repeatedly, seeking a car to take us. We returned as we went, but driven by a young Englishwoman who was just a little fearful of meeting armed Germans or a shell-burst round the next corner. She was plainly under no such vow as one Woman's Corps is said to have taken, not to speak to any officer. Her tongue never rested : we brought her into the Mess for a cup of tea, and could scarcely get her away. When the A.D.M.S. heard that his car had searched Le Tréport for me all afternoon he damned me for not waiting to be fetched.

July 29th.—Thunder plumps: one damped devotion on church parade; the men passed the time between them singing Welsh songs. A Battalion Mess Meeting, supposedly quarterly, decided *July 30th*—not to revive the Band. The Transport goes north by road. The R.S.M., two C.S.Ms., and four other old N.C.Os. are applying for commissions in self-defence, so many of our duration privates are being recommended. Later on when one of our corporals was thinking of a commission his companions couldn't always catch what he was saying, he was cultivating such a very nice twang—almost the Oxford touch: sometimes he forgot himself and lapsed into broad Cardiff.

Yesterday the Brigadier said laughingly that he would "perhaps look in" to see us training: he has never done so here. An orderly had to be kept at H.Q. all this morning to show the party where the training ground is; but the Brigadier didn't come. Few know that Brigade is in the town, so little is seen of any of them.

July 31st.—A fine morning that clouded later. The Deputy Mayor called to express regret at our going. We marched to Pont Remy; arriving at 4 p.m. we hung about, entrained and left at 6. In Abbeville I saw the Women's Army Auxiliary Corps, "Waacs," for the first time. If they don't speak to officers they seek and find ample solace with other ranks.

August 1st.—After quite a good journey we arrived at Dunkirk at 4 a.m. Railway travel on main lines had been on the level of our own local lines since railway staffs from home replaced the R.E. who used to be in charge, and we became less dependent on the French. Our farther journey was by barge on a canal to Bray Dunes. Never in Europe have I seen a heavier downpour of rain than fell on us.—Rumours of great gains and captures at Ypres were soon discounted by 600 per cent.

For a month we were on a strip of coast on which Elizabeth's scurvily treated men, and Cromwell's men, fought gloriously. No move was made for two weeks. H.Q. squeezed into a cottage which had for foreground ideal golf country, covered by the tents of a brigade, and the Dunes. It was a great contrast to the dusty *Place* at Airaines, and the watchmaker's opposite us, the window

of which, or a vision within, fascinated one of our General officers.
What was well-nigh unique for a whole Formation, come to these
yellow sands, was sea-bathing. The picture from the Dunes of
the shimmering rays of afternoon sunlight on a broad strand, a
belt of surf beyond and the pink skins of 2000 or more men
splashing in it, backed by an immensity of blues and whites of sea
and sky, was unfailingly delightful. And the men were delighted
to feel clean every day, not just once a week, if so often. Room
was still found on the Transport for the polo sticks of Bois Grenier
days; the sands were all right, not so the ponies or the officers'
horsemanship. Paper-chases among the Dunes were better fun.
A dash of sport attended dinner in Dunkirk. At any moment
electric alarms might sound. They were rung by spotters at
Nieuport of a big gun at Ostend. Two minutes elapsed between
the flash and the fall of the shell, two minutes in which to find
a *cave* and plunge into it: besides cellars, there were bolt-holes
dug in some of the streets. Twice Dunkirk was bombed in our
time; we heard stories of 20 and 30 casualties from each raid.
There were a great many aircraft about; they were said to be
partly for the air-defence of London. The Naval fliers who
entertained us at Camp 13 were our neighbours. They practised
firing into the water, and once hit a bather. A real joy was to see
the White Ensign on its proper element. There were always some
ships off Dunkirk. Once in a while a monitor would slip its
moorings, steam sedately along the coast, fire a few shots with
provoking deliberation, and sedately return. For two days the
Drums were on passive resistance because Dyer, their Sergeant,
put Hedges, the Big Drum, under arrest.

August 5th, our first fine day. The weather broke just after we
entrained to come north. Until yesterday it has rained almost
continuously, at times very heavily, but with a blessed absence of
mud, the soil being pure sand.—A great strafe has started Ypres
way: it did not quieten down for 48 hours.

August 6th.—R.S.M. Boreham rejoined. Leave is going strong
in the Division, and while Mills is overdue the Canteen is going
to pieces in—perhaps more trusting hands. A surprised owl could
not have blinked more than did his proxy when I went to check
the stock and found that more than the last barrel of beer was
empty. There was no accounting for the deficiencies, unless some

of the Old Sweats had sapped in this time to test their saying that one might burst but never get drunk on French beer.

Sassoon's quixotic outburst has been quenched in a "shell-shock" retreat. He will be among degenerates, drinkers, malingerers, and common mental cases, as well as the overstrained. It is an astute official means of denying our cold-blooded, cold-footed, superior persons the martyr they are too precious to find from their own unruly ranks. Sassoon gave a moral flavour to a gibe everywhere current at the front for a couple of years, that a lot of individuals in cushy jobs don't care how long the War lasts. It used to be said laughingly, now it is said bitterly. But for one in the Army with an interest in the prolongation of the War there are now hundreds of "indispensables" at home in well paid war-jobs. The affluence and the squeals of the indispensables have made it hard for the serving-men's families, and exasperated the serving men, many of whom have been taken from increasing affluence for service. But I have not heard any stop-the-war talk among front-line troops, whatever may be spoken among the Base tribe : Base canteen workers have told me that the talk there is pretty alarming. On that point Sassoon did not speak the feeling of those with most to lose by the War. . . . J.'s remark that 'the country is ripe for revolution' would have been better unsaid in Mademoiselle's hearing, but there is much substance in it. The most sober-minded of the men, whatever their circumstances and wherever they live, return from leave with one story of popular feeling : so I am hearing from all quarters. There is great unrest, and an intensity of feeling and determination that make certain the coming of great political and social disturbance after the War, the early phase may precede the end of the War. That feeling was being expressed by officer drafts who joined three months ago.

August 7th.—The Guard at Fourth Army H.Q. at Malo is being found by our August 1914 men.

August 8th.—The most brainy exercise Brigade has risen to is route-marching. To-day, under G.1's stimulus, it set a battalion attack, which turned out a good bit of a farce as we were made do it. With G.1's going on leave his programme was dropped, and Brigade turned to thought again. There's room for a rifle-range here, that's something to be thankful for.

The reason the Government has given the House of Commons

for the large sum needed for personnel in the War Office vote is the best public joke for many a day. They say that the exceptional number of men on charge is owing to casualties having fallen short of the estimate. So they haven't done in enough of us to keep the Budget within moderation! We often grouse at the Staff work.

August 9th.—The camp, flooded by thunder plumps, has been a comical sight. Everything that could float floated. The men turned out barelegged, or more, swearing and mirthful. One party worked for two hours on a drainage scheme for their tent-floor before realizing that water won't flow to a higher level. One of the Drums, in his shirt only, squatted on an island hummock playing, "The end of a perfect day."—This evening, with good visibility at last, the Mont des Cats and other heights and the tower of St. Omer Cathedral could be seen from a dune.

August 10th.—The Division being so close to Corps and Army, there have been comings and goings and the note of wires being fingered. It looks as if a brigade or other plum were an attainable vision for some. The C.O. went off this morning well groomed, self-conscious, inscrutable. When he mounts his eyeglass he means to impress someone. After several hours absence he returned walking on air and containing himself with an effort.

All the Company officers think we need more training; our Generals say "the men are getting stale" and that "there is to be less work," but they never come to find out what we are like. Kearsley has been getting some rational work done. He was *August 12th*—inspecting the cookers this morning. On being told that Jones, the sergeant-cook, was "on a Course," he asked, "Who is answering for him?" Plainly no one was, but Corporal Goulder hazarded, "The Medical Officer, sir." When Ruby was brought round for Kearsley, Poore having gone on leave, he remarked that she was "fidgety." "She wasn't always that," Griffiths said, "she's got fidgety waiting for Major Poore, it's never less than half an hour." Recently I overheard Owens, a Company cook, say of Poore, "The old gent's all right, just gettin' old and a bit fussy." It gave me, who am only a few months younger, something to ponder. He can be repressed. A week ago after helping himself from a dish he asked for a potato. "That's a hontree, sir," the Mess waiter told him with heightened colour, and in a tone Poore was not too deaf to hear, or bold enough to gainsay.

August 13*th.*—The fourth rainless day since we came. Our landlady told me that her potatoes were very good until the heavy rains, now they are "*purée.*" "*C'est la guerre,*" she added with resigned inconsequence. She's a buxom decent soul; we have pumped her cellar dry for her.—The people hereabout are Flemish in appearance, and bilingual; a few speak Flemish only, though the district has been politically French for 250 years. "Dull Flemings" they are not, but a talkative lively people, more so than those of any part I have been in yet. The cottages are gaily painted in vivid blues, greens, red and yellow, within and without: doors, window-frames and a cornice are generally white. There is nothing of the scented air and unsightliness of the French midden, but, in a very porous soil with a high ground-water level, the nearness of the open cottage well to the cottage privy is gruesome. The flea and the gnat outnumber the louse in the billets here.

August 14*th.*—Thunder and a deluge after dinner. The eve of our departure. We are going up with a trench strength of 20 officers and 460 other ranks out of a ration strength of 900.—Battle Surplus was left near Coxyde Bains, in a large house near the shore, a quiet spot. A senior N.C.O., who hailed from a Welsh mining valley, went on leave. He was asked, after his return, what it was like at home. "I don't know," he said, "I got drunk the night I arrived, and was back in France again before I got sober."

August 15*th.*—Réveillé 2.15, marched 4.15. I contrast the two hours we are allowed to move with the half-hour given us in South Africa, where everyone had a horse as well as himself to see to. We were kept dawdling on the road in rain, then hanging about for a half-hour outside our billets in Oost Dunquerque, a busy little place though it's shelled. We saw for the first time horses with gas-masks, worn at the "alert"—fixed to the noseband of the head-stall. A draught-dog of the village, wounded in both forelegs, hobbled only a step or two at a time. He submitted trustfully to be handled, and looked grateful. Several medical officers and orderlies must have dressed him since he was hit, and given him food. I thought his tongue would be the best *August* 16*th*—dressing now and left off the bandages. At 4 o'clock gas-shells wakened me, none were near enough to worry about. The population has gone since gas-shelling began here recently, only two or three civilians remain; a donkey-cart carries as much as is taken: even the milk-cows have been left behind. The dog has gone. Dogs are like a lot of the wounded, think themselves unfit as long as they are made, or allowed, to wear a bandage.

We moved at dusk by road, then by a raised stone causeway over a bog, to Nieuport. The town was all ghostly, tottering walls, and powdered brick exhaling gas faintly. Nasturtium describes the smell of mustard gas. A few 4·2s dropped harmlessly as we passed through, or were delayed in, a long arcade of splinter-proof timber. We were held up to weariness by a fear-ridden subaltern having bolted from the Company he was deputed to lead. It was the third time he had done something of the sort: he said someone said he had a floating kidney, and put it down to that.

The Yser was rolling rapidly when I came to its bank at dead *August* 17th—of night. The tide was nearing full ebb. The floating bridges and their approaches were being shelled. In the dark men shouted orders, others alarm; yet others shouted encouragement from the far side of the river. A crossing was practicable, but there was not darkness enough to hide its frightening look, for the chesses gaped, tilted and clattered as the pontoons rocked in a gurgling rush of water. When I was committed to it some biggish shells burst near by, and cries of "Gas" were raised. To be stifled in vapour or water: that was a clamant question when one's feet were being jerked together or tugged apart on grinding timbers, and one fumbled with a mask. The river was a dread reality, and anyone in a mask was as likely to stumble into it as step on to a foothold. "Gas" might just be "wind": so I left my mask loose and shouted to those behind to do the same and come on, perhaps to hearten myself as much as them. On regaining solid earth, and breath, there was a shell-burst, and more cries of "Gas" came from out its dust. It was a "K" shell, bromine, one just to hurry past. Before going to roost some much-needed gaspirator drill was done.

The alarm that the first use of mustard gas caused had partly passed, fortunately. Meanwhile our kilted regiments wearing full-length grey woollen drawers, for the protection of bare parts, beat any burlesque of the garb of old Gaul ever seen on the stage.

H.Q. is in the Palingbrug, or Redan, a small, brick fort of Vauban's time, kept in repair, and lately reinforced with concrete. The Store is called the Rubber House, so impervious is it to all shell so far: beside it is a shell-hole 32 feet across. It is lighted by electricity. Its permanent occupants are fleas, lice, and a cat now about to have kittens. H.Q. of two battalions, (four during a relief), and what not more use it. The air in it is like that of a common lodging-house before the sleepers have gone out and the windows have been opened. Lombardzyde Right was a breastwork area in marshy land crossed by dykes and raised stone causeways. We shared it with the 5th S.R. Our front had been knocked about in July, and was still in disrepair. The line consisted of posts in staggered echelon. It was easy to slip between them; once Mann's orderly put his head round a corner and saw some Gerries at supper : he got away unseen. Company signallers spent miserable minutes, that seemed hours, laying their forward lines in the twilight, for they chanced snipers as well as traversing machine-guns rather than risk losing direction in the dark. No-mansland was 70 to 100 yards wide, but our left post, Geleide, on the river bank was within bombing distance. The Belgians were on the Division's right. The 66th Division, on the other side of the Yser, was between us and the coastline. Lombardzyde and its golf course and Westende were completely destroyed.

During the first months of the War there was heavy fighting here between French Marines and Germans. Since then this had been a very peaceful front. There was a legend of the opposing garrisons being used to exchange dinners at Dunkirk and Ostend. The operations at Messines and Ypres were begun to clear the way for a combined naval and military push up the coast, to deny it as a Base for submarines which were working havoc among our merchant ships. We heard at Croisilles that our Division would be in it. At midsummer the B.E.F. took over the coast sector. Our 1st Division infantry relieved the French on the sea-board: the French artillery had withdrawn, ours was delayed in crossing the Yser by a spring tide. If the French, on the spot, and we didn't know about that tide the Germans did. They struck hard and drove our unsupported infantry into or over the river. The line here bent, but held. [The consequent abandonment of the amphibious scheme was a main factor in bringing about the heroic naval adventure at Zeebrugge on St. George's Day, 1918.]

August 18th.—Lane has told the C.O. that one of the Company Commanders is windy; only the C.O. has been unaware of it. Too many of our men are gun-shy, duck for any shell however wide of them.—H.Q. cat has been joined, for quarters and rations, by a bitch in the same condition: she was a friendly creature, but she soon wandered off, likely in search of privacy. Two *August 20th*—bridge repairers walked over a broken end in the dark, and have been no more seen. The bridges, like those at Béthune, are named after London bridges. Watching them being shelled is one of my pastimes until it is dark enough to visit the front. One can recapture something of small boyhood's joy in stoning a floating tin or bottle, or just stoning the water to see the splash. I never had the luck to see a hit, but two hits a day were usual, so good was the German shooting; one day our signallers repaired their Brigade line seven times after direct hits. To the official directions the bridge staff has added these typical examples of Army sarcasm: "You may loiter on the bridge, it inspires confidence"; "Don't spend time looking for the handrail, there is none"; "N.B., all wood is required for repair of bridges, there is none to spare for crosses."

August 21st.—The Aid Post sergeant remarked, when a man was brought in dying, "I never see a man now what's goin' to die, but what he's got one of these bloody things on 'im." He was running the pages of a small khaki-covered book through his fingers. "What things?" I asked. "Noo Testimint."—Electric light in the Aid Post is a great convenience, but I'd swop it for a little more resistance on top of my sleeping cubicle, long and often as I've felt no concern under less or nothing at all. The idea of cover acts strangely on the mind. Men will sit calmly under no more than a corrugated-iron sheet, or even a groundsheet, when shells are dropping about, whose eyes would be starting were there nothing over them. Absolutely safe quarters, like the Hindenburg Tunnel, spoil one, even make one a bit windy in quarters that leave something of safety to pray for.

At dusk a listening-post reported the enemy deploying to attack— or occupying an advanced position to meet an attack. His *August 22nd*—artillery was active all night as if he feared attack. He used a good deal of "K" gas, and, for the first time since Loos, I was made weep and sneeze with "pepper." In the afternoon a venturesome German airman flew low along our front, so low that he could be seen working furiously to get his machine-gun going. He was fired on, and a lot of black smoke came from his fuselage : he turned sharply to his right and just managed by a switchback movement to clear his own breastwork before his machine crashed and burst into flame. What happened to the flier couldn't be seen.—To-day's instance of the any-and-everyday waste that goes on everywhere : a fatigue-party shovelled some tons of soil on to a partly blown-in dump without salving any of the many undamaged tools in it.

On our immediate front things have been pretty quiet this tour, bar some interpost bombing, although minutes were few when a shell did not sough or swish past. Our artillery got most of the shelling ; they are said to be having nearly 50 casualties a day : seems a lot. A high-velocity gun laid on H.Q. compound made movement there chanceful. A section of 5·9s had a spite at a spot quite close to the Aid Post ; the fall of the shell could be watched by standing aside.

"Geleide Post rushed by the Boche." That message caused a wind-up just after midnight. We were being relieved. The *August 23rd*—Cameronians were in everywhere but relief was not reported "complete," so the C.O. was responsible. Mann halted our left Company, and Kearsley went up to look into affairs. The raiders had killed two Cameronians and left four of their own dead in the post. When all was quiet again The Cams. had to flee from our artillery fire, for which the C.O. had S O S'd. We were glad to get over Putney Bridge in safety : there is no chance in the water, weighed down by one's kit. We settled in burrows in the south bank of the river, west of the sluices that control the drainage of these parts : they were used to flood the Germans in 1914.

August 24th.—A wet night has broken a succession of fine fresh days, and of nights with a touch of frost. Many American medicos have been hired to make up our shortage. One, who is attached to the Field Ambulance for a few days instruction, boiled over after being sent sanitating to the Rubber House. He said, "A corporal could have done that," it was "risking too much technical knowledge" to expose such as he to a chance shell.

August 25th.—Things are warming up on this front. The Cams. *August 26th*—and Germans have had a second night-and-day ding-dong strafe. In the forenoon the Germans fired with 7·2-inch on the Rubber House, and cracked it, and on Brigade H.Q., a reinforced house in Nieuport. The Staff scattered to any likely-looking temporary refuge, leaving the office boy and some signallers to

carry on the War. The amused unconcern with which we viewed
the Brigadier's discomfiture was disturbed by a threat of eviction
from our peaceful quarters to accommodate him. Just before
dinner the Brigade fugitives invaded us, hungry and scared. It
appears that the trench-mortar officer who, with his sergeant,
blundered into the German post opposite Geleide four nights ago
had a map showing all our tender spots.—Poore and Mann sat
out a strafe on the peninsula; it was a self-imposed penance for
having run away from one shell yesterday.

August 27th.—A wet night and day, but quiet. The Division
is coming out. We go to the Second Army, Plumer's, to be put
in, as usual, when and where it's sticky—and it's been sticky as
blood beyond Ypres.

August 28th.—After an unconscionable time in getting away
we marched, in a high wind and showers, via Oost Dunquerque to
La Panne. "H.Q. is in the Hotel Terlink," was all Poore and I
were told by a voice out of the dark. Poore's way of finding his
room was to open each door in turn, shine his torch on the bed
and say, "W'—hat!" when the roused sleeper asked who the devil
he was. His hand was on a door outside which were a woman's
shoes, he cannot have noticed, and I was standing by hoping for
a Pickwickian scene when his servant arrived and pulled him away.
In a street doorway on which Yates flashed his torch sat two nurses
each with a squire in very close attendance. Yates was told to "get
out," was damned for "contravening regulations by showing a
light." "I'm an officer, I'm a lieutenant," said one of the squires.
"Well," said Yates in his diluted Lancashire, "I'm a captain, but
I don't want to spoil sport, just to find my billet."

August 29th.—Still heavy showers and high wind.—After breakfast, while an A.S.C. camp was being shelled, crowds of our
infantry sat on the Dunes at adjoining Coxyde, delighted and
cheering, and singing:

> We are Fred Karno's Army,
> We are the A.S.C.
> We cannot shoot, we cannot fight,
> What bloody use are we?
> But when we get to Berlin
> The Kaiser he will say,
> Hoch! Hoch! mein Gott! What a bloody fine lot
> Are Ally Sloper's Cavalry.

The tune is "The Church's one foundation." There are variations in the words, and adaptations.—Many horses in these parts die of sand-colic.

After long uncertainty how and when we would move we went by barge from Adinkerke to Coudekerke. An informing bargee, an old sailor and Royal Naval Reserve man, helped me to pass the time. "Plenty of us on the Canals, and land-lubbers doing the cross-Channel trade!" he scoffed; but I suspect "us" of having found the cushy jobs. About 1500 barges of all sorts are on all the kinds of trade. A crew of two is enough on the Canals, but even "the small boats have five according to Army Order No. . . . Hah!" It's an easy life, no drill, inspections or nightwork, but they've "only 6.30 to 8 p.m. for shoregoing!" Few of the officers are sailors, or know anything about handling any kind of craft. "The other day an officer shouted 'go astern there,' but we knew what to do. Then he came and told us that he 'had to say something because there was a Brass Hat passing.'" For eighteen months our munition barges returned empty from Béthune, although we were paying French barges 3 and 4 shillings a ton for bringing away coal. Road metal for repairs in our area comes from Middlesborough or Guernsey. And much else he told me. 'A [1] barge we met was in charge of another ancient mariner, one who had travelled the globe. Like many sailors he had hankered after a shore job, and became a berthing master in one of the Welsh harbours before the War. He resembled very many others who were usefully employed far from the area of active operations, for later on in the day he spent a long time trying to convince me that his job was a most dangerous one, and that he carried his life in his hand while going up and down the Canals in his barge. I understand that after the War he blossomed forth as a leading member of the British Legion, and was a great stickler for what he called his "rights."'

August 30th.—The Transport has gone ahead by road. For us it was a slack day in this indifferent suburb of an indifferent town.

August 31st.—We marched four kilometres, for the last two of them alongside the buses we boarded at 11.45, and then did not start until one o'clock. How like our Brigade staff work. At the other end we were dropped three kilos short of our billets, to

[1] M. Jones.

the outspoken astonishment of the Corps Commander, Lieut.-General Fanshawe, V Corps, who was waiting for us in the village. These were London General Omnibus Company's buses, their red repainted khaki of sorts. The Transport Company's sign is the reverse of a penny, and the motto "All the way." It would have the first prize from me among the many signs I've seen. Our Divisional sign is the double-three domino. The Brigade sign is a butterfly, which one of the men defined as "an insec' that does as they does, it flies from one (obscene) flower to another."— The run was most interesting. Although these parts are fully cultivated and very flat we rarely saw an inhabitant. An unclouded sun showed us, at their richest, the colours that follow harvest, and of much fine old Flemish brickwork. For several miles we travelled through a bit of France that is the back area of the Belgian troops; not an impressive-looking lot. Petite Synthe lay to the right of our route, a short distance away: the church spire has a balustrade collar. Bourbourg church, of mellow brick, has a heavy square central tower with a balustrade at its base. One sees that unornamental enrichment on some old Scotch spires, I have not seen it anywhere else until now. Bourbourg was the first place of any size we passed through. It is barely raised above the plain, as if on the refuse of its past, and probably an ancient site. Beyond it was a R.E. dump employing mostly Chinese labour. Egyptian labourers squeal and run when they are shelled; the Chinese carry on, and laugh when any of their number are killed. At Watten we overtook the Transport. From the canal bridge the water could scarcely be seen for barges. There the country becomes undulating, and yet more pleasing. We found good but crowded billets in farms and cottages at Houlle and Moulle, adjoining hamlets not far from St. Omer.

September 1st to 14th.—We had come to a very pleasant place where we stayed for two weeks. Except for a couple of sultry, thundery days at the end of the first week, and a day of gale and rain a week later, we had very fine September weather. There were no inter-battalion competitions now, not even in the Brigade ; units saw each other only at reliefs. Our own recreations were not encouraged and organized as formerly. There were many partridges in the fields, and it is likely that our farming and mining men got birds by surer and less tell-tale means than shooting.

Although we were limited, and do-each-as-you-please, for recreation everyone enjoyed Houlle and Moulle.

Above us two changes occurred that might have been fraught with important consequences. The G.O.C. went to hospital. That raised hopes in some, it caused anxiety to others for a few days; then it was said that his place had been taken by a merely Acting G.O.C. A day or two later the G.S.O.1 was seriously wounded when visiting the Ypres front. He was a loss. Not helped by some puritan stodginess, he was an earnest, capable worker in a Division whose General Officers, many of us thought, were not notable for earnestness or capability. His successor was Maxwell Scott of Abbotsford.

The mornings were, as always, the working hours. Poore and Kearsley had charge of training, and gave it cohesion and purpose. It was interrupted once or twice when Brigade awoke from contemplation, had a brainwave and planned a route-march. The marches had the merit of letting many who would not otherwise have stirred from the billets see something of our delightful surroundings. A couple of miles away, at a rise of a road bordering the plain, one came unawares to an outlook over an immense patchwork of harvested fields, patterned with woods and villages, and crossed by straight tree-lined roads, that faded into a purple haze near the sea some twenty miles off. Spread in sunshine, canopied in September blue and drifting cloud, it was a scene of exquisite restfulness. Trees in the north are planted about fields as we plant them, not just cooped in woods as farther south. The Flemish hamlets hereabout are homely, but the cottages are not old and quaint like our native English cottages, and they are shoddy. The broad effects are better than any of the details, for a flower-garden is uncommon, a creeper on a wall, a growing plant or a bowl of flowers in a window, is rarely to be seen.

The other local activity was on the part of the Germans. There were few nights on which we did not hear their air-raiders. They bombed from Cassel to St. Omer, or passed over untrammelled to Dunkirk, Calais, and Boulogne. Our hospital townships on the route were not touched: the medical, surgical and convalescent parts were freakishly named Dosinghem, Bandagehem, Mending-hem, the last syllable being common in the district. In the clear moonlight, it was nearly full moon when we arrived, our Archie-guns fired without searchlights; one night their puff-ball shell-bursts made the only cloud in the sky. A bomb, dropped quite near our billets, killed three R.A.F. officers; they had gone out of their cottage and lain down in the garden to look up at the raiders. Those of us who slept near poultry had timely warning of aircraft we could not hear or see; the restlessness of the roosting hens and the loud quacking of the ducks was a sure sign of their coming. Dissatisfaction with our Air Force came to a head about this time. The complaint was that our fliers were going in too much for solo ribbon-hunting stunts, to the neglect of contact, spotting, and helping counter-battery. The rural population was scarcely disturbed by air-raiding, their risks were very small. They were in high spirits; well might they be, so greatly was the War enriching many of them. My landladies, two nice old souls of 60 to 70, were of those to whom the small billeting allowance meant a great deal; they slept in some sort of loft while two of us had a room each.

St. Omer is only about 5 miles distant. We enter it by a road lined with sycamores. They make a fitting approach to a little old-world town of sixteenth, seventeenth and eighteenth century houses, clustering round a Cathedral set on a hill; there is scarcely a bit of modern building. Many easily effaceable evidences of a vanished order survive in it. High-pitched roofs and gabled fronts abound. Here and there are pilasters with heavy capitals and dentelled cornices above them. The Hospital, a restored early baroque building dated 1592, was the first House of the English Jesuits. The ruins of St. Bertin's well repay a visit; the remains of St. Denis and of St. Sepulchre are outrages in brick preservation of old stone walls. St. Erkembode's tomb in the Cathedral is the venerable thing in St. Omer. The saint was an Irishman. On the equivocally worded testimony of the bishop something about the rough-hewn altar tomb of this missionary of 1200 years ago has a magical effect on the rheumatism of the faithful and on the tuberculous joints of their offspring. The Cathedral is small, like one of our smaller abbeys. Excepting Amiens it is the finest church I have seen in France these two years. In contrast to Amiens it is sombre, but it has an air of reverence Amiens has not. The building is twelfth and thirteenth century, with a square tower at the crossing. The material is all stone of a beautiful grey, like the rain-washed, sun-bleached parts of our Banqueting Hall and a lot of the City churches, but there is none of the grime to which the London buildings owe so much of external light and shade. All the side chapels have discordant, sometimes gaudy, neo-classical furnishings. On my first visit one of the clergy took me round: a middle-aged, merry-eyed amusing fellow. Neither of us had much time, so we stepped out and he talked at the double. The best restaurant in the town is "Le Bœuf," transferred from Armentières where it was a familiar rendezvous in Houplines days. Teashops are many and dear; their custom is cakes yesterday and cakes to-morrow but never cakes to-day.

Anywhere we have been there is a whole realm of interest in the estaminet names. They may equal English names in variety, but not in quality. Such inevitable and universal urban names as 'the station,' 'commerce,' have their rural and agricultural counterparts in 'the true labourer' or he may be 'merry,' 'the bundle of straw,' 'the ear of corn,' and so on. One tree only can I place, 'le gros tilleul,' and not a flower except the rose and the heraldic 'fleur de lys.' The rest is history, legend, piety, sentiment, wit and bucolic fun. Unlike as at home heraldry seems rare. Perhaps that is why the estaminet bestiary is not large. 'Le Paon d'Or,' 'Au Lion Blanc,' must be heraldic, 'Le Cerf' may be; 'Le Bœuf' recurs: 'Au Repos du Renard' and 'Le Nid du Rat' are typical names; 'chat maigre' is not uncommon, why? Bird names are few: 'l'hirondelle' is quite popular, only less so is 'rossignol'; 'au chants des oiseaux' must have been named when thrushes and linnets were more valued for their song than for eating, the birds themselves are very rare to my observation. 'Au Véritable Coucou' seems a bit out of this context. It is remarkable that the 'Écu de France,' displaying the Crown, the Valois blue, and the golden lilies, should have survived revolution and the destructive theorists of three republics; I have seen it twice or thrice between here and the Somme. Could anything be less expected than 'Au grand Malbrouck'?—an old house not far from here. It gives a clue to the near-by 'Reine d'Angleterre,' doubtless Marlborough's Queen, Anne. So these two names belong to the six or eight years before 1713; their survival of the Franco-British wars of more than 100 years is striking. Can "à la réunion des franc-tireurs" belong to the last Franco-German war? Then there are 'rendez-vous' for field workers, fishers and other sportsmen. Some of France's small overseas wars are commemorated, perhaps by *patrons* who served in them; they run 'au retour de Tonkin,' and such like. 'Au trois Empereurs' I identified with their pious Majesties of Köln, not with any political alliance, until it was suggested to me that it is an allusion to Austerlitz; but the 'Trois Rois,' not far off, must be the Magi. 'Allons à la Grâce de Dieu' I have seen; and several Saints 'petit' or 'grand,' and a 'chanoine solitaire.' 'À la petite Cendrillon' is much too good for an estaminet. 'Au point du jour' is a popular name. 'Au paradis des enfants' is thoroughly French; so is 'Le soleil luit pour le monde,' and thoroughly pompous, it is scarcely imaginable in England. 'Aujourd'hui pour l'argent, demain pour rien' turned up several times. In a village that is a maze of narrow lanes is 'au chemin perdu.' Who would not pass a mere 'bon coin,' possibly even a 'grand verre,' when 'la chaumière' beckons? In another mood one might prefer the 'vrai cœur joyeux.' There should be fun in a 'coin menteur,' but 'l'habitude' has the stale breath of the toper.

A man who joined us eighteen months ago as a private is now a sergeant. Before enlisting he was butler to an officer in the Regiment. He declined to be a servant when he came to us, said he preferred duty and hoped for promotion. Now he is up for a commission. (He was killed on the 26th.) He is a capable, good fellow, very different from one whose record this is. Conscription was imminent before he joined the yeomanry. When a rude change from the even tenor of home service loomed up he transferred to the A.S.C., and was sent to France. One of his earliest experiences was seeing some men take a tin of sardines off one of the dead, and eat its contents. "His nerves gave way at the sight." Family influence got him home, and a job on the east coast. And here is the war service of two brothers in an equally good way of business. A is one of a triumvirate who control one of our great war departments for transport; B is a private picking up bits of paper on a sharp-pointed stick; so their nephew told me.

September 15th.—A warm day. Going forward, we marched north over hilly country to Wulverdinghe. We were at the rear

of the column. All the Brigade transport, which was in front
of us, stuck on the steeper hills, so the beauty of the road was
partly lost in the irritation of constant jolts and halts. Watten
has a large German-owned factory: the sort of place that
journalists taught popular fancy to picture as a battery position
planned by a far-seeing enemy. The meaning of the name of an
estaminet was likely lost on the men—"*Assurance contre le soif*,
10, 20, 30 *Cmes. l'action*"—or many would have had to fall out
just there. There were few within my range of seeing who did
not look wistfully at a wayside house of red brick and tiles, built
to an English design, and set in an English garden with a front
lawn and rosebeds in it. We passed a party of men of another
battalion threshing. I doubt if a dozen of them with a machine
will do as much in a day as one Frenchman, such as I have watched,
with a flail.

September 16th.—Why was réveillé 4.30? We didn't start until
7.30. A 14-mile march took us through Noordpeene and Zuytpeene. At noon there was a merciful dinner-halt of 80 minutes
in a meadow. Then on by Oxelaere, skirting Cassel. To a medley
of red gables and tile or slate roofs among orchards that cling to
and cap a hog's back, add a church having a squat pyramidal tower,
as solid looking as the hill it crowns, and windmills turning giddily
on skylines, to find in Cassel a very perfect picture recalling Rye
of old, for now the windmills round Rye are still. We reached
Steenwoorde at 4 o'clock. March discipline went to pieces towards
the end, one Company fell out almost in a body at the start of the
last lap: 80 had straggled in by 5 o'clock, others were coming in up
to 6: a lot had sore feet, not a few were dead beat. A feature of
this wooded district is the graceful brick steeple, solid or fretted,
on the heavy church tower that is characteristic of the rest of the
country around. It is a Flemish-speaking part. The farms look
to be larger than is usual out here.

The Area Commandant, an elderly Temporary R.W.F. Captain,
saw that we had the best billets. Queer chap: his story that he
has sailed before the mast, canned salmon in Vancouver, served in
the American Army, adventured in Klondike, been lumberjack,
correspondent in Paris and music critic at Bayreuth for an American
paper, and what-not-more, ought to be true if it isn't. He accepts
the tribute of a dinner from those who pass through his area in

return for a lecture on the "Strategy of the Western Front," which he has got up with transatlantic assurance and the journalist's facility.

September 17th.—Réveillé 4.15. The Brigadier would not let us use the lorries the Area Commandant sent us to carry the men's packs. The march was short, to Thieushouk, a hop-growing centre. The plant looks of heavier growth than ours, but far fewer poles and less cord are used than in Kent and Hereford. A few oast-houses had conical hoods like ours, but the kilns are mostly in undistinctive buildings. One billet is given free in return for attention to the fires; and 3 francs a day are offered to men of passing battalions to get in the hops, since there is practically no local labour to be had.

September 18th.—High wind, a grey sky and fine showers.

September 19th.—Still resting at Thieushouk: hop picking and nursing sore feet are the only occupations.

On each of these afternoons I took a short ride round a country in which every prospect pleases. In the next village, Eecke, a cluster of cottages on a flat hillock, the church has a detached wooden belfry like some in our south-eastern and Welsh border counties. A modern monastery perched on the Mont des Cats is, in part, used by the B.E.F. as a hospital. As I passed, a young bearded friar, wearing the brown gown of his Order over khaki trousers, worked in one of its fields of roots. Jogging along, as delightful a surprise as I have had yet in France was coming on a few acres of ling and bracken on a hillock, and near by was honeysuckle trailing over a hedge. Bailleul has much of the air of Béthune, but its site and buildings are better. A lot of pillow lace is on sale, and British tastes are well catered for. Its church, an ill-assortment of Gothics and Baroque, is large. Time, painted on the sundial of the exotic Town Hall, is a most dissolute-looking old fellow. The Germans were lengthening the range of their guns about this time. A medium large shell that hit a façade, one of the many decorated façades in the town, beside the Officers Club, shortened my short visit. Although it did not explode, it made Dolly frantic until she was clear of the shelled area: she was wounded on the hip by a shell-splinter three weeks ago. A year later I was again in this neighbourhood. So great was the destruction that followed the eruption of the Germans in April

1918 that not much of the villages was left standing, or of Estaires
and Meteren. Bailleul suffered less, but on a hasty view it looked
doubtful if there was a house fit for habitation until repaired.

In this charming country of moulded hill and hollow the rumble
and reverberation of gun-fire beyond Ypres sounded all day and
night long. Gun flashes blinked in the dark. From higher ground
near us the line of Verey lights could be followed through Bois
Grenier, La Cordonnerie, Neuve Chapelle, Festubert, Givenchy,
Loos, and up the fall of Lorette Ridge to Vimy, rising and bursting
into brilliance, hovering, fading, falling, and burning brightest
before flickering out. It was a weirdly fascinating spectacle,
arresting to those most aware of it and its meaning.

The Base Censor may open any letter. Two from senior
officers out here reached me with his marks. The two of mine
you complain he has opened will make him thoroughly con-
versant with one important source of our income and one minor
source. A third I have heard of, to Mr. Mann, contained a Canteen
payment and further orders. Base censoring will be very different
from mine. I don't even pretend to read the letters of the H.Q.
servants, or of the Aid Post and Canteen Staffs. A little while
ago my sergeant handed me an empty unaddressed envelope and
asked, would I "mind censoring it. I want to write to the girl,"
he added, "you know, sir—the usual stuff."

September 20th.—We were up before 4 o'clock: the sky clear
and star-spangled after heavy rain. The march began in daylight;
it was drizzling, and the rain became fairly heavy again. Only
C Company was wearing groundsheets as capes when the Brigadier
came upon the scene. He took in the situation at a glance. Here
was a breach of march discipline. His initiative in the crisis was
swift as intuition, and effectual. Radford was told off, and ordered
to countermand his own order at once. After that the C.O., in
whose prerogative is the wearing of groundsheets, was not so
tactless as to order all Companies to put them on, so the men
arrived at Westoutre about equally wet.

In a pocket of silence evidently, we heard nothing of this
morning's push, and of the aborted German counter-attack that a
prisoner had given away. A sergeant of our 10th Battalion, captured
not long ago, seems to have given away a good few grains among
much chaff.—There is this compensation for the ghastly Ypres

Show, the capture of one more ridge will give us a good jumping-off ground for next year—if Russia give us the chance next year. . . . A M.G.G.S., a notorious pessimist, can now conceive the War being over in six months, certainly in twelve. His peers have given him a cold douche.

The 1st Battalion and another have been at Etaples suppressing rioting. It began when some W.A.A.Cs. showed a partiality for Maoris. Our fellows, taking no account of the fascination the abnormal and the exotic male has for many females, resented it. Authority intervened. The Maoris retaliated with provoking humour; they trundled a brigadier in a handcart, and asked for a civil speech before releasing him. A Red-cap shot a Jock by mistake. It was then that trouble arose, and other real or supposed grievances were aired.

CHAPTER XV

The Ypres Salient: Behind "Menin Ridge"—"Polygon Wood"—Messines—Hewers of Wood—Passchendaele, unrestful—Christmas in "Pop."—Chinese Justice—Passchendaele, at ease—Drawers of Water—Dissension in high places

Contributors:—CHARLTON; DOCHERTY; LL. EVANS; HUGHES; CUTHBERT JONES; E. R. JONES; M. JONES; KEARSLEY; KENT; MOODY; SMITH; H. SPENS; RADFORD

Sketches:—4, 5, 20, 21

September 21st.—The Division is now in X Corps reserve: brought in, as on the Somme and at Arras, when and where progress tarries. The Brigade is in reserve; and the Battalion, in reserve as usual, is finding working-parties galore. After lunch Mann and I rode among the dwarf oaks of Mont Rouge to its top. South, west and north there is a tumble of hill, wood and waste land, all in fine colour. Our curiosity was in the east. Not far off some of our heavies were firing. The stumps of Ypres could just be seen in a haze that hid everything beyond. Uppermost in my mind rose scenes of a visit the autumn before the War. It was about this time. The children were playing conkers, and throwing chestnuts at each other and, slyly, at passers as we came along the street from St. Jacques.—In the evening one of our sausages was brought down in flames. At night there was a clear sky with stars and no moon. In these conditions an air-raid is more of a fireworks display than ever, for tracer-shell has been added to tracer-bullet and searchlight. The raider glistened like a moth in a beam of light; unlike the moth he doubled and doubled to escape it.

September 23rd.—Between 4 and 5 a.m. there was a lot of gun-fire. Our first cases of mustard gas have occurred in a party digging a buried cable last night. Fifteen have gone to hospital with redness or blistering of sweaty parts, streaming eyes, vomiting, and a few have some cough. Our casualties of all sorts so far are 30. When a party was going out this evening, and I suggested some possibly preventive means, a man said to his neighbour, "I don't mind the (obscene) gas if it'll rid me of the (obscene) lice." In the morning *September 24th*—more of the original party reported with scalds, seemingly from gas held in the clothes. The weather is still very fine and warm.

In the afternoon I rode to Poperinghe. At the entrance to the town a large coloured poster, in French, bids everyone "visit the Belgian coast." An estaminet, "In Pretoria," a South African war-time gibe at us, is derelict. A few shells are fired into the town at times, there was a burst of shrapnel near the Post Office during my visit, but a large civilian population is doing a roaring trade in many goods, for the place is alive with our troops. On returning to camp I met one of the happenings that repay in moments days of unrest—not here alone, and remain a joy. About and beyond the bivouac fir and birch grow sparsely, making a perfect stage before which I reined-in Dolly, and looked on enchanted. A rich glow from the west filled the wide hollow among wooded heights where the Battalion rests. Duty was over for the day. The men were taking their ease, or were busy with their own affairs, among rows of old tents, of piled arms and equipment; and the smoke from their green wood fires rose through faintly opalescent light in blue-grey curls; long shadows lay in sharp outline on purple and browns of ripe grass and bare sandy soil: behind and irradiating all was the resplendence of a late-September evening sun—a glory of old gold flushed with crimson. In few moments the shadows on the foreground had faded, and its undertones deepened. The sun had gone down: and the western background was set for the wonderful sublimity of after-glow. The "hush of evening" felt real. Dolly, feeling hungry, and always impatient, broke the spell: then Proud came for her, and told me I was wanted at the Aid Post.

The Third Battle of Ypres was in its third month. It began at the end of June with the recapture, after more than two and a half years, of the Messines and Wytschaete ("White Sheet") Ridges. The German front was obliterated by the blowing of huge mines. That cleared the right flank of the Salient. Since then there had been the most dogged fighting. Men in thousands and shells in thousands of tons had been expended to advance the line one and a half miles on a small front. Sometimes the weather was fine, at other times men were being mired, and wounded men drowned in shell-holes. The Division has now relieved the 23rd Division between the Menin Road, where it crosses the Tower Hamlets Ridge, and Black Watch Corner. Roughly the line ran northwards from the 6 kilometre mark on the Menin road to cross a west to east road to Reutel at a point about 250 yards west of Polygon Wood; the crossing was called Black Watch Corner. The 100th Brigade plus the 4th King's of the 98th is south of the Reutelbeek: the 98th is north of the Beek. Our Brigadier is left out again: his battalions are to be attached to the other brigades as required. On our right the 39th Division is to capture the ridge overlooking the low ground south of Gheluvelt: on our left the 5th Australian Division has the east side of Cameron Covert and Polygon Wood as objective: the Division is to straighten the line between.

September 25th.—At 3 o'clock the Germans counter-attacked in the centre; the 100th and 98th Brigades lost considerably in men and ground. 3.30—réveillé, clear starlight. We marched by La Clytte, Dickebusch, where the Transport remained, and the Café Belge to the Bedford House area, a smelly spot south of Ypres, where the railway bends east round Shrapnel Corner. It was strange to see the volume of traffic at high noon on roads on which for so long men hurried in the dark. We occupied flimsy old shacks that gave shelter from splinters when shells came over. The Battalion was detailed at once for carrying duty.—Having known Ypres before the War I was curious to see it in its stricken state. An orderly was sent with me. He is 19, English born of Scotch parents. He told me that before being called up he was being paid £2 and £3, 10s. in alternate weeks, making corrugated-iron sheets. Conditions before the War would have given him a few shillings weekly as an apprentice. He commented that much more of such hot, hard work as his would have made him old before he was young. He intends to go into the Navy if he survive the Army. Ypres is a ghost: the grubby little town will have to be rebuilt, every house, from its foundations. The ramparts are scarred, but stand. Only the moat is unchanged. On its calm surface there floated, so stilly as to make scarcely a ripple, two swans preening themselves languidly in the brilliant, oppressive sun of a fine day.

There were many instances of men who, on the eve of going into action, had an unshakable idea, a premonition, that they would not come out alive. Morgan Jones tells of one of his fellow-signallers, an intelligent, well-read man. 'He asked me to go for a walk with him in the evening after tea. When we had gone a little way he turned to me and said, "Look here, '95, I know something is going to happen to me to-morrow. I am not going to get through this business alive. I want you to take charge of my letters to-morrow; I'm expecting some money." . . . My arguments failed to persuade him not to give room to such gloomy thoughts. When H.Q. Company led the way into the line next day one of the first to be killed was '91 Davies.'

8 o'clock: first by road, then by tracks we went round the south of Zillebeke Lake, a dirty pool now, past Hellblast Corner, the Dormy House, and through Sanctuary Wood to Stirling Castle where we were beside 98th Brigade H.Q. The march in the dark was without any disturbing incident. One or two men "fell out" successfully, others didn't. We arrived just after midnight. Brigade *September 26th*—advised us to dig-in well, because the battle was to be resumed in the morning. Some earlier troops had begun digging; the men were tired, they could not be bothered to carry on and make cover for themselves, they just lay down and slept. Sleep on so chilly a night is an enviable gift, I had to walk about for warmth. Over the quiet of one part of the bivouac rose a voice, "Where is that wise virgin going with that lamp?" Second voice (piano, tremolando), "I'm going to the latrines, sergeant." First voice, "Yes, and if Gerry sees your lamp you'll want the latrines too."

The 4th Suffolks and 5th S.R. had been given the part of the Argylls and Middlesex, on whom the Germans had fallen heavily. The orders were to pass through the Argylls and Middlesex, wherever found: because their whereabouts was unknown, there could be no creeping barrage, but tanks were to lead and cover the attack. The 98th Brigade guides sent to take the assault troops to their line of deployment wandered them in strange woods, on which there was an uncommonly good German barrage. It was said that the Suffolks were hard hit and became disorganized.

Zero was 5.25. Stirling Castle and our bivouac were peppered with shells for a short time, and we had a few needless casualties. Only two companies of the 5th S.R. got off the mark on time, another half-company was 20 minutes late. Some Suffolks also took part in the advance. Parties of Argylls and Middlesex were found in, and on the line of, Lone Farm, which is about 400 yards southwards of Black Watch Corner. The S.R. were stopped there, and later they dug-in. (It was 10.30 before their missing company and a half rejoined.) They were in touch with the 31st Australians H.Q., who were in a pill-box at Black Watch Corner. A tank clattered up the Reutel road after they had settled down; it was cursed heartily for turning up then, "only to draw fire," and went away willingly. It was the only tank of which anything was seen.

The 100th Brigade, across the Reutelbeek, was waiting for the 98th to conform: the Australian right had not advanced, and was blaming the 33rd Division for failing to come up with it. That was the situation at 8.15 when, Division having put us under 98th Brigade, we were ordered to attack at noon. We were required to deploy on the Reutel road east of Black Watch Corner, to advance across the front of the 5th S.R., and establish a new Brigade front facing south of east, its left being near the south-east corner of Cameron Covert—a point about 1400 yards eastwards of Black Watch Corner. Poore called a conference of Company Commanders: the C.O. had gone on leave when we came out of rest. C and D Companies were under their own commanders, Radford and Coster; but owing to leave, Battle Surplus, and the inexperience of subalterns, Moldy Williams had been transferred from C to B, and Hywel Evans from B to A, both only the previous day. A shortage of maps caused some difficulty to begin with. Then there was a long discussion before Poore was persuaded, but not convinced, that the succession of advances and changes of front through a right angle which he proposed were too complicated to be practicable in action, even if any of them had ever been practised. With time pressing it was given out that B and D would lead and bring up their right until that of B was directed on Polderhoek Château, that A would follow B in echelon so that its left was brought on to the Château, and then the three Companies would continue the advance in line.

At last, at 10.5, H.Q. led off, followed by D, B, A, and C Companies. The advice of the O.C. 11th Field Company R.E. about a route was invaluable; although a time-consuming detour round Glencorse Wood was entailed we were screened in great part from observation and we avoided the barrage on Inverness Copse, where the early morning advance lost cohesion, and the direct approach north of it. One of the other battalions was said to have had two or three hundred casualties in the Copse. We crossed the Menin road east of Clapham Junction, on the fringe of the barrage. The surface was soft before that point was reached. It was boggy behind Inverness Copse, where half a dozen foundered tanks lay, and the bog extended a great part of the way behind Glencorse Wood. Delay was caused by having to cross much of it in single file, choosing bearing footholds and jumping soggy bits. The track was traced by Lewis-gun magazines and rifle-grenades cast aside by their carriers. When I, having been delayed by a badly wounded man, crossed the Menin road the Battalion was out of sight but for one individual, who, it was plain, did not mean to see it again if he could help. (A week later the Calais police reported his arrest there.) Between Glencorse Wood and Nonne Bosschen the ground rises and comes under observation from higher ground in front. The howitzer barrage had to be gone through there, then a track, about which shells were dropping, had to be followed. We had casualties in the barrage, but reached our jumping-off ground without serious loss. The ground over which we were to operate was found to be as bare as tidal sand; not a wild flower, not a blade of grass grew on it; the surface was churned up soil, which nearly masked the roads, and shell-holes. Trees, all of them small, had survived, and there were short lengths of hedge. All the farms and houses named on the map were pill-boxes on the sites of dwellings. H.Q. details were left in a pill-box shell-hole position on the road running north-west from Black Watch Corner. Poore and Mann, with a few runners, went forward to the line of deployment.

At 11.45 D Company was forming up under some machine-gun fire. Two platoons of B arrived in time to advance with D at zero, noon. The only covering fire given was a few ineffectual smoke shells, because it was still thought that there were parties of the 98th Brigade in front, and there was no definite German position. Mann had just seen the other two platoons of B away when he was shot through the throat, and died almost immediately. Coster was shot through the head as his Company was entering a scraggy orchard, enclosed by a scraggier hedge, north of Jerk Farm: it is about 550 yards eastwards of Black Watch Corner. At this early stage the two Companies were losing touch. The extent of hedge, orchard and pill-box, and the consequent obstruction to view and control of movement, was underestimated on the map which had been our only source of information. As A Company came up Poore ordered one platoon, then a second, into the gap he saw on B's left: there they remained in echelon, never getting into touch with D. When the other half of A arrived Poore ordered it to cover B's right, according to the original plan. By that time B had got clear of a crescentic row of pill-boxes which embraced Carlisle and Jerk Farms in its horns. Coming into the open the Company was met by machine-gun and rifle-fire from the Polderhoek Château direction, and brought to a standstill facing south-east, with its left on Jerk Farm. Williams, Colquhoun and a number of others had been hit. A few Australian dead and German wounded lay about; these were the leavings of earlier operations. The two platoons of A on the right edged off under the small-arms fire, merely extending the line south-west-wards; they came to a standstill with their right in front of Lone Farm. Evans was wounded there; he died in a few hours. D Company had not kept direction through the orchard and farm enclosures. There was easy egress on the left, on which each platoon closed, changed front quickly, and advanced due east. They found some of the 31st Australians in shell-holes; with them the Company arrived at a north and south trench about midway between Carlisle and Jerk Farms in rear, and Jut Farm and Cameron House in front. There they spent the afternoon firing to their right front. Nothing of this was known at H.Q.; they could not be seen, no message was received from them; they were "missing." That was the situation in front from before one o'clock. Williams, who had stayed in command of B, was sent to hospital at one o'clock. Colquhoun, whose wound was not bad, stayed and directed the fire of an abandoned German machine-gun till it jammed. On his way to hospital he called at H.Q. It looked as if we were in front of a screen of a few machine-guns and rifles, most of them on the higher ground between Polderhoek and

Reutel, skilfully hidden among the leafy trees. When the Companies lay low the Germans held their fire, but any movement, even by one man, drew a very accurate fire. In these circumstances A and B ceased to shoot at their unseen enemy.

Whereas the front Companies were quite untroubled by shell-fire, the German gunners respecting the area in front of Lone Farm, between the Reutel stream and road, as scrupulously as did our own, a 4·2 or 5·9 was always on the way to the ground from Polygon Wood rearwards. The Australians had their Aid Post as well as their H.Q. at Black Watch Corner. Their many wounded were spread about awaiting removal, and the German observers could not but see the amount of movement there. Our H.Q. details added a little to it. Two signallers had begun to enlarge and deepen a shell-hole, but finding it far too hot a spot they went to a shallow trench in rear which others of them already shared with some Australian details. 'Within [1] seconds a dud shell buried itself close behind us, lifting us clean off the fire-step on which we sat. My companion, Harry Golder, was due to leave for England in a couple of days for a commission, so perhaps he was rather sensitive. I shall never forget him turning his dark eyes on me, and, with the most serious look that ever I saw, saying, "This is no bloody place for me." I could not help a hearty laugh, which relieved the tension. Within a few yards of us a wounded German was trying to crawl behind our lines.' And Kent 'well remembers that dud shell arriving. It was one of the few I actually saw in the air and at the point of contact. We were looking over the parapet when it came along whining miserably. It landed in the trench, breaking down the parapet and burying one of our Australian comrades. He was unconscious when we pulled him out, and remained so. It was apparent to all of us that Harry Golder's hair turned much greyer during the two days he and others were in that wretched hole. I happened to speak to one of the prisoners during the later part of the Show and was struck by his white and haggard appearance, but on taking a look at my own cronies they were no better—and I am sure I was the same.'

At 1.30 Poore told Radford, who had reported personally to him at our line of deployment, to take C Company to less exposed,

[1] M. Jones.

lower ground in a northerly direction. Poore himself then went and sat down in the half-improved shell-hole that Golder and '95 Jones had quitted, to await events and instructions.

After sending Colquhoun away and attending to one or two others, I, finding nothing more to do for the time being, and having had no food since last night's dinner, was sent in the same direction to seek my servant. He and another man, with the heedless coolness which was so common, had lighted a fire on the enemy side of a pill-box, and made tea. They were about to give some to a young Australian with a bad belly wound. After stopping them I was trying to placate him when Signaller Barrett came and told me that while Colquhoun was talking to Poore and Casson, the Assistant Adjutant, a 5·9 burst among them, killing all three. That happened about 2 o'clock. Thereupon I went to look for Radford about the Reutel road where I had seen him an hour before. On the way, two men suddenly rose into the air vertically, 15 feet perhaps, amid a spout of soil about 150 yards ahead. They rose and fell with the easy, graceful poise of acrobats. A rifle, revolving slowly, rose high above them before, still revolving, it fell. The sight recalled, even in these surroundings, a memory of boyhood: a turn that thrilled me in a travelling circus at St. Andrews. I found Radford, accompanied by Sergeant Frost, behind B Company. He 'had come up again about 2.30 to have a look at things.' We went to the H.Q. area and sat in a shell-hole while he made out a report for Brigade. The writing was interrupted several times by the quantity of soil that was thrown about us.

About 3.30 the report was sent off; and a German plane came along the line of the Reutel road low enough to be fired on. It circled round Black Watch Corner and Lone Farm, and went back over our Companies. A commotion on the Australian front, at the west side of Polygon Wood, led an Australian officer to turn his men and our H.Q. details out of their trench to be ready to deal with what he thought was a German infantry attack. They were lying out when the German plane, which had gone only as far as Becelaere, came back. It flew on the same course as before, amidst a fusilade. This time it seemed too low to be under control. It turned north-east at Lone Farm, and glided unsteadily past our details who joined in firing at it. Kent tells how 'the pilot looked over the left side of the cockpit, with a view to making trouble for us I expect. He was wearing a black flying-helmet and goggles. I rolled over on my side with the idea of presenting a smaller target in firing.' The plane crashed not far from C Company. The pilot was seen to have been shot.

After the report to Brigade was sent off I went again to see if any tea was to be had. Where the Australian youth had been there was a fresh shell-hole. '37 Jones told me that a krump had burst on him just after I left, and he hadn't seen any more of him, and another shell had done in the tea pans. Next, I went to the Aid Post. The Staff had settled in a bit of trench behind our line of deployment; it was probably a relic of October–November 1914 because digging had exposed a rusted rifle barrel. When I got near, Sergeant Hogben shouted, "Look out," and pointed to the Fokker which was coming round for the second time. It was not a hundred feet up, and fewer yards away by then. "Get down," he shouted again, "the bloody thing's hit me." Very soon he was showing me the nose of a German bullet sticking out between two of his ribs in front. He was sure the airman had hit him, although the airman never seemed to fire, and he had no notion that the bullet had come through from his back. It had most probably been fired from Polderhoek. He did not feel ill, but septic pneumonia was to set in. Ten days later he died close to Beachy Head. He had told me of his home, and of his father, a Devon man, one of generations of Bluejackets, who had been a coastguard there; and near there the girl lived to whom he wrote "the usual stuff."

Hours passed, just as in other battles, unmarked except by a rare incident not often as striking as these. The enemy did nothing to ruffle the quiet where the Companies were, and on our side nothing more was done to call down retribution from his machine-gunners. The shelling slackened everywhere. Among a few pill-boxes that lined our part of the Reutel road a rare shell broke long spells of quiet. Once a signaller had just stepped out when a shell burst on him, leaving not a vestige that could be seen any-where near. The day's casualties were 140-odd; upwards of 100 occurred during the hour or so about midday. Nothing was seen this day, or next, of any 98th Brigade parties, but in a trench at Carlisle Farm were many Middlesex dead. There was a story of the Middlesex and Germans being at feud. Of its source I never heard, but it was said to have been the subject of an official correspondence in which the Middlesex were accused of shooting some captives in cold blood early in the War.

When the light failed A and B Companies were reorganized, and two platoons of C came up into close support. After dark a sudden commotion was caused by D Company falling back on the Reutel road. They reported that the enemy was massing in Polygon Wood, and that they had very little ammunition left. The decision to fall back was made in consultation with the O.C. their Australian comrades who fell back with them, and remained mixed with them during the night. D Company's movement induced A and B to swing back also, except two sections of A on the extreme right. The rations and S.A.A. which Yates sent up to the rendezvous were not collected, since no one surviving knew what the supply arrangements were. An urgent request for S.A.A. was made to the 5th S.R., and perhaps a little was gleaned from abandoned equipment. Twice between dark and midnight the S O S went up in the Reutel direction, and was repeated by other units. It was a red-over-green-over-yellow parachute grenade at the time, a pleasing combination of colours hanging above the fretted outline of pines that stood in dark relief against a clear night sky. Each time the gunners on both sides opened promptly on their night lines, firing their rapidest as though frenzied to add to the stupendous tempest of sound. It was as a rending of our part of the firmament. The staccato of the machine-guns filled the intervals of the larger reports and of the shell-bursts, and the overhead rush of bullets through the nearly still, crisp air was like the whistle of a great wind. A veil of acrid smoke drifted over us, tainting the freshness of the autumn night. Neither time was there any movement on the Battalion front, and none of us joined in the tumult. After the second spell of drum-fire ceased C.S.M. '10 Jones of D Company arrived with others off leave. They brought with them their Company's mail and one jar of rum. One! Many of us were not tantalized with a knowledge of this meagre windfall until it was, at most, only an exhalation from the lucky.

September 27th.—About 1 o'clock an Australian officer arrived at H.Q. with the news that the Australians had "orders to attack in the morning in conjunction with the Imperial troops on the right." "Are you them?" he asked. He could only be told that we had no orders. Between 2 and 3 o'clock Siddall, who was patrolling the front, reported a small enemy patrol or listening-post in front of Jerk Farm. Otherwise there was no sign of the enemy during the night. At dawn there was a preventive barrage by our artillery, followed by quiet. Rations were collected from a Brigade fatigue party. Radford, being still without orders, went to the 5th S.R. H.Q. at Fitzclarence Farm to learn by telephone what Brigade intended. He was told that Kearsley, who had been kept in reserve, was already on the way to take command, with orders to advance in conformity with the Australians. In anticipation of this, and because the Australians were concentrating in Polygon Wood, the Battalion had closed somewhat to the left. When waiting there it was lightly shelled. One 4·2 that burst among 3 men sitting in a shell-hole killed them with no more visible mark than some singeing of their clothing. Kearsley arrived at Fitzclarence Farm while Radford was there. On their way up they met the Australian Brigadier, Elliot, called "Pompey" by his men. He told them that there were few, if any, Germans in front of our position, he had "been to look." The Australian A.D.M.S. came up too to see for himself how their wounded were being handled. Was one of ours ever within the shelled zone when there was the greatest need for him to know how things were being done, and what might be needed?

At 8 o'clock Kearsley arrived. After having the position explained to him he moved the Battalion yet farther east, and sent to have the alarming deficiencies in Lewis-gun magazines, rifle-grenades, and S.A.A. made up. At 9 o'clock a patrol was sent to learn the state of affairs east and south-east of Jerk Farm. At 11 C and B were sent to the trench D occupied yesterday and withdrew from at night. The Australians had been on the move early. Seemingly they became impatient because we had not kept pace with them, and their right was again uncovered. Kearsley's concern was that we were so terribly short of every kind of ammunition. At 11.30 he received a Brigade message to push forward at once, and a report from his patrol that the Australians were in Cameron Covert and that German machine-guns were firing into Polygon Wood. Officers commanding Companies were summoned to H.Q., now in a pill-box north of Jerk Farm. They were told that what loose ammunition lay about was to be collected, and how to proceed without artillery or machine-gun covering fire. D Company, McChlery's, of the 5th S.R. had been lent to us; and the 5th S.R. had moved up to the line of Carlisle Farm.

At 12.30 McChlery's Company and D began to dribble forward by twos and threes, supported by C and B in the same formation. Except for a little small-arms fire at the beginning there was no opposition. As the advance developed the support Companies came in between the leading Companies, and men of both C and B got mixed with D. Jut Farm was seen to be occupied when C's right approached it. Sergeant Moon was the active member of the small party who rushed in on the blind side. There was no fight in the garrison of 14, they came up at once when called on to surrender: this pill-box had a cellar. The slightly lower ground in front of Jut Farm was the Battalion's objective, whatever the colour used to mark it on the Staff map. By 1.30 the Companies had settled in a shell-hole line. The S.R. Company faced south-wards, having a bend of the shallow and sluggish Reutelbeek to cover its right, and Jut Farm on its left rear. From Jut Farm C, B, and D Companies extended north-eastwards; D was in touch with the Australians in the Covert in front of Cameron House. The idea was to go forward another 100 yards after dark. Through-out the advance the formation was a loose line. "Worms"—sections in single file, a Verdun model which G.H.Q. copied from the French instruction in Spring, and specially recommended against pill-boxes—can have been used rarely when it came to the bit. Here there was no opposition to test any formation. McChlery was the worst of the two or three casualties. One of his men came and announced, "Sirr, Cap'n McChlery's mor-rtully woundet, Sir-r-r." The final "r" was still rolling when McChlery limped into view, looking not displeased, and showed a flesh wound of the mid-thigh. Long afterwards he told me that there were some three dozen fragments of metal spread about him.

On hearing of the progress of the Companies Kearsley went and satisfied himself with their position. At 3.15 Division's Intelligence Officer came to H.Q. to ask about it. At 4 o'clock the acting O.C. of the S.R. Company reported movement on his front which made him uneasy. Two platoons of A Company, which was in reserve at Jerk Farm, were moved closer up: the Sapping Platoon was moved from reserve at H.Q. out to the right. After issuing the orders for this adjustment Kearsley went to inspect the flank. He was barely clear of the Jerk Farm enclosure when he was wounded in the foot, and had to be sent away; so the command devolved again on Radford, at 5 o'clock.

The Companies continued to enjoy the quiet of their advance. Everything suggested that the Germans had gone back after making their counter-attack on the 98th Brigade, and that they were settling into another position. Until the late afternoon a battery of howitzers was enough for the shelling which was dispersed in and behind Polygon Wood, with bursts about H.Q. A couple of snipers cross-firing from Polderhoek and Reutel provided what small-arms fire there was; the Companies were in dead ground to them, H.Q. area got all of it. In a lull not long after 5, a delusive lull, I went out to look for Mann's body. Some Australians told me where about it was, and added that "one of our fellows is taking care of his ring." There has been time [1938] for the ring to become an heirloom in an Australian family. Radford seemed to be amused at the game of I-spy among shell-holes that followed; doubtless the snipers enjoyed it, and perhaps a German artillery observer; I didn't, much, until it was over. It was the longest quarter-hour of my life. Beginning near 6 o'clock there was half an hour's sustained shelling of H.Q., so accurate, so concentrated, that my confidence in a new shell-hole as the safest shelter was shaken. I came to date a failure of nerve from impressions taken then.

Through scattered trees at a distance, the sun was seen sinking amid clustered cloudlets barred with red and black when a York and Lancs officer from the 23rd Division came to talk relief. After he had gone a S O S went up on the left. "For an hour" the gunners on both sides and our machine-gunners did their worst on a pretty narrow front. H.Q., luckily, was among pill-boxes of sound German build in which all took shelter except Radford, Signaller Tom Jones, who was a bank clerk, and another self-constituted look-out. Thus far I had not been under such a drumming. As the shells burst redder in the falling darkness, and doubt crept in and grew of what might be happening in front, the fascination to watching eyes and ears became tremendous. At last the uproar lulled for a little, then, as if by agreement, ended.

The echoes had barely died down when the head of our relief came along. There being no trenches the change-over was a quick one. The Companies, it was learned, had been untouched by all the shelling, and there was no hostile movement they could see; but when they got back into the zone of desultory shelling two or three men were wounded. The fourteen prisoners were given as many of their wounded compatriots, of whom 6 to 8 had been found in Jerk Farm, as they could carry. There was scarcely a man, younger or older, of good military type among these Germans. Once clear of the barrage line the officers were astonished, less or more, at the strength of their Companies. In the afternoon Ramsay, commanding B, accounted for his Company having a very short front by its strength being only 25. Casualties could not have caused such a wastage. After relief that Company's strength rose, one by one, to 60. Over and above some sorting out, the shell-holes in rear had given up their secrets. Not long afterwards a German prisoner, under examination, said that only eleven of his company had followed their officer in an advance. About that date the trench strength of a B.E.F. company was 100, of a German company 60. At 10.5 H.Q. got away. When we neared Inverness Copse a friendly little black cat fell in between Radford and me, and seemed to try to keep in step, taking long graceful paces like a cat's strokes in the water, which are so different from a dog's fussy strokes. After two hundred yards it stopped, mewing piteously, and turned back, likely to some bare site that had been its hearth. Radford called at 98th Brigade H.Q. in passing, and was wreathed with congratulations. I waited outside thinking how efficient the German artillery and machine-gun fire was these days, almost ideally economical for its purpose: compared with it ours seemed sheer overwhelming mass of metal. On by Clapham Junction and the Embankment to our destination, four kilometres beyond Dickebusch, was a long way to go, ten miles in all, but the surface was good and we were in a spell of fine weather.

September 28th.—By 4 o'clock the last of us was in. Radford had to be helped at the finish. After fifty-six foodless hours, and seventy-three sleepless hours of almost incessant movement, I could take only some clear soup before sleeping. At 11.30 I was called, and breakfasted on a plump young partridge someone had sent up. Was food ever more enjoyed!

The Battalion casualties were one-third of the trench strength with which we went in: more than 60 were dead. Mann was the greatest loss. He was an outstanding figure during the two years to a day he served with the Battalion. There was much discrimination in Col. Williams's early and, at the time, not very popular choice of him for work at H.Q. Of shortish, athletic build, he was purposeful activity in all he did. When he joined he was a gay chatter-box. "Knib" wrote of him in 1916:

> Captain Mann, when work is ended,
> Sees the proverb is amended;
> Golden Silence! that is wrong,
> Talk is gold the whole day long.

But as time passed the gaiety which had bubbled over gave place to increasing taciturnity. Most able and conscientious of Adjutants, he was devoted to his Battalion and Regiment. At any time in 1917 he might have gone to Brigade or Division, where he was wanted; but his loyalty to the Battalion rose as its efficiency fell, and he would not be influenced to leave it, thankless though his task in it had come to be.

At one o'clock we marched 2 kilometres, then waited on the roadside until 7.30 for buses which carried us through Hazebrouck to billets near Blaringhem, between St. Omer and Aire. The last *September 29th*—4 kilometres were done on foot. Arriving dog-tired at 2.30 I sat up until 5 with the C.O., who had awaited us with Surplus. H.Q. was in a pleasant little modern chalet in a clump of trees; it had a short grass-grown drive with a rose and marigold border.—By the light of a nearly full moon St. Omer was seen being bombed, and next night too.

October 1st.—Two signallers making a midnight-raid on sacks of newly-dug potatoes were thwarted by the watchful, voluble, and scarcely placable farmer.—The days and nights are still very fine; and the scenery around is most pleasing, especially the colourful view from the Mont d'Hiver.

October 2nd.—The Division, in tremendous repute, is draining the fount of awards. But one becomes more impressed by the all-round economy of the German operations, the few men used to hold us up. Pill-box garrisons are betaking themselves to shell-holes at a little distance. That is an obviously good ruse, for it is the pill-box that magnetizes the attack, but thought and faith are needed to carry it out.

October 3rd.—Commander-in-Chief's Inspection. At 7.30 sections were being inspected by their N.C.Os., then the whole Battalion hierarchy in ascending order made inspection. The Brigadier had us on the ground two hours before zero. This was to be his hour in a war that had interrupted his professional life as A.D.C. and Secretary. Tall, goodly, golden—if getting fleshy—fair and blue eyed, he was to that manner born. His study, we felt, had been the pomps of military service. Of the niceties of ceremonial he had nothing to learn; to-day he was all confidence, for his mind was moving in accustomed channels. It was interesting to see him take each battalion in turn; sometimes he moved the files about to get his front-line effects, and sometimes he adjusted the set of men's collars and the skirt of their coats. The C.-in-C. rode on to the ground at 12.30, twenty minutes late. After pinning ribbons on a few he remounted and passed along the lines of Infantry. Then we marched past, uninspired, on our way back to billets. We were told that "these inspections are his only recreation." He looked as if he took it sadly to-day. The day was dull, felt as if rain were not far off.

October 4th.—Radford is to be Adjutant. How long will he stick it?

October 5th.—Off at 6 o'clock; we marched by Arques, Longue-nesse and Wisques—"Whiskers" in Atkins' speech—to Acquin: a 16-mile march on which no one fell out. A street in Arques is named "Edith Cavell" after an English nurse in Brussels who was shot by the Germans for spying and helping prisoners to escape. Our route was mostly in changeful, pleasing country. Acquin lies at the bottom of a hollow, wide, shallow, and bare, but the trees that embower it and the warm red of its roofs gave it a cosy look from a distance. It will be remembered for its dirt. Instead *October 6th*—of staying for a week, as we expected, we were roused at 5 to pack up and let the Transport get away. It would be interesting to know what, if anything, is behind the relegation of the Division to an inactive Corps after all the praise-singing. As for the Battalion, I have not heard of any that did better, if as well, although it is a rabble compared with the Battalion that went through High Wood.

Before starting a few of us learned at the smithy how, by heating and chilling, the iron tyre is fixed on a cart wheel. We marched at 10.15 by Wisques to Wizerne, in a lime-stone district. There was more or less rain nearly all the way. To have some warmth and comfort to-night I carried a full pack and a bundle, and wondered all the time how the men carry what they must, let alone rations, dixies and what not as well. We waited about from noon until 4 to entrain. News came in of a lucky stroke at Passchendaele Ridge, plainly quite a good Show. The whole of the line attacked was thrown into confusion, the front overrun, the reserves staggered. The local civilians know all about the tactical idea of the Ypres moves; they are in high spirits, and talk about a German withdrawal from Belgium. To us the disquieting factor is that our Cavalry has been brought up. Our train started at 5. A journey that should be done in about one and a half hours took five hours. We ended the day with a 5-mile march to Kortepyp Camp, where we arrived at midnight. The night was *October 7th*—fine, so we were dry before lying down.—Summer time was changed to solar, and Winter came in the night—so cold. *October 8th*—The Transport rejoined—slept warm and well.

'Stories of ill-treatment of prisoners and wounded at the Front ought not to be believed unless the teller's character is known; your informant speaks like a rotter. Inevitably nasty things happen, for frenzy or fear may lead to anything on either side, and in action it is unavoidable that the wounded should be unattended for a varying time. But Atkins treats his prisoners decently and, as far as I can learn, Fritz treats our fellows decently. What Atkins swears at roundly is seeing prisoners carried in lorries when he is on foot; and he objects to carrying wounded prisoners, he thinks the Medical Corps should do that when no unwounded prisoners are available.'

It was raining when we moved off at 4.45, and went through Neuve Eglise to the foot of Messines Ridge by road, thence on uneven and greasy single duckboards in the dark, the very dark, and more rain. 'In[1] front of me walked an officer's servant who carried a sand-bag full of foods. It was all I could do to keep his silhouetted form between me and the little light that was showing. Of a sudden he disappeared into a water-logged shell-hole, from which I gave him a hand back to the path. A bottle of H.P. Sauce had been broken in the fall. From then it was easier to follow

[1] M. Jones.

the scent than to strain one's eyes peering into the darkness.' We
were all partly or wholly wet through on reaching the support
line just north of Messines.

October 9th.—The village is only foundations, brick rubble, and
a few stark pill-boxes. The ridge was captured early in June at a
heavy cost to the Australians, and to the Germans who counter-
attacked again and again. The dead of both were still where they
fell. From their attitudes it was easy to reconstruct the fighting
round the pill-boxes. It had been a fierce affair at close quarters,
mostly with bombs. The cost of one of our field-gun batteries
in the action was—for shell fired and blown up, half and half, and
2 guns knocked out, £240,000 : the gunners killed and wounded
were not costed.

The Cams. were raided last night and lost 2 men, prisoners, so
the Division has been identified its first night in. It sounded as
if there were guns all round us this morning : a queer acoustic
effect of what was only a strafe to the north.

October 10th.—Damp and drizzle. A pair of sparrows and of
starlings come to be fed ; likely enough they've been on the ration
strength of H.Q. pill-box since it was German. Heavy carrying
October 11th—fatigues are our portion here. A fine fresh October
day : quiet.

October 12th.—Partial success in the north is reported of the strafe
that woke some of us before daybreak. News of revolutionary
trouble in the German Navy sounds true.

We are in the VIII Corps, Hunter-Weston, alias Hunter Bunter,
alias Hunty Bunty, the peripatetic Brigadier of the day at La Ferté-
sous-Jouarre. He is a rum 'un. As many absurd stories are told
of him as of all the other Generals put together. He soon visited
Brigade and went into the kitchen, called for a frying-pan, and
made its greasiness the text of a harangue. Again, he was lecturing
—when isn't he ?—when news of his election to Parliament arrived.
He announced the news and asked to be heckled ; on going away
he insisted on shaking hands with an unwilling sentry, told him
who he was, and how he had been honoured by his fellow-citizens.
The man probably doubted his sobriety.

Our relief of the 5th S.R. in front was a long, sticky affair in
rain, pitch darkness, and the red burst of shells on Fanny C.T.
We had 11 casualties all told. D Company had 4 killed when one

shell dropped right into the trench : there was just not a panic in the Company. Troops following along a trench in the dark when, as now, their dead lay in it, were warned to "step over the sand-bags." Dead Germans are an unpleasant ingredient of our parapets.

October 13th.—Nomansland is crawling with German patrols. They expect us to make a sudden attack : so say 2 prisoners taken in a scotched raid on the Middlesex. The captured Cams. must be men with imagination, they have told tales.—The latest evolution of German tactics here is to have 800 yards of impediments to break up an attack before the line of resistance is reached.

Why did the intelligent German shell a bare field for two hours this morning ?—there are only turnips in it. There are turnips of his sowing all round here ; they are now a large part of his dietary. After an hour's quiet, it was his dinner hour, he lifted 500 yards on to H.Q. pill-box, which he sees as we see his lairs from it. Lunch was just finished. Cuthbert had strolled over from his Company, and put his head past the door. There was no time to offer a drink when a shell burst in front, then one behind. "A bracket," I said, and invited him to go for a walk. The C.O. and others sat still. For over an hour 5·9s rained down, two every minute. There were several direct hits ; they only chipped the German concrete ; the heavily steel-sheathed oak door was partly wrenched off its hinges ; an apple-pie was made of the surroundings. To the end the servants squatted against the lee wall in a huddle of crockery, pots and pans, and stores. The only loss after all was a half-bottle of whisky, and the balance of Lane's eyes—until he slept it off. The C.O. moved H.Q.

Leave to a summer Rest Camp at Wimereux is being offered : well, if this is to be our winter home it's dry on top of a ridge. It's a treat to be on the high ground and look down on the damp hollows to which Fritz has been driven, and to see in the distance the long white plume of one of his trains. To sit and watch his guns firing is something almost new : not that we are going to have too dandy a time even with the higher ground in our possession. . . . The possibility of doing anything further on this front, comparable to the capture of Passchendaele, has faded in mist, rain, and mud. We have now all the high ground in the north except one or two spurs, but, having direct observation, we ought to take them during Winter when spells of better weather allow movement. If the Germans retire on a wide front I fancy it will be, as in Spring, in their own time; but if only Russia can hold together until next year's operations we should have a walk-over everywhere. In any case a substantial gain in the West before the Yankees come into action effectively would be good. They may be able to do great things, but it will be best if they don't have the chance. The Gallic cock, strutting and crowing, is going to be insufferable enough after the War without having the American eagle flapping around too.

October 14th.—In the early morning a gas-sentry was scared limp by the emergence of a white cat from Nomansland. Relieved at night to Neuve Eglise: billets not bad. Our relief was raided *October 15th*—within an hour; our covering party, if it functioned, must have been as good as followed in.

Plainly no action whatever is to be taken against our habitual deserter, clear as is the evidence of wilfulness if it were offered. And yet, what use? To gratify a mawkish humanitarianism two or three score mean fellows are encouraged to slip away every time there is risk to their skins, so more and more average men learn to shirk with impunity; attacks fail, and losses run into untold thousands, because the most dutiful of our men are not backed up.

When my servant was on leave recently his place was taken by a lady-like individual who is quite a good fellow; now he has gone to Le Tréport, to Kearsley. When he joined us the usual question about his civil occupation was put to him; he answered in a mincing manner, "I have independent means, sir, and am interested in agriculture." His brother is said to have been High Sheriff of his county not long ago.

October 16th.—Dull but fine. From a neighbouring height one looks down on Steenwerck, where I joined the Brigade, and Armentières, and, in the receding distance, Estaires, Béthune and Vimy Ridge. The old hands say it is about three years to a day since first the Battalion came to these parts.

October 18th.—We left Neuve Eglise at noon in lorries, and travelled by Dranoutre, Vlamertinghe, the Asylum and Place of Ypres to a bivouac just outside, and on the right of, the Menin Gate. The A.S.C. subaltern in charge of the lorries supplied the needed ginger to timorousness that would not have taken the lorries so far. A flight of Gothas appeared while we were debussing. The Place was as busy as any London street, but it was empty bivouacs at Potijze that were bombed.

October 19th.—A chill night, a damp day with some rain. After more than a day's quiet the guns woke up in the afternoon and made a lot of noise for hours. The Brigade is attached to the Anzac Corps. Our strongest possible numbers are navvying. It's strange that the "storm troops" of three weeks ago should now be hewers of wood for others. Engineers are directing the labour of thousands of men repairing roads, laying down miles of railway-sleeper corduroy for the supply of guns, and raised duckboard tracks across a couple of miles of shell-holes full of foul water, to let infantry be moved to flounder to yet another fold of the sodden, battle-scarred slope that rises east of Ypres.

October 20th—The holding of the old front line, only some hundreds of yards from the town, for upwards of two years is a monument to our national obstinacy. How many know that 6000 of Cromwell's men—"The immortal 6000"—captured Ypres by assault in 1658? That the Cloth Hall and Cathedral were scarcely damaged until March 1915 shows how the German gunners in the early days had to limit their fire to the front positions. Now there is not a room above ground that even troops can live in, yet I doubt if the town has been as busy for a couple of centuries or more. A long search of the fallen masonry of the Cathedral for a volute or some such ornament was bootless, although that is not the sort of souvenir to be taken readily. A party of Belgian troops, sent to salve a bell, armed itself with hammer and chisel and offered chips at a price. I saw no buyers. This is the most drying day we have had for long, but there is mud galore even back in the town.

October 21st.—One of the men reported with a scratch on an elbow and a few slight bruises; he looked pallid. He and other oddments coming from work jumped a G.S. wagon: a big shell burst between the horses: he is the sole survivor. Movement in front has not quite ceased, but most of the casualties occur in the back areas, B Company had about a dozen two days ago. A high-velocity gun, called "Slippery Dick," is laid on the Gate with damnable accuracy. After three dry days there was drizzle and *October 22nd*—greasy mud for this morning's partly successful attack. In the dusk of afternoon sparks were flying from bombs near enough the bivouac to make one wonder where the next would drop. German bombers have been all over the place these nights. The moat in moonshine must be a good landmark.

October 23rd.—Wet and muddy.

October 24th.—Clear and sharp. The swans from the Lille Gate sailed round this morning. The cob, a great beauty, appears to have been wounded; one of the digits of his left wing looks as if it had been broken and had set badly. These birds have become legendary. Their appearance at the Menin Gate foretells a peaceful day, their disappearance, no one knows whither, portends a bombardment.—The good stuff used for shelling the Menin road and other tender spots turns out to be mostly our own ammunition, fired from our own guns, captured from the Russians. Shelling has, however, greatly lessened these last two days, since it became possible to get our counter-battery guns into position. Our job here is over for the present. The Anzac sappers are most *October 25th* — complimentary about the men's work. We marched through Ypres to buses, a terribly windy pother being made of it, and so to Bulford Camp near Neuve Eglise: the huts are comfortable. Our casualties have been 20.

October 26th.—A wet night and day. The push for Gheluvelt and Passchendaele was gone on with: a ghastly failure, by report.

October 27th.—The ingenuity of the Battalion is ordered to conciliate the good opinion of the Corps Commander. Our predecessors, actuated likewise, have painted some sententious mottoes on doors; we are to improve on them. It is thought to fetch him with "Cleanliness is next to Godliness" on the kitchen door. "Prevision and Provision in all things" on the Orderly Room door is quite in his style. "If you can't smile don't come in" has gone up on the medical hut. That counsel, seen by the preacher on a hospital door, and a succession of comic scenes, is all my memory holds of the many sermons and homilies I have sat through.

October 28th.—We are still in a succession of unsettled days: rain, sometimes heavy, at some part of the 24 hours.—A draft of 70 of our new conscript class has joined, eighteen-year-old boys. With a few exceptions their physique is good for their age, but they are no better trained than their predecessors of the last 18 months. How will they stand an average winter? According to Napoleon they won't.

October 29th.—Full moon: a bitterly cold night and a fine day.

"Chopper" Lee is in trouble with a Middlesex officer; called him "a (obscene obscenity)," and his Q.M.S. "one of these (obscenities) who don't go into the line."—Five Divisions are going to Italy to stiffen the Italian Front after Italy's defeat by Serb-Croat troops and four German Divisions. The Italians complain that Austria *October 30th*—sent her best troops against them! Our move back to support at Messines makes it unlikely that we will be one of the five.

October 31st.—Fine and milder. The Brigadier wants a support line dug, and a communication trench to the front line H.Q. His only reason seems to be that the G.O.C. strafed the other Brigadiers for "doing nothing." The Count has been put in charge: he has *November 1st*—indented for stationery. A start was made on the new trench in broad day. We turned a few sods in full view of the German observers; their gunners carried on the good work.

November 3rd.—H.Q. came in for some very unpleasant shelling in the early dusk. Possibly the smoke of the signallers' tea fire drew it, because, perched on a hill as we are, Gerry can see us. The C.O. was more than annoyed. He ordered two pigeons to Corps, immediately, to put on counter-battery. Half a gale blew into the east: the birds, when last seen, were being carried into the distance—and the darkness—behind the German line.

Cats seem to cling even to the sites of their homes. They have increased on this now bare ridge-top to such numbers that the eldrich shrieks of their courtships can drown an ordinary shelling. The young ones, having never known a human home, are quite wild. And where do the flocks of sparrows that chirrup and chatter about these few pill-boxes find food and roosting place?

After dark we moved into the front line peacefully. At long, long last location calls are to be used instead of battalion calls when telephoning.—Of two American subalterns, who are attached to us for instruction, one aspires to shoot the Kaiser from the fire-step. His companion wants only to be told how to know a shell in flight that is wide of him from one that may burst near him; meanwhile there is no getting him to stir outside company headquarters.

November 4th.—A strafe up north at dawn, the rest of the day exceptionally quiet: grey and raw. A sprinkling of gas shell in the evening.

As O.C. Works the Count is in his element, he spends the day among sheets of paper. He conceives the new trench in cubic yards, which he has reduced to feet; he has reduced subalterns and sergeants to distraction, and the work accomplished to next to nothing. The last reduction has the hearty co-operation of the men and occasional encouragement from the German gunners. *November 5th*—Four bays have been dug in four days. All round here there is slackness, and want of any efficient supervision from *November 6th*—above.—At dawn someone in the north attacked or had the wind up. The bursting shell and varied signal lights made *November 7th*—a grand play of colour. We are again patrolling to see if Fritz has gone back.

This year more than last I have missed the fall of the leaf; for a second autumn we have been where trees are naked stumps. It is two years to-day since I joined the Battalion. Of the officers, only Yates and Radford have remained throughout, Barkie has been wounded and returned. The turn-over of the other ranks is probably less; the great change is in quality.

November 8th.—We were back in Bulford Camp by the small hours for routine of baths, work, training. Corps is interesting itself in our training—on paper. Brigade can do that much.— Another attached American is Dundee born, and a live man. He told us that the cinema is used largely for their instruction; formations, deployments, movements are shown and explained to great advantage.

November 9th.—At 11 o'clock my leave warrant came in: packed up at once. Another draft of about 200 was parading for inspection when I left. All but a score are eighteen-year-olds,[1] although many thousands of men are being kept in the camps at home to shield our only possible war-winners from the phantom of a German invasion. The train left Bailleul at 2, and was two hours in reaching Hazebrouck, $7\frac{1}{2}$ miles. A man explained that we had an "engine of 120 horse-power, but 119 of the blighters is dead." This single-line railway is of our building; the material was lifted from our own Black Isle. It makes a loop through Arques and Wizerne, and carries 70 trains a day. Boulogne, 52 miles, was reached in nine and a half hours. A Portuguese officer in the compartment said with quiet assurance, "The Italians are very *November 10th*—poor soldiers." We crossed in the afternoon. A

---

[1] Orderly Room reckoned that of the two drafts of 240 boys fewer than 40 were left by May.

kindly R.T.O., a fellow-trooper in South Africa, had booked a cabin for me, 15s., and a seat in the Pullman at Folkestone: home 4.15 afternoon.

November 14th.—The Battalion marched through Bailleul to Strazeele, and remained there three days.

November 17th.—To the White Château area, Ypres: working on *November 19th*—the Menin road was its portion for two days. Then it crossed over to Potijze to find large working-parties in front for *November 24th*—five days. At night we moved to Passchendaele left support; we were shelled going up and had casualties. B and D Companies were in Hamburg, A and C on Abraham Heights. The men would go about, contrary to orders, until a shelling and resulting casualties induced immobility. But there was no real cover, only a few badly constructed dug-outs, and on each of three days all the Companies were shelled frequently.

The end of my leave—two weeks of dramatic, historic events. In Russia the realists of revolution evicted the theorists, and the Russian Army went to pieces: Russia became a potential [unrealized] source of food supply in Germany's dire need. The Italian front was built up again, and stiffened by strong British and French contingents. Our Army in Palestine arrived within striking distance of Jerusalem. At last, for once, an organized surprise blow was struck at the enemy; the Cambrai Show opened well at least. Our Prime Minister made a speech in Paris he dared not make at home, and when challenged he rehabilitated himself and lulled the public with the boast that his "indiscretions" were "calculated." He had committed us to French control by a trick.

The cross-Channel passage was rough; chairs and their occupants were thrown about the deck, and the spindrift whipped it. The boat manœuvred off Boulogne for an hour. Someone started the idea of having to anchor outside until daylight, whereat a Base bug kept up a moan about submarines; however, the harbour entrance was made in the dark at the third attempt. Having given the midnight train a miss, and had a comfortable night in Boulogne, *November 25th*—I left for Poperinghe, via Calais, at 10 o'clock and arrived at 6. Dining at "La Poupée," I contrasted the abundance of food in this part of "poor Belgium" with the meagreness and makeshift at home. Dinner cost 4s.: a good soup, whiting, roast chicken and potato, cauliflower au gratin, coffee; bread, butter, sugar without limit—no margarine, saccharine or other substitutes as at home. London can't offer anything like it. There was also a large choice of good wines at quite moderate prices. There are tempting shops full of Ypres lace.

November 26th.—Breakfast at the B.E.F. Club; a major, as honorary secretary, runs it : then to Division and got a car to our Transport. The Pop.–Ypres road carried, as always, a procession of vehicles. Our padre piloted me to Boethoek, where H.Q. is in an unsavoury pill-box in which one is bent double. The Aid Post has the only pill-box anywhere near in which one can stand ; most of the others have sunk unevenly into the saturated soil. Judged by the map, the district is given over to typical Belgian small holdings. Now there is "death, desolation, ruin and decay." The whole country round is a waterlogged waste, barely passable but on raised footboard tracks and corduroy roads : the guns are ranked on corduroy, practically in the open. There is safety in numbers in this high place of sacrifice, because there are rescuers for the wounded ; a lonely wounded man may perish in a shell-hole or in the mud beside a track before help arrives. Breakdown gangs are employed constantly keeping the tracks in repair. As destructive as the enemy's guns is the pilfering of the wood by the troops for fuel and making shacks.

November 27th.—After dark we scrambled to the front at the apex of the Salient, winding our way among shell-craters until the Broodseinde-Passchendaele pavé was reached ; then the posts had to be sought in darkness. ' D [1] Company had halted near to some ruins when a shell dropped close to a party of another unit that was going down. They were a good way off, but I could hear one of them shouting in thorough fright, "I've been killed ! I've been killed !" Then another, likely his N.C.O., said in the gruffest manner, "If you are killed don't keep up such a (obscene) row about it." '

Our system of defence is now small posts distributed in depth. D and A Companies are in front of the village, C is in support behind it, and B is in Crest Farm. The whole position has a bad reputation. The C.O. abandoned Hillside which has been H.Q. He thinks that our land-wire telephone messages may be picked up from there by enemy planes hovering overhead, so we are in

[1] M. Jones.

November 8th—the hollow half-way back to Tyne Cot. Hillside has direct observation of the Battalion area, and an excellent view of Crest Farm which is the vital spot. To-day was damp and raw, and quiet for these parts; there were only bursts of shelling, 'one hour on and one hour off.'

November 29th.—At dawn I went with Radford round part of the line. Many scarcely recognizable dead lie about, a few of them Germans. Passchendaele is not quite levelled. Its fields are a shell-crater swamp. It is hard to know where among the craters is the group of holes, or where among cottage debris is the nearly hidden cellar, a section occupies. Mud flows through entrances, and rain drips through the cracked cemented-brick floors roofing the cellars, on to the occupants. Some cellars were crowded to suffocation. A shell on the roof of one, that scared out some of the occupants to seek another, gave the remaining men a chance to stretch their legs if not to sleep. Where the position is overlooked the men are pinned down by day, and numbed with cold by day and night. In places, as behind Crest Farm, freedom to move about unseen is abused—and paid for dearly. In the morning some of our planes came over in an objectless-looking way. Fewer Germans were active and aggressive. In the afternoon one of them was shot down in flames near H.Q. Ll. Evans, just appointed Assistant Adjutant, helped to take out the dead pilot, Boehm, who wore the ribbon of the Iron Cross, First Class, given him by the Kaiser a few days ago. The guns have been so active all day that a S O S didn't make much difference. The Aid Post near Hillside remains a favourite target. A rapidly filling cemetery beside it is a most unrestful place. It is the labour of a squad to keep the dead in their graves. A sapper officer was killed and buried in the morning; his tormented body had to be reburied twice during the day. But for all the havoc up here the effect of a glint of sunshine on the waste is magical.

November 30th.—Another S O S by our windy neighbours meant more casualties for us. We are in an unpleasantly acute angle. Crest Farm is the highest point in the Salient. Its retention is a matter of anxiety to the High Command, so the intermediate commands live in an atmosphere of expected attack by the enemy, and so they keep the Battalion wire buzzing. On our front German Moorslede is separated from Passchendaele by a hollow that is an almost impassable sea of mud and of the flood-water of a meandering stream. In that hollow a few German posts somehow exist, but until the ground dry or freeze neither side can hope to advance.—The last windy warning of an impending German raid that Brigade sent us arrived at the same time as our relief. One heart went into a state of flutter, but the Companies in front recked nothing of that, they were let depart in peace to Potijze.

Our old G.O.C. has come back to us; he is said to have much influence. The Corps Commander fell foul of his substitute for belittling some of his eccentricities or not knowing someone's name, but he was alive to this job, and was waking up this Division.

Moody's Narrative.—'I rejoined the Battalion when it was at Ypres before going up to Passchendaele, where it was my lot to command C Company. Three days there were the worst three days I experienced during the whole of the War. C Company occupied a freshly dug, and very narrowly cut, strong-point near Passchendaele Church which was a well-known range mark. We had orders that on no account was anyone to move by day, because the position was not to be given away. The outgoing company commander told me that he had been heavily shelled, and often for hours at a time. We were treated at times to shelling which was like the bombardment before an attack. Under this ordeal one of my officers lost his nerve and had to be sent away : he was the only officer casualty. A draft of young soldiers who had just joined were, naturally, very nervy. Standing up hour after hour under heavy shell-fire, unable to move about, all in extremely trying weather conditions, is a severe test of anyone's morale, and this was their first experience of war conditions. Then ration-parties were not regular; most of the food arrived sodden with mud and water. Dealing with casualties was pathetic. In that part of the Salient at that season many of the wounded died from exposure and inattention owing to the difficulty in getting them away; stretcher cases had to remain until night, and four bearers were required for each stretcher. The second morning the Company had casualties from the machine-gun fire of two aeroplanes that flew over less than a hundred feet up. In the afternoon of the third day, during one of the heavy shellings, C.S.M. Cumberland

and I, who shared a hole covered with a waterproof sheet, were
buried; we had a minor experience of the kind the day before.
We were dug out little the worse, but the same shell killed or
wounded some of the Company. To approach Company H.Q. in
daylight was forbidden; to find it in the dark was not easy, a
wire fixed on stakes had to be found first and followed. The
relief took place about midnight; it was a quick one because there
was nothing to hand over but a few boxes of ammunition and the
battered trenches. I heard afterwards that the relieving company
of the 2nd Worcesters lost 50 per cent. of its strength the first night
of its tour.'

Our casualties since Polygon Wood have exceeded those there.
For these three days they are 47 killed and 43 wounded to hospital,
18 slightly wounded remain at duty: just not all are owing to
shell-fire: many are newly-come boys. No one fired a rifle except
at an aeroplane, or saw a German except the dead flier. For the
men Passchendaele was, perhaps, the most disheartening period of
the War, of which some of them saw a good deal. 'It was bad
enough in support, but that was a tea-party compared with the
village itself. The mud, the shelling, and the inadequate protection seemed to them to point to the hopelessness of the
situation.'

December 1st.—Two men were killed and 2 wounded by a
shell bursting in a shack. Another shell pitched in the
Signallers tent without hurting anyone. The incident caused
talk because two of the occupants had leave warrants in their
pockets. For anyone with his warrant to remain within the
shelled area is a defiance of Providence; the superstition dates
from the beginning of leave, it is supported by innumerable
cases of death. After a short march to St. Jean we went by
tramway to Erie Camp near Brandhoek. The huts are quite
good; H.Q. is in a farmhouse.

There's a rumour that Russia's Bolshevik Government has been
upset. In any case Russia was out of the War, because the Commander-in-Chief—his previous rank was cornet—had the support
of two armies for the Bolshevik policy. . . . The extremist faction
that had seized office in Russia had done nothing to rally the
country. It sought to advance a politico-economic theory by
recommending a "fraternal armistice" to the belligerents. An

armistice may have been necessary to Russia in collapse. Naturally Germany took advantage of it to occupy the chief communications and cities: the Bolsheviks eventually accepted a peace of the defeated. Serbia and Roumania had been overrun in 1916, so, except in the malaria-infested valleys of Macedonia, there was no longer a battle front in Eastern Europe, and German troops were being transferred to the west to strike before the American Army could be a decisive factor. America did not come into the War until the spring of 1917; before then its Army was paltry in numbers. Plainly the Spring Offensive is going to be run by Germany.

For the next four months intensive work was in hand along and behind the British Front preparing for a new phase of the War. The Battalion had its share in that, but the dispositions of G.H.Q. and the fortune of war spared it from involvement in the great actions of March and April. The next eight months show a like number of deaths to three years ago. They are as wanting in battle incident as the same months were then, but there was no pleasure in them. The world drama, however, was absorbingly interesting.

December 2nd.—A very cold night: we rose to a powdering of snow. I dined with Stanway in Poperinghe. He has a battalion Mess in the refectory of a convent where there is every convenience. His Mess-sergeant was a steward on the *Lusitania*. Next day Stanway sent his Band, the 6th Cheshires, who played to us a typical army programme: "Welcome to the King of Spain": "Marche Indienne": "Friend of Mine": "The way to win": "Sérénade d'Amour": selections from "Poet and Peasant," "Maid of the Mountains," "Chu-Chin-Chow": "God save the King."

December 4th.—Clear, and the frost holds, the surface is icebound. A very good French-made corduroy road, the Chemin Militaire, leads to Elverdinghe; we have a Tank hospital on it.—The Chocolate Soldiers sent their Concert Party: not a bad show: charged us 50 francs.

December 5th.—What is to be thought of the Cambrai affair the Staff seemed so proud of, and of which others were so hopeful until word of the stickiness of the cavalry, and of their mishandling, leaked out? We were left in a bad salient. And now! Above—slackness and want of supervision, below—panic affecting several brigades, have undone everything; the fleeing infantry uncovered their guns.

December 7th.—Thaw. The end of six days when little could be done, and that little was done slackly. We moved to a miserable camp on the Menin road, between the Cemetery and the White Château. More bays of the Cloth Hall have fallen since last we were here, and others totter.—It was odd to see a Canadian polling-booth in Ypres. At this election Canada adopted conscription. The old Anglo-Scotch provinces on the Atlantic seaboard supported the minority against the new provinces which, although they have a largish foreign element, gave the majority. At a plebiscite soon afterwards Australia kept to voluntary enlistment.

December 8th.—Fritz is putting heavy stuff into the town. The men are grousing at the large working-parties we have to find daily. An epidemic of diarrhœa is abating.

December 10th.—A clear day after yesterday's damp and drizzle, so there is much Air and Artillery activity. In the morning two Gothas came and bombed the camps at Potijze, scarcely checked: in the afternoon five came over the area; our rations had a narrow escape. "What's become of our Flying Corps?" everyone asks. In the late afternoon our Mess Sergeant was killed close to the Menin Gate, hit on the shoulder by one of "Slippery Dick's" shells. There has been no more popular man in the Battalion than Ginger Owens: a very faithful fellow.

December 11th.—We travelled in cattle trucks from St. Jean, at 6 p.m., to Abeele, and reached our billets, farms between Steenwoorde and Watou, at 9. Two shells burst near the station; that's the Railway Service's notion of being "shelled to (obscenity)."

December 12th.—The C.O., as acting Brigadier, is being met in the area escorted by the Brigade Staff in force, self-consciously rehearsing the part. In his absence de Miremont, not long back from a Commanding Officers Course at Aldershot, is acting C.O. He has revived the practice of an earlier regime so far as to issue a training programme. A copy of it has somehow escaped my periodic destruction of papers.

PROGRAMME—14TH TO 16TH DECEMBER 1917

Friday, 14th

	9–9.45 a.m.	10–10.45 a.m.	11–11.45 a.m.	12–12.30 p.m.	5.30 p.m.
A.	Close order platoon drill	Bayonet fighting games	Extended order drill	Saluting drill	Lecture on Sanitation for Officers and N.C.Os.
B.	Extended order drill	Bayonet fighting games	Close order drill	Dismissing	
C.	Bayonet fighting games	Extended order drill	Close order drill	Platoon marching past	
D.	Bayonet fighting games	Extended order drill	Close order drill		

Saturday, 15th

	9–9.45 a.m.	10–10.45 a.m.	11–11.45 a.m.	12–12.30 p.m.
A.	Close order platoon drill	Bayonet fighting games	Artillery formation — Section columns extension as a drill	Saluting drill
B.	Artillery formation — Section columns extension as a drill	Bayonet fighting games	Close order platoon drill	Dismissing
C.	Bayonet fighting games	Artillery formation — Section columns extension as a drill	Close order platoon drill	Platoon marching past
D.	Bayonet fighting games	Artillery formation — Section columns extension as a drill	Close order platoon drill	

Sunday, 16th

Divine Service—Divisional Band will play if possible immediately after Church.
Platoon Conferences will take place daily. Recreational training to take place daily 2–3 p.m. Infantry Training, Bayonet fighting, Recreational Training Books to be read carefully. Chapter V. *Infantry Training* to be taken on parade.

December 13th.—Rode to Vogeltye for money. Poperinghe has a large suburb of shacks fashioned from packing-cases and biscuit-tins by refugees who ply numerous home industries and small commercial ventures. I strayed into another Corps H.Q. where all was still as the grave, and unapproachable on horseback for a wide distance, that it might escape aerial notice and bombers.—Divisional H.Q. in the ramparts of Ypres has been burned out: 3 officers and 3 men [or more] are missing: the flames closed behind one officer who went back for something, he was dug out through an uncompleted exit.

December 14th.—Sick parade at 7.30 these mornings is a perishing business for all concerned. Steenwoorde, to which I rode for beer for the Canteen, is a little town of seventeenth- and eighteenth-century houses.

December 15th.—Rode with Radford to Cassel. Only the site is picturesque. A crisp breeze made its many windmills hurtle round merrily, most exhilarating. The sleepy little town has eighteenth-century buildings. It is 2nd Army H.Q., which does not liven it. The Great Ones occupy the Casino, a dull building, by day; at night they leave clerks to mind the office, and go to bomb-proof dug-outs in the surrounding woods. We had lunch and an excellent Corton at the "Sauvage."

December 16th.—Snow showers. Kearsley's return at midday was very welcome: he buckled to work at once.

December 18th.—Keen frost has followed yesterday's rain, rawness and bitter cold. The men have been burning gates, farm utensils, latrine seats, any combustible, for a little warmth. Hop-poles were specially favoured, some were more like telegraph poles; to pinch and get away with them was an art; the Pioneers lent their saws ungrudgingly to cut them up.

December 19th.—Ice is bearing, the children are sliding on the ditches. Mistletoe grows in profusion in all the orchards here. It is among the prohibited articles of import at home: posted a small bunch.—The C.O. rejoined from Brigade two days ago, and is off on a month's leave to recover from the intellectual strain of these two weeks.—The G.S.O.1 promoted: his successor is Cyril Gepp, a fellow-trooper in S. Africa who was given a commission.—Radford's adjutancy is in the Gazette.

December 20th.—Radford is interviewing the Brigadier about chucking the Adjutancy.—The G.O.C. is bubbling over with news and gossip about the "regrettable incident" at Cambrai, as it would have been called in S. African days. Some Generals find an unholy joy in the disasters of others. Praise be we were not there. Two of our Regimental Brigadiers were in the collapse; they appear to have come out with credit; it's all one of them came out with, for he had to set fire to his H.Q., kit and all. The Government Enquiry would be more promising of good if an outspoken coroner and a candid finding were feasibilities. It is plain that the southern re-entrant was so thinly held that it invited attack. German preparations were reported on each of the three previous days; the G.O.C. who reported them had his Division stand-to each morning. Will the Enquiry show why nothing of the sort was done, no move was made, by others? Why gunners were killed in pyjamas?—the Germans did not attack until daylight: why a G.O.C. had to escape in pyjamas, leaving his Yellow Book and other confidential papers to be captured? Do the High Commands know of the unfitness of not a few of their immediate subordinates? Is it owing to the continual circulation of divisions through Corps that duffers escape detection, or deletion if detected?—yet a good average G.O.C. may be dismissed rather arbitrarily.

December 21st.—Up at 5.30 to go to Poperinghe to navvy: the chance we hoped for to spend Christmas in Pop. The country is most wintry-looking under a coat of rime. The whole Battalion is in a convent, with a blow-in gable, off the rue de Cassel.—We left our Surplus at Watou. The food situation there made bread easy to buy, in fact the number and importunity of the children offering bread was a nuisance. Quantities of vegetables were grown. The men sought potatoes, of which they were rather skimped, mostly in the dark, because activity by day led to wordy warfare with the natives. There was a surfeit of parsnips—'I have not been able to touch any since.' Nationalist feeling on both sides of the Franco-Belgian frontier was interesting. The people are Flemings and speak Flemish, but the nearest neighbours, divided only by an arbitrarily drawn line on a map and a post on the road, despise each other.

December 22nd.—Daily sick parade is to be 6 a.m. These days see-saw from frost to thaw, snow to slush, but are always cold; and it's colder in the billet than outside. Clear nights bring bombing visitors.

December 24th.—Corps, to which I rode to draw the Battalion's pay, does itself as well as the others I've seen. The roads around are swept and garnished, and sanded lest the august slip—again. There is a story which connects highly polished parquet with a perfectly staged but most undignified entry to a conference by the Corps Commander.

The Companies set out each morning in the dark to start work at daylight on another light railway to supply the Salient, but Pop. makes any employment tolerable and any billet acceptable. This billet is just accepted. Its spaciousness, shoddiness, and the bareness of the rooms aggravate the effects of chilling currents from large broken windows and ill-fitting or ever-open doors, of tiny fire-places and, at first, lamentably little fuel: thanks to the diversion of a wagon of coal we no longer perish. The town is a sight. There is daily movement of troops through it, a lot of troops are billeted in it. The whole atmosphere has been Christmassy for days; nothing so like Christmas-tide at home has been known out here. The men have an extra pay-out, and most appear to be getting postal orders from home. Christmas shopping is in full swing. One sees that there are no women and children, and scarcely misses them. All the shops, and there are lots of them, are full of goods and buyers, and doing a roaring trade. There's no need for Army French or shots at Flemish; in three years every native has become fluent in English.

December 25th.—Christmas, grey and misty. There were showers of snow that did not lie until night, then there was an inch of it. In the morning the G.O.C. called with Gepp. He was told by Radford, with characteristic bluntness, that we had no word of to-day's holiday until last night, which was too late to arrange a dinner for the men; he went away swearing he'd "twist someone's tail," for the Corps telegram giving a holiday is dated the 22nd. Money to spend and three hours extra opening of the estaminets made up to most men for the want of extras to eat. There was any amount of liquor in the town; there were cinemas and several Divisional Variety Companies. All went well until the men's dinner hour, when an urgent message called for two armed parties of 100 men each to deal with an outbreak—"mutiny," "insurrection" were words one heard—among the Chinese labourers. By the time our parties reached the Chink camp the Chinks were strolling in by twos, threes, and half-dozens, as quietly satisfied as men coming from a Band of Hope Meeting. They didn't understand what all the pother was about. The half company here had just walked over to Reninghelst, and joined their other half company in killing the sergeant-major. They said that he squeezed them too much, took 5 francs from each man on the voyage, and flogged them too readily; he was a bad man, the son of a half-caste woman, and better dead. They had beaten him until he was nearly dead, then shot him. They had not handled the two English officers more roughly than was needed to prevent them protecting the sergeant-major, who had fled for shelter to the officers quarters. The Chinese are not liked by the civilians. They handle and taste anything in the shops and may not buy; their curiosity is boundless, they push through any open door into family quarters to have a look round. It is said that some of them have vanished into domestic service with officers in side-show jobs who can hide them.

The Signals and Runners subscribed for a dinner of their own, so did the Drums. Kearsley and Radford had to drink the Signals' cocktail, a tumblerful of beer and sweet champagne: they jibbed at the Drums' neat whisky, and were given "porto." There was plenty of jollity and a few black eyes. Each officers Mess was on its own. Four of us at H.Q.—Kearsley, Radford and "Yanto" Evans—had hors-d'œuvre, clear oxtail soup, fresh whiting, dressed cutlet and celery, stuffed turkey and trimmings, plum pudding (Parry's making), angels on horseback, dessert—apples, oranges, dates, walnuts: Veuve Cliquot, Kümel, coffee. The turkey, at 3s. 2d. per lb., cost 30s. Everything was bought locally. I don't suppose anything like the dinner could be got at home. Besides my share of Mess festivities, boxes and subscriptions will come to over £7.

December 26th.—The reason why we had no Christmas mail: it had been strewn along the Watou road before the tipsy driver was arrested.

"The Bells of Hell" is one of the best, and least known, of the snatches heard out here:—

> The bells of hell ring ting-a-ling-a-ling
> For you but not for me;
> The herald angels sing-a-ling-a-ling,
> They've got the goods for me.
> > Oh death, where is thy sting-a-ling-a-ling!
> > Oh grave, thy victoree!
> > The bells of hell ring ting-a-ling-a-ling
> > For you but not for me.

It may be Canadian in origin. None is so expressive of the men's cynical stoicism, which is always cheerily, and usually blasphemously expressed. The best-known snatches are short, four-line pieces that some vocal, inglorious Milton has been delivered of suddenly. They are fitted, as a rule, to a hymn or metrical psalm tune. They can hardly be called songs, they're not songs. Their drollery makes them catch on, and they get an extraordinary circulation just to be hummed or trolled at odd times, with more or less variation according to individual taste and ingenuity. Send some—I can't without bowdlerizing, and that would be emasculation. Here is one that is merely vulgar; it illustrates the inconsequence and clowning that give most of them their distinctively English flavour.

> You can wash me in the water
> In which you've washed your dirty daughter,
> And I shall be whiter
> Than the whitewash on the wall.

She may be the "Colonel's," "Quarter's," or "Sergeant's," daughter.

At sing-songs the man with a voice sings "Mother Machree," "Tarpaulin Jacket," and others such: the man with no voice whines "Oh where is my boy to-night?" or bawls "I am a bandolero": the comedian may sing or patter anything clean, soiled or unclean: the operatic aspirant, who never got off the ground and is becoming stout, "will oblige" with "La donna è mobile"—if a couple of front teeth are missing it is extra funny.

Since the Mess servants were having a dinner and an evening off I dined at Skindle's, where a substantial civilian clientele guarantees the food and cooking. The favourite B.E.F. resort is Cyril's; it is best known as "Ginger's," after the flame-headed, tart-tongued youngest daughter of the house.

December 27th.—"The Pedlars" at the "Alhambra," said to be

the best Divisional company in the town, played to a full house:
seats 1 and 2 francs. My neighbour (until his turn came) was in
"the profession"—a jealous spiteful person who should be returned
to duty. Topical skits were followed by "Buckshee," a revue
mostly lifted from *Topsy Turvy* (which was running in London).
"The Leave Boat" and "The Garden of Eden" were good
scenes: the "girl's" arms gave him away.

December 28th.—Clear and frosty, then thaw: snow in the
evening. Officers released from Germany say that the Germans
get their French and Russian prisoners to work, but our men
won't work in spite of the consequent punishment and hardship.—
The Fiji Labour Company are said to be volunteers without pay;
all are over 6 feet. An officer said "Good morning" to one with
a great mop of hair, clad in a loin cloth, scrubbing a dixie. The
savage replied, "Good morning," and spoke pure English: asked
to account for it, he said he was a Cambridge graduate, a barrister,
a member of Lincoln's Inn.

December 29th.—Marched back to the Watou area: the country
is under the Christmas snowfall: the billets are cold barns and
stone-floored rooms.

December 30th.—All day a raw, sound-deadening fog lay upon
the countryside, depressingly. In the afternoon I bestirred myself
to ride out, and found pictures in the bare trees and forms of
homely things looming through the fog. When jogging back in
the fast failing light I pulled up at a shrine by the gate of a village
church because there was a tablet on it, the first I had noticed.
The sense of the Flemish was plain enough from its likeness to
German and the Taal, but the idiom of the last line was baffling
me when a girl of 18 or so came along, of whom I asked a French
translation. She plunged into English. "It mean, 'the man that
loff the girl in there' . . ." with a stab of her thumb at the image
within the shrine. Possibly she misunderstood a natural look of
astonishment at the freedom of her rendering and gesture, anyhow
she stopped, caught her breath, exclaimed "Oh," and bolted.

Die hier passeert	[*Whoso pass here*
En Maria eert,	*And St. Mary revere,*
Zoo wel te paard als te voet,	*As well on horse as foot (be ye),*
Lees een Weesgegroet.	*Say a Hail Mary.*]

December 31st.—"The greatest possible number" of officers of the Brigade was ordered to attend a lecture by the Corps Commander, so I joined the crowd of combatants who expected a morning's fun. He orated on a high platform among blackboards on easels, on which were chalked the headings and a summary of his discourse on "Training," mostly in alliteration and mnemonics. "Teach the teachers how to teach before they teach the Tommies" was the refrain. His matter was distilled wisdom, his manner histrionic to a degree. The lecture was followed by an outdoor scheme, platoon work, for which I could not wait. It began by the General taking a flying start in a race with his officers across a field: a county three-quarter back said he had to extend himself to make up on him. I went on to St. Omer by lorry to lay out a Battalion fund on extras for the men's dinner which had to be put off from Christmas to New Year's Day. The wind was very snell, the roads were icy, there was scarcely a soul but ourselves on them; the bare, wintry scene had a hard, cold beauty. A good few houses in Hazebrouck were more or less damaged three weeks ago by a new German long-range gun. The people have gone, or are going as stocks are sold off. The tradesmen at St. Omer, like those at Pop., have done and are doing famously out of the B.E.F. Tangerines and oranges, both unpurchasable in England, can be had by the case: tangerines retail at $2\frac{1}{2}$ to $4\frac{1}{2}$ pence each, Seville oranges at 3 to 6 pence each. Sugar (beet) is 2/5 the pound. Butter costs only 2/10 the pound at our farms, and is plentiful: eggs are 3/6 a dozen, and milk $4\frac{1}{2}$ pence the quart. A goose cost 2/9 the pound. Whiting is dear, 4/6 or 5/- the pound. [At home the price and distribution of sugar and butter had been under Government control for months: in the towns buyers waited in queues, often the stocks were too small to go round: rationing was of later date.]

A year ago it was assumed that everyone would drink beer. This year forty per cent. of one Company have asked for coffee, two other Companies have twenty-five per cent. and one thirty per cent. of coffee drinkers. The number of Old Army men remaining in the Companies is negligible, there have been "duration" sergeants for the past six months. The Transport, Old Army almost to a man, are beer drinkers; so are the Drums. Among the Signals, half of them Old Army, and H.Q. Runners, mostly sporting young miners, three chose coffee. The Battalion which arrived in France was largely English, the "Birmingham Fusiliers" it was chaffingly called, with a sprinkling of Irish. [Of the killed of 1914-1915 there are about two English for one Welshman.] By the beginning of this summer it had become about eighty-five per cent. Welsh, and there were fewer Irish. Three officers and two or three men, in my time, were Scots. Down to the Somme period only defaulters, detailed to make a congregation, attended a voluntary church service. At Airaines the Chaplain told me he got a real voluntary congregation of 30; the number reached 70 to 80 later still—Carnarvonshire was largely represented in these numbers. We had a much respected Chaplain at this time.

January 1st.—Tuesday, a holiday. A fine frosty morning with high wind: turned raw later. The occupation of an estaminet was hotly disputed by our senior N.C.Os. and those of the 5th S.R. Called in to arbitrate, I decided that the Scots had an indefeasible claim to anything of the sort on Ne'ar Day nicht, our fellows to have it during the afternoon for their dinner. Our billets are so scattered that each Company and Mess had to make its own arrangements for cooking dinner and supper, and for a sing-song. Some of the dinners were very good, others ill-cooked. Left so much to themselves now, the Companies don't function as they used to. A very quiet day with sporadic trouble in some billets at night.

January 2nd.—Everyone went through the gas hut.—The Power Above requires all battalions to train a special platoon to be a model and incentive to the others: Ll. Evans is to organize one of men picked from all Companies. Three weeks later this platoon-on-paper was disbanded, and Clarence Jones's platoon made to serve the purpose. Affairs in the Battalion and in the Field were against results ever being got, but if someone Jones had not taken to chaffed him about his model sparks flew.—Decorations in the New Year's dish-out are counted by hundreds and thousands; nearly every General has something. Is peace coming? We had Giraud to lunch at H.Q. He is for ending the War now, being very doubtful of the French people sticking it much longer: he says the bulk of their rank and file, and their Labour officials want peace, the old people want revenge, trade wants annexations and privileges: France distrusts Ll. George—says he is all for personal kudos. [That was the French President Poincaré's opinion, as stated in his Memoirs.]

January 3rd.—Breakfast at 6. We left Abeele at 9.30 for Brandhoek. Frost and snow after yesterday's thaw made all but the main roads icy: falls were many, language and laughter ran free. Toronto East is a poor camp. The cold increased as the day advanced, becoming the coldest we have felt this winter. Bombers visited the neighbourhood after dark.

January 4th.—Breakfast at 7: by bus to the Square at Ypres, marched to Alnwick Camp, a poor spot at Potijze: clear and cold. There is great activity everywhere preparing rear defensive positions. The 4th Army is determined on its queer notion of frostbite prevention: feet dusted with camphor and talc, and no puttees. I observe, with a blind eye, that a lot of the men are wearing their puttees below their trousers.

At dusk we went to Passchendaele left support by a wide raised footboard track. For twenty-four hours the sector was quite *January 5th*—quiet. The policy is now non-provocative. After dark we went on to our former position at Passchendaele village. The outgoing battalion has had no casualties. C and B are in front; A, at Crest Farm, shares with rats and standing water a large and deep dug-out in a pocket of sand; D is in reserve. Kearsley, back from a visit to the Flying Corps, is commanding. Radford has dropped the adjutancy, Moody has taken it on.—The *January 6th*—wind, gone south, has brought a dead thaw and greasy surfaces. There is no war. At night gross darkness covered us; objects loomed in it and took unlooked-for shape as one gazed, only on closing with them did one know if they had substance or were fancy-formed.

January 7th.—At dawn I went out with Moody, and found the line as nebulous as before; we were yards in front of our posts, and were walking over to the enemy when a shout recalled us. The wind is back in the east, the night clear, freezing. D relieves *January 8th*—C, and A, B.—There was a S O S on our left at 5 o'clock; it soon blew over. Between 7 and 8 an inch of snow fell. Flakes danced in the wind most of the morning, but a Cameronian stripped to the waist and went over his shirt for lice—"chatted," as we say. Kearsley helped H.Q. to while away the time with tales of his recent stay with the R.A.F. He was one of a number of infantry Brigadiers and C.Os. for whom the Powers Above arranged visits to restore the Infantry's lost confidence in the Flying Corps. They were done well by in Mess.

The joy rides were adventures. Kearsley was thrown out on his head in landing. In the next course two machines collided, pilot and visitor in each being killed. The comedian of the air is a pilot transferred from a Highland regiment, who will fly in his kilt. In making a bad landing he threw a brigadier out, and himself was caught by the tail of his kilt on the wing of the machine; there he hung, tucked up like the lamb of the Golden Fleece, a bare-breeched Jock.

January 9th.—Still some frost, and fine snow in the wind. During a two-and-a-half-hours strafe round H.Q. in the morning I realized with dismay that my nerve was failing. Any confined space under shell-fire had always been hateful: now, sitting in a pill-box, the entrance of which faced the enemy, I became possessed by a picture of each oncoming shell bursting in it, and shrank within myself. The way one of the party, who has a reputation for windiness, looked at me was the most disconcerting part of the ordeal. (Four months later this loss of the sense of placing and timing shells had become a horrible worry: two months enforced absence from the shelled area, but not from a sometimes bombed area, restored self-confidence.) In the afternoon the wind changed to south-west, and more snow fell covering all tracks. At night the relief was held up for a couple of hours because two posts could not be found. Relief in the Salient still had a character of its own. On other fronts relief was welcomed, but men would tarry to hear a yarn, to have a drink, or they might just dawdle. In the Salient they waited the moment of relief, then stood not on the order of their going. The padre is light footed, but G. Parry far outdistanced him. Snow had become sleet, and it was dripping off the roofless, broken walls of Ypres when we got into icy cellars in the rue de la Boucherie. We have come in for a fair amount of shelling, and have had just over a dozen casualties this tour, half of whom are dead.

January 10th.—Up at 7.30: we came to St. Lawrence Camp, Brandhoek, in open light-railway trucks, to rest and bath.

January 12th.—Thaw, mud and slop yesterday, then frost in the night. Scott of The Cams. dined at H.Q. He told stories of the Corps Commander's inspection of his billets; nothing about the sanitation was overlooked; it's not their head that others put where he put his.

In these parts there is a lieutenant-colonel who was formerly an Old Army sergeant-major. He will not allow that he is "lucky," says he is what he is just because there is not a better man for the job. His habit on going round his line is to postulate situations that might arise, and get rid of company officers who can't suggest intelligent action. Would that all commanding officers were competent to do so, and did it.

January 13th.—Up at 5.45, we waited two hours for our light-railway train to take us back to Ypres, and so to tents, each within an anti-bomb sand-bag parapet, at Witley Camp, St. Jean. Coal, at 3 francs a bag, offered two weeks ago to supplement the cut-down battalion ration, is forthcoming at last.

A second Decauville line to the front is being laid: thanks probably to a Corps Commander who is an Engineer. The *January 14th*—Battalion will be taken up in open trucks over the completed part of the line to the present railhead near the Augustus Wood area. As the work went forward we came to be in the Crest Farm area. Digging and levelling spongy ground into which one was liable to sink was hard work. Shell-holes had to be drained and filled in. Cutting channels from hole to hole and watching the water run took some of us back to spade-and-pail *January 16th*—days. A second day of heavy rain and increasing high wind has suspended work. H.Q.'s corrugated-iron shack is threatened with being blown to bits; tent-pegs won't hold, the *January 17th*—drenched tents fall on the inmates; crazy walls in Ypres are tumbling down. To-day snow, then sleet, then rain: water is oozing from the ground everywhere, and there is mud, mud.

January 19th.—Kearsley, appointed yesterday to command the 10th S.W.B., has sprained or fractured his knee; his horse came down with him on loose macadam: bad luck dogs him and us, and others flourish.

According to a recent Order Pioneer battalions are to consist of high-grade category men. Our Divisional Battalion has eighteen with double rupture, the sort active battalions are to have for their water-carts. We have plenty of weeds in the Companies as things are, for the grading of men at Home and at the Base is passing strange. In the afternoon somebody's water-cart skidded into a ditch and caught in a hedge. Two hours later the mules were exhausted and the Bis were no nearer getting the cart out; none had thought of manhandling it back two or three feet to clear the obstruction.

A train laden with timber for the front area chanced to halt beside our Camp. I never saw our men work so hard as did those who pinched stacks of wood with the evident approval of the fatigue party on the train, who would unload the remainder on delivery. No one minded when 1100 tent floors, besides all wood on latrines, ablution benches, and such like, round Ypres were being burned during the cold snap about Christmas; and the burners cared not who would have to lie in mud when the thaw came, they were perishing and there was no ration or other fuel to be had.

The finding of the Cambrai Enquiry: no one who matters is to blame, the dismissal of some senior officers is not to be talked about, that's all. An Admiralty Enquiry finds that responsibility and the provision of escort for convoys belong to it; that the escorting ships and responsibility for a convoy belong to the Fleet; therefore neither and no one is to blame for the loss of the Scandinavian convoy and its escort that the Germans did in: and that's all. Lo! there came out this calf.

January 20th.—Mild, with a drying wind. A plane, to all appearance one of ours, flew exceptionally low over the valley where our men were working. Very soon afterwards German shells were dropping in the middle of groups; only one man was wounded, but fatally.

January 24th.—One of two planes attacking our observation balloons was brought down. These days are mild with sunshine and showers. Munitioneers wages have been raised again. The Army's pay remains at a mere 33 per cent. increase since 1914. And our rations have just been reduced: it was only tea last time. Our new scale is:—

Bread, 1 lb. or biscuit, 10 oz.: Tea, $\frac{1}{3}$ oz. reduction:

Fresh meat, 12 oz.—in practice it has fallen sometimes to 200 lbs. among 800 men: Bacon, unchanged:

Sugar, 3 oz.—and $\frac{1}{2}$ oz. additional is to be deducted if the milk is sweetened. Potatoes have become so scarce that rice, 2 oz., oatmeal, currants, etc., may be substituted. For weeks unused dripping has been exchangeable for cash, which must be spent in buying extras.

The latest German scale of rations—Bread, a poor quality of rye, 1$\frac{1}{2}$ lb. Meat, $\frac{1}{3}$ lb.: no sugar or milk.

Fantastic stories circulated, with circumstantial detail, of the German dead being collected that the fat and other useful derivatives might be extracted for the making of munitions, and of nutriment. (On Armistice day Kent and the Brigade Interpreter were told the current story by the Municipal Engineer at Aulnoye. He pointed to one of the factories, and declared that he had seen the naked German dead, wired in threes, lying in trucks in its railway siding.) But the German people were encouraged to endure hunger and cold by the belief that our people were suffering more than they. At a farm where four of our captured men, two Scots and two Australians, were employed the arrival of 17 parcels with food at Christmas 1917 disillusioned the whole district. My informant of that party told me his most valued war-souvenir is the wrapping of a parcel that, owing to an error in the address, did not reach him although the German authorities forwarded it from one distributing centre to another, as the postmarks prove: finally it was returned to the sender in Scotland.

January 25th.—The C.O. rejoined off a month's leave. He says there is no food scarcity, or scandal, in Ireland. But the abundance of everything and the free market is a scandal when food supplies in the English towns get worse and many people are feeling hunger. Rural England has ample farm produce; the farmers are as exasperated with Government control of it as the urban would-be consumers. Sorely needed sugar is said to have been thrown into the sea by a jack-in-office because it had been landed at the wrong port, and tons of bacon let rot on Liverpool quays—to be sold at a penny a pound to the soap boilers. A tale told by one given to good deeds: the speakers were two London women overheard in a food-queue. A. "Is there a Gawd above? thet's w'ot I sez to meself." B. "O'corse there's a Gawd above. Don't you da'aht it." A. "Then w'y, I sez, if there's a Gawd above, are things so for us pore people?"—Officers and men rejoining off leave say that "fighting is over," according to common talk on the home front. It looks like a toss-up if the Anglo-French home front doesn't crack before the German.

January 26th.—The last day of two monotonous weeks of 3-in-the-morning réveillé and doing uncongenial navvy work, although there was plenty of interest, much of it painful, in the political game in which the conduct of the war was floundering. In notes and letters I made seven references to politics during the fortnight. The peace feelers, which began to be protruded in 1916, had been protruded further and more actively during recent weeks. The stimulus was widespread food shortage in Europe, an open letter from a former Foreign Secretary, Lord Lansdowne, and the accession of an Austrian Emperor in the prime of youth. Now it looked as if the feelers had been withdrawn again. Antwerp was the latest stumbling-block to peace which rumour discovered or created. In Eastern Europe Germans and Bolsheviks split hairs over Poland and the Baltic lands. At home Mr. Lloyd George, as Prime Minister, found unlimited scope for his genius for intrigue, and for short-sighted deals and expedients. The wretched Irish-Ulster imbroglio was up again; there were fresh talks along old lines, and it was being said that the Prime Minister had tried to diddle both sides. Earlier in the month a number of senior officers out here were retired. There are more changes at G.H.Q. which are said to have been forced on the C-in-C., the hand that squeezed being the Prime Minister's: but who is his adviser? The P.M. was said to be behind the Northcliffe newspapers' attacks on the C.-in-C., as he was behind the attacks on Lord Kitchener, his Cabinet colleague, from the same quarter; his animosity had long been common talk, but the attitude of the House of Commons in November assured the C.-in-C. against dismissal unless a pretext could be made. A military publicist, a former attaché, left the Northcliffe-owned *Times* to write "unmuzzled" articles in another paper: disappointingly uninforming they proved to be; the censorship would see to that.

Suggestions had reached the public over a long time, from probably untraceable sources, that regular soldiers had an interest in prolonging the War, and that no regular was too incompetent to be preferred to others for appointments. There were promotions which gave support to the latter suggestion. In all professions and crafts there are those who, having scraped in, have a great repugnance to learn anything more about their job; but it is remarkable, to say the least, that in tragic times like these there should be any regular officer who professedly "don't care a damn" what is not done if only he is "not found out and strafed." Juniors have speculated on the number of their professional seniors who lean on civilians for the practical details of operations and complacently reap the credit. The question, "How do they mop-up?" has been heard asked with a silly laugh, and answered only with a laugh as silly. A small group once listened with savage interest to a revealing recital of examples of the successful use for professional gain in the War, as in peace, of eyewash and sycophancy. —Now it has been announced that Territorial and New Army officers are to be given preference for certain promotions and appointments. That is the kind of vindictive folly that a type of administrator resorts to. It won't get rid of one incompetent place-holder, it will limit the choice for new appointments.

A Despatch caused uneasiness to those whose minds were troubled by its implications, because it veiled more than it revealed of the C.-in-C.'s mind. "There must be something big behind so pointed a public reference to training by the C.-in-C., more than the Trade Unions' standing obstruction to recruiting. . . . Out here the C.-in-C. is ultimately responsible for Training, but he is too far removed from actuality to know what goes on. There are divisions where the G.O.C. and brigadiers are keen about it, and competent. There are also spectacles of detachment that have to be seen to be believed." That was written on the 17th. On the 25th there is, in substance, this note : 'A reorganization is afoot; brigades are to be reduced to three battalions. Are we to have more divisions? Divisions made up of the cast-offs of existing divisions and staffs are too awful to think of; either our numbers are drying up, or there's mismanagement or underhand dealing at home. German battalions on our front can, or do, put only 60 men per company into the line. . . . This development sheds light on what was behind the C.-in-C.'s reference to training. He is defending himself before the public against the consequences of our heaven-sent war-winner's refusal to call up sufficient men in time for training, such as it is. That Despatch will stand alongside unpublished representations on the subject. It's a terrifying atmosphere in which we await the German onslaught.'

On all that disquiet there obtruded, as ever, the eternal feminine. Orderly Room often has to deal with domestic problems ; a letter that arrived yesterday illustrates many of them. Marked "urgent" and addressed "Commander," it runs :—

DEAR SIR I beg you to asked you would you be so kind sir

to tell me where must I send for my money as I be waiting over four months for them.

as I got married on the 14th day of September 1917 and my child was born on the 6th day of December 1916 can I get pay from the day the child was born as I been brought up with my grandparent and they are getting great ages.

I havent got nothing to live on.

I would be very glad if you be kind enought Sir as to write me a letter for me to send up myself as you know better what to say in it Sir.

my husband address Pte. . . . No. . . . R.W.F BEF France

Please let me know how much for your trouble Sir I will send by return

      if you be kindle send by return of post

           I remain   Your Mrs. . . .

CHAPTER XVI

*All Welsh—Bois Grenier and digging again: Flight from home:
London: March 21st, 1918, "Michael Day"*

Contributors:—BRIERCLIFFE; LL. EVANS; CUTHBERT JONES;
M. JONES; KENT

Sketches:—4, 5, 7.

January 27th.—A thick mist: not a shot to celebrate the Kaiser's birthday. We entrained in the afternoon at St. Jean for St. Omer, and marched in bright moonlight to billets at Longuenesse, within half an hour of St. Omer; our cookers joined at Vlamertinghe, the rest of the Transport went by road. H.Q. is in a very good villa. The old dames whose house it is are deuced particular: we are asked to be in our rooms and have lights out by 10.30, and all servants off the premises; and we just feel like complying. (We did, in effect, comply.)

January 28th.—On rising I looked down on a lawn of vivid green, sparkling with dew, which continues into a glade in the trees that surround the house; closing the glade, framed in black stems and branches, was the weathered grey Cathedral, aloft on its hill, standing in relief in liquid winter sunlight against a clear blue sky. It was an enchanting scene, awakening visions of faerie. Billets very good: everyone cheerful: there is training of sorts alongside the billets.

January 29th.—An Edinburgh hospital has been set up in St. Omer. An old class-fellow is in charge; a favourite, as ever. He operated, unperturbed, on a man's innards when the hospital was being bombed on September 29th; there were 100 casualties, including 4 nurses killed and 2 wounded. I watched that bombing from near Wardrecques. Since it has been the German prisoners hospital there has been no bombing of St. Omer. The day was the nurses' usual Tuesday At Home.

January 30th.—A draft of officers and men are Yeomanry trans-

ferred to Infantry: for age and physique they are the best that
have come to us since before the Somme. Embodied since 1915
and the early months of 1916, the backwardness of their training
shows up the rottenness of the Home Establishment. They appear
to have done only the simplest routine garrison duty, more and
more perfunctorily, on a low standard of discipline. One man
told me they had not work enough, or of a kind, to keep them
interested and occupied; he was ashamed to take all the leave that
was offered because, for the past year, he was met each time he
went home with the remark, "So you're not away yet." At least
one of the officers had the confidence to say that overseas service
is scarcely more serious—only anyone can get a decoration for it
by applying to Orderly Room. (I don't remember hearing what
became of him.) Why, with these men and others like them
available, were boys sent out to front-line service in November?

January 31st.—Reduction and reorganization are upon us. What
the Brigadier told the C.O. in confidence D.A.D.O.S. proclaimed to all and sundry at Refilling Point: we transfer to the
38th Division any day. We go with somewhat mixed feelings,
though the men on the whole seem pleased enough. The 19th
Brigade, as an improvised formation at the outset, has been
the step-child in every Division to which it has been attached
or of which it has been a part. It has never been given a place
in the glow of the footlights in the Greater Shows except at La
Boutillerie, where it acquitted itself in a way second to none.[1]
From Somme days there has been a feeling of belittlement.
When the Division operated in two columns its Brigadier was
left out; it has been the Brigade lent to other divisions—
auxiliaries ever. Always to be odd man out is disheartening;
and Heaven knows how the qualities that gain trust, and inspire,
have been wanting. We are going to a division begotten in Welsh
parish politics: one on which the War Office looked askance until it
had to send it overseas, and which has been in G.H.Q.'s bad books
since the Mametz muddle—though some excellent officers have been
given command of its units.

February 1st.—With others I rode to Wisques, 2nd Army School
Prize-giving: a noisy affair: the new M.G.G.S.'s address seemed
rather pointless.

[1] The *Official History*, in the detailed volume of that period, scarcely mentions it.

February 2nd.—Frosty, moonlit nights and beautiful days: Candlemas. An American aeroplane, the first to be noticed, flew over the area. The morning was spent rehearsing for our Farewell Inspection. Since the C.O. couldn't agree with his technical advisers, the R.S.M. and Clarence Jones, it was a box up.—The A.D.M.S. has followed yesterday's reminder that I am divisional, not battalion, personnel by offering a choice of several battalions. Some of the men have come and asked me to stay.— Our Chocolate Soldiers are disbanded. The 2nd Royal Fusiliers, getting a draft of 300 of them, sent a party to pick and choose. They took the Band, football team, and "Ruffles"—the Concert Party, and after that anyone for makeweight. All the rest of the Division tried, and failed, to get some of their horses, which go to Remounts.—The Brigadier came to dinner: one of Parry's extra good ones, and on short notice: it was a rather stiff affair. The price of fresh fish is down 30 per cent.

February 3rd.—We quit to-morrow, too sudden for farewells. Our place in the Brigade is to be taken by the 1st Queen's from the 100th. A rumour persists that an American battalion is joining each British brigade. (Nothing came of it.)—In the afternoon, under duress, officers attended a concert in the school: a poor affair, it was only meant to raise some money. Gepp dined with me in St. Omer: we reminisced, and talked about present intimacies.—"À La Betterave" is the only vegetable I have seen on an estaminet sign.—At home the engineers are on strike; the papers don't mention it. The strike is said to have been brought about mainly by a semi-skilled lot who fled into engineering as an indispensable's refuge from service, a well-paid refuge: they have waxed fat, and kick.

February 4th.—Our old dame was most complimentary when I went to bid her au revoir. We paraded at 12.30. The Brigadier made a scrupulous inspection, shook hands, and said "Good-bye" in a short, graceful speech. Referring to his knowledge of the Battalion since July '16, he said its service at High Wood, Croisilles and Polygon Wood equalled, or excelled, anything in the Regiment's history. Next, the G.O.C. arrived. After observing that we had been a long time on parade, he spoke a few correct words, but he hasn't the Brigadier's art of making felicitous remarks. Then we marched past. The Pipes of The Cameronians and the

5th S.R. played us out of the Brigade area. When they fell out and the C.O. thanked the Pipe-Majors, he expressed regret to The Cam. that a comradeship beginning in August 1914 had ended. The Cam. replied, "Yes, sir—and if they had to take anyone out of the Brigade I don't know why they didn't take that lot," glowering at his opposite number. The march was via Arques to billets in farms near Renescure. On a crucifix at the gate of the church is this inscription :—

Crêtien ! Rapelle toi	[*Christian ! Bethink thee*
Ce que coûte l'âme, et voi	*What thy soul cost, and see*
À quel prix elle a été	*At what price it was (deem'd)*
Rachetée.	*Redeem'd.*]

February 5th.—Very fine and mild. We marched by Wardrecques and Blaringhem to Thiennes. H.Q. landlady is a very agreeable schoolmarm, an unknown for whom the C.O. chanced to do some little service when returning off leave : everything about the house is spotless. After lunch I went to have another look at Aire, and found it given over to Portuguese and Chinese. The mass and simplicity of the church is fine, and there is a quiet dignity about the large unpretentious square. English street architecture of the eighteenth century is far ahead of French.

February 6th.—Sunny with haze. We marched at 9 o'clock by Le Sart to billets at Robermetz. The country is flat, but attractive in this day's light. Two estaminets with apt names—"à la Clef du Bois" and "au Feuillage vert," are beside the Forest of Nieppe. We were played through Merville by the Drums and Band of the 17th R.W.F., (Lt.-Col. Cockburn), and the 10th S.W.B. These are the other components of our new Brigade, the 115th, Gwyn Thomas's. Merville shops are well stocked, notably the butcher's. The C.O. told the men to remember we are the only regular battalion in this Division, and to behave accordingly. When the Bands struck up at the approach to our billets we were passing the led horses of the Divisional Artillery ; the horses stampeded, and some of the riders were thrown into the roadside ditch. "We've begun to put the wind up the new Division already," was one man's remark.

February 7th.—Morning rain, mild and muggy. Chaplains without number are rolling up ; they shake hands unctuously, and bid us individually and collectively a most genial welcome. The

Battalion has never received chaplains gladly, but Padre Jones has enjoyed an unusual measure of goodwill. When he left at Longue-nesse for "a Course" his return was applied for. Large minded and evangelical, he had been let in for a "retreat," an affair of seclusion, fasting and abasement. He set out with the sympathy of all, and a haversack of foodstuffs from the Mess. His servant sought strength at an estaminet before facing privation. The Padre has returned after experiencing a terrifying vision of his short-comings, but a more liberal table than he expected. His servant, who had to share some of his austerities, says "It was like Sunday every day"; to get himself normal again he went off to an estaminet for four hours: no penalty is incurred, it is deemed that there are extenuating circumstances.

February 8th.—Drizzle. At Estaires: the front is 5 miles away, points of defence are being dug 5 miles in rear of the town. I looked up the Ambulance Mess of August 1915 in the wine mer-chant's house, and my billet above the bonnet shop. Everyone not already gone is preparing for an ordered flight, and bearing up bravely. The cutting down of trees was a greater sorrow to the old woman of a little stationery shop; her look when some limbers rattled past loaded with the trunks of elms, and the tone in which she said, "There will soon be no trees left in Le Nord," gave an unforgettable touch of poignancy to an impression of overhanging doom.

February 9th.—We are in the XV Corps again: Lt.-Gen. du Cane has succeeded Gen. Haking who commands in Italy, he inspected us: he looks urbane, and was complimentary. The G.O.C. looks a *bon vivant* first and last, possibly a sick man. Officers reconnoitred a line behind Laventie, in support of the not overcleanly Portuguese. One of the most amusing G.R.Os. was aimed at Atkins's playful habit of calling the Portuguese the "Pork and Beans." Our ancient Ally felt hurt and said so.

February 10th.—Sunday. In bright sunshine I rode to Béthune. Its best approach is from the north, the skyline is good; and to-day the colours of brick and stone were at their best, but the town looked dead, not a chimney smoked. Some ancients of the 2nd Division are still on traffic control, but I saw no traffic; the bustling little town of two years ago was as quiet at midday as formerly at midnight. Damage is far short of the accounts we had; only a dozen or so houses have been smashed in the main parts of the town. The barber's at the base of the very Flemish-looking Belfry is a gaping void. The barber and the customer he was shaving were taken out, both dead: the rubble remains. Most shops are open, although their windows are boarded up and doors generally are half-closed. The magnetic, reserved presence has gone from the boot shop. Sharp-featured Madame is still at the barber's in the main street to bid "Bonne chance, M'sieu, Goot loock," to buyers, blushing or brazen, of her specialities. Lunch at the Hôtel de France, where a gable is blown in, was indifferent. My *vis-à-vis*, a very German-looking, American Young Christian, came to England originally to set up a motor-engine plant in Birmingham; the plant was up ten months ago, it hasn't turned out an engine yet, he told me. Returning by Beuvry and Le Quesnoy, I called on Selina—or should it be Alida?—who appeared to be presiding at a mother's meeting: she's become bunchy. Gorre, Le Touret, La Couture, Lestrem are unchanged. Portuguese are all over the place; two lots were playing football. Their command has undergone changes as senior officers were on the winning or losing side in the most recent revolution at Lisbon. Their front is to be reduced. Our Corps Staff was out studying a scheme in case it break. The only gun heard all day was "Grandma" at Gorre, once.

February 11*th.*—The Battalion is still digging. Officers have poured in from disbanded battalions, we have over 50 now. Radford is back off a month's leave. A scheme for sending home the "war-worn" for 6 months rest is functioning: Walter Fox, "out since Mons," goes with everyone's goodwill.—The O.C. 12-inch showed me round the big gun position: a survey adept, he measured the universe to find the exact site of his gun in it. There are lots of "silent" guns in the area. All batteries have wireless, they receive only—to prevent casual talk all day long. Before Cambrai all infantry telephones in front of battalion head-quarters were withdrawn that there might be nothing for an eavesdropper to pick up. Artillery lines had to be left in. The night before the "surprise" an artillery observer, passing the time with his battery signals, asked, "any news of our creeping friends." The chat was picked up. German Intelligence deduced a reference to tanks, and took action. Such was the tit-bit of a Corps lecture I attended later on.

February 12th.—The Welsh Division played disappointing Rugby against New Zealand, and was beaten by 14 points to 3.

February 13th.—We marched in a vile drizzle via Doulieu and Steenwerck to a good camp of half-moon huts at Hallebeeke Farm near Erquinghem. A new public building in Steenwerck is pure Flemish, not a French element in it : remarkable after two hundred years of the pressure of French administration.

February 14th.—Thursday, very cold. de M. is very much commanding, otherwise there is nothing doing. Our Government, greatly daring, has prosecuted one of the most pestilent of the superior people for saying that American troops are to be used to crush strikes in England. How he must despise his audiences. Who is to prosecute the Government for telling the poor silly people that the reduction in our numbers is a means to strengthen us ? Divisions have been pared to the bone, Corps are too weak to find a reserve.

February 15th.—The Battalion is on the range : officers are going over the Fleurie–L'Armée area.

Few civilians and no industry remain in Armentières, which smells of neglect and gas ; the Rest House is ruinous. After lunch Moody took me over the Battalion area of three years ago, hallowed by mostly pleasant memories to some of us for whom there has been a welcome from the remaining inhabitants. L'Armée and Chapelle are sore stricken, Bois Grenier is broken walls at the best. Streaky Bacon is occupied, but the roof has been knocked in ; Dead Cow and Moat Farms are ruins. Ration Farm stands ; there Binge Owen met Stockwell, and was taught how to command his platoon. The green paint on the tub at each side of the entrance to Shaftesbury Avenue looks fresh, but the orange tree in each is dead. Last of all we called at 17th Battalion H.Q., and Moody introduced me to Welton. After greetings Welton spoke of the officers of to-day. "What do you think of them, Percy ?" he asked, concern on his face ; and himself answered, "Damn it, Percy, they don't even know Mess etiquette." He touched on the great decline in efficiency and the actual unfitness to command of many, but "their ignorance of Mess etiquette"—that was the sorrow. In agitation he walked to and fro in the pill-box, hands in pockets, deploring what the officering of the Army had come to. There was a cigar on the table. He eyed it once or twice in passing; then he paused to handle it, more critically each time; he sniffed it; he wondered whose it was: finally he said, glancing towards the entrance and listening, "Well, perhaps it isn't just Mess etiquette—but that's a damned good cigar," and put it carefully into his pocket.

February 16th.—A very cold night, in the huts sponges and brushes froze; the day fine: occasional shoots.

February 17th.—Frost: the clearest day we have had hereabout; balloons are up and there's a fair amount of shooting. C. S. Owen came to lunch. There was some talk of his Cambrai experience: his summary is, "too few men all through." The diversion of divisions to Italy may have thinned us. We have the feeling now of being few.

February 18th.—At dawn the German guns opened a strafe which might have been the beginning of the battle. Our guns kept quiet. Perfect peace reigns in the trenches these days. We moved at 1 o'clock: H.Q. to Artillery Farm, scene of the rape of Suzanne's piano, B Company to Gris Pot, the others to La Rolanderie, and the Transport to L'Armée; all comfortable, if crowded.

February 19th.—Keen frost, clear and sunny: quiet. Robertson, Chief of Staff, resigns: the best plum to be shaken down. The chief of the Prime Minister's backstairs military staff has Robertson's job. How will he act now? The whole business, judged by such parts as have leaked out, is most unsavoury.

February 21st.—Clear and bright, after a day of thaw and drizzle. To-day's gun-fire again looks like registration. All transport has been withdrawn behind the Lys. At dusk we took over Wez Macquart centre and left: C and D in front, B and A support. These are good old peace-time trenches—in a breastwork area: the men have to be shaved by 9 o'clock, French newsboys sell papers at the entrance to C.Ts.; limbers bring rations to H.Q.— 1100 yards behind the front. H.Q. is a pill-box with good reinforced concrete walls but the roof is fragile—the sort of defect that is in so much B.E.F. work.

February 22nd.—At 4.45 it was dark and damp, and too cold for sleep, when the C.O., having been ordered to report on his front, took me with him. The dilapidation of the old breastwork gave me a shock, front and support have been wholly neglected for a year or more. Our lines consist of posts of 10 or 12 men at intervals of

150 to 200 yards: in early 1915 men worth ten of these—were something like one to the yard. The wire would not keep sheep out, except at the posts where it is indifferent. Nothing is being done in front. The men seemed only half alive; the scuppering of a post should be a simple matter. (A 17th Battalion post was lifted a few days earlier.) If the Germans have the enterprise of those at Messines patrols must be examining our new "line of resistance" in front of H.Q. At this period of the War it should be a crime to put out wire in a straight line; diagonal belts in front are what is needed to break up an attack and shepherd it to destruction before it has gained momentum. Pray heaven Fritz doesn't attack here, or he'll gobble the posts and be breaking through the new support (resistance) line before H.Q. knows that its front has gone. There are 300 yards of Nomansland. The German front is held by posts too. Our whole position is over-looked by high ground. Tanks are reported to be lying behind Aubers. Posts are all "Cissie," "Daisy," "Decima," "Evelyn," "Fifi," and so on, named by a brigadier whose wife is a stage favourite. His G.O.C. is the brother of two stage favourites. An eccentric C.O. in that division carried a catapult in his pocket; he shot at anything, once at his Corps Commander holding a conference.

February 23rd.—A very fine day, so the guns, especially Fritz's, are active. Our jumpy Staff wanted to turn on even our silent guns. This Brigade seems as futile as the one we've come from, and meddles more. It thinks a Lewis gun can keep a gap in wire, and has ordered one in the support line to fire on a gap made for Cockburn's raid, although our breastwork masks it—a fact none of Brigade seems to have come forward far enough to see.

February 24th.—Getting old, but I had a prowl round the whole line. Work has become a drowsy pastime. What was once routine repair of immediate damage has now been transferred to the "company task" list, to wait its turn of appearing in Battalion Orders. Little is being done except on the new "resistance" line. Is there anyone who cares to know how much of the 1000 yards of wire each battalion should put out nightly is thrown out on the reel?

Our area was pretty well strafed to-day. Every enemy shell *February 25th*—has to be spotted, counted and reported. Fritz has begun to shell our communications. It's odd he has done so little of that hitherto. Pray he may not copy our machine-gun barrage: he has copied our Stokes mortar action. The civilians just behind us have been cleared to Erquinghem to await transport to the south of France, there's no nearer stopping-place. Many fields were just ploughed when trenches were dug and wired in them.

There are wild rumours that the German push will be made any day now. Rumour favours St. Quentin–Péronne as the centre of it: from here to Ypres is second favourite. We have relieved a French Army beyond the Somme: the French had done next to no work on that front, and we are terribly thin on it: that should settle the debate, and it will be second Cambrai over again. G.H.Q. has been absorbed for months in a humiliating controversy thrust upon it by Downing Street, which has ended in us being put at the mercy of the French. The Versailles Council, which is Foch, commands the Reserve, which is French. Reserves and the control of reserves determine everything. Foch has been made arbiter of our fate, subject only to the political considerations which determine French action. That is the core of the Robertson affair. That is what our Prime Minister, unstable, and shortsighted in so much of his contrivance, has done for us; and the political consequences will be serious and lasting. Our people are being deluded with specious falsehoods when French, Italian and German papers are publishing the facts.

The C.O. ordered out again: I went with him at 11.15 p.m. and visited posts on the left. Our fellows seem to sleep by night as well as by day. It's awkward getting through the small opening of the shelters: one at a time makes for easy capture.

February 26th.—Fritz has done the obvious asked-for thing: luckily for us it's on our neighbours. A party of 9 scuppered a wired-in post of 7: killed 1, wounded 1, and captured 5: one dead and one wounded were left behind. The wounded raider gave an account of the whole operation. Four parties crossed our wire on footboards, divided, and enveloped 4 posts: one party having attacked and signalled a capture a white rocket recalled the other 3 parties: meanwhile a fifth party had pushed on, crossed the support line wire and divided right and left: a green rocket recalled all. Q.E.F. . . . At home all food is now rationed. Will our pampered munitioneers stick food-tickets and privation half as long as Germany has done already ?—Slight frost at night, the day clear : larks aloft, sparrows and cats all round.

February 27th.—Repeated patrols have failed to reach a gap made for Cockburn's raid owing to the repairers being well covered. Last night's patrol reported a big fighting party and a small decoy. But why have we gone on sending only one patrol, and at about the same hour each night ? After much futile talk at H.Q. Moody asked the artillery and machine-guns to fire unofficially, and they agreed; the roving gun is to be used. A well-led patrol then went out before dawn and did the job thoroughly. When the Brigadier got to hear of it he strafed !—Fritz is reported to be withdrawing guns from opposite.—Thought I heard a blackbird.

February 28th.—It was a blackbird, not yet in good voice : so Winter has gone though Gerry is coming.—I was immersed in arranging to-morrow's dinner when all preparations were thrown out of gear : there's a whisper of impending attack, so relief is uncertain; and the Mess Corporal has been arrested by the police in Estaires : Mills says he has no head, he had only one glass of "red wine."

March 1st, St. David's Day.—Friday. All quiet, and relief promised. Sergeants Horton and Mills, and Parry worked hard. The only possible hut, close to La Rolanderie, was occupied until after dark by Englishmen who knew not David and didn't want to hear about him. Horton did wonders in the short time left to him, but only the largest of the holes, through which a raw cold wind swept, could be closed. At half-past eight it was not known where plates, glasses and cutlery could be got; however, one of the remaining estaminets at Erquinghem was persuaded to lend what had been packed for removal, to eke out the contents of the company boxes, and clean bed linen to serve as tablecloths. Midnight was near when the C.O. invited our old-maidish Brigadier to be seated. Parry, as ever, sent in first-class fare in the most adverse conditions. The menu, in the French of Kitchen cum Orderly Room : "Consumme of Gallos; merlan Duglers; Escallops de Veau Vilanairese; Gigot de Mouton Roti, pommes Rissoles, Choux Bruxelles; Pudding au Chocolat; Scotch Woodcock; Dessert; Cafe: Veuve Cliquot, Benedictine, Kümmel. At Gris Pot." Only port was wanting, even the Portuguese canteen had none—or said so. Of 31 at table 23 ate the Leek in the odour of the Goat and to the roll of the Drum. The toasts were proposed by the C.O.—"St. David," "The King," "Other Battalions"; Cuthbert—"Toby Purcell and his Spurs"; Moody—"Shencin ap Morgan"; French—"The Ladies"; Radford—"The Guests." As usual I had to reply for The Guests, though I'm responsible for the dinner and pay my whack. After the Brigadier and the C.O. had gone the younger members of the Mess resumed, and made merry *March 2nd*—until near daylight.—A biting wind, some snow in it; thaw later. Digging is to be got on with, everyone at it.

March 3rd.—The attack of which there was warning two days ago fell on the Portuguese. Driven behind Neuve Chapelle, they counter-attacked and recovered the lost ground: so at least the story goes. The Germans are making many raids on the French, and on Sammy who has a Corps in the line now.—Cockburn's raid appears to have been a costly affair owing to the wavering of O.C. raiders, but one German let himself be captured when the others ran. He said the big attack is not wanted in Germany, that his battalion does not mean to go over the top, that they had petitioned successfully for the removal of their C.O. for striking a man. He's a bad type.—A Mess meeting: decision, to carry on as we are.

March 4th.—Going on leave, I saw in Steenwerck the latest class of French conscripts leaving home for their depots. Dressed in their Sunday best, beflowered, beribboned, beflagged, befuddled, they were calling at every friend's house and being given liquor. Poor boys. The train arrived at Calais at 7.30 in pitch darkness. I had to share a top room in the Terminus Hotel on the Quay. A light and a scuffle in the room, near midnight, awoke me; my companion was scrambling into his clothes to go to the cellar. Bombs were swishing past and bursting not far off. Chancing it *March 5th*—in bed, I fell asleep. The return of my room-fellow awoke me at 6.30, so I rose and went out to see the results. A large dump had been burned, and other less damage done on the quay and near.—Calais is historic, but doesn't look it.—A lot of my travelling companions took home joints of beef and mutton, butter and sugar. We had a good crossing to Dover, and I was home soon after 2.30. An immediate errand was to a Food Control office to get tickets for a daily modicum of meat, sugar, etc. As it happened the day was the last for the free purchase of poultry, and of offal—sweetbread, tripe, liver, etc. Before returning I looked up a friend and found him perplexed; he was dining out and had no ticket to give his hosts for his scrap of meat, his tickets were locked up and his sister had gone out with the key. Such is "rationing." Two nights later when coming out of Baker St. Station after 11 o'clock I had to ask the ticket collector about the crowds, whole families, who jostled me. The warning that air-raiders were expected had sent them hurrying down to the safety of the station platforms and lower stairways. The neighbourhood of Lord's Cricket Ground was bombed. This was said to be the first moonless raid on London. The play of our searchlights was like a brilliant aurora. A medical friend told me the story of a talk between two London girls overheard on a bus-top the following day. "The first time the maroons went off he put his arm round my waist. The second time they fired—well, he kissed me. Now that's all very well, but what I want to know is, when I meet him on Thursday do I bow."

Work on the line of resistance occupied the four days the Battalion was in support. Gas projectors for an intended stunt were carried up.

March 9th.—Some shelling of H.Q. billet, Artillery Farm, delayed our return to the front; there was plenty of wind at the centre of the disturbance, but no one was hit.

March 10th.—All day the whole line was under a dispersed shelling.

March 11th.—To-day the back areas were heavily shelled; there was some trouble in bringing up rations. Next day was quiet as things are.

March 13th.—At 5.30 in the morning, when our guns were doing a time-table shoot of the line opposite, a party of fully 20 Germans attacked two of D Company's posts. Clarence Jones was on duty. He got very excited, as usual, but he did the right thing—took charge of the Lewis gun. The attackers bolted, except one man who entered our line by a gap between "Eunice" and "Evelyn," and was collared by Jones. The prisoner, who was very ready to talk, said that a party of 300 was assembling to raid us when our guns opened on them and broke up their formation, but the operation was gone on with. The shoot was a lucky coincidence for us, but the most was made of our part in the affair since it gave the men some conceit of themselves. The Brigadier came

up next day "to hear all about it." He did. Jones had still much
of the child in him. The number of his slain grew with each
telling, although the Company's patrols had not been able to find
any corpses. After relief D Company officers occupied a small
canvas-walled hut at Rolanderie. One day chaff about the slain
warmed to abuse, followed by a scrap between Jones and another
subaltern during which the side was knocked out of the hut, and
the scrap was continued among the debris to the amazement of
D Company's braves. Almost as entertaining to a smaller audience
was a lesson in French pronunciation which the C.O. gave an
A Company subaltern who would call de Miremont "de Merry-
mount."

March 16*th*.—There was a mixed explosive and gas shelling of
the area. C Company's H.Q. was blown in. We got off with
one casualty.

March 17*th*.—During a sudden strafe of a too-fragile company
H.Q. there was a hurried reaching for tin-hats. Butler, who has
rather an outsize in heads, was accused of having on a hat which
was much too small to be his. "Damn it," he told his accusers,
"it's that my hair's standing on end." Relief was a relief indeed
from a very harassing tour, for messages and enquiries about the
expected big attack poured in day and night from the Staff.

March 18*th*.—Yesterday and again to-day the front and rear
areas were shelled, gas and heavy stuff being used.

Briercliffe, on coming fresh from a Lewis-gun course, had been
put in charge of D Company's guns. He found that only two of
the four were complete with equipment, a state of affairs that H.Q.
could not be told about except in the last resort. Clarence Jones
came to the rescue by telling how the Guards made good and
were never found deficient of anything. A few selected men
were initiated, it being stipulated that nothing was to be found
in the lines of the other Companies. Before returning to the line
D had seven guns and the makings of an eighth. The other Companies made up: and the Battalion was complete, perhaps suspect
too, when the Brigadier had a Lewis-gun deficiency strafe in his
command a little later.

March 19*th*.—The end of leave.—London was never so unpleasant as it has become. Darkened streets and restricted supplies
are mere galling inconveniences. But the day of the theorist and

faddist, fatuous and dangerous, has come. And everywhere one sees or hears of the same things—great numbers of people out only for pelf, or place and its emoluments; public money and time diverted to individual self-advancement; self-seekers assailing administration without, and eating it up within. There are, of course, very many noble exceptions. When Mann rejoined off his last leave he met me with the passionate exclamation—"Thank God, I'm back. London's awful." He was by no means singular in feeling and expression; of places at home not London alone is thought "awful." London has worsened since my November leave, and become yet more profit and pleasure seeking. I too am glad to get away to the wholesome humanity of the front.[1]

The Germans have all the luck of the weather; for two months it has been wholly at their service, and plenty of added mist hides a lot of their doings. Comparing the two armies, both are to be distrusted. I believe that whichever can be gingered to go forward, every man as if he meant it, will drive the other before it—given a reasonably well-launched attack. Of the outlook: there are those like me who think the immediate outlook very bad, but I fancy that the men as a body look on with the incomprehension that has saved so many situations. Anyhow, we'll know soon; and we'll win in the long run if the home front hold. The poisonous atmosphere there is disheartening. Intrigue and chicanery and inspired half-truth are the media through which the most important decisions affecting us are come to. . . . In quests for a scheme of "rededication" I can't help. I doubt if the men out here are more drawn to religion; I'm sure they are more than ever repelled by the clergy.[2]

The train left Victoria at 8 a.m. We had to wait at Dover until 2.30 for the boat which brought the home-coming leave party: their haversacks were bulging with foodstuffs. (Soon afterwards a G.R.O., issued at the request of the French Government, put a stop to that.) The Dover–Calais crossing was much more interesting than the more usual Folkestone–Boulogne route. It gave one a passing glimpse of the Navy's work. There was a wreck or two on the beach; there were destroyer flotillas in Dover and Calais harbours; the boat sailed close to the anti-submarine boom and net that was laid from coast to coast, and

[1] Written at Dover.   [2] Begun at Dover, finished in France.

to the airships—blimps—that patrolled it. On the journey from
March 20th—Calais an Anzac, off Paris leave, said, "The Yankees
are holding the Boulevards in great strength." Passing through
the back of the front in a car I saw large fresh shell-holes beside
the bridges at Bac St. Maur and Berry au Bac, and other bridges
and culverts had just escaped a hit. A lot of civilians were on the
roads, tramping to the rear. Each family had a cart or hand-cart,
no more, with such bedding, utensils and personal chattels as are
most needed. The women mostly carried some small thing, likely
a cherished article picked up at the last moment; one had a looking-
glass, and one her wedding wreath. All were resigned, dry eyed.

Rejoining, I found H.Q. packed into La Rolanderie with C
and D Messes; this is the only time for a year that H.Q. has not
kept itself to itself. Artillery Farm had been given to a Company
this time. The Battalion has been on fatigue on L'Armée Switch:
réveillé is at 3.30 each morning.

March 21st.—Thursday. At 4 o'clock a dispersed shelling of our
area, and the muffled rumble and dull thudding of very heavy
gun-fire in the distance, woke me. From the door of the hut I
saw our working-parties going out. There was a trace of bromine
in the outside air. The morning was ideal for getting all the moral
effect of gas shelling, windless with a ground mist. Visibility may
have been 100 yards, not more. The drum-fire was in the south
and not nearer than Arras. It seemed plain that there was no
infantry attack on our front, so, after dressing partly and seeing
that my gaspirator was in order, I lay down again. At 7 o'clock
I rose and dressed. The working-parties were returning; they
had worked in gaspirators. Two men had been killed and one
wounded slightly by a shell; these were our only casualties for
the day. The enemy was now putting over more distinctly
mustard-gas shell, but in such small amount that gaspirators had
not to be worn; it didn't harm the poultry. On a tree-top in
the pure air a blackbird sang rapturously. The shelling of our
area ceased at 8 o'clock, and the mist soon cleared. The rest of a
fine sunny day passed in quiet round the billets. The gunners
estimated that there had been two field batteries, one 5.9 how.
and one 4.2 how. in action on our front. Heavier stuff was fired
on gun positions and communications all day; some 11-inch shell
fell in Armentières, and a naval gun fired on Aire. Our Artillery

did not reply. In the afternoon we learned that German guns were in action from the Swiss frontier to the Channel, and there were hushed references to an "obscure situation" down south. Two large and four small German destroyers were reported sunk off Dunkirk. The affair took on a much more modest guise later. By evening there was quiet everywhere, and a waxing moon shone in clear air.

March 22nd.—A bright genial day: very quiet. The buds of the big, early trees are beginning to open; hedges and shrubs are about a week behind those in Kensington Gardens. A white cloud in the south is as if a great mine had been blown, more likely it is a fire or fires: the situation there is very bad. A big white cock in the farmyard puts the wind up some of us; his conversational voice, and Spring has come, is like the coming near of a heavy shell.—A raid is in rehearsal by A and B Companies and a platoon each of C and D. The idea is Moody's, the detail and its exposition Radford's. I foresee trouble over rational artillery co-operation, the authors won't be allowed to arrange it directly. Two days after this the Brigadier came to a rehearsal, questioning and axing, and pulled the scheme to pieces: everyone was fed up, its authors went on strike, and there was no more about it.

March 23rd.—Like a day in June, with a slight haze: two bats flying about must think it is June, or has their winter sleep been broken by removals. The furniture has been taken out of La Rolanderie. The occupants of Streaky Bacon are most indignant at having to go. Not a shot has been fired on this front for two days. More gas projectors are being carried into the line. Our Germans had a gas alarm the other night, whistling and banging gongs. The evening mist rising from this reclaimed marsh had deceived and scared them.—A division has been taken from the Corps to go south. The German claims, where our front down there has crumpled up, are not excessive measured in frontage and with 30 divisions attacking. We are back on the old Somme line; so the Germans have recovered in two or three days what we needed months of toil and slaughter to take from them. They *March 25th*—called the 21st Michael Day, it has been the German infantryman's day. He has been checked now, or is waiting for guns and supplies to come up. Our Third Army claims to have inflicted four casualties for one.

All our leave is stopped, officers on leave have been recalled; all Courses and Army Schools have closed down. The miners and engineers officials, not satisfied with having held up recruiting for three months, are making more trouble. And when every command in the Army has its hands overfull some fatuous person has found it a fit time to thrust a General Education policy on G.H.Q. Divisions are to become hot-beds of culture; lectures are to be organized on a University Extension model and to a matriculation standard, it is said, although instruction in the urgent job we have on hand is suspended. It's a scream. Yanto has been appointed Brigade Dominee. (This absurdity was held in abeyance till operations had ended. Carried out on a modest scale, it helped our small Army of Occupation to pass the time on the Rhine.) Amid so much that is depressing the sight of a uniformed peasant, on leave, at his plough heartens me. That was not how the men saw it. The prevalent feeling among them was that the civilians round about were so cool in the midst of what had been happening, ploughing and sowing in view of the German observation balloons, that they were "not genuine." Nowhere did our men take greatly to the French people, and in some places they disliked them.

Because of the withdrawal of divisions from here about, the G.S.O.1 came and arranged a new disposition which will keep us in the line for twenty days on end. One man is to pretend to do what was once the job of a section. There is said to be nothing between us and the sea but a raw American division near the coast.—After dark we went up to the front by tracks over the top: all Companies in. The state of the trenches proved the accuracy of the German Intelligence; the evidences of his shelling on the 21st showed that the site of our every dump, water point and trench mortar was known.

March 26th.—Yesterday was showery and chilly, to-day is clear and sharp. C Company has been sent back to Fleurie Support. Our orders are to potter away at the new resistance line although the German patrols are as free as they were weeks ago to circulate about our posts to a depth of 800 yards. A most informing note on "wiring," circulated by G.H.Q., is a scathing indictment of the method on this front. The Third Army had strong outposts and strong wire in front: it withstood attacks until it had to withdraw, its right being outflanked. For the Fifth Army, which took

over a very poorly wire-defended position from the French and
was very thin on the ground, the plan was for the outposts to fall
back on their supports. That may have been the best makeshift,
but it is the beginning of "retire" for the quality of troops we
have now, and the movement gains momentum if the attackers
follow up.

March 27th.—Still pools have a film of ice: the wind is south-
west, but it won't rain. The Companies are short of water owing
to difficulty in distributing it so widely.—Four days ago Corps
issued a warning that German agents, dressed as British officers,
were sowing alarm and disaffection in the villages in rear. To-day
a chit from Division says that "two suspicious looking officers"
are at large asking for various H.Q.; they bolted when covered
by a revolver. Wasn't it loaded?

March 28th.—The German claims are 40,000 prisoners so far,
guns and machine-guns by the hundred. The Kaiser spills over
appropriate pious bombast. There are two gaps of unknown
width in our retreating line; we had no Reserves to put in, and the
French won't move theirs. The Prime Minister, who heralded any
success we have had hitherto, has—characteristically—let Bonar
Law announce our disasters in the House of Commons; now he
has had Gough, G.O.C. Fifth Army, dismissed for a disaster that
lies at his own door.

During the night a S.W.B. patrol went through a retrenchment
on the railway, an old gap with new wire behind it, and identified
a fresh division opposite. We are sending a platoon of A Company
to learn what division is on its front north of the Armentières–Lille
road. They will have to cross two belts of very old wire. The
senior Company stretcher-bearer is too drunk to help with arrangements, but up to any heroism. We go south to-morrow. That
was told to half a dozen of us at H.Q. as a great secret, it was to
go no further lest a man be lost on the raid and give it away under
examination. The whole Transport heard it at Refilling Point,
and gave it out with the rations.

March 29th.—Two signallers were sent over in advance with a
line ready to be picked up by the raiders: needlessly, because it was
to be a dash-and-grab raid. With the unconcern our men usually
showed they put a round iron bar through the square tin hole of
the drum and clattered across, anxiously but unharmed. On

second thoughts the raiders did not take a telephone.—There was a clouded full moon at 3.25 when our guns opened. They had fired only a few shots when a German gun replied, and with rapid fire traversed our jumping-off ground, missing by feet only : it was quite unpleasant while it lasted. At 3.30 two officers and 35 other ranks dashed over. On getting near the post they heard the garrison bolting along the duckboards; a fat man, who fired a Verey light, was seen at the rear. Our guns' preliminary puff, which was imposed on us, was enough to give away the Show. Except at the post the breastwork was found more dilapidated than our own, there was little but the brushwood revetment; much of our communication trenches consists of no more than that. When all was quiet again a German signaller lamped a general call and a message in German, followed by the remark in English, "We made you suffer." We had three casualties. As one of two Lewis-gun teams which covered the flanks was following the raiders in "Eileen" fired on it : two men were wounded, both on the left ear. A little later a gas guard at Mosquito Palace, 800 yards behind the front, was hit by a traversing machine-gun—on the left ear. After seeing the last man away, something broke under my feet and I hung from the arm-pits in the man-hole of a sewer.

A North Lancs battalion of the 34th Division, come from the south to convalesce, relieved us. Their Brigadier, Chaplin, lately O.C. The Cameronians, looked us up. They were at Croisilles, the left of the German onslaught. Although they got a mauling and had to draw back he's sure they gave more than they got. The R.T.O. at Frévent told him of a wounded officer prisoner saying that the attack had not gained enough ground to bury their dead in—which was hyperbole.

March 30th.—The relief was very badly arranged. Our last Company was straggling into Sailly-sur-la-Lys at 5.30 a.m. Half the Battalion is at Bac St. Maur. Both villages are crowded with refugees, so billets were hard to find. Looking for mine, I saw a notice on a door—"private, 2 Ladies"—whatever was behind it. Everyone is feeling a bit done in. Working hours have been long, sleep little and broken; my sleep for three days—2, 2$\frac{1}{2}$, 3 hours, and on the go nearly all the time bar meals.

' This [1] was a most unpleasant tour for the Companies in front.

[1] Briercliffe.

They had been fretted by the long suspense and by frequent warnings that Fritz was coming over. They knew what he had done in the south, and felt that our poorly defended, thinly held line was at his mercy. The schemes for forming defensive flanks, if the line broke anywhere, were looked on as so much paper, for there were no troops behind to bring up. We discussed these things and the consequences with the devastating frankness which our very doubtful position engendered. We had no illusions. . . . A number of D Company had lost their voices from gas shelling, so it was a most nerve-racking job to go round the isolated posts, which were so few and far between, with the knowledge that a jumpy sentry who couldn't challenge might just as readily fire at one as not. The only way, on approaching a post, was to make a noise to assure the sentry, but, as one never knew that a German patrol was not hanging about, the method had its drawbacks. . . . I spent the night of A Company's raid prowling round those miles of unoccupied trenches. It was my birthday. Some comforting pessimist, after commiserating with me on having to spend such a day in such a place, said that I need not worry since if Fritz attacked, and everybody said he would, I would not have such another. The backwash of the raid seemed, at first, to our jangled nerves to be the beginning of the inevitable. . . . I have never felt more thankful than when night brought the relieving division. I spent most of it searching for a young cousin in the relieving battalion, and arrived at D Company's billets with the milk. It seemed all wrong that such a weak and badly knocked-about division should be put in where our comparatively strong and fresh division had been lost in space. They must have been just walked over, though they put up as good a show as they could. My cousin was killed a fortnight later leading his company in a counter-attack.'

The Companies marched from Bac St. Maur at 10, from Sailly at 11, to billets at Le Sart which were good, but terribly crowded owing to refugees. Not much damage had been done at Estaires and Merville except to the windows. Their inhabitants had all gone, or were going, to the Bordeaux area. H.Q. roadside lunch was stuffed chicken: a belated celebration of Yanto's birthday. "À la Fleur de Printemps" is much too poetic for an estaminet name; but "L'Arche de Noë," Noah's Ark, might be any old pub at home. We left behind a R.F.A. canteen called "The Step

Inn"—to which had been added "and stagger out" : quite in the French style. There is some rain, not enough to check the movement of German guns and transport.

March 31st.—Easter Day : blue sky and sunshine, grand black and white cloud effects. A morning mist seemed to rest on the Forest of Nieppe ; the reality was the charming effect of sunlight on opening buds. Civilians filled the parish church to the door for morning service. In the afternoon they sat out of doors in groups, gossiping and drinking beer. Our voluntary services did not draw one worshipper among them all, to the padres' unholy indignation. —We are adjured to practise rapid loading. Such is G.H.Q.'s woeful discovery of our Army's training.—At long, long last the French reserve has moved and recovered a little ground.

CHAPTER XVII

The Ancre Valley again—Albert–Hamel: The Germans in
Bois Grenier: A spent blow: Wind and Gas—An Opera-
bouffe raid—Tom Fool's errands: Hamel raid: Ancre crossings

Contributors:—BRIERCLIFFE; CHARLTON; CHICK; LL. EVANS;
      E. J. GREAVES; CUTHBERT JONES; KENT; MOODY; NICKSON
      RADFORD; RICHARDS; TURNER; YATES

Sketches:—5, 11, 22, 23, 24

April 1st.—Up at 5.15, we marched at 7, entrained at Calonne,
and started at 9. St. Pol has been shattered by German bombers
since I saw it. An adjoining wood is glorious with daffodils. We
arrived at Doullens at 3 o'clock. As at Calonne, the Divisional
Canteen handed out cigarettes, chocolate and biscuits. For a cup
of tea which tasted like our ration, sugar and jam which were
certainly our ration, a mouthful of bread and omelette, a couple
of resetting sluts in a café charged 3 francs. Since the Transport
is going by road all the way the men carry a blanket each, dixies
and Lewis guns. As dark fell a halt for tea was made at Beauval,
a large factory village. We marched off again in starlight, the
moon not up. The navigation lights of a procession of our bombing
planes going on their baleful mission were like constellations adrift.
An estaminet on a breezy height is well named "Au Bon Air."

It is told of our douce Scotch Commander-in-Chief that, coming
from a big Conference at Doullens in the Summer of 1916, he
stopped at this point, the highest on the Amiens road, to enjoy
the beauty of the scene while he ate his sandwich lunch. The
valley of the lower Somme was in front, and behind him the
ridges to the battle zone. After finishing, he looked at the house,
humble as any other wayside estaminet, and sent his A.D.C. to
ask if they could be given coffee. They were welcomed, and
served in the usual public room, all bare plain deal. Car after
car passed carrying Generals and officers of their Staffs from the

Conference. Mightily tickled they all were to see the C.-in-C.'s car, distinguished from every other car by the Union Jack on the bonnet, drawn up at that door, and to think that the C.-in-C., of all men, was inside. Everyone but he knew that half a dozen daintily appointed rooms lay beyond that in which he sat. The house was owned by a notorious Parisienne who had staffed it with some winsome daughters of Rahab, and ran it as a select house of the kind. It had turned out a profitable investment.

We arrived at Villers-Bocage after midnight. The men marched well; less than a dozen fell out, two of these have mild influenza of which a few cases have appeared again. There was a remarkable absence of gun flashes. Fritz has been quiet for several days, but we are not to have the promised and needed two days rest. The entrance of the C.O. and myself caused two Ordnance youths to scramble out of comfortable beds; the one who gave place to me looked quite amiable about it, because of my greying hair perhaps.

April 2nd.—Up again at 7.30, having slept like a log for six hours. The village is full of troops, and refugees from the area up to the line, ten miles off. Our landladies, two handsome middle-aged women of superior type, expended themselves to help us. They put up with discomfort cheerfully, gave the men their own pillows, sewed on buttons for the C.O., did sundry other little obligements; and they were not given the loaf of bread they might have liked. Instead of the ordinary refugee's goods, some bedding and utilities, they have packed for removal their fine linen and other dainties. They bade us smilingly "chasser les Boches," and did not know quite how to take it when I answered lightly, if the Boches don't "chassent" us. We started at noon. The head of the column took a wrong turning, adding three and a half miles to the route. The detour to Rubempré took us through Rainneville too: then on by Hérissart, Contay and Warloy-Baillon. Warloy was gaudy with large English posters advertising a whisky, custard powder, railway excursions to Edinburgh, Colwyn Bay, and our "breezy East Coast." During a halt our former Brigadier, Robertson, came along; his Division was coming out of the line. It is "one of three that fought back from the Cambrai front for days," he told a few of us whom he recognized, "lost only 2500 men and took a big toll of Boches." He was very jaunty about it all. We passed eighteen dead horses and two broken limbers, the result of a direct hit which exploded the ammunition in a limber. For much of the way we were passing the country people clearing out. A woman, still in her second youth, very fat and quite composed, shared a cart with a breeding sow and a caged parrot; an ageing woman, wan, patient-looking, stooping, led the horse. The day was hot and the march trying; the men got fed up with being told—"it's only one kilometre more," they ached with every weary pace: sore feet, that had not been washed for a week or more, and fatigue, caused 60 to fall out. The Drums played wonderfully, as last night when Hedges burst the big drum. "What's the use of worrying" always met with some response. We got into Hédauville at 8 p.m. very tired: billets filthy. New unwashed socks are not the best to march in.

April 3rd.—I slept from 11 till 8.30 in a quaint bed, a full-size, high-sided wooden crib, likely made for an adult imbecile or a demented grandparent. We watched the sudden departure of our hosts. Our breakfast was cooking, the table was laid, when stove and table were taken without a word and put on the farm cart. A sack, or two, was filled with potatoes. The daughter held the hen-house door while her mother went in and tied the fowls by the legs in threes, in which bundles they were put in baskets and loaded on top of the furniture; a few fortunate fowls were tied singly to various articles on which they squatted. Then a heifer calf was tied behind the cart, and, struggling violently, was belaboured out of the yard by the grandmother. She had been wailing all morning, "No bon la guerre! No bon la guerre!" The home was on the road in fifteen minutes. The young woman remained behind. Why?—or why not? She is a "useless mouth" returned from the other side of the line, expectant to a German, she says, and vows she will destroy the child.

The G.S.O.1 2nd Division, Clayton, formerly O.C. 5th Scottish Rifles, came to lunch. He gave a good deal of real detail of fighting back from the Cambrai front, and was not at all jaunty about it. After the first day the German artillery played little or no part; the infantry advance was made with machine-guns at regular hours, 9.30 a.m. to 4 p.m.: he had no more than 1000 rifles on a brigade front, so it was not possible to prevent gaps through which the enemy filtered, compelling farther withdrawal: the 2nd Division was Third Army's right flank; the flank was open, there being always a gap of 2 or 3 miles between them and the Fifth Army : the long and the short of it is that our Army is not trained to real fighting. Bearing on his last remark, a recent note of Ludendorff's is the acutest comment I have yet seen on the conduct of operations— too much trust is put in mechanical means to the neglect of manœuvre of men. Although the criticism is of the German push it is more applicable to our operations ; it needs exposition, but it goes down to the root of the matter.

We are in V Corps, Fanshawe's. The Division is broken up as Corps Support ; our Brigade supports the 2nd Division which now has the Ancre between it and the enemy. The Brigadier has *April 4th*—gone sick, Cockburn is commanding. Rain is not an unmixed blessing. More than half the Battalion strength is digging, the others are practising loading—loading! Officers are reconnoitring at Englebelmer.

April 5th.—The Brigade has been on an hour's notice to move since midnight, but no one slept less soundly. Our other Brigades have gone to meet a German attack between Albert and Aveluy ("Aveloy") Wood, made at 7 this morning. Early reports understated the German success ; the counter-attack failed. Our Brigade has been transferred to Army Reserve. Companies are on the range at last. Officers are reconnoitring again. The day is gloomy, there's more rain. The new "Cavalry" Tanks, "whippets," are armed with machine-guns only, are easy to manœuvre and do fifteen miles an hour instead of three, like the old heavily-armed pattern.

April 6th.—A peculiar acoustic effect here made a local strafe sound as if it was behind us. The Brigadier has gone home. Carton de Wiart, V.C., D.S.O., sans an eye, an arm, and with only one sound leg, has come to command : sharp work. He was wounded again about a week later, his sound leg being broken. In the meantime he had left us, he had come to the wrong address, and Cockburn commanded again.—Digging has gone on by night ; all nights have been dark, and sometimes wet ; the diggers have been shelled and had a couple of casualties.

April 7th.—At 6.30 p.m. we marched by Warloy and Contay to Hérissart ; still showery, the roads very muddy ; lorries carried packs, and the men marched well. Aveluy is now reported recaptured. (Erroneously.) Bombers came over after dark.

April 8th.—Wet. The Battalion purchase of War Savings Certificates for March—£5, by Corporal Maggs.

'TIS HUMAN TO ERR,
TO BULLY A MAN WHO ERRS IS INHUMAN.

When on a sanitary round I found this cry from the head, written in block capitals by an artist's hand, in a privy: the first time I've seen any writing or drawing in such a place used by the troops. Has some sensitive, useless soul in the ranks been put on sanitary duty, or a feckless officer been told off by an efficient C.O.? It's of earlier date than our coming here.

"Champagne" containing raw spirit, at 10 francs the bottle! and wine fortified with illicit rum, are causing a lot of drunkenness. Half a mile from the billet the senior stretcher-bearer lay for hours, quite incapable. A notoriously thirsty sergeant returned off a month's re-engagement leave to find strangers to him as C.S.M. and C.Q.M.S. He arrived in a reckless mood, and had made himself more reckless before a difference arose on pay-parade about his seniority and credit. At the end of it he emptied a dixie of hot stew over the Orderly Officer, also a stranger to him. On personal grounds there was more sympathy for the aggressor than the aggrieved, but he was given a five years sentence. In peace time he never would have been anything but a private, often in trouble. There were misgivings when he was promoted, and he was one who oscillated in rank as occasion raised him and temptation led to his fall. When others were anxious he stood square looking to his front, and, seeing nothing, would speak words of comfort. His was the repose of the blessed, the bedrock people who know that troubles, coming from within or from without, are a part of all life, and hold that it befits a man to stand up to them, and time enough, when they come.

April 9th.—Last night was too damp and misty for air-raiders. A postulant has come to the Brigade, and been chased away by the G.O.C.; he was not a success in his last brigade.—The meat ration at home has been reduced.—French ill-will is overcoming French greed. In shops at Doullens, and in billets, the people are refusing our men attendance; they blame us for letting them down: "Anglais no bon," they say with scorn. They are confirmed in this notion by the partial success of the French divisions from reserve which counter-attacked near Amiens when the German advance had been overstretched.

April 10th.—Practice in rapid loading is again enjoined by the Powers Above. A new German onslaught is reported. From Givenchy to Fleurbaix "the situation is obscure," which means that our divisions up there, already battered down here, are being *April 11th*—swept in front of the advance (Stockwell's fresh Brigade held Givenchy.) The German front is at Lestrem, the situation is obscure at Croix du Bac, near where we rested for a few hours ten days ago ; the Germans are in Plug Street and on Messines Ridge : so the ground that cost the sweat and blood of months last autumn has been lost in a day. (A premature report, and reflection ; the Germans failed to take the Ridge until the 12th, our Army was not withdrawn from Passchendaele until the 17th, or back to Ypres until the 27th.) Where will he butt in next ?— All the guns captured from the Russians, Italians, French and us are not saving the tuneful bells of Belgium if it's true that they are for smelting. But Fritz is not taking the leaning statue off Albert Cathedral. Does a dash of superstition prolong its giddy pose ?

We moved off at 5.30 a.m. The C.O. remained with our Surplus of 160 who were dropped at Contay. When we passed the Drums they played "Good-bye-e-e," which some thought in bad taste. Our trench strength is about 95 per Company. The day became warm by noon. Dark was falling when a tranquil march ended between Hénincourt and Millencourt. H.Q. rusticates in a spinney ; the Companies bivouac in the open. The men have had no great-coats since coming to these parts.

April 12th.—The night was too cold for sleep, then the Companies were kept on stand-to for three hours. The dawn magnificent : an azure sky and glorious sunshine all day. Spring's touch is on the land and birds sing. The young grass and the sprouting crops that are little likely to be harvested are brilliant green, spotted with red or slashed with white where shelling or trench digging has thrown up the surface soil or underlying chalk. Our spinney is bursting into leaf ; there are catkins on a willow, a blackthorn brake is in flower, and anemones deck the ground. Below, in a small park, ducal coronet on the gate, is a large winged-château, as featureless as a factory, like quite a number of the less old French country houses. An estaminet in Hénincourt, "Au Petit Caporal," has a portrait of Napoleon on the signboard.

There are 600 to 1000 yards of Nomansland here, and both sides are wiring themselves in. The line is much as it was before July 1916, but villages are being shelled that were spared then; they have been cleared of their inhabitants now. Most of the artillery activity is ours, especially at night. Our reserves must have been enormous to replace our loss of guns and munitions, and allow such a volume of fire. If Lloyd George's speech about our numbers is true his refusal to maintain our strength three months ago is the material cause of our disasters, for the men were there, as is now proved, and it cannot be pleaded that they were withheld in ignorance. Except for the moral effect of the arrival of men many of the reinforcements won't have much value; they will be men with such long service at home only that they have no notion of serving out here. A good many of that kind, both officers and men, have not been long in wriggling home again. The new levies will consist largely of men who have been profiteering for far too long to accept this life with even the needed minimum of readiness, and their training will be sketchy in the extreme. As for the proposal to raise the service age to 50, no small part of my occupation, and most of my worry, comes from the men round 40. They do well for trench routine if severe weather does not last long and wake up their latent "rheumatism"; also, the strain of marching with pack for two days running causes them to give out if under the pressure of march discipline, although they could do it if grouped and allowed to come on in their own time. For want of a simple practical means of dealing with them for a day or two when they have been overtried they have to be sent to hospital, which is terribly wasteful. Our organization is for the trained Regular, it is not to be trusted to use the older men profitably. According to Orderly Room, of our eighteen-year-olds who joined in October–November, the largest number now left in any Company is 9. . . . It's odd that Jellicoe and Haig should have sons after a lapse of years, having had daughters only. Hereditary peerage must belong to God's providence, and no Salic Law nonsense. But "odd" is not the word for this: the Franco-British line, with a superiority of about 3 to 2, took months to gain ground which the Germans, with about equal numbers, have retaken in as many days. True, they were training during the months when we were all digging, because we were beggared of available men, and their training has been in field operations, not specialism on the square like our own.

There was a prolonged strafe south of us in the evening. A *April 13th*—starry night, and very noisy. A misty day was almost silent here, but the strafe to the south kept breaking out. Our Divisional Ambulance arrangements being seemingly nil so far, the Australians on our right have agreed to clear us if necessary. An Anzac medical officer asked about the morale of this Division. Significant. Is every Anzac sick at the failure of the Imperial Troops, as they call the B.E.F., to hold? Is the issue of rifles to the heavy artillery, coupled with a hint not to pull out so soon another time, a G.H.Q. reflection on them or on the infantry?

The C.-in-C. tells us "our backs are to the wall." His men are asking, "Where's the . . . wall?"

April 14th.—A wet night: the day misty, raw and wet. The Battalion was digging all morning: extra Lewis gunners are being trained.

April 15th.—The quietest night here so far; and a stove in the shack makes life better, for both days and nights are chilly: Spring hangs back.—At last we have a Brigadier, a genial pleased-to-meet-you man, Hulke by name. Inactivity is most boring when a very limited kit leaves no room for books. The men digging, as yesterday. Harrowing the plough round the guns to efface tracks contrasts with a preference for visible skylines by detachments coming and going. On a calm evening three days ago a ration-party, straggling through scattered trees on a crest, made a wonderful silhouette in an atmosphere suffused with rose from a glorious western sky.

April 16th.—The morning being misty our neighbours, the heavy guns, were extra active before daylight on likely assembly positions. —A rest day for the men. The C.O. and the Count are embroiled in a squabble between Brigade and Division over A. and Q. affairs. There's been a great to-do at H.Q. over ammunition deficiencies. Yates has made up, although scrounging is not so easy as formerly.

'The [1] outstanding event of the six days at Hénincourt occurred

[1] Moody.

during an extra active shelling of Albert. I saw a direct hit on the already damaged tower of the Cathedral, which brought the leaning Madonna crashing to the ground. It happened about 4 in the afternoon. The incident caused a certain amount of gloom among those who thought there might be something in the saying that when the Madonna fell the War would end soon in the defeat of the people who perpetrated the deed.' . . . One of our six-inchers did it. Our prestige with the French people has fallen so low that it would be worth hearing what they say about it. The stump of the modern Byzantine tower still rises above the Millencourt ridge.

April 17th.—Our guns were distractingly active again all night.— The appointment of a generalissimo of sorts is long, long overdue. Conferences and Councils have nearly brought us to ruin. The more recent have been the most pernicious, because of their personnel perhaps. It's an old saying that a Council of War never fights. After this it may well be said that a War Council of Prime Ministers sets its own fighters by the ears. We will have to see how Foch works, for all or for France. He won't dare again to see an Army of ours put in a false position, and look on while it is being overborne. At the worst Clemenceau's adviser and the controller of the only reserve, a French reserve, will have to come into the open. He has the great advantage of coming to the front when Germany has probably overstrained herself. . . . It's possible, too, that with a Frenchman in Supreme Command we will be spared a repetition of the spectacle of a British Prime Minister pressing for a strategy that is impossible without Solomon's magic carpet, and addressing to an assembly of foreign journalists in a foreign capital sneers at a British C.-in-C.—not that the home public felt humiliated by it.

April 18th.—A wet night, the day dull and raw. Yesterday the enemy was reported in Merville and Bailleul. The 33rd Division has been in action near Neuve Eglise.—Our casualties for 20 days are 2 slightly wounded.

At 10 p.m. we made a peaceful move into the front line, C and D Companies, each on a two-platoon front; B is in support, A in reserve: our right is on the Doullens–Albert road. Bouzincourt ("Boosy") is a thousand yards behind the front. My quarters are the cellar of a damaged house in the village, a less safe but much more comfortable spot than H.Q., from which I am separated for the first time since joining the Battalion. The policy here is to refrain from adventures, and wait to see what the other side will do. A lot of work on the line awaits doing, by night—for the position is under observation and machine-gun fire. Our snipers *April 19th*—did not get into their hides until it was light, so they were seen; already half of them have been hit.

The people must have fled from here as they stood, so hurriedly that dishes have been left unwashed; I have not yet seen dishes left lying, or set aside, dirty in a French house. This morning two men, civilians, drove up in a cart, they were followed by three girls with hand-barrows, who chanced the single shells and rafales, and collected from houses. All the houses had been gone through before our coming, every cupboard and drawer ransacked; every floor is a litter of personal and household articles, and the odds and ends people hoard. Looting of a sort is allowed. A man changed out of a very lousy shirt into a frilly female linen garment. The Aid Post has a cow; she gives two quarts of milk a day except after a big strafe, when she may go dry for a day— "with shell-shock." There are a few hens and pigeons left which the men are catching. The cats always remain; and I've been adopted by a dog; he may have been tied up, like nearly all French dogs, and forgotten.—There was a sprinkling of snow last night, and slight snow showers throughout a sunny day.

April 20th.—Bright and keen.—One of the Brigade chaplains, who shares our cellar, defied his bishop, enlisted in the artillery, and was a bombardier when he was reclaimed and transferred. To save his gold denture and best kit from roughing it down here, he left them in the Divisional Dump up north which the Germans have captured, all but ten lorry loads. Now he wants to kill Germans.

The value of our loss of Ordnance Stores on the Fifth-Third Army front is put at £100,000,000: that includes 20,000 miles of telephone cable, 8000 of it in Albert. Seven Y.M.C.A. huts, 5 Church Army huts, and E.F. Canteen Stores are not included. Atkins chortles over the Canteen's huge losses: its prices are not popular. Mills's bills show that the devils have put the prices up further, many articles are cheaper in French shops. Ten days after this the Canteen was recouping itself with a vengeance. Under the guise of "giving a preference to the troops in front" its lorries were coming up as far as the Transport lines; for biscuits that had been priced at 4.75 francs 6.15 was charged, and so on. Later on it was learned that the large stocks of eatables captured in the Canteens were a great factor in demoralizing the German Army, for they proved that we were not so short of food as Germany.

April 21st.—At 6.30 a R.A.M.C. orderly roused me and said there was "something wrong" with my men. With nothing worse than rum in mind, although there never has been any such trouble, I hastened and found it was carbon-monoxide from the slow burning of our very poor coal in the ill-drawing kitchener our predecessors had dragged down to the Aid Post cellar. Our fellows would use it in spite of warnings of the danger, for there was no ventilation when the trap-door was closed since all openings had been blocked to exclude shell-splinters. The orderly had done as so many people do in circumstances of the kind, he dropped the trap-door again before looking round to learn where I was. Sergeant Jones, "Ol' Bill," was blue and stertorous; his assistant and '37 Jones, my servant—a faithful little fellow, were dead; they slept nearer the floor level and in the far end of the cellar. Wrapped in blankets and laid in the open with a fresh wind blowing over him, Jones came-to in a couple of hours and fell asleep. On waking he said he feared he would not get such a good job again if he went to hospital, so I kept him; he was almost himself again in a week.

Activity is restarting. The German line is the Ancre and the steep bank on the other side. It is covered by a widish belt on this side running up to a slight ridge which is occupied at night by strong outposts with machine-guns; these are in part withdrawn throughout the day. A Corps operation, centred about Martinsart, is planned to advance our line to that ridge, and therefrom have observation of the river. The 113th Brigade, made up of our 13th, 16th and 14th Battalions, and the 35th Division on its left, are to be engaged. In the forenoon the A.D.M.S. revealed to a conference of medical officers an alarming expectation of the German counter-action. His orders are frankly based on the idea that "everything on the front will be blotted out." His intention therefore is to subordinate everything to saving as much as possible of the medical personnel and material from destruction, so orders did not admit of discussion or amendment, for all their absurdity. Although the Battalion has quite a minor part in another Brigade's action we are put in charge of a single battle Aid Post: the medical officers of the battalions in action are to be in cellars upwards of a mile behind: the Field Ambulances, but for a few squads at the Aid Post, will be in the blue beyond. The difficulty in settling on a site for the Aid Post is that no one taking part in the operation knows where the German barrage line is; Cockburn, than whom no one is more likely to know, is sulky at being left out of the Show and won't speak. A small chalk pit on the lee of a slight rise was chanced, and the ordained evacuation route to the flank was pegged after dark: a long heavy carry it will be for the bearers even if dry as now.

April 22nd.—Up at 2.30 and out at 3 to put the bearers in position in the dark: a needless interference with sleep. During the night the 13th Battalion relieved C Company, which dropped back into support with B. To-night A Company will go from reserve to support the 16th Battalion: C—it was joined eventually by three platoons of B—supports the 13th: D, with the remainder of B, will occupy our original front. To minimize the chance of Fritz getting wind of what's afoot, zero was withheld even from Company Commanders until 3 p.m.; but everyone knew it from early in the day, an ambulance driver having told it in Bouzincourt.

7.30 p.m. The infantry went over when the artillery opened fire. There was no preliminary bombardment, but the machine-guns opened fifteen seconds ahead of the guns and of time; the front and volume of their fire proclaimed an attack. The German barrage dropped within seconds of our own. I went up to see the start, and watched one company of the 13th Battalion: the men soon gathered into suicidal little bunches. Our artillery barrage looked quite good, it was however very ragged: guns detailed to deal with well-known, vital machine-gun positions never got near some of them. There were many shorts; as I ran back to the Aid Post one of our 4.5s burst near me, 400 yards behind our jumping-off ground. Infantry representations had no effect while the action lasted. The Aid Post, as I found on reaching it, was in the back fringe of the German barrage, but because the first walking-wounded arrived on my heels we had to carry on. Although plenty of splinters flew about the pit during the night, and a few shells burst in it, no one was hit. The slighter early wounded came in the usual rush; the first stretcher-case was brought down in forty minutes. A. Company passed us; it was led by Cuthbert, who is "Five Franc Jimmy" to his men. I watched them go through the barrage. They did go well: little men overladen with Lewis-gun magazines stepped out gamely with heads up.

At 10 o'clock it began to rain. The ground became greasy, so the long cross-country carry over plough-land on a slope was more of a toil for the ambulance bearers: squads did not return. Ambulance men don't like the whizz of shells which sound as if close over their heads. These ones said they ought not to be worked so near a barrage. The few remaining hid in a shack which had to be pulled down to get them out, and when not watched they crept under its ruins. Their N.C.O. carried until he collapsed, but his men would do nothing for him. After one of their number had been wounded slightly they disappeared. For want of bearers a dump of wounded had to be made on the Albert road. By midnight 30 lay there. The number rose to 50, and remained at that for 3 hours although German prisoners and our Pioneer squads worked untiringly. Stores and ration limbers clattered up and down the road which was never shelled, but neither the prayers nor the imprecations of commanding officers brought an ambulance car, a bearer section, blankets or dressings. In the end infantry squads carried down the forbidden road into Bouzincourt in daylight, the last journey was made at 8.45 in the morning. It was learned later from the padres that the shelling in rear was negligible. The clearing scheme was clogged with groundless fear and aimless ingenuity; a little horse-sense would have got the stretcher-cases away six or eight hours earlier.

April 23rd.—At 2 o'clock the quiet of a couple of hours was broken. Things were quite lively for a bit, but no change took place in front. The 13th Battalion had gained an important point at Lone Tree, on our left, which gave observation of the river. Elsewhere little material gain had been made. One commanding officer said as much could have been got at trifling cost by walking out in the dark and digging-in. The width of Nomansland had become from 600 yards to 30 or 40 at Lone Tree. Brigade casualties were said to be 700, of which the 13th Battalion's share was 300-odd—our C Company did good work in bringing them in. Our casualties were 20. We passed back 40 prisoners. The

German infantry behaved badly. Two or three score came over
with hands up as soon as the attack developed; a party walked
down the Albert road and sat there waiting to be shown in, after
which their very youthful officer talked gaily to our equally
youthful "Babe" Ainge. German machine-gunners are splendid
as ever.

At dawn five enemy planes shot out of a low cloud, and flew
close and boldly over our lines: the Lewis-gun fire opened on
them was a feeble effort. In the afternoon when a German was
flying high just behind us his wings folded over his head and he
dropped like a stone. Half a dozen crashed or disabled planes of
ours, and one German, lie in the fields in rear. Our planes are
nearly always in the air, a German slips over just once in a while
on a special mission. Richthoven, the greatest of fliers and leaders,
was shot down the other day in the New Zealand lines. He is
claimed by one of our fliers above him and by the troops below;
the wounds of entrance and exit should show whose bird he is.

After dark some of the 13th Battalion's "missing" came from
hiding and asked for their rations. An officer of the —— Battalion
who also was shy last night had to be reported on: he pleaded
constipation. The Old Testament symptom is commoner.

April 24th.—At stand-to two parties of Germans appeared on
the front of C Company and the 13th Battalion, about 20 opposite
C. They tried to get back as soon as they were fired on. C was
steady, the sections well in hand: they're quite pleased with themselves. The Germans were in marching order, shaved and clean.
It's hard to think what was intended. The incident generated the
wittiest and most caustic story to which the Battalion has given
birth during the War, but it is wholly unrecordable. It also
disclosed our new S O S line, for some windy one beyond our
left fired the rocket. Our only casualties were from our own
6-inchers and 18-pounders. When the S O S was reported orders
came for the whole Transport to stand-to, ready to hook-in;
Hérissart was to be the first halt, they were not to be caught on
any account. So ammunition limbers are to be saved although
the infantry is reduced to throwing stones. It has always looked
as if men were of less account than wagons.

Official complacency over the Show is reminiscent of April 23rd
last year,—"South of Aveluy Wood we advanced 250 yards on a

1000 yards front." Had the return for the cost been less poor, and the margin between intention and achievement less wide, we might have had a ballad. At the best the enemy would still have had the high ground, and his snipers are deadly. His morale, however, has sagged badly. Fritz does not now just believe what it is thought fit to tell him. He had heard of our Cabinet changes as soon as we. Lord Derby's farewell letter to the War Office Staff makes it fairly plain that he has been let go now, the refusal of his tendered resignation when Robertson "resigned" having served its purpose. It is a sorry game that Downing St. plays; its backhanders are the Army's tragedy. It blames the weakened Army for not standing; its vaunted provision of reinforcements is its own condemnation.

To-night's expected relief is postponed: a prisoner says that one of their captives of two nights ago spoke about it. The H.Q. of all the 113th Brigade's battalions were shelled when rations came up. The enemy has got a lot of information somehow. And it is being said that a deserter, not from us, warned them of the attack.

April 25th.—A night's sleep at last, and feeling like it.—de Miremont's defence scheme goes on growing daily, there are now over twenty sheets of the squared notebook. He may know it, but Company Commanders have been getting so many orders, counter-orders, amended orders, that they don't. An offer to index its bewildering tangle was taken ill.—Relief by the 10th S.W.B. was not over until after midnight. de M. damned and blasted because their O.C. insisted on being taken round the line, *April 26th*—and made a five hours job of it. We went to cubby-holes in the sunken road south-east of Bouzincourt. H.Q. was dug into the bank, a space 16 feet by 4, and 6 feet high, lined with wood stripped from cottages. There was some shelling during the night. Our casualties for the tour are about 50, a large proportion from snipers and our own guns. Even I am lousy. The men have had one bath in five weeks and no change of under-clothing. The life is harder than it has been, and harsh conditions last longer. So far our health keeps good despite discomforts, very broken rest, and not quite satisfactory feeding; rations are no more than enough for the demands of temperature and work; quite a lot of the men are only 19 and 20. The French have in being a large unused Army. They know how to look after themselves while we hold the baby. Our tired divisions can't get rest, but there's a quiet confidence that we'll wear Fritz down. The Allied and German Armies are as they were last autumn, when a determined attack by either succeeded. A moral impulse tips the balance. Villers-Bretonneux seems to have been a brilliant little affair. Is it the turn of the tide ?

The day has been very misty, and the quietest we have had in these parts. The people behind think we may be counter-attacked. The Anzacs are relieving the 10th S.W.B. across the Albert road. Are the powers above as sceptical of the morale of this Division as are the Anzacs ? It is told of an Anzac battalion on coming here that the fur-coated Area Commandant pointed to a bare field as their quarters : they threw him into a neighbouring stream. Braithwaite, one of our Regimental officers, has a command with the New Zealanders. One of them, looking at his ample girth, called to another, "Say, Alf, that's where our rations goes."—Relief, *April 27th*—again by the 10th S.W.B., was complete by 4 a.m. We spent the day in a bank behind Hénincourt Château. In the evening we moved to another sunken road, south of Senlis.

April 28th.—The loss of Kemmel by the French is good, we held it anyhow, it should make them less uncivil ; but it has brought us back on to the walls of Ypres. And it has had another grave result. Since 1914 there has been a meteorological post near Ravelsberg where a wind-gauge had to be read every two hours. A staff of three Engineers grappled with the task—working in reliefs, two days off and one on. According to report Fritz has been shameless enough to bust it up. The more one hears through escaped prisoners of the poverty of the German transport, its few motors, its carts drawn by Russian ponies, by donkeys and dogs— all in poor condition, the more one admires what they have done. They have a splendid, flexible light-railway and trolley system to supply every bit of their front.

April 30th.—"The Ambulance is resting." That was the only reply to an indent on our Field Ambulance for dressings. Poor devils ! What next ?—The Battalion has been on short notice since coming out, but three Companies navvy each night on the Senlis Windmill line : nothing is done by day but overtake arrears of sleep.

Battle Surplus is It. The C.O. went off to some untroubled

spot, taking the surplus company commanders with him, after deputing the senior surplus subaltern to draw up a training programme and get on with it. Into the second day's work there butted a New Army major having political connections and official authority, but no obvious qualifications to exercise it, as subsequent days were to show. There was confusion, confounding, and threats of arrest were uttered. The C.O. was written to. He came and fulminated, first on the side of authority, then on that of his subaltern, whose programme and argument he made his own when bespeaking Division's approval, and getting it. Now we hear that surplus is being taken from the restored calm of Contay to the greater calm of Domqueur le Plouy in the Abbeville area. At this rate they ought to be home soon.

de M. took me over the Support battalion's position: very fagging on greasy slopes in a Scotch mist and drizzle. We came on a hare killed by a shell, the first small creature I've seen so killed since the woodlark. Truly we'll be thin on the ground, and we have had no training at all in manœuvre. The notion is just to fix the men in trenches, the siting of which takes for granted the direction of the enemy's attack. We argued: I that nowadays a company commander cannot control his platoons when attacked if they are in line—as is planned; he may have some control if they are in depth.

May 1st.—Still navvying: still grey and raw, the mist chills us.

May 2nd.—The Sun, the stranger! The first swallow; and the air is filled with the song of larks; the pall of mist has muted them for days, or muffled their song—and the guns. Now that we have shivered for a month "The G.O.C. has approved the issue of greatcoats."—In the afternoon Corporal Richards was overheard rebuking the language in the shack next the Aid Post lest it "put the Aid Post in the family way." At night we relieved the 17th Battalion between the Albert road and Lone Tree: A and B Companies in front, C support, D reserve.

May 3rd.—The G.S.O.1 came to H.Q. and discoursed on the Staff's latest scheme of a defensive battle. A battalion commander has done his part when he has placed his platoons on the ground, and even a company commander becomes a passive spectator of his subalterns' action. It affirms the point of the argument with de M. that the official defence is an affair of platoons, each for itself;

it is as if there were a virtue in unco-ordinated platoons in line that the same controlled strength in depth lacks, and the counterpart of our mechanical mass attack is just fixed defence. Operations, consequently, are made void of movement to meet thrusts or seize openings; the more is it so that the battalion reserve, the company a C.O. had to keep under his own hand, has now been put under Brigade, and Brigade, like The Happy Land, is "far, far away." One subaltern when told of the scheme spoke with rising indignation, and concluded, "I'm to stand and fight while everybody behind is legging it to the coast and the transports. No bloody fear!" What answer is there?

May 4th.—After early morning rain there was a fine growing day. Quiet enough here, but day and night the gunners to the south are as unresting as ever. Albert is strafed every day, and gas-shelled most nights. This afternoon it was smothered in dust by bombs: over 70 of our planes were counted in the air at once, as active as a swarm of gnats, and they returned later.—An officer of the 47th Division, which has just relieved the Aussies, spied tanks coming out of Albert. It was a hallucination, but the report of it caused violent quaking behind, and everyone was put on the alert. The best tank yarn belongs to a Corps H.Q. at the beginning of April. Hearing that the enemy had "broken through, and was advancing behind rapidly moving tanks of peculiar construction," Corps put its large force of camp followers in position for defence, and prepared itself for flight. The fact was that some farmers were salvaging machine-implements from their abandoned farms. Many stories of those days are more informing than satisfying. The people of Doullens seem to have seen the worst side of things of the sort. Plainly there was a bit of a rout about the 5th Army's "withdrawal": one division did not bring out a single telephone, so we are all on a reduced allowance.—One of Cockburn's men has been found in a shell-hole in front: three days ago he was told to dig, he has been digging at intervals ever since: he is inclined to grumble because no rations were sent to him.—The C.O. has gone to a brigade, taking "Mugwump" as his charger. de M. seems to have a pull at Division that looks like getting him the succession.

May 5th.—A heavy drizzle nearly all day.—The proprietor of "Charlie's Bar" at Amiens is said to have been shot: a wireless outfit and other incriminating discoveries are alleged. And there's a story of the shooting of a cheque-changer at Béthune.—Fraternization on the Division's front is to stop. Front and rear have never looked on such incidents from the same angle. To give point to the Order our guns are more active on the German line. Our ringleader in the exchange of news, views and cigarettes, that has gone on at Lone Tree, is the one-time confidant of commanding officers; he has been returned to duty after falling from favour, and falling foul of the Sergeant-Major. (Like other older men he ended his service on the Railway, waving a red flag at a crossing.) Saxons have relieved the Naval Division that was opposite us.

May 6th.—D Company had two posts blown in during the night, and two stretcher-bearers knocked out. Although we were over-officered to about 60 per cent. in February there was now a shortage in the line. D had only 2 officers on a front of about 400 yards. The Count broke off a strafe of a sleepy subaltern and beat it when he was told, to his surprise, that he was at Lone Tree, and could be overheard by the Germans. Officers from Battle Surplus were promptly sent for. Besides an officer's watches and fatigues, the list of daily routine reports and indents he had to send in, and their times, were now:—a.m. 2.30, one: 5, two: 7, two: 8.30, one: 9, one: 10, one; p.m. 2, two: 5, two; besides odd and emergency messages in and out.

The night was inky, and heavy rain set in at 9 o'clock, but de M. had B Company go on with a small raid on a post. The rain *May 7th*—continued; there were inches of water in the trenches, streamlets on roads and tracks. The raiders drew off on spying guns flanking their objective.

J. T. S. Evans and a man of A were lost last night. The other 4 members of the patrol say they were outflanked and fired on from a 'communication trench' 15 yards off, and that Evans sent them back saying he would get the wounded man in. Something of the sort was bound to happen. A, like their predecessors, have sent a patrol every night at the same hour, from the same spot to the same objective. Evans was never heard of again.

A strong patrol came to have a look at D. It was chased off by the moral effect of Lewis-gun fire rather than its accuracy, for no dead or wounded German could be founded afterwards; a casualty might have been carried away.

Radford, just back from Surplus, was jumped on, because of a report from the Brigadier, for allowing "most of" his men to lie about without equipment. An apology from Brigade soon followed ; the defaulting company belonged to another battalion. The Brigadier's inspection took him into D Company's line. He was alone. He had never been seen by Briercliffe, who 'was full of tales of impersonation, so he was shown little respect when he appeared, and a good deal of suspicion when he asked to see the Lone Tree posts. But he seemed quite a human person for a General, and rather amused at my close attention until he was identified.'—A Yankee captain, and a sergeant, arrived for three days instruction. "This is my birthday in hell," he began. He seemed a good fellow, said that Yankee divisions are rolling over.

Company officers are again fed up with the daily alarms—"an attack is expected"—which come from behind. Report says one day that cavalry have come to support us, another day that a division is being sent up in buses ; so it goes on ; and always that the French are behind. The latest alarm, "sure this time," is of a *May 8th*—big attack to-day. Pending its onset I sat, if the midges allowed, or strolled in the cottage gardens. Forget-me-not is the favourite flower, there's a lot of a white variety. The swallows here prefer chalk to clay, whether ready puddled or not, as building material ; one came nearly to my feet for it. Four cock-sparrows were rivals for a hen. Is there sex disparity, for one often sees such rivalries, or has she an alluring personality? She looked on the display of bravery aquiver with desire, just like a little kiss-me-quick who does not care who is her mate if only she is mated. After much strutting, posturing, pecking and shrilling the rivals flew off noisily, the hen after them, so I didn't see more of the comedy.

Relieved by the 17th Battalion : there was a good deal of shelling when we were going to the bank behind Senlis. We did not reach *May 9th*—the bivouac until 2.30, and I was kept from rest until 4 o'clock by intemperate axing.—de M. is to be C.O.—odd, when such very competent seniors are available.—The Germans had made a local attack astride the Albert road. The 17th Battalion stood. The Londoners didn't. And no wonder. J. O. Smith went over to their lines some nights ago ; he could find no sentries, and all the officers were asleep, facts which he mentioned to their company commander: going back later he found sentries awake, but not at their posts.

A glorious May day: the sun and atmosphere would gild any landscape; this landscape needs no gilding.

May 10th.—The Londoners are said to have retaken their line. Grey and drizzling again.

May 11th.—Fine: quiet by day, but we are too near the big guns to have anything but noise at night.—Two days of cold and wet followed: the whole Battalion was digging on each of them.

May 14th.—While it was yet early morning a flier slipped over in the clouds, dropped on to one of our sausages and set it alight: the observer escaped. The German could not go for a second sausage because five of our fliers were already after him. He made for home, all out. The chase was good to watch. He was brought down, but not until he could land inside his own lines: good man. In the afternoon the small area round the Aid Post was strafed, unaccountably, with 5·9s and 8-inch.—A number of the men are getting a bit out of condition, but to send them away will only make things worse for the others.

We relieved the 10th S.W.B. on the left front of Bouzincourt: C and D in front, A support, B reserve. This part of the line looks *May 15th*—on the ravine and Aveluy.—A cantankerous bitch with a small litter was found under a broken bed on to which the gable of the house had been blown: food and water from the Aid Post were arranged for, the family to be handed over on relief. Things *May 16th*—are very quiet, the weather still very fine. German planes came bombing in the moonlight.

May 17th.—In full day one of our airmen flew very low and deliberately to the line opposite, close to his targets, and dropped two or three bombs: one of his wheels was shot off as he came away. There are no complaints now of our observing planes. One flight amuses itself looping the loop, and with other antics, over the German lines.—To-morrow or the 20th is the next "sure" date for a big German attack here: no one in front of Brigade, bar the C.O., cares a damn.

May 18th.—Going round his line during the night one of our Company Commanders found seven out of twelve sentries asleep: one result of our discipline having gone down and down for long

months. In the morning our left was shelled because our neighbours were raiding.

We have a new Corps Commander, Shute, who is reputed a
tremendous strafer of his Command. When he was a brigadier
"S O S (an ordurous monosyllable)" was the code that passed
from signal office to signal office to give warning of his movements.
He is to inspect the Division when it goes out. A Divisional Order
to spit, polish and burnish has been issued in spite of G.H.Q.'s
standing order against burnishing. And a real training programme
is foreshadowed. The men are not fit to stand an eight-hour day
of the kind talked of, they need rest.

The days are gloriously fine. We endure in shirt-sleeves; the
village is being rifled for white shirts or chemises; I exist under a
black flowered-silk sunshade, having lost the blue-and-white cotton.

May 19th.—At dawn there was some shelling. At night, at 10.30,
there was a panic in rear on both sides, even our silent guns fired.
I did not notice who started it, so prompt was the reply, and no
one noticed what it was all about.

May 20th.—The unwonted quiet of the day and the methodical
gas shelling of our immediate communications, which began at
10 p.m., roused suspicion of Fritz. The hollow behind the village
was well saturated, and the gas drifted into the sunken road where
H.Q. details burrow. So little was it felt that no special precautions
were taken. A pleasant breeze diluted the mixture, and I preferred
the open to the horrible fug and opaque tobacco-laden air of
H.Q., a heavily gas-curtained den. The relief, by a 35th Division
unit, proceeded slowly because the incomers were chary of the gas
and of being mixed up in a night attack on new ground. There
was, however, nothing of that sort on Fritz's part. It was well
May 21st—after midnight when the appearance of one of our
Companies at H.Q. led me to send to divert others. The last of
us got away at 3 in the morning. The march was mostly across
country. It took us through the new unfinished lines of wired
trench on Senlis Ridge, which must need a lot of labour. A halt
was made beside Harponville aerodrome, which had been hurriedly
deserted. The sun was still below the horizon when we climbed
the ridge on which it was built, and it grew upon us. Its austere
lines and form fitted the site on top of a bare down. The half-
light, the solitude and the stillness gave to its rude simplicity so

strange a grandeur that one could forget it was an empty thing of deal and cloth, and colour camouflage; it might have been a relic of a bygone race or of some forgotten rite. At sunrise there was a scene of splendour as a vast expanse of downland, falling to the west, was unfolded from the shroud of mist rolling slowly off the hollows, and the early sunbeams lighted up here a field, there a wood or red roof, until all was colourful. The fresh night wind fell, and the morning was becoming warm when, marching again, and meeting no one, we came at 8 o'clock to a tented camp beautifully placed beside a coppice between Contay and Hérissart, and found Battle Surplus awaiting us. On the march a growing number of H.Q. men became troubled with watering eyes, a few with vomiting : gas cases plainly, and there were more during the day. There was a morning sick parade ; in the afternoon parties were seen from time to time. By then I had passed from the stage of blinking to finding the shimmering light unbearable, and having to keep in the sun-mottled shade of the young trees with other gas cases, hoping that the irritation would lessen and wear off. Later on candle-light could not be borne. In the morning I shaved *May 22nd*—with closed eyes, and took food through tears. An officer of the Ambulance had to be called in to see the sick. The total of cases sent away by the end of the day was about two score, I believe ; I was the last of them.

May 23rd.—A bath, and the passage of all clothing through a Foden oven, afforded much-needed comfort; the latter process got rid of all retained gas as well as vermin.—'Parry [1] found some edible snails, and served them up at H.Q. dinner. I can't say I liked them.'

Two weeks were spent in some mild training, gas drill, and rifle competitions ; and there was plenty of complete leisure to enjoy a very pleasant bivouac situated far enough from Hérissart, where the Transport was, to escape the night riders of the German Air Service. The weather was splendid, a couple of thunderstorms *May 27th*—cooled the air. Our new Corps Commander's inspection proved a good show, and brought the Battalion special compliments for its general-turn out. Yates scored by his unique doing-up of all steel helmets, and some subtle fancy-work in brightening-up the Transport caused the Corps Commander to

[1] Ll. Evans.

remark that ours was "the only clean turn-out in the Division."
The General's approval led to some easing of the tension at H.Q.
under which Company Officers had been suffering, but orders con-
May 28th—tinued to be untimely and contradictory.—The Battalion,
taking part in a tactical scheme, had its first experience of tanks. At
May 29th—a Divisional shooting competition we did so badly that
the other battalions, who had hated us for outshining them at the
Corps Commander's Inspection, forgave us their hatred.

Touche died, mourned by the whole Transport. Since he joined
the Battalion, by purchase, he had enjoyed a standard of living
unknown to the working dogs of the Continent. After the Summer
of 1915 he did no work. Age, ease and good living made him fat.
He was run over upwards of a year before this; he survived, a
cripple, cared for and carried from place to place on a wagon.

May 31st.—Our mild training was varied next by a pretentious
Brigade scheme for officers, runners and signallers—indifferently
June 2nd—executed. A voluntary Church Service was the next
variant. There had been no church parade for a long time.—The
June 3rd—long spell of fine weather broke.—A little excitement
was caused by the King's Birthday Honours List. There was some
grumbling at a mere "mention"; everyone approved Yates's M.C.
The G.O.C., Blackader, went sick during this rest: he was
succeeded by T. A. Cubitt.

Battle Surplus went off to Hiermont, on the Abbeville-Auxi-St.
Pol road, in charge of James Cuthbert. In the late afternoon the
Battalion marched to a hut-bivouac camp in Acheux Wood.

June 4th.—We took over the Mesnil front from the Hawke
Battalion of the Royal Naval Division. The enemy was quiet;
but among ourselves much confusion, and amusement, was caused
by the Hawke's "ratings" insistence on using naval nomenclature
for everything: thus—"quarterdeck" for headquarters, "Chief
Petty Officer" for R.S.M., "heads" for latrines. Their quarterdeck
was an ancient dug-out in chalky soil; its "heads" were on an
uncomfortably exposed eminence subject to a good deal of
"backwash."

The north-west of Aveluy Wood was in the Battalion's charge,
our right penetrated to a depth of about one-third. The Ancre,
bordered by swamp or drainage dykes, was 1500 to 1000 yards
distant at the bottom of a slope, and overlooked by our left.

At first A and B were in front, C was in support and D in reserve: the whole position was held by posts. All work was done by night, even in the reserve line where everyone was digging. Subalterns were again, after two years, required to work with their platoons. One, who had chosen a shell-hole to rest in rather than the unrestful company H.Q., looked up from sleep to see a very beautiful, shining youth who was poking at him superciliously with a stick. The sleeper arose, and was using his outsize to back the rude words with which he assailed a recoiling A.D.C. when, on turning round, he saw a very large and fierce-looking major-general, with two rows of ribbons, and a gleam in his eye. He was the new G.O.C. Charlton had been made wise about the G.O.C.'s obsessions, and had tutored his juniors. After asking some pointed questions, personal and tactical, the large personage leapt on to his hobby: "How many trench latrines are there, and where are they?" The R.Es. had installed the pattern he approved. He and the gilded one were piloted round them all. Having pointed to their simple mechanism he strode off seemingly pleased, though saying with a snarl that he would "remember" his guide.—Although the enemy artillery had been active only spasmodically on the front, the rear of the sector was under nearly continuous shelling, especially with gas that hung *June 8th*—about the sunken roads.—'The [1] Aid Post was across the narrow valley behind H.Q. I called on Christofferson[2] in the morning in time to assist at an operation on the spot, detaching a man's foot from a shattered leg.' In the evening two 17th Division battalions on our left made a raid. We co-operated by discharging rockets and adding to the general confusion, for which we were shelled.—The weather was again fine.

A raid in Aveluy Wood was proposed for us, to the amazement of those who knew the Wood—our part of it at least. There were those who, it seemed, never learned that warfare inside a wood is a totally different proposition from warfare in the open. D Company was now in the right front. In daylight and when in our own posts we knew the approximate location of the German posts, but when visiting posts at night it was the easiest thing to lose direction. The Wood was dense, and there was a thick undergrowth which made movement difficult except in the rides, but

[1] Ll. Evans.   [2] The New Medical Officer.

they were unhealthy to walk along, for Fritz had snipers in trees which overlooked them, and they were not innocent of pitfalls. To get from point to point through the trees direction had to be changed every few steps, because of some obstruction which would not give to the body. One's compass was in constant use to pick up direction again. The snapping of twigs underfoot, entanglement in barbed wire dropped on to bushes or hung from the lower branches of trees, were other troubles that had to be overcome. One man might possibly reach an enemy post unheard, a party couldn't reckon to get anywhere near a post. 'I[1] took out a patrol of four men. We lost touch at once, and I lost half the patrol after five minutes : lost myself for half an hour, wandered about, was fired at several times, beat hasty retreats, took compass bearings, tore my clothes and self on barbed wire, imagined every bush a Boche, and finally arrived in our own line to find that the rest of the patrol had got back somehow. I took another patrol out the next night : it was inky black. We made enough unavoidable noise to awake the dead over whom we often stumbled. I sent in an adverse report, and was chided by the Count who said Brigade might think we were shirkers ; but we heard nothing more of that proposed raid.'

June 11th.—The tour ended without incident, and we moved to *June 12th*—the reserve line. During the night we marched to a rest area, called the Purple System, at Forceville. The camp was a hut-tent-bivouac-cubby-hole conglomeration of dwellings. A much-used and very dusty road ran through it ; at the western end was a notice—"Please drive slowly," and at the other end "Thank you, P.B.I."—But for one shower the weather was still fine.

The Battalion was warned for a big raid on returning to the line. There is no doubt it was intended as a test, from Division's point of view, of this Regular Battalion that had been transferred to what was an entirely New Army Division. We were a Regular Battalion in name only. After a discussion in D Company Mess at this time Charlton took a census of his command actually in the line ; only six were Regular Soldiers, they were nearly all N.C.Os.

The area to be raided was the half-mile of road, and railway embankment immediately north of Aveluy Wood. We were to

[1] Charlton.

attack on the right, on a three-company front; our 14th Battalion
was to attack with us on our left: the approach was to be made
in two waves; the first of these would deal with the sunken
Aveluy–Hamel road, the second would pass through and deal with
the (supposedly) strongly held railway embankment beyond the
road: artillery and machine-gun barrages were provided. The
scheme, whosesoever it was, was handed out to us, we were given
no say in the arrangements. Because of that, of the circumstances
in which the order was carried out, and of the consequences, this
raid requires to be described at length. To the Company Commanders and their subordinates the operation seemed farcical from
its inception. They knew that the Germans had strongly-held
bridgeheads at Aveluy, Authuille and Hamel: that the eastern
part of Aveluy Wood was held as a salient, and that strong-points
at its re-entrants covered the Aveluy and Authuille bridgeheads.
Further, the Authuille strong-point still included an old Prisoners
of War cage of ours, which was on the front of our right Company,
and from it our objectives could be enfiladed; but between it and
Hamel there were no Germans by day, and only a patrol or patrols
by night. Apart, therefore, from the Authuille strong point there
was nothing to raid. The Brigadier apparently had not the courage
of his convictions to say that the Show was not worth while.
The new G.O.C., a fire-eater with a marvellous flow of language,
had never, as far as we could learn, inspected the ground or
considered the reasonable prospects of getting anything.

For six days we practised the raid *ad nauseam* near Caterpillar
Wood, on the sloping ground towards Lealvillers. The carefully-
laid-out tapes and direction signs made our trial runs look quite
fine, but the ground was unsuitable, and no one who mattered
suggested that anyone should go and look at the actual place.
The men were told no more than that the raid was to last about
45 minutes; and that the signal for withdrawal was a thermite
bomb, a large luminous shell or light of some description, fired
by a trench-mortar, its appearance was left to the imagination of
June 20th—each and all of us. On the seventh day we rested.
D Company was cast for the rôle of maid-of-all-work to the
other three Companies, the actual raiders. Charlton, F. L. C. Jones
and Pte. Tibbs 'were [1] the unhappy ones who had to spend five

[1] Charlton.

nights laying guiding tapes in Nomansland. After a fairly long day of company and battalion training we set out about 6 o'clock, arriving in the front line about 9. Sentries and any patrols had to be warned that we were going out in front. Laying tapes over ground sounds delightfully simple; but throw in innumerable shell-holes and small ponds, wire and iron stakes, the possibility of "stopping one," or of meeting prowling Germans; mix all these on a dark night, and the operation of distributing "millinery" —as Jones called it—by the compass was, to our minds, a good sample of hell. The tapes must not be too short, or they would not guide sufficiently. If they were too long they might be discovered, and the whole show given away. We laid over thirty tapes, some of them twice as we found they had been shifted— patrols were not too careful when they crossed them. Wire had to be cut away, or cleared to one side to make a path, as the tape had to be run out straight; someone had his work cut out to stop sentries loosing off when the tins, cans and old iron rattled on the wire when we cut it away.'

June 21st.—As the appointed day approached the weather turned wet. On the afternoon of our move there was a colossal thunderstorm with torrential rain. Everyone thought the raid would be washed-out in every sense of the term. About 9 p.m., however, we moved off. Everything was soaking wet. Throughout the seemingly interminable march of several miles a cold drizzle fell. Sometimes we had to wait for twenty minutes in the C.Ts., up to our knees and higher in water and mud, owing to blocks caused by stretcher cases coming down or stores going up; consequently the men persisted in climbing out on top, and every rifle got caked with mud. We took over from the 13th Welch Regiment. They were surprised the raid had not been called off owing to the appalling weather conditions; and they reported, encouragingly, that a strong German patrol had lifted one of their men from a listening-post a couple of hours earlier.—C Company was on the right, the strong-point was its special bit, then A, then B. The Companies were under strength, so D Company was divided among the other three, but Briercliffe was the only one of its officers detailed to go over, he was attached to B Company. About two hours were spent huddled in the front line, standing in water, shivering with cold, wet and dispirited; our bombs and

Lewis-gun equipment sank into inches of mud and slime; and the rum ration arrived too late to be dished out. About three-*June 22nd*—quarters of an hour before zero the covering-parties went out, and the final arrangements were made.

Nearly a minute before zero, 2 a.m., the trench-mortars opened fire. That gave the enemy notice to think, and when our artillery opened his guns replied instantly. As C Company was scrambling out of its overcrowded trench the covering-party, who had forgotten their rôle, came tumbling in among them. When the Company did get to its jumping-off line it found an enemy barrage just in front of it. While the men were contemplating what they had to go through a large phosphorus-like bomb exploded high over our lines, it was a huge affair. Quite naturally many of the Battalion took it to be the much-discussed signal of recall, fired at this time to signify that the operation was cancelled. C Company returned to its trench in confusion and would not be induced to get out again; so its contribution to the operation was the Company Commander, his runner and one other, who were joined by Sergeant Gill of D Company. A party of four could not involve itself with the strong-point, but it went down the slope, waited about the road and railway embankment, saw nothing of the enemy, and returned. A. Company were equally bad starters, so many did not leave the trench that those who did went back to it. B Company's trench was cut in chalk, very narrow and deep, and there was over a foot of water in it; the little men could not get out, they had to be lifted or pulled out. Then 'the Company started across as if on parade, in spite of some shells and an infernal din.' Going down the slope it accelerated to the double, and found the sunken road by falling into it—ahead of the 14th Battalion. The road was empty, obviously unoccupied for weeks. Every section was accounted for, and the second wave was sent on. No signs of recent occupation were found on the railway embankment. 'Within five minutes we were enfiladed by machine-guns in Aveluy Wood, and later a most accurate trench-mortar bombardment commenced.' About twenty casualties were incurred in the road and on the railway. The second wave went on through the trees to the river, and still found nothing. When it was time to return the trench-mortars had ceased firing, but the Germans had started traversing machine-gun fire along our line. In the labour and risks of getting the casualties 'over a skyline and through the wire as day was breaking, Charlton, as usual, turned up trumps, for he came out with a stretcher-party; and a young Nonconformist padre, called Jones, stood in a gap in the wire directing the party which way to go.' The 14th Battalion was said to have walked down to the river unopposed, and walked back; one of them chanced on a rusty machine-gun of doubtful origin, and took it in.

The worst of a raid is not always felt in front. Evans had arranged all signal communication, lights, codes, advanced stations, runners, etc., into what seemed a perfect scheme. 'My[1] own observation-post, carefully selected, was in a trench immediately behind our front line. When the guns opened I found myself in a German barrage, and there I spent the longest hour of my life. We were four or five men crouched in this trench; flashes, smoke and earth filled the air; the raided area to be observed and the raiders' light signals were completely blotted out; and all rearward lines were broken. The trenches around crumbled under the terrific counter-bombardment. Every second we expected a direct hit on the spot we were imprisoned in. Every moment seemed an hour, every minute an age. I feared to look at my watch for it seemed to be motionless. One of my men fainted under the strain. The relief we experienced when the guns lifted must be unbelievable to any but those who have lived through a similar experience. Compared with the raiders, the guides posted at trench junctions and crossings suffered disproportionate casualties during the counter-shelling. After the raid we returned to Forceville. The start was difficult because of the obliteration of landmarks by flood and shell, so due west over the top was the easiest way.'

It was a thoroughly bad Show from start to finish. It was futile in its aim, just a blow in the air. The organization was bad, for the guns and trench-mortars did not start together; the men were left in doubt or ignorance about things, and were, therefore, very windy. Finally, the raid should have been postponed because of the weather conditions. For all that, the indifferent morale of the Battalion at the time probably accounts for a good deal. Over a longish period Companies, with which H.Q. was little in touch,

[1] Ll. Evans.

had been tending to become coteries. The loss of seniority which the disbandment of battalions and the large influx of officers in February entailed caused much heartburning; transfers to the Machine Gun and Flying Corps were much discussed, and were being made. The senior N.C.Os. had long ceased to complain of slackness, they acquiesced, shared in it; and King Stork reigned. Men of D Company who were questioned said the machine-gun barrage upset them. It is doubtful if they had been told of it. It seemed to be only three or four feet over their heads, and its curious swish caused most uncomfortable feelings; they felt as if they were stepping out of the deep trench into a stream of our own bullets, and they did not like the idea of being shot at from behind.

In spite of the general fatigue a move was made in the evening to the support position at Englebelmer. Before the Battalion moved off the C.O. had it formed up, and delivered his verdict on the post-mortem he had held on the raid. His remarks were addressed to the men. Coming from him they were indiscreet, and were received with sounds and expressions of derision that were audible to the Company officers if not to the speaker. Morale *June 23rd*—was not improved by a visit from the G.O.C. in the afternoon; everyone was feeling sore enough before it. The Battalion was paraded by his order, but he had the men dismissed —"I don't want *them*." Addressing the officers he expressed his dissatisfaction in no uncertain manner. He questioned those who took part in the raid individually as to what each had done, where he had gone, and so on, and oftentimes cast doubt on the veracity of replies. A. Company was cross-examined first, then C. Radford was rash enough to mention the phosphorus-like bomb. He was promptly told he had invented it—Division explained it away subsequently as a "premature." His decorations were pointed to ironically. "You are a much-decorated young man, but I frankly disbelieve you," was the G.O.C.'s conclusion. 'In [1] truth, when Radford's Company would not move he said, "Well, I'm going alone then." His runner and one or two others followed him round the objectives of his front. To my mind this little band going out into the night, to meet they knew not what, for the honour of the Battalion is one of our real epics. Reward, however,

[1] Charlton.

is often in inverse ratio to the deed.' When the G.O.C. had
questioned Montgomery he passed by the other B Company
officers. Montgomery was an old soldier who had mastered the
art of putting a good face on a bad case ; here he had an unanswer-
ably good case. The facts of the operation were plain enough.
As the G.O.C. saw them, however, ' we damn well had to do the
raid over again, and damn well see that this time we made a proper
job of it, or else, by God ! we'd damn well go on raiding till we
damn well did.' As those addressed saw the parade ' it was a
contemptible exhibition for a General Officer to make of himself
in addressing others of very junior rank.'

Retribution in the form of a raid, or a series of raids, was decreed.
"One officer and a platoon will make a surprise raid on the enemy
line west of Hamel." A. Company found the scapegoat : try
though they did it's all they found, for there was no enemy there
to lay hands on. The fact was that after dark the Germans had
only a movable post or roving patrol between Aveluy and Hamel ;
it rarely went to the same place twice, and possibly did not go out
every night. Some of us thought one man was used to fire a
parachute light, lie low for an hour or so, then fire another light
half a mile away. He had a stretch of nearly 2000 yards in which
to play this game. "Joe" was the name we gave the sportsman.
It was this bit of work which gave the Staff the notion that the
Aveluy–Hamel road and railway were occupied.

June 24th.—"290 men for working-party under R.E. supervision
on rear defences" was not part of the retributory design, it was the
tale of the nightly corvée.

June 25th.—"Two officers and 32 other ranks" of B Company
were sent to attempt a cutting-out raid near Hamel. Germans
were seen ; the best that could be done was to fire on them,
casualties were inflicted but there was no possibility of getting a
prisoner, it was enough that the party got back without loss.
Two officers and a strong patrol of D Company sallied out on their
own, intent on freeing their fellows from the curse that had been
put upon them : beyond finding a few corpses, and being bothered
by the light operator, they achieved nothing.

June 26th.—C Company was given a turn with "Two officers
and 20 men." Unofficially all four officers went out, making four
parties. After beating an assigned area to and fro for four hours

they came in soaked with dew; that was all. The irritation in the Companies was not assuaged when it was found that no one at H.Q. had sat up, or been detailed to sit up, to receive their report.

June 27th.—"An officer and 20 men of B Company"; actually two officers went out. They made up their minds to catch "Joe" alive. They saw him coming, just one of him, and firing a light on the roadside. The two parties closed on him silently, but some-one was too eager, made a noise, and "Joe" bolted. He ran in such a way that neither party dared fire for fear of hitting the other. By the time the parties had located each other he had escaped among the trees. They chased him along the road to Hamel. In the dark and the eagerness of pursuit they found themselves almost on top of a strong-point at the road junction south of the village. A machine-gun opened fire, and bombs were thrown from the post. As the patrol had gone out lightly armed to get this one man they were in no case to tackle an alarmed strong-point; they were lucky, as was the patrol two nights earlier, to get away without damage. de Miremont was feeling the chill, badly, of our continued failures to get an identification; his jumpiness was common to the whole Battalion, whose morale was not improving. We continued to find the large nightly working-parties, and any R.E. officer's regular greeting was, "Caught your prisoner yet?" for the situation had become a joke in the whole Division.

June 28th.—After digging most of the night Briercliffe, who had been given charge of A Company, told the signallers to call him at a certain time, and retired to rest in his dug-out which was small but very deep. 'They certainly called me next morning, but they had to dig a way in as the dug-out had had a direct hit—and I slept through it.'—Moody was borrowed by Brigade as an extra Staff Officer, so Evans combined the Adjutancy with his own Signalling Duties temporarily.

At night we moved up to the front again: the night was quiet, the relief a good one. We were closer to the Wood than when last in the sector. There were two Companies in it, one in front —D, and A in close support; both were distributed in posts in short lengths of shelter trench.

June 29th.—A, B, and C Companies arranged a co-operative effort starting at 10.30 p.m., to get the elusive identification, and *June 30th*—a second at 1 a.m.; still without success.

'Living,[1] off and on, in a wood was a new experience for most of us. It gave us a primitive feeling to wake up after a few hours sleep and find trees and bushes all around and birds singing. There was still plenty of animal life; rabbits were fairly common, but I never heard of anyone having the luck to knock one over. Although the Wood was heavily shelled frequently it had not suffered very much, the foliage and undergrowth were still very dense. Gerry seldom used heavy stuff; he realized that spraying a wood with shrapnel produces better results from the flying pieces that cannon off the trees and cause ragged wounds. The sound of shrapnel as it strikes the leaves is very unpleasant, it is just as if an almighty hailstorm was going on. In the usual trench line or outpost we were always short of firewood, and it was not unusual for ammunition boxes and other public property to be burned, contrary to standing orders. Here there was fuel in abundance, but, as it was Summer, care had to be taken that the premises were not burned down.

In the daytime things were comparatively easy, it was a fairly simple matter to find the posts. At night, when out on the rounds, it was only by the sheerest good fortune that one stumbled into a post; to find one we were often reduced to standing still and shouting as loudly as we dared, praying that any answering call would not be by a German. The danger to guard against was surprise attacks. The field of observation and of fire was very restricted; the depth of clearance of the undergrowth in front of each post was only from three to seven yards, so a rush by the enemy was always on the cards. The only effective field of fire was along the rides, three to four yards wide, which traversed the Wood at intervals, but surprise attacks were made away from them because both sides had them well taped.—Sniping was one of the usual pastimes. Generally D Company had two men a day sitting up in trees, but from all accounts their bag was negligible. Our fellows never ran after the job, nor were they much good at it, as extreme patience is not a strong point with the Welsh. We thought the Germans were better at the game; we were obliged always to take advantage of all cover, otherwise they got busy; they scored several direct hits.—During this tour both Companies in the Wood sent out a couple of officer's fighting patrols each

[1] Charlton.

night. Noise was unavoidable and made these patrols risky, so
the Company Commander was always relieved when his patrols
got back safely.

One day there came to Company H.Q. a Battalion runner with
a memo. urging all ranks to buy War Savings Certificates. To
encourage the others I signed for a few and sent a cheque to
Battalion H.Q. I forgot all about the matter until some months
after the War when I received a book of certificates from the
Assistant Adjutant of the time of my purchase. I presume it was
made out then, as all particulars are entered in pencil; I hope no
doubt will be cast on their authenticity when I have to cash
them.'

July 1st.—A Divisional reshuffle was taking place, the 113th
Brigade coming in. Some good fun was provided in the afternoon
by de Miremont and his opposite number of our 13th Battalion
being unceremoniously chased out of Aveluy Wood by some
astute German shelling, and making remarkably good time over
the open to the sanctuary of H.Q. dug-out.

About 10 o'clock, just as the light was fading, a furious bombing
broke out at an isolated post on D Company's extreme right.
F. L. C. Jones, who was on duty, was in the second line at the time.
He jumped out, and, accompanied only by his batman and another,
ran towards the sounds, firing as he ran. When he got within
sight of the post a dozen or more Germans, under an officer, had
got hold of an undersized boy of 19. But for Jones's timely and
offensive arrival they would have taken more prisoners, for the
other five men of the garrison were wounded. The raiders withdrew, throwing bombs to cover their retreat. Charlton was very
early on the scene with a few men quickly collected. He found
Jones behaving like a heroic madman, dashing in and out of the
trees and bushes throwing bombs, shouting, and encouraging the
less wounded to follow him and counter-attack. As the raiders
had vanished he agreed it would be better to stand fast and prepare
in case they came on again. We all thought they would come
again when, a few minutes later, a heavy bombardment fell on
our front and right. It was so suggestive of an intended attack
that A Company moved up to reinforce D, and take over the
wiped-out post. As A was moving the guns lifted and laid a
barrage on our rear positions: that put the enemy intention

beyond reasonable doubt. It was now dark. S O S rockets went up along the threatened line of the Division on our right. The attack was made on our neighbours, and was beaten off. A. Company had a few minor casualties. Before this Charlton had been taking risks to clear his wounded that not everyone would take. Often, as now, in that closely planted Wood stretchers could not be handled, and the clearing of the mangled was a long and distressing affair. A hammock had to be improvised, by tying jackets together, to move a corporal with a painful and hopeless-looking belly wound, whose struggles must have lessened what little chance of life he had, a chance that was not realized. For the Germans to get so near the post unnoticed, to inflict casualties and slip away without loss, was a praiseworthy effort in a wood bristling with obstacles both natural and man-made. And Jones did extraordinarily well, his fearlessness was an inspiration to everyone. Relief, in the circumstances, was not completed *July 2nd*—until 4.15 in the morning.

The Battalion returned to the Camp at Forceville. Acheux housed the Divisional baths and the Canteen. In and round it there was a concentration of heavy stuff, large-calibred naval guns, that made conditions in the area most unpleasant at all times. During the day an extra heavy shelling cost the Battalion two of its best N.C.Os., Sergeants Mills and Jones. In a fine endeavour to rescue some wounded officers of another unit from a shelled billet Mills was killed and Jones died of wounds. Mills had been the very capable manager of the Canteen from its start, and Jones was the Medical Officer's right-hand man.

July 4th.—Our M.O. was determined to celebrate the Fourth of July with fireworks of some kind. In contravention of the Geneva Convention the Heavy gunners let him fire a round, so sending Fritz his message that "America is here."

The general tone and health of the troops was not good. In the uncongenial conditions of Forceville an insidious form of influenza attacked large numbers. It seemed to run its course in three or four days; its symptoms were a feeling of general weakness, and an extraordinary depression while the weakness lasted. Although cases were many evacuations to hospital were few; Christofferson, combating it valiantly, found that treatment and rest sufficed to pull the men round. All this time the weakened Battalion found personnel for a working-party up the line, the remainder doing some rifle practice.

July 5th.—A new C.O. arrived in the evening, Lt.-Col. J. B. Cockburn from the 17th Battalion. He was "Cocky" to everyone, behind his back. His transfer was felt to be an effort by Division to pull the Battalion together. de Miremont reverted to Acting Major, Second-in-Command. The Orderly Room worked late starting the new regime. There was to be company training : parades before breakfast were to be revived—these had obsolesced for two years, some theorist at home having pronounced them unhygienic : and servants, cooks and other details used to having a slack time had to parade and furbish up their drill against a day when they might be wanted.

July 6th.—The Adjutant's start under the new regime, 'which [1] I had planned to be impressive, was rather humiliating. When I took the C.O. out to show him the Companies at work we found them waiting to know where to go. The R.S.M., who had succeeded Boreham, was not on parade although I had been at extra pains in giving him his orders overnight about allotting the ground. When he turned up he said he had "slept in." The facts were not probed too deeply, but he got a good choking off after Orderly Room.'

Another raid was ordered, a Battalion affair. Its objective, Hamel, was known to be occupied, and recent experience had made many of us familiar with the ground. The village was a salient covering a practicable river-crossing. Two attempts to raid it by frontal attack had been made by other units : they had broken down on wire, machine-guns behind hedges, and the German barrage ; so it was decided that we should advance against the right face in the expectation of taking the main defending lines in flank. This approach, however, was enfiladed by a strong-point south of the village, where the road forked to Mesnil and Authuille. A. Company was detailed to scupper that strong-point and any other post on the road-railway embankment re-entrant, and, by occupying the embankment, to guard against a counter-attack or reinforcement from across the river. The Companies carrying out the main attack were C, B, and D, to whom Engineers for demolitions were attached. They were to advance in line, each

[1] Ll. Evans.

having two assault platoons on a front of 175 yards and two mopping-up platoons at distances of 20 and 30 yards. Assault platoons consisted of a bombing section on each flank and a Lewis-gun section between, the sections to advance in "worm" formation. The C.O. allowed Companies a large latitude in making their dispositions, but he supervised everything, and by a tactful general gingering-up soon made everyone feel that a long-absent efficient authority had been restored to the Battalion. Corps and Division interested themselves in the Show, but there was no interference in the arrangements this time. The C.R.A. made a special visit to concert and perfect plans, and to explain the barrages. Field-guns and a machine-gun company of another division, and the Corps heavies, reinforced the Divisional artillery, trench-mortars and machine-guns. For three days, besides company training, we practised the raid on specially prepared ground towards *July 10th*—Lealvillers. A new spirit and keenness and a new thoroughness were evident. The Corps Commander came to see the final practice. We were shelled when returning from it, and two or three men were the joyful recipients of blighty wounds.

July 11th.—In the early hours the Battalion, about 460 strong, moved up through Quaker—commonly called Quacker—Alley, to Barn Trench, our former front line, which was already manned by a company of the 17th Battalion. No movement was allowed during the day. 'But [1] the C.O. was anxious about the road junction strong-point, and unsatisfied with another unit's patrol report that it was empty. The whole German position was, in fact, held by mobile posts. He took O.C. A Company with him and spent the afternoon observing the spot from various angles. Since this involved crawling about Nomansland in broad daylight, under very inadequate cover, one of the observers was not too happy.' During the afternoon another terrific thunderstorm broke over the area. The support line was soon knee-deep in water. Everyone was very dispirited, thinking there would be a repetition of failure; but in the evening the weather cleared, there was a fine star-lit night with just light enough to pick up landmarks. By 10 o'clock the Battalion had side-stepped to its assembly position north-east of Mesnil. The tapes were run out. O.C. A Company, with Lance-Corporal Hill and another man, laid theirs as the C.O.

---

[1] Briercliffe.

had suggested in the afternoon. By 10.45 all Companies lay outside the wire of Hamel Outposts. The password was "Reggie." The C.O. appeared, not unexpectedly in his case, and had a look at A, who were hidden from possible prowling Germans by some handy hedges or trees. When a Company Commander is waiting, like as then, he wonders if the gunners' watches are properly synchronized.

At 11 o'clock, with a sudden terrific uproar, a hurricane bombardment and an intense overhead machine-gun fire, perfectly timed, fell on Hamel. The Battalion rose to its feet and started. 'Hamel was a mass of red flames and flashes, and one began to feel a tremendous exultation.' After C Company got off the tapes the C.O. and his runner were met in Nomansland. His remark, "You'll have to go into the village for your prisoners; I've been down to have a look, and there aren't any outside the wire," acted as a magnificent tonic, and sent the men forward lightheartedly. Going down the slope it seemed for a bit as if we were walking into the bombardment, and one tried to think that the guns would lift in time and form the barrage. In two minutes all approaches were barraged, communication trenches to Beaumont-Hamel being specially dealt with. Our main line of advance was north-east; it was well chosen, for the German barrage fell due west of Hamel and we escaped it altogether.

'A.[1] Company advanced in columns of platoons, which had somewhat independent rôles to play before forming a continuous line on the embankment. No. 4, on the right, had to deal with whatever might be found at the road junction; it was commanded by a sergeant, so I went with it. Realizing that the sooner we got to our objective the safer we should be, No. 4 made for the junction at the double, leaping over half-filled-in trenches, stumbling, falling over wire. The final rush was over an old British cemetery in which the wooden crosses loomed up white in the lurid glare of the artillery. We found nothing. As we were congratulating ourselves on this, and preparing to form a defensive position, a parachute light was put up from the road about a hundred yards on our right, and a machine-gun opened fire with tracer bullets over the ground we had crossed, and more lights were put up. It looked as if what the C.O. had feared had happened, that the

[1] Briercliffe.

Battalion was being enfiladed. We had to act quickly. A section was left at the road junction. A sergeant was sent with two sections to get round and attack this strong-point from the rear. Company H.Q. went straight for it. We avoided some barbed-wire knife-rests on the road, and crept through the trees which were on our left. We could see the Germans, five of them, working their gun for all they were worth, so it seemed imperative to silence them without waiting for the sergeant's party. Before we could get near enough to rush them we were attacked in flank by a bombing section. Some quick work with bomb, revolver, and bayonet made casualties on both sides, and I was one of them. At that moment the sergeant's party attacked with the bayonet. The Germans bolted with No. 4 Platoon after them, chasing them into the road, killing some and capturing others, and becoming so excited that they roamed over Nomansland looking for victims, and forgot all about the machine-gun, which was not brought in. The subaltern in charge of No. 3 lost himself and half his platoon; the other half, led by Lance-Corporal Hill, found some Germans to chase. No. 2 ran into a machine-gun post near the clump of trees it was making for; the post bolted for the river, taking their gun with them: they had to be let go as A Company's orders were explicit, to occupy the embankment and not to go beyond it. No. 1, advancing in echelon on C Company's right, had a scrap too, and drove off some Germans who were said to be among C's captures.'

Where C Company attacked the German front line was found unoccupied, but the support line, on the south of the village, had a small garrison who promptly surrendered when they realized how many enemies were swarming round them. The Company's right party went too far, and got into trouble beyond the village; the platoon officer was killed, and his corporal was wounded and captured. Progress in the village was not as fast as had been hoped for, owing to the enormous amount of wire entanglement. Perhaps B Company met with more opposition than the others. A German officer kept a machine-gun in action single-handed until he was put out with bombs: he was surrounded and our men wanted to take him unhurt, but he would not give in. ' As [1] D Company entered the village we saw dim figures moving about in front.

[1] Charlton.

We gave chase, and there was much letting off of revolvers and bombs. Marvellous we did not blow each other up. There was not much wire in D's area, but there were hedges and tombstones, broken tombstones everywhere in the wrecked churchyard. From among the tombs suddenly arose two very frightened little Gerries, they were only 17 or 18 years old. With hands above the head they kept up a perpetual chant of "Kamerad."' Charlton and his runner 'took them along while we explored farther; they trotted beside us causing no trouble at all.' The din had become indescribable. By now the Sappers were blowing up strong-points and dug-outs, some 20 were demolished; they dealt with the village thoroughly. One bungling Sapper blew up himself and some of us. Trench-mortars across the river had also started up and were making the village unhealthy for us. These were the two main sources of our casualties. When Hamel had been combed from front to rear, from the railway to its western limit, and no more Germans could be found the Companies were with- drawn; they had been out for an hour. As Charlton brought away his rear 'a dug-out blew up almost under our feet, quite upsetting us, so we hared it home up the slope.'

During the raid Evans ' was with the Colonel in the Hamel Outpost line. Later we went into Nomansland to meet the returning raiders.' 'The [1] C.O. held a kind of reception. He was *July 12th*—in great spirits, laughing and talking; he needed only a little encouragement to hold an officers conference there and then, but we merely left a card, so to say, and went on.' 'He [2] rounded up stragglers, helped in the wounded, and remained roaming in Nomansland so long after the "all clear" that Brigade became anxious about his welfare, and sent up for news and to search for him; we, however, met these enquirers on our way back. We called at Brigade, where an excellent breakfast was much more satisfying than even the hearty congratulations of the Staff.'

Nineteen prisoners and a machine-gun were brought in. Over fifty Germans were estimated to have been killed; many were found dead and dying in the village, especially at the cross-roads. We learned later that our guns and machine-guns caught relieving troops and ration-parties coming up, and upset them badly. The Battalion casualties were:—killed, 1 officer and 3 other ranks;

[1] Charlton.   [2] Ll. Evans.

wounded, 3 officers and 44 other ranks; missing, 8, of whom 3 were wounded.

As a raid the operation succeeded in all its objects; prisoners were taken; the men's morale was further improved—since Col. Cockburn's arrival morale had been raised to a level it had not been on for a year or more; and the notion which had grown up in many quarters since March that the German was unbeatable was definitely dissipated among us. 'I think the casualties were greater than the operation itself warranted'; the Higher Command, however, seemed uncommonly well satisfied. We returned from the raid to our position in reserve. The G.O.C. visited us and went about the lines congratulating and commending everyone from the C.O. to the Company Cooks. Complimentary messages from Corps and Army followed; and the home papers spared space for a one-line mention.

July 13*th*.—After baths the Battalion went into the intermediate support line. The Count commanded, since the C.O. was in temporary command of the 113th Brigade. We enjoyed a succession of fine and quiet days, and supplied working-parties to strengthen the reserve line. The establishment of S.A.A. and water reserves in all trenches—front, support, and several reserve lines— was apparently the latest stunt. These reserves were cached in hollows in the trench walls at regular and frequent intervals.

The passing of another familiar figure from the Battalion added to the dullness of these dull days. Radford went to England on six months exchange after almost three years of sterling service with the Battalion, leaving behind him a fine record as a soldier and leader.

(On June 9th and July 15th the Germans had made ineffectual attempts to improve the precarious position which they had gained on the Marne at the end of May.)

July 18*th*.—To-day's French counter-attack on the re-entrants of their salient proved to be the beginning of the end.

The Welsh Division was being relieved: the Battalion moved *July* 19*th*—to a tent and hut encampment at Hérissart. Battle Surplus rejoined after a respite of six weeks in delightful conditions. Its H.Q. was in a farmhouse, all serene with lake, ducks, geese, animals and midden complete; the others were billeted at Hiermont. James Cuthbert proved a tiger for work. An intensive programme of drill, musketry, Lewis guns, etc., was acted on. A lot was done before breakfast, but there could be no complaint of want of leisure. Abbeville is only 19 kilos distant on a main road, so lorries could be jumped. "Jimmy's," as one of its resorts was called, was the sort of place where old acquaintances were unexpectedly met. At óne such meeting an R.T.O. contrasted, with real conviction, the precarious life from shell-fire the Railway Service led, only the wooden roof of a railway carriage for protection, with the advantage, such as deep dug-outs, which the infantryman enjoyed: poor devils, in their happy ignorance. Those who, in a previous existence, had known the Aberdovey Hotel found its assistant Manageress similarly employed at the Officers Club. After two weeks a change was made to farms and tents at Valheureux. Doullens, 6 miles to the north-east, is the nearest place of any consequence. A chance meeting there let one of the party recover an eighteen-years-old debt of half-a-crown from a borrower who had gone off to Argentina. A strolling Army cinema visited the area, so did the influenza epidemic. Squadrons of the Air Force were established around, from whom "flips" were to be had. On Col. Cockburn's welcome appointment Cuthbert departed on transfer to the 14th Battalion as Second-in-Command. Five officers and all the N.C.Os. in camp went to make up the casualties of the Hamel raid, and fourteen of the slightly wounded raiders arrived. Drafts came in, not a few of them of conspicuous physical unfitness for front-line service.

Radford's going made vacant the command of C Company. Before it was filled, by Cuthbert Jones, certainly one Company Commander applied to be transferred to it. The lure was the Company charger, a placid, easy-pacing nag. For two years there had been no Young Officers Riding School, not even such as would have been acceptable to the humane ideas of 1918.

There were days of training and nights of discomfort at Hérissart: a full moon meant much night bombing all round by the enemy. The aspects of training that were stressed were the platoon in attack, tackling machine-gun nests, and "the spirit of the bayonet"; the C.O. was keen on patrolling, and by precept and example was a well of information. He was one of the old school of Regular Officer, and the old Regulars of the Battalion, who had had experience of the other sort of commanding officer during the

War, valued him for it. Under his command any who had served in the 1st Battalion found little or no difference as the two Battalions were made up by that time. To one Platoon Commander, an Old Army promotion from the 1st Battalion, who joined about now, it was a rare satisfaction to have an Old Army platoon sergeant in Varcoe (wounded April 25th, 1916, and recently returned).

July 26th.—' All [1] leave was still closed except for urgent family reasons, so I was fortunate, through the C.O.'s good offices, to get away on condition that Moody returned temporarily to the adjutancy, and on my solemn undertaking not to seek extension in any circumstances, but to be back within fourteen days. I started in pouring rain, the following day too was wet. Cross-Channel traffic had greatly dwindled, apparently only special cases were on board. A distinguished figure on the bridge, going home, was Admiral Sims of the U.S.A. Navy. On my return Yates was at Senlis with the Transport. There I got the Battalion news and gossip, and, as usual, some philosophy and much grousing, and a thundering good tea.'

July 29th.—A holiday: Brigade Sports at Rubempré.

July 30th.—The Battalion marched to a camp between Forceville and Acheux. The heat was sweltering, consequently there was a lot of straggling. The Wynnstay Goat died, the vet. said of heatstroke. He was buried near Toutencourt. His head, which it was hoped to preserve, could not be seen to properly. After dark a civilian was found prowling about C Company H.Q., and run-in. He turned out to be the owner of the farm, who had walked many miles to see how it was faring. During our time in support we *July 31st*—were to find large digging-parties near Beausart, and training went on in tropical heat. The only rest from digging was *August 3rd*—a half-day allowed to attend a Divisional Sports Meeting.

August 4.—Baths, and a Divisional Horse Show. "Girlie" was the favourite as usual, but she failed badly in one race with the Count up—or down; later in the afternoon she won well when ridden by Montgomery, a subaltern promoted from the Cavalry.

The C.O. had inspected the front with Company Commanders on the afternoon of our move. On a dull evening the Battalion *August 5th*—relieved a battalion of the Dorsets in the Bouzincourt

[1] Ll. Evans.

subsector. Since the Anglo-French Armies regained the initiative
an active German withdrawal had been taking place. Locally the
Germans had recrossed the Ancre, on which they held only the
bridgeheads in seemingly reduced strength. We were in what
had once been their support line. Sections were distributed in
short lengths of tolerably habitable trench with no real communications. The position looked down on the river, but since it was
overlooked from the higher ground opposite, movement was forbidden by day. The Germans were as still as we. There was
plenty of artillery activity, but very little of any other arm. A
great many dead, especially Germans, lay in Nomansland; most
of them had been there since Spring. Americans were again
attached for instruction. What was chiefly impressed on them
was that they were a bit late in coming over.

For the first time Companies were supplied with carrier-pigeons.
An old and a young bird had to be released together. It was understood that they would fly to Corps, and that the message would
be wired back to Battalion H.Q. Fatality seemed to attend the
Battalion's post-pigeons. One Company had no orthodox pigeon-
food, and it feared that experimental food might impair their
flight. Explanations to H.Q. would be difficult whatever the event.
A taciturn mess-cook probably knew most about their last phase.

With the coming of darkness each day the front awoke. Some
very heavy showers during five otherwise fine days made a lot
of extra work. Patrolling was never so active. Long stretches of
the railway line were examined in moonlight without any enemy
being met. The track was surprisingly little knocked about. One
patrol came in greatly excited after touching off one of several
booby-traps that were found. Patrols penetrated farther each
night. The river, its approaches and possible crossing-places were
searched. Charlton and Keepfer, besides others, ' found [1] an old
boat and got into it, but had to return hurriedly because it leaked—
the river looked fairly deep and the water unpleasantly cold and
black. Another night we turned south and went into Albert,
which was quite near on our right front. It was not known if any
part of it was still held by the enemy. I shall always remember
the eeriness of creeping through the streets—the houses, surprisingly
intact, standing gaunt and white in the moonlight—and trying to

[1] Charlton.

make out if the shadows moved, wondering if we should be leapt upon suddenly. But the enemy had apparently packed up and gone.'

August 8th.—All quiet here, but there was a great din on the right. From our ridge we could see with glasses that our troops were advancing. It was the Fourth Army's Battle of Amiens. Movement continued next day. Bouzincourt was heavily shelled in *August 10th*—the afternoon.

August 11th.—Moody had been awaiting Evans's return to "proceed to the United Kingdom on six months' exchange," so, after handing over, he waited not upon the order of his going. 'It [1] was remarkable how the departure of some fellows left a blank, whereas the passing of others as casualties, exchanges, promotions, and so forth, made no impression on the corporate life of the Battalion. In my time Dunn, Radford, and now Moody each left a definite gap not easily filled, the Battalion feeling not being quite the same after his going. Each time, somehow, it had left us who continued a little poorer, a little lonelier, and made everything for the moment less worth while. Moody was one of the first three temporary officers, it was "on probation" then, to join the Battalion, and his service of over three and a half years was an outstandingly good one.' He had held a regular commission for two years.

On relief the Battalion went back to Senlis. Company training *August 12th*—was entered on under the C.O.'s supervision. Llewelyn Evans became Adjutant.

August 15th.—In the afternoon officers, N.C.Os. and guides went to reconnoitre the line to be taken over. O.C. C Company sent his party ahead, with orders to keep well apart in crossing a ridge where they would be in view of the German line and in range of guns. On the crest the G.O.C. met them and stopped to speak to them, when they closed-in to fours; next, meeting the Company Commander, he cursed him roundly for letting his men "straggle"; when it was pointed out to him that they were on a skyline he cursed more wildly—they should have spread out more.

It was a beautiful evening when the Battalion took over the centre sector of the Division's area, Aveluy Wood–Martinsart, from the 114th Brigade. B and C Companies were in front, supported by A and D. The Germans no longer held any of the Wood, but their patrols or movable posts still came west of the

[1] Ll. Evans.

Ancre. The Wood was in our charge, and we patrolled its rides
down to the river. The Companies were fairly strong for this
period of the War, and the general morale was rising owing, no
doubt, to the improved war situation and the encouraging news
generally. We were, however, thinly officered in the Companies,
and a goodly proportion were new to the rank. 'The [1] C.O. was
indefatigable these days. I've never known a man who could do
with so little sleep, three hours in the twenty-four seemed ample
for him.'

We had entered on a tremendously busy time. The impulse
eastwards which the Western Front had been given was gathering
mass and momentum. Since the line immediately south of Albert
was being straightened preparations for a big advance on the
Divisional front were being improved. Company Commanders
had frequent summonses to H.Q. for conference, and to be given
instructions about likely developments. The two support Companies
were finding daily working-parties of 120 on roads and machine-
gun emplacements with the Engineers, and carrying up stores.
There was considerable aerial activity on both sides, day and night.
One afternoon a plane of ours thought fit to drop a bomb about
a yard from one of our trenches, then turn back over our lines.
The Germans did nothing untoward beyond subjecting the whole
area to periodic shelling. Sometimes they used gas shell, so the
C.O. required the men to be practised frequently in gaspirators
for ten or fifteen minutes at a time. Our night operations were
interfered with a good deal by the dropping of brilliant parachute
lights of greatly improved pattern, which were effective over a
wide area and burned for a long time, compelling us to stand still
August 19*th*—until they went out. An inter-company relief
brought A Company in front of Aveluy and D of Authuille. C
went to Bouzincourt and B to Martinsart, both to supply large
working-parties. Meanwhile reconnaissances of the approaches to
the river bank, of the causeways and any possible crossing, were
being made nightly for Intelligence, and to gain familiarity with
the ground; and occasional scraps took place. This night an
officer and 7 other ranks of B Company left the south-east corner
of Aveluy Wood at 10.30 to examine a projected crossing-place
400 yards north of the broken road-bridge at Aveluy. It was a

[1] Ll. Evans.

duckboard footbridge which led to a track running eastwards to the Authuille road. An identification was to be got if possible. The password was "Raffles," but no crib was cracked.

August 20th.—After a warning order the detail was issued for a crossing by A Company at Aveluy, and by D at Authuille. It was expected that the Germans would withdraw overnight from these places. Both Companies posted a "patrol platoon" on the railway embankment in readiness to go over behind its patrol, and hold the crossings while the other platoons followed. A and D were then to advance and occupy the ridges east of the Ancre to a depth of twelve to fifteen hundred yards; there C and B were to leap-frog, and carry the advance another 1500 yards. So the day passed in the bustle of preparation, and in uncertainty.

August 21st.—During the night Smith and 7 other ranks of A Company repeated last night's patrol by B at Aveluy, at a cost of one man killed. Another man, who was stalked and seized by a German, knocked his would-be captor into the water and escaped. D Company sent over a patrol, not the first, at Authuille. The approaches there were longer and much more intricate than at Aveluy, owing to the extent and overlapping of the areas of marsh on both sides of the river. To-night's password was "Rodger." During the day operation orders underwent two changes owing to the apparent strength with which the Germans stood their ground, and to the need to keep C and B Companies on work in rear. Order after order, and amendments to orders, had put a great deal of memorizing upon Company Officers and N.C.Os. A code of signals to and from contact and reconnaissance aeroplanes by ground signs, which were reintroduced after two years disuse, had also to be learned. The sending of vital news and orders between front and rear was always the great difficulty in conducting operations. A one-way wireless from the front to Advanced Brigade H.Q. at Martinsart was provided for the first time. The latest attempt to overcome the difficulty of supplying ammunition was by parachute from aeroplanes, called for by ground signals.

There was news of good progress by the Corps on our right, and that on our left. The shelling by the enemy on our front suggested that he was ill at ease, he was firing frequent bursts all over our area. It was expected that he would cover his retreat by sousing the river valley with gas, so, except for the patrol platoons, the front Companies remained on the ridge behind. The patrol platoons worried less about possible gas than about getting their rations.—At night our working-parties were called in.

August 22nd.—Patrols, with orders to avoid scrapping, tested the two crossings every four hours during the night. The intention was to cross if conditions were favourable to an advance, so everyone was in readiness to follow up. There was, however, no encouragement to press matters at either point; at Authuille heavy small-arms fire was met. Throughout the day snipers fired on our advanced positions, and machine-guns repeatedly sprayed our back area. The German artillery was also active: every shot had still to be observed and reported.

Amidst all these alarms and excursions the life went on. A subaltern might hope to get a run into Doullens. Leave was open again. There were Courses once more, to and from which officers and men went and came; Companies were being called on to make nominations for vacancies a week in advance. The eligibility of "duration" men for membership of the Comrades Association was up again, and again the Regulars maintained their exclusive attitude.—A Regimental War Memorial was under discussion, and the amount of individual subscription—three days pay was suggested. At 8 at night the C.O. met Company Commanders to hear the views of their men.—One of the surest signs that a large-scale operation is impending is the settlement of officers Mess accounts. Details of these show that the price of the tinned foods commonly consumed in the front line had risen 12 per cent., on average, in two years. Whisky, the usual alcoholic drink, had risen about 25 per cent. in the same time. Purchasable out of bond it was costing 4 shillings (5·55 francs) a bottle; the price at home was 12/6; (the pre-war price of a much better whisky was 4/-).

By an order issued at night the Authuille crossing was given up, and A Company was to make a crossing at Aveluy. A corporal's patrol, sent forward in advance, had two casualties. Next, a sergeant who reconnoitred the position reported that it would not be possible to get the Company over. The enemy fire came from Crucifix Corner which our artillery had bombarded earlier, so Chick, who now commanded the Company, ordered a light trench-mortar battery which had been put at his disposal to fire on it. Still the patrol advised that no attempt to cross be made.

CHAPTER XVIII

The German Retreat—Across the Ancre : Astride Bazentin Ridge—High Wood revisited : ("Bapaume") Morval and Lesbœufs again : Sailly-Saillisel—a dead end : Gouzeaucourt : Echoes of "Epéhy" : A patrol : Villers-Outreaux : The Selle— Le Cateau revisited : Englefontaine—winkling : Mormal Forest : Across the Sambre at Aulnoye : November 11th

Contributors:—AINGE ; CHARLTON ; CHICK ; COCKBURN ; CRAB-TREE ; DOCHERTY ; H. EVANS ; LL. EVANS ; E. J. GREAVES ; HUGHES ; CUTHBERT JONES ; E. R. JONES ; M. JONES ; KENT ; KIRKBY ; McKAY ; NICKSON ; NORMAN ; TURNER

Sketches:—2, 11, 13, 15, 24, 25, 26, 27

On our right the 17th Battalion was making good, and farther along the 113th Brigade was crossing at Albert, but on our left the 114th Brigade was having trouble at Hamel.

August 23rd.—In the early morning the C.O. resolved that there must be no more delay. Chick accordingly went down himself and, taking a party of 5 or 6 men, waded over at dawn. On a signal from him the Company began to follow. Hughes, the Intelligence Officer, went with the first platoon. They used the old duckboard causeway belonging to a long-ago time in the War. It was about eighteen inches above the water, and led to the track Morris and Smith had reconnoitred. There was a gap of about 6 feet in the middle where the laden men had to drop into about 2 feet of water, and clamber on again. A distant machine-gun on the high ground about Authuille Wood played on the gap, but it was firing high and did no harm. The platoon ran and took up a covering position under one of the convenient banks of the Somme country, about 50 yards beyond and to the right of the causeway, where it had a very quiet time until a further move was made. Another platoon, searching the area, rushed a couple of machine-gun positions, whose crews surrendered without resistance; and some occupants of dug-outs were quite agreeable when a sergeant called on them to come out. Our guns covered these doings; they strafed Crucifix Corner until half-past six. The German artillery was very quiet, it was probably being pulled back.

Crucifix Corner was occupied later on; it is a cross-roads fully 500 yards north-east of the church. After that the men became so casual that they had to be checked for strolling about without equipment. The severest casualty in the Company had been to Chick's breeches, which were torn on wire right across the seat. An S O S was sent to Yates to supply at once from Store a replacement of "trousers, khaki drab"; until he could comply the injured officer preserved the decorum of his rank in a German greatcoat.

At noon Cuthbert Jones took half of C Company over. The main body of A was then 400 yards beyond the river. A big dug-out in the area, which had been overlooked so far, was found to contain Germans. Chick and Jones tried to get them out, 'but apparently they were being restrained by one man, so at last we had to throw two Mills bombs, one each, into the dug-out and await results. In a few minutes eight men emerged, with the cheeky one doing all the talking.' Our captures were then— 4 machine-guns and about 30 prisoners. The remainder of C Company crossed after dark and wheeled to the left, the Company's position being on the left of A. The Albert district was being heavily shelled then; there were large fires in the town, as there had been for several nights.

D Company had moved from the ridge down to the railway embankment just south of Aveluy Wood at dawn, encountering only slight shelling: 'the men in great spirits.' At 3 o'clock we had orders to send a patrol over the river, so Lieut. Diggle, a cheery, round-faced Lancashire boy, took out three or four men. We watched them cross; they were up to their knees only in one or two places. They moved about for a while on the other side but drew no fire; the place was seemingly deserted: we learned otherwise at night. When they were within yards of the embankment on their return the Germans began dropping heavy stuff about. Diggle was hit on the head; he was brought in but nothing could be done for him. After dark we crossed the river by the causeway used by the other Companies, with no greater mishap than that some of the men fell in the water. The Company assembled north of Authuille where it was on C's left. B Company was attached to the Brigade's reserve Machine Gun Company to carry for it. By midnight the assembly was complete, and seemingly unknown to the enemy. A. Company's strength was 91; the other Companies were much the same. There had been two or three minor casualties during the day.

'In[1] the afternoon the C.O. went scouting through the Wood down to the river, boyishly demonstrating to his Adjutant, as we dodged through the undergrowth, how he had learned in West Africa to move, take cover, and crawl along. When we crossed in the early hours next morning his amazing nonchalance in making the passage, stopping frequently on the way to examine various points and features which hitherto we had observed only from our front line, made the journey most uncomfortable for me. By that time the nervous enemy had realized that a big move was afoot, and was plastering the river bank on both sides with great thoroughness, chiefly at the crossing, but also the road and railway beyond it—our very recent front.'

The 113th and 114th Brigades, on the right and left respectively, moved at 10.30 p.m. The latter had great difficulty in holding its bridgehead. Our rôle was to mop up the triangle that would be formed by these Brigades converging attack. The triangle had a base of 3000 yards, extending from Aveluy to north of Authuille, on which A, C, and D Companies were deployed; its apex was 1000 yards north-east of Ovillers-la-Boisselle. The steep eastern bank of the Ancre is broken, on the left of A Company's area, by a re-entrant, Nab Valley, from which the ground rises, steeply on the right and more gradually on the left, to its highest point on D Company's front. In C Company's area were the remains of Authuille Wood and village.

August 24th.—The night was pitch dark at zero, 1.30, when our three Companies moved off. They were in battle formation: two platoons in front and two in support, all in "worms" of five to seven men. Our barrage was well placed, whereas the German barrage was on the river bank behind us. A. Company found abandoned machine-guns, and took inoffensive prisoners as

[1] Ll. Evans.

it moved up Nab Valley. Except for some shelling, which hurt no one, there was no opposition. A. never was in touch on its right where the 17th Battalion, supported by the 10th S.W.B., was moving. In the centre Turner's platoon was involved at once with some Germans in a sandpit, who threw bombs causing two or three casualties before they were scuppered or driven off. There and on the left the advance began with a rocky ascent of about 100 feet, which was more rather than less steep. It was a fortunate circumstance that the enemy position was on the crest; C and D therefore were in dead ground almost until they closed with the defenders whom they could see on a skyline. Turner was within revolver range when machine-gun fire was opened on his platoon of C, which went for the guns in approved fashion. Our men attacked with confidence, and the defenders generally did not put up much of a fight, although there were isolated instances of hand-to-hand encounters. Cuthbert Jones shot one hefty German who had seized his runner and was about to strike him on the neck with a stick bomb. Fire was opened on D, where Charlton was, at a range of only six or eight paces. His runner, on his right, and a man on his left were killed, and he was laid out for a time by what proved to be a ricochet lodged in his back.

After the capture of this, the main, German position there was no organized opposition, but at 2 a.m. the advance was suspended short of the intermediate objective until daylight because the troops on the flanks were said to be in difficulties. When it became light the German heavies were the first to get busy, 'they plastered us well and truly for some time,' causing a few casualties. When the mopping-up was resumed it was not carried beyond the trench system we were in. Groups of Germans were found in deep dug-outs. For the most part they were thoroughly shaken, and let themselves be taken like lambs, being only too willing to be made prisoners. Several of Charlton's men showed him 'German watches which they said had been given them as peace offerings— I wonder.' Until well on in the morning D Company's left flank was in the air, so slow had been the progress the 114th Brigade could make. With daylight and leisure Charlton and Clarence Jones examined the German position on the crest, and concluded that the machine-guns had been trained on the river, too high therefore to hit any but the leading assailants. 'We followed the river bank north, then went east for some distance and discovered, on referring to the map, that we were in Thiepval; it was only discernible by brick rubble and flints. We did not see a German, going or returning. . . . It was like a stroll on Sunday morning, but without the dog.'

On completion of the operation the Companies were withdrawn to the road east of the river for stocktaking, breakfast and sleep. Altogether over 200 prisoners were taken, but there was not an officer among them. One lot said they could not understand why we had not come over four days sooner, since when they had not had proper food. Seventeen machine-guns and trench-mortars were sent back as spoil. Our casualties were under thirty, but they included two experienced officers, for Charlton and Turner had to go to hospital. The latter had a wound of the eye, caused as several of our casualties were: he was not seen in the dark by one of our men who threw a bomb from a flank. The Adjutant returned to our former H.Q. west of the river with instructions for the Transport, and to bring along the Details. When the Battalion advanced again the Transport was still on the western bank, waiting until the Sappers could make a passage for it through Aveluy and repair the road-bridge, 'so [1] the C.O. ordered me to remain as guide until we caught up with the advance. While waiting there I used what Details were with me to collect some thirteen of our dead. As no padre appeared handy, and I had a Prayer Book in my pocket, I read portions from the Burial Service over them as their common grave was being filled in.'

At 4 in the afternoon the Battalion, leading the Brigade, moved off again in the same order, and over the same ground to begin with, as in the early morning. No Germans were found where we had mopped-up already, but there were a few, who gave themselves up very readily, in a trench west of Blighty Valley. This Blighty runs north-eastwards beyond Authuille Wood, and is a continuation of Nab Valley. Across the valley was a trench system in which A Company linked up with the 13th Battalion. A halt of about an hour was made there. An anxious sub., asking about tanks, was told to "keep smiling." Another advance of about 1000 yards brought us just east of the line of Ovillers-la-

[1] Ll. Evans.

Boisselle. Again we halted for about an hour. There was some machine-gun fire close at hand but none of us were involved in it. Going on again, more or less in touch with the flank battalions, there was a short delay west of Pozières before we went to ground on the Albert road to the right of the village, about 11.30, to await orders. Across the road was a railhead, and in a dug-out was a wounded German; he was the only sign of the enemy A Company had encountered since the early morning. During the halt of about three hours a man of C Company who had made himself scarce on a previous occasion repeated the manœuvre. At midnight Company Officers were summoned to H.Q. A general move was being made, beyond the original objectives, against a line the Germans were understood to be holding 1000 yards east of where we were. It was hoped to get astride the ridge on our front at High Wood. The advance was going to take us off our maps very soon, and there were no maps of the new ground for issue, so the C.O. indicated the direction and told us to keep in the closest touch possible.

August 25th.—When we did move, at 2.30, progress and keeping touch were difficult owing to our Companies marching off at different times, to the intense darkness, shell-pitted ground, narrow-gauge railways, innumerable trenches and dug-outs, trees and road-screens. Added to all these there was, ahead of us, a very heavy bombardment of roads and other spots vital to the Germans. Until after daylight C Company was never in touch with A or D, but it ran into B near the chalk-pit on the Bailiff Wood–Pozières road. Next, when three-quarters of a mile south of Pozières, there came towards it a company of another battalion whose officer said his line of advance was north of Pozières: so far was it easy to go astray.—To Hughes, as to most, 'all that is retained of that march is blundering and stumbling along interminably, and a very vivid impression of men marching in extended order, silhouetted against the light from burning huts and dumps. This was in the earlier part of the night, later there was complete darkness. To me it was an eerie experience and most exciting, because we fully expected—at least I did—to bump up against the enemy somewhere beyond the burning dumps.'—'It was getting dusk,' Evans says, 'before the road-bridge at Aveluy could carry transport and guns. We went forward not knowing any

location for junction with the Battalion, just "somewhere in front," following the general direction of the obvious battle-front. The going was rough as there was no road or track of any continuity ; detours had to be made frequently owing to cross-roads having been blown up. Some time in the darkness, and somewhere near Pozières I imagined, we ran into our Brigade H.Q. ; they, however, could give me only a general direction along which to proceed. Later on in the night progress with the wagons became impossible, the roads and tracks were so broken up, so all available men man-handled as much water and rations as they could, and we carried our loads thus for what appeared to be many weary miles. Before us it was as if battle waged all night, much shell-fire and noise, flashing explosions, burnings ; and tremendous activity was apparent in a general move forward of guns and ammunition, all cross-country fashion. Eventually, just after dawn, my small party stumbled upon the Battalion, gone to ground since just before dawn, in shell-holes and in the sunken road north-west of Mametz Wood, having Bazentin-le-Petit Wood in front. We shared out what little provision we had been able to carry.'
The Battalion had reached Contalmaison without any opposition. C Company had, however, overstepped the general line. Passing north of Contalmaison they made contact, in a trench line on their left, with a company of another battalion who were going forward, and went with them. It was then dawn. Two men were spotted across a valley, with glasses they were seen to be Germans, so the Company was ordered into a trench near by. While they were still above ground machine-guns, in posts in the foreground, fired on them inflicting loss. Cuthbert Jones and another officer we could ill spare were among the Company's 30-odd casualties before it was extricated. This happened on the fringe of Bazentin-le-Petit Wood.

'A [1] little over two years ago the Welsh Division was engaged on practically the same ground, and I was a unit in the 13th R.W.F. of its 113th Brigade. Then we attacked *en masse* from the south-east, and fought for yards of ground thickly held by an enemy with no thought of retreat. Now the front in movement was wide and elastic, the fighting was open, and we were attacking positions from the flank. On our immediate front were only

[1] Ll. Evans.

courageous rearguards, well supported by artillery, covering their retreating main body.'

During the morning the Transport arrived at Contalmaison. Rumours, excursions and conferences occupied the day. H.Q. exchanged its shell-hole for a rickety German structure, without much advantage. This was done on the C.O.'s account. He was feeling the strain of the hard going, his old wounds making exposure and fatigue doubly trying. But he was all agog to go scouting into Mametz Wood when a proposal was made that we should attack it. At night he could scarcely be roused from sleep when Brigade Orders were taken to him. We heard no more about Mametz Wood. In the afternoon someone else cleared out a few posts in it which covered the German line east of the Happy Valley.

The 113th Brigade was to attack due east from in front of Mametz Wood with Bazentin-le-Grand, Longueval and Ginchy as its successive objectives. The Order attached us to the 113th as reserve battalion, and required us to take position just east of the Wood for the advance in the morning. The Brigade's right would be uncovered as it progressed, because the 18th Division, on its right, was not attacking towards Montauban until later, so we were to form a defensive flank until the 18th conformed. To do this B Company, which had been detached earlier in the day for duty with the 113th, and D were detailed to follow the advance and drop posts facing outwards.

August 26th.—Thanks to the C.O. waking at 3 o'clock we got off the mark in time. Zero was 4 o'clock of a very misty morning. Before daylight the Brigade came against serious machine-gun opposition which gradually increased. Although quite a lot of German posts were rounded up some escaped notice. The C.O., following the advance and accompanied only by the senior runner, Lance-Corporal W. Evans, came on a machine-gun post quite unexpectedly. Evans, who was a little in front, was covered suddenly by the revolvers of two Germans. He was as ready with rifle and bayonet as always with tongue or fist. The revolvers were dropped. Several more of the team were flushed from shell-holes near, to fall into the hands of one of our groups at a little distance.

'My [1] instructions were to proceed along the defensive flank to

[1] Ll. Evans.

see that every post had been established properly and at appropriate intervals, then to rejoin the C.O. when I caught up with the advance which he was following. Pierpont, permanent adjutant's runner since Mann chose him, and whilom professional golfer, accompanied me on this job. We found post No. 1 quite all right, but, because of the mist and early morning darkness, we veered out of line in the direction of Caterpillar Wood. Soon realizing this, and fearing we were beyond our outpost line, we worked inwards towards our left over some ruined buildings, damaged emplacements, and the stumpy undergrowth of Flat-iron Copse. Here we stumbled on some very recently killed and wounded Germans, were deafened by very immediate firing, and moved towards some ghostly figures looming in the mist. We realized that they were our men, but they knew nothing of us, for they had just been dealing with that party among the ruins. It was a tense moment when they sighted two fresh figures appearing through the mist in which everything was so ethereally vague, so our relief was great when a voice was heard, "Let's take the b——s prisoners. Come on, Gerry." To them Pierpont and I went with our arms fully extended in true Kamerad fashion. "Good God, it's the Adjutant," said our captor, the O.C. post, one Perkes, a diminutive lance-corporal whose spoken, humane impulse undoubtedly saved our lives, and who, I regretted to find, was killed later in the day. I made sure we would keep inside our line all right from then on, and it was not long before we caught up with A and C in a little copse on the western edge of Bazentin-le-Grand Wood. Here there was some vigorous mopping-up going on, since the copse was being held strongly in defence of the Wood and the village, Bazentin-le-Grand, behind it.

I now rejoined the C.O., who next sent me to get to the advancing troops and order them not to proceed beyond the Montauban–Bazentin road, which was parallel to our front and between the Wood and the village. This time I saw to it that I did not get outside the flank of the attack, so I followed the Longueval–Contalmaison high road, on which our left rested, with the intention of reaching the ordered halting-place at the same time as the first wave. In a quarry on the left of this road we saw Christofferson and his Aid Post staff up to the eyes in work, dealing with casualties of all units of the Division as well as of attached troops. The M.O.'s case at the moment was a cavalryman who had lost a leg, but who mourned entirely for his beloved charger, the missing leg being a matter of no moment with him then. Pierpont and I reached the sunken road we were making for before our troops got there. We found it seemingly empty, but there was a cubby-hole in its western bank with a door which opened outwards; it gave up to us eleven very scared Gerries, who came out in single file to see what the fates had in store for them. Fortunately the front wave of the 113th Brigade began dropping on to the road, and released us from an embarrassing situation. Just as I gave these troops their orders a beautifully placed barrage came down plumb on the road. Fortunately, again, a deep and wide ditch ran along its eastern bank, so, thanks to its excellent cover, the whole line, together with the phlegmatic Pierpont and me, lay snug while the strafe lasted.

Returning by the same route, and to almost the same spot as where I had last seen the Colonel, I found him a stretcher case. Shortly after his encounter with the M.G. post the C.O. got a ragged wound in the thigh when he was on the Caterpillar Wood ridge, learning the situation on the right and getting his dispositions adjusted to deal with it. In going to his help Lance-Corporal Evans had to pass through a zone of heavy machine-gun fire. The C.O. had continued on his feet somehow until he arrived at H.Q., trying to make light of his wound, but when the leg stiffened he handed over, and the last we saw of him was being carried down the road, waving to us cheerfully and shouting an encouraging "Carry on." '

It was approximately midday, and the Division seemed to have come to a halt. On taking stock we found our numbers considerably depleted of both officers and men. Enfilading machine-guns on the ridge above Montauban, outside our area, had done a lot of mischief. The loss of the Colonel was the culminating blow; his departure left an enormous gap, for the time we all felt lonely and dispirited. The Division's front was a convex curve on which we remained until next day. B and D Companies were swung into line on its right, in touch with the 18th Division which had moved forward. A and C Companies rejoined the 115th Brigade, and were attached to the 10th S.W.B. and 17th R.W.F. respectively. H.Q. was on the western fringe of Bazentin-le-Grand Wood, in a recess in the bank on the roadside, half filled with road metal; we spent the night there.

When it was barely twilight a rumour, rather than a message, came to H.Q. that "the 2nd are falling back." Greaves and Evans took Lance-Corporal Evans and a couple of other runners, and visited the whole of the line held by our men; they found everything normal, and nothing at all in the scare. But they were in time to observe preparations for an enemy counter-attack by troops massing opposite and slightly to the right of our front. The Germans had assembled in Trônes Wood, and were streaming out of it exactly like a crowd leaving a theatre, moving parallel to our front and towards our left. They were harassed right along by machine-gun and rifle-fire from our line. Eventually they turned down the road from Longueval against a sector of the front held by our 13th Battalion. The 13th went forward to meet them with the bayonet, but opened out to let a squadron of The Carabiniers through. The Cavalry had a rare gallop and an exciting dash at the counter-attacking enemy, who broke and cleared back before doing any great damage beyond making The Carabiniers pay for their ride. Cavalry was operating in the advance at this time, though almost wholly as liaison units and gallopers.

August 27th.—The night passed without incident for us, but pressure on the flanks forced the enemy to abandon his line, Trônes Wood to west of Longueval and Delville Wood, overnight. H.Q. and B and D Companies made an early move on Longueval–Ginchy with the 113th Brigade, but were ordered, *en route*, to rejoin our own Brigade which was in close support to the 113th and 114th Brigades. By noon the Battalion had side-slipped to east of High Wood. Later it moved into derelict trenches between Delville Wood and Flers. The Divisional front was from short of Longueval to north-east of High Wood. We were subjected to much heavy and uncomfortable shelling, as was the whole area. 'In[1] the *August 28th*—morning Greaves and I visited High Wood of doleful memory to the 2nd Battalion. Like Mametz Wood it was in a much worse state than when a few of us saw it in 1916, having been more fought over since then. Its tree stumps were fewer, and the ground was a tangle of undergrowth, shell-holes and wire.

[1] Ll. Evans.

We found the graves of several men of ours who had fallen there in 1916, and recalled the tales we had heard from survivors of that sanguinary period. We met the Brigadier who had gone there with the same object as we, for he had fought over it in those days.'

At 10 o'clock de Miremont and 7 subalterns came up from Surplus, but rank and file reinforcements were far from adequate. The strain of this long stretch of more or less active warfare—we had been in the line since the first week of the month, and moving forward and fighting for six days—was beginning to tell on those who had been in it the whole time. Fortunately the weather had been good although the nights were cold, and rations and water had never failed; but the only topic of interest was "when are we likely to be relieved." There was little hope for the time being, for it was said that all divisions were in the line and none in reserve. (The Germans too had all their divisions deployed in line.) At H.Q. we were given some light relief during the evening. A recommendation for the award of a M.C. was submitted from one of the Companies on behalf of its very temporary Acting O.C. It was signed by some of the sergeants. Enquiry found that the recipient-to-be had written it himself and got these N.C.Os. to sign it. He joined us five days before, direct from England, and had been acting O.C. Company for a matter of hours. Good work!

Late in the day the Germans withdrew from their Longueval position, so orders came in to follow up. "You'd better hurry and change your pretty clothes, the big push is soon after dawn," said Evans to Ainge, just off leave. These were the first words spoken to many a one on return off leave.

The education scheme was to the fore again. Hairy-eared propagandists were going round. The men took them for post-war employment agents.

August 29th.—Zero 5.45 a.m. The 115th Brigade moved east on Morval and Lesbœufs, the Battalion being in support. After passing through the 13th Welsh we found posts to cover the left flank of the advance. Virtually we were moppers-up, following close on the heels of the 10th S.W.B. and our 17th Battalion. The advance was just a Brigade route-march in four waves, close behind a creeping barrage, on open undulating ground. There was no resistance until a railway south-west of Lesbœufs was reached; there we came under artillery fire, 5.9 mostly, which slackened down later. Morval and Lesbœufs were both strongly held, and all further progress was resisted along the slight rise on which they are situated. The S.W.B. got into Lesbœufs, but were forced back on to its western edge. A Brigade line was consolidated in the north-and-south sunken road that runs west of both villages. About 20 prisoners were passed back. We had been well under way before it was noticed that H.Q. Company, the signallers, most of the runners, the orderlies and other details, were not with us. The R.S.M., who was in charge of them, had his orders overnight to follow up and be available at any moment as a reinforcement or for any other duty that might arise. The check in front and the evidences of serious resistance increased anxiety at their continued absence. After we had settled down they appeared. The R.S.M. had "overslept" again. He reported "sick," and was advised by de Miremont to avoid rejoining in a hurry or serious trouble would be awaiting him. The Battalion went to ground in the sunken portion of the Ginchy–Lesbœufs road, near where H.Q. was in 1916. The appearance of the surface was much altered; all over the district there was a network of tram-lines that did not exist then. H.Q. established itself partly in an old trench of the Flers Line where it crossed the Ginchy road, and partly in a recently cleared German Field Hospital, an unhealthy structure of wood and sheeting. At 6 p.m. our dispositions were: C Company attached to the 10th S.W.B., B in close support, D in reserve, A on carrying fatigue. D and A occupied shell-holes and old fallen-in trenches, which they improved and a heavy shower made nasty, almost a mile north-east of Ginchy.

August 30*th*.—Orders were issued in the expectation that the Division, taking part in a wide sweep forward, would march to Fins, but as yet the leading battalions were unable to get their battle patrols through the villages in front. The Germans were making good use of cycle machine-guns, and were shelling the Brigade position continuously and fairly heavily. The Companies had casualties; two of the reinforcement officers of two days ago were wounded, one was at the front for the first time; and H.Q. had to quit the hospital for trenches farther west.—C Company was making the most of its inactivity in expectation of an early move. 'Idly[1] we listened to the buzzing of a telephone wire over-

---

[1] Crabtree.

head, and it dawned on me that the wire couldn't possibly be
connected with the War on our side of the line. Without more
ado my batman, Rothwell, shinned up the pole and cut the wire
down. Possibly an hour afterwards our reveries were disturbed
by two German linesmen who came, riding on bicycles, to find
and repair the damage. They were promptly bowled over and
sent to Battalion H.Q.'—The heavy shelling continued. The
August 31st—Brigadier, visiting his line, was wounded by a shell
outside H.Q. and attended to by our stretcher-bearers.

Although the position was unchanged things became easier in
and about Lesbœufs. Later in the day it was given out that the
Corps was to advance the line along a front St. Pierre Vaast Wood–
Sailly-Saillisel–Le Transloy, our Division's move to be made
several hours ahead of the flank divisions. The 17th Battalion
was to advance with us, on our right, the 10th S.W.B. would be
in support; troops to be in position, 15 minutes before zero,
5.45 a.m.: meanwhile the 114th Brigade would be clearing the
remaining Germans out of Morval; the 113th Brigade would
then pass through, and our 13th and 16th Battalions coming up
on the right of the 17th at 6 o'clock, the four R.W.F. Battalions
would continue the advance in line.—Our strength was considerably
less than when we crossed the Ancre, in spite of some dribbling in
of reinforcements. There were only two officers per Company,
all of them subalterns. Chick was still with A; Tunnicliffe had B,
its fourth acting commander in a week; Crabtree, who'd been with
us six months, had C; F. L. C. Jones, an experienced man, had D.

September 1st, Sunday.—Overnight the Germans withdrew from
Lesbœufs.—The road leading to the assembly was being shelled
when we went forward. At 3.30 we began forming up just east of
the village in the sunken road which, coincidently, had been
occupied by D Company in October 1916. D and C, each formed
in two waves of two platoons, were our front line, A was in close
support; because our left would be unprotected B's job was the
defensive-flank business once more. To mask our advance the
artillery was to make a smoke screen of a battalion frontage on
our left. From 4.45, when the 114th Brigade attacked Morval,
we lay under an intense barrage. de Miremont, having seen the
Companies assembling, had returned to H.Q. details in the ruins
of the village.

The route to be taken rose before us ; it was over open undulating country. From Lesbœufs the ground rises for nearly 1000 yards, then runs evenly on the left for about 1000 yards, but a somewhat higher spur projects on the right : there follows a dip of some 400 yards, through which the Frégicourt–Le Transloy road runs— the road was our first objective and second pause : another rise for 300 or 400 yards to a second spur on the right is succeeded by a shallow dip, fully 1000 yards wide, having Sailly-Saillisel on a height on the farther side. The levels vary by fully sixty feet. All the way there is a slope from right to left, and the ground falls to yet lower levels farther to the left. The general effect of the contours is the creation of re-entrants on the left of the route. On the right also of the Battalion's line of advance there is a downward slope. C and B had to cross what was A Company's support position in October 1916, and skirt B Company's junction with the French on the Morval–Le Transloy road. This old trench system, which ran parallel to and near the route, combined with the contours, was of supreme importance during the next couple of hours. An artillery programme divided the advance into four stages of 800 yards, to each of which 40 minutes was allowed, including 10 minutes when the creeping barrage rested to let the infantry conform. Just before the start a small splinter humming through the air hit Chick in the neck. In this interval, too, F. L. C. Jones confided to Crabtree that he was "going all out for a V.C." He was a Mons man, a Grenadier, commissioned in France ; he intended to remain in the Army after the War, and he knew the value the Cross would be to him. Decorations was a very frequent subject of his talk.

At 5.45 the Battalion began its nearly 4000 yards advance on a front of 500 yards, behind a very indifferent creeping barrage. The Companies were in clumps, nominally "worms." As D Company made the ascent Sailly-Saillisel came into view. Several buses that had apparently brought up reinforcements were seen on a road on its right. A pause was made on the first of two roads from Morval to Le Transloy ; the first leap-frog was made there, the second wave of D and C passing through to take the lead. Some small-arms fire came from the left and increased in volume. A. Company was seeing less and less of the 17th Battalion, and was being troubled by long-range small-arms fire from the right as the first objective was approached. To D Company it seemed that things had gone well when, at the crossing of a road (Frégicourt–Le Transloy) and railway track, the Company Commander told his signaller to send a message to H.Q.—"The first objective has been gained." So far our artillery's shorts had caused one or two casualties; now machine-guns on the ridge ahead played on the Company, but ineffectually, because few guns fired and the range was a mile. 'For [1] C Company at the start it was just an early morning stroll, punctuated occasionally by one of our own shrapnel shells bursting short. One of them burst quite close behind me, and I was knocked down by a terrific blow on the seat of the trousers. Gingerly I put a caressing hand on my posterior and drew it away to try and estimate at what rate I was bleeding. My hand was wet and sticky, but it was just mud. A little later, when we had gone about 1000 yards, we began to be really troubled by Germans about 500 yards away on our left, who kept up a continuous fire, enfilading us. Whilst it became more and more unpleasant I realized that, firstly, I was responsible for the direction of the attack, and secondly, we could not afford to delay the advance by dealing with the blighters : B Company could do that. Apart from these diversions all went well.' D and C were in close touch, the fire from the left had inclined C inwards. Having paused, they advanced at 7 o'clock ; now the slope of the spur over which D was passing inclined them towards C. Meanwhile the eccentric movement of the main body of B Company, about 40 of them, was watched by some of D and A with surprise, and other feelings, for it was bearing to the left quite out of touch with C, and as if in passive touch with Germans. The leading Companies had gone another 400 or 500 yards, D had crossed the railway track and was on a skyline, A was close behind, when 'the [2] great hold-up brought us to a standstill. We could not say what had happened, but we came suddenly face to face with an inferno of machine-gun fire while we were yet in very open country. There was a general scattering of the two leading Companies, and we took cover wherever we could. I dropped into a shell-hole in the middle of an open field, and the other signallers near me did likewise.' C Company 'was [1] suddenly met with an appalling and withering outburst of machine-gun

[1] Crabtree.   [2] M. Jones.

and rifle fire from the front and left front—the west and north-
west of Sailly-Saillisel. Our fellows went down like ninepins,
and soon all was confusion. F. L. C. was close to me; he said,
"Here's my chance, I'm after that V.C." With a shout to his
men he was off, making for a machine-gun straight to his front.
He got 20 yards, and went down shot through the head. Our
only hope was to get on, to stay was to be slaughtered. I shouted
to the men to rush to the railway, and started towards it myself.
I got perhaps 50 yards, when I crumpled up with a bullet through
the leg, which split the tendon. Rothwell, my faithful batman
and runner, was close on my heels, and he and I were alone, about
40 yards in front of the rest of the Company. He bandaged me,
and, even amongst the bullets flying about, managed to envy my
luck in getting such a perfect "blighty." I scribbled a line to
H.Q. telling them of the situation, and ordered Rothwell to take
it back. He flatly refused to leave me, bless his heart!—until I
forced him, by alternate blasphemy and threats. I could then
see the survivors making their way back. I tried to follow, but
was like a winged partridge. Our barrage had ceased, and, to
my horror, I saw Germans coming out of their position and
advancing towards us. They came from a line in front of their
machine-guns and in lower ground. With a despairing look
around I saw more advancing from the left rear. I wasn't left
long in doubt as to my fate. I was soon a prisoner, hustled by
two men to a battalion H.Q., and the Great War ceased to be
interesting.' Ainge describes the blast of fire as coming from
D Company's left front, later from the left rear; Chick agrees
about these directions.

Besides these two officers, J. O. Smith and Larson were still
on their feet; they set about extricating their men. West of the
railway Ainge came upon Rothwell, who told him where Crabtree
lay wounded. They set out by the side of the line with the notion
of bringing him in, but, coming against Germans who were too
many and close to be wholesome, they had to scramble back.
Counter-attacking Germans were all about. Isolated shooting,
bombing and some hand-to-hand fights took place over a fairly
wide area. Under pressure, men of A, C, and D Companies
worked and fought their way, with loss, to a position on the right,
just below the crest of the spur that looks over to Sailly-Saillisel;

it was an old trench and sap, recently improved by the Germans, two to three hundred yards east of the Frégicourt–Le Transloy road. There were about fifty men with Ainge and Larson, and an officer and possibly ten men of the 17th Battalion who had become detached. They mounted their Lewis guns and fired to their left and left rear mostly, for they had not much trouble from the front. The small-arms fire they were under died down, but after a little the enemy resorted to trench-mortars which fired from the left front. As this new offence was finding them they had to wage a fresh battle. It used up a lot of ammunition before there was quiet again. Morgan Jones, D Company's senior signaller, who has been quoted as having dropped into a shell-hole in an open field, continues, 'For a long time it was impossible to raise one's head above ground without making oneself a target for the German machine-gunners, who seemed to be in complete command of that part of the line. How long we lay in the shell-hole I cannot say, it felt ever so much longer than it really was. At last, looking round, I saw a few men of D Company in a shallow trench. Picking up my rifle and signalling apparatus —and my dwindling courage—in both hands, I made a series of dashes across the open and eventually dropped headlong into the trench. . . . What impressed me at the time was the admirable coolness of the officers; I can see Mr. Ainge now [1932] sitting on the side of the trench, wearing a thick comforter round his neck. I learned that Mr. Jones had tried to rush a machine-gun post almost single-handed, and that he and his batman, Davies, had been shot in the attempt; also that Signaller '88 Jones had been shot. I had asked '88 not to leave me as I feared for his safety in a place of that kind, he was very awkward, a care to others, but he elected to go with Napper, apparently to the undoing of both. Napper was found dead, bayoneted in several places; he was a great souvenir hunter. On reaching the trench I made an attempt to get into touch with H.Q. by means of a Lucas lamp. Unfortunately, or otherwise, while fixing the lamp on the parados I happened to lift my head a little too high, and a bullet passed through my steel helmet and cut its way along my scalp. I was very thankful then for a thick head. I was not knocked out, but merely stunned, so I continued to manipulate the lamp and to send out messages while some friend was kind enough to dress my wound. (Ainge's recollection is that Morgan Jones was raising his lamp to try to attract a contact aeroplane, that was taking no notice of them, when he was hit.) I remained in the trench for sometime after I was wounded, and I remember very clearly a newly-made young sergeant of D Company saying, "Something has happened to the Battalion on our left, boys; we are nearly surrounded by Gerries." At the same time he put a fresh clip of cartridges in his magazine, for it was a dark hour then.'

The direction of the German counter-attack drove A Company also to the right. Chick and Smith organized, as they could, a withdrawal along the railway line. They had not gone far west of the Frégicourt road when the fire from the right became heavy, and they could see movement about the Morval–Sailly road, which threatened their right rear. Sergeant Mays was put in charge of a party, with orders to push ahead and occupy a position from which this threat could be held off while the withdrawal of the main body was being effected. For a time A Company was completely isolated, held up by small-arms fire from the right, rear and left. Men of B, C, and D had been picked up or had joined. All of them reported disaster and the loss of their officers. That was the burden of a message Chick got through to H.Q. The concern of later messages was to learn the situation on his left, he could see to his right for himself. Eventually the remains of the Company, and parties of the other Companies and of the 17th Battalion, got back to the outskirts of Morval. Smith was one of their considerable number of casualties. The sergeant's post was left in position out on the railway, and the sergeant received a nasty wound, 'he was shot through the mouth—he was a tremendously forceful talker.'

Some further impressions of events in front were gleaned by the Adjutant during a reconnaissance. D Company's Acting C.S.M. said that when they were met with the blast of small-arms fire they formed a shell-hole line; attacked by the enemy in large numbers, they were ordered to fight their way back: only he and two others had succeeded in doing so. But Evans found another party of D not far off. They told him of Germans who played the Kamerad trick as they passed them on the forward rush, then fired into them from behind, doing a good deal of damage as well as escaping back to their own side of the fence. From a

SEPTEMBER 1918 529

party of A Company he learned that one of their sections had been captured by a ruse. Some Germans came forward with their hands up, but when our fellows approached about fifty other Germans surrounded them. No clear account of what happened on the left was got from the men of C and B who were spoken to. B Company was in difficulty before the first objective was reached. The smoke screen was an imposture, it was no more than a thin mist at the start of the advance and the breeze soon dispersed it. The Company was met and followed by fire from the left, enterprise was felt to be wanting in the handling of it, it became disorganized, and was shepherded away into captivity. These details, which round off an account of events in front until noon, anticipate events in rear.

H.Q. followed the Companies. With E. J. Greaves, who was Acting Second-in-Command, and the Adjutant were Hughes, the Intelligence Officer, a few runners and a signaller or two; and Padre E. R. Jones had attached himself. Greaves was "wounded at duty," a shell splinter had entered his neck. The going was good. 'We[1] observed as we went that B Company had already placed one of its flank defence posts, and the Companies ahead had disappeared over the dip at the far end of the plateau. Our first surprise was experiencing that uncomfortable sensation of being fired at from behind, from our left rear to be exact. Some fifty yards in that direction were 3 or 4 wounded Germans in a shell-hole. Suspecting them of this unsportsmanlike potting I went and inspected their shell-hole, but found them unarmed and one or two of them armletted stretcher-bearers. Very shortly afterwards some of our men on the left, the defensive flank party, were seen to be falling back rather hurriedly towards our starting-point; so our little party linked up with them in some ragged trenches (on the west side of the re-entrant we were in, and about 800 yards from Lesbœufs). It was about 7 o'clock. Just then an enemy machine-gun force appeared at a point our men had come from, about 400 yards away. They settled down without delay to get their light machine-guns at work, while we got equally busy with our rifles, and a providential machine-gun team, at this time attached to every infantry battalion, got busy. Some details of the 17th Battalion had somehow got mixed up with us. Quite early one of them, firing at my elbow, was shot

[1] Ll. Evans.

through the head. We had no means of getting him or any of our other casualties away, and he eventually died in the trench. Our C. of E. Padre assisted us by dodging back to the village to our H.Q. details for ammunition, and to Brigade with a message to push out the supporting troops to deal with this menace to our exposed flank. While we kept up a lively fusilade with the German party, two companies of the 10th S.W.B. were very shortly seen coming out from a point in rear of our left and moving, in open order, on this enemy "stronghold." Some little time later they returned past our post with a good bag of prisoners. The Gerries had thrown in their hand in good time. Indeed, as Hughes says, their attack was half-hearted.

So far there was no news of the Companies apart from the evidence of this section of B which had fallen back when threatened with being cut off; it had previously lost touch with the rest of the Company. Later in the morning, rather after 8 o'clock probably, a runner appeared with a message from Chick reporting that he was in difficulties and needing help. de Miremont had just arrived. He looked round his staff and said to me, "I think, Yanto, you had better go and see what's happened." So I took up a rifle and some ammunition, the phlegmatic, ever-ready Pierpont went with me, and we had quite an adventurous time of it altogether. Aiming for Morval, on the right, with Chick as a first call, I got in touch with a battalion of the 113th Brigade some 300 yards north-east of Morval: their left was in the sunken road leading to Morval Mill, their right was in front of the village. Going east along the railway line a post manned by A Company was found, and an isolated party farther out was heard of. The sniping and machine-gun fire from the right, that was still active, made a visit to that post too foolhardy a task in the circumstances. Returning along the railway, and inclining to my right, elements of all four Companies were found in packets in a trench facing east of north-east, some 200 yards in front of the 113th Brigade line already mentioned. There were half a dozen men of B, a dozen of C, and two parties of D, including their acting C.S.M., from whom an impression of the nature and extent of the disaster in front was got. The trench was under the fire of machine-guns and snipers, and was being shelled pretty heavily. Just behind the right of these groups, in some entrenched ruins, was Chick with the remainder of his Company, along with elements of the 17th Battalion. Chick was in a bad state of shock, hanging on by his nerves and quite unfit to carry on longer. (Thus a portion of the Battalion was so far south as to be in the 113th Brigade area, the rest was all in the 17th Battalion area, excepting H.Q.) Returning now to H.Q., a situation report was written and despatched to Brigade. It was timed 2.5 p.m. By then the 10th S.W.B. had been moved out to the left, and was in touch with the 17th Division. Chick had been sent to hospital; (the morning's strain had been too much for one who for two weeks on end had done strenuous work excellently in responsible and hazardous conditions). Hughes relieved him; he collected and sorted out the remains of the Companies. Rothwell turned up at H.Q. with Crabtree's message.'

Between one and two o'clock D Company's wounded signaller, Morgan Jones, had been persuaded to make his way back. 'Things had quieted down by this time, and I managed to get well away during a very quiet interval. I must have kept well to my left, and I came across some of our men. I made a bee-line through quarries and orchards, making good use of my legs. I met Padre E. R. Jones, who was looking for the doctor as he had collected a number of wounded, ours and German. He directed me down a road on which were some dead horses, and soon I reached an advanced dressing-station where the doctor gave me a cup of tea, for by this time I was feeling very faint.' A message to H.Q. had been given to Jones, although the senders thought that he was as likely as not to fall into German hands, or by them. It was delivered direct to Brigade where the pitifulness of its appeal moved Colonel Norman, the Acting Brigadier, almost to tears, but he had no troops to send to the succour of his suppliants. The trench-mortar bombardment of these isolated elements was followed later by whizz-bangs fired from Sailly-Saillisel. The gunners had the position taped, and fired bursts for a good bit of the afternoon, 'finding us all right.' Although these bursts caused only a few slight wounds they were more nerve-racking than any of the previous fire had been. After the whizz-bangs ceased there was a period of real peace. Our 17th Battalion comrades left us then, and made for the rear. Towards dusk there was a lot of movement about the German position. Two or three hundred men formed up in close column of eights, and marched through the village from right to left. They were followed by several vehicles, the last of which was a Red Cross wagon. The light was failing, the range was long, and our supply of ammunition was very short, so they were let depart in peace. About half an hour later lines of troops in open order appeared from behind our right. There was no creeping barrage covering them, and no bombardment of Sailly-Saillisel, consequently our impression was that they were Germans. The question of using up the remaining ammunition on them was under discussion when they were recognised as our own people. They advanced to our objective of the morning without being opposed. After that Ainge and Larson withdrew their party along the railway to Morval. Casualties in the composite detachment they had collected in the morning amounted to about 50 per cent. When Ainge went to H.Q. to report Evans looked up and exclaimed, "Hullo, Babe, I'm just returning you as 'missing, believed killed.'"

During this hectic time our American M.O. was fully occupied. He showed that day that he had the infantry outlook, and had made himself one of the Battalion. He set up his Aid Post well forward. Owing to the inability of the Battalion to supply bearers he borrowed squads from the Ambulance; learning, as did others, that these men have not the enterprise of the infantry in clearing casualties, he went up himself, and several men besides J. O. Smith, who was lying out on the railway, owe much to his action.

The day had been disastrous to the Battalion; 36 were dead, there was practically no B Company. The causes of the disaster became clear enough after the event. The Battalion advanced with both flanks in the air and found itself in a cul-de-sac. The uncovering of the right flank was owing to the failure of the 113th Brigade to overcome the opposition to its emergence from Morval earlier in the morning, it could make no headway against the enfilade fire from its right, and the frontal fire, to which it was exposed: its failure uncovered the 17th Battalion, which came under similar fire and was held up. On the left, our line of advance being parallel and close to an old trench system which the enemy occupied, it needed only an enterprising officer there to seize the chance that was offered, for there were still in the retreating German rearguards men with plenty of fight in them when they were well led.

The Germans at Sailly had played their part by the late afternoon, so the situation had become easier when renewed action by the 18th Division contributed to the clearing of the ground on the 113th Brigade's front and flank south-east of Morval. At 6 o'clock that Brigade began the sweep which brought our Division on to the line of the main north-and-south road through Sailly. By then the delayed 17th Division had advanced on Le Transloy; the 10th S.W.B., in touch with it, straightened the line; and our attached machine-gun kept touch with the S.W.B. At 8 o'clock the 115th Brigade advanced, in extended order, to a line of old trenches in the low ground 800 yards west of Sailly. At 9 o'clock Hughes had orders to organize our 120 remaining men in two Companies of four platoons each, one to be commanded by himself, the other by Ainge. Already the scene of the morning hold-up had been searched. H.Q. betook themselves to a quarry-like hollow having some crude shacks and cubby-holes in its sides.

September 2nd.—For the greater part of the day the Division stood fast. In the later afternoon orders, expected since last night, came in. Again the whole Corps would move. The Brigade was to advance two and a half miles to a trench line, presumed to be the nearest enemy position, between St. Martin's Wood and Le Mesnil-en-Arrouaise. The dispositions were—ourselves on the right, the 10th S.W.B. on the left, and the 17th R.W.F. in support, the 113th Brigade being on the left. The Companies had about an hour in which to prepare, to form on a north-and-south line where the road from Saillisel forks to Mesnil and Rocquigny, and be ready to advance at 5 o'clock. A few minutes before our start, Larson, whom Hughes had sent forward to reconnoitre the jumping-off position, reported that he had been fired on before reaching it. The different units had orders to move to their assembly independently. Our orders were to go up in column of route, with a point well forward, and to be ready to deploy before getting to where we might be fired on. When we were still in the ruins of Sailly-Saillisel, and in close order, heavy machine-gun fire scattered the column. Hughes 'got[1] in touch with two or three sergeants, and 20 or 30 men were collected in adjacent shell-

[1] Hughes.

holes. We worked our way to the jumping-off ground, and waited under cover in a bit of wood on the edge of the open country. Ainge was not far off with some of his men. Shortly afterwards our barrage began. The counter-barrage, or an unpleasant portion of it, for one could not distinguish the bursting of individual shells, came down on our position.

At zero we moved off. The ground was found ideal for our purpose; there were plenty of shell-holes, mostly old ones. We were no longer worried by shell-fire, but machine-guns on our right front became troublesome, and some machine-guns were firing from a village behind us. We, however, had the pleasure of firing at an extended line of the enemy retiring in good order down the slope; the range at first was 400 yards. Pushing on we came very close to a machine-gun nest right in front of us. Machine-guns were firing from both flanks also, and we could get no farther. Our distance from the village was then about 600 yards. I sent a message back to H.Q. giving our position, but unfortunately it did not arrive in time to stop a fresh barrage by our own guns, which passed over us.'

The village in rear of Hughes's Company from which fire had come was Saillisel, which is east of and contiguous to Sailly-Saillisel. It had been reported clear earlier in the day, so it was not included in the artillery programme. The troops on our right found it occupied, and cleared it only after considerable scrapping. Parties of the 17th Battalion were formed to try to work round the machine-guns on Hughes's right which had checked his Company's advance at the start. The barrage which passed over him was meant to cover that movement, of which he did not know owing to the usual difficulty and delay in getting messages through. Little progress was made, so about 9 o'clock a line was formed from a point about 200 yards east of Saillisel, running north-westwards. When darkness fell, and it was a very dark night, Hughes 'got in touch with the troops behind us; we brought our wounded back; and the enemy retired.' Before midnight the 17th Battalion had taken over the front of our short advance. Our right Company was withdrawn somewhat to an old trench south-east of the fork of the roads, and the left Company to the ruins of Sailly. The whole Brigade was bunched into a small space, its front was very narrow. Overnight the H.Qs. of its three battalions and other elements of each were in a commodious but stuffy dug-out. The scene was comic. de Miremont waged hectic warfare, handling the Brigade with a Napoleonic touch; Welton, commanding the 17th, would be damned if he'd subscribe to the Count's strategy; Sykes of the 10th S.W.B., a one-time English international Rugger forward, just lay low. In *September 3rd*—the small hours Hughes was summoned hurriedly to the Council of War which still sat, and decided nothing.—The 113th Brigade, on the left, was attacked during the night. In the morning the enemy shelled the villages with guns behind the Tortille.

The longed-for relief was not forthcoming, but the spirit of the troops was extraordinarily good in spite of the arduous fighting of the last two days. A new spirit had possessed all ranks since the crossing of the Ancre and the seeming end of trench warfare. A fresh attack was to be made with the same immediate objective. The only change in yesterday's dispositions was that we and the 17th Battalion changed over. Our advance, which was made in the morning, had its humorous side. de Miremont took charge in person of our operations, and we were honoured by the presence of a number of Brass Hats who came to witness the show. Portents surely. Marching on the road, again in close order, we were treated to a particularly heavy and accurate dose of shelling, mostly gas shells. The men scattered all over the place. Two attached officers of a Lancashire regiment were among the casualties; they were such recent arrivals that their particulars had not been taken by the Company. The shelling was asked for, because the German guns were visible on a hill crest and must have been firing over open sights. There was an anxious interval as we approached the objective, but the trench was found unoccupied. By two in the afternoon the Battalion had settled down on a sheltered ridge near St. Martin's Wood, within hearing of the efforts of the 114th Brigade to push across the Tortille. Company officers and men were dead beat from fatigue and want of sleep. Ainge, when he could, threw himself down in a dark, fusty old dug-out in which his servant had put his stuff. He awoke at length to find it was no trance that had overcome the German on whom he had pillowed, mistaking him for the roll of his kit. 'The[1] conjoint H.Q. resting-*September 4th*—place in this hollow was unique. For two nights

[1] Ll. Evans.

we slept—de Miremont, Welton, Sykes, myself and several other officers—in a rectangular hole in the ground, some four feet deep. A huge tarpaulin, salved from somewhere near by, covered us. So tight a fit was this communal bed, and so exactly did our counterpane cover us, that it was literally a case of "when father turns we all turn," father being usually the Count.'

The Battalion had a strength now of about 90. It was formed into one Company of four platoons fully officered, a draft of three officers having arrived. The weather was fine, and the day's rest most welcome, but with the halt the desire for relief became an obsession The men as a whole were patient, but they were listless, having almost reached the limit of endurance. A youngster, one of a group of 30 among whom a shell burst, harmlessly, became violently mad with shock; he was like a hysterical child, and had to be restrained forcibly from running wildly towards the enemy. The Count would have had him tied to a post, but the M.O. took charge and sent him to hospital. Evans 'ventured to remark on the men's patience and endurance, and how one couldn't at heart really blame them if they said they'd reached their limit and couldn't go a step farther. The Count completely misunderstood the humanity of the remark, and stormed—"never let me again hear my adjutant expressing such sentiments."

September 5th.—Relief at last. One battalion of the 21st Division took over our Brigade area. We marched back to hutments west of Le Transloy. Even the heavy rain which came on towards evening failed to damp our spirits.' The order now was for troops to glean their route for equipment and stores, and to dump surplus at cross-roads for other units to pick up.

September 6th.—With the coming of a new Brigadier, H. de Pree, a Gunner, Lt.-Col. C. C. Norman from the 17th Battalion, who had been Acting-Brigadier, took command. The old Regulars congratulated themselves on having 'another of the Old School, and of the Regiment.' Before de Miremont went on leave he and Evans advised the C.O. whose names should go forward for decorations earned during the recent period of fighting. Lance-Corporal W. Evans was strongly recommended for the V.C. (see August 25th), for he had saved the C.O.'s life, and perhaps other lives. Col. Cockburn, from hospital, supported and amplified our representation.

September 7th.—Surplus rejoined, bringing with them strong reinforcements of officers and men. They had been waiting close to Delville Wood. For one of them at least, the remains of Ale Alley, Beer and Stout Trenches, and the Sugar refinery at Ginchy held memories of the rough times our 1st Battalion had there in 1916. Ainge was made Assistant Adjutant in place of Corney, who had to go to hospital as soon as he rejoined from Surplus.

The Battalion enjoyed a well-earned rest for three days. Since we went into the Aveluy Wood sector early in August there had been practically a continuous performance of trench warfare, followed by more or less open fighting. None of us had taken off our clothing during that time, and we had been wet many times since we waded the Ancre. Our casualties had been nearly 360, and we had come out of action as one company. Baths, *September 8th*—change of clothing, hair-cut and sleep were badly needed. All these joys were ours now. A gift of several barrels of beer from the Division, and a visit of The Welsh Wails, an excellent Concert Party, afforded real entertainment. The relaxation was most beneficial. Refitting and reorganizing, a little Lewis-gun practice, practising an expected attack—it included firing a rocket, as B Company was soon amused to remember—filled in the short working hours. The strength of a company was now 58 exclusive of men specially detailed to remain at the Transport; the Staff consisted of signallers, 2; runners, 2; cooks, 3; servants, 2 (average); stretcher-bearers, 4; sanitary man, 1. Of 25 battalion officers 9 might be on leave or on a Course at one time. Some of our reinforcement officers were slow to absorb existing conditions, so Greaves, never the most patient, was inclined to be irritable, but "Uncle" was loud in his praises of two very young and keen subalterns he had been lucky—his usual luck—in getting to his Company. The new C.O. showed a zeal for all-round efficiency and smartness that was bracing. He revived the practice of falling in to the Drum that had died out since we were at Airaines. He surprised and shocked our junior officers by finding out personally how much each knew of map reading. It was characteristic of him that he could do smartly the things that every man in his Command had to know. Because this was his first tour in front with us the Adjutant gave up his turn at Surplus to go in with him.

September 10th.—The Battalion and Transport marched in the afternoon, in torrential rain, to German huts east of Lechelle. A considerable move forward had been made since we were in the line. Cambrai is a bare twelve and a half miles north-east of where we were. The march was memorable for one new Company Commander who had risen from the ranks and felt justifiably proud of his promotion. 'I[1] was called on to get astride the Company charger. My only experience had been with a wooden horse at a Fair. After nearly going over the other side of the beast when mounting, I managed to remain seated until we arrived at the first halt when I handed it over to the groom, feeling much more comfortable on my feet.'

September 11*th*.—Bad weather continued. In the morning officers went to reconnoitre the position we were to take over just south of Gouzeaucourt. Later on we relieved the 7th East Yorks. The front line was near the village. H.Q. was on the main road to Fins, beside Gouzeaucourt Wood and near Metz-en-Couture. We were on the ground where the 3rd Army's surprise attack last October might have pulled off a big success. A and B were in front, C and D in support. The area was a network of old trenches dating from 1917. Our front was an old British support line, Heather Support. It was much broken down and quite shallow in places, the wire was very sketchy and there were no dug-outs. B Company's only shelter was a cubby-hole on the left, with a tin roof, that Kirkby and Nickson shared. Owing to the length of front and the weakness of Companies the line was held by scattered posts in the least dilapidated parts. Visiting the posts by day was most unpleasant, the longish stretches between them were so filled in. Our predecessors had a number of men sniped; since their bodies had been left unburied they served as a grim injunction to us to keep low. The Germans were in the corresponding old British front line. There was a bulge forward of B Company's line on the left, where the distance from the enemy was only about one hundred and fifty yards, but the line ran straight and at a greater distance on the right. 'Although[2] it looked as if the enemy was up on a skyline and we in dead ground to him he could see into our trench all right, as I learned in after years, and we couldn't see him.'

The enemy was offering a determined resistance again, his

[1] Turner.   [2] Nickson.

September 12th—artillery being particularly active with gas and high explosive. For several hours in the early morning until 7 o'clock there was heavy shelling of the front line, and a dispersed fire behind. We had about 20 casualties, including an officer killed. About a dozen of the casualties were in B Company, there would have been more but for the bulge of the trench on the left, the shells fell behind that part of it.—A subaltern in the support line, whose first twenty-four hours of the actual war this was, longed so audibly and persistently for 'the fleshpots of Piccadilly' that to his seasoned companions 'it seemed ridiculous to be moaning so soon,' and he was rudely bidden to 'shut up.' To one veteran the best remembered feature of the tour is the want of firewood, and the day-long puffing and blowing by his servant at a candle and sand-bags to cook a dinner, and the three-course triumph that 'gem of a batman, Dale, put up.' Sand-bags cost half-a-crown a piece by then.

September 13th.—During the night the German machine-guns were active enough on the Brigade front to interfere with our patrols. 'In [1] B Company several sentries, men of the latest draft, were found with unloaded rifles. Two of them, on being questioned, said they didn't know how to load.

The morning was that of a perfect early autumn day with bright sunshine. It was very quiet and still, not a shot was being fired along the whole front. Perhaps the quiet was rather ominous. We had finished breakfast in B Company H.Q., and Thomas, our cook, an old soldier, was in his shirt sleeves washing up. Suddenly, at 9.20, we heard in the distance what sounded like a long ripple spreading in a wide arc along our front, and almost simultaneously a hurricane of shells descended on us. Uncle and I lay down in our shelter, biting the dust. We realized at once that this was something quite different from yesterday's shelling, and was almost certainly the prelude to an attack. Where we were the shells were falling as yesterday, about 20 yards behind the trench. This intense bombardment lasted 40 minutes, then it lifted as suddenly as it had started. No one in our post had been hit. We scrambled up, and heard shouts from the trench—"Here they come." Someone fired the rifle holding the S O S rocket: it popped out of the muzzle about a couple of feet and burned out on the ground. The Germans were coming over the skyline in extended order, in

[1] Nickson.

sections, on each side of the communication trench which entered our line at this point. Two men were carrying a light machine-gun, one firing the gun from the hip as he walked and the other holding the box with the cartridge belt. There were others away on our left. It looked as if the 10th S.W.B. were being attacked too. In front of us the first lot was quite close. Thomas jumped up from among his pots and pans, where he had been crouching, and shot the nearest man in the hind quarters as he was about to get down into the trench. The Hun jumped high in the air, turned round and ran as fast as he could. The nearest post of the unit on our left had disappeared along the trench, leaving a long stretch empty, and our flank in the air. A section or so of the attackers got in there, but Sergeant Lee picked up a Lewis gun, jumped out on top, and, getting a position for the gun, shot eight of them. Lee was a very stout-hearted little fellow; he was acting C.S.M. since the previous day's reshuffle consequent on casualties.

Uncle told me to go quickly to the far end of our line and see what was happening there, so I ran off down the trench: it had been almost completely blown in. I picked my way over masses of broken earth, and could not find a man alive. Three of our posts had been wiped out. At the far end one small post had survived, and, in spite of the men who could not load their rifles, was firing away quite merrily. The Germans on their front were just beginning to appear in an extended line on the crest. Our artillery was now putting over a very effective shrapnel barrage. These raiders began to waver, some lay down, then they got up and all ran back. I could hear firing and bombs bursting at the end I had come from, but after a time that ceased, and all was quiet there. I had left the fight in a very open state, with the Germans coming along strongly against our isolated post of about a dozen men. I listened intently but could hear no sound. It was impossible to know what had happened. The post at my end numbered eight or ten sound men, a few wounded men who were able to move had joined them from the next post. All the rest had been wiped out, I knew. As far as I had been able to see no Germans had come over in the middle part of our sector, but only against the two end posts. The question was, who was at the other end.

I started to go back along what was left of the trench, stopping frequently to listen. When I had gone about half-way I heard stealthy steps approaching. Whoever it was had evidently heard me and was playing the same game; he too stopped frequently, then came on a few steps when I was not moving. We were stalking each other. As we got closer the pauses became longer, and the moves shorter. At last the point came when we were bound to meet round the next bend. I felt that the tactical move was to be round the corner first so as to have "the drop" on the other man: so, getting ready to shoot at sight, I stepped round the traverse. Simultaneously a large figure leapt round the other end. We both made a kind of half lunge with our revolvers, then shouted "don't shoot,' in the same breath. It was Uncle. The whole thing was quite dramatic, it would have looked really well on the films.

The main part of the raid had been repulsed, thanks chiefly to Sergeant Lee and a few others of the Old Army in the post. When I got back to them they were sitting in a group calmly cleaning their rifles, and discussing the morning's shooting. Thomas, still in his shirt-sleeves, had gone back to his pots and pans. A German N.C.O. was lying almost on the parapet. When his section began to fall back he ran forward alone, and threw a bomb which hit the back of the trench and burst: under cover of this he had got right up to the post and was standing on the edge of the trench with another bomb in his raised hand when someone shot him. It was a stout effort. B Company's losses had been heavy; we were reduced to about 20 men all told. D Company sent up 2 Lewis guns to reinforce the position.'

The C.O. was making his morning round with Evans 'when we ran into a perfectly hellish bombardment which covered the whole of our front and support lines. It was impossible to seek shelter forward, so we had to try to work our way back to H.Q. The C.O. showed an uncanny instinct in dodging the shell-fire, some subtle intuition guiding him and controlling his pauses and dashes. Following his lead blindly I got back unharmed, like him, to find that H.Q. area also had been severely shelled.' Although B Company bore the brunt of the raid, A was involved, and the support Companies suffered under the shelling. D escaped with 3 casualties. Sergeant Gill was not included among them. He had spun like a top on one foot from the impact of a piece of shell on the great toe of the other; he had a similar whack on it at Nieuport.

The German troops were very mixed dismounted cavalry, prisoners were clothed in a variety of headgear and uniform. Besides some half-dozen prisoners, they left 13 dead among us, whatever other casualties they may have had. Our losses were probably greater under their bombardment, but the honours were with us. Nickson, a newly joined subaltern fresh from school, carried on like a veteran, showing any amount of pluck and resource.

An enemy aeroplane came over very low indeed, presumably to see the result of the raid. We all blazed away at it ; even a man with no idea of shooting at a moving object could hardly have failed to hit it. It turned, made several uncertain movements, then appeared to crash just over the skyline. The R.A.F. subsequently confirmed our claim to it.—During a dispersed shelling in the evening, of which H.Q. had an extra share, a shell burst in the Signallers flimsy shack when a card game was being played. Of the four occupants two were wounded, and Corporal "Paddy" Barrett, "out since Mons," was killed ; Richards, another original, escaped untouched.—At night C relieved A, and D, B. 'Hughes,[1] commanding D, was very upset that B had failed to move all their dead ; he said it was bad for the morale of his men, which was no doubt true, but we had all we could do to get away our wounded, for, to add to our difficulties, two of our stretcher-bearers had disappeared. As far as I know they were never heard of again. They had made several journeys between the trench and the Aid Post before they left us with a wounded man, and failed to turn up at the other end. To take a wrong turning and go into the German line was quite an easy thing to do, but an odd shell may have caught them in the open.'

September 16th was the third of three fairly quiet days but for some gas-shelling, mostly of our rear position. Trench routine, such as it had become, was the order. Any enemy patrol that was seen was a strong one. A sniper put on a road Gerry was using denied him its use, for there still were men among us who could shoot.

September 17th.—In the small hours the 10th Lancs Fusiliers completed a very slow relief. To save time a number of C Company started to go across country, and got some salvoes of gas shell when tied up in wire. Putting on their gaspirators they learned, as many had learned, how helpless one is in these blinkers

[1] Nickson.

in the dark: but no one was any the worse for removing them.—
A day and a night were spent in cubby-holes in the Canal du Nord
embankment and adjoining sunken road north of Equancourt. We
had baths, and made up a bit from Battle Surplus. Suggested by
the swank of one of his Lewis-gun teams, Turner, to excite healthy
rivalry, hit upon the notion of naming his Company's guns, and
had the names painted on the barrels. "Spitfire," "Wildfire,"
"Gunfire" and "Hellfire" were the right half-company, and
"Viper," "Adder," "Cobra" and "Asp" the left. It pleased the
teams immensely, but possibly it did not conduce to veracity in
their reports.

September 18*th*.—A march to trenches on Fins Ridge took us
through our Heavy Artillery positions. One of the howitzers had
burst, knocking out the entire team. By relieving the 2nd Argylls
we found ourselves associated again with the 33rd Division. We [1]
were part of a brigade in reserve during 'a full dress Show (the
Battle of Epéhy) by the 4th and 3rd Armies. As darkness fell the
stupendous volume of the bombardment for this attack was
apparent. It was the greatest show of fireworks I had yet seen.
The front was a line of flame, the explosions were so numerous
that they combined into one continuous earsplitting crash.'
While this was going on we were side-stepped to the left at
8 o'clock into trenches north-east of Dessart Wood. Our recent
Gouzeaucourt trenches were just over the ridge in front of us, but
the enemy had been driven back since we were there. Rations
were late in coming up because the Transport Officer's party had
a particularly bad time from shelling on the way, but it escaped
the casualties with which rumour had thinned it. The night was un-
September 19*th*—disturbed; and we spent pleasant, idle hours lying
in the sun and listening to the battle in the distance. Long streams
of prisoners came past us all day. In the late afternoon we were
under orders to be relieved. Rumour had it that we were going a
long way back into Corps reserve, so we were much elated. One
party was singing lustily "Shipmates o' mine" when an order for
the front line came in, and the singing stopped. We had no idea
there was any front line within miles. A reshuffle was taking place
among the Brigades of our Division. After being kept hanging
about in front of Dessart Wood for a long time, then following

[1] Ll. Evans.

guides up sunken roads and communication trenches "for hours," we arrived in some trenches crossing the main road into Gouzeaucourt village. B, A, and C Companies were in front, and D in support. 'B [1] was at a very unpleasant place called Queen's Cross. The trench was the continuation to the left of the one we were in a few days ago. A strong enemy pocket had held out here. Our 14th Battalion, whom we relieved, had made an unsuccessful daylight attack and had been severely mauled. During the relief the line was heavily shelled, and our artillery retaliated, which made matters worse. Both sides gradually worked up to such a pitch that Fritz, evidently expecting an attack, put down a regular S O S barrage on us. We had a fairly substantial dug-out here, which was fortunate since trench-mortar shells arrived on top of it with some frequency. A message came up that a fighting patrol of one officer and fourteen men with 2 Lewis guns was to go at midnight to the enemy line, find out if it was still occupied, and, if the enemy had left, take possession and send back word. The order ended with the usual exhortation to kill and capture large numbers of the enemy, which nobody in his senses ever took any notice of.

September 20th.—The first difficulty was to get out of the trench and through the barrage. We lumbered along, getting more and more strung out as we went. Even with the shelling going on, the noise of the patrol sounded to me like the whole British Army on the move. The men with the Lewis guns kept falling into shell-holes with tremendous crashes, and crawling out cursing. Progress was very slow After a time I decided to park my cumbersome command and go forward with the sergeant and one man. Having gone what seemed several miles, actually I expect about a hundred yards, we came to the wire and lay down to have a look at it. It seemed more than adequate—a thick black mass. A Verey light which went up fell almost on top of us, and burned on the ground beside us for an incredible time, lighting up everything as clearly as daylight—or so it seemed. And it seemed impossible that we were not seen. We saw a number of heads in coal-scuttle helmets just beyond the wire, looking over the top and moving up and down. When the light burned out it was so dark I couldn't see my sergeant lying at my side. We discussed the situation in whispers. The question was, should we go back and get the patrol and start a

[1] Nickson.

fight. My sergeant was very much opposed to this, and the more I thought about it the more I was inclined to agree with him. We reminded each other that we really ought to be back in Corps reserve. Finally I decided that honour would be satisfied if we went in and reported what we had seen. We found the rest of the patrol with some difficulty; most of them were fast asleep. On the way back we came across several wounded men of the 14th Battalion lying out in Nomansland, and took them in. It was beginning to get light when we reached the trench. Apparently we had been away a very long time, because Uncle was having a tremendous row over the 'phone with Battalion H.Q.; they wanted a report about his patrol in the worst way. No doubt Brigade was worrying them. As soon as the news went back that we were in everyone seemed satisfied, and what we had to report didn't seem of any consequence. After writing out a lurid account of all we had seen and done we turned in for a little sleep. The shelling of the trench had been very severe while we were out; probably it was just as well that so many were in front of it. We were lucky to escape with only a few casualties. The whole of one post were dazed, a large shell had blown in the trench and half buried them but no one was actually wounded.'

During the day several more wounded men of the 14th Battalion found their way into our lines. There was again a heavy strafe of our front line in the evening. At night we were relieved. ' B [1] Company marched organized as two platoons with nominally 100 yards between them. The men went at a tremendous pace down the slope to Dessart Wood, particularly those behind, and the hundred yards dwindled to about ten, we were in fact all in one tight bunch when a 5·9 shell landed in the very middle of us. We all fell flat, then got up slowly—feeling ourselves. Not a single man was touched. Why half the Company was not wiped out I don't know. On Fins Ridge the cookers were waiting for us with a meal of porridge. I don't remember ever tasting anything so good. We marched on most of the night to good huts at Lechelle. Uncle and I took it in turns to ride our fat pony. The men were in tremendous form, singing hymns all the way. We were all glad to have seen the last of Gouzeaucourt and district. *September 21st*—After being on the road most of the day we finished,

[1] Nickson.

over rough and sodden ground, in very comfortable huts, an old Casualty Clearing Station, just north of Beaulencourt, on the Péronne–Bapaume road. The G.O.C. was passed on the road-side; he offered congratulations on the Gouzeaucourt Show, and shouted to the men, "Well done, B Company; did you get the bayonet to work?"'

A week was spent refitting, reorganizing and training. The arrival of large drafts, there were 9 officers, almost brought the Battalion up to strength. Some old friends from Limerick turned up. The 3rd Battalion had been sent there after an uprising in Dublin in 1916, and owing to the continuance of unrest in Ireland. One of the new officers distinguished himself by shooting his servant in the foot with his revolver which, he said, he was trying to clean. The man at once shouted, "Thank God for that," and hopped away to the medical hut. Besides ordinary all-round training—drill, shooting, classes and practice attacks, the C.O. had the officers on compass work and map reading. There remained time to ramble about; there were excursions into Doullens; there was basket-ball. A Battalion Mess was set up again: that there had been none when practicable since Col. Crawshay's time was one of the Battalion's misfortunes.

September 28*th*.—It had long been a conviction in the B.E.F. that when buses came to carry the P.B.I. to the front, or a new front, they were for it. We bused to a hut-and-tent camp at Sorel-le-Grand, south-west of Gouzeaucourt. Stirring events were taking place a few miles ahead. The Hindenburg Line had been broken through on the 27th, to the general surprise. Gerry was on the run again, but Company officers and men who had been meeting him off and on for several years could not believe that his whole front was crumbling, and the War ending. Some day he'll stand again, they said, and we'll get it in the neck.—There *September* 29*th*—were rumours of disaster to the Americans on our right. The Battalion was standing-by at one hour's notice while Company officers reconnoitred the forward area. That unsettled state continued for four days, during which there was training, 'but not too serious, on a bomb and rifle-grenade range that ad-joined the camp. B Company found a dump of German stick-bombs, and sneaked off to divert themselves. The entertainment was not without excitement, some of the men threw so badly and so short. The Brigadier came on us one morning and stayed quite a long time, entering thoroughly into the sport.' Those who had seen several Brigadiers thought him the best we had had. Although the G.O.C. will never be forgiven the Hamel raid affair, many thought him the best the Battalion had served under, admitting that the War was going swimmingly for us by his time; anyhow, he made the Division.—For the first time in France the Battalion took part in Rugby games, playing matches against the 10th S.W.B., and a Field Ambulance team. One of the last batch of officers, A. C. F. Griffiths, was a prime mover in the matter, he aroused genuine enthusiasm among the men. During one of these matches the referee was interrupted, more agreeably than is usual for referees, by a message from the Staff-Captain telling him that he had been awarded the M.C.

October 3rd.—In the evening the Battalion marched via Epéhy to trenches near Lempire. The Division was in reserve while the *October 4th*—Schelde Canal was being attacked. At 7 o'clock we were on the move again. Our route was on top of a high bare plateau which was being shelled with bursts of 5·9s, so we had to get into artillery formation. It was hard to keep direction over the broken ground in that formation, there had to be frequent halts to check up. The enemy must have had a line in front of his main position here, because the ground was thick with American dead. We came on a long line of tanks, twelve or fourteen, all blown up and out of action. They had been manned by American crews. We heard that they had been supporting the Yanks' attack, and had run on to one of the anti-tank minefields laid in 1917. The mines had done their work well, the line of derelicts was as straight as if it had been dressed by the right. Deprived of the cover of their fire the Yanks came in for heavy casualties, and had to be extricated from their difficulties by the Australians. A long halt, from 9 until 3.45, was made. B Company, anyhow, used a tank as H.Q. Major Clegg-Hill, from the G. Staff of the 21st Division, looked us up and had a drink with Uncle, the only officer except Yates who had been with the Battalion in his time. From where we were the ground fell in a long gradual slope. The Hindenburg Line was about a mile in front; it extended like a long snake as far as we could see in either direction. Three thick and broad belts of wire with a space between each protected it. At this part the line was sited on the reverse slope of a ridge, and in such a way that our artillery was denied good positions unless it came into view. It looked about as impregnable as a trench line could be made, but the enemy had not been able to occupy it at his own time, or before he was definitely on the run. Far away in the distance we could see the smoke and bursting shells of the battle in progress. In the late afternoon we moved on again, came to Bony, and spent the night in part of the Tunnel of the Hindenburg Support Line. The machine-gun emplacements were particularly interesting. They were of thick concrete, each communicated with a dug-out below for the crew. The gun was clamped to a swivel arrangement by which it could be raised and lowered.

October 5th.—Our next move, to a line west of the outskirts of Le Catelet–Gouy, was a short one like yesterday's; we started in the late afternoon. Again the position was a very strong one; it was well wired, and covered by a highish cliff on top of which had been a line of machine-guns which had taken a heavy toll of the attackers; there were a great many of our dead on and in front of the wire. Here too, although the defenders had been under a tremendously concentrated shell-fire, the position might have been held almost indefinitely. As it was, the masses of gear and stores of all sorts left behind showed that the deliberate retirement was not going according to plan, but that, after holding out for a time, the defenders had suddenly cracked and made a run for it. We felt that the retreat was being accelerated to the point when it must fairly soon become a rout.

A pill-box that had been used as a dressing-station was full of dead; when the bodies were removed it made very comfortable quarters. 'B [1] Company occupied a large broken-down house with a very good cellar. As it was under the lee of the cliff there was no possibility of being worried by enemy shells. Altogether it made a most desirable billet. The men were in the upper part, and we had our Mess in the cellar. Some parcels had arrived, and we settled down to enjoy quite a good dinner from the contents. We had just started when a battery commander came in to say that he had planted two of his hows. in the street outside, and was going to fire seventy rounds during the night at some

[1] Nickson.

distant cross-roads, and, since he was obliged to point his guns over the house, he was afraid we might be rather disturbed. He then went away leaving a subaltern in charge. At the first shot the roof fell in, burying most of our men and causing several casualties; part of the cellar ceiling came down blotting out our dinner beyond recovery, and coating us with plaster; all the candles went out, leaving us in gloom. And there were sixty-nine more shots to go. We went out and discussed the situation with the gunners: but, orders!—business before pleasure!—in any case all that was going to fall had fallen at the first shot. It was not a pleasant night. In the morning we found that their tractor, which had brought up the guns, had been placed too near them and had also been wrecked.'

October 6th.—A short march in the morning brought us to the south of Basket Wood near Pienne, where we were close behind the line, in Brigade reserve. We were now beyond the old Somme battle-field, so conditions were less trying. The countryside alone was a pleasing contrast to the much fought-over ground that had been our habitation and our outlook for so long. Of late the German rear-guards had given little trouble, even the crossing of the Canal of the Escaut (Schelde) had not been strenuously resisted, but it was said that resistance was stiffening. The 38th Division had not been seriously engaged recently. Now, however, it was facing a strong position west of Villers-Outreaux, on the Beaurevoir–Masnières Line. It was long since the Germans prepared this reserve line, their next main line, $2\frac{1}{2}$ miles behind the Hindenburg Line. Not all the trenches had been dug, but concrete machine-gun emplacements had been built, deep dug-outs had been prepared, and a thick, double, barbed-wire entanglement ran along the whole length. For the most part the line was in open country, so it had a wide field of fire. Villers-Outreaux was one of the fortified villages on it. Like so many French villages it is mostly length. There are houses on both sides of a main road for probably one and a half miles, and the greatest width is not more than five hundred yards. Villers Farm, standing on a high feature south of the village and behind the trench system, was held by machine-guns which commanded Aubencheul and the approaches to Villers. In these circumstances a daylight attack could be carried out only under a heavier bombardment and barrage than was practicable,

and after wire-cutting had been completed; a night attack had,
therefore, been decided on.

October 7th.—'In [1] the evening Uncle was summoned to a
Company Commanders conference. He brought back word that
we were for it early next morning, but only, he thought, in a
mild sort of way. (The 115th Brigade was to capture Villers-
Outreaux in the dark by a north-east movement which would
envelop the village. The 10th S.W.B. and an attached Company
of ours, A was detailed, were to break through on the south,
dispose of Villers Farm, and join hands behind the village with
our 17th Battalion: the 17th were to break through towards the
high ground on the north-west, on which was Pierre Mill.)
When the S.W.B. and 17th had accomplished their part, for
which they were given three hours, B and C Companies were
to go up and, with the help of some tanks, enter the village by
the front door, and mop-up any of the defence who had failed to
get away before the back door was closed. The front door, a
sugar factory just beyond the wire, was to be held open by D
Company advancing with the 17th Battalion. C was to be
accountable for the south-east side of the main road through
Villers, B for the north-west side. We were told that the enemy
would probably try to make a big stand because he had no other
defensive position except a line many miles back, which was only
in course of preparation, and that if we could push him out of
here the War was as good as won. As prospective moppers-up
we quite realized that some little unpleasantness might well attend
the process, for Villers is a largish place, and the Germans in it
might need to be convinced by us that there was no escape for
them. Having retailed to the men as much of this as seemed
necessary, and particularly the part about winning the War, we
turned in to get some sleep.'

October 8th.—Zero 1 a.m. The attacks of our sister Battalions
and our own attached Companies, A and D, failed completely
against undamaged wire and heavy machine-gun fire. The 113th
Brigade, on the left, had some measure of success against the wire,
but could not advance beyond it against Pierre Mill and Angelus
Orchard. H.Q. was not aware of the failure until it moved into
the sunken road just south of the east end of Aubencheul-aux-Bois.

[1] Nickson.

The road was found choked with parties of the 10th S.W.B., our A and D Companies, machine-gunners, and advanced parties of the 114th Brigade, which had orders to carry the attack beyond the 115th and 113th Brigades' objectives. They were all seeking cover from the rain of machine-gun bullets which swept over the top. The postulates on which the advance of C and B Companies was founded had not been realized. There seemed to be a complete deadlock. 'In [1] the meantime B and C were moving up. They were due, according to plan, to push off from the sunken road at 4 o'clock. To get to it we had to march through Aubencheul, which is built on an eastern slope overlooking Villers. The night was very dark and wet. As we came over the ridge and through the main street we saw many lights going up from the direction of the German trenches in front of Villers and on our left front, and a good deal of machine-gun fire was coming into or going over Aubencheul. This was our first indication that all was not well.

Col. Norman met us at the end of the sunken road. He told us that the attack had failed, that our supporting tank had not turned up, but B Company was to go ahead and do its best to get into the village. (The C.O. had taken the situation in hand, and acted in this on his own responsibility.) The Company pushed off. It was organized as two platoons. There was no time to make any elaborate plan of advance, and no object in doing so; we did not know what to expect, and we were not being fired on. Leading to the village was a long straight piece of pavé road alongside which was a light railway. The ground along the railway was very broken, so we marched straight up the road in fours, fixing bayonets as we went. Ware's platoon, which was leading, got right up to the wire across the road. Suddenly German S O S rockets went up all round and we were fired on heavily from a trench just ahead. Almost at the same moment our belated tank came lumbering up behind, spitting fire into our backs. We scattered in all directions, taking cover as best we could. The tank came right into the middle of us and circled round, shooting at anything moving it could see against the lights of the Show. A lot of our men were hit. Uncle was lying on the ground riddled from the trench in front and the tank behind, but he kept on shouting to the men to "get on with it," and to the tank to get

[1] Nickson.

elsewhere. (He is so large that he could harbour a good many missiles without any important part being touched.) By this time Fritz was barraging the road heavily with hows. and trench-mortars. The shells burst with tremendous crashes on the hard pavé; one of them hit the tank and, most happily, put it out of action. Just before that, one of our men had attempted to lead it against the wire by putting his tin-hat on the butt of his rifle and walking ahead with his rifle held up in front of him. He was killed at once. It was impossible to see in the half light who he was, but it was a most gallant act.' Nickson was among the wounded: a bullet through the leg laid him out for a time. Willie Ware, meanwhile, had found a gap in the wire, and got some of his platoon through. He was new to the front, little more than a schoolboy, and this was his first time in action. At the head of his men he disappeared into the village. Directly afterwards several Germans came out of the trench and gave themselves up. Nickson was on his feet again. Our men were so scattered that it took him some time to collect what were left of them; but when this was done they 'went [1] on into the village and joined Ware. He was making a house-to-house canvass with his men, and had collected several prisoners. We went on doing this for some time, and found quite a number of Germans in the cellars of houses. Why they were there, and the entrance to the village not more strongly held I don't know, unless they relied on their exceedingly strong flank positions to cover the direct approach, and thought an attack up the main road impossible; or they may have thought that only the usual early morning strafe was going on, and didn't bother to come up.

As it was still rather dark, and difficult to keep control in the streets and houses, we of B decided to get out and work our way along the light railway round the north-west outskirts until we could see better. Turner arrived now with C Company, and made off towards the south-eastern part of the village. By the time we reached the railway station it was beginning to be light. We were fired on from Pierre Mill, on the left, and from the trenches directly behind us, which the 17th Battalion had attacked unsuccessfully earlier; so, turning round and taking cover behind the railway embankment, we returned the fire with our Lewis

[1] Nickson.

guns. It was rather an open question then if we or the enemy were surrounded. They, however, evidently felt it was time to be moving, because after a bit a number of them came out of Pierre Mill and ran away across the open, and we could see others slipping away down communication trenches in the direction of Angelus Orchard. While this was going on we were, of course, on the wrong side of the embankment relative to our front; and next, we were fired on by a field-gun on the rising ground just behind the village. Through a gap in the houses we could see the gun, and the men loading it and firing over open sights. We had several casualties from the first two or three shells before we got back into the sunken road between the brickfield and the station. Very soon one of our planes came over, so we lit a ground-flare to show where we were. It replied by dropping two bombs into the brickfield! Next our own artillery started shelling the village, so things were not too comfortable. A runner was therefore sent to the C.O. to tell him how we were situated. A message came back from him to say he was having the artillery stopped, and directing it on to the German gun; that, at 11.30, another tank, followed by D Company, was coming up to help by working round the north of the village: at the same time he would return to us 32 of the Company who had been "missing"—to put it kindly—since we found ourselves between the German trench and our own tank. They had been rounded up at H.Q. One of them was my servant; when questioned about his movements he said he had gone back to see about getting me some lunch.

We pushed into the village again, and met a runner with a message from Turner saying he was hard pressed, being surrounded in the south-east corner of the village, and wanted help. At the same time we could hear the second tank rumbling towards us, and indulging in some rather indiscriminate shooting—like its predecessor, so there was every inducement to go on rather than back. On the way we were fired on from the entrance to a house. One of our men ran forward and threw a bomb at the open door-way, but the bomb hit the side of the house and bounced back right among us. Miraculously no one was hit. We took a few prisoners from the house. One of them, a very fat sergeant, was very pressing with his cigar case. By the time we reached C Company they had got the best of it, and taken about 20 more prisoners.'

'When[1] C Company was ordered to follow B they advanced in file until the village was entered. Parties were then sent to right and left with scouts ahead, and connecting files. Our left got into touch with B Company. There were barriers across the roads, but there was no opposition in the village itself. We found a solitary, half-demented little Gerry in one of the cellars, who gave himself up readily enough. When we arrived at the Market Place our artillery began to drop a lot of heavy stuff in our midst, so we withdrew until it should lift. At this time an enemy machine-gun post was reported on our right rear. It and Villers Farm were about equidistant from, but on opposite sides of, a road running southwards from the village. Fire was opened on the post, and, after a time, it was rushed, 20 prisoners and 4 machine-guns being taken. These Gerries were greatly surprised at being taken in rear, but the readiness with which they surrendered was a bit of a surprise to me. When they were lined up for my inspection fire was opened on us by two field-guns that had escaped my notice so far, about 500 yards away on our right front. The gunners could not see us, because the prisoners were drawn up in a lane, but they had seen what had happened and guessed rightly where we were likely to be. Several of the Company were knocked out, including Sergeant Varcoe who had a bad thigh wound. I still have the message I shot back to H.Q. by a rocket apparatus, informing the C.O. of the situation and asking for stretcher-bearers. It is timed 10.40 a.m. The rocket, I was told, landed within 50 yards of H.Q. which, I estimated, was 1000 yards in rear. The prisoners were so docile that only one man was sent to H.Q. with them as escort, besides that I could not spare more. He was one too many. On the way down he fell into a shell-hole, accidentally bayoneting his leg, and was half-carried the rest of the way by his charges. The Company returned to the village and got into touch again with B.'

When C and B joined up they took stock of their resources. They had too few men, and too little ammunition for the number of Lewis guns they were carrying. It was seen that the second tank had soon run into the side of the sunken road near the station and become a casualty, so the surplus guns were dumped in it: it was useful for that purpose at any rate. A decision to work

[1] Turner.

through the remainder of the village had been made, and to meet in the sunken road at the far end, which was the Brigade's original objective. It was carried out without any further opposition being met. As C Company was going forward it had a view from the crest over a big stretch of open country on the right, and saw a disordered crowd of all arms of the enemy retiring. There were gun-limbers, horse-drawn wagons and motor lorries. 'It [1] was most exhilarating, the best thing I saw during the War. It made one wish for a regiment of cavalry.' The Company opened fire, but the excitement hardly lent itself to good shooting. There was a great deal of gear of all sorts lying about the exit from the village, all evidence that the main force holding the place had made a hasty departure. A motor lorry had solid iron tyres, for the Germans could not get rubber owing to the naval blockade. Near the south-east corner there was another windmill; a direct hit by our artillery had brought down a wooden platform at the top, killing the observer whose body lay among the debris inside.

Some of A Company had been seen in Villers at noon. By 4 o'clock the day was over as far as the Battalion was concerned. The 10th S.W.B. and our 17th Battalion, who had got going after noon, had joined us on their original objective. The 113th Brigade, on the left, was by then on its objectives. Again on the left, the 114th Brigade, from reserve, had advanced and dealt with the strong and troublesome machine-gun position at Château des Anglais. We had been at it for twelve hours, and were glad to watch the 114th go through and up the slope towards Malincourt, scarcely fired on. An occasional shell from a long-range gun was all that came over. And so, by penetrating the village B Company, and C, had turned the German defence on both flanks, and an awkward situation into a great success.

Christofferson had his Aid Post going promptly in a house in the village, and was busy with a great many wounded, our own men and Germans. In the late afternoon when Nickson was sitting in H.Q. reporting his Company's doings, his leg became stiff; he suffered later from a very bad attack of tetanus. His going from the Battalion was dramatic, like the deeds in which his was so active a part, and about which he has written such vivid passages. 'General [2] Cubitt came up in his car and, on his

---

[1] Turner.   [2] Nickson.

way back, picked me up and took me to the Field Ambulance in Aubencheul. The road was blocked with a mass of odd transport, and we were held up by what appeared a hopeless deadlock; but the General stood up on the back seat and withered them with such a magnificent gush of language that they scattered hastily, leaving a way through.' As dramatic was the chance identification in hospital by Kirkby of the commander of the first tank. The manuscript account of what Kirkby said to him is milk and water; anyhow, the original is quite unprintable. Our losses during the day were heavy. Griffiths, an outstandingly good officer, was killed, as was our Nonconformist padre. The padre should not have gone with A Company in the early morning. He was told that he would be an embarrassment to them; but he was impulsive, he insisted on going, and was killed when seeking a M.C. to please some fool of a girl in Liverpool who had taunted him with having no decoration.

In the late evening the Battalion formed camp; and our own reserves and the back-area troops began to swarm into the village. Our old friends of the 33rd Division passed through to take over the new line beyond Malincourt, three miles ahead. The night was spent in Villers-Outreaux. 'I[1] could not help contrasting this kind of warfare with that we had been used to during the preceding years. I never believed that we could lose the War, but I knew, like many more, that Gerry could hit very hard, and I expected that he would do so again. Here we had been advancing from the Ancre, and the opposition was becoming weaker at every scrap. His readiness to give in to-day showed that his morale was gone.'

October 9th.—The line to which the Germans had withdrawn was 7 or 8 miles east. The 33rd Division advanced across country in artillery formation, accompanied by field-guns, and preceded by cavalry who cleaned up some machine-gun rear-guard posts. Our 113th and 114th Brigades moved to Clary in support. *October 10th*—We marched to Bertry, and were the first Allied troops to rest there since the fight at Le Cateau on August 26th, 1914. We had come to country untouched by operations since the Retreat. The villages were inhabited. They had been occupied by the Germans as rest billets for four years. Only a few days

[1] Turner.

earlier Turner's billet sheltered a German officer who, it seemed, had been most hospitably entertained. In general, however, hatred of the Germans was deep; a man would spit on their dead who were laid out for burial. The people were friendly and kind to us, but they seemed as yet too dazed to realize that the German occupation was actually a thing of the past. They were badly clad, looked sadly and emaciated. What they craved was meat. They asked for the carcass of a horse that had been killed in our lines. It must have been a British horse, because all the German horses we came upon had been stripped of the best of their flesh. Seemingly every German on finding a dead horse took out his jack-knife, cut himself a steak—preferably from the loin, and put it in his haversack for a future meal. The inhabitants stripped the bones; groups of old men, women and children could be seen round the carcasses. Mules were not eaten.

A draft of 150 arrived. The number of men of poor physique was exceptionally large, in full equipment they were sorry objects. *October 11th*—"All troops of the 115th Brigade are granted a day *October 12th*—of rest." The Battalion and Transport marched to Troisvilles, three and a half miles west of Le Cateau.

The German retreat was speeding up, although a stand was being made on the Le Cateau–Solesmes road and railway parallel to our front. Our Brigade relieved the 100th Brigade on the river Selle, facing the railway embankment; we were about midway between Montay and Neuvilly. C and D Companies were *October 13th*—in front; C's posts were reached through a ravine that was much shelled: A and B were in support. The situation was similar to that on the Ancre. There was no movement by day and great activity by night; the river was patrolled, and examined for the establishment of posts on the eastern side. The sector was, at first, somewhat ahead of the general advance, but movements on the flanks brought them into line during the five days the Battalion was in the position. H.Q. shared Rambourlieux ("Rumblebelly") Farm with Brigade H.Q. The farm is on high ground, a landmark for miles round. It was less comfortable than where the Companies were, traffic about it being hazardous, for it was shelled constantly with gas and high explosive. de Miremont was in command with Ainge as Adjutant; the C.O. and Evans remained with the Transport at Troisvilles.

October 15*th*.—The railway embankment was treated by our heavies and by gas projectors. The Germans replied with an unusually heavy volume of fire for these days on our river positions. A shell burst on one of C's posts, killing or wounding everyone in it. One C Company man's scheme for an undue leave, on the plea of his wife's health, was wrecked by an unsympathetic police report from home. What does a wife's health not cloak or explain? After dark the Engineers began work on light causeways *October* 16*th*—at chosen crossing-places. Our Divisional Artillery and the 17th Division's, on our left, carried out another gas bombardment. At night A and B Companies relieved C and D, and C was withdrawn to the Le Cateau road as a reserve.

The war of movement upset the accustomed trench economy established during years of siege warfare. Picks and shovels were not now trench stores, companies had to take their own in and out on relief. Billhooks and axes had been issued to cut brushwood for flooring posts and trenches. Thermos food containers came into use again; and bivouac sheets appeared as a store on company charge.

October 17*th*.—The 66th Division, attacking on our right, took Le Cateau station and about 400 prisoners.

October 18*th*.—After dark the Battalion returned to Troisvilles. *October* 19*th*—Baths had been fitted up, so we became clean, and rested.

October 20*th*.—At 1 a.m. We were on the move to support the 113th and 114th Brigades in an attack across the Selle on the Amerval Ridge. In the evening we returned to billets without having been in action.

Troisvilles had been shelled continuously since first we came to it, and casualties were of daily occurrence. The Transport was in a field at the western outskirts of the village. During a vigorous strafe one evening a shell exploded in the field; fragments of it killed a horse at one extremity, its driver in his bivouac at the other extremity, and damaged their cart which was many yards away from both.

October 21*st*.—The crossing of the Selle was accomplished by the 114th Brigade against a stout resistance. The high railway embankment, not the river, had been the enemy's main line. It was held by numerous well-placed machine-gun posts which our artillery, with the co-operation of the 33rd Division's artillery and machine-guns, smothered. An exceptional number of machine-guns were found abandoned, both damaged and undamaged, along the embankment; and the large number of German dead beside them was eloquent testimony to the high total of the defender's losses. The amount of recent rain had made the ground so soggy that our tanks could not be used in this attack, but the Divisional pontoons, after being laboriously trundled about France and Belgium for over two and a half years, were used to bridge a crossing for the first and last time.

Our Brigade relieved the 114th. The Battalion was in reserve; but C Company was lent to the 17th Battalion, and B to the 10th S.W.B., from whom they took orders. A and D Companies were on the railway. R.E. fatigues occupied them all. H.Q. remained in Rambourlieux.

October 22nd.—Relieved by the 2nd Argylls, we returned to Troisvilles and were ordered to be ready to move in the morning. A very spick-and-span division, just out of rest, passed us on its way up. Our old soldiers had another fit of pessimism; they felt that Gerry would stand yet.

October 23rd was a day of action on a large scale. The whole Third Army moved forward. Our Brigade was supporting the 33rd Division. We left Troisvilles at 5.30 for the assembly position on Amerval Ridge. At midday we advanced in artillery formation. An enemy aeroplane swooped on us, but his aim was so bad that we had no casualties then; later we had a few from long-range shelling. Richemont was our first halt. At dusk we reached the neighbourhood of Croix and settled in for the night, but were on an hour's notice.

October 24th.—H.Q. was in the village. Croix straggles along the straight road that bounds the vast Forest of Mormal. All day we were standing-by, ready to fill a possible gap between the 18th and 33rd Divisions. Companies were dropped on for untidiness and untidy billets. Billet routine orders were revised and reissued: all the inspections that had fallen into disuse, and a few additional inspections, were to be made henceforth; and special orders were issued about saluting.

Since the Battalion left Troisvilles the Transport had been at Montay, fully a mile north of Le Cateau. The village was derelict, although earlier villages, and later, along our route eastward were comparatively undamaged, and inhabited. Possibly Montay had suffered in August 1914, and the recent fighting had only added to its ruinous state. One of its cellars yielded some very charming tumblers for the Mess, and a huge well-bound ledger to replace the much-worn volume containing the Battalion's nominal roll which had become almost illegible, so many were the alterations and erasures. From Montay Yates revisited Le Cateau, accompanied by Evans. 'It was inhabited but most dead-looking, seeming as if its four years of enemy occupation had completely broken its spirit and sapped its vitality.' The inhabitants of some places were being given entertainment by divisional Concert Parties.

October 25th.—Relief orders were suspended for twenty-four hours to let the 33rd Division complete, if it could, the capture of Englefontaine on the western edge of Mormal Forest. We practised scouting and close-country work. The district is very like the rural parts of the Midlands of England. Hedges and trees suited the sniper, and we were to find that the Germans were taking full advantage of the conditions.

October 26th.—Our Brigade relieved the 100th. At 4.30 p.m. we began taking over from the 2nd Worcesters and a company of the 9th H.L.I.; then the arrangements were changed and our dispositions were extended to include the 1st Middlesex front as well; eventually, after a very protracted relief, we occupied the right half of the Division's front. The code for "relief complete" was Chartreuse. H.Q. was in the Brasserie at the extreme west of Englefontaine, a village which stretches for about two and a half miles along the Bavai high road. C and B were on a line which ran through the western part of the village: D was on B's left by the tile-works road. A. was in the open. As the C.O. was again Acting Brigadier, de Miremont commanded. The Battalion had a twofold rôle: to hold a front, and to push in the screen the Germans had so far maintained to cover their latest intended line of resistance. Our posts were few, at varying and very wide intervals: thus C Company had two posts, and a liaison post with the 18th Division unit on its right; the remainder of the Company was under cover, ready to move at the shortest notice. Posts were relieved night and morning; such as were not fixed of necessity changed position frequently. The Germans had similar posts, so the Companies had patrols out every night to locate them, and strong enough to attempt their capture.

October 27th.—A very heavy strafe at 6 in the morning looked like the prelude to an attack. Nothing happened on our front, but our neighbours were raided; one of their posts was lifted. We had a few casualties. Among the killed was the civilian owner of C Company's H.Q. billet. He was lying on a bed in one of the cellars when a tiny shell-splinter came through a very small ventilation hole and entered his brain.

Sniping from house-tops, street corners, and cellars was the chief activity in villages through which the front ran. In places there was safety on one side of a road and sudden death on the other. Winkling these lairs and little strongholds was a popular pastime— less or more. Otherwise operations consisted largely in what was humorously called "peaceful penetration," a species of the German infiltration. It was altogether a queer sort of warfare for troops bred to war in trenches, but the technique, in its essentials, is as old as warfare. It consisted in creeping up to a post and watching for a favourable chance to surprise it; the gain was then used to attack the next enemy post in reverse, or threaten it, so that one's own next post could come up into line. Sometimes a stout resistance would be met with, as happened to-day to B Company's effort to drive in two posts some 300 yards ahead in houses on the rue d'Hecq near the church. Foiled for a time by machine-gun fire the B's gained their objectives at dusk, and their neighbours advanced 150 to 200 yards. Sometimes a converse procedure was adopted. Thus, posts and patrols were encouraged to let pass enemy patrols they could cope with, who did not see them, and then to close on them from behind. Later in these operations the Germans captured a small post of ours by another ancient stratagem : the occupants were deluded by friendly talk in fluent English from the other side. A macabre device was used by a blunt-mannered officer of ours to induce a recalcitrant prisoner to give his particulars ; a German wooden cross and a pencil were handed to him.

The chief opposition to our forward movement was on C Company's front. 'About [1] 300 yards in front of Company H.Q. the Germans had a barrier on the main road beyond the centre of

[1] Turner.

the village. As the Company's best sergeant was peeping round a
corner to observe it a sniper got him. That sniper was a watchful
fellow and a good shot. Butler, now O.C. B Company, and I
decided to investigate a house about half-way to the barrier.
We began at the front. The sniper promptly put a bullet through
and through my tin-hat about quarter of an inch above the cap
badge and the same distance above my skull. His next shot went
through my shoulder-strap. As it would have been a pity to have
"paid" put to my account so near the end, after having gone out
with the 1st Battalion in October 1914, we went round to the
back to examine the cellar. There we found about 20 civilians,
who shouted excitedly, "Anglais," and embraced us. They had
been crammed in that cellar for several days. Very pleased they
were to be evacuated during the night.'

October 28th was a quiet day. But C was pressing on its preparations to establish a post at the barrier, a small operation to
which the Staff attached importance. The orders issued for the
co-ordination of the arms employed make strange reading to
anyone who had seen the destruction of everything, regardless of
its use, value, and associations, on every front from the Somme to
Nieuport. The trench-mortars had to blow a gap in a garden fence,
but all care was to be taken that no damage was done to anything
beyond the needed width of the gap!—C Company got its barrier
October 29th—post. The Battalion was thanked, and ordered to
stand fast behind mobile patrols who were to be watchful of
chances to make small snatches. On our left the 17th Battalion
made a remunerative raid. Poix and Englefontaine were shelled
heavily by the Germans, who always fired in front of their posts
with great confidence and accuracy.

Villages shared by the Germans and the B.E.F. were being shelled
by both artilleries, so the clearing out of all remaining civilians was
ordered yesterday. Hitherto civilians known to be in Englefontaine
had been discouraged from coming out of their cellars except at
night; the German gunners generally rested then, but their every
morning strafe was something that had to be remembered. An
incident of to-day was the firing by Germans on a group, including
aged and infants, whom some of our men were helping to remove.
There were several casualties in the group and among our men.
As the desire of refugees to take the most needed of their chattels

tied them to the roads, and these were always liable to be shelled, instances of loss of goods and of life were not uncommon those days.

In the evening we were relieved by the 15th Welch, and returned to Croix, being heavily shelled on the way. The operations had cost the Battalion two subalterns of whom no trace was then, or since, discovered. They were not wounded or made prisoners. Representations to the enemy through The Hague by the parents of one of them, Ware, failed to throw any light on their fate, although the troops opposed to us at the time were identified and questioned.

Bulgaria was already out of the War; Austria-Hungary was suing for peace, and not to be put off this time; now Turkey had asked for an armistice, so our old soldier pessimists came round to the notion that our prospects were brightening.

October 30th was fine. There were the usual baths, cleaning up, and so on. A wet day followed, but we practised fighting in enclosed country. In anticipation of an advance through the *November 1st*—Forest of Mormal to-day's practice was fighting in a wood; Vendegies Wood, a copse between Croix and Englefontaine, was the venue for the exercise. We had a fine day for it.

November 2nd.—The Battalion returned to the line, which had scarcely changed. H.Q. was again in the Brasserie. Since the C.O. was still Acting Brigadier, de Miremont commanded; a subaltern commanded each Company.

A drive of the Forest by the 18th, 38th, and 17th Divisions had been planned. We were the right flank battalion of the Division, the 10th S.W.B. was on our left, our 17th Battalion on theirs. We were given a line of 500 yards on which to form up: during the advance our right had to conform to a meandering stream, the ruisseau des Eclusettes, imposing on us a contracting and expanding front which varied between 300 yards at its narrowest and 800 yards at its widest; the final objective, a north and south line through Locquignol, was 120 yards wide. The leap-frogging laid down for units and formations had to be modified to meet these conditions. Also, we could not keep in step if Companies, which were not strong enough to drop mopping-up parties, waited to mop-up, so H.Q. details were organized to do that, and our whole forward movement was made continuous.

November 3rd.—A lovely morning : a quiet day of preparations— inspecting rifles, ammunition, bombs, and giving instructions. There had been many pow-wows at H.Q. : maps and aero- photographs were studied. So excellent were the photographs that when we came on to the ground it seemed familiar to us. In the afternoon Howells Evans, now commanding C, and Keepfer, D, whose Companies were to open the attack, went out with Butler reconnoitring. Keepfer did not like the look of a farm on his right, and asked Evans to help from the flank. On their return Keepfer, an able Welsh-speaking platoon officer for all his German name, expressed a feeling that the chances of living to a ripe old age were distinctly rosy for those who came through this show, since the present opposition looked much like being the German's last despairing stand, and that their collapse was very near. Whatever truth his prophecy held Keepfer was to be one of the first to fall. And Howells Evans had the shock of learning that one of his two subalterns had gone sick, and had been sent down the line ; in the evening a substitute reported, a youngster come to the front for the first time.

November 4th.—The 17th Division opened the attack at 5.30. Zero for our Brigade was 6.15. C and D Companies were in position in front of the Landrecies road and just south-west of Englefontaine, ready to move off. Our artillery opened on time. 'In [1] spite of repeated warnings, the only officer with any experience I had, dashed forward too soon and was wounded in our barrage. Almost as the action began we became enveloped in a thick fog. I rushed down the trench to see that everyone was out, and, on clambering out myself, found I was alone and unable to see more than half a dozen yards. Here was a situation ! A company commander who at the start of an operation had lost his company in a fog. However, I blundered on in the direction the Company should have taken, and soon came across a sergeant and 14 men. We went on together. Soon we found a hedge leading in the line of our advance, and followed it through fields and orchards. Suddenly, when we had gone some distance, we heard a shout, "Kamerad." Looking through the hedge we saw a German machine-gun post. We dived through to get away from the gun's biting end, but the crew had the wind up, and surrendered

[1] H. Evans.

meekly. We managed to get out of them that there were other machine-gun posts, so we went in search of them and found seven. They were approached from the rear, and gave us no trouble. After that mop-up we went over to the house that Keepfer had not liked the look of. Its only occupant was all that remained of him. (D Company had had a clean run through; but in the fog it ran into our barrage and had casualties. A piece of a shell bursting behind him had penetrated Keepfer's heart.)

The fog was clearing. Although it had made the keeping of direction difficult it helped the attack and hampered the defence. I shall always feel as if it was sent to protect and help me, as it most certainly did. Our meeting with the machine-guns, and the flank move we made, had delayed us. When we got to the first objective, the Hecq–Englefontaine road, the rest of the Battalion was already there, for everyone had just gone ahead. They only began to have opposition from houses on the road. (A tank which had been allotted to us had failed to turn up, but a wandered 18th Division tank was found in the road. It was willing to be adopted, and rewarded us by doing valuable work in dealing with these houses.) I had the fright of my life in one of them. I was about to enter when a German threw a "potato-masher" at me from the top of the stairs, and at the same time Butler fired his revolver at him past my head. The masher fell behind the door; its bang on one side of me and the burst of Jim's revolver on the other made me wonder what had happened.'

After mopping-up these houses a realignment of the Battalion was made. B Company came up on C's right, on the left A took the place of D which fell back into support. The second stage of the advance was through the Forest of Mormal. It started off behind a fresh barrage. The mist had lifted. B Company was soon in trouble with a machine-gun post, and did not overcome it until several minor casualties had been incurred. B and C then got going again, but at the edge of the Forest B was held up by trench-mortars. Howells Evans, hurrying forward with C to take the mortars in flank, found that the whole of H.Q. was in front of his Company, and heard that A was well ahead of them. After the mortars had been scuppered there was no real resistance. Throughout the advance there was a gap of more than 400 yards between our right and the 18th Division. There again the tank was helpful, for it kept down the mortar and machine-gun fire from that zone which was not otherwise engaged. There was more trouble when the Locquignol objective was reached. It was of a kind we had not bargained for. The artillery of the 18th Division, intent on protecting the left flank of its own infantry, shelled us, with the result that we had to withdraw to the lower ground until it could be diverted to some better use. D Company, meanwhile, had formed a defensive flank along the Eclusettes. It was now sent across the stream into the gap, which it mopped-up from in front of Locquignol back to Hecq.

The German defence had broken down during the morning. The enemy was in rapid retreat, and was being followed by 33rd Division troops who passed through us in the afternoon, and reached their objectives without meeting any opposition. On relief we returned to our billets in Englefontaine. Our casualties during the operation were 1 officer and 10 other ranks killed, 4 officers and 65 other ranks wounded or missing. 4 officers and over 100 other prisoners were passed back. Next day we collected our trophies—1 field-gun, 6 trench-mortars, 26 machine-guns—light and heavy: we cleaned up and reorganized.

November 6th.—In cold and heavy rain we marched to a bivouac in the heart of the Forest; everyone was soaked to the skin. The *November 7th*—night, which was spent in the open, afforded the acme of discomfort and misery. So continuous and drenching was the rain that no fires could be lit, not even in the cookers which had come up.

Movement in the Forest was a hazardous business, since booby-traps for the unwary abounded. Special explosives experts from the Engineers were attached to infantry units to look out for and render harmless all such snares laid for the careless and the inquisitive. Passage for transport was likewise a problem because the main tracks were mined, or blown up. Much R.E. re-construction work was necessary before heavy vehicles and guns could use the rides and tracks.

The Battalion moved on to Berlaimont where we halted for four hours. Then, under considerable shell-fire, we crossed the Sambre to Aulnoye, a mile or two beyond the river, and billeted, relieving the 33rd Division. Outside the town there is an important junction on the railway line on which Germany's armies to the south depended. The town was almost undamaged, but our bombers and long-range guns had done their work well on the railway. Huge coal dumps along the sidings had been fired by the Germans; they burned for a week or more. The front was well beyond the town.

November 8th.—Early in the morning the Battalion moved out in the direction of Pot de Vin. 'My[1] last impression of the War is the advance across fields, and the enemy fighting a rear-guard action with rifles and machine-guns. Just in front of Pot de Vin I came upon the Count, who had made a captured N.C.O. stand on a hump and point out the position of machine-guns that were holding us up. With every question he asked he poked his revolver into the unfortunate fellow's ribs.' At noon we returned to our billets. The Transport, which had been at the curiously named village of Sart-Bara, came up.

It was plain that the War was fizzling out. Rumour of an Armistice was from now the general talk. For the rest, we spent *November 9th*—the day cleaning up and making ourselves comfortable. In case of some strenuous marching the Brigade turned out *November 10th*—on a practice route march, for operations had become a pursuit. A few reinforcements joined. Among them was Morgan Jones, who was wounded on September 1st. '. . . it was almost like going to a new battalion.' The last two and a half months had seen nearly as many changes as all the months on the Somme two years ago.

November 11th.—There had been so much talk of an armistice that a Brigade message in the morning telling us of its having been signed at 8 o'clock, and that hostilities were to cease at 11, fell somewhat flat. The event was anticlimax relieved by some spasmodic cheering when the news got about, by a general atmosphere of 'slacking off for the day,' and by the notes of a lively band in the late afternoon. The men betook themselves to their own devices. There was a voluntary Service of Thanksgiving in the cinema which the Germans had built; the spacious building was quite full. The local civilians were overjoyed. They dug out some drapeaux des Alliées in astonishingly quick time. And they were hospitable with their poor means. They brewed an awful decoction of baked and ground oats in place of coffee which had been

[1] Kent.

unobtainable for a long time. 'To [1] me the most remarkable feature of that day and night was the uncanny silence that prevailed. No rumbling of guns, no staccato of machine-guns, nor did the roar of exploding dumps break into the night as it had so often done. The War was over.'

The 33rd Division.—Not even on this day did the G.O.C. allow his men a tot of rum.

At a Signal School.—'If there is one thing in particular that I shall remember about the Armistice it is that we, six officers, were given a case of whisky by the C.O. Nothing more need be said than that we had to parade for flag drill at 7 o'clock next morning.'

In London.—During the closing weeks of the War I was in London, mending after being wounded at Messines at the end of September. The evening of November 10th was spent by most people in tense expectation that would have become wild ecstasy had news of the cease-fire come through. On the morning of the 11th all went to their accustomed place of work or resort, and made-believe to carry on as usual. In the middle of the morning the firing of maroons proclaimed that an armistice had been signed. Great numbers of the people were not aware of the changed meaning of the signal. Thinking it was a warning of the approach of German bombers, for such it had been for three years, they made for basements, cellars, underground railway stations and other like places of refuge. But soon everyone was in the streets cheering, yelling, and dancing: hats were thrown in the air, and often lost, handkerchiefs were thrown from windows: from the innumerable temporary government offices paper-forms, thousands and thousands of them, were floated out over the crowds below. Everything with which a noise could be made was in use. Some people went to the churches. No more work was done that day. Everyone was alternately anyone's host or guest. As the day advanced the vast number of men in uniform doubled, trebled, in the streets, for trains and vehicles of all sorts brought in men, with or without leave, from the Camps for miles round. Every man in uniform was the centre of a demonstration. The jollity increased after dark. Bonfires were lighted in Trafalgar Square and other open spaces; any combustible was used, a motor lorry if nothing else was at hand.

[1] Ll. Evans.

The experience of one regimental officer, Moody, is typical. After three and a half years spent in France he had been sent home for six months rest as an Instructor at a Corps School. 'With three colleagues, officers in the Royal Scots, Argyll and Sutherland Highlanders, and Rifle Brigade, I went to see what London was doing on Armistice night. Parades had been ordered for next day, the 12th, but they were cancelled tacitly, then formally. We arrived in town early in the evening of the 11th in rain, and it continued to rain. Thinking it necessary to book a table for dinner we made a weary round of restaurants that were full up before coming to rest at a little place in Wardour Street, owned by a Frenchman. Very bedraggled we were, for the London populace was in a state of wild excitement, especially the feminine part, who seemed to think that anyone in uniform was fair game. The doors of the restaurant were closed immediately after we got in, and customers were told that Monsieur X., the proprietor, wished to make a speech. Standing on a table he spoke partly in French, partly in broken English, with much gesticulation. He said that the doors had been closed because of the crowds, and that it would be unsafe for those who had been fortunate enough to get in to leave until late at night. He had an eye to business! Dinner was ordered, but before the fish had been eaten it was obvious that no more food would be served owing to the waiters' preoccupation with the opening of champagne bottles. Songs were started by the French community and rendered with excessive noise, fervour overcoming the singers. The Scottish officers could not stand it; they insisted on providing real music; so every Scottish song ever written was given in turn. The popularity of the Scots overcame all thought of food. Everyone in uniform had to be the guest of the civilians. All present were soon on the best of terms. The scene of amity was indescribable. We danced. We toasted the entente cordiale many dozens of times. But as time wore on the novelty of the experience wore off; so we contrived to give our new-made friends the slip, and have a look at what the rest of London was doing.

Outside, the scenes were extraordinary. Coventry Street and Leicester Square were packed with people of every description, whose chief object seemed to be to shake the hand of any service-man. Girls formed rings, in the centre of which was pushed and pulled any officer or man they could seize. By this means the four of us got separated for a time, but by good luck we met again in Coventry Street. The feeling of the people was really genuine, there was no disorder. Everyone was extraordinarily kind and generous; it seemed that most of the better-off people were taking a personal interest in each soldier they met. About 1 a.m. on the 12th I found myself alone, having seen the going of my friends. Number One had taken strong objection to an undersized Jew, and expressed his intention to ask the little man "what he had done in the Great War." His victim, sensing that something out of the ordinary was about to happen, turned and bolted through the crowd closely pursued by Number One. Number Two disappeared on the roof of a private limousine, dancing a reel. Number Three was left giving a good exhibition of squad drill, using a squad of policemen who had just come out on duty from Vine Street. A space had been cleared, and the police were willingly carrying out his orders to the amusement of the crowd. Number Four, his hand black and swollen with much handshaking, arrived at the Piccadilly Hotel which was more than overcrowded. After a clean-up I descended to the grill room where most of the occupants seemed to be dancing on the tables, or steeplechasing over the furniture which had been pushed against the walls. I had not been in the room a second before a party of perfect strangers insisted that I had been a friend of the family for more years than they cared to remember, and compelled me to be their guest for the rest of the night. So there I was among about twenty people, being hilariously entertained. Having had nothing to eat since lunch time I tried to impress on my new-made friends that food was all-important. The protest was ignored and more champagne was ordered.

A day or so later the original party of four met again, and tried to reckon up the number of people who had ordered champagne on their behalf. It had been quite impossible to share in all that had been offered, many dozens of bottles must have been wasted.' . . .

CHAPTER XIX

Demobilizing—The Channel recrossed—Home

Contributors :—H. EVANS ; LL. EVANS

Sketches :—1, 2, 11, 27

November 12th.—Baths were a first concern. In the afternoon the Brigade paraded to be addressed by the G.O.C. At a Mess meeting next day it was decided to re-form the Battalion Mess. Working-parties converted the huge waiting-room at the railway station into a Mess. Soon junior officers were falling over each other, for all Base reinforcements were cleared to their Units. Colonel Cockburn rejoined, but he left again in a few days.

November 17th, Sunday.—There was a Thanksgiving Service for Divisional H.Q., the Royal Artillery, and the 115th Infantry Brigade.

November 21st was our first Guest Night, when the G.O.C., the C.R.A., and their Staffs were among the guests.—The G.O.C. had *November 23rd*—a Divisional Parade of all recipients of awards gazetted since we crossed the Ancre, and pinned on the medal ribbons. Ginger Evans of the Runners got a D.C.M. in lieu of the hoped-for V.C., but there was satisfaction in the M.S.M. for grey-haired, perky, quarrelsome little Sergeant-Drummer Dyer. All this time pre-war routine and observances struggled with influences that made for disintegration.

November 26th.—"Demobilization," a word to harass executive officers for many months to come, appeared first in an order for the medical inspection of all miners : they were the first category for release. Among the first to go were Private Richards, a signaller, one of the few remaining "old originals," not in a Battalion staff job, to serve throughout the War, and Ginger Evans.

November 27th.—The Education Scheme which was launched on top of the German Spring Offensive was brought out. Its authors and sponsors were woefully scant in providing material, and plainly the Staff did not take it very seriously. The bulk of the men were quite indifferent; to get home, not to prepare for a nebulous job on getting there, was all they cared about. Units, however, gave a sort of lip-service to it. Some officers took up the work from sheer boredom, others, with no definite prospect, as a means of prolonging their Temporary Service. Baits were laid to induce duration men to extend their service, so many were wanted for garrison duties abroad; and much literature, which had to be hurriedly digested, and given forth in the form of a "Lecture by the Adjutant on Extension of Service," flowed into the Orderly Room. The object was not helped by a tightening-up of discipline, company training, an ambitious effort at battalion drill, *December 2nd*—and Brigade route-marches twice weekly.

December 3rd.—H.M. The King passed through Aulnoye on his tour of the Units of his Army in the Field, accompanied by T.R.H. the Prince of Wales and the Duke of York, and a numerous Staff. H.M inspected the Battalion drawn up in "loose fatigue order" along the roadside. de Miremont, who was Acting C.O., presented the Company Officers and the Adjutant. The King reminded us that he was Colonel in Chief of the Regiment, and spoke a few words of gratitude for splendid work done by the Battalion.

de Miremont decided that a rapidly shrinking Battalion could not do without the Colours, which a G.R.O. authorized Regular Units to send for if they wanted them. So two officers and a few deserving N.C.Os. had a pleasant jaunt to Wrexham. The safe-keeping of these valuable possessions in inflammable quarters was to cause anxiety until their return home, but the men were never shown them and told their significance.

More reinforcement officers joined after another Base clearance; some of them had not arrived in France until after the Armistice.

December 25th, Christmas Day.—Morning Church Parade, then Dinner under Company arrangements. The Quartermaster, Company officers and Mess President had combined to give the men a first-class dinner, with plenty of beer to wash it down. At 8 o'clock there was a concert in the Recreation Huts, which were converted railway sheds, but no specially talented item can be recalled. The Mess Dinner was as usual.

December 26th.—The daily routine duties, and the drill the men

did so reluctantly, were resumed. The last Brigade route-march
December 28th—in this area was through Petit Maubeuge. The
weather had been bad, especially during the two middle weeks of
the month.

December 29th.—The Battalion began to move west by route-
march through the Forest of Mormal, and Englefontaine. Since
the day was wet and stormy the going was bad. Junior officers
were detailed in pairs to carry the cased Colours, and found the
honour somewhat overshadowed by the task. One night was
spent at Hecq where the inhabitants were most hospitable. Our
December 30th—next stopping-place was Inchy. Billets were
found in comfortable houses which had been occupied by the
German High Command; Battalion H.Q. was in what had been
Hindenburg's quarters until late October.

December 31st.—The last stage of the move was made in buses.
Starting at 7 o'clock we crossed the familiar devastated Somme
area, passed through Cambrai, Bapaume, Albert, and reached the
new Brigade Camp near Blangy-Tronville, between Amiens and
Villers-Bretonneux, in the late afternoon. An advance party
having been sent on, our move in was very comfortable. We
had large wooden huts with a slow-combustion stove in each.
A good deal of ingenuity was needed to keep warm in them,
for really cold weather had set in. The Camp was incomplete,
much work was required to finish it, so the Count never at any
time failed to find a job for Major Adamson. New paths were
made, duckboard tracks were laid. The equipment of a Recreation
Hut included a Dry Canteen and a chip-fryer, the latter a very
popular innovation. Meanwhile a Court of Enquiry had sat,
with pre-war solemnity, to find out how we came to be one
government bicycle short.

After a week of fatigues and ordinary camp duties a Brigade
January 8th—route-march was quite a welcome leg-stretcher.

January 9th.—At 3 in the morning we were ordered to send at
once two Companies, armed and with Lewis guns, to Sailly Laurette.
A nest of Australian deserters, who had been terrorizing and living
on the neighbourhood, was reported to have been located on an
island in the Somme west of that place. A and B Companies
sprang a surprise on the picnickers, two in number, who were
found in snug dug-outs, sleeping in pyjamas of striking pattern.

They were led back to Camp, and handed over to the Australian authorities.

January 20th.—An inspection by the G.O.C. had been preceded by several practice parades and one cancellation of date.

From now on Units were visited by itinerant lecturers sent by Army or Corps to relieve the monotony. The topics were various, and of varying interest; as for examples, "My experience as a Prisoner of War in Germany," by an Army padre—"Adventures in Egypt"—"Re-enlisting"—"The purpose of the Service of the Divisional Advisory Board"; and similar dry themes. Educational classes were continued, sometimes regimentally, sometimes as Brigade classes; later they were worked by Division.

The appointment of a Brigade Field Officer made for co-operation between the three battalions in games and recreation. *January 29th*—At an Inter-Brigade Tournament the Battalion represented the Brigade against the 13th Battalion representing the 113th Brigade.—We had marked out a full-sized Rugger field close by. Our games were often watched by crowds of Gerries from a large prisoners-of-war camp across the road from ours. They apparently thought we were quite mad playing such a rough game in such biting weather, for the early months of 1919 were drab, wet, and for the most part intensely cold. The Germans possessed a really excellent string orchestra, and they gave concerts to which the officers in charge occasionally invited our Brigade officers. Their huts were just such as ours, but it seemed to us that they were allowed an infinitely more generous issue of coal.

January 30th.—A final Honours List was published.

By the end of the month 1 officer and 365 other ranks, of whom 206 claimed to be miners, had been demobilized. The demobilization of horses was going on too. A G.R.O. offered officers the option of purchasing their chargers, subject to veterinary inspection as to fitness for importation. 'I[1] negotiated for Jenny, the Adjutant's hack; but my sentimental gesture fell through as she was graded "for sale on the Continent." Yates got Girlie.' James Ormrod kept her for him pending his eventual settlement. She was ridden with the Wynnstay Hounds, and reared a foal which was ridden with the Wynnstay; she lived until 1931.

February 3rd.—The new Men's Recreation Hut was officially

---

[1] Ll. Evans.

opened with a Battalion Concert, but with no Band we had to do what we could with Dyer's Fifes for our music.

During a week which the Prince of Wales spent with the *February 7th*—Division as General Cubitt's guest, he came to luncheon. Fox, the Mess President, rose to the occasion splendidly. In the ante-room, before lunch, all officers were presented to H.R.H. He was interested to meet our Yankee M.O., Christofferson, and chatted with him about Chicago, his native city. After lunch the Prince expressed a wish "to have a look at the men," telling the General he didn't want "a damned tail with him." So the Count sent Evans to take him round. The Prince was interested in the Recreation Hut. He had a word with most of the men wearing medal ribbons. When he came across Sergeant-Drummer Dyer he recalled having seen him on a previous visit to the Battalion. Dyer gave him chapter and verse, waxing loquacious and bursting with pride. Returning to the Mess, the Prince chatted with the Count and others, and did much leg-pulling at the G.O.C.'s expense.

February 14th.—A week later the Battalion route-marched to Querrieu, Corps H.Q., to view the "Presentation Shield to H.R.H. the Prince of Wales." This was a huge wooden affair, 4 or 5 feet in height, on which had been arranged, symmetrically and in pleasing pattern, the shoulder-straps of various German Units, elements of which had been captured by the 38th (Welsh) Division during its 56 miles advance from the Ancre. Enscrolled on the shield were the Division's Battle Honours, Crests and Badges, and a dedication to H.R.H. The whole of the work had been done by some Divisional Engineers. After viewing this "work of art" the Battalion marched back to Camp; the chief topic was not the wonderful shield, but the magnificence of the "chatoo" in which the great ones dwelt.

February 16th.—The first batch of officers left: six went to the 26th Battalion for duty with the Army of Occupation, others to various duties in the devastated area: some went on Courses!

February 17th.—A really welcomed event was the arrival of the Battalion Band from Wrexham, under Bandmaster Clancy. This also was the consequence of a G.R.O.; it authorized Regular Units to send home for their Mascots and Bands. With our Band came a Windsor Goat, presented by H.M. The King to replace the one which died the night that training was interrupted by the Shadow of War. It was very young, unprepossessing, and troublesome on its arrival, and it did not shed any of these attributes. The Band was at full strength, 53 men and boys. It came with the reputation of having been the "best Band in the Western Command." Its arrival at the Camp was unheralded by any martial airs, since it was utterly fatigued and dispirited, having foot-slogged from Villers-Bretonneux, some 5 miles distant. In three days all were fully recovered, and it headed a morning *February 20th*—route-march on which we were joined by the 17th Battalion.

The Band Boys had promptly put up the blue chevron for overseas service. Special arrangements and regulations had to be made for them. They were quartered in a separate hut in charge of Sergeant-Drummer Dyer, who ruled them with complete pre-war severity. "School" was set up for them, and "bounds" were enforced. Band funds and Control were added to the Adjutant's duties, and proved no sinecure. Orderly Room was henceforth enlivened by Dyer marching in some of his charges, crimed with "not washing cleanly," "breaking Camp bounds," petty thefts from comrades and the Canteen, and similar juvenile delinquencies. Clancy would come for orders, or submit the Programme for Guest Night. Requests were soon pouring in from Division and Brigade for "the loan of the Band" for varying periods. It certainly brightened the dullness of Blangy very *February 28th*—considerably. 'Division [1] lent us some lorries to take it for a tour of the battle area. We visited Albert, Mametz Wood, and High Wood, went nearly to Lesbœufs, and came back through Bapaume. Souvenir collecting was most fancied by the newcomers. Some of the senior Bandsmen had served with the 1st or 2nd Battalion during the earlier stages of the War; they were interested in visiting battlegrounds they knew. We came across the wreck of one of the German monster guns and of its concreted emplacement.' Twenty-three men straddled the barrel without crowding, and with room to spare. It was reputed to have been used to shell Paris the previous summer, but Amiens was its target; its fourth shot was a premature which wrecked it.

By the end of February the Battalion was a mere skeleton.

[1] Ll. Evans.

March 1st—"Taffy's Day"—the fifth the Battalion celebrated in France. The Drums and Fifes heralded dawn with "Old Mother Reilly" and other traditional airs, awakening the whole Camp. Leeks were distributed to all ranks according to custom, and the Dinner Rites were resumed. In the evening the 2nd and 17th Battalion Messes dined together. Our guests included Major-Gen. T. A. Cubitt, Commanding the Division, and Brig.-Gen. H. de Pree, Commanding the Brigade. Colonels Cockburn and Norman were the Senior Regimental Officers present. Col. Harvey, then commanding the 17th, though not a Fusilier, was very much one on this occasion. The function lacked none of its peace-time ceremonial, other than commodiousness of building, plate and Mess Dress, for we had our Band and Goat, and the menu would stand comparison with that of many in peace-time. The uninitiated ate their leek; our Yankee M.O. ate his with gusto, but the G.O.C. excused himself on the plea of recent indisposition.

March 2nd, Sunday.—Summer Time came in. Church Parade was made more interesting by the presence of the Band. The concert it gave later in the day was a pleasing innovation. We were not to have it to ourselves for long at a time; it had been borrowed in the area frequently before leaving us on a three *March 9th*—weeks engagement at a theatre in Paris.

March 15th.—General Cubitt paid us a farewell visit on leaving to command a brigade on the Rhine. He was in cheerful vein, albeit regretting parting with his "bloody little Welshmen," swearing that he never wished for better troops to command. Col. Norman had already gone to command a composite battalion of Welsh troops on the Rhine, where also were Colonels Owen, the Adjutant of early days, and Stockwell.

March 17th.—The remnant of the 113th Brigade moved into the Camp from Warloy; increasing accommodation made such a concentration easy. Next, our lines and huts were shared by our *March 23rd*—17th Battalion and the 10th S.W.B. A joint Brigade Mess was thereupon formed in what had been our Officers Mess. By the end of March the Battalion had demobilized 5 officers and 614 other ranks, besides sending 8 officers and 87 other ranks to the 26th Battalion, and other officers to odd jobs in the old battle area.

The monotony of camp fatigues, baths, Church Parades was

relieved somewhat by the enthusiasm shown in Rugby matches between battalions, and now between brigades. The Count discovered a flair for the full-back position, and spent many odd half-hours on the parade ground or Rugby field practising fielding and kicking. Evans captained a 115th Brigade team which won *April 4th*—against the 113th. The Count performed creditably, if with some characteristic eccentricities which did duty for rules of which his knowledge was elementary. A "popular" concert in the Recreation Hut wound up a happy day. Our next match *April 5th*—was with the 114th Brigade. Col. Brock Williams, an old Swansea player, was their last line of defence. The referee was Padre Williams, formerly of the Llanelly team, and very West Walian in sentiment. In their pack were faces extraordinarily like those of gunners who somehow had been in our pack the previous day. It was a jolly game which we lost handsomely.

Fatigues included carrying wood from the Somme Valley, and an attempt was made to level some ground sufficiently to allow of tennis later on, for as yet there was no indication of a move homeward. By this time everything was cadre. In the morning *April 7th*—it was the skeleton Division that went off for a route-march, headed by our Band.—Col. Brock Williams of the Welsh Regiment, a real music lover, had, with our Bandsmen as a nucleus, got together all the instrumentalists, and formed a Divisional Cadre Orchestra, which gave the first of a series of Symphony Concerts *April 15th*—in the 114th Brigade Recreation Hut: a most enjoyable affair.

April 17th.—Things were literally brightened up in our lines at night. The fish-fryer in our Canteen went ablaze, and burnt the hut down. There had been a smaller fire in a Band-hut some time before, but this was a complete "Brock's Benefit." No one was injured, although the hut and its contents became a total loss. *April 18th*—A Regimental Court of Enquiry found that it was purely accidental, and Authority was satisfied when it was established that the hut had been adequately protected by having the regulation number of sand-filled fire buckets. There was, however, no more frying of fish and chips while we were at Blangy.

April 20th, Easter Day.—Parade Services with Band, and a Band programme in Camp in the afternoon.

The Band was again in demand in the Corps area. It played

April 24th — at the V Corps Concentration Camp Sports at Saveuse, and at Moutieres in the evening. Next, a deputation of Australian officers begged the loan of it at the A.E.F. Sports at Villers-Bretonneux. This area had gone completely Aussie, for large numbers of troops were engaged in burying or reburying their numerous dead, left where they fell since their historic advance on August 8th, 1918. Most of the actual work was done by troops freshly drafted from England, men who had not previously been in France. Their battle-wise N.C.Os. and the veteran rankers called them Rainbows: they had come out after the storm. Several of us accepted their invitation to attend *April 25th* — their Sports on Anzac Day, and were entertained splendidly at their big Mess afterwards. The following Sunday the Band went to Villers-Bretonneux again, to play at the Memorial Service the Australian troops held there.

April 26th.—On the Saturday evening, meanwhile, tragedy visited our Camp. In spite of rigorous bounds having been enforced the Band Boys had broken them on several occasions, without mishap until now. They strayed to a large dump. Some bombs were accidentally exploded. One boy was killed and three others wounded. The dead boy was buried with full military *April 28th*—honours at Austral Cemetery on the Amiens-Villers road: he was 15, probably the youngest British soldier to be buried in France. When his companions rejoined at Wrexham, from hospital, they were wearing wound stripes!

Lieut.-Col. de Miremont had been in Acting Command since Col. Norman's departure. While on leave he had negotiated for service with the North Russian Expeditionary Force, and was offered command of a company of the 46th Royal Fusiliers. He returned to Blangy to hand over, and left again the same day. 'Having [1] served with him off and on since June 1917 I had come to know him pretty well, and found much that was attractive and naïve mixed up with his characteristic irascibility. During these last months a threat to "demob" myself and leave him to it worked like a charm.'

We had demobilized 8 officers and 628 other ranks, besides sending more officers and other ranks to the 26th Battalion, when the next incident in our vegetative existence was Sports. The

[1] Ll. Evans.

May 6th—day was fine. The prisoners of war from across the road, and a large contingent of Australians attended. 'I[1] had taken what turned out to be my last leave from France three days earlier, so I missed them, as well as a visit which the Prime Minister, the Rt. Hon. D. Lloyd George, paid to the Divisional Cadre on *May 16th*—the day of my return. Prior to going on this leave I had put my name down for a Staff job at Army H.Q. Urgent orders to report at once awaited my return, and, at long last, Orders had arrived for the return of the Battalion Cadre to England. An opportune lift by D.A.D.O.S. got me to Army very quickly. After an interview a job as Staff Lieutenant was offered me, and the use of a car "to conduct Distinguished Visitors round the Battlefields." On consideration I turned it down, for I had a sincere, though perhaps sentimental, desire to see the War through with the Battalion I had served in so long, and to proceed as part of it on its homeward journey.

Camp routine and preparations for the move occupied us for a week. Albutt had been our dependable R.S.M. for some time. Yates had been busy for weeks with Army Form G. 1098, which imposed on him the making up of a complete Mobilization Store for a battalion down to the last horseshoe and strap. This was to be taken to England, apparently as the most satisfactory way of clearing out stores held in France. It was, of course, packed on our Mobilization Transport. In addition there was a complete German light mortar he was taking home *sub rosa* for the Brigadier, and innumerable brass shell-cases of all calibres which he and I had been collecting for months. That he got them all secreted and securely packed speaks volumes for his resource and experience in such matters.'

May 24th, Empire Day.—The Imprest Account was closed. The move commenced. All material, labelled as ordered for Gosport, *May 25th*—was loaded in trucks at Longueau. Cadre, Band, Goat and Colours entrained. But we were not to get away without fickle fortune spoiling someone's homegoing. Belfield, one of the Old Originals, had rejoined from detachment some weeks previously. Naturally he was confident that he would go home with the Battalion, with which he came out, after having been with it so long. At the eleventh hour, actually at about 3.58,

[1] Ll. Evans.

a message got to him ordering him to report for duty with the Army of Occupation. Our train left Longueau at 4 p.m. It arrived *May 26th*—at Havre at 2 a.m. After unloading the Transport we proceeded to No. 17 Embarkation Camp at Harfleur. The personnel passed through a Delousing Station, where baths and a complete change into clean clothing were given, and blankets *May 27th*—were handed in. The Cadre then moved to No. 2 Wing, Despatch Camp, Harfleur. Orders were received to "prepare to *May 28th*—move to the United Kingdom" on the following day, but to Blackdown Camp, not Gosport. The change entailed a night-long labour altering destination labels on all baggage and vehicles.

May 29th.—Loading parties put the Transport and baggage on to H.M.T. *Iona*. Personnel embarked on H.M.T. *St. George*. There were 5 officers and some 75 other ranks all told. Ten of them had disembarked at Rouen on August 11th, 1914. Yates and the rank and file had an uninterrupted service except for ordinary leave. Fox was a Sergeant then; as A Company's marker he was one of the first to step ashore : now he was Captain Commanding the Cadre. Roberts Morgan, who carried the Regimental Colour, was Post-Corporal in 1914, and the first casualty, for he was carried off the *Glengariff* sick.

'Before [1] we could sail the Goat Business started. Weeks before this a permit, in accordance with Orders, had been obtained from the Board of Agriculture to bring over the Regimental Goat, but the Skipper would not allow it to set foot in his ship. He had no use for any "Authority" from England, one had to come from the port of embarkation. There was nothing I could do but taxi from the quay in search of some "Competent Authority" : the ship, all ready to cast off, waiting for me meanwhile. The local Embarkation Officer was traced to his lair, only to be found dubious of his authority to issue a permit; so off to someone higher up; thence higher up still. Regulations and Orders had to be brought out and consulted every time, while I held my paper tightly in my hand; it was too laborious a process to put it into a pocket and take it out again, so much in demand was it, and so much did I fear losing it or seeing it retained as a curious souvenir. Eventually I got the necessary chit, and sped with all haste to the

[1] Ll. Evans.

impatient Transport. There all was set except that our Bandmaster and his opposite number of the 1st Lincolns, whose Cadre and Band shared the boat with us, hadn't even then decided who was senior, and therefore entitled to conduct the Massed Bands as we put off from the French shore.'

At 4 o'clock the *St. George* sailed. The Bands, conducted by the Lincolns' Bandmaster, struck up "Auld Lang Syne," "The Marseillaise," "Men of Harlech," "The Lincolnshire Poacher," *May* 30*th*—and other appropriate Airs. In the morning the Battalion slipped into Southampton as silently and unmarked as it had slipped out that fateful August morning in 1914. Disembarkation commenced at 8 o'clock. We were surprised to discover that there had been kept under guard in the hold a large gang of Australian military prisoners. They were marched from the dock under an armed guard with fixed bayonets. 'Such tough-looking desperadoes I've never seen, they looked capable of any crime.' What became of them we never heard. We went to a very comfortable hut encampment on the outskirts of the town, on the Winchester road. Unloading was to begin on the morrow. But now the Goat wasn't allowed to be landed. The Port Authorities would not be convinced that our two chits were sufficient. While the controversy was in temporary suspense the obstinate creature was somehow or other smuggled on to the dockside, and stealthily lugged to the Camp.

June 1*st.*—Having completed the unloading we entrained for the Military Camp at Blackdown, not far from Camberley. The Goat was smuggled, since apparently station-masters and guards equally objected to its conveyance, pleading some restrictive Orders, foot and mouth disease or other impediment. We were accommodated along with a battalion of the Loyal North Lancs, who were preparing to proceed on a tour of overseas service, and to whom we were to hand over our "Mob. Stores." There we remained for five days, having nothing to do, while Yates was making a ritual of the transfer of Stores, checking them off on G. 1098, item by item, with his N. Lancs *vis-à-vis*. Some of us whiled away these pleasant, idle days paddling up and down long stretches of the Basingstoke Canal.

June 6*th.*—On a Saturday the Cadre proceeded on the final stage of its journey home to Wrexham. There was a last altercation over the Goat with the station authorities. A minor welcome was given us on the platform at Birmingham, where friends and relatives came to meet us, demonstrating the close connection of the Regiment and that City. Belfield's folk were there in force, and Yates had much to do explaining his non-appearance.

Arrived at Wrexham we were met at the station by Major Kearsley, commanding the Depot, by Col. Cockburn and the Band of the 1st Battalion, who were preparing at Oswestry for service in India, by the Mayor and Corporation in their robes, and by officers and men from the Depot. We marched to the Guildhall to receive the Town's official welcome. The streets were beflagged, and all the townspeople lined them. A cinema-camera made news and record of us. On the way Yates saw his wife among the crowd; forty years of Army discipline were forgotten, he dashed from the ranks, and greeted her heartily and unblushingly. At the Guildhall speeches were made to which Fox and Evans replied; and on calls for "The Soldiers' Friend," Howells Evans rose bashfully and spoke. Then we proceeded to the Depot, where a hearty welcome awaited us, and much-needed drinks. Chick, who was last seen in such bad case at Morval, was Mess President, and he did us proud. In the evening a Dinner was given to the Cadre by the Corporation at the Wynnstay Arms. There were more toasts and speeches, and the hospitality was "of the most lavish."

June 7th.—The returned troops and those at the Depot attended Service in the Parish Church. Canon Davies, the Vicar, made a welcoming reference to our return. And he told the congregation that a hundred years ago, on Whitsunday 1819, the then Vicar, later Bishop Heber, conducted the Service, and his hymn, "From Greenland's icy mountains," was sung for the first time. We also sang it on this Whitsunday.

In the evening another returned officer reported at the Depot, Compton Smith, who had commanded one of our Service Battalions. He was to be foully murdered by Sinn Feiners in Ireland, whither the Battalion proceeded in a few weeks, again commanded by Col. O. de L. Williams.

During the week, after some commemorative photographs had been taken, the Cadre and Band were sent away on a month's leave. Howells Evans, who had carried the King's Colour, rushed off to get himself demobilized that he might join his newly-come first-born. The other officers went on the Regulation "two months leave on return from foreign service." When leave was ended some would go back to duty; and some would go forth to take up again the daily work from which Duty had called them, or to search for work, often with wandering quest: and the Goat had died.

APPENDIX

A postscript to May 22nd, 1918.—The effect of gas was trifling in the overwhelming majority of cases. No factitious or hysterical symptoms delayed my recovery. In two days a little reading and writing were possible with ordinary tinted glasses. In eight days I was at duty although slight throat and chest signs appeared, and three weeks of simple treatment was needed before the effects of the irritant on the eyes had passed. In the meantime a sharp attack of the widespread June epidemic of influenza supervened, without unfitting me to see daily upwards of 200 fellow sufferers. Service with the 2nd R.W.F. had been interrupted. The Battalion had fallen upon a not very happy period. It is a fairly easy matter for an attached medical officer to get release, but it is difficult for the regimental officer, even if every subordinate feel that he is being rubbed the wrong way. My return to the front at the end of June was to a battalion in another division, but interest in the Royal Welch has not abated—hence this Chronicle. Some further reference to the non-commissioned officers who were my principal professional assistants and colleagues may not be amiss before my contribution closes. The following sketches are a compound of scattered notes and of memories:

The work, the outlook, of a battalion medical officer is not purely medical and surgical, certainly not in war-time. As much knowledge of one's fellow-man as of medicine is needed; indeed knowledge of one's fellow counts for more than in all the other aspects of practice, except compensation, of which I have had experience. The position is not one for the newly fledged practitioner, because the necessarily limited means of investigation is always having to be made up for by experience when there is no obvious urgency for a more technical investigation than is at hand. There were two or three men on my first sick parade; in identical circumstances there were quite two dozen next day. Nothing more gratifying could befall the civilian doctor, but I was to learn that nearly all had come to test the gullibility of the new M.O. That some had come to make my acquaintance was soon plain; there was such a group sameness about the terms and the tone in which symptoms were reeled off. I turned to Sergeant Roberts—he was Corporal then—to give directions about one of the first comers, but the cloud on his somewhat saturnine countenance froze my sympathetic intention. He lifted censorious eyes from mine to dart an angry glance at the man, on whose face I thought I detected a repressed smile. My frozen intention dissolved into awkward evasion; but I did not flatter myself I had saved face by adding "one day only" to the "Excuse duty" already entered on the report sheet. The "sick" man was one of our best boxers; he had a reputation, of which I had abundant subsequent corroboration, for not expending himself in any way outside the ring. I saw a good deal of him, but we were never on easy terms: he was an Irishman wanting in versatility. There are those of my teachers—not a few—who won my respect. Roberts demanded it with an accusatory look: "mug" that look said with more contemptuous emphasis than there is in speech. Other help had I none from him. His Army life began with boy service. He was one of those soldiers from whom it is impossible to extract an opinion until his officer has spoken, and then the tone, not the words, conveys it. I got no satisfaction from asking him "what sort of fellow is so-and-so." He just stood at my elbow menacing me with his scorn if I let a scrimshanker get away with it. I devised cunning tests to save my reputation with my orderly. I could not look up at his face for aid, but one day I noticed a contraction of the ring and little fingers of his hand that was within my sight, as I neared deep water. My embarrassment in his presence fell away after that. When I had learned the technique of malingering, and of its detection, and its motives, I ceased to be afraid of his censure, and we became good friends. He had taught me that the first duty of a battalion medical officer in War is to discourage the evasion of duty. That has to be done not seldom against one's better feeling, sometimes to the temporary hurt of an individual, but justice to all the other men, as well as discipline, demands it.

Lance-Corporal, later Sergeant, Hogben succeeded Roberts. Some generations of his forebears served in the Navy. He too was as close as an oyster if asked about a man's reputation with the others. "I don't know," was Hogben's invariable answer to a pointed question, and he met a feeler with a far-away look. But I never felt uncomfortable with him. I had been well schooled before he came on, and had learned to make enquiry in the man's Company. In contradistinction to the malingerer is the man who deceives to his hurt unless the M.O. go outside the Aid Post for information.

When Jones arrived as a draft in the early autumn of 1917 I looked him up and down, looked at his South African ribbons and asked, "What induced a man of your age to come as far up as this?" "Oh, I'm just an old fool, Sir, couldn't keep out of it": then he added, "I thought I might get a job in your department, I'm a chemist's assistant." Very soon one of my staff went on leave, so Jones was asked for. He and Hogben were at daggers drawn from the first hour. I was glad when the leave-man returned, and Jones automatically returned to duty before I was embroiled.

I had nearly forgotten him when a crisis in our relations arose at Westoutre. When we were warned to move he was brought to me on a stretcher. He was apparently paralysed, scarcely conscious, speechless. The needless emission of an unnatural groan hardened my heart. The flicker of a loosely closed eyelid showed he was watching my manipulations; I made a feint and he mistimed a reflex badly: anyhow, his symptoms would not fit any picture of disease known to me, so the bearers were told to take him back to his Company. His Company Commander must have left him behind, likely enough he thought hospital the proper place for him. When we came out of Polygon Wood Jones was one of the first men I saw, he was hanging round eyeing me. Everyone knew Hogben was wounded, and his assistant missing. Someone had to be got for the Aid Post; only Jones knew anything about it. I asked for him, fully intending to dismiss such a "damned old soldier" as soon as a likely man could be found. He seemed to have other views, and he proved so efficient that I was glad to overlook his trick. He had two periods of pre-war service, about which he was not very communicative. He could be as punctilious as his predecessors, and he was—with interjections. Number and name would be called formally, but often as the man was coming forward Jones added in my ear, " Our old friend, Sir," or " Workin' his ticket, Sir," or "Hav'n't seen him for three days, Sir," or " Swingin' it again, Sir." His reports on doubtful complaints of bowel disturbance and fever, detained for observation, were graphic and conclusive. These were asides. About an error or misjudgment on my part he was out-spoken. Thus, of a lumpish man, a notorious slacker, who came after an unusual absence, he said in an undertone, "He's tryin' something new, Sir." The man's complaint was so vague, and remained so vague under examination, that I failed twice or thrice to find a basis for it, and warned him not to come again till he had something to show. He came next day, but gave no further clue. However, a test, made at a venture, revealed a malady. "By Jove," Jones exclaimed aloud, "well done ——. You've stuck it. Well done." When over-exposure to gas irritated my eyes, of the dozen surgeons and nurses who handled me, none had a lighter, more purposeful touch than Jones. Not long after my going to hospital he and Mills, the Canteen Sergeant, a first-rate man, ran to aid some officers in whose billet a large shell had burst: another shell burst in it while they were inside, wounding both mortally.

Although the Aid Post is the scene of much that is painful to witness, and of something that is ignoble, it provides, too, plenty of sheer fun. Belonging to my next battalion was an orderly it is a privilege to have known; he was a master-tailor in a Yorkshire town, a good citizen, an observant man and a very fine one. His manner was paternal to the would-be dodgers who came with a wry face, barely able to utter, "There's something the matter with my heart." After my examination he would say softly, "Go away back to your Company, laddie, your heart's in the wrong place, that's all that's the matter with it." It was my custom to have men stand aside until the others were disposed of if they needed more of me than an ordinary examination, or than a "number nine"— a compendious term applied to all the pill and tabloid contents of the monkey box. One morning I looked round sure there was something for me to do, but forgetting what it was. "Isn't there someone I have to attend to, Sergeant?" I asked. "You were going to draw a tooth, Sir," he replied; "I've done it," he added, with an air of conscious satisfaction. Following his look, I saw a strapping youth sitting on an upturned bucket, clasping his head; he was rocking to and fro and from side to side, and at intervals he muttered, "Gosh!" After a time he rose unsteadily, still clasping his head: "Aa thawght ma toe-nails was draaw'd," he gasped. Still unsteady he walked away, saying, "Gosh! Aa'm fair ——'d!"

INDEX

Page numbers preceded by † *refer to Billets, Camp or Bivouac. o.o. = Operation Order.*

Abbeville 69, 248, 287, 289-90, 370, 502
Abeele 221, 430
Aberdovey 503
Abraham Heights 415
Acheux †362, 496. Acheux Wood †484
Achiet-le-Petit 347
Acoustics 224, 257, 264-5, 408
Acquin †406
Adamson, Maj. 573
Adinkerke 380
A.D.M.S. *See* Medical Corps
Age and service 260, 272, 412, 414, 467, 475
Agincourt 223, 245, 257
Ainge, Capt. 474, 510, 521, 526-7-8, 532-533-4, 535, 537, 557
Air Force, R. 14, 115, 139, 146, 178, 181, 194, 229, 239, 302, 330, 344, 371, 383, 417, 421, 431, 481, 503; dissatisfaction with 383, 421, 431, 481; transfers to 491; bombing 461, 478, 481, 507, 553
Air fights 239, 250, 293, 330; observation *q.v.*; photography 218, 564; planes and animals 265, 383; planes, protection from, 22, 66, 178, 272, 371, 377, 382, 390, 423, 433, 474; raid shelter 451, 568
Airaines 282, 284, †364-70, 537
Aire 442
Aisne 38, 61; battle 61-3
Alarms 25, 34, 66, 114, 316, 334, 417, 480; German 254, 455
Albert 245, 464, 478, 505, 507, 510-11, 573; Madonna 466, 469
Albutt, Maj. 580
Allenby, F.M. Lord 19, 20, 327, 346, 349, 358
Ally Sloper 126
Alphabet 62, 87
American aeroplane 441; Army 410, 420; Army troops 445, 450; 546-7; Eagle 410; Munitions 116
Americans 360, 444, 454; attached 378, 413, 414, 480, 505. *See* Christofferson

Amerval(les) 558-9
Amiens, A. Company in 12-†16; 69; 247-8; 284; 304; 307; 324; 366; 466; 478; Battle of 506; Cathedral 222, 383
Ammunition:
 Shell *q.v.*
 S.A.A.: shortage 410, 468; supply by aeroplane 508; surplus 21; tracer 390, 499
Ancre 223, 265; 464, 471, 484, 504, 523, 537; bridgeheads 487; crossings 505; 507-8-9
Anecdotes 6, 22, 27, 28, 29, 30, 59, 60, 72, 74, 78, 79, 92, 93, 97, 98, 109, 114, 116, 117, 124, 135, 138, 146, 150, 158, 162, 164, 165, 169, 170, 171, 174, 175, 177, 178, 179, 183, 186-7, 194, 196, 198, 199, 200,-1,-2, 203,-4,-5, 230, 247,-8,-9, 252,-3,-4, 257, 260,-1,-2,-3, 268,-9, 270, 273,-4, 278,-9, 280, 286, 288,-9, 290,-1, 294, 310, 324, 330, 345, 347, 354, 357,-8, 360, 365, 373,-4, 378,-9, 380, 391, 393, 397, 408, 410, 416, 425, 428, 431-2, 435, 442, 444,-5, 447, 451,-2, 461, 465, 470, 476,-7,-8, 482, 512, 521, 539, 541, 546, 548, 558, 588
Angelus Orchard 550, 553
Animals: Bats 455. Cats 166, 376, 404, 410, 413, 449, 470. Cows—abandoned 84, 375; Aid Post's 470; casualties among 84, 98; refugees' 44, 463; Stockwell's 79, 91. Deer 310. Dogs 262, 374-5, 377, 470, 481. Frogs 183, 201, 348. Goats q.v. Hare 477. Horses q.v. Pigs 92, 257. Rabbits 43, 64, 66, 366, 494. Rats 178, 198, 259, 431
Transport 39, 47, 62, 65, 249, 274, 285, 325; mules 274, 310, 342, 433, 557
Annequin, North (Tourbières) 145, †177, †179, †182, †194
 South 145, †180-1, †205
Annezin 145, †160, †193
Anniversaries 410, 414

Antipathies 109, 343, 424
Antwerp 436
Archbishops 11, 150
Armour, R.S.M. 222, 233, 239
Army Service Corps, R. 36, 47
  personnel 34, 59, 262, 385, 410; age of 272
Artillery : men 27, 33, 228
  officers 86, 107, 192, 195, 218, 228, 248, 253; officers to guns 291; F.O. 86, 107, 121, 131, 269, 297
  action 26, 50, 82, 84, 86, 107, 110, 116, 122, 125, 135, 146, 178, 218, 231, 248, 266, 269, 274, 280, 294, 296, 298, 333, 350, 376, 378, 408, 412, 464, 505, 549, 554, 566
  barrage 123, 180, 196, 266, 336-7, 350, 400, 403, 417, 451, 474, 482, 499, 512, 521, 524, 534, 564-5; creeping 253, 336-7, 344, 524; for raids 192; 195-6; 219, 221; 296-7-8; 458; 490; 499
  bombardment 113, 133, 149, 150, 151, 152, 153, 156, 158, 177, 180, 202, 217, 219, 221, 227-8, 230-6, 240, 250, 253-4, 265, 266, 269, 331, 349, 458, 472, 489, 499, 509, 511, 543-4, 548; gas 354, 369, 558
  comparative inferiority 81, 86, 91, 94; comparative superiority 288, 404, 467
  costing 408
  Divisional : 6th 110. 33rd C.R.A. 296, 298; casualties 248. 38th 571; C.R.A. 498, 571.—Div. casualties 378
  guns and howitzers : anti-aircraft 66; 178, 382, 390; captured 412, 466; heavy 62, 126, 177, 271-2, 279, 318, 340, 390, 468, 496, 498, 558; 6-inch 84, 184, 469, 474; 12-inch 444; 15-inch 149, 444; L Battery R.H.A. 41; 13-pounder 253; 72nd Battery R.F.A. 116, 130; 18-pounder 157, 266, 366, 474; roving 449; silent 444, 447, 482
  registration 146
  rôle of 224, 339
  Shell q.v.
  shooting short 84, 116, 177, 232, 240, 252, 267, 270, 350, 359, 378, 472, 525
  smoke-screen 354, 395, 523, 529
  wire cutting 150-1, 192, 344; 550
Artois 260
Attichy 38
Attwater, A., Capt. 95; quoted 107, 111, 114, 115, 121, 125, 126-9
Aubencheul 549, 550-1, 556

Aubers 447
Audrecque Dump 259
Aulnoye 435, 566, †572
Australia 421 ; Australians 261, 288, 362, 407, 454, 468 573
  Anzac Corps 411-12; 476, 547, 579, 580, 582; 5th Div. 392; 31st Regt. 393, 396-9, 400-3
Austria-Hungary 159, 250, 563
Authie 257, 261, 265
Authuille 487, 495, 507-9, 512. Authuille Wood 510, 512, 514
Aveluy 151, 487, 507-9, 512, 514-15. Aveluy Wood 464, 484-5, 487, 493-495, 511, 537; raid 486
Ayette Races 342

" B " 38, 64
Bac St. Maur 454, †458-9
Backs to the wall 468
Bailleul †70; 88; 387-8; 414-15; 469
Bailleulval 341, †354, 356
Baird, Bdr.-Gen. 330, 360
Baisieux, cavalry skirmish 20
Baldwin, Sgt. 320-2
Bale, Sgt. 181
Bandagehem 382
Bands 160; 33rd Div. 365, 422; 1st Lincolns 582; 1st R.W.F. 355, 358; Welsh Pioneers 250
Bangalore Torpedo 192-3
Banks, 2/Lt. 208, 213-14
Bantams 260
Bapaume 359, 573
Bardolph 223
Bargees 380
Barges 38; coal 380; hospital 160; travel 370, 380
Barkworth, Capt. 231, 234, 288, 414
Barling, C.S.M. 3, 194, 198
Barrage : Artillery q.v.; rifle 88; machine-gun q.v.; trench-mortar 353, 552
Barrett, Lt. 180, 208
Barrett, " Paddy," Corp. 398, 542
Base 10, 63, 147, 245, 259, 356, 372, 415, 581
Bass 72, 138
Basseux †311, †340
Bathing : Aisne 38; canal 198; sea 371
Baths 62, 92, 114, 280, 284, 475, 537, 543, 571, 577; coffins as 148
Baylis, Pte. 210, 217
Bayonet 91, 214, 245, 503, 520; broken 85; tool 11
Bazentin-le-Grand 239-40, †250, 254; 517-18-19. Bazentin - le - Grand Wood 518-†19

Bazentin-le-Petit 228-9, 233; cemetery 226, 228, 240. Bazentin-le-Petit Wood 240; 516

Beaulencourt †546

Beaurevoir 29

Beaurevoir–Masnières Line 549

Beausart 504

Beauval †309, 461

Beauvoir †257

Becelaere 398

Bécordel 225, †249, †256

Bedford House 392

Beer 31, 72, 127, 138, 287, 357, 365, 371, 423, 537, 572; drinkers 429; French 138, 365; German gift of 101

B.E.F. 3, 13, 14, 25, 112, 117, 290, 339, 353, 376, 404, 429, 453, 460, 464, 468

B.E.F. Army :
  First 122, 207, 341
  Second 379, 423, 440
  Third 259, 327, 340, 341, 455, 456, 462-3, 538, 543, 559
  Fourth 223, 263, 373, 431, 506, 543
  Fifth 244, 248, 341, 456, 457, 464, 478
  New 7, 113, 133, 134, 161, 167, 170, 176, 179, 199, 202, 289, 429, 430, 484
  Old, 5, 46, 72, 91, 129, 161, 167, 176, 185, 202, 205, 244, 252, 253, 264, 284, 289, 296, 353, 354, 372, 429, 430, 486, 503, 536, 538, 539, 540-1, 542, 571, 581, 585-6. See Old Soldiers
  of Occupation 456, 575
  of Pursuit 344

B.E.F. Cavalry (see Regiments) 18, 19, 22, 33, 40; 69, 71, 73; 224, 225, 239, 303; 325, 407, 420; 520, 555, 556
  Cavalry Generals 162, 163, 172, 325, 358

B.E.F., nationalizing 245
  reduced 440, 445
  Reserve 163, 457, 521; material 467

Belfield, Armr.-Sgt. 23, 580, 583

Belgian civilians 19, 73, 391, 423, 425, 426, 427; coast operations 357, 376; food plenty 415, 424-5-6; frontier 19, 72; troops 369, 376, 381, 411

Belloy †363

Bennett, Corp. 130, 139

Bennett, Lt.-Col. 232

Bennett, Pte. 335

Berlaimont 566

Berlancourt 32

Berlin 75

Bernaville †257

Berry au Bac 454

Bertry 26, 28; †556

Bethisy St. Pierre 68

Béthune †141, 145, †146-7, †151, 160, 162, †164-†5, †171, †174, †183, †184, 194, †198, †200, 205, †206, 212, 222; 255; 443, 479; capture of 142; life in 147, 160-1, 185-6

Beuvry 145, 164, †174, †176, 182, †188, †201, 444; life in 186

Bienvillers †259

Billet fires. See Fuel

Birds : Blackbird, 310, 330, 449. Crow 200, 301. Cuckoo 198, 343. Ducks 383. Goose 173, 284, 287. Hens 85, 197, 383, 463. Kestrel 182. Lark 184, 187, 200, 201, 296, 302, 449, 477. Woodlark 325. Magpie 200. Nightingale 200. Owl 182. Partridge 64, 381. Pheasant 64, 101, 178, 336. Pigeon 311. Robin 325. Rook 343. Sparrow 408, 413, 449, 480. Starling 301, 408. Swallow 201, 206, 358, 477, 480. Swan 392, 412. Thrush 310. Turkey 164, 173, 284, 287, 426. Waterfowl 294. Yellowhammer 325

Birmingham 583

"Birmingham Fusiliers" 429

Blackader, Maj.-Gen. 443, 465, 484

Black Isle 414

Black Prince 364

Black Watch Corner 392, 394-5, 397

Blair, H., Capt., 141, 192, 198, 216-17, 224, 228, 249; quoted 147-8, 149, 155-6, 207-12

Blairville †325

Blangermont †257

Blangy-Tronville †573-80

Blaringhem †405, 442

Blasted Tree 234

Blighty Valley 514

Blimp 454

Boer. See South African War

Boethoek 416

Boiry Becquerelle 338-†9

Boiry St. Rictrude 344

Bois Grenier †104, †106,-7, †109, 115, 126, 129, 133, 135, 136; †445

Boisleux-au-Mont 325

Boisleux St. Marc 325

Bolshevik 419, 420

Bomb (hand grenade) 103 (jam-tin); cricket-ball 152; egg 321; Hale's stick 105, 119, 124; Mills 148, 332; German stick, potato-masher 244

Bombing 123, 128, 134, 178, 180, 193,

195, 220, 236, 241 ; 320-1 ; 332-4 ; 349, 351, 352 ; 359 ; 360 ; 495 ; 500 ; 511 ; 514 ; 540 ; 553 ; accidents 148 ; practice 105, 119, 124, 171, 207, 546

Bonnières †257

Bony †548

Booby-traps 71, 326, 505, 566

Boots 7, 21, 32, 44 ; 175 ; fitting 46

Bordeaux 459

Boreham, A., R.S.M. 49, 68, 95, 222, 243, 274, 371, 441, 497 ; *quoted* 1, 3, 4 ; 6, 7, 8, 10 ; 11 ; 17, 18, 23 ; 29, 30, 32, 37, 38, 43 ; 57, 60 ; 71, 73, 74, 75, 76, 80, 89, 91, 93 ; 253

Bottles 59

Bouchavesnes 285, 295

Boulogne 69, 304, 324, 382, 414

Bourbourg 381

Bournemouth 2

Bouzincourt 469, 472, †475, 481, 504, 507

Bowles, Lt. 237, 246

Boxers 100, 195, 199 ; French 185 ; boxing 199, 368

Boy Scouts 8

Boys. *See* Band

Boyelles 330

Bracey, Prov.-Sgt. 283, 358

Braddel Point 166

Braithwaite, Bdr.-Gen. 476

Brandhoek †419, †430, †432

Bray Dunes †370-4

Bray-sur-Somme 246, †284, †290

Bresle 369

Brétencourt 343

Brickstacks 143. *See* Cuinchy

Brie Comte Robert 48

Briercliffe, Capt. 439, 452, 461, 488 ; *quoted* 458-9, 480, 493, 498-9

Brigade 339

Brigade Major 260, 263

Brigades :
 4th—140
 6th—154, 168
 11th—50-1-2, 56, 58, 268, 279
 12th—55
 15th—30
 16th—72
 19th G.H.Q. Reserve—15 ; Mons 18 ; att. Cavalry 19 ; II Corps 26 ; 5th Div. 27 ; III Corps 43 ; Marne 50 ; Aisne 63 ; 6th Div. 68 ; G.H.Q. 72 ; III Corps, 6th Div. 74 ; " La Bassée "-Fromelles 75 ; La Boutillerie 77 ; Houplines 97 ; Bois Grenier 109 ; 27th Div. 134 ; 8th Div. Laventie 136 ; ceases to be G.H.Q. Troops 2nd Div. 140 ; Loos 146 ; 33rd Div. 168, Béthune 169 ; Ancre 222, High Wood 230 ; Somme 265, Morval-Lesbœufs 268, Clery 291 ; Arras-Croiselles, Hindenburg Line 327 ; Belgian coast 370 ; Ypres Salient 390
 19th—(*Hon. N. G. Drummond* q.v.) 20, 26, 29, 37 ; 50 ; (*Hon. F. Gordon* q.v.) 58, 66, 76, 95, 106, 113, 114, 116, 122, 125 ; (*Sir P. Robertson* q.v.) 137, 144, 153, 158, 166, 172, 175, 188, 213, 218 ; (*C. C. Mayne* q.v.) 224, 232, 233, 245, 249, 252, 257, 270, 271, 289, 291, 296, 297, 298, 303, 326, 327, 328, 329, 335, 341, 344, 348, 353, 372, 378, 380, 381, 382, 390, 392, 405, 406, 408, 413, 414, 421, 440, 441, 442
 19th—Transport 33, 41, 227, 328, 338, 386
 22nd—105
 62nd—313
 92nd—205
 98th—(*J. D. Heriot-Maitland* q.v.) 226, 238, 250 ; 329, 330, 331, 335, 338, 345-6 ; 392-3-4, 398, 401, 403, 404
 100th—(*A. W. F. Baird* q.v.) 226, 238, 250, 254 ; 275, 278-9, 300 ; 329, 330-1, 345, 360, 392, 394, 441, 557, 560
 113th—471, 475, 494, 502, 510, 512-513, 517, 519, 520, 523, 530-1-2-3, 535, 550, 555-6, 558, 577,-8
 114th—506, 510, 512-13, 516, 520, 523, 535, 551, 555-6, 558-9, 578
 115th—(*Bdr.-Gen. Gwyn Thomas* q.v.) 2nd R.W.F. joined 442 ; Bois Grenier 442, 447, 464 ; Ancre 465, 468 (*Bdr.-Gen. Hulke* q.v.) 484, 486, 501 ; across the Ancre 512, 514, 516 ; Bazentin 519, 520-1-2 ; Sailly-Saillisel 523, 530-1, 533-4-5-6 (*Bdr.-Gen. H. de Pree* q.v.) ; Gouzeaucourt 538 ; 545 ; Villers-Outreaux 550 ; R. Selle 557 ; 559 ; Englefontaine 560, 562 ; Forest of Mormal 564 ; Armistice 567 ; Blangy-Tronville 571-2-3, 578

Briqueterie (Brickworks) 272, 280

Broadsheets, *The Times* 172

Brushwood 111, 121, 458, 558

Buckley, Pte. 220

" Buffalo." *See* Jones, Tudor

Buire †223, †244, 256, 282, 287

Bulgaria 563

Bullecourt 308, 326, 345-6

Buller, Gen. Sir R. 205
Burbure 143, 158
Burials 80, 126, 157, 221, 225
    by mine 148, 175, 193, 217; by shell
    93, 254, 419
Buried valuables 138
Busigny 28
Busnettes †165
Butcher, Prov.-Sgt. 122, 274
Butler, Capt. 452, 562, 564-5
Buzancy †60
Byng, F.M. Lord 358

Cadet School 356
Caestre 70
Café Belge 392
Calais 364, 382, 415, 450
Caldwell, J., Lt. 4, 80
Calonne 139, 461
Cambrai 415, 420, 424, 444, 446, 538,
    573; Enquiry 424, 434
Cambrin 142; Mayor of 175
Cambrin Trenches 142, 149, 174, 181-2,
    187, 200, 202
Cameron Covert and House 392, 394,
    396, 401-2
Camouflage 107, 343, 483
Camouflet 193, 207, 209
†Camps: "A" 359; Alnwick 431;
    Blackdown 581; Bovington 1;
    Bray (111) 286, 290; Bulford 412,
    414; Erie 419; Kortepyp 407;
    Sailly Laurette (13) 287, 302, 306-8;
    St. Lawrence 432; Suzanne (17)
    293, 300; Toronto East 431;
    Witley 433
    Rest: Hardelot 259; Havre 304;
    Rouen 356; St. Nazaire 62;
    Wimereux 409
    and cages, prisoners of war 344, 487,
    574
Canadians 90, 115, 117, 130, 192, 324
Canals: Aire-Béthune 160, 381; Bas-
    ingstoke 582; Béthune-La Bassée
    142-3, 198, 217-18; Coast-St.
    Omer 381; Condé 18; Dunkirk-
    Nieuport 370, 380; du Nord 292,
    542; Schelde 547, 549
Canche 248, 257
Candas 257
Canly 69
Canteens: Battalion 184, 203, 249, 287,
    368, 371, 423, 470, 496; Church
    Army 249, 470; Division—8th
    139; 38th 461, 537; Expeditionary
    Force (E.F.C.) 96, 204, 249, 470;
    French 291; German 244; R.F.A.
    459; Y.M.C.A. 288, 470

Carbon-monoxide poisoning 292, 471
Cardonnette †223
Carnoy 265
Cars, armoured 73
Cassel 382, 386, 423
Casson, 2/Lt. 309, 312-13
Casualties: French 75; German 57, 85,
    94, 501, 542, 559; Neuve Chapelle
    124; picking fruit 137; souvenir-
    seeking 136, 165, 179, 216
Category, men and units, 246, 433, 467
Cathedrals: Amiens 222, 383; Arras
    344; Albert 245, 466, 468; Rouen
    12; St. Omer 373, 383, 439;
    Ypres 411
Causeways 375, 507, 558
Cavalry. See B.E.F. and Regiments
Cavalryman 519
Cavan, Earl of, Lt.-Gen. 265
Cavell, Edith 406
Cayeux 248
Cemetery 126, 300, 343, 417, 579
Censorship: letters q.v.; movements
    7; newspapers 436
Cerfroid 60
Certigny (? Germigny) 60
Channel crossings 9, 10, 582; Dover-
    Calais 450,-53; Folkestone-
    Boulogne 179, 283, 304, 324,
    414-15; Newhaven-Havre 304
Chapelle d'Armentières 445
Chaplains 72, 124, 205, 289, 294, 345,
    430, 442, 453, 470, 473
    Jones, E. R. 390, 430, 432, 510, 529,
    530-1
    Jones, — (Nonconf.) 490, 556
    M'Shane,— (R.C.) 234
    Williams, — 578
Chaplin, Bdr.-Gen. 158, 299, 319, 322,
    354, 458
Charcoal 92; burning 369
Charlton, Capt. 390, 461, 485, 490,
    495-6, 510, 513, 514; quoted 486,
    487, 491, 500-1, 505, 513, 514
Châteaux: Buzancy 60; Gorre 206;
    Hénincourt 466, 476; Pierrefonds
    39; Perrouse 52; Polderhoek 394,
    396; Renescure 69; Suzanne 294
Château des Anglais 555
Chemin des Dames 63, 326
Chérisy 327, 345
Chevry 48
Chezy 60
Chick, Capt. 461, 509, 510-11, 523-4,
    526, 528, 530-1, 583
Chilblains 270, 283, 285
"Chinese" attack 122
Chinese labour 381, 426, 442; justice 426

Chocolate Soldiers. *See* Regiments: R.F. 20th

Chouy 60

Christmas Day: (1914) 101-2; (1915) 173-4; (1916) 287; (1917) 424-7; (1918) 572

Christofferson, Capt. 485, 496, 518, 532, 555, 575, 577

Church Army huts 186, 240
 parades 111, 124, 289, 571, 577, 583; services, 430, 460, 484
 spires and towers in Flanders 381, 386; as O.P. 84, 137, 246

Cider-making 283

Citadel †265

Civilians 6, 206, 304, 305, 309, 324, 372, 435, 451, 452-3; wages 392; French *q.v.*

Clapham Junction 395

Clary †556

Clayton, Lt.-Col. 299, 345, 463

Cleanliness 96, 258, 289

Clegg-Hill (Lord Hill), Lt.-Col. the Hon. C. R. 49, 56, 68, 83, 87, 89, 94, 108, 117, 122 151 ; 547; *quoted* 88

Clemenceau, G., Mons. 469

Clery 290, 292-3, 301

Clewly, L/Corp. 127

Clothing 130, 136, 158; coat, goatskin 100; jerkin leather 100

Coal. *See* Fuel

Coast defence 23
 operations 374-9

Cocherel 60

Cockburn, J. B., Lt.-Col. 449, 450, 472, 497, 498-9, 500-1-2-3-4, 506-7, 510, 515, 517-18-19; 536; 571, 577; 583

Code 560

Cojeul 314,-5

Collins 129

Coltart, J. S., Capt. 95, 222, 324 ; *quoted* 235

Colquhoun, Lt. 396, 398

Combles 285

Comforts Committee 96, 174, 287, 340

Comic Cuts 197, 224, 360

C.Os. at variance 109, 114; 249, 263

Commings, Maj.-Gen. 357

Commissions : other ranks 89, 196, 259, 370, 397; Temporary 108

Compiègne 35. Compiègne Forest 39

Comrades (R.W.F.) Association 284, 509

Conning, Capt. 209, 215-16, 232, 234, 239, 241, 242, 287, 288, 298, 307, 322, 327, 348-9, 350

Conscription: Australia 421; Canada 421

Conscripts : boys 412; first 245

Contalmaison †516-17

Contay, 462, 464, †466, †477, †483

Contrasts 235, 309, 354, 360, 374, 385, 455, 467, 468

Convoy 434

Cook's tourist 206

Cooker 3, 33, 566 ; D Company's 286 ; Tommy's 293

Cooper, Lt. 352

Corbie 223, 245, †308

Corney, Lt. 537

Corps :
 I—133
 II—14, 26, 27, 74, 76, 223
 III—43, 50, 52, 65-6, 72, 74, 76
 V—381, 464, 471, 482, 498, 502, 523, 533, 563, 579
 VI—326
 VII—258-9, 326, 334, 340, 354, 357, 370, 373
 VIII—408, 414, 425, 429
 X—390
 XI—181, 185
 XIII—257
 XIV—265, 280, 295-9
 XV—223, 226, 230, 244, 248, 285, 443,-4
 XVII—326
 XVIII—303, 309
 Indian 82, 133, 137

Cosh 221

Coster, Capt. 188, 193, 239, 241-2, 274, 276, 288, 357 363, 365, 394, 396

Costing 373, 408

Coudekerke †380

Couloisy 38

Count. *See* de Miremont

Coureau de La Grande Chapelle 126

Courses (*see* Schools) 289, 421, 509, 537, 575

Cover (*see* Barrage *and* Camouflage) Contour 87, 274, 336,-7,-8, 353, 513 ; craters, houses 83, 154, 219 ; night 68, 80, 83, 92, 106, 146, 176, 549 ; smoke 253, 395, 523 ; tin-hat and groundsheet 184, 377; trench 199, 278, 393 ; tunnel 361

Cox's Bank, 203

Coxyde †374, 379

Crabtree, Lt. 510, 523-4; *quoted* 522, 525

Craig, Capt. 121, 197, 215

Craters 142-3-4; Etna 142 ; Midnight 188; Red Dragon 217; "R.W.F." 181; Vesuvius 142

Crawshay, C. H. R., Lt.-Col. 126, 206-7, 216, 218, 222, 224, 229, 232,

234, 237, 241-2, 246-7-8-9, 251, 253-4, 256, 257, 259, 261-2, 263, 268, 271, 273, 275, 277, 280, 283, 285, 286, 287, 288, 291, 293, 303, 346

Crécy, 364. Crécy Forest 369

Crockett, Lt. 222, 236

Croisilles 317, 327, 345, †347, 376 ; 458

Croix de Guerre 366

Croix du Bac 466

Crombie, Capt. 222

Cromwell 370, 411

Crosland, 2/Lt. 208-9, 217

Cross (flank) fire 112, 277-8, 339

Crown and Anchor 248

Crown Prince 75

Crucifix (Calvaire) : Jaulzy 38 ; Renescure 442

Crucifix Corner : Aveluy 509, 510 ; Bazentin 234, 250, 254

Cubitt, Sir T. A. 484, 485, 487, 491-2, 502, 506, 546, 555, 571, 577

Cugny 32

Cuinchy (Brickstacks) Trenches 142, 143, 145, 177, 182, 184, 195, 198 ; triangle 172

Cuirass 56, 59 ; 75

Cumberland, C.S.M., 352, 418

Curgies, Fort of 21

Curlu 291

Cuthbert, J., Maj. 110, 115, 127, 164, 288, 295-6, 409, 472, 484, 502-3

D.A.D.O.S. 440

Dai and Evan 134

Dale, Pte. 539

Dammartin 44

Daours †223

Darling, Justice 4

Darling, Lt.-Col. 169

Davies, Canon 583

Davies, Picton, Capt. 49, 63, 68, 87, 324, 340, 349, 350, 352 ; quoted 81, 82, 86, 87, 89, 90 ; 350

Davies, L/Corp. 114

Davies, '90, Lt. 82, 122

Davies, '91, Pte. 393

Davies, Pte. 527

Davies, "Teg", Lt. 261, 346, 350

de Miremont (Count), Maj. 259, 269, 275, 288, 327, 329, 353, 413-14, 421, 445, 452, 468, 475, 477, 478, 479, 481, 486, 491, 493-4, 497, 502, 504, 521-2-3, 530, 535-6, 557, 560, 563, 567, 572-3, 575, 578, 579

de Pree, Bdr.-Gen. 536, 547, 577, 580

Dealing, Lt. 61, 194, 251, 278

Decauville Railway 285, 433

Declaration of War 4

Decorations 73, 116, 255, 335, 354, 405, 430, 524, 547, 571, 574 ; Birthday 1918, 484 ; New Year 1918, 430 ; final 574

Defence Scheme 137, 475 ; High Wood 230, 238

Deficiencies 3, 33 ; 63 ; 400-1 ; 452, 468, 573

Delettré, Suzanne 131

Delousing, 289, 581

Demobilizing 571, 574-5, 577, 579

Denison, Lt.-Col. 176

Depot. See Wrexham

Derby, Lord 475 ; Derbyites 245

Deserters, 358, 395, 410, 475, 515, 573 ; returned 7

Despatch Riders 15, 38, 87, 175

Despatches 360 ; Loos 163, 165 ; Somme 288

Dewhurst, Lt. 162, 179, 180, 186

Dickebusch 392, †404

Diggle, Lt. 511

Discipline 15, 64, 410, 440, 480-1. See Regiments : R.W.F. 2nd

Divisions :

Cavalry 1st—19

Guards—160, 280

1st—252, 255, 376

2nd—(Maj.-Gen. Horne q.v.) 140, 142, 154, 164, 165 (Maj.-Gen. Walker) 168 ; 443, 463-4

3rd—20, 27, 31

4th—23, 33, 42, 55, 59, 60, 118, 266-7

5th—25, 26, 31, 32, 230, 244

6th—23, 69, 70, 99, 134

7th—94, 117, 159, 225, 230, 244, 347

8th—136, 139, 279

9th—151

12th—205

17th—276, 278, 462, 485, 531, 533, 558, 563-4

18th—517, 519, 533, 559, 560, 563-5

19th—244

21st—228, 326-7, 344, 535, 547

23rd—392, 403

24th—152

27th—134

30th—312, 326, 331, 337

31st—222

33rd—168 (Maj.-Gen. Landon q.v.), Béthune XI Corps 169 ; Ancre–Somme, High Wood, XV Corps 222 ; Humbercamps VII Corps 256 (Maj.-Gen. Sir R. Pinney q.v.) ; 260 ; Somme – Morval – Lesbœufs XIV Corps 267 ; Somme–Clery XV Corps 290 ; XVIII Corps 302 ;

Divisions—*continued*:
　Arras–Croisilles VII Corps 319;
　Nieuport, XV Corps 376; (*Maj.-
　Gen. Wood* q.v.) V Corps 382;
　Ypres Salient–Polygon Wood X
　Corps 390; Salient VIII Corps 408;
　(*Maj.-Gen. Sir R. Pinney*) 418
　33rd—Command: 190, 212, 218;
　226-7-8, 234, 238, 244, 248, 252,
　253, 254; 256, 257, 260, 263; 265,
　267, 271; 284, 285, 289, 290, 292,
　295, 296, 297, 300, 302, 303; 326,
　327, 330, 331, 334, 340, 344, 349,
　352, 357, 359, 360, 361, 366, 372,
　373, 376, 379, 390, 392, 394, 402,
　405, 408, 416; 418, 423, 425; 556,
　559, 560, 566, 568
　33rd—Casualties, July 1916, 248
　34th—458
　35th—260, 471, 482
　38th (Welsh)—223, 225, 226; (*Maj.-
　Gen. Blackader* q.v.) Bois Grenier,
　XV Corps 440; Ancre V Corps
　464; (*Maj.-Gen. Sir T. A. Cubitt*
　q.v.) 484; across the Ancre 512;
　Bazentin-le-Grand 517; Sailly-
　Saillisel 522; Gouzeaucourt 543;
　Villers-Outreaux 549; Selle 558;
　Sambre 566; demobilizing 571
　38th—Command: 440, 442, 456, 464,
　468, 471, 474, 477-8, 486, 491, 493,
　496, 498, 502, 504, 518-19, 520, 522-
　523, 533, 543, 547, 549, 563, 566,
　571, 574-6, 578
　39th—201, 392
　46th—126, 259
　47th—478, 480-1
　50th—341
　51st—244, 248
　63rd (Naval)—484
　66th—202, 376, 558
Dixie (dechse) 3, 407, 461
Docherty, C.S.M. 141, 324, 390, 510
Dolling, Capt. 170-1, 178, 180, 247, 252
Domestic problems 437, 558
Domqueur le Plouy †477
Dorchester 2, †5, 6, 8; Assizes 4
Dormy House 393
Dosinghem 382
Doullens 260-1, 263, 310, 324-5, 461,
　465, 478, 503, 509, 546
Doulieu †140, 445
Dover 369, 450, 453
Doyle, Conan 206
Dranoutre 73, 410
Drinks 11, 31, 60, 72, 119, 138, 146, 173,
　191, 195, 247, 261, 262, 282, 307,
　308-9, 423, 425-6, 465, 509, 583

Drinkwater 247
Drums. *See* Regiments: R.W.F. 2nd
Drummer, American 24
Drummond, Bdr.-Gen. 15, 36, 37
Dublin Rising 546
du Cane, General 285, 443
Duckboards 166, 272, 280, 573
Duck's Bill 208, 215
Dugouts 148, 154, 178, 214, 348, 359 475,
　538; French 285, 302; German
　220, 229, 249, 325
Dunkirk 370, 371, 376, 382
Dunn, Capt. 307, 323, 506
Dupont, Mons. 21
Dury †32
Dysentery 261

Earnshaw, L/Corp. 196
Easter Day: (1916) 195; (1917) 311;
　(1918) 460; (1919) 578
Eclusier 294, 301
École des Jeunes Filles 148
Ecuiry †61, 65.　Ecuiry Wood 65
Edge Hill 287
Edge, Pte. 253
Education Scheme 456, 521, 571, 574
Edward III 364
Edwards, Pryce, Capt. 206, 208, 217
Eecke 387
Egypt 246, 356
Electric Supply, 98, 117, 249, 329, 375, 377
Elizabeth, Queen 370
Elouges 19, 33
Elverdinghe 420
Englebelmer 464, 491
Englefontaine 560, 562-3-4-5-†6, 573
Epéhy 547; Battle of 543
Epidemics: diarrhœa 421; influenza
　191, 283, 496, 503; German
　measles 200; measles 290
Equancourt †543
Equipment: obsolete 3; modern 63;
　machine-gun 117; Lewis-gun 452;
　salvage 536
Erquinghem †103, 110, 445, 449
Escaut (Schelde) 18, 547, 549
Esprit de corps 246, 347
Estaires 113, 138, 388, 443
Estaminet-life 118, 141, 169, 186, 425
Estaminet names 107, 184, 290, 326,
　384-5, 386, 391, 441-2, 459, 461, 467
Estrées-Maretz †30, 34
Estrées St. Denis †69
Etaples 69, 248, 283, 389
Eu 369
Evans, H., Capt. 510, 565, 571, 583;
　quoted 564
Evans, Hywel, Lt. 309, 313, 365, 394, 396

Evans, J. T. S., Lt. 479
Evans, Ll., Capt. 324, 390, 417, 426, 430, 439, 456, 459, 461, 490, 493, 510, 520, 528, 532, 557, 571; 575, 578, 583; *quoted* 356, 490, 497, 501, 504, 506, 507, 512, 514, 515, 516, 517-19, 520, 529, 535, 536-7, 541, 543, 560, 568, 574, 576, 579, 580, 581
Evans, W., Corp. 517, 519, 520, 536, 571
Exchange, franc 97, 184, 204
"Eyewitness" 55

Falstaff 252
Fanshawe, Lt.-Gen. 381, 464
Farms: Artillery 446, 457; 454; Carlisle 396, 399, 402; Carrière l'Evecque 61; Cellar 78, 84; Corbière 59; La Cordonnerie 77, 94; Crest 416, 417, 433; Culvert 106; Dead Cow 445; Fitzclarence 401; Grande Flamengrie 104; Hallebeeke 445; Hillside 416-17; Jerk 396, 401; Judas 330, 344; Jut 396, 402; Les Briques 151; Lone 394, 396,-7,-8; Moat 104, 445; Rambourlieux 557, 559; Ration 445; Rolanderie 104, 446, 449, 454; Streaky Bacon 104, 117, 454; Tyne Cot 417; Villers 549, 554; Water 104, 107
Farm midden 74, 202, 258, 283, 374, 502
Fascines Road 129
Fatigues 6, 106, 112, 143, 146, 147, 165, 177, 230, 238, 250, 272, 285, 296, 317-18, 390, 392, 408, 411, 421, 425, 433, 444, 454, 468, 476, 481, 492, 504, 507, 559, 577-8; mechanical substitutes for 143, 272, 285, 329, 433, 476
Fauquissart 74, 137
Ferguson, Sir C. 31
Ferrières 48
Festubert 207; Battle of 133
Feud: Scotch 343; Middlesex-German 399
Feuillères 301
Ficheux 312
Field Cashier 63, 260, 316
  Punishment 119
  Service Regulations 314
Fifty-Seventh. *See* Regiments: Middlesex 1st
Fijians 428
Fins 522, 538. Fins Ridge 543
Fishing 218
"Fizzer" 158, 193
Flame-thrower 187, 251, 255
Flare. *See* Rocket
Flash 13, 198, 264

Fleas 69, 374, 376
Flemings 374, 424
Flemish buildings 374, 445; speaking 19, 374
Flers 230, 255. Flers line 266, †520, †522
Fletcher, Lt. 49, 68, 87, 120, 121, 122, 125; *quoted* 66
Fletcher, C. R. L. 174
Fleurbaix 78
Flixecourt 263
Flying Corps, R. *See* Air Force, R.
Foch, Marshal 314, 448, 469
Foden oven 483
Fokker 239, 254
Folkestone 179, 324
Foncquevillers 259
Fontaine-lez-Croisilles 326, 346, 353. Fontaine Wood 313
Food 450; abundance 424-5, 435; contrasts 415, 435, 471
  control: British 448, 450-1; German 200
  cost 200, 429, 441, 509
  scarcity: British 285, 435, 465; European 436; French 369, 442, 453; German 415, 470
Forceville (Acheux) †486, †490, †496, †504
Forceville (Airaines) †282,-3, 287; Mayor of 283
Forster, R.E., Lt.-Col. 263, 297, 360, 367, 368, 372, 382
Fort Rouge 69
Fortnum and Mason 14, 32
Fouling furniture 71
Fouquereuil †179, †205
Fouquières †222
Fournes en Weppes 75
Fox, d'Arcy, Capt. 283, 288
Fox, Walter, Capt. 133, 192, 201, 222, 256, 258, 274, 276, 356, 365, 444, 575, 581, 583; *quoted* 219
Francis, Sgt. 293
Fraternizing 101, 479
Freeman, C., Capt. 88, 152, 154-5
Frélinghien 97
French, F.M. Lord 13, 33, 35; 172
French, Lt. 450
French Air Force 292
  Army 31, 74, 246, 268-9, 276-7, 376, 448, 476, 480; attacks by 133, 149, 326; counter-attack 502; local 267, 277; postponing 269
  Artillery 45, 291; "Seventy-fives" 63, 76, 159, 227, 276, 291, 376
  Cavalry 74, 75, 79
  canteens 291
  communications 290-1

French conscripts 450
    construction 74, 291, 302
    control of operations 161, 326, 415, 469
        Divisions: 17th 290; 30th 284; Marine 376; at Valenciennes 34, 35
    insubordination 324, 326
    officers at Amiens 324, La Cordonnerie 79, Le Cateau 34, Fromelles 75-6, Morval 269, St. Quentin 35
    organization 291-2, 303
    prisoners, treatment of 246; prisoners in Germany 428
    raids on 450
    rations 291
    Regiments: 90th 291; 125th 268-9; Chasseurs Alpines 75; Cyclist 74
    reliefs 75, 292
    Reserve 303, 448, 457, 460, 465-6, 469, 475
    Reservists 12, 13
    soldiers 36, 294, 324; physique 227, 272
    telephones 290-1
    Territorials 14, 21, 42; General of 194
    training 303
    transport 240
    uniforms 75
French boxer 185; building 200, 260, 359; civilians 10, 18, 25, 26, 84, 144, 160, 186, 218, 289, 304, 324, 407, 445, 456, 460, 470, 504, 557, 560-1-2 (*and see* refugees *and* women); disliked 456; farm labour 223, 363; food supply *q.v.*; furnishing 258, 363; Gendarmes 10, 12, 324, 336; ill-will 465, 476; mining villages 141, 145, 205; miners 141; money exchange 97, 184, 204; National Festival 366; refugees (*and see* civilians) 44, 45, 47, 205, 304, 374, 423, 448, 454, 458-9, 460, 462-3, 470, 562; sanitation 12, 80, 284; shops 96, 470; ways 12, 256, 266, 269, 470; French women: landladies 66, 169, 179, 256, 257, 261, 363, 365, 366, 374, 383, 439, 442, 444, 462; others 10, 11, 25, 26, 44, 57, 71, 96, 161, 171, 175, 206, 247, 358, 369, 443, 444, 470
Fresnoy †43
Frévent 458
Friar in khaki 387
Fricourt 225, 227. Fricourt Wood †249, †255
Frise 294, 302
Froissart 364
Fromelles 74, †76, 81, 91

Front, Franco-British 467
Front and Staff 77, 177, 290, 339, 361, 478, 479
Frostbound 291-2, 296
Frost, Sgt. 398
Fryatt, Capt. 295
Fuel: coal shortage 292, 425; scrounged 283, 293, 416, 423, 434, 494; supplied 92, 292, 433, 539, 574
Fuse: accidents 136, 165; German 359
Fyson, Capt. 222

Gallic cock 410
Gallipoli 161, 261
Gamaches 369
Game 64-5-6, 101, 381; shooting 64, 366
Games: at Beuvry 187; Blangy-Tronville 574, 578; Bois Grenier 110, 133. *Basket-ball* 546. *Football, Association* 110, 169, 187, 444. *Paper-chases* 371. *Polo* 110, 131, 371. *Rugby* 445, 547, 578. *Sports* 139, 357-8, 367-8, 504, 579. *Quoits* 131
Garnett, Bdr.-Gen. 298, 301, 310, 335, 348, 353, 359, 363, 365, 367, 368-9, 373, 376, 378, 388, 394, 405, 409, 413, 416, 421, 423, 435, 440, 441-2, 446, 448-9, 450, 452, 462, 466, 468, 476-7-8
Gas: drift (chlorine) 146, 151, 153-4-5-156-7, 161, 178; shell 354, (phosgene) 369, 558
    effects of 178, 390-1 483, 585; in farmyard 197-8, 454
    masks 133, 152, 165, 283, 375, 507, 542; for horses 374
    officer 258
    prevention 156, 375; projectors 451
    R.E. Company 153, 157
Gas, German: alarm, 178, 455
    drift 132, 197-8, 206
    shell: bromine (K) 226, 228, 374, 375, 377; mustard 369, 374-5, 390-1, 413, 452, 454, 482-3, 485, 507, 535, 539, 542; tear (pepper) 157, 377
Gaudiempré 325
Gazette 116, 255, 423
Geiger, Maj. 1, 68, 280; *quoted* 2, 4, 5, 8-10, 11-16, 17, 20-26, 28-9 30-3, 38-9, 42, 44-7, 49, 51-2, 56, 58-9, 61
Geleide Post 376, 378-9
G.H.Q. 75, 113, 145, 163, 194, 218, 252, 288, 303, 340, 342, 349, 353, 355, 420, 436, 440, 448, 456, 460, 468
Generalissimo 469

G.R.O. 66, 78, 140, 233, 266, 289, 342, 443, 453, 482, 572, 574-5

George, Rt. Hon. Ll. 245, 303, 415, 430, 436-7, 446, 448, 457, 467, 475, 580

Gepp, C., Maj.-Gen. 423, 425, 441

German Army 46, 63, 68, 94, 112, 288, 376, 420, 453, 455, 517, 533, 546, 548 ; First Army 19, 48

attack (1918) 420, 450, 454, 458, 463-464, 466, 502, 539, 540

attack formations 81, 91 ; 241-2, 244 ; 463

German Air Force :

activity 21, 22, 139, 146, 178, 184, 194, 239, 279, 301, 330, 348, 377, 382-3, 390, 398, 417, 421, 434, 465, 474, 481, 542, 559

bombing 66, 181, 259, 265, 280-1, 296-7, 371, 382, 405, 411-12, 431, 439, 450, 481, 503 ; 568

signals 181

German Artillery :

accuracy 235, 377, 562

activity 22, 27, 44, 49, 50, 62, 75, 79, 81-2, 85, 88-9, 90-1, 93-4, 107, 132-3, 150-1, 159, 179, 181, 184, 198, 201, 216, 224, 226, 249, 250, 252, 254-5, 267, 274-5, 279, 281, 334, 353, 375, 392, 397-8-9, 401, 403, 404, 409, 413, 416-17, 419, 432, 447, 448, 451, 452, 454, 458, 464, 468, 480, 485, 493-4, 498, 505, 511, 513, 520, 523, 530-1, 535-6, 542, 545, 547, 553, 555, 558-9, 562-3, 566

barrage : cover 225, 228, 231-2-3-4, 236, 254, 277, 350, 395, 400, 404, 472, 482, 489, 490, 495-6, 499, 512, 519, 523 ; creeping 240 ; for raids, 213, 302, 495, 561

bombardment 9, 153, 155, 162, 180, 202, 213, 221, 227-8-9, 230, 240, 243, 251, 337 ; 377, 393, 395, 403, 495, 515, 521, 534, 539, 541, 544 ; gas q.v.

captured 43, 44, 226, 228, 284, 566

heavy 159, 162, 296, 347, 378, 411, 421, 481, 576

long-range 387, 429, 454, 576

registration 302, 348, 446

shells spotted 447, 509

German Cavalry 23, 33, 39, 40, 42, 52, 56, 59, 69, 71 ; 4th Div. 44 ; 8th Hussars 40-1-2

Divisions and Regiments : Bavarian 113, 198 ; Guards 302 ; Marine 479 ; Saxon 98, 101, 113, 126, 479 ; Prussian 113 ; 24th 279 ; 81st 279 ; Jaegers 198, 217

German hand grenade 103, 244, 321 ; bombing 123, 132, 148, 180, 195, 213, 220, 236, 241, 320, 352, 359, 360, 493, 540-1, 565 ; screen 254, 360

intelligence 140, 186, 216, 444, 456

machine-guns 52-3, 55, 58, 69, 83, 117, 125, 151, 153, 154, 158, 193 ; 195-6 219, 266 ; 231, 235, 236, 238, 242 ; 277, 297, 300 ; 332, 334, 336, 338 ; 346, 349, 351 ; 396, 401 ; 472, 474 ; 489, 497, 499, 500 ; 509, 510, 513, 516 ; 517, 519 ; 525, 526, 529, 530 ; 533-4 ; 539, 540 ; 548 ; 549, 550 ; 554-5-6 ; 558 ; 561, 564-5 ; 567 ; Cycle machine-guns 522

morale 85, 224, 288, 471, 473, 475, 514, 517, 533, 548, 556

physique 221, 245, 404, 501, 554

prisoners 40 ; 42, 89 ; 220-1, 224, 245, 278-9, 284, 307, 332, 338, 340, 397, 402, 501, 511-12-13-14, 519, 522, 542-3, 552-3-4, 558, 564 ; hospital 439 ; orchestra 574

raids 203, 209, 302, 378, 408, 409, 410, 448, 450, 474, 480, 494, 561

rations 344, 409, 434

snipers : sniping 83, 84, 86, 88, 98, 112, 115, 135, 199, 202, 251, 293, 322, 403, 475, 494, 538, 560, 562 ; co-ordinated 83, 135

stragglers 59, 65-6

transport 133, 145, 476, 555

treatment of prisoners 244, 279, 353, 407 ; in Germany 428 ; 435

trench strength 404, 437

ways 59, 71, 74

withdrawal (1917) 295, 300, 302, 325-6 ; (1918) 505, 546, 548

work 220, 229, 409, 549

German navy : destroyers 455 ; mutiny 408

Germans 40, 59, 72, 84, 89, 98, 101, 102, 137, 174, 199, 220, 244, 279, 337, 353, 458, 481, 492, 500, 501, 511

Germany's Peace offer 284

Gheluvelt 392

Gibbs, P. (Journalist) 247

Gill, Sgt. 489, 541

Ginchy 266, 273 ; 517, 520, 522, 537

Giraud, Corp. Interp. 430

Gittens, Lt. 286, 336-7

Givenchy 133, 255, 466 ; trenches 142, 144, 148, 169, 209, 218

Glasgow Highlanders 369

Gleichen, Lord E. 30

Gnat 374

Goat. See Regiments : R.W.F. 2nd

Golder, H., Corp. 397-8
Goldsmith, Capt. 156, 267
Gommecourt 300
Gonnehem 167, 169
Gordon, Hon. F. 58, 66, 74, 76, 95, 113, 116, 117, 122, 125
Gore, P. K., Lt.-Col. 2, 71, 129
Gorre †206, 444
Gosport 580
Gough, Gen. Sir H. 141, 162, 457
Gouzeaucourt Wood 538, 543-4-5
Government 290, 373, 445
Graves, R., Capt. 146, 166, 228, 231, 246
Greaves, E. J., Capt. 461, 510, 520, 529, 537
Greaves, R., Lt. 271, 274; 307-8, 318, 324; quoted 333
Grenade: hand see Bomb; rifle 104, 116, 181, 200, 333, 395
Grierson, Lt.-Gen. 14
Griffiths, A. C. F., Lt. 547, 556
Griffiths, L/Corp. (Goat-Major) 53
Griffiths, Pte. 373
Gris Pot 104, 126, 446, 449
Grisy †48
Grouche 261
Ground, use of 28, 87, 88, 219, 338, 388; groundsheets 377, 388; signs 508, 553
Guémappe 337
Gueudecourt 278
Guides 315, 327, 393
Guillemont 266, †271
Guiscard 32
Guise Lamotte 39
Gum-boots 169, 172, 298

Haggis 287
Haig, F.M. Lord 172, 314, 461, 467, 468
Haisnes 151
Haking, Lt.-Gen. 181, 185, 443
Hall, Sgt. 101
Ham 36
Hamburg 415
Hamel 487, 492, 510; raid 497-502
Hamelincourt (Camp A) †359
Hamilton, Maj.-Gen. 26
Hangest 364
Hanmer, Lt. 336
Hannescamps 259
Hansom 283
Happy Valley 227, 230, 243, 517
Harbison, Capt. 135, 165
Hardelot 259
Harfleur 581
Harley St. 144, 152, †165
Harponville 482

Harries, Capt. 259, 288, 356, 365, 368-9
Harvey, Lt.-Col. 577
Hate 116, 148
Haussy 22
Havre 9, 62, 147, 290, 304, 356, 581
Hazebrouck 131, 405, 414, 429
Heastey, 2/Lt. 208, 221, 237
Heath Robinson 194, 255
Heber, Bishop 583
Hebuterne 263
Hecq 565-6, †573
Hedauville †463
Hedges, Drummer 371, 463
Heligoland 39
Hellblast Corner 393
Helmets: steel, shrapnel 164, 180, 184, 452; gas q.v.
Hem 291
Henin 326, 347; Hill 327; Ridge 337
Hénincourt †466, 468
Héninel 312
Hennessy 101
Henry V 223, 294, 364
Hérissart 462, 464, †474, †483, †502-3
Herlies 76
Hesdigneul 200
Heywood, Bde.-Maj. 58, 66
Hiermont †484, 502
Higginson, Capt. 192, 194, 218-19, 237, 239; quoted 220, 224, 228, 249
High Wood 225-6, 229, 230, 244, 250, 515, 520
Hill, L/Corp. 498, 500
Hindenburg, von, Marshal 573
Hindenburg Line 307, 326, 338, 361; 546-7-†8; construction 316-17-18, 328-9, 347; 547-8; barricade 329, 330-7; Front Trench 346; The Hump 345-6; Tunnel Trench 329-335, 346-7; Plum Lane 347-54
Hinder, Sgt. 236, 241
History Drama 415
Hogben, Sgt. 377, 388, 399; 586
Hog's Back 273
Hohenzollern Redoubt 158, 160, 185
Holden, Capt. 188
Holmes, Maj.-Gen. 1, 17, 20, 33, 80, 87, 88, 354; quoted 4, 23
Home Establishment 246, 440
    Front 435, 448, 453; French 435; German 435
Honnechy 28
Hop-growing 387
Horne, F.M. Lord 141, 223
Horse: casualties 42, 47, 325, 380, 519; flesh 557; masks 374; racing 342; shoes 47, 65; shows 139, 206, 259, 367, 504

Horses 79, 286, 325, 441 ; *François* 342
2/R.W.F. : *Billy* 367 ; *Dolly* 347, 387,
391 ; *Girlie* 42, 259, 260, 308, 342,
504, 574 ; *Jenny* 367, 574 ; *Mug-
wump* 367, 478 ; *Rabbit* 367 ; *Ruby*
373
Horton, Sgt. 300, 449
Houlle †381
Houplines 95, 98
House 161, 207
H.P. Sauce 407
Hughes, Capt. 390, 510, 529, 531, 535,
542 ; *quoted* 515, 530, 533-4
Hughes, J. R., Q.M.S. 79
Hughes, T., Sgt. 124, 127, 333
Hulke, Bdr.-Gen. 468, 487, 521, 464
Hulluch 197
Hump, The 345-6
Hunter-Weston, Lt.-Gen. 50-1-2-3-4-5,
408, 412, 418, 425, 432-3
Huts, Army : cost 286 ; French 284

Ibbotson, Sgt. 353
Idylls 357, 364, 365
Inchy †573
Incompetent tents 424, 433, 436
Indispensables 290, 324, 372, 441
Industrial conditions 392
Inscriptions 428, 442, 465
Intelligence 120, 135, 140
Interpreters 12, 18, 24, 257, 430
Ireland 23, 43, 56, 546
Iron Cross 293
Italy 413,-14,-15
Itchas, Gen. 206
Ivergny †258

Jack Johnson 75
Jackson, Lt. 336-7
James, L/Corp. 335
Jaulzy †38
Jellicoe, Lord 467
Jenkins, Pte. 198
Jenlain †21, 33
Jerusalem 415
" Joe " 492-3
Joffre, Maréchal 284
Johnson, Bombr. 33
Johnson, Bde.-Maj. 15, 20, 21, 29
Johnson, Sgt.-Shoemaker 293, 301
Jones, C., Lt. and Q.M. 222, 235, 236
Jones, Cuthbert, Capt. 390, 439, 461,
503, 510, 513, 516
Jones, F. L. C., Lt. 430, 441, 451-2, 487,
494, 496, 513, 523-4-5-6-7
Jones, J., Lt. 235-6
Jones, Rhys, Lt. 333
Jones, Tudor (" Buffalo "), Lt. 46, 57, 64

Jones, '10, C.S.M. 239, 336-7, 400
Jones, Sgt.-Cook 264, 373
Jones, L/Sgt. 471, 496, 586
Jones, '45, Morgan, Signaller 282, 324,
390, 398, 439, 510, 528 ; *quoted* 380,
393, 397, 407, 416, 525, 527, 531 ;
567
Jones, Tom, Signaller 403
Jones, '37, Pte. 398-9, 471
Jones, '42, Pte. 329, 338
Jones, '88, Signaller 527
Jossigny 49
Jutland, Battle of 205

Kaiser 12, 457 ; Kaiser's birthdays 113,
178, 293, 439
Kearsley, Maj. 368, 373, 378, 382, 390,
401-2-3 ; 410 ; 423, 426, 431, 433 ;
583
Keepfer, Lt. 505, 564-5
Kemmel 73, 476
Kennedy, A., Col. 141, 234
Kent, Corp. 282, 390, 435-9, 461, 510 ;
quoted 397-8 ; 567
Kilt 164, 375
King, H.M. the 13, 97, 249, 572, 575
King's Rules and Regulations 4
Kirkby (" Uncle "), Capt. 95, 183, 195,
307-8, 312-13, 315-16 ; 510 ; 537-8-
539, 540-1, 545-7, 550, 551, 556
Kit : burned 293, 424 ; carried 68, 407,
461 ; cast 21, 25 ; eked out 158 ;
fighting kit 86, 152, 225, 466, 477 ;
lost 32, 36, 37, 45, 307 ; some kit
167, 206 ; summer (1915) 136 ;
weight of 25
Kitchener, F.M. Lord 141, 205, 436
Klück, von, Gen. 19
" Knibb," Capt. 190, 258, 405
Kut 198

L'Armée 104, 124, 126, 445, 446
La Bassée 142, 145 ; Battle of 74. La
Boutellerie 77, 440. La Bréarde 69.
La Clytte 392. La Couture 444.
La Ferté-sous-Jouarre †52-3, 55.
La Guernerie 104. La Haute Maison
†49. La Panne †379. La Vesée 104,
†124, 126, 134
Labour : Annamese 369 ; B.E.F. char-
coal-burning 369 ; Chinese *q.v.* ;
Egyptian 381 ; Fiji 428
Lagny †46
Lamp (Lucas) signal 233, 458, 527
Landscape 38, 39, 68, 182, 199, 223, 257,
266, 282-3,-4, 292-3, 337, 343, 349,
364, 381-2-3, 388, 390, 406, 439,
466, 468, 482, 560

Landon, Maj.-Gen. 169, 187, 249, 258, 260
Lane (" Hammer "), Pte. 199, 214, 376, 409
Language, difference of 96-7
" Lanoline " 118
Lansdowne, Lord 436
Larson, Lt. 526-7, 532
Latrines 207, 328, 393, 485 ; French 80, 291
Laventie †74, 117, †137, 443
Law, Bonar, Rt. Hon. 457
Lawrie, C.S.M. 148
Layes, rivière des 83, 104
Le Cateau †23-39 ; 556, 558, 560. Le Catelet–Gouy †548. Le Cornet Bourdois †171. Le Lenthe 70. Le Mesnil-en-Arrouaise 533. Le Mans 51. Le Pilly 76. Le Plantin 207, 217. Le Préol 145, 217. Le Quesnoy 145, 169, †182-†3, 444. Le Sart 442, 459. Le Touret 444. Le Transloy 266, 276, 279 ; 523, 533, †536. Le Tréport 368, 410
Lealvillers 487, 498
Leave, Home 96, 179, 283, 304, 340, 374, 414, 450, 509 ; stopped 194, 456 ; undue 558
   Warrant 304, 419
Lechelle †538, †545
Lectures 262, 429, 572, 574
Lee, " Chopper " 413
Lee, Sgt. 540-1
Legend 171, 341, 376, 412
Lempire, 547
Lesbœufs 266, 270, 274 ; 521-2-3-4 ; 529. Lesbœufs Wood 275
Lestrem 444, 466
Letters 32 ; domestic 437 ; from the Front 65
   Censorship of 22, 65, 388 ; Base 162, 388
Lewis Guns 165, 207, 213-14-15, 239, 270, 277, *333*, 334, 338, 395, 401, 447, *451-2*, 458, 461, 468, 474, 479, 498, 527, *540*, 543-4, 552, 554
Lewis, Pte. 288
Liencourt 258
Lille 98, 113, 125
Lillers 171
Limerick 90, 546
Limon 60
Lindenhoek 73
Lindsley, Lt. 293
Lines of Communication 11, 13, 247
Litherland 356, 358
Lloyd, Sir F. 145
Lloyd, Pte. 221

Locquignol 566
Lombardzyde 376
London, 96, 98, 283, 371, 416, 451-2-3, 468-9, 470
Londoners 480-1
Lone Tree 473, 477, 479, 480
Longperrier 44
Longueau 222, 580
Longueil Ste. Marie †68
Longuenesse 406, †439
Longueval 230 ; 517, 520-1
Loos, Battle of 149-163
Looting 60, 110, 470
Loopholes, steel 99, 135
Lorette Ridge 388
Lorries : abandoned 27, 30 ; jumping 62, 159, 325, 358 ; moving troops 48, 68
Louâtre 60
Lucheux †260-4, †310
Ludendorff, Gen. 314, 464
Lusitania, S.S. 365, 420
Luynes, Duc de 12, 13 ; family 364
Lys 97, 111, 446

McChlery, Capt. 353, 402
Macedonia 420
Machine Gun : Battalion Sections 3, 63, 87, 117, 178
   Brigade Companies 201, 236, 239, 241-2
   Corps 183, 353
   barrage 400, 448, 472, 491, 499, 559
   gassed 154
   on whippet tanks 464
Machine implements 478
McKay, Lt. 181
McKay, Pte. 95, 164, 510
Maconochie 92, 307
Madame, P.C. †293, †299
Maggs, Corp. 465
Mair, Lt. 278-9
Maisnil 77
Maison Rouge 330
Maitland, Heriot, Bdr.-Gen. 330
Malincourt 555-6
Malo 372
Maltby, Capt. 130
Mametz Wood 223, †226, †243 ; †516, 517, 520
Manchester Grammar School 171
Mann, J. C., Capt. 170, 178, 180, 224, 231, 265, 283, 287-8-9, 296, 298, 300, 311, 335, 337-8, 340, 348, 368, 378-9, 390, 395, 403, 405, 453, 518 ; his father 204, 368, 388
Manœuvre of men 339, 464, 477
Maori 389

Map 17, 39, 52, 54, 112, 218, 379, 394, 515; planning by 77, 339, 396; reading 537, 546
Maretz 27, 29
Margarine 72
Marizy Ste. Geneviève †60
Marks, C.S.M. 334
Marlborough 142
Marne 45; Battles of 52-8; 502
Marseillaise 12, 21, 582
Martinpuich 225-6
Martinsart 471, 507
Maunton, Sgt. 80
Maurepas †284
Maurois 27, 28
Maxim-Nordenfelt 66
Maxse, Lt.-Gen. 303, 309
Mayne, Bdr.-Gen. 224, 232, 245, 249, 263, 269, 275, 296, 298, 299, 329, 330, 344, 349, 363, 367, 379, 387, 388, 392, 406, 413, 424, 440, 441
Mays, Sgt. 528
Méault 224, 249, 256, 272, †280
Medaille Militaire 73
Medical Corp., R. Army 163, 407; A.D.M.S. 401; 33rd Div. 368, 441; 38th Div. 471-2
Ambulance: 38th Div. 468, 476, 547, 556; 19th Field 72, 137, 141, 157, 226, 246-7, 257, 269, 304, 443; bearers, 33rd Div. 353, 38th Div. 473, 532; Auxiliary, Woman Driver 369
Australian, A.D.M.S. 401
Memorial, Regimental War 509
Mendingham 382
Menin Gate †410; Road 392, 395
Mercatel †312, †329, †330
Meredith, Sgt. 286
Méricourt l'Abbé †265, 284
Mers Touquet 369
Merville 442, 469
Mesnil 484, 497-8
Messages, 4, 127, 172, 226, 232-3; 349; 531, 547, 567; sending 233, 243, 508, 527, 534, 553, 554
Messines 74; 354; 376, 391, 408, 413; 466
Meteren 69, 388
Metz-en-Couture 538
Michael Day 455
Millencourt †466, 469
Mills, Sgt. 203, 368, 371, 449, 496, 587
Minenwerfer. See Trench-mortar
Miners, C.S.M. 11, 43, 71, 74, 76, 92, 241
Miners 125, 130, 141, 368, 381, 429, 571; Army 193, 207, 214

Mines 191, 207, 391; German 148, 175, 193, 210, 218; mining 145 in sea 179, 304, 324
Miniature 33
Mistletoe 423
"Missing" 474
Mobilizing. See Regiments: R.W.F. 2nd
Modera, Lt.-Col. 222, 296
Mole, hydraulic 251, 254
Moncel 257
Moncheaux 258
Monchy-au-Bois 341, †361
Monchy-le-Preux 326, 337
Monro, Lt.-Gen. 207
Mons 19; Angels of 61
Mont de Cats 373, 387. Mont d'Hiver 405. Mont Rouge 390. Mont St. Quentin 292
Montagny 44
Montauban 230, 255, 280; 517, 519
Montay 557, 559
Montdidier 69
Montgomery, Maj. 238, 338, 342, 402
Montgomery, Lt. 492, 504
Montmorency Barracks †151, †181, †183, †184, †198
Montigny 26
Moody, Capt. 95, 111, 141, 164, 192, 197, 208, 215, 218, 222, 234, 235, 250, 282; 304, 324, 348-9, 351-2-3, 357, 365; 390; 431, 445, 449, 450, 455, 461, 493, 504, 506; 568; quoted 154, 156, 194, 198, 224, 418, 468
Moon, Sgt. 402
Moorslede 417
Moral values 100, 440
Morale (Retreat) 47, 50; (1916) 228, 288; (1917) 353, 404, 410, 420; (1918) 468, 490, 493, 502, 507, 535. See German
Morgan, Pte. 201
Morgan, Roberts, Capt. 68, 95, 286, 581
Morin, Grand 49
Mormal, Forest of 559, 563-6, 573
Morris, H., Lt. 180, 181
Morris, L/Corp. 210, 216-17
Morris, Lt. 510
Morval 266, 270, 274, 279; 521-2-3, 528, 530, 532-3
Mostyn, Sir Pyers, Capt. 17, 95, 114, 120, 122, 126, 130, 134, 135, 139; quoted 121
Moulle †381
Moutières 578
Moyenville †354
Moyvillers 69
Mullens, Pte. 32

Murphy, 2/Lt. 10, 24, 32, 37, 72, 78, 80, 89, 105, 109, 115, 119, 124, 132
Music 3, 5, 367, 420, 463, 466, 582
Myths 335, 365

Nab Valley 512, 514
Names of Posts 447
Napoleon 161, 412, 467
Napoo 19, 201, 223
Napper, Signaller 527
Navy, Royal 3, 371, 453; in action— Destroyers 455; Cruisers 65; Heligoland 39; Jutland 205, 250
Bluejackets in trenches 181
Enquiry 434; terms 484
Nerve, loss of 253, 432, 531
Néry 41-2
Neuilly St. Front 62
Neuve Chapelle 122-4, 450; casualties 124
Neuve Eglise 72-3, 407, †410, 412, 469
Neuville †282
Neuvilly 557
Newspapers 46, 96, 161, 162, 165, 172, 250, 290, 386, 436, 441, 502; *Daily Mirror* 367; *Daily News* 125; *Morning Post* 346; *London Mail* 172; *Sporting and Dramatic News* 342; *The Times* 217, 436; foreign 448
New Year's Day: (1915) 104; (1916) 174-5; (1917) 287-8; (1918) 430
New Zealanders 445, 474, 476; Maoris 389
Nicholas II, Czar 304
Nickson, Capt. 461, 510, 542, 552, 555; *quoted* 538-9, 542, 544-5, 548, 550-1-552, 555
Night: defence 84; marching 2, 45, 68; relief 176; soup 176; work 80, 83, 92, 106, 470, 505, 557
Nightmare 243; 254
Nivelle, Gen. 326
No going back 78-9
Nocturne 355
Noordpeene 386
Norman, Col. 510, 531, 537, 541, 546, 551, 553-5, 557, 560, 563, 577
Northcliffe, Lord 290
Novion 369
Noyelles 369
Noyon 32, 35
Nurses 160, 162; 379

Oakley, Maj. 119
Oblinghem †169
Observation 77, 131, 295; aeroplane 21, 22, 115, 139, 178, 184, 194, 229, 239, 279, 348, 377, 398, 417, 421, 434, 474, 542; balloon 20, 224, 301, 390, 434, 481, 490; Posts 76, 84, 131, 143, 146, 228, 246; search-light 115
Officers Clubs 71, 415, 503
Official History of the War 28, 33, 44, 52, 58, 94, 440
Oil drums 251, 255
Oise 37, 39
Oisemont 368
Old Soldiers 7, 43, 78, 79, 81, 138 (158, 193), 174, 181, 186, 196, 203, 248, 252, 254, 274, 278, 282, 287, 371, 373. *See* B.E.F.: Old Army
Older men 197, 467
Ollezy 32
Omnibus: London General 380; move by 73-4, 286, 380, 405, 546, 573; French 265
Onions, Sgt. 353
Onnaing 33
Oost Dunkerque †374, 379
Operations 177, 339, 464, 477
Orchestras 574, 578
Ordnance Corps, Royal Army 2: repairs 286
stores 3, 63, 116; clearing 580, 582; lost 470; traffic in 186
Orme, E. L., Lt. 348
Ormrod, J., Capt. 85, 139, 172, 174, 198, 574
Ormrod, L., Capt. 349, 352
Ostende 376
Oswestry 583
Ovillers-la-Boiselle 512, 514
Owen, C. S., Bdr.-Gen. 1, 4, 7, 17, 29, 33, 49, 54, 68, 119, 121, 125, 136, 141, 154-5-6-7-8; 164, 171, 178, 446, 577; *quoted* 27
Owen, J., Capt. 108, 111, 178, 180, 265, 295-6, 307, 331-2-3, 445
Owens, Bob, Sgt. 286, 373
Owens, Sgt. (Mess) 347, 421
Oxelaere 386
Ozoir la Ferrière 48

Packs 17, 21, 46, 257, 280, 387; cast 21, 25
Palestine 415
Parasites, body 2, 96, 97, 184, 259, 261, 289, 374, 431
Parcels 96, 195, 344, 435, 548; German 344
Paris, 48, 64; leave 362, 454
Parker, Maj. 55-6
Parks, Pte. 110
Parliament 3, 249, 303, 372, 436, 457
Parry, G., Capt. 432

Parry, N., Lt. 231
Parry, N., Pte. 206, 283, 288, 301, 345, 426, 441, 449, 483
Parry, Sgt. 352
Parsons, Sgt. 5, 80
Passchendaele 409; 415-16-17-18-19; 431; 466
Passwords 499, 508
Patrol Platoon 508
Patrolling 87-8-9, 99, 100, 116, 120, 181, 201, 251, 253, 401, 414, 449, 494, 498, 503, 557, 561
Patrols 120, 121, 127, 130, 134, 139, 149, 275, 278, 479, 486, 492, 505, 507-508-9, 554-5
    German 23-4-5, 41, 70, 71, 90, 134, 293, 409, 449, 456, 479, 488
Pattison, C.S.M. 146, 154-5, 209, 213
Pay 13, 197, 425, 434, 465; Pay-book 3, 4, 63; Paymaster 63
Peace Talk 284, 436
Perkes, L/Corp. 518
Péronne 292, 304, 307, 448
Pétain, Maréchal 326
Petit Maubeuge 573
Petite Synthe 381
Petrol 247
Phillips ("Tiger"), Capt. 87, 88, 90; Mrs. 288
Phillips, Lt. 336
Phonetics 170-1
Physique 245-6, 272, 286, 309, 503, 557; French q.v. ; German q.v.
Pianos 118, 131, 308
Picardy 260
Picquigny 248
Pienne †549
Pierpont, Pte. 376; 518-19; 530
Pierre Mill 550, 552-3
Pigeon Post 186, 290, 413, 505
Pill-box 263, 339, 342, 395
Pinney, Sir R. 260, 263, 271, 297, 299, 319, 328, 329, 340, 341, 342, 346, 354, 357, 366, 367, 368, 381, 382; 418, 424, 425
Pistol 252
Pithon †32
Platoon : resting 92, 96, 107; sapping 129, 130, 180, 216, 402; special 430; training 288, 303, 306
Plum Lane 347-54
Plumer, Lord 379
Poilu 294, 324
Poincaré, Pres. 430
Poix 562
Poland 436
Polderhoek Château and Wood 396, 399, 403

Political soldiers 303; unrest 305, 372
Politicians 303, 435
Polo 110, 371
Polygon Beek and Wood 392-404
"Pompadour Fritz" 96
Pom-pom 66
Pont Fixe 144, 165
Pont Remy 287, 290, 370
Pontcarré 48, 49
Pontoise †32, 36
"Pontoon" 172
P.B.I. 269, 309
Pontoons 559
Poore, Maj. 246, 301-2, 310, 325, 340, 354, 356-7, 359, 365, 367, 368, 373, 379, 382, 394-5-6, 398
Poperinghe 391, 415, 420, †423-5
Poppies 199; cultivation of 369
Portland, 1, 2, 3
Portuguese 442-3-4; officer 414
Pot de Vin 567
Potatoes 285, 405, 424
Potijze †411, †415, †417, 431
Poulainville 223
Powell, D., Lt.-Col. 1, 7, 18, 30, 32, 37, 49, 53, 71, 76, 104, 107
Powell, F., Pte. 122
Powell, R., Q.M.S. 1 17, 49, 68, 164, 222, 256, 220-1 ; quoted 4, 26, 31, 37, 60, 72, 74, 83, 90, 94, 95, 101, 168, 228, 241
Pozières 515-16
Precocity 364
Premonition 393
Preston, Pte. 24, 30
Prime, Lt. 350, 352
Prime Minister. See Ll. George
Prisoners 457 (and see Regiments : R.W.F. 2nd); escape 344
Profiteering 223, 305, 309, 453, 467; soldiers' 436
Promotion, preferential 437
Proud, Pte. 347, 365, 391
Pugh, Pte. 174
Punch 188
Punishment, No. 1 Field 119
Pyjamas 424, 573

"Quail." See Thomas, Capt.
Quéant–Drocourt Line, 343-4
Querrieu 575
Quetta 5, 82
Quiévrain 19, 33
Quillebœuf 9

Race for the Sea 68
Radcliffe, Delmé, Lt.-Col. 4, 9, 17, 27,

33, 37, 39, 42, 48, 49, 55, 58, 64-5, 75, 77, 78-9, 83 ; *quoted* 50-1-2, 54-55, 62

Radford, N. H., Capt. 141, 164, 180-1, 192, 222, 251, 256, 282, 287-8, 299, 324 ; 331-2-3, 340, 363, 365, 366, 388, 390, 394, 397-8, 401, 403, 406, 414, 417, 423-4-5-6, 431, 444, 450, 455, 461, 480, 489, 491, 502-3, 506 ; *quoted* 233, 276, 278, 335

Radinghem 76

Raiding 192

Raids (*see* Regiments : R.W.F. 2nd) 300, 359, 360, 450, 457 ; German 203, 302, 378 ; 408-9-10, 448, 450, 480, 496, 561 ; R.E. part in 193, 219, 497

Railway : light 285, 425, 432-3, 476 ; service 421, 479, 503 ; T.O. 259, 415, 421, 458 ; travel 222, 282, 304, 324, 370, 414, 450, 461

Rainbow 151

" Rainbows " 579

Rainneville †256, 462

Ramrod 85

Ramsay, Lt. 404

Rancourt 285, 302

Raray 43

Rations (*see* Regiments : R.W.F. 2nd) 130, 246, 293, 300, 418 ; reduced 434 ; sardines 302 ; German 409, 434

Ravelsberg 476

Reading matter 172

R.E. (Royal Engineers) 144, 147, 291, 381, 411, 433, 476
  Chemical Company 153, 157-8
  6th Div., C.R.E. 112 ; 33rd Div. 242 ; 38th Div. 485, 492-3, 497 ; 507, 514 ; 558-9, 566, 575
  11th Field Company 80, 97-8 ; 103 ; 106 ; 111-12, 121 ; 193 ; 219, 240 ; 230-1, 237 ; 326 ; 348
  Mining *q.v.*
  officers 227, 268 ; 351 ; 395 ; other ranks 273, 476, 501

Recreation (*see* Games) 132, 147, 381

Red Cross Flag 5

Red Cross Sisters 57

Red Lamp 161

Red Lamp Corner 137

Redan 375

Rededication 453

Regiments and Battalions :
  Carabiniers 520 ; Household Composite Cavalry 42 ; Hussars 15th 76, 18th 33, 19th 289 ; Lancers 9th 20

  Argyll and Sutherland Highlanders 2nd 9, 17, 18, 20, 26, 52-3, 74, 77,

81, 89, 99, 109, 114, 124, 129, 134-5, 153, 156, 206 ; 227 ; 251 ; 331-2, 335-6 ; 338 ; 393 ; 573, 559 ; C.O. 206 ; M.O. 151
  Artists Rifles 108
  Berks 1st 145
  Black Watch 1st 255
  Cameron Highlanders 29
  Cameronians, The 9, 17, 18, 26, 27, 29, 50, 52, 73-4, 81, 97, 104-5-6, 109, 111, 114, 119, 123, 136, 156, 158, 168, 211, 216 ; 230-1-2, 237, 241, 270-1, 299, 318-19, 320-1, 327, 329, 331, 333, 335, 346-7, 348-51, 359, 378, 408-9, 431-2 ; 441 ; Pipe-Major 441 ; Private 31, 114 ; R.S.M. 169
  Cheshires 245 ; 6th 218, 420
  City Imperial Volunteers (C.I.V.) 168
  Civil Service Rifles 255
  Devons 2nd 279
  Dorsets 24,-504
  Dublin Fusiliers 95,-270
  Gordon Highlanders 2nd 231, 239
  Guards 452 ; pace 280
  Guards, Coldstream 58, 272
  Guards, Scots 2nd 94
  Hants 268 ; Hants Yeomanry 301
  Hawke (R.N.D.) 484
  Hon. Artillery Company (H.A.C.) 188
  Highland Light Infantry 9th 350, 360, 560
  Imperial Yeomanry 168
  Irish, Royal 76
  Irish Fusiliers, Royal 95
  King's 4th 228, 392
  King's Own 4th 54-5
  King's Royal Rifle Corps 165 ; 16th 168, 243, 275, 331
  Lancs, East 1st 58 ; South (T.) 6 ; North 458 ; Fusiliers 10th 540
  Leicesters 110
  Lincolns 1st 582
  London Scottish 69
  Loyal N. Lancs 159 ; 582
  Manchesters 17th 312
  Middlesex 1st (57th) 9, 17, 18, 19, 23, 26 ; 41-2, 50-1-2, 76, 81, 96, 109, 124, 126, 129, 134-5, 138, 145, 149, 153-4-5-6, 164, 168, 274-5, 331, 333, 335-6, 393, 399, 409, 560 ; M.O. 151 ; Sgt. 333 ; 18th (Pioneers) 215, 242, 286, 299
  Northumberland Fusiliers 13th 315
  Queen's 1st 243, 331-2 ; 441 ; 2nd 225, 232
  Rifle Brigade 33, 56

Regiments and Battalions—*continued*:
Royal Fusiliers 2nd 441; (Sportsmen)
168; 20th 168, 170, 179, 187, 203-4,
216; 230-1-2, 234, 236-7, 239, 240-
241-2, 268, 276, 278,296-7-298-9;
329, 330, 337, 346, 352, 441; 46th 579
Royal Welch Fusiliers 1st 13, 73, 97,
105, 107, 117, 133, 166, 226, 239,
240, 262, 284, 307-8, 345, 347-8,
354, 368, 389, 504, 537, 583;
casualties 133, 345
Royal Welch Fusiliers 2nd (L. of C.
Troops; 19th Bde. 15; 115th Bde.
440):
    Actions and Raids:
Le Cateau, rear-guard 27
La Ferté-sous-Jouarre 50; o.o. 51,
52, 55
*La Cordonnerie 77; o.o. 78; raid 88
" Chinese " raid 122
Loos, 151; o.o. 152
R.W.F. Crater capture 180
Cambrin raid 192
Cuinchy raid 195
*Duck's Bill 209
Givenchy Warren 218
High Wood 230; o.o. 230, 234,
238; raid 252
Lesbœufs 276
Hertzfeldt Trench (cancelled) 295;
o.o. 295, 297, 298
Hénin Hill (company bombers)
319; A and C Companies 330;
o.o. 327, 330; B and D Com-
panies 335; o.o. 336
Croisilles, Plum Lane 348; o.o.
347-8
Polygon Wood 392; o.o. 392, 394,
401
*Wez Macquart raid 446
Lille road raid 457
*Lone Tree 474
Albert road 479
Ancre raid 486; o.o. 487
Aveluy-Hamel raids 492-3
*Aveluy Wood 495
Hamel raid 497
Ancre crossing 510; o.o. 510-11-12
Bazentin 517
Sailly-Saillisel 523
Saillisel 533
*Gouzeaucourt 539
Villers-Outreaux 549; o.o. 550
Englefontaine : minor actions 561-
562; o.o. 562; and Forest of
Mormal 563; o.o. 563, 565
Pot de Vin 567

    * Denotes German attack.

Royal Welch Fusiliers 2nd—*contd.*:
Aid Post 298, 399, 417, 470-1, 472-
473, 477, 481, 485 518, 532, 562;
586; Staff 267, 271; 377, 399,
471; 496; 585-7
bakery 100
band 2, 3; 575-8, 580; boys 7,
576-7, 579; service 194, 370
battle surplus 256, 309, 356, 374,
394, 405, 424, 466, 476, 480, 483,
484
cadre 580
canteen 184, 203, 287, 368, 371,
496, 573, 578
casualties 21, 58, 83, 85, 89, 114,
134, 154, 158, 165, 167, 178-9,
180, 196, 217, 221, 228-9, 237,
243, 254, 404, 412, 419, 432, 454,
458, 469, 473, 475, 483, 489, 501,
514, 516, 532-3, 537, 539, 542,
549, 556, 566; conditions 83,
151, 268, 279, 337, 353, 418,
472-3, 496
changes 201-2, 245-6, 249, 414,
429, 430
colours 572, 580
conjurer 186, 262, 272, 278, 282
cooking 264, 270, 292, 430, 566
Court of Enquiry 573, 578
cyclists 70
dinners 11, 14, 56, 104, 152, 174,
247, 261, 288, 365, 415, 583.
See Christmas Day, St. David's
Day
discipline 91, 119, 404, 481, 559
drafts 49, 50, 63, 60; (New Army)
199, 243, 245, 255-6, 259, 264,
286, 306, 339, 348, 358-9, 363,
368, 412, 414, 439, 467, 503, 537,
546, 557, 571-2
drums 2, 3, 183, 263, 280, 290-1,
371, 426, 429, 463, 466, 575;
Drum-Sgt. Dyer 290, 371, 571,
575-6; Drummer Hedges 371
fatigues *q.v.*
flash *q.v.*
games *q.v.*
glees, Welsh 187
Guard to Fourth Army 372
guest nights 263, 571
health 256, 296, 412, 467, 475, 481,
496
horses *q.v.*
inspections 97, 119, 141, 185, 245,
345, 406, 443, 483, 572, 574
laundry 100
Lewis Guns *q.v.*

Regiments and Battalions—*continued*:
  Royal Welch Fusiliers 2nd—*continued*:
    Machine-Guns *q.v.*
    march discipline 257, 386, 388, 406, 467
    marching 2, 6, 18-62, 68-74, 223-5, 246, 272, 308-12, 362-3, 462-3, 467, 567
    Mess 11, 56, 64, 110, 121, 187, 256, 261, 546, 571; bills 509; cart 60, 256; meeting 370, 450, 571; shacks 129; subscription 103, 187, 261
    Mess, Sergeants 3, 5, 105, 287, 430
    morale *q.v.*
    mouth-organs 114
    nominal roll 560
    officers 179; few 479; many 444; Temporary 108, 357, 506
    oldest man 260, 267
    originals 185, 444, 542, 571, 581
    patrols *q.v.*
    physique *q.v.*
    prisoners 30, 221, 242, 244, 352-3, 526
    rations 30, 31; 130, 270, 293, 300, 302, 312, 338, 341, 418, 475, 509, 521
    records 7
    recruiting 430
    Regular soldiers 179, 429, 486, 503, 536
    reliefs 176, 198, 302, 432, 535-6
    Reserve, Special 185
    Reservist 6, 13, 185
    Rest House 118, 135, 445
    Retreat: straggling and missing 21, 25, 30; summed up 46-7, 65
    Riding School 110, 160, 188, 201, 207, 503
    Sick Parades 181, 249, 265, 288, 348, 423, 585
    sickness 256, 289, 296, 299, 481; dysentery *and* epidemics *q.v.*
    Strength 7, 63, 222, 304, 374; trench 301, 340, 347, 404, 446, 466, 488, 512, 523, 533, 536, 537, 546
    Transport 12, 17, 33-37, 41, 47, 49, 64, 78, 244, 265, 270, 283, 285, 326, 338, 370, 380, 392, 406-7, 416, 429, 439, 457, 461, 483, 504, 514-17, 537, 557-8-9, 567, 580-1
  Royal Welch Fusiliers 2nd (Garrison) 246; 3rd 300, 345, 356, 546; 4th 340; 8th 7, 368; 10th 248, 388; 13th 471-2-3-4, 494, 514, 516, 520, 523; 14th 471, 487, 489, 490, 503, 544-5; 16th 471-2,

523; 17th 172, 226, 442, 445, 447, 449-50, 477, 480, 497-8; 510, 513, 519, 521, 523-4, 527-8-9, 531-2-3-4-535, 550, 552, 555, 559, 562-3, 576; 26th 575
  Royal West Kent 171
  Scottish Rifles 5th 109, 135, 137, 216; 230-1, 233, 235, 237, 239, 241-2, 268, 271, 285, 293, 296, 299, 310, 327; 334-5-6-7, 339, 345-6, 348, 350-1, 353, 358, 376, 393-4, 400-1-2, 408, 430, 442
  Seaforth Highlanders 60, 97
  Shropshires 245-6
  South Staffords 125; 159
  South Wales Borderers 245; 10th 433, 442, 457, 475-6, 481, 513, 519, 521-2-3, 530-1, 533, 540, 546, 550-1, 555, 559, 562, 577
  Suffolks 4th 209, 331-2, 334-5, 393-4
  Vaughan's Rifles (Sikhs) 82
  Warwicks 159
  Welch 6th (Pioneers) 250; 13th 488, 521; 15th 563
  Worcesters 2nd 148; 230; 346, 360, 419, 560
  York and Lancs 403
  Yorks, East 181; 7th 538
Reinforcements. *See* Regiments: R.W.F. 2nd (Drafts)
Remounts 5, 286, 441
Renescure †69, †442
Reninghelst 426
Reports and returns 224, 479
Respirators, box. *See* Gas
Restaurants and Cafés: Le Bœuf 384; Comte d'Egmont 95, 117; Cyril's (Ginger's) 427; The Globe 147, 160, 183, 255; Godbert 247, 307, 367; Hôtel de France 160, 444; Hôtel du Rhin 13, 241; Jimmy's 503; Café Mollard 14; Paon d'or 160; de la Poste 11; La Poupée 415; Quatre fils d'Aymon 261; Sauvage 423; Skindle's 427
Retaliation 116, 137
Reumont 26
Reutel 397, 403; beek 392, 394, 402; road 392, 394, 397, 399, 400
Rhine 456
Rhymsters 188, 205, 258, 264
Ribemont †256, 265
Richards, Lt. 352
Richards, F., Pte. 1, 49, 68, 95, 347, 461, 542, 571
Richards, Corp. 477
Richardson, Lt. 68, 86, 88; *quoted* 89, 90, 93

Richardson ("Tracker") 117
Richthoven 474
Rifle : care of 299, 541 ; damaged 84 ; fire 342 ; loading 245, 306, 460, 464, 466, 539 ; practice 355, 372, 445 ; S.A. cross fire 278, 339 ; shooting 117, 245, 342, 355, 483, 484
Rifles issued to R.G.A. 468
Road : control 273 ; metal 380
Robermetz †442
Roberts, F.M. Lord 205
Roberts, Owen, Lt. 222, 236 ; *quoted* 237
Roberts, Sgt. 267, 271, 585
Roberts, Pte. 213
Robertson, Sir P. 137, 153, 159, 188, 218, 225, 475
Robertson, F.M. Sir W. 446, 448, 475
Robertson, Capt. 148, 173-4, 175, 178, 198
Robertson, Lt. 288, 365
Rochford Boyd, Lt.-Col. 192, 195, 218
Rockets (Verey, etc.) 136, 218, 291, 338, 388 ; improved 507 ; message by 554
Rocquigny 533
Roderick, R.S.M. 1, 49, 57, 68, 95, 126, 141, 164, 192, 222, 232 ; *quoted* 7, 88, 120-1-2-3 ; 146, 213, 234-5-6
Roisin 33
Romainvillers 49
Roman Road 27-9
Rombies 18, 20
Rose Garden 48, 386
Rothwell, Pte. 523, 526, 531
Rouen 9-11, 15, 17 ; 307
Rouge Bancs 77
Rouge Croix 69
Roumania 420
Rubempré 462, 504
Rucourt 69
Rue : d'Aire †164, †165, 206 ; de Biez 104 ; du Bois 104, 134 ; de la Boucherie †432 ; des Corps nues sans Testes 14, 247 ; de Lettrée 104 ; Michelet 174 ; Tilleloy 138 ; des Trois Cailloux 15, 247
Rugg, Capt. 156, 206
Ruisseau des Eclusettes 563, 566
Rum 63, 124, 130, 152, 271, 400, 465 ; stolen 124 ; illicit 119
Rumour 6, 19, 34, 37, 43, 44, 63, 70, 114, 115, 140, 164, 184, 194, 202, 286, 304, 341, 344, 357, 362, 370, 441, 447, 517, 543
Ruse 354, 405, 529, 561
Rush, Sgt. 216

Russia 64, 90, 304, 389, 410, 415, 419 ; North Expeditionary Force 579 ; Steam Roller 64, 90
Rye 386

Saillisel 533-4
Sailly-Labourse †159
Sailly Laurette 573
Sailly-Saillisel 268, 277 ; 523-4, 526, 531-532-3-4
Sailly-sur-la-Lys 94, †458-9
St. Erkembode 383. St. Jean 419, 421, †433, 439. St. Leger 330, 342, †344, 346. St. Martin-Cojeul †312, 314, 317. St. Nazaire 62. St. Omer †69, 382-3, 405, 429, 439. St. Pol 257, †308-9, 356, 461. St. Python 22. St. Quentin 31, 34 ; 448 ; St. Quentin, Mont 292. St. Remy †68. St. Valery 248, 369. St. Venant 171-2. St. Wolfram's 248
St. David's Day : (1914) 105 ; (1915) 117 ; (1916) 183 ; (1917) 300-1 ; (1918) 449-500 ; (1919) 577
St. George's Day : (1917) 331-8 ; (1918) 376
Salient 162, 416-432
Salisbury Plain 1
Salisbury, Sol, Pte. 120
Sambre 566
Samson, Capt. 11, 14, 25, 42, 57, 75, 81, 86, 106, 108, 111, 112, 121, 124, 127, 149, 156
Sand-bags 158, 166, 409, 539
Sanitary man 359 ; utensil 109, 114
Sanitation 12, 80, 284
Santines 68
Sappers. *See* R.E.
Sarcasm, Army 252, 377
Sart-Bara †567
Sassoon, S. L., Capt. 329, 346, 372 ; narrative 306-321
Saulty †310
Sausage. *See* Balloon
Saveuse 578
Sawyer, Pte. 101
Scapegoat 248, 492
Scarborough 99
Scarpe, Battle 324
Schelde 18, 567, 569
Schools 103, 263, 456, 509. *See* Courses
Scott, Maxwell, Maj.-Gen. 382
Scott, Maj. 432
Scouts 51, 253
Scrounging 43, 452, 468
Searchlight 110, 272, 451 ; German 107, 115
Sebourg 21

Secrecy 68, 440, 444, 457, 472
Seely, Sir J. 55
Seine 9, 31
Self-inflicted wound 96
Seline (Alida) 169, 444
Selle 23, 31 ; 557-8
Senlis 43 ; near Albert 476, †480, †482, †504, †506
Sensée 326-7, 348
Sentries 13, 410 ; asleep 480-1
Sepmeries 22
Septmonts †62-68
Serbia 164, 420
Serches 66
Serre 222
Seth 158-193
Shearsby, Corp. 236
Sheldon, Clifton, Capt. 34, 36, 65
Shell 391 ; 13-pounder 235 ; 18-pounder 336 ; blind 182, 254 ; gas q.v. ; H.E. 176, 192, 339 ; smoke 178, 354, 395, 529 ; star 82 (see Rockets) ; thermite 331 ; tracer 390
    counted and reported 477, 509
Shell-hole : defence 268, 348, 359, 360, 405 ; safety 403, 404 ; shallow 359
Shell-shock 100, 250-1
Shell shortage 83, 86, 94, 116, 346 ; German 94, 411
Shelley, Lt. 352-3
Shrapnel Corner 392
Shrewsbury 7
Shrine (Calvaire) 38, 174, 301
Shute, Lt.-Gen. 482, 483-4, 498
Siddall, Lt. 401
Siege Warfare 63, 103
Signs and badges 140, 262, 381
Signy-Signets 50-1, 58
Sims, Admiral 504
Singing 5, 107, 118, 152, 160, 255, 264, 545 ; German 102, 107
Sing-songs 102, 110, 187, 188, 427
Slackness 64, 413-14 ; 2/R.W.F. 180, 327, 354, 491
Sleep 23, 29, 30, 38, 45, 62, 91 ; 227, 250, 272, 404, 458, 462-3, 466, 472, 535, 550 ; sleepers 38, 227, 313
Sloper. See Clegg-Hill
Smart, Corp. 321-2
Smith, Compton, Lt.-Col. 583
Smith-Dorrien, Lt.-Gen. 26, 27, 35
Smith Hyde, Lt.-Col. 222
Smith (L.N.L.), Lt. 180
Smith, J. O., Lt. 480, 510, 526, 528, 532
Smith, L/Corp. 222, 390
Smith, Pte. 110
Smoke-screen 354, 395, 523, 529

Snipers and sniping 82, 84, 107, 117, 178, 200, 470, 494, 542 ; German q.v.
"Snookie" 287
Snow, Sir d'O., Lt.-Gen. 33, 42, 354
Snow. See Weather
Socks, 81, 100, 298, 340, 463
Soissons 64
Solesmes 23, 33
Solly-Flood, Maj.-Gen. 28
Somme 223, 248, 290, 292, 347, 364 ; 573
Songs (see Singing) 5, 118, 152, 278, 282, 373, 379, 427, 463, 543, 583
Sorel-le-Grand †546
Souastre †260
Soues 364
Soup containers 176, 558
South African War 1, 66, 168-9, 339, 586. See Boer
Southampton 8, 356, 582
Souvenirs 15, 19, 61, 87, 179, 188, 411, 435, 527, 580-1
Spens, H., Col. 390
Spens, T., Capt. 222, 235
Spies, and "Spies" 17, 24, 38, 65-6, 73, 93, 98, 135, 139, 170, 406, 457, 478 ; "No Spy" 40
Spring tide 376
Stable, Lt. 60
Staff, and Front 77, 232-3, 290, 303, 339, 477
    job 65, 177
    staff nerves 95, 114, 338, 417, 452, 459, 478, 480-2
Stand-to 66, 148, 466 474
Stanway, W., Lt.-Col. 25, 30, 51, 54, 84, 89, 107, 129, 132, 178, 180-1, 192, 195, 205, 216, 218 ; 420 ; quoted 214-15
Staple †69
Steam Roller 64, 90
Steenwerck 70-1, †72, 74, 136 ; 410, 445, 450
Steenwoorde 386, †421, 423
Stirling Castle †393-4
Stockwell, C. I., Bdr.-Gen. 49, 62, 65, 68, 69, 74, 82, 95, 112, 115, 126, 129, 133, 222, 226, 445-6 ; 577 ; quoted 66, 75, 81, 85, 87, 89, 94, 97-8, 101, 108, 110, 121, 125
Straggling 23, 44. See R.W.F. 2nd
Strazeele †70, †415
Strong, Maj. 130
Submarines 181, 304, 376, 415 ; anti-submarine 453
Subsidiary Services 246
Suicide 299
Summer Time 201, 407, 577

Sunrise 266, 282, 483 ; sunset 218, 343, 391 468
"Sunny Jim" 253
Superstition 148, 419, 466, 469
Suzanne †293, †300, †302
Suzanne Delettrée 131, 446
Sykes, Lt.-Col. 535-6

Tactics 302, 416, 477, 561 ; Boer 339 ; French 288 ; German 346, 405, 409, 498 ; of mine craters 144, 145
Talmas †362
Tancrou 60
Tank 255, 267, 331, 393-4-5, 478, 484, 551-3 ; Cavalry 464 ; German 447 ; minefield 547
Tapes 219, 488, 498
Tea, Army 18, 307 ; tea-shops 117, 147, 171, 384
Telephone : blocking 172 ; calls 413 ; new 348 ; shortage 478 ; tapping 360, 416, 444
wire 146, 292 ; cut 216, 233, 377, 490 ; laying 376, 390, 457 ; French 291-2
wireless 233, 444, 508
Tetanus (lockjaw) 293, 555
Thiennes †442
Thiepval 514
Thieushouk †387
Thomas, Capt. 5, 73, 130, 157
Thomas, B. (Correspondent) 247
Thomas, Pte. 539, 541
Thomas, Gwyn, Bdr.-Gen. 449, 452, 455, 464
Thomson, Lt. 58
Tibbs, Pte. 487
Tin-hat. See Helmet
Tobacco 38, 47, 204, 312
Torkington, Lt. 352
Tortille 292, 295 ; 535
Touche 130, 484
Toutencourt 504
Tower Hamlets 392
Townshend, Maj.-Gen. 198
Townsend, Sgt. 195
Tracy le Mont 38
Trade Unions 305, 456
Training 171, 207, 245, 249, 262, 263, 283-4, 288, 342, 347, 357, 366, 370, 373, 382, 414, 429, 437, 440, 460, 464, 468, 477, 483, 498, 503, 506, 537, 539, 546, 572 ; platoon 288, 303 ; recreational 249, 303
Transport, Army : civilian vehicles 15, 18 ; French 266 ; German 133, 145, 476
officer 5, 206, 330
vessels 8, 307, 581

Trench : construction 78, 81 ; 97-8 ; 106, 111, 121, 125, 129 ; 359 ; French 74, 285, 294 ; German 112, 316, 328, 348
economy 558 ; floor 106, 129, 138, 166 ; maintenance 166, 182, 447
life 83, 86, 96, 129, 136, 167, 182, 202, 270, 292-3, 298 ; 446
names 363 : Ale Alley 337 ; Antelope 268 ; L'Armée Switch 454 ; Back Street 177 ; Barn 498 ; Beaurevoir-Masnière Line 549 ; Beer 337 ; Black Road 230, 239 ; Boritzka 269, 277 ; Dead Man's 207 ; Dewdrop 274-5-6-7 ; Fanny C.T. 408 ; Fiddler 329 ; Flers Line 266 ; Fleury Support 456 ; Friedrich 329 ; Frosty 268 ; Hamel Outposts 499, 501 ; Hazy 268-9, 271 ; Heather Support 538 ; Hertzfeldt 295-9, 300 ; High Wood Switch 226, 230, 244 ; John Bull 275 ; Mackensen 219 ; Montauban Alley 259 ; Misty 268 ; "Nellie" Lane 350 ; Old Boots 187 ; Ox Support 268 ; Plum Lane 347-354 ; Quaker Alley 498 ; Queen's Cross 544 ; Serpentine 266 ; Shaftesbury Avenue 120, 445 ; Slush 268 ; Snow 268 ; Stout 337 ; Summer 274 ; Tunnel (see Hindenburg Line) ; Wimpole Street 153 ; Windy 274 ; Wood Lane 230, 250, 255
practice 259, 263, 498
visitors 146, 206
Trench fever 118, 296
foot 99, 285, 431
Trench-mortar 103, 117 ; (Stokes) 104, 148, 183 ; 237 ; 298 ; 332-53 ; 448 ; 527, 562 ; German 103, 107, 114-15, 148, 177, 200, 489, 501
Troisvilles †557-†8-†9
Trones Wood †265, †271, 520
Tubby 78, 110
Tugny †32
Tunnellers. See Miners
Tunnicliffe, Lt. 523
Turkey 563
Turner, Lt. 461, 510 ; 513-14, 543, 552-3, 557 ; quoted 538, 544-5-6, 561
Turnips 124, 409
Twigg, C.S.M. 252
Twyman, Pte. 92

Uhlan 23-4-5, 65, 70, 72

Vacquerie 257
Valenciennes 17, 21, 33

Valheureux †503
Varcoe, Sgt. 504, 554
Variety Parties 425 : *Follies* 118 ;
    Pedlars 427 ; *Ruffles* 420, 441 ;
    Shrapnels 186, 342 ; *Welsh Wails*
    537 ; 8th and Meerut Div. 138 ;
    for civilians 560
" Vaseline " 118
Vauban 21, 375
Vauchelles-les-Quesnoy †287-290
Vaughan, Jones, Lt. 34
Vaux-sur-Somme †284
Venizel †61-2
Ver Touquet 77
Verberie †39, 68
Verdun 284, 303
Verey Light.   See Rockets
Vermelles 149, 157
Verne Fort 2, 5
Versailles Council 448
Vez †68
Vicq †18
Villeneuve St. Denis †49
Villeselve 32
Villers Bocage †308, †462
Villers-Bretonneux 476, 576
Villers-Helon 60
Villers-Outreaux 549-†556
Villiers-sur-Morin 49
Vimy Ridge 324, 326, 388
Vingt-et-un 172
Vlamertinghe 73, 410
Vogeltye 423
Volunteers 245

Wakelin, Pte. 115
Wales, Prince of (H.M. King Edward
    VIII) 97, 288, 572 ; presentation
    to 575
Walsh, Bandsman 213-14
Walwyn, F., Lt.-Col. 4, 21
Walwyn, Norah 6
Wancourt 312
War Office 5 ; 168 ; 245 ; 440
War Savings Certificates 465, 495
Ward, Lt.-Col. 37
Wardrecques 442
Ware, W., Lt. 551-2, 563
Wareham 5
Warloy-Baillon 462, 464, 577
Warren, The 144, 148, 207 ; Raid *q.v.*
Waste 106, 130, 340, 378
Watchmaker 370
Watches, wrist- 89, 158, 187, 216 ; 513
Water 295, 457 ; withheld 73, 362
Waterloo 17
Watou †421, †428
Watten 381, 586

Weather 18, 22, 23, 28, 39, 81, 83, 84, 86,
    96-7, 103, 106, 115, 121, 136, 148,
    157, 158, 164, 169, 178, 182, 183,
    198-9, 218, 228, 239, 255-6, 258,
    261, 267, 270, 271, 276, 279, 280,
    288, 298-9, 300, 310, 317, 330, 342,
    357, 359, 364, 371, 374, 379, 381,
    388, 404-5, 407-8, 411-13, 417, 421,
    423, 425, 428, 431-2-3-4, 441, 442-
    443-4-5, 446, 447, 454, 455, 456,
    457, 460, 464, 465-6, 468-9, 470, 473,
    477-8-9, 481-2-3-4-5, 488, 498, 504,
    521, 536, 538, 539, 543, 551, 559,
    563-4, 569, 573-4 ; freezing 10, 12,
    113, 265 ; snow 108, 183, 282, 290-
    291, 295, 312, 325, 431, 470 ; and
    frost 96, 169, 292, 311, 420, 450 ;
    Ypres III 392
Weight, increase 108
Welton, Maj. 36, 37, 78, 89, 114 ; 445, 535-6
Westende 376
Westoutre †388
Weymouth 2, 3
Wez Macquart 115, 446
White Château.   See Ypres
Whitsunday : (1916) 205 ; (1917) 348-
    354 ; (1919) 583
Whizz-bangs 76, 277, 553-4
Wiart, C. de, Bdr.-Gen. 464
Wild-boar shoot 365
Willcocks, Sir Wm. 113
Williams, Brock, Lt.-Col. 578
Williams, Lt. 180
Williams, J., Lt. 335
Williams, Jones, Lt.-Col. 345
Williams, Moldsworth, Capt. 180, 216,
    239, 270, 394, 396
Williams (" Shem "), Lt. 105
Williams, O. de L., Bdr.-Gen. 1, 2, 8, 17,
    20, 31, 33, 40, 49, 55, 57-8, 61, 68,
    71, 74, 79, 83, 85, 95, 103, 107, 111,
    114-15, 120, 121, 126, 135, 137, 141,
    147, 149, 155, 159, 162, 169, 171,
    180, 184-5, 187, 190, 192, 195, 199,
    201, 202, 205, 222, 405, 583 ;
    quoted 10, 27-8, 47, 50, 53-4, 56,
    122, 124, 154
Wilson, H. F. M., Gen. 50, 55
Wilson, Capt. 252
Windmills : Bazentin-le-Petit 233 ; Cassel
    386, 423 ; Mormal 530 ; Pierre
    550, 552-3 ; Senlis 476 ; Villers-
    Outreaux 555
Windy Corner 144
Wine 80, 103, 285, 350, 369, 447, 538 ;
    bottles 59
Wire 80, 103, 285, 350, 369, 447 ;
    German 224, 328, 348, 359

Wire-cutting 150-1, 192, 344; 550
Wiring 112, 193, 456, 467
Wisques 406-7, 440
Wizerne 407, 414
Women: Ambulance driver 369; Army
  Auxiliary Corps 370, 389
Women's voices 134
Wood, Maj.-Gen. 382, 413, 418
Wool 1
Woolman, C.Q.M.S. 74
Woods and forests: life in 494; opera-
  tions 485; patrolling 486; raids
  485-6, 495-6; sniping 486, 494;
  stragglers 59, 65; wounded 496
  Acheux w. q.v.; Adinfer w. 341,
  343, 357; Armainvillers f. 48;
  Augustus w. 433; Authuille w.
  q.v.; Aveluy w. q.v.; Bailiff w.
  515; Basket w. 549; Bazentin-le-
  Grand w. q.v.; Bazentin-le-Petit w.
  q.v.; Bernafay w. 271; Bouleaux
  w. 266; Caterpillar (Lealvillers)
  w. 487; Caterpillar (Mametz)
  w. 227, 518-19; Compiègne f.
  q.v.; Crécy f. q.v.; Delville w.
  238, 520, 537; Dessart w. 543,
  545; Ecuiry w. q.v.; Flat Iron
  Copse 230, 518; Fontaine w.
  q.v.; Fricourt w. q.v.; Glencorse
  w. 395; Gouzeaucourt w. q.v.;
  High w. q.v.; Howitzer w. †295;
  Inverness Copse 395, 404; Lesbœufs w. q.v.; Leuze w. 266;
  Mametz w. q.v.; Montlognon w.
  44; Mormal f. q.v.; Nieppe f. 140,
  460; Nonne Bosschen w. 395;
  Pigeon w. 259; Ploegsteert w.
  99, 101, 466; Polderhoek w. q.v.;

Polygon w. q.v.; Road w. †293;
  Rossignol w. 263; Sanctuary w.
  393; St. Martin's w. 533, 535;
  St. Pierre Vaast w. 285, 523;
  Trônes w. q.v.; Vendegies w.
  563; Villers-Cotterets f. 68
Work 359, 414, 446, 447
Working Subalterns 317-18, 485
"Worms" 402, 512, 524
Wrexham 6, 7, 572, 575, 583
Wright, Capt. 318-19, 320
Wulverdinghe 385
Wynne-Edwards, Capt. 53-4, 57-8, 125
Wytschaete 391

Yates, H., Maj. 1, 4, 17, 32, 49, 68, 92,
  129, 183, 204, 227, 247, 286, 288,
  300, 307, 325-6, 338, 342, 354, 365,
  367, 379, 400, 414, 461, 468, 483-4,
  504, 510, 547, 560, 574, 580-1-2-3;
  quoted 33-37, 41, 47, 48, 65, 73
Yeomanry draft 439
York, Duke of (H.M. King George VI)
  572
Ypres: 73, 371, 376, 392, 411, 418, 421,
  423, 425, 431-2, 434, 448, 466, 476;
  Cloth Hall 411, 421; Lille Gate
  412; Menin Gate †410; Moat 392,
  412; polling-booth 421; White
  Château †415, †421
  Battles, I 73; II 132-3; III 370, 379,
  389, 391; IV 466
Yser 375-6, 377-8

Zeebrugge 376
Zeppelin 133, 357
Zillebeke 73; lake 393
Zuytpeene 386

SKETCHES

SHEET I

THE CHANNEL AND B.E.F. AREA OF OPERATIONS IN FRANCE AND BELGIUM.

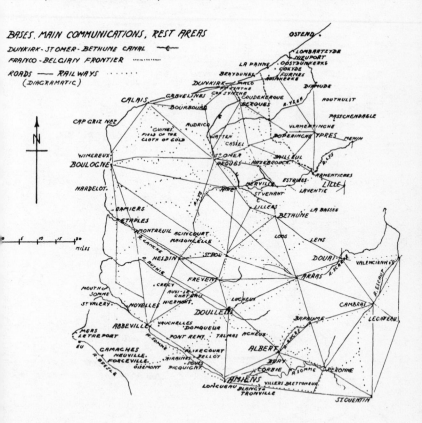

BASES, MAIN COMMUNICATIONS, REST AREAS

DUNKIRK-ST OMER-BETHUNE CANAL
FRANCO-BELGIAN FRONTIER
ROADS ——— RAILWAYS ·········
(DIAGRAMATIC)

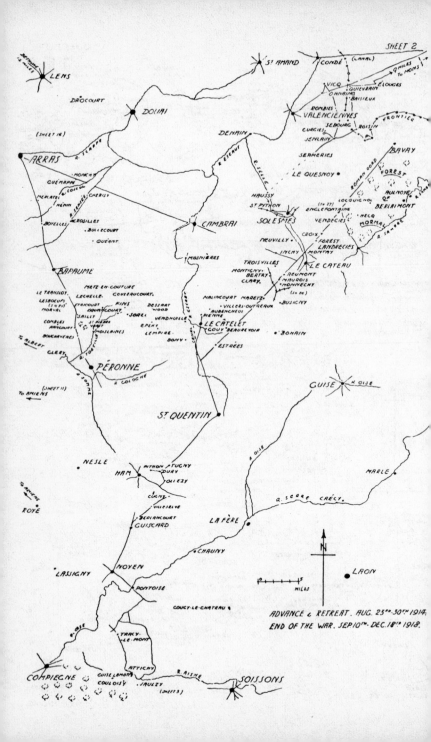

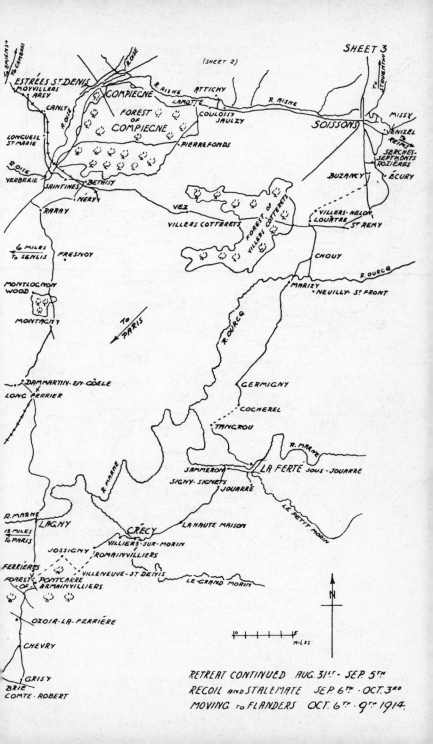

SHEET 3

(SHEET 2)

To BAPAUME + To CAMBRAI

ESTRÉES ST DENIS
MOYVILLERS
ARSY

CANLY

R. OISE
COMPIÈGNE

R. AISNE   ATTICHY
LAMOTTE
COULOISY
JAULZY

FOREST OF COMPIÈGNE

R. AISNE

To ST QUENTIN

MISSY
VENIZEL
REIMS
SERCHES
SEPTMONTS
ROZIÈRES

SOISSONS

LONGUEIL
ST MARIE

PIERREFONDS

BUZANCY

ÉCURY

R. OISE
VERBERIE   SAINTINES   BETHISY
NÉRY

VEZ

VILLERS-HELON
LOUÂTRE
ST REMY

RARAY

VILLERS COTTERETS

FOREST of VILLERS COTTERETS

6 MILES
To SENLIS   FRESNOY

CHOUY

R. OURCQ

MONTLOGNON
WOOD

MARIZY   NEUILLY ST FRONT

MONTAGNY

To PARIS

R. OURCQ

GERMIGNY

DAMMARTIN-EN-GOELE
LONG PERRIER

COCHEREL

TANCROU

R. MARNE

R. MARNE

SAMMERON

LA FERTÉ SOUS-JOUARRE

SIGNY-SIGNETS

JOUARRÉ

LE PETIT MORIN

R. MARNE

R. MARNE
LAGNY

CRÉCY   LA HAUTE MAISON

13 MILES
To PARIS

VILLIERS-SUR-MORIN

JOSSIGNY   ROMAINVILLIERS

FERRIÈRES
FOREST PONTCARRE
of ARMAINVILLIERS

VILLENEUVE-ST DENIS

LE GRAND MORIN

OZOIR-LA-FERRIÈRE

N

CHEVRY

1   5
MILES

GRISY

BRIE
COMTE-ROBERT

RETREAT CONTINUED AUG. 31ST - SEP. 5TH
RECOIL and STALEMATE SEP. 6TH - OCT. 3RD
MOVING to FLANDERS OCT. 6TH - 9TH 1914.

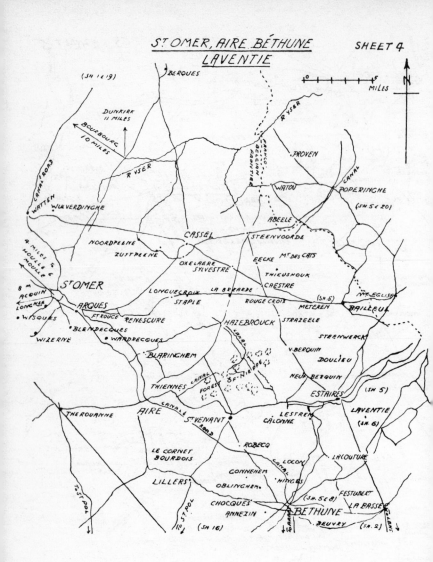

St. OMER, AIRE, BÉTHUNE LAVENTIE

SHEET 4

BÉTHUNE, ARMENTIERES SHEET 5
YPRES

MILES.

PROVEN · ELVERDINCHE · WELTJE · PASSCHENDAELE · MOORSLEDE (SH.21)

WATOU · ST JEAN · ZONNEBEKE

(SH.20) YPRES · VLAMERTINGHE · POTIZZE · BECELAERE

DOPERINCHE · BRANDHOEK · TO MENIN

CAFÉ BELGE

ABEELE · DICKEBUSCH · RENINGHELST

LACLYTTE · CANAL

WESTOUTRE

Mt DES CATS · KEMMEL · WYTSCHAETE

LOCRE · LINDENHOEK · MESSINES · (SH.20) · COMINES

CAESTRE · DRANOUTRE · WARNETON

METEREN · RAVELSBERG · NEUVE EGLISE · LA DRULE

BAILLEUL · LE LENTHE · PLOEGSTEERT WOOD · FRÉLINGHIEN

STRAZEELE · LA CRECHE

STEENWERCK · NIEPPE · HOUPLINES

ERQUINGHEM · ARMENTIERES · LA Cte ARMENTIERES

(SH.4)

(SH.7) · GRIS POT · WEZ MACQUART

SAILLY-SUR-LA-LYS · FLEURBAIX · BOIS GRENIER

ESTAIRES · LA BOUTILLERIE · LILLE

CALONNE LESTREM · LAVENTIE · PICANTIN · RADINGHEN

FRAUQUISSART (SH.6) · LE MAISNIL

FROMELLES

AUBERS

LA COUTURE · NEUVE CHAPELLE · FOURNES

LOCON · HERLIES · LE PILLY

FESTUBERT

(SH.8) · LA BASSÉE

BÉTHUNE · GIVENCHY · CUINCHY

(SH.16) · BEUVRY · ANNEQUIN · AUCHY

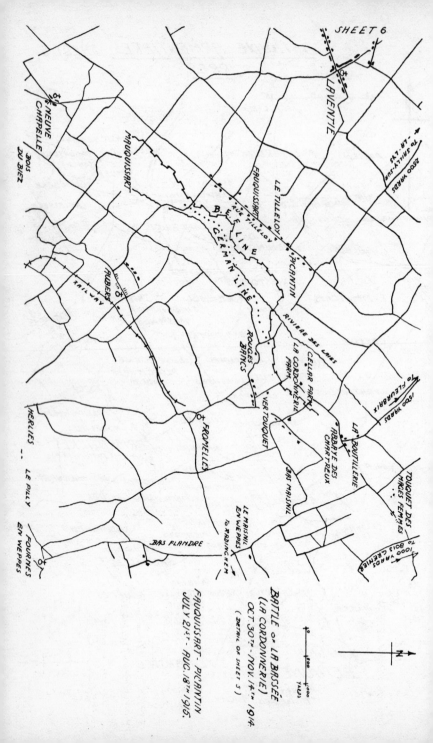

SHEET 6

LAVENTIE

NEUVE CHAPELLE

BOIS DU BIEZ

MAUQUISSART

To STEENWERCK - LA LYS

2500 YARDS

LE TILLELOY

FAUQUISSART

ALE TILLELOY

PICANTIN

B.F. LINE

GERMAN LINE

RIVIÈRE DES LAIES

AUBERS

RAILWAY

To FLEURBAIX

1500 YARDS

ROUGES BANCS

CELLAR FARM

LA CORDONNERIE FARM

FROMELLES

VER TOUQUET

ABBAYE DES CHARTREUX

LA BOUTILLERIE

HERLIES

LE PILLY

FOURNES EN WEPPES

BAS MAISNIL

LE MAISNIL EN WEPPES

To RADINGHEM

BAS FLANDRE

TOUQUET DES TROIS FEMMES

To BOIS GRENIER

1000 YARDS

N

10   1000

YARDS

BATTLE OF LA BASSÉE
(LA CORDONNERIE)
OCT. 30TH - NOV. 14TH 1914.
(DETAIL OF SHEET 5)

FAUQUISSART - PICANTIN
JULY 21ST - AUG. 18TH 1915.

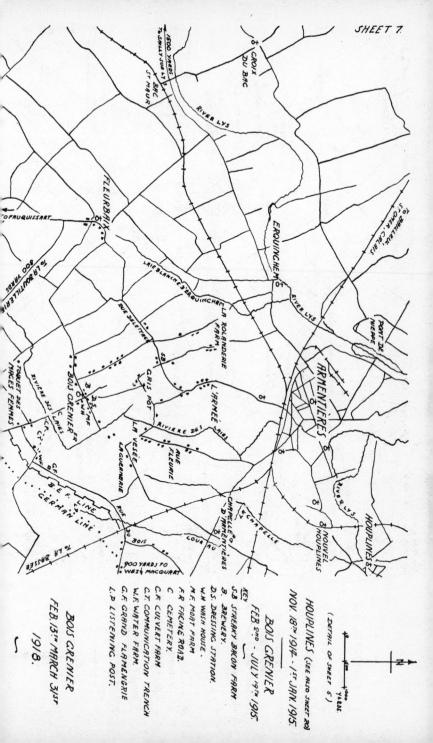

SHEET 7.

(DETAIL OF SHEET 5.)

HOUPLINES (SEE ALSO SHEET 20)
NOV. 18TH 1914 - 1ST JAN. 1915.

BOIS GRENIER
FEB 2ND - JULY 19TH 1915.

KEY
J.B. STREAKY BACON FARM.
B. BREWERY.
D.S. DRESSING STATION.
W.H. WASH HOUSE.
M.F. MORT FARM.
A.R. FRICNE ROAD.
C. CEMETERY.
C.F. CULVERT FARM.
C.T. COMMUNICATION TRENCH
G.F. GRAND FLAMENGRIE
W.F. WATER FARM
L.P. LISTENING POST.

BOIS GRENIER
FEB. 13TH MARCH 31ST
1918.

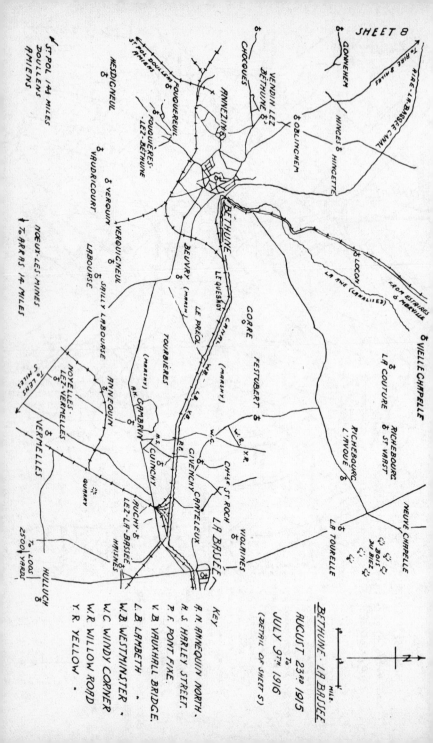

SHEET 8

To AIRE 8 MILES

GONNEHEM

CHOCQUES

VENDIN LEZ
BÉTHUNE

HINGES

HINGETTE

St POL DOULLENS
St AMIENS

FOUQUEREUIL

FOUQUIÈRES-
LEZ-BÉTHUNE

ANNEZIN

OBLINCHEM

HESDIGNEUL

VERQUIN

VIRUDRICOURT

BÉTHUNE

AIRE-LA-BASSÉE CANAL

RICHEBOURG
LA COUTURE

LOCON

FROM ESTAIRES
To MERVILLE

LA AWE (CANALISED)

VIELLE CHAPELLE

RICHEBOURG
L'AVOUÉ

RICHEBOURG
St VAAST

St POL 74 MILES
DOULLENS
AMIENS

VERQUIGNEUL

BEUVRY

LE QUESNOY

LE PRÉOL

GORRE

FESTUBERT

RICHEBOURG
L'AVOUÉ

SAILLY LABOURSE

LABOURSE

TOURBIÈRES
(MARSH)

CANAL
W.B.
L.B.
(MARSH)

W.C.

W.R.

Y.R.

NEUVE CHAPELLE

NOYELLES-
LEZ-VERMELLES

ANNEQUIN

AM. CAMBRIN

CUINCHY

M.S.
P.F.

GIVENCHY
CANTELEUX

CH LES St ROCH

VIOLAINES

LA TOURELLE

To LENS
9 MILES

VERMELLES

QUARRY

AUCHY-
LEZ-LA-BASSÉE

HAISNES

LA BASSÉE

BOIS
DU BIEZ

HULLUCH

To LOOS
2500 YARDS

NOEUX-LES-MINES
To ARRAS 14 MILES

N

KEY

R.N. ANNEQUIN NORTH.
H.S. HARLEY STREET.
P.F. PONT FIXE.
V.B. VAUXHALL BRIDGE.
L.B. LAMBETH   "
W.B. WESTMINSTER "
W.C. WINDY CORNER
W.R. WILLOW ROAD
Y.R. YELLOW   "

BÉTHUNE - LA BASSÉE

AUGUST 23rd 1915
to
JULY 9th 1916
(DETAIL OF SHEET 5)

MILES

To AIRE 8 MILES

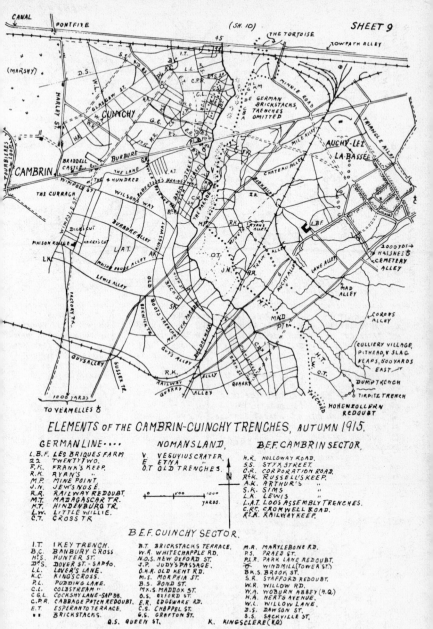

ELEMENTS of the CAMBRIN-CUINCHY TRENCHES, AUTUMN 1915.

GERMAN LINE····	NOMANSLAND	B.E.F. CAMBRIN SECTOR.
L.B.F. LES BRIQUES FARM	V. VEGUVIUS CRATER.	H.R. HOLLOWAY ROAD.
22. TWENTYTWO.	E. ETNA	S.S. STYX STREET.
F.K. FRANK'S KEEP.	O.T. OLD TRENCHES.	C.R. CORPORATION ROAD.
R.K. RYAN'S.		R&K RUSSELL'S KEEP.
M.P. MINE POINT.		A.K. ARTHUR'S "
J.N. JEW'S NOSE.		S.K. SIMS "
R.R. RAILWAY REDOUBT.		S.K. LEWIS "
M.T. MADAGASCAR TR.		L.A.T. LOOS ASSEMBLY TRENCHES.
H.T. HINDENBURG TR.		C.RC. CROMWELL ROAD.
Lw. LITTLE WILLIE.		R&K. RAILWAY KEEP.
C.T. CROSS TR.		

B.E.F. CUINCHY SECTOR.

I.T. IKEY TRENCH.	B.T. BRICKSTACKS TERRACE.	M.R. MARYLEBONE RD.
B.C. BANBURY CROSS	W.R. WHITECHAPPLE RD.	P.S. PRAED ST.
H.S. HUNTER ST.	N.O.S. NEW OXFORD ST.	P.L.R. PARK LANE REDOUBT.
D.S. DOVER ST.-SAP40.	J.P. JUDY'S PASSAGE.	⦶ WINDMILL (TOWER ST.)
L.L. LOVER'S LANE.	O.H.R. OLD KENT RD.	B.K.S. BROOK ST.
K.C. KING'S CROSS.	M.S. MORPHIA ST.	S.R. STAFFORD REDOUBT.
P.L. PUDDING LANE.	B.S. BOND ST.	W.R. WILLOW RD.
C.L. COLDSTREAM "	Mx.S. MADDOX ST.	W.A. WOBURN ABBEY (H.Q.)
C.S.L. COCKSHY LANE-SAP38.	O.S. OXFORD ST.	H.A. HERTS AVENUE.
C.P.R. CABBAGE PATCH REDOUBT.	E.R. EDGEWARE RD.	W.L. WILLOW LANE.
E.T. ESPERANTO TERRACE.	C.S. CHAPPEL ST.	D.S. DAWSON ST.
·· BRICKSTACKS.	G.S. GRAFTON ST.	S.S. SACKVILLE ST.
	Q.S. QUEEN ST.	K. KINGSCLERE (H.Q.)

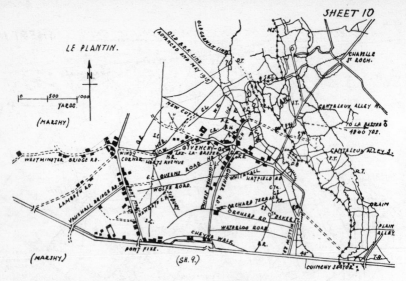

SHEET 10

LE PLANTIN.

N

0 500 1000
YARDS

(MARSHY)

(MARSHY)

(SH. 9.)

B.E.F. TRENCHES & POSTS.
FROM A MAP OF DECEMBER 1915:

⚹ D.T. DEADMANS TRENCH.	H.R. HILDA REDOUBT.
P.L. PARK LANE.	L.L. LAVENDER LANE.
R. THE ROCKERY.	Wᴿ.R. HERTS. REDOUBT.
U.C. UPPER CUT.	B.C.W. BIRD CAGE WALK.
W.R. WARE ROAD.	Hᴵᴿ.R. HITCHEN ROAD.
C.L. COLDSTREAM LANE.	G.R. GRENADIER ROAD.
A. THE AVENUE.	S.C. SUEZ CANAL (DITCH)
P.R. POPPY REDOUBT.	C.Tᴿ. CAMBRIDGE TERRACE.
B.H. BUNNY HUTCH.	G.S. GLASGOW STREET.
C.R. CALEDONIAN ROAD.	F.R. FINCHLEY ROAD.
K.W. KILBYS WALK.	S.S. SHORT STREET.
C.H. CONSTITUTION HILL.	O.T. OXFORD TERRACE
P. PICCADILLY.	B.R. BAYSWATER ROAD
C.S. CURZON STREET.	D.B. DUCKS BILL.
K.R. KINGS ROAD.	(I) B.E.F. GERMAN (r)
I.C. INNER CIRCLE.	
G.K. GIVENCHY KEEP	
⚹ ABANDONED IN NOVEMBER.	

GERMAN TRENCHES.

M.T. MACKENSEN Tᴿ.	
S.R.T. SUNKEN RD. Tᴿ.	
A.W. AUSTRIAN WAY.	
P.W. PRUSSIAN WAY.	
S.W. SAXON WAY.	
S.T. SUPPORT TR.	
R.T. RESCUE TR.	
P.N POPE'S NOSE	

SAPS, THOUGH NUMBERED LATER, WERE BEST KNOWN, AS AT CUINCHY, BY THEIR ORIGINAL NAMES, E.G. BANBURY ROAD (41), SHAFSBURY AVENUE (57), REGENT ST, BOND Sᵀ, BERKLEY Sᵀ (60) CLARGES Sᵀ, HALF MOON Sᵀ, DOWN Sᵀ (63).

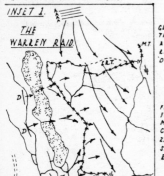

INSET 1.
THE WARREN RAID

INSET 1
GERMAN SALIENT AT THE WARREN, FROM A GERMAN PLAN: RAIDED 6/7/16. BY 'D' AND 'A' COMPANIES

INSET 2
FROM A GERMAN PLAN FOR THE DUCKS BILL MINE (RED DRAGON CRATER) AND RAID OF 22/6/16: THE CRATERS SHEWN WERE OF EARLIER BLOWING.

INSET 2.
THE DUCKS BILL RAID

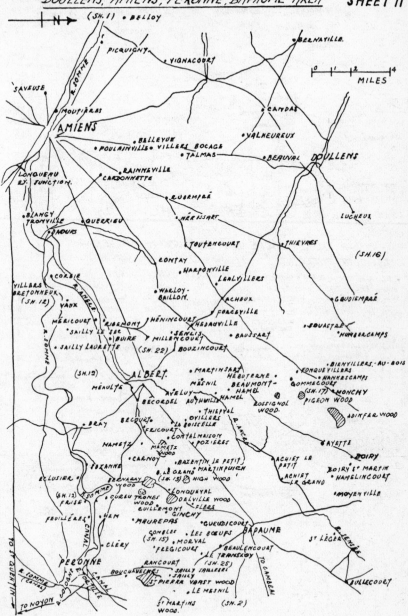

(SH. 1) • BELLOY

N →

BERNATILLE.

PICQUIGNY
VIGNACOURT

0   1   2   4
MILES

SAVEUSE

MOUTIÈRES
CANDAS

AMIENS
VALHEUREUX

BELLEVUE   DOULLENS
POULAINVILLE • VILLERS BOCAGE   BEAUVAL
TALMAS

LONGUEAU
RY. JUNCTION.
RAINNEVILLE
CARDONNETTE
LUCHEUX

QUERRIEU
BLANGY
TRONVILLE
DAOURS
QUERRIEU

QUERMPRÉ
(SH. 16)

NÉRISSART

TOUTENCOURT   THIÈVRES

CONTAY

HARPONVILLE
LÉALVILLERS

CORBIE
WARLOY-
BAILLON.
ACHEUX
GAUDIEMPRÉ

VILLERS
BRETONNEUX
(SH. 12)
VAUX
FORCEVILLE

MÉRICOURT
RIBEMONT
HÉNINCOURT
HÉDAUVILLE
SOUASTRE

SAILLY LE SEC
BUIRE
SENLIS
BAUSSART
HUMBERCAMPS
MILLENCOURT

SAILLY LAURETTE
(SH. 22)
BOUZINCOURT

(SH. 12)
ALBERT.
MARTINSART
HÉBUTERNE
BIENVILLERS-AU-BOIS

MÉNELTE
MESNIL
BEAUMONT-
FONQUEVILLERS
HANNESCAMPS

AVELUY
HAMEL
GOMMECOURT
(SH. 17) MONCHY

BECORDEL AUTHUILLE
HAMEL
ROSSIGNOL
WOOD.
PIGEON WOOD

THIEPVAL
ADINFER WOOD

BRAY
BECOURT
OVILLERS
LA BOISSELLE
R. ANCRE.

MAMETZ
FRICOURT
CONTALMAISON
POZIÈRES
GAYETTE

CARNOY
BAZENTIN LE PETIT
ACHIET LE
PETIT
BOIRY
BOIRY ST MARTIN

ECLUSIER
BECNAFAY
WOOD
LE GRAND MARTINPUICH
(SH. 13) HIGH WOOD
ACHIET
LE GRAND
HAMELINCOURT

FRISE
(SH. 13)
SOMME
CUREU TRONES
WOOD
LONGUEVAL
DELVILLE WOOD
MOYENVILLE

FEUILLÈRES
HEM
GUILLEMONT
FLERS
GINCHY

MAUREPAS
GUEUDICOURT
BAPAUME

COMBLES
LES BŒUFS
ST LÉGER

CLÉRY
(SH. 15)
MORVAL
FLÉGICOURT
BEAULENCOURT

PERONNE
RANCOURT
LE TRANSLOY
(SH. 25)

BOUCHAVESNES
SAILLY SAILLISEL
SAILLY
TO CAMBRAI

R. SOMME
(CANAL)
ST PIERRE VAAST WOOD
BULLECOURT

TO NOYON
CANAL
LE MESNIL

TO ST QUENTIN
ST MARTINS
WOOD.
(SH. 2)

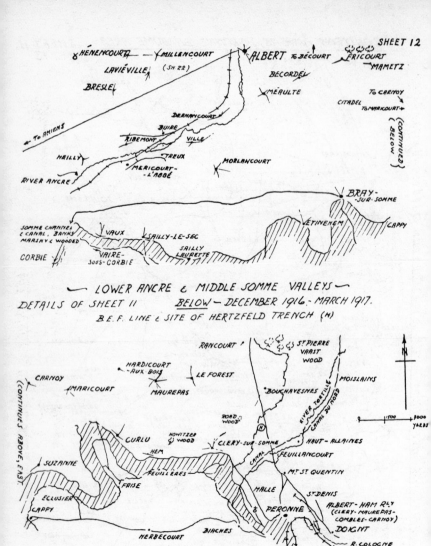

SHEET 12

HÉNENCOURT — MILLENCOURT — ALBERT — To BÉCOURT — FRICOURT — MAMETZ

LAVIÉVILLE — (SH 22) — BECORDEL

BRESLE — MÉAULTE

To CARNOY

CITADEL — To MARICOURT — (CONTINUED BELOW)

DERNANCOURT

BUIRE

RIBEMONT — VILLE

NEILLY — TREUX — MORLANCOURT

RIVER ANCRE — MÉRICOURT-L'ABBÉ

BRAY-SUR-SOMME

ÉTINEHEM — CAPPY

SOMME CHANNEL & CANAL, BANKS MARSHY & WOODED — VAUX — SAILLY-LE-SEC

CORBIE — VAIRE-SOUS-CORBIE — SAILLY LAURETTE

~ LOWER ANCRE & MIDDLE SOMME VALLEYS ~

DETAILS OF SHEET 11   BELOW — DECEMBER 1916 - MARCH 1917.

B.E.F. LINE & SITE OF HERTZFELD TRENCH (H)

RANCOURT — ST PIERRE VAAST WOOD

HARDICOURT-AUX-BOIS — LE FOREST — MOISLAINS

CARNOY — MARICOURT — BOUCHAVESNES — RIVER TORTILLE — CANAL DU NORD

MAUREPAS

(CONTINUES ABOVE, EAST.) — CURLU — HOWITZER WOOD — ROAD WOOD — (H) — HAUT-ALLAINES

1500   3000 YARDS

HEM — CLÉRY-SUR-SOMME — FEUILLANCOURT

SUZANNE — FEUILLÈRES — CANAL — Mt ST QUENTIN

FRISE — HALLE — ST DENIS

ÉCLUSIER — PÉRONNE — ALBERT-HAM RLY (CLÉRY-MAUREPAS-COMBLES-CARNOY)

CAPPY — DOINGT

HERBÉCOURT — BIACHES — R. COLOGNE

ST JUST-CAMBRAI RLY

N

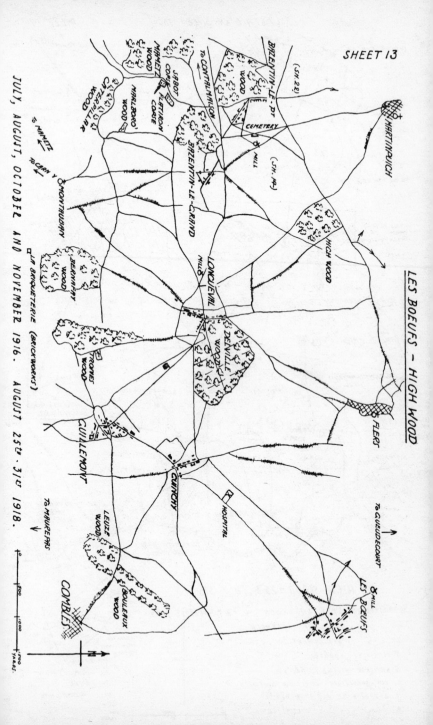

SHEET 13

LES BOEUFS – HIGH WOOD

JULY, AUGUST, OCTOBER AND NOVEMBER 1916. AUGUST 25th-31st 1918.

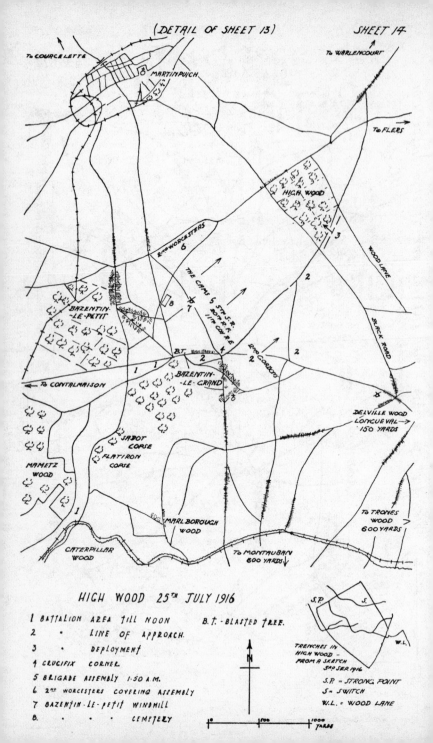

(DETAIL OF SHEET 13)   SHEET 14

To COURCELETTE

To WARLENCOURT

MARTINPUICH

To FLERS

HIGH WOOD

2ND WORCESTERS

6

THE CAPS 5 STH. S. R. 20TH R.F. 11TH CORPS

WOOD LANE

3

2

BLACK ROAD

BAZENTIN-LE-PETIT

8

7

2ND GORDONS

2

2

B.T.

1

2

2

BAZENTIN-LE-GRAND

To CONTALMAISON

DELVILLE WOOD
LONGUEVAL →
150 YARDS

SABOT COPSE

FLATIRON COPSE

MAMETZ WOOD

1

MARLBOROUGH WOOD

To TRONES WOOD 600 YARDS

CATERPILLAR WOOD

To MONTAUBAN 800 YARDS

HIGH WOOD 25TH JULY 1916

1 BATTALION AREA TILL NOON
2   "   LINE OF APPROACH.
3   "   DEPLOYMENT
4 CRUCIFIX CORNER.
5 BRIGADE ASSEMBLY 1·50 A.M.
6 2ND WORCESTERS COVERING ASSEMBLY
7 BAZENTIN·LE·PETIT WINDMILL
8   "   "   "   CEMETERY

B.T. - BLASTED TREE.

N

S.P.

S.

W.L.

TRENCHES IN
HIGH WOOD –
FROM A SKETCH
3RD SEP. 1916

S.P. = STRONG POINT
S = SWITCH
W.L. = WOOD LANE

0   500   1000 YARDS

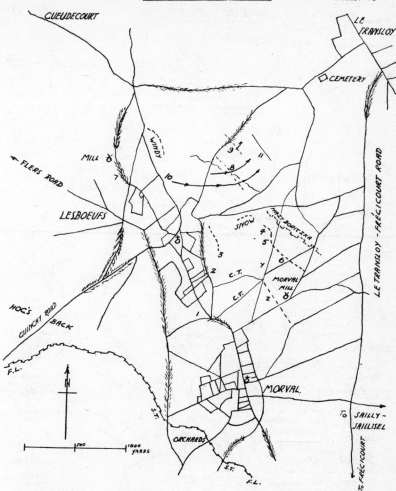

MORVAL · LES BOEUFS

SHEET 15

CUEUDECOURT

LE TRANSLOY

CEMETERY

MILL

WINDY

FLERS ROAD

LESBOEUFS

9
11
8
10
7

SNOW

HAZY BORITZKA

4
5
6

3

2 C.T.

C.T.

MORVAL MILL

1

HOG'S BACK

GUINCHY ROAD

F.L.

S.T.

MORVAL

ORCHARDS

S.T.

F.L.

To SAILLY-SAILLISEL

To FRÉCICOURT

LE TRANSLOY - FRÉCICOURT ROAD

N

500   1000 YARDS

F.L. FLERS LINE   S.T. SERPENTINE TRENCH   C.T. COMMUNICATION TRENCH

OCTOBER 1916.

1 BATTALION H.Q.
2 "D" COMPANY.
3 "A" DITTO. (OX SUPPORT)
4 "C" DITTO. (FROSTY)
5 "B" DITTO. (SLUSH)
6 THE FRENCH (ANTELOPE)

1st SEPTEMBER 1918.

Y BATTALION H.Q. FROM 7 AM.
Z LINE ON WHICH ELEMENTS OF COMPANIES WERE ORGANIZED AFTER NOON.

NOVEMBER 1916

7 BATTALION H.Q.
8 "D" COMPANY (FIRST POSITION)
                    (DEWDROP)
9 "B" DITTO. (SUMMER)
10 "C" DITTO. (JOHN BULL)
11 LINE OF OBJECTIVE

NOTE. GERMAN TRENCHES WERE SHELL-
-HOLE POSTS · OURS WERE MADE
CONTINUOUS, SO WERE THE
FRENCH.

ARRAS - DOULLENS

↑ N

MILES

R. AUTHIE

AUXI - LE - CHATEAU

R. CANCHE

AGINCOURT
TO ST OMER
30 MILES

MAISONCELLE

MONCHEL

VACQUERIE-
LE-BOUCQ

BLANGERMONT

BONNIÈRES
BEAUVOIR

FREVENT

R. TERNOISE

TO AIRE
12½ MILES

DOULLENS

R. GROUCHES

ST POL

MONCHEAUX

LUCHEUX

IVERGNY

(SH. 11)

LIENCOURT

(SH.ᵗ 4 & 8)

GAUDIEMPRÉ

SAULTY

BRUAY

R. CLARENCE

HUMBERCAMPS

BAILLEULMONT
AU-BOIS

BIENVILLERS

BAILLEULVAL

BETHUNE

HANNESCAMPS
(SH. 17)

MONCHY

BASSEUX

NOEUX-LES
MINES

LANSART

BRÉTENCOURT

ADINFER WOOD

BLAIRVILLE

AYETTE

FICHEUX

GRENAY

VERMELLES

BOIRY-
STE RICTRUDE

BOIRY-
ST MARTIN

BOISEUX-AU-MONT

MOYENVILLE

ARRAS

HAMELINCOURT

MERCATEL

B. ST MARC

LOOS

BOYELLES

BOIRY BECQUERELLE

VIMY

LA BASSÉE

R. SCARPE

HÉNIN

ST MARTIN

HULLUCH

ST LEGER

R. SENSÉE

(SH.17)

P. COURT

LENS

WANCOURT

HENINEL

CROISILLES

GUÉMAPPE

FONTAINE

MONCHY LE PREUX

CHÉRISY

(SH. 2)

BULLECOURT

TO DOUAI

TO DOUAI

DROCOURT

R. COJEUL

R. GY

R. SCARPE

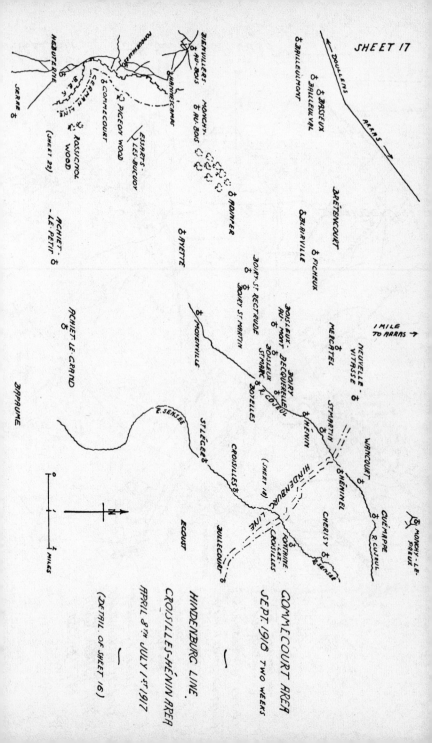

SHEET 17

DOULLENS

ARRAS →

HÉBUTERNE

SERRE

BIENVILLERS-
AU-BOIS

BRIARMONT

BAILLEULMONT

BASIEUX

BAILLEULVAL

BRETENCOURT

NEUVILLE-
VITASSE

MERCATEL

MONCHY-
AU-BOIS

HANNESCAMP

CONNECOURT

B.E.F.
LINE

GERMAN
LINE

PIGEON WOOD

ROSSIGNOL
WOOD

ESSARTS-
LES-BUCQOY

ADINFER

BERVILLE

FICHEUX

ROSSIEUX-
AU-MONT

DOSSIEUX-
BECQUERELLEOL

DOISY-ST RECTRUDE

DOISY ST-MARTIN

ROSSIEUX
ST-MARC

ST-MARTIN

BOYELLES

HÉNIN

HÉNINEL

WANCOURT

GUÉMAPPE

R CUSUL

MONCHY-LE-
PREUX

ACHIET-
LE-PETIT

AYETTE

MOYENNILLE

ST-MARC
& COTEOL

HINDENBURG LINE

FONTAINE-
LES-CROISILLES

CHÉRISY

R SENSÉE

ACHIET LE GRAND

R. SENSÉE

ST-LÉGER

CROISILLES

ST-LÉGER

CROISILLES

(SHEET 16)

BULLECOURT

ECOUST

BAPAUME

0   1   2 MILES

N

1 MILE
TO ARRAS →

(SHEET 22)

CONNECOURT AREA
SEPT. 1916 TWO WEEKS

——— HINDENBURG LINE.

CROISILLES-HÉNIN AREA
APRIL 8TH JULY 1ST 1917

——— (DETAIL OF SHEET 16)

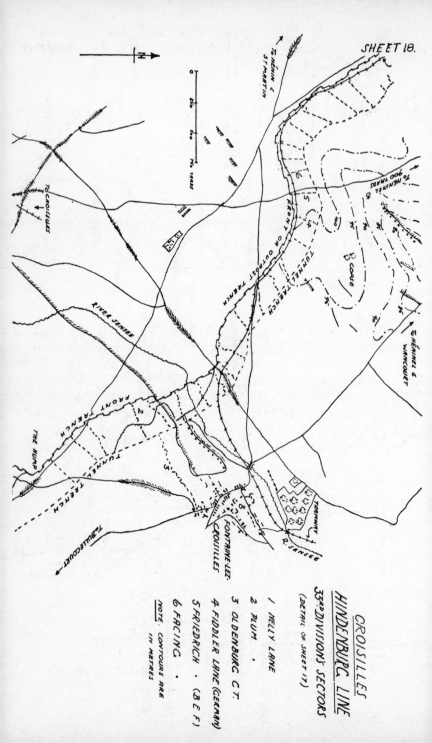

SHEET 18.

CROISILLES
HINDENBURG LINE
33RD DIVISION'S SECTORS
(DETAIL OF SHEET 17.)

1 NELLY LANE
2 PLUM „
3 OLDENBURG C.T.
4 FIDDLER LANE (GERMAN)
5 FRIEDRICH „ (B E F)
6 FACING „

NOTE. CONTOURS ARE IN METRES

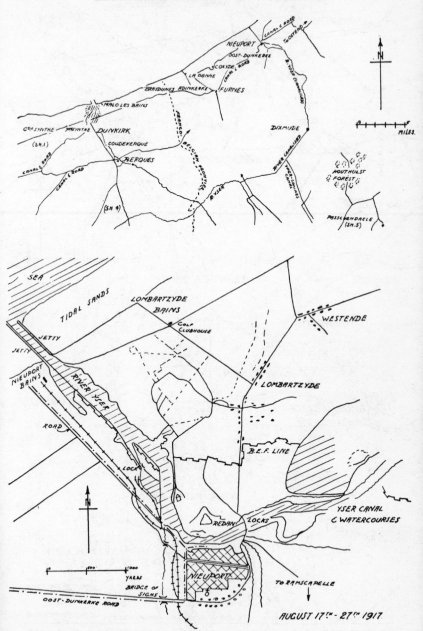

NIEUPORT · DUNKIRK · PASSCHENDAELE   SHEET 19

CANAL C ROAD
To OSTEND
NIEUPORT
OOST-DUNKERKE
COXYDE   CANAL C ROAD
LA PANNE
BRAYDUNES ADINKERKE   FURNES   R. YSER (CANALISED)
MALO LES BAINS
DUNKIRK   DIXMUDE
G^{de} SYNTHE   P^{te} SYNTHE
(SH.1)
COUDEKERQUE   N
CANAL C ROAD
BERGUES   MILES.
CANAL C ROAD
RIVER YSER (CANALISED)
R. YSER
(SH.4)   HOUTHULST
FRANCO BELGIAN FRONTIER   FOREST

                                         PASSCHENDAELE
                                         (SH.5)

SEA
TIDAL SANDS   LOMBARTZYDE
                     BAINS
                        GOLF   WESTENDE
                        CLUBHOUSE
JETTY
JETTY
NIEUPORT   LOMBARTZYDE
BAINS
        RIVER YSER
ROAD   B.E.F. LINE
                LOCK
                                  YSER CANAL
        N   C WATERCOURSES
                        REDAN LOCKS

                                  TO RAMSCAPELLE
YARDS
BRIDGE OF
SIGNS   NIEUPORT
OOST-DUNKERKE ROAD
                        AUGUST 17TH - 27TH 1917.

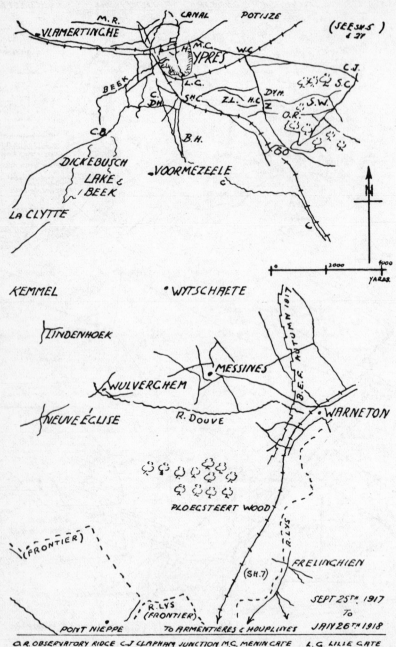

YPRES - PASSCHENDAELE : MESSINES

SHEET 20

(SEE SH.S & 21)

SEPT 25TH 1917
TO
JAN 26TH 1918

O.R. OBSERVATORY RIDGE	C.J. CLAPHAM JUNCTION	M.C. MENIN GATE	L.G. LILLE GATE
H.C. HELLBLAST CORNER	S.C. STIRLING CASTLE	Z. ZILLEBEKE	C.B. CAFE BELGE
S.W. SANCTUARY WOOD	W.C. WHITE CHATEAU	Z.L. D? LAKE	H. CLOTH HALL
H.L.C HELLFIRE CORNER	D.Y.H. DORMY HOUSE	D.H. DOLLS HOUSE	C. CANAL
S.C. SHRAPNEL CORNER	B.H. BEDFORD HOUSE	60. HILL 60.	M.R. MILITARY ROAD

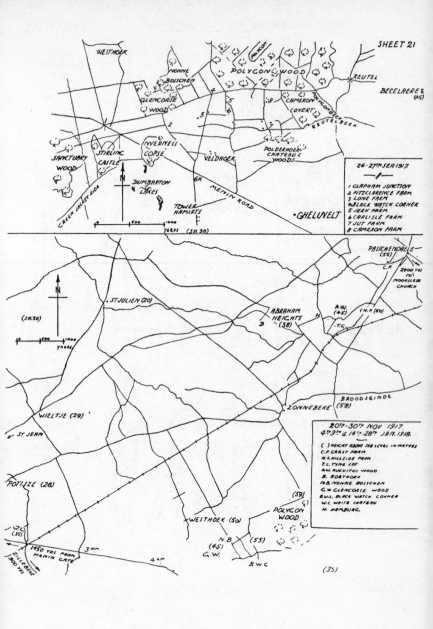

SHEET 21

WESTHOEK

YVONNE
BOSSCHEN

GLENCORSE
WOOD

POLYGON WOOD

POL. COT.

REUTEL

BECELAERE
(45)

CAMERON
COVERT

POLYGONBEEK

REUTELBEEK

SANCTUARY
WOOD

STIRLING
CASTLE

INVERNESS
COPSE

VELDHOEK

POLDERHOEK
CHATEAU &
WOODS

N

DUMBARTON
LAKES

6K

MENIN ROAD

GREEN JACKET RIDE

TOWER
HAMLETS

•GHELUVELT

500   1000
YARDS   (SH.20)

26-27TH SEP.1917.

1 CLAPHAM JUNCTION
2 FITZCLARENCE FARM
3 LONE FARM
4 BLACK WATCH CORNER
5 JERK FARM
6 CARLISLE FARM
7 JUT FARM
8 CAMERON FARM

PASSCHENDAELE
(55)

C.F.

2900 YDS
TO
MOORSLEDE
CHURCH

N

ST.JULIEN (20)

(SH.20)

500   1000
YARDS

ABRAHAM
HEIGHTS
(38)

A.W.
(45)   C.H.P.(50)

B   H   .T.C.

BROODSEINDE
(58)

WIELTJE (29)

ZONNEBEKE
(58)

•ST JEAN

20TH-30TH NOV. 1917.
4TH,9TH & 14TH-28TH JAN. 1918.

( ) HEIGHT ABOVE SEA LEVEL IN METRES
C.F. CREST FARM
H.H.HILLSIDE FARM
T.C. TYNE COT
A.W. AUGUSTUS WOOD
B. BORTHOEK
N.B. YVONNE BOSSCHEN
G.W. GLENCORSE WOOD
B.W.C. BLACK WATCH CORNER
W.C. WHITE CHATEAU
H. HAMBURG.

POTIZIE (26)

(50)

POLYGON
WOOD

T.C.
(35)

WESTHOEK (50)

N.B.
(45)   (55)
G.W.

ZILLEBEKE
300 YDS

1450 YDS FROM
MENIN GATE

3 KM

4 KM

B.W.C.

(35)

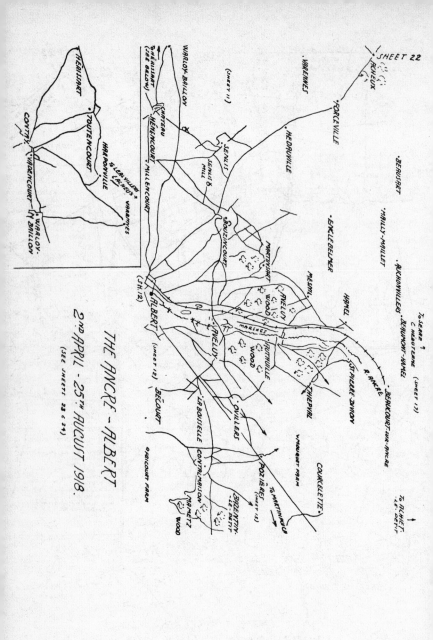

THE ANCRE - ALBERT
2ND APRIL - 25TH AUGUST 1918.
(SEE SHEETS 23 & 24)

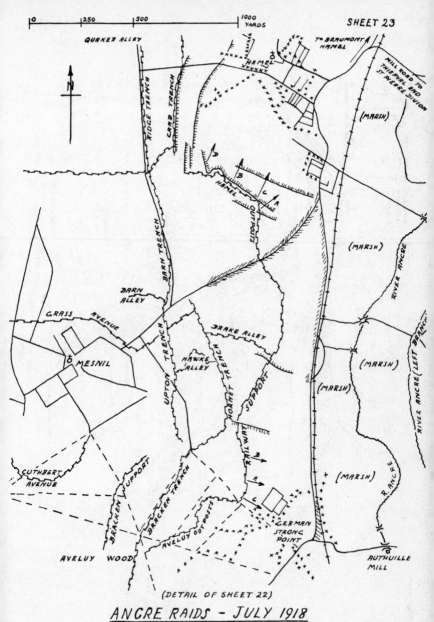

SHEET 23

QUAKER ALLEY

0   250   500   1000 YARDS

N

To BEAUMONT HAMEL

MILL ROAD TO THIEPVAL AND ST PIERRE DIVISION

HAMEL

(MARSH)

RIDGE TRENCH

CARD TRENCH

D

B   A C

HAMEL OUTPOSTS

(MARSH)

RIVER ANCRE

BARN TRENCH

BARN ALLEY

GRASS   AVENUE

MESNIL

UPTON TRENCH

HAWKE ALLEY

DRAKE ALLEY

HORNET TRENCH

RAILWAY SUPPORT

(MARSH)

(MARSH)

(MARSH)

RIVER ANCRE (LEFT BRANCH)

CUTHBERT AVENUE

BRACKEN SUPPORT

BRACKEN TRENCH

HAWKE ALLEY

B

A

C

GERMAN STRONG POINT

(MARSH)

R. ANCRE

AVELUY OUTPOSTS

AVELUY WOOD

AUTHUILLE MILL

(DETAIL OF SHEET 22)

ANCRE RAIDS - JULY 1918

THE "DUD" RAID 22/6/18.   HAMEL RAID 11/7/18.

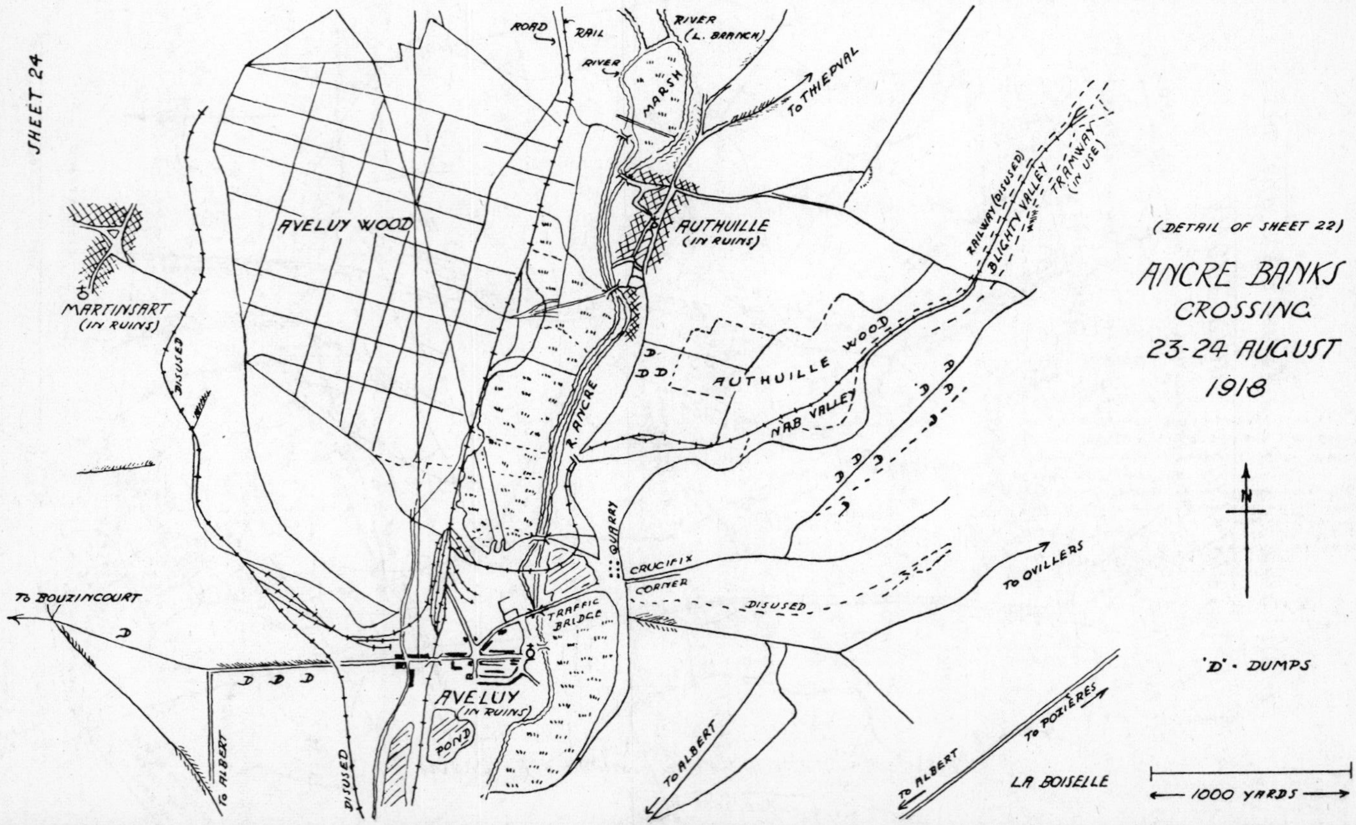

SHEET 24

TO BOUZINCOURT

MARTINSART
(IN RUINS)

DISUSED

TO ALBERT

AVELUY WOOD

DISUSED

AVELUY
(IN RUINS)

POND

TRAFFIC
BRIDGE

R. ANCRE

ROAD TOLL

RIVER

MARSH

RIVER
(L. BANK)

QUARRY

CRUCIFIX
CORNER

DISUSED

AUTHUILLE
(IN RUINS)

TO THIEPVAL

TO ALBERT

AUTHUILLE
WOOD

NAB VALLEY

RAILWAY (DISUSED)

BLIGHTY VALLEY

TRAMWAY
(IN USE)

TO ALBERT

TO POZIÈRES

LA BOISELLE

TO OVILLERS

1000 YARDS

'D' DUMPS

(DETAIL OF SHEET 22)

ANCRE BANKS
CROSSING
23-24 AUGUST
1918

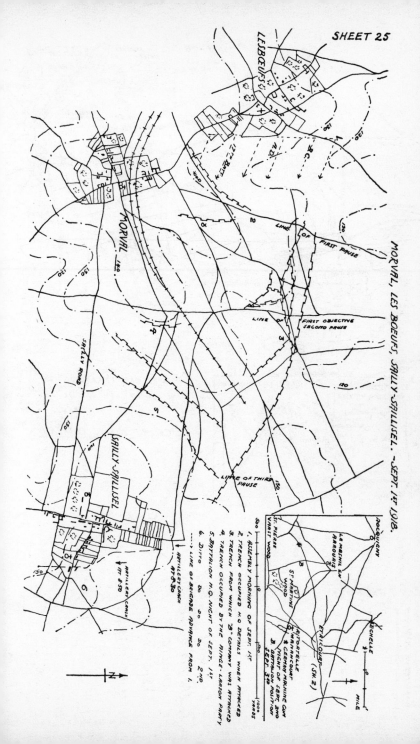

SHEET 25

MORVAL, LES BOEUFS, SAILLY-SAILLISEL. ~ SEPT. 1st 1918.

LESBŒUFS

MORVAL

SAILLY-SAILLISEL

SAILLY ROAD

LINE OF FIRST PAUSE

LINE OF FIRST OBJECTIVE SECOND PAUSE

LINE OF THIRD PAUSE

ARTILLERY CAIRN AT 8·30

1. ASSEMBLY MORNING OF SEPT. 1st
2. TRENCH OCCUPIED H.Q. DETAILS WHEN ATTACKED
3. TRENCH FROM WHICH "B" COMPANY WAS ATTACKED
4. TRENCH OCCUPIED BY THE RINGE-LARSON PARTY
5. BATTALION H.Q. NIGHT OF SEPT. 1st
6. DITTO DO DO DO 2ND
→ LINE OF BRIGADE ADVANCE FROM 1.

ARTILLERY CAIRN AT 8·30

N

ST. PIERRE VAAST WOOD
ROCQUIGNY
LE MESNIL EN ARROUAISE
RETORTELLE
ST. MARTIN'S WOOD
MARRANCOURT
ÉTRICOURT (SH. 2)
LECHELLE

A. CAIRN MACHINE GUN
B. NIGHT OF SEPT. 2ND
C. BATTALION POSITION SEPT. 3RD

500   1000 YARDS

½   1 MILE

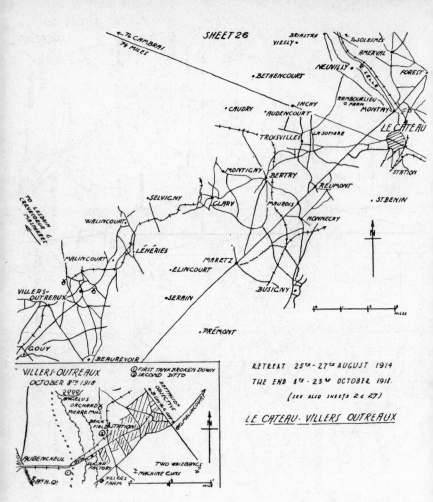

SHEET 26

← To CAMBRAI
74 MILES

• BRIASTRE
• VIESLY
→ To SOLESMES
AMERVAL
NEUVILLY
FOREST
• BETHENCOURT
RAMBOURLIEU
FARM
MONTAY
• INCHY
• CAUDRY
• AUDENCOURT
LE CATEAU
TROISVILLES
LA SOTIARE
STATION
MONTIGNY
BERTRY
REUMONT
• SELVIGNY
CLARY
MAUROIS
• St BENIN
WALINCOURT
HONNECHY
TO LECROIN &
CREVECOEUR
MONTIGNIES
LÉNÉRIES
MARETZ
MALINCOURT
• ELINCOURT
VILLERS-
OUTREAUX
• SERAIN
BUSIGNY
• PRÉMONT
GOUY
• BEAUREVOIR

VILLERS-OUTREAUX
OCTOBER 8TH 1918
① FIRST TANK BROKEN DOWN
② SECOND DITTO

ANGELUS
ORCHARD
PIERRE MILL
BATTALION
OBJECTIVE
TO MALINCOURT
BRICK
FIELD
STATION
AUBENCHEUL
SUGAR
FACTORY
TWO WHIZBANGS
8TH H.Q!
VILLERS
FARM
₹ MACHINE GUNS

RETREAT 25TH - 27TH AUGUST 1914.
THE END 8TH - 23RD OCTOBER 1918.
(SEE ALSO SHEETS 2 & 27)

LE CATEAU - VILLERS OUTREAUX

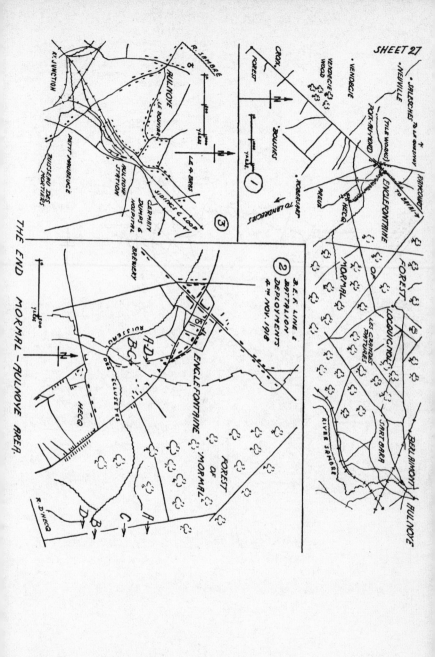

SHEET 27

THE END   MORMAL-RULNOYE AREA.

ON HISTORY

Eric Hobsbawm

In these stimulating and engaging essays, Eric Hobsbawm reflects upon the theory, practice and development of history and its relevance to the modern world. Covering a wide range of topics, they reflect Professor Hobsbawm's lifelong concern with the relations between past, present and future. He deals, among many other subjects, with the problems of writing history, its abuses and the historian's responsibilities; with Marx and current historical trends; with Europe, the Russian Revolution, and the descent into a world-wide barbarism that threatens to destroy the civilisation we have inherited from the European Enlightenment.

'For sheer intelligence, Hobsbawm has no superior in the historical profession . . . *On History* is of great interest for the light it throws on one of the most powerful minds of our time. It should be read by anyone who cares how history should be written and why it matters'
Guardian

'Brilliant'
Sunday Times

'Crisp, clear, logical, mordantly witty, splendidly aloof from British class assumptions, and untarnished by ancient university snobbery'
Ben Pimlott, *Independent on Sunday*

Abacus
978-0-349-11050-9

THE AGE OF REVOLUTION

1789–1848

Eric Hobsbawm

'A brilliant account of Europe in its revolutionary age . . .
No one could ask for more'
A. J. P. Taylor

'A harsh, brilliant, powerful, fascinating book'
Peter Lasslett, *Guardian*

'The work is challenging, learned, brilliant in its analytical
power, wide-ranging in its lucid exposition of literary, aesthetic
and scientific achievements and packed with novel insight'
English Historical Review

'Brilliant'
Times Literary Supplement

Eric Hobsbawm traces with brilliant analytical clarity the
transformation brought about in every sphere of European life
by the Dual Revolution – the 1789 French Revolution and the
Industrial Revolution that originated in Britain. This
enthralling and original account highlights the significant sixty
years when industrial capitalism established itself in Western
Europe and when Europe established the domination over the
rest of the world it was to hold for a century.

Abacus
978-0-349-10484-3

THE AGE OF CAPITAL
1848–1875

Eric Hobsbawm

'Excellent. Professor Hobsbawm writes extremely well . . . A
book of great originality and learning which gives a coherent
picture of a period in which so many of our own problems
have their roots'
New Statesman

'This brilliant book sparkles on every page . . . With a power
of decision that commands a terrified admiration, he selects
basic themes, illustrates them with a wealth of reference,
European and global . . . What a book! For heaven's sake,
and your own, read it.'
Guardian

'A book filled with pleasure for the connoisseur and the
amateur alike'
Economist

The first thorough major treatment of the critical years
1848–1875 – a penetrating analysis of the rise of capitalism
throughout the world.

Abacus
978-0-349-10480-5

THE AGE OF EMPIRE

1875–1914

Eric Hobsbawm

'This is history writing grand in ambition, excellently and wittily written . . . its sheer synoptic power and eloquence will make this book a classic'
Observer

'A superbly rich and erudite portrait of a society which was evolving rapidly under a variety of pressures – economic, technological and political'
Times Literary Supplement

'It takes far greater gifts – and far greater nerve – to simplify and to scintillate than to criticise and to complicate. This oustanding book displays both these admirable qualities in abundance. As in the previous volumes, the prodigious learning is lightly and lucidly borne, the range of example and breadth of allusion could not be bettered, and the illustrations have been admirably selected in order to complement the text'
New Society

The splendid finale to Eric Hobsbawm's study of the nineteenth century, *The Age of Empire* covers the era of western imperialism and examines the forces that swept the world to the outbreak of World War I – and shaped modern society.

Abacus
978-0-349-10598-7

THE AGE OF EXTREMES
The Short Twentieth Century
1914–1991

Eric Hobsbawm

'Magnificent' *Independent*
'Dazzling' *Financial Times*
'A masterpiece' *Guardian*

Age of Extremes is eminent historian Eric Hobsbawm's personal vision of the twentieth century. Remarkable in its scope, and breathtaking in its depth of knowledge, this immensely rewarding book reviews the uniquely destructive and creative nature of this most troubled century, and makes challenging predictions for the next.

'The power of Hobsbawm's exploration of the age of hot and cold wars lies in its brilliant synthesis of familiar, though sometimes forgotten, facts and ideas. It combines an Olympian, multi-lingual erudition and an addictively readable style'
Ben Pimlott, *Independent on Sunday* Books of the Year

'Quite simply the best book of the year'
Richard Gott, *The Guardian*

'The best account of our calamitous century . . . A marvellously imaginative set of essays on the period from 1914 to the collapse of Communism. For Hobsbawm, this constitutes virtually the history of his own life-time and ideas; and he draws the threads together with subtlety, compassion and a gentle, quizzical wit'
John Simpson, *Spectator* Books of the Year

'A magnificent piece of historical exposition . . . an essential read . . . Hobsbawm is a master historian and his version of events is thrilling'
Bryan Appleyard, *The Independent*

Abacus
978-0-349-10671-7

THE BOER WAR

Thomas Pakenham

The war declared by the Boers on 11 October 1899 gave the British, as Kipling said, 'no end of a lesson'. It proved to be the longest, costliest, the bloodiest and the most humiliating campaign that Britain fought between 1815 and 1914.

Thomas Pakenham has written the first full-scale history of the war since 1910. His narrative is based on first-hand and largely unpublished sources ranging from the private papers of the leading protagonists to the recollections of survivors from both sides. Out of this historical gold-mine, the author has constructed a narrative as vivid and fast-moving as a novel, and a history that in scholarship, breadth and impact will endure for many years.

'Not only a magnum opus, it is a conclusive work . . .
Enjoyable as well as massively impressive.'
Financial Times

'Hypnotically readable . . . A tremendous feat of research
. . . this is grand-scale history with heroes and villains . . .
hot, impassioned work, and I recommend it wholeheartedly.'
Newsweek

'Both a richly researched book and one that makes delightfully easy reading . . . deserves a huge success.'
Times Literary Supplement

'This is a wonderful book: brilliantly written . . . the reader turns each page with increasing fascination and admiration.'
A. J. P. Taylor

Abacus
978-0-349-10466-9

THE NEW CENTURY

Eric Hobsbawm

Following on from his worldwide bestseller *Age of Extremes*, Eric Hobsbawm continues his analysis of the twentieth century, asking crucial questions about our inheritance from the century if conflict and its meanings for the years to come.

The New Century looks back over the last decade to learn something of the new era: the disappearing distinction between internal and international conflicts; the crisis of the multi-ethnic state; the distortions of history involved in the creation of its myths. Questioning the cornerstones of current international relations and assessing the impact that popular global culture has had on every aspect of life, *The New Century* is a concise, challenging account from one of our pre-eminent historians.

'Its refreshingly sober perspective on contemporary trends gives it an interest that many more pretentious volumes lack . . . Hobsbawm shows he possesses to an extraordinary degree the historian's gift of identifying what is old and what is genuinely new in the present time'
Independent

'Excellent . . . Hobsbawm's characteristic erudition and charm underwrite his bracingly provocative viewpoints on subjects ranging from the Kosovo war to globalisation'
Guardian

'A bold little *tour d'horizon*'
Sunday Telegraph

Abacus
978-0-349-11336-4

Now you can order superb titles directly from Abacus

☐	The Age of Revolution	Eric Hobsbawm	£13.99
☐	The Age of Capital	Eric Hobsbawm	£14.99
☐	The Age of Empire	Eric Hobsbawm	£14.99
☐	The Age of Extremes	Eric Hobsbawm	£12.99
☐	On History	Eric Hobsbawm	£12.99
☐	The New Century	Eric Hobsbawm	£13.00
☐	The Boer War	Thomas Pakenham	£14.99

The prices shown above are correct at time of going to press. However, the publishers reserve the right to increase prices on covers from those previously advertised, without further notice.

──────────── ⬭ ABACUS ⬭ ────────────

Please allow for postage and packing: **Free UK delivery.**
Europe: add 25% of retail price; Rest of World: 45% of retail price.

To order any of the above or any other Abacus titles, please call our credit card orderline or fill in this coupon and send/fax it to:

Abacus, PO Box 121, Kettering, Northants NN14 4ZQ
Fax: 01832 733076   Tel: 01832 737526
Email: aspenhouse@FSBDial.co.uk

☐ I enclose a UK bank cheque made payable to Abacus for £ . . . .
☐ Please charge £ . . . . to my Visa/Delta/Maestro

☐☐☐☐☐☐☐☐☐☐☐☐☐☐☐☐

Expiry Date ☐☐☐☐   Maestro Issue No. ☐☐

NAME (BLOCK LETTERS please) . . . .

ADDRESS . . . .

. . . .

. . . .

Postcode . . . . Telephone . . . .

Signature . . . .

Please allow 28 days for delivery within the UK. Offer subject to price and availability.